EPIC

MASTERING
UNREAL®
TECHNOLOGY

VOLUME II:

Advanced Level Design
Concepts with Unreal® Engine 3

Jason Busby, Zak Parrish, Jeff Wilson

Sams Publishing, 800 East 96th St., Indianapolis, Indiana, 46240 USA

POWERED BY™

UNREAL
TECHNOLOGY

Mastering Unreal® Technology, Volume II

Copyright © 2010 by Epic Games, Inc.

ISBN-13: 978-0-672-32992-0
ISBN-10: 0-672-32992-1

Library of Congress Cataloging-in-Publication Data:

Busby, Jason.
  Mastering Unreal technology / Jason Busby, Zak Parrish, Jeff Wilson.
     p. cm.
  ISBN 978-0-672-32992-0
  1. Computer games—Programming. 2. Entertainment computing. 3. UnrealScript (Computer program language) I. Parrish, Zak. II. Wilson, Jeff. III. Title.
    QA76.76.C672B8685 2009
    794.8'1526—dc22

                                                              2009003414

Printed in the United States of America

Second Printing December 2009

Trademarks

Warning and Disclaimer

Bulk Sales

Sams Publishing offers excellent discounts on this book when ordered in quantity for bulk purchases or special sales. For more information, please contact

   U.S. Corporate and Government Sales
   1-800-382-3419
   corpsales@pearsontechgroup.com

For sales outside of the U.S., please contact

   International Sales
   international@pearson.com

Editor-in-Chief
Karen Gettman

Executive Editor
Neil Rowe

Development Editor
Mark Renfrow

Managing Editor
Kristy Hart

Project Editor
Anne Goebel

Copy Editor
Bart Reed

Indexer
WordWise Publishing Services

Proofreader
Julie Anderson

Publishing Coordinator
Cindy Teeters

Multimedia Developer
Dan Scherf

Interior Designer
Gary Adair

Cover Designer
Chris Bartlett

Compositor
Nonie Ratcliff

Table of Contents

About the Authors

Jason "Buzz" Busby is the president and chief executive officer of 3D Buzz, Inc., a company dedicated to teaching the world the arts and skills behind today's hottest technical industries, including 3D animation, programming, and game development. Through his website, www.3DBuzz.com, Buzz distributes his signature Video Training Modules (VTMs), which contain hours of training content that is professional, informative, and entertaining. His site also boasts one of the most robust, friendly, and helpful online communities in the world of 3D animation.

Zak Parrish is 3D Buzz Inc.'s chief of operations. For the past six years, he has worked with Jason Busby and 3D Buzz, Inc. to help provide top-quality education to students across the world. His work can be seen on many of the 3D Buzz VTMs, as well as in the Unreal Tournament 2004: Special Edition and Unreal Tournament 3 Limited Collector's Edition training video series. He is also an aspiring student of graphic design and is in the process of wrapping up his Bachelor of Fine Arts degree at Austin Peay State University.

Jeff Wilson is a student at the University of Advancing Technology, where he is pursuing a degree in game design. He has been studying the Unreal Engine for four years, while creating various modifications for Unreal Tournament 2003 and Unreal Tournament 2004. During his period of self study, Jeff developed a thorough understanding of the internal workings of the Unreal Engine, allowing him to create several unique gaming applications using his programming skills and 3D artistry. He has since become a professional consultant working for 3D Buzz, Inc., aiding in the development of many training videos over Unreal Technology.

Dedications

Acknowledgments

Jason: I would like to thank my family and my mom for putting up with me throughout this project and providing the love and support that allowed me to get the job done. I'd like to thank Zak for dealing with me through all my ups and downs and using his incredible writing talent to help make this book run as smoothly as possible. I also want to thank Jeff for his professionalism, his seemingly endless knowledge of the Unreal universe, and his indomitable will in seeing this project through to its completion.

Zak: I would like to thank Jason for seeing potential in me and helping me see it in myself. Without his vision and insight, I could never have learned or achieved so much. Thanks certainly go to Jeff for helping all of this make sense when it seemed that nothing else out there possibly could.

Jeff: I would like to thank Jason first and foremost for taking a chance on me and for allowing Zak to talk him into writing this book in the first place. I can't really imagine where I would be right now if he hadn't. I would also like to thank my parents for instilling in me the work ethic and determination I have needed to make it this far in life. I never made things easy on them, but they were always there for me and encouraged me when I needed it the most.

All Authors: We would all like to extend a most hearty thanks to those who helped make this book a reality from behind the scenes. First, thanks go to Logan Frank, who can always be counted on for technical assistance, no matter how complex the problem. We'd also like to thank Terry Wilson, for his countless hours of testing and screen capturing. Thanks also go out to Lee Jae Chi, for his amazing drawing skill and help with illustrations.

We would also like to thank Mike Capps and Mark Rein for making this book a reality, as well as Tim Sweeney for designing the Unreal Engine and starting this gaming phenomenon. Special thanks to the people at Epic who also reviewed this book: Chris Bartlett, Jim Brown, Andrew Bains, Dana Cowley, Scott Dossett, Jay Hosfelt, Wyeth Johnson, Mike Larson, Chris Mielke, Greg Mitchell, Maury Mountain, Mikey Spano, Ken Spencer, Jordan Walker, and Alan Willard. Finally, we would like to give a very large thanks to the Unreal community, which has been a massive source of support and inspiration in all our Unreal projects.

We Want to Hear from You!

As the reader of this book, *you* are our most important critic and commentator. We value your opinion and want to know what we're doing right, what we could do better, what areas you'd like to see us publish in, and any other words of wisdom you're willing to pass our way.

You can email or write me directly to let me know what you did or didn't like about this book—as well as what we can do to make our books stronger.

Please note that I cannot help you with technical problems related to the topic of this book, and that due to the high volume of mail I receive, I might not be able to reply to every message.

When you write, please be sure to include this book's title and authors, as well as your name and phone or email address. I will carefully review your comments and share them with the authors and editors who worked on the book.

Email: feedback@samspublishing.com

Mail: Neil Rowe
           Executive Editor
           Sams Publishing
           800 East 96th Street
           Indianapolis, IN 46240 USA

Reader Services

Visit our website and register this book at informit.com/register for convenient access to any updates, downloads, or errata that might be available for this book.

Chapter 1

Introduction to Advanced Level Design

Welcome to advanced level design in Unreal Engine 3! Whether you've read our previous two volumes, created your own games and levels, or just played games built with Unreal Engine 3, you probably realize just how powerful this game engine can be. You've seen Unreal Engine 3 create vast worlds with lush environments that stagger the senses of your players. You already have some idea of the power the Unreal Editor gives to game artists.

Now, it's time to kick things up a notch. Heck, *more than a notch:* It's time to take Unreal Engine 3 to the limits, and make your gaming experiences even more stunningly believable.

If you want to shake your players to the very core, you're gonna have to master the heavy-duty stuff: particle systems, custom animations, physically reactive dynamic objects, advanced materials, and more. All that stuff's built into Unreal Engine 3—and we're going to show you how to use it. Not just a little: *to the fullest.*

1

Who Is This Book For?

A little housekeeping first. (Just a little.) As you've probably figured out by now, this isn't intended as a beginner's book.

Now, if you're a beginner or have only limited experience, let's be clear: We are *not* blowing you off. Quick learners should be able to follow along: just go slow, and take it a bit at a time. The tutorials are written in an easy-to-follow, step-by-step manner that should allow users of just about any experience level to participate—and we know, because we've been training Unreal developers for years.

But if you're already comfortable with the Unreal Editor, and you've done basic Unreal programming, you'll definitely be able to move faster.

What Should You Know Before You Start?

This book is intended to be used with the game *Unreal Tournament 3*.

Many of the basic concepts we teach you apply to other Unreal Engine 3–based games that provide access to the Unreal Editor. However, many of our tutorials rely on game assets that come with *Unreal Tournament 3*. What's more, other games sometimes change the engine and the editor, which could make them work differently—or at least confuse the heck out of you. We wouldn't want that!

As we've already said, we do some handholding throughout the tutorials, but you'll be better off if you're at least basically familiar with the Unreal Editor's key concepts and controls. Ideally, it'd be way cool if you've already explored:

- Navigating perspective and orthogonal viewports
- Creating additive environments using BSP brushes
- Navigating and creating assets within the Generic browser
- Loading and unloading asset packages within the Generic browser
- Placing objects into levels from the Generic and Actor Classes browsers
- Adjusting actor properties within the Actor Properties window
- Setting up basic Kismet sequences
- Creating basic materials with the Material Editor
- Simple keyframe animation using Matinee

Haven't done all that? As someone once said, *don't panic*. As we keep saying, you'll still be able to follow along, just more slowly. But you'll definitely have a smoother, faster learning experience if you're already familiar with Unreal Engine 3 and the Unreal Editor. To that end, you might want to check out the following training resources:

- ***Mastering Unreal Technology, Volume I: Introduction to Level Design with Unreal Engine 3***—The first volume in this series, this book gets you up-and-running with the Unreal Editor. It's specially designed for anyone just getting their feet wet with Unreal Engine 3 modding.

- ***Unreal Tournament 3: Collector's Edition***—The Collector's Edition version of *Unreal Tournament 3* includes a separate DVD that contains many hours of Unreal Editor training—including several videos geared specifically for beginners.

- **www.3dbuzz.com**—That's us! 3D Buzz, our company, delivers hours of professional-quality video training content covering Unreal Technology, programming, 3D graphics, and more! Get started right away by watching our Video Training Modules, or dig through our forums for tons of valuable information. And, since this site's staffed and run by this book's authors, it's a great way to get in touch with us. (Come, say hello—really!)

What We Mean By "Advanced" Level Design

The Unreal Editor brings together a vast toolset and immense power. Some of its tools are simple, straightforward, and haven't changed much over the years. Others have changed dramatically in Unreal Engine 3, offering far more power and flexibility than ever before. And some are brand-new to game editing: They bring elements of high-end film and special effects production into gaming for the first time.

In this book, we focus primarily on the tools that are either new or dramatically improved in Unreal Engine 3. But we also show you breakthrough techniques for making the most of commonly used tools like the Material Editor, so you can create more powerful assets than 99% of the people who are using it right now. (Hey, it's a competitive world. These days, average just won't cut it anymore!)

Included Assets and Game Assets

Beyond your sparkling personality, you need plenty of other assets to complete the tutorials in this book. Textures. Sounds. Images. Stuff like that.

Fortunately, you'll find many of those assets on the DVD we've bound into the back of the book. There's a folder for each chapter that requires these assets.

1

The other assets you need are installed with the *Unreal Tournament 3* game. You'll find them within packages (UPK files). After a default installation, you'll find those packages in the following installation folder:

C:\Program Files\UT3\UTGame\CookedPC

If you've installed to a different drive or folder, your path will start out differently, but once you drill down to the UT3 folder, everything underneath it should follow the same folder structure.

Within the CookedPC folder, you'll see several subfolders, each containing several packages. The subfolders you care about most are:

- **Environments**—Here are the assets used to build the levels that shipped with *Unreal Tournament 3*, such as static meshes, textures, and materials. These packages are organized into themes, which makes it easier to find the assets you need, based on what you're trying to create.

- **Characters**—Need a UT3 character for a cinematic sequence? They're here, and each type of character is itself divided into various packages.

- **Maps**—Need to change an existing map? Want to see how an effect was created in one of *Unreal Tournament 3's* built-in maps? Those maps are here.

- **Effects**—Here are the packages you need to create particle effects (explosions, fire, and so on), lens flares, vehicle and weapon effects, and other special effects.

> **NOTE**
>
> Keeping things simple for you isn't the only reason for Unreal's folder and package structure. There's an equally important reason: memory usage. When you load a package, its contents are all placed in memory. Since you don't have infinite memory, you don't want to load more packages than necessary. The folder and package structure helps you load only what you need right now. (How many packages is too many? That depends on your system's specs. But if you're noticing a slowdown or occasional instability, you just might have too many packages in memory. Unload a few!)

Working with INI Files

A few of our tutorials require you to alter an *Unreal Tournament 3* INI file in order to see the result in-game. When this happens, we tell you exactly which files to alter and how to do it.

These INI files can be found within your local Documents folder. If you've performed the default *Unreal Tournament 3* installation on a Windows system, that'll be here:

Documents\My Games\Unreal Tournament 3\UTGame\Config\

Unlike, say, Registry entries, INI file changes are dead simple to remove. Just delete your altered INI file. Next time you launch *Unreal Tournament 3* or the Unreal Editor, it'll create a new, replacement INI file using the default settings.

By the way, when you create a full modification for *Unreal Tournament 3*, players can include INI files that pertain only to their mod, so other gamers can view their creations.

Future Software Changes

Finally, if we had lawyers, they'd probably tell us to say this: We've done our best to make sure this book's tutorials and concepts are up to date and accurate at the time we wrote them. They reflect everything we know about writing accurate, reliable Unreal code. We've been darned careful. But we can't predict the future. (Find someone who can, and we'll hire them ASAP!) Bottom line: If someday, some patch or software update changes the way these tutorials behave, hey, that's out of our hands.

With that, let's say goodbye to the lawyers, and get down to work.

Chapter 2

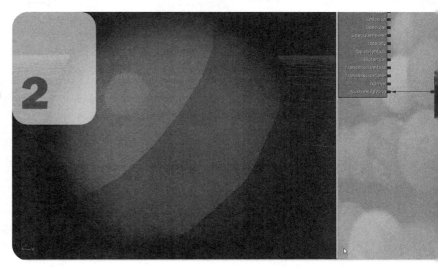

Advanced Material Construction

Over the next several tutorials, we explore some of the effects that can be achieved by creating more complex networks of expressions as well as creating customizable materials through the use of parameters. This is where the true power of the material system provided in Unreal Engine 3 begins to shine. Throughout this chapter, you create materials putting these effects and principles into practice. Many of the materials created use several of the methods mentioned to achieve the desired result.

Material Instancing and Parameters

Perhaps the most powerful aspect of Unreal Engine 3's material system is the ability to use parameters inside of materials that can be modified at runtime or used in conjunction with material instancing. Modifying parameters at runtime allows for controlling the appearance of a material or animating effects in response to in-game events. Material instancing can be used to create multiple different materials from a single template, thus saving a great deal of

2

time when many materials are required that have a similar underlying structure or purpose. This makes final adjustments for the artist extremely easy because material instances update according to any changes made in real time.

Material instancing is often used when several variations of a material are needed using different colors. Instead of creating multiple materials, one material is created using a parameter for the color and instanced. This technique is also used, although in a much more sophisticated manner, when dealing with materials for the characters in a game. One base material will be created that contains the node network that is to be used for all of (or at least the majority of) the characters in the game. Parameters are used for pertinent properties and textures so that values can be adjusted or textures swapped out on a per-instance (or per-character, as the case may be) basis. The use of instancing may go even deeper because a small number of base materials may be created for the entire game from which most other materials will be derived. This allows the game to keep a unified look and feel in addition to making material creation for numerous meshes much more efficient.

As mentioned previously, parameters can be used to allow materials to respond to in-game events. These parameters are dynamic, and modification to these parameters is done through Kismet, Matinee, or with code. Effects such as emissive areas of a material being ramped up or switched on, textures being swapped out, and controlling the panning or tiling of texture coordinates are all possible through the use of parameters.

Another type of parameter, the static parameter, is used only with material instancing because it provides no ability to be modified at runtime, hence the name *static*. These parameters, whose names are prefixed with "Static," allow modification within instances inside of UnrealEd, but are set in stone once play begins. These parameters—StaticComponentMaskParameter and StaticSwitchParameter—allow certain channels of a texture to be masked or make the masking of entire networks within a material possible. This technique is used in the fur shader constructed later in this chapter (see **FIGURE 2.1**).

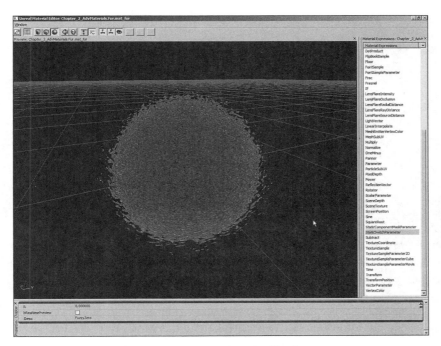

FIGURE 2.1   The fur shader we create later in this chapter

Blending

Through the use of the LinearInterpolate expressions or texture masks, materials can blend between different values, colors, or textures (see **FIGURE 2.2**). This effect could be used to apply a lower specular power value to the skin of a character, while applying a much higher value to the eyes of the character all within the same material. Another possibility would be to use the rendered-out (using a 3D application) vertex colors of a mesh as the Alpha input of a LinearInterpolate expression to re-create the material blending ability of terrains on a static mesh.

2

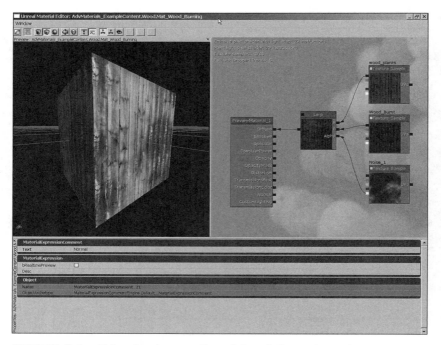

FIGURE 2.2   This network uses a linear interpolation system setup.

UV Manipulation

The material system allows the texture coordinates (or UVs) to be manipulated or modified in several ways, providing the ability to create a multitude of effects. Via Panner expressions, textures can be moved along one or both axes to create flowing rivers, pulsing waves of energy, or even a rolling counter display. Rotator expressions, not surprisingly, rotate the UVs and consequently the textures they are applied to. These expressions can be used to create effects such as the rotating blades of a helicopter, a large industrial fan, or the spinning hands of a clock. Another expression that modifies the texture coordinates is the BumpOffset expression. This expression is used to increase the appearance of depth on surfaces beyond that which a normal map provides by simulating the displacement of the pixels and actually causing the material or texture to occlude itself (see **FIGURE 2.3**). This is often used when creating materials for stone walls or walkways, but can also be used to create protruding slats of a vent or even effects such as fur.

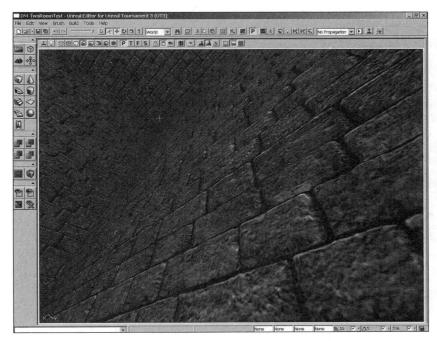

FIGURE 2.3 Bump offset allows for materials to occlude themselves.

Normals

Materials use normal maps to create the appearance of high-resolution geometry when applied to low-resolution meshes. The normals of meshes can also be used in conjunction with the Fresnel expression to create effects based on the orientation of the surface normals to the camera. This expression can be used to create a material that mimics the look of objects viewed with an electron microscope or the behavior of water that is mostly transparent when viewed straight on but becomes opaque when viewed at an angle, or the appearance of a glass ball that is less transparent around the edges (see **FIGURE 2.4**).

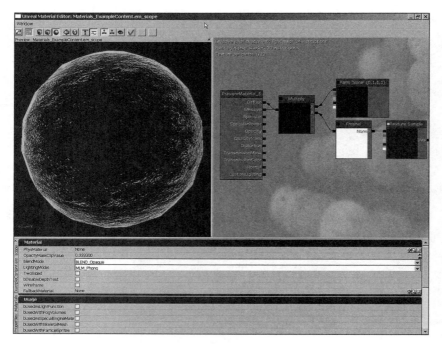

FIGURE 2.4   An example of an electron microscope shader

Depth

A few different types of depth can be used when creating depth-based effects in materials. First, there is the depth of the material itself from the viewpoint. This is accessible using the PixelDepth expression and is used to create effects based on the distance the object is applied to and the current camera (see **FIGURE 2.5**). This might include causing the object to become transparent as it gets farther from the camera and becomes too small to be seen (or even as it gets extremely close to the camera so as not to obstruct the player's view). Another type of depth is the distance from the material to the surface behind it. This is accessed through the use of the DestDepth expression and can be used to create pseudo-volumetric effects such as water becoming murkier where it is deeper. The last kind of depth is accessed through the SceneDepth expression and is used when creating material effects for post processes. This is discussed later in Chapter 8, "Post-Process Effects."

FIGURE 2.5   This hallway gets darker as it progresses due to depth effects.

Special Lighting

When you're forced to use unlit materials to create transparency, especially on dynamic objects, being able to give the material the appearance of being lit or adding specular highlights is often desirable. There are also times when character meshes need accent lighting in order to stand out during cinematic sequences. Knowledge of how lighting is calculated and the clever use of networks of expressions can allow these types of effects to be created. Some common game situations where these effects might be used include faking the lighting on the particles of mesh emitters because of the expense of calculating the dynamic lighting on a large number of meshes or adding specular highlights to an unlit transparent water material.

There are some limitations with these types of effects, however. For instance, you may recall that the LightVector expression provides the direction of the current light being calculated. This expression does not work when using the Unlit LightingModel, which makes it useless in cases such as this. This means that any light source used in the calculation must be added in the material's network of expressions using a vector expression. It also means that the direction of the light is either going to be constant or must use a parameter in order to be modified. Assuming these limitations are acceptable, these methods can be extremely useful in creating efficiently lit visuals.

2

Reflections

Whether they are real time or static, adding reflections to surfaces can provide a more realistic feel to the world you are creating (see **FIGURE 2.6**). Reflections are added using TextureSample expressions, just as regular textures are added into a material, but they require their texture coordinates to be set up in a specialized manner in order to appear correctly. Often, this requires using a ReflectionVector expression, which is then transformed to world space using a Transform expression and finally applied to the UVs of the reflection's TextureSample expression. For some effects, the ScreenPosition expression may be masked using a ComponentMask expression and then applied to the UVs of the TextureSample expression. The method used is dependent on the desired result, but many potential effects are at your disposal.

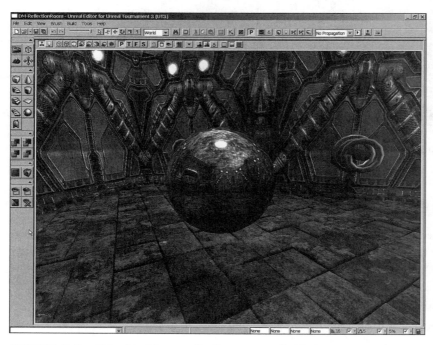

FIGURE 2.6   This object has a reflection map applied to it.

Distortion

The material system provides the ability, through the use of the Distortion channel, to distort the pixels behind the surface to which the material has been applied. This effect can be used to re-create refractive elements commonly seen in the real world, such as water and glass, as well as other effects such as heat distortion (see **FIGURE 2.7**). Creating these types of effects can be as simple as connecting a Constant expression to the Distortion channel of the material, but the use of textures, especially normal maps, can make for a much more visually pleasing result.

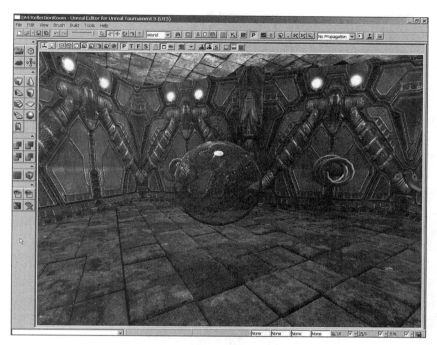

FIGURE 2.7   Distortion allows for the refractions that you see in this material.

Transparency

Simple transparency is often used when creating particles or materials for other see-through surfaces, but it can also be used in conjunction with more complex networks and specific expressions to create some interesting effects. The DepthBiasedAlpha expression can be used to make transparent surfaces blend with other surfaces they may intersect with, making for a smoother transition from one to the other. This is very beneficial when creating materials for particles because they almost invariably find a surface with which to intersect. It is also possible to create a holographic display or simulate very realistic volumetric lighting by using some clever math involving vectors.

Subsurface Scattering

Some surfaces, although not transparent, do allow some light to pass through, causing the surface to emit a soft glow when lit from behind. This effect is commonly known as *subsurface scattering* (see **FIGURE 2.8**). Although the calculations required to perform true subsurface scattering are too intensive for real-time applications, this effect can be approximated with the Transmission and TransmissionMask channels of the material. When you're creating realistic skin for characters, this can be the difference between a good material and a great material, especially if the character is to be used in cinematic sequences where lighting and camera angles can be controlled to really show off the effect. Typically, this involves connecting the character's skin texture to the TransmissionMask channel. It is also possible to create other materials, such as wax or plastic, that allow only some light to pass through.

FIGURE 2.8   Subsurface scattering is perfect for translucent objects such as wax.

Custom Lighting Models

One of the most powerful aspects of the material system in Unreal Engine 3 is the ability to create your own lighting model directly within the Material Editor. This gives you as the designer the ability to decide if the lighting model the engine uses, Phong, is satisfactory and replace it if not (see **FIGURE 2.9**). Using the expressions available with the material system, you can completely re-create other lighting models, such as Blinn or Lambert, or you can create other effects such as cel shading. To make this even more powerful, the use of parameters can be employed to easily use your custom lighting model throughout an entire map, mod, or game. The main expression making this possible is the LightVector expression. This gives you access to the current light being calculated against the surface. In conjunction with the CameraVector and ReflectionVector and through the use of the vector math expressions, DotProduct and CrossProduct, virtually any lighting model can be produced.

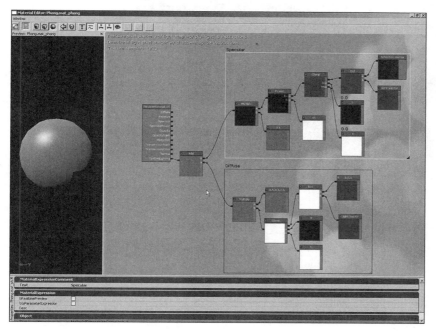

FIGURE 2.9   This network shows the re-creation of the default Phong lighting model.

Over the course of **TUTORIALS 2.1** through **2.5**, you construct a burnt wood planks material that is smoldering (see **FIGURE 2.10**). This requires the use of two separate blends—one for the diffuse texture and one for the normal map—between the texture for the regular wood and the texture for the burning wood.

NOTE

All expressions are named by setting their Desc properties and are referred to by those names throughout these tutorials. When dealing with naming parameter expressions, it is assumed that naming refers to setting both the ParameterName and Desc properties.

2

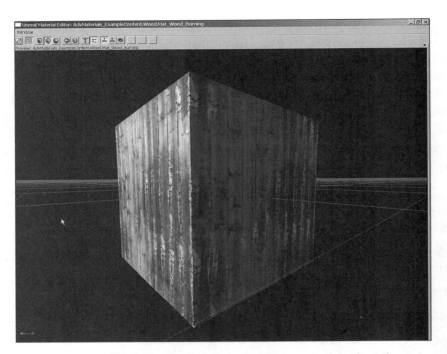

FIGURE 2.10   This is the result of the material we create throughout the next several tutorials.

TUTORIAL 2.1: Burning Wood Material, Part I: Diffuse Blend

1. Open the Generic Browser and right-click in the background. Choose New Material from the context menu, enter the following information in the dialog that appears, and then click OK:

    ▶ **Package**: Chapter_2_AdvMaterials

    ▶ **Group**: Wood

    ▶ **Name**: mat_smoldering_wood

2. Select the wood_planks texture from the Chapter_2_AdvMaterials package in the Generic Browser and press T while left-clicking in the Material Editor to place a TextureSample using the texture. Name this expression by entering **DiffuseTex** in the Desc property. The names entered in the Desc property will be how expressions are referred to throughout the tutorials.

3. Select the wood_burnt texture in the Chapter_2_AdvMaterials package and place a TextureSample using that texture. Position this expression directly below the previously created expression. Name this expression **DiffuseBurntTex**.

4. Select the noise_large texture from the Chapter_2_AdvMaterials package and place a TextureSample using that texture. Position this expression directly below the previously created expression. Name this expression **LerpTex** (see **FIGURE 2.11**).

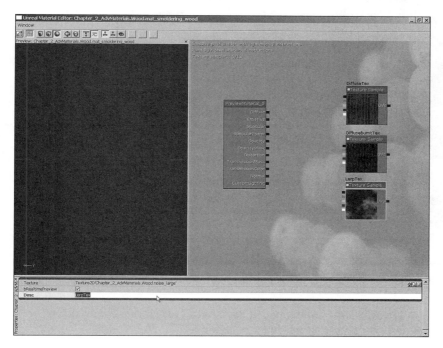

FIGURE 2.11 The new LerpTex has been created.

The alpha channel of this texture is used to blend between the regular wood texture and the burnt wood texture. The black areas cause the regular texture to be visible, whereas the white areas cause the burnt areas to be visible.

5. To the left of the TextureSample expressions, hold down L while left-clicking to place a Linear Interpolate (referred to as Lerp) expression. Name this expression **DiffuseLerp**. This expression will use the values of the LerpTex to perform the blend between the two diffuse textures.

6. Make the following connections (see **FIGURE 2.12**):

- ▶ DiffuseTex-RGB → DiffuseLerp-A
- ▶ DiffuseBurntTex-RGB → DiffuseLerp-B
- ▶ LerpTex-Alpha → DiffuseLerp-Alpha
- ▶ DiffuseLerp-Output → Material-Diffuse

2

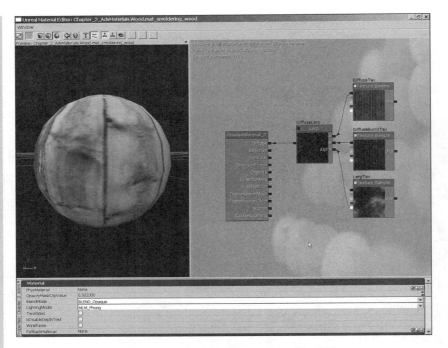

FIGURE 2.12   Your network should look something like this.

7. Click the Cube button ⬡ in the toolbar to use the cube preview mesh. The blending between the two textures should be visible in the preview.

8. Commit the changes to the material and save the package to preserve your work.

END TUTORIAL 2.1

Continuing from **TUTORIAL 2.1**, open the mat_smoldering_wood material in the Material Editor. If you have not completed it, you may use the mat_smoldering_wood_01 material provided in the Chapter_2_AdvMaterials package. In **TUTORIAL 2.2**, you create the network that blends between the normal map for the regular wood and the normal map for the burnt wood.

TUTORIAL 2.2: Burning Wood Material, Part II: Normal Blend

1. Select the wood_planks_normal texture in the Chapter_2_AdvMaterials package and place a TextureSample using the texture. Position this expression below those from **TUTORIAL 2.1**. Name this expression **NormalTex**.

2. Select the wood_burnt_normal texture in the Chapter_2_AdvMaterials package and place a TextureSample using the texture. Position this expression below the previously created expression. Name this expression **NormalBurntTex** (see **FIGURE 2.13**).

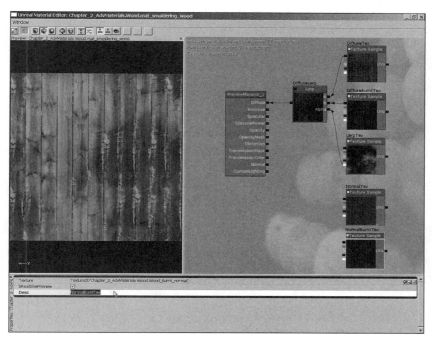

FIGURE 2.13   This second normal map is used for the burnt wood.

3. To the left of the new TextureSample expressions, place a new LinearInterpolate expression. Name this expression **NormalLerp**. Just as in **TUTORIAL 2.1**, this expression uses the values of the LerpTex to perform the blend, only this time between the two normal map textures.

4. Make the following connections (see **FIGURE 2.14**):

  ▶ NormalTex-RGB → NormalLerp-A

  ▶ NormalBurntTex-RGB → NormalLerp-B

  ▶ LerpTex-Alpha → NormalLerp-Alpha

  ▶ NormalLerp-Output → Material-Normal

The effects of the normal maps should now be visible in the preview.

5. Commit the changes to the material and save the package to preserve your work.

2

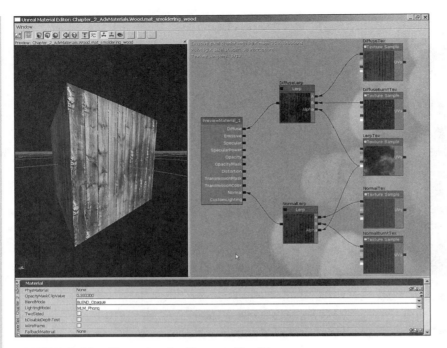

FIGURE 2.14   Your network will appear like this.

END TUTORIAL 2.2

Continuing from **TUTORIAL 2.2**, open the mat_smoldering_wood material in the Material Editor. If you have not completed it, you may use the mat_smoldering_wood_02 material provided in the Chapter_2_AdvMaterials package. In **TUTORIAL 2.3**, you set up the specularity of the material.

TUTORIAL 2.3: Burning Wood Material, Part III: Specularity

1. Hold down the 1 key and left-click to place a Constant expression. Set the value to 2.5, name it **SpecPower**, and connect its output to the material's SpecularPower channel.

2. Place another Constant expression. Set its value to 0.75 and name the expression **SpecConst**. This expression is simply used as a way of adjusting the amount of specularity for the material (see **FIGURE 2.15**).

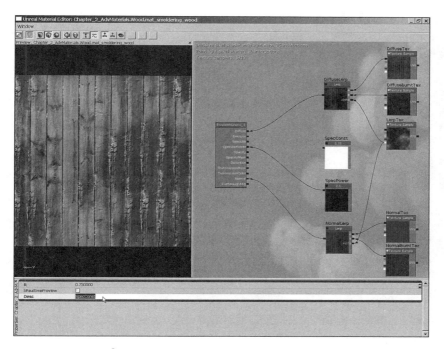

FIGURE 2.15   Create a second constant.

3. To the left of the SpecConst expression, place a Multiply expression by holding down M and left-clicking. Name this expression **SpecMult1** (see **FIGURE 2.16**).

4. Connect the Alpha output of the DiffuseTex to the A input of SpecMult1. Then, connect the output of SpecConst to the B input of SpecMult1. The alpha channel of the DiffuseTex texture holds the specularity data for the material. Multiplying it by a Constant expression allows the values of the alpha channel to be adjusted if necessary (see **FIGURE 2.17**).

5. Just above the SpecMult1, place a OneMinus expression by holding down O and left-clicking. Name this expression **SpecMinus**. Then, connect the Alpha of the LerpTex node to the input of SpecMinus.

This reverses the colors of the LerpTex, allowing it to be used as a mask for the specular amount and allowing the specular highlight to only be visible on the nonburnt areas of the material. This reversal of the color is necessary because, as was mentioned in **TUTORIAL 2.1**, the white area of the texture is associated with the burnt area of the material. Using the texture without reversing the color would cause the specular highlight to only be visible in those areas.

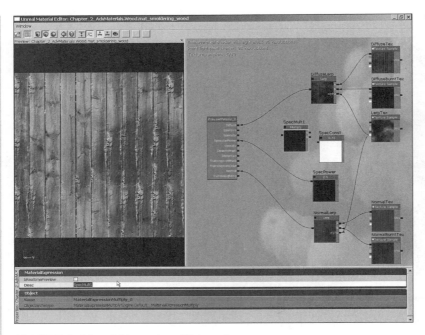

FIGURE 2.16   Add a new multiply node.

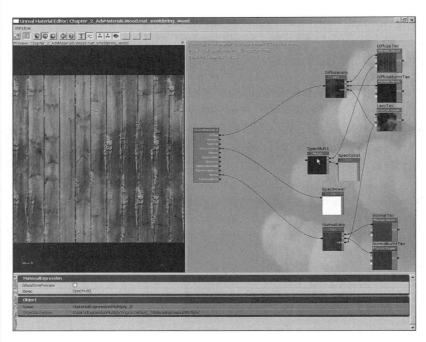

FIGURE 2.17   Connect the nodes as shown.

6. To the left of the SpecMinus, place a Multiply expression and name the expression **SpecMult2** (see **FIGURE 2.18**).

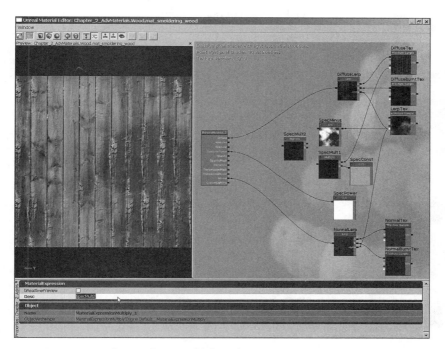

FIGURE 2.18   Create a new multiply node.

7. Connect the output of SpecMinus to the A input of SpecMult2. Then, connect the output of SpecMult1 to the B input of SpecMult2.

8. Connect the output of SpecMult2 to the Specular channel of the material.

9. Commit the changes to the material and save the package to preserve your progress.

END TUTORIAL 2.3

Continuing from **TUTORIAL 2.3**, open the mat_smoldering_wood material in the Material Editor. If you have not completed it, you may use the mat_smoldering_wood_03 material provided in the Chapter_2_AdvMaterials package. In **TUTORIAL 2.4**, you create the part of the network that is responsible for creating the noise of the smoldering embers.

TUTORIAL 2.4: Burning Wood Material, Part IV: Noise

1. Place a TextureCoordinate expression by dragging it from the Material Expressions panel or select it from the context menu. Name the expression **TexCoord** (see **FIGURE 2.19**). This expression provides a method of adjusting the size of the noise of the glowing embers.

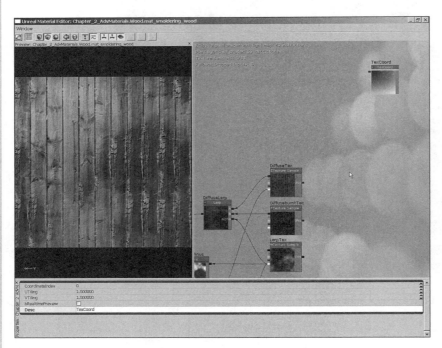

FIGURE 2.19   Create a new Texture Coordinate node.

2. Create a Panner expression by holding down the P key and left-clicking. Name the expression **Panner1**.

3. Duplicate Panner1 three times to make a total of four Panner expressions. Name the new expressions **Panner2**, **Panner3**, and **Panner4**. Position them in a column to the left of the TexCoord expression (see **FIGURE 2.20**).

4. Set the following values for the Panner expressions:

   ▶ Panner1

      ▶ **SpeedX**: 0.09

      ▶ **SpeedY**: 0.05

▶ Panner2

  ▶ **SpeedX**: −0.075

  ▶ **SpeedY**: 0.05

▶ Panner3

  ▶ **SpeedX**: −0.09

  ▶ **SpeedY**: −0.04

▶ Panner4

  ▶ **SpeedX**: 0.1

  ▶ **SpeedY**: −0.08

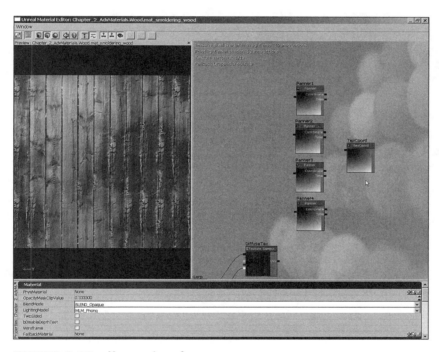

FIGURE 2.20   You now have four panners.

5. Make the following connections (see **FIGURE 2.21**):

  ▶ TexCoord-Output → Panner1-Coordinate

  ▶ TexCoord-Output → Panner2-Coordinate

  ▶ TexCoord-Output → Panner3-Coordinate

  ▶ TexCoord-Output → Panner4-Coordinate

2

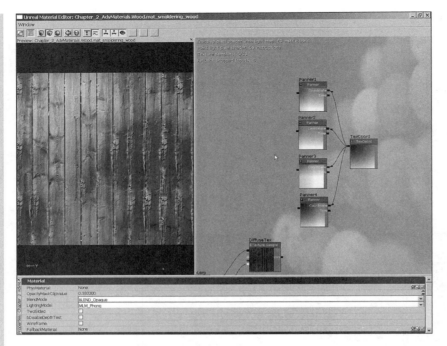

FIGURE 2.21   Connect the Panners like so.

6. Create a new TextureSample using the noise_large texture. Name the expression **NoiseTex1**.

7. Duplicate the TextureSample expression three times for a total of four TextureSample expressions. Name the new expressions **NoiseTex2**, **NoiseTex3**, and **NoiseTex4**. Position them in a column to the left of the Panner expressions (see **FIGURE 2.22**).

8. Assign the noise_small texture to the NoiseTex2 and NoiseTex3 expressions.

9. Make the following connections (see **FIGURE 2.23**):

  ▶ Panner1-Output → NoiseTex1-UVs

  ▶ Panner2-Output → NoiseTex2-UVs

  ▶ Panner3-Output → NoiseTex3-UVs

  ▶ Panner4-Output → NoiseTex4-UVs

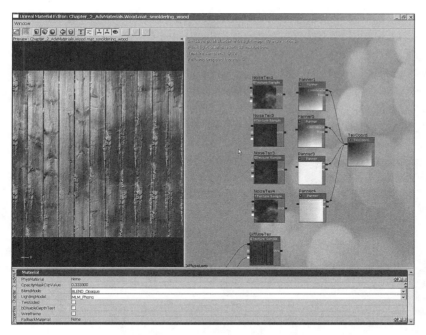

FIGURE 2.22   You should now have four texture samples.

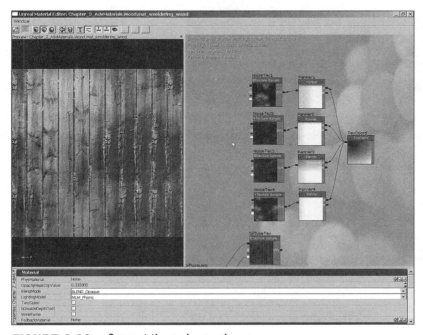

FIGURE 2.23   Connect the nodes as shown.

2

Panning the noise textures causes the glow of the burning embers to have some movement to it. Using four separate textures moving in different directions allows the movement to appear random.

10. Create an Add expression to the left of the NoiseTex1 and NoiseTex2 expressions by holding down the A key and left-clicking. Name the expression **NoiseAdd1**.

11. Create another Add expression to the left of the NoiseTex3 and NoiseTex4 expressions. Name the expression **NoiseAdd2** (see **FIGURE 2.24**).

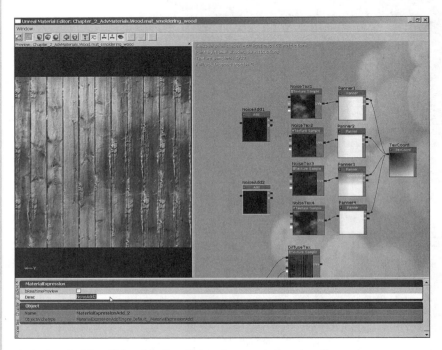

FIGURE 2.24   This adds the other noise expressions together.

12. Make the following connections (see **FIGURE 2.25**):

- ▶ NoiseTex1-RGB → NoiseAdd1-A

- ▶ NoiseTex2-RGB → NoiseAdd1-B

- ▶ NoiseTex3-RGB → NoiseAdd2-A

- ▶ NoiseTex4-RGB → NoiseAdd2-B

In order to create a random wave-like appearance, we first add each set of panning textures to build up the values. Over the next few steps, the results of those two additions will be multiplied, thus lowering the values and producing a much more random appearance.

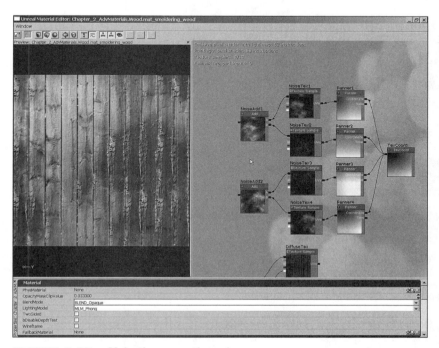

FIGURE 2.25   Make the connections shown.

13. Create a new Multiply expression to the left of the NoiseAdd1 and NoiseAdd2 expressions. Name the expression **NoiseMult1**.

14. Create another Multiply expression to the left of the NoiseMult1 expression. Name the expression **NoiseMult2** (see **FIGURE 2.26**).

15. Create a new Constant expression below the NoiseMult1 expression. Name the expression **NoiseConst** and set its value to 0.5 (see **FIGURE 2.27**).

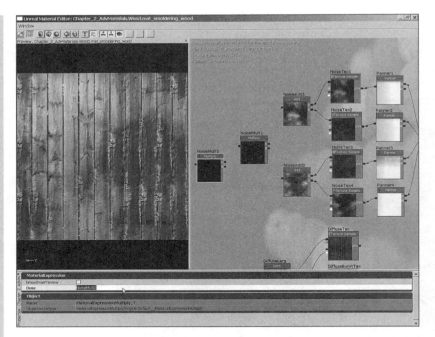

FIGURE 2.26   Create a second Multiply.

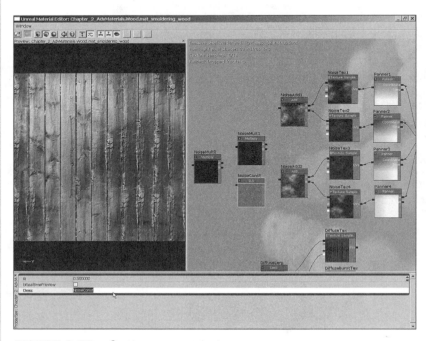

FIGURE 2.27   Create a new constant.

16. Make the following connections (see **FIGURE 2.28**):

   ▸ NoiseAdd1-Output → NoiseMult1-A

   ▸ NoiseAdd2-Output → NoiseMult1-B

   ▸ NoiseMult1-Output → NoiseMult2-A

   ▸ NoiseConst-Output → NoiseMult2-B

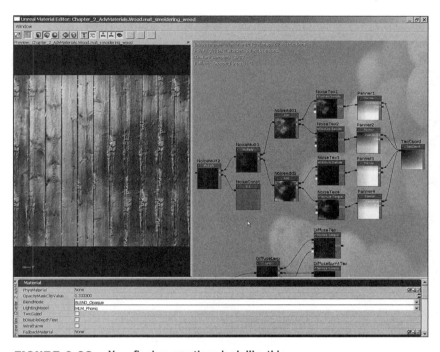

FIGURE 2.28   **Your final connections look like this.**

17. Commit the changes to the material and save the package to preserve your work.

END TUTORIAL 2.4

Continuing from **TUTORIAL 2.4**, open the mat_smoldering_wood material in the Material Editor. If you have not completed it, you may use the mat_smoldering_wood_04 material provided in the Chapter_2_AdvMaterials package. In **TUTORIAL 2.5**, you create the remainder of the network that produces the smoldering embers effect.

2

TUTORIAL 2.5: Burning Wood Material, Part V: Burning Embers

1. Create a Constant3 expression above the NoiseMult2 expression by holding down the 3 key and left-clicking. Name the expression **EmberColor**. Set these values:

   ▸ **R**: 4.0

   ▸ **G**: 1.0

   ▸ **B**: 0.5

   This expression controls the color of the burning embers of the wood material (see **FIGURE 2.29**).

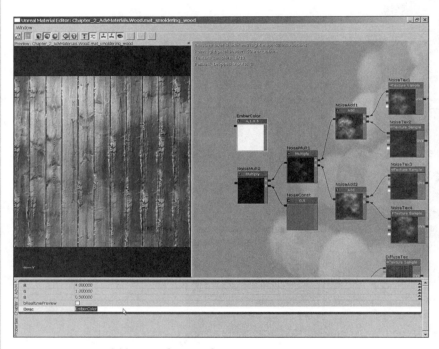

FIGURE 2.29   Add a new Constant3 vector.

2. Create a new Multiply node to the left of the NoiseNult2 and EmberColor expressions. Name the expression **EmberMult1**.

3. Make the following connections (see **FIGURE 2.30**):

   ▸ EmberColor-Output → EmberMult1-A

   ▸ NoiseMult2-Output → EmberMult1-B

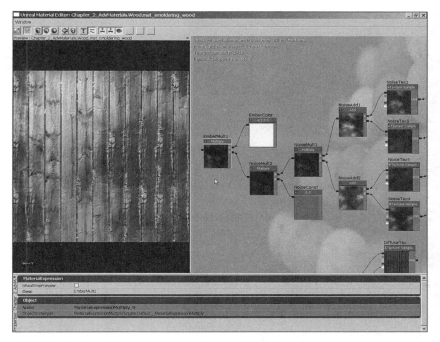

FIGURE 2.30   Create and connect a new Multiply node.

Multiplying the color by the result of the noise network masks the color to only the parts of the material where the noise is located.

4. Create a new TextureSample expression using the noise_large texture above the EmberMult1 expression. Name the expression **EmberMask1** (see **FIGURE 2.31**).

5. Create a new Multiply expression to the left of the EmberMask1 and EmberMult1 expressions. Name the expression **EmberMult2**.

6. Make the following connections (see **FIGURE 2.32**):

   ▸ EmberMask1-Alpha → EmberMult2-A

   ▸ EmberMult1-Output → EmberMult2-B

This multiplication effectively masks the color even further so that it only appears in the areas of the material where the burnt diffuse texture is visible.

7. Create a new TextureSample using the wood_burnt texture above the EmberMult2 expression. Name the expression **EmberMask2**.

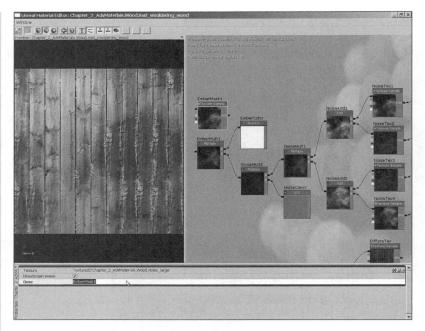

FIGURE 2.31   Create a new TextureSample.

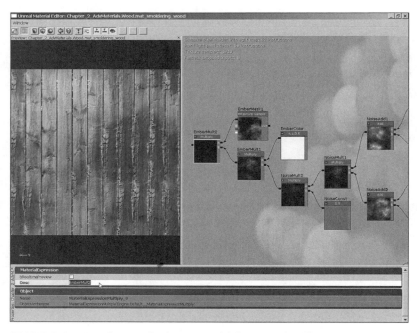

FIGURE 2.32   Connect in the new multiply expression like so.

8. Create a new Multiply expression to the left of the EmberMask1 and EmberMult2 expressions. Name the expression **EmberMult3** (see **FIGURE 2.33**).

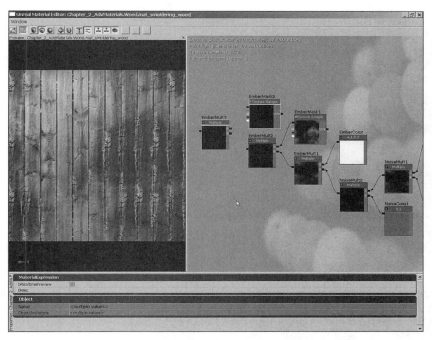

FIGURE 2.33   A new TextureSample and Multiply have been added.

9. Make the following connections:

- ▸ EmberMask2-RGB → EmberMult3-A
- ▸ EmberMult2-Output → EmberMult3-B
- ▸ EmberMult3-Output → Material-Emissive

The color is masked yet again to only be visible in the white portion of the burnt diffuse texture and connected to the material's Emissive channel (see **FIGURE 2.34**).

10. In the toolbar, make sure the ToggleRealtime Material Viewport button ⬛ is toggled on. You should see the completed material with the glowing area of the burning parts moving because of the noise (see **FIGURE 2.35**).

11. Commit the changes to the material and save the package to preserve your work. If you'd like the embers to glow more brightly, increase the value of the NoiseConst constant expression.

2

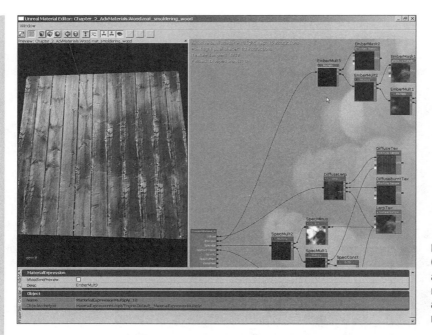

FIGURE 2.34
Connect the nodes as shown. Note that nodes were moved around to accommodate readability.

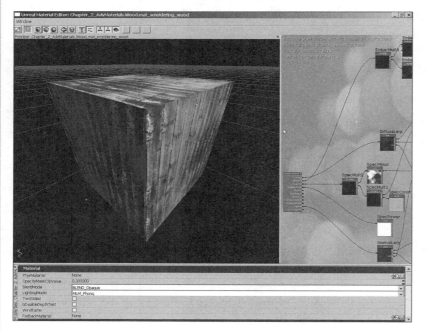

FIGURE 2.35
The final material.

END TUTORIAL 2.5

In **TUTORIALS 2.6** through **2.9**, you are shown how to use the TransmissionMask and TransmissionColor channels of the material to create a wax material that simulates subsurface scattering as well as how to use the CustomLighting channel to re-create this effect.

> **NOTE**
>
> All expressions are named by setting their Desc properties and are referred to by those names throughout these tutorials. When dealing with naming parameter expressions, it is assumed that naming refers to setting both the ParameterName and Desc properties.

TUTORIAL 2.6: Candle Wax Material, Part I: Standard Lighting Version

1. Right-click in the Generic Browser and choose New Material. Enter the following information in the dialog that appears and then click OK.

   - **Package**: Chapter_2_AdvMaterials
   - **Group**: Wax
   - **Name**: mat_candle_wax

2. Create a Constant3 expression by holding down the 3 key and left-clicking. Name the expression **WaxColor** and set the following values:

   - **R**: 0.9125
   - **G**: 0.8
   - **B**: 0.475

3. Connect the Output of the WaxColor expression to the Diffuse channel of the material node (see **FIGURE 2.36**).

4. Below the Wax Color expression, create a Constant expression by holding down the 1 key and left-clicking. Name the expression **WaxSpecAmount** and set its value to 0.125.

5. Connect the Output of the WaxSpecAmount expression to the Specular channel of the material node (see **FIGURE 2.37**).

6. Below the WaxSpecAmount expression, create another Constant expression. Name the expression **WaxSpecPower** and set its value to 20.0.

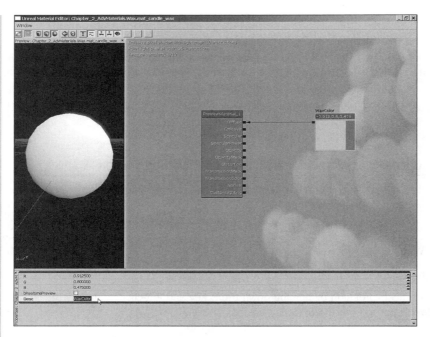

FIGURE 2.36   Start with a new Constant3 connected to the Diffuse channel.

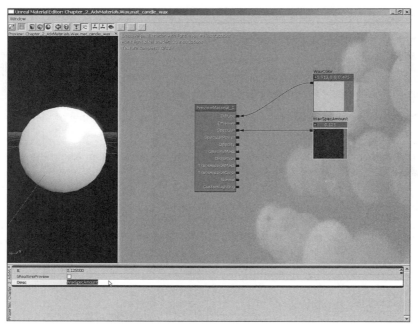

FIGURE 2.37   Add and connect a new Constant expression.

7. Connect the Output of the WaxSpecPower expression to the SpecularPower channel of the material node (see **FIGURE 2.38**).

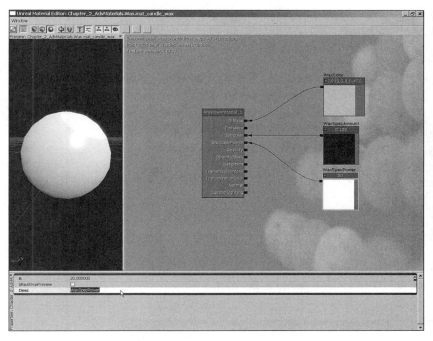

FIGURE 2.38 This new Constant controls the specular power.

8. Below the WaxSpecPower expression, create a Constant expression. Name the expression **WaxTransAmount** and set its value to 0.625.

9. Connect the Output of the WaxTransAmount expression to the TransmissionMask channel of the material node (see **FIGURE 2.39**).

10. Below the WaxTransAmount expression, create another Constant3 expression. Name the expression **WaxTransColor** and set the following values:

▶ **R**: 0.725

▶ **G**: 0.425

▶ **B**: 0.025

11. Connect the Output of the WaxTransColor expression to the TransmissionColor channel of the material node (see **FIGURE 2.40**).

12. Commit the changes to the material and save the package to preserve your work.

2

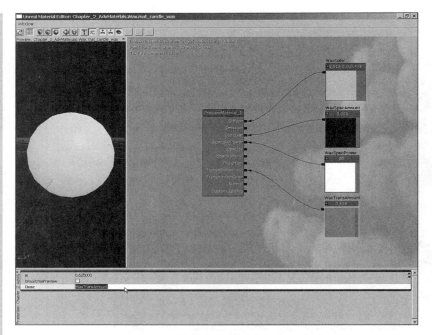

FIGURE 2.39   You are now driving the Transmission Mask.

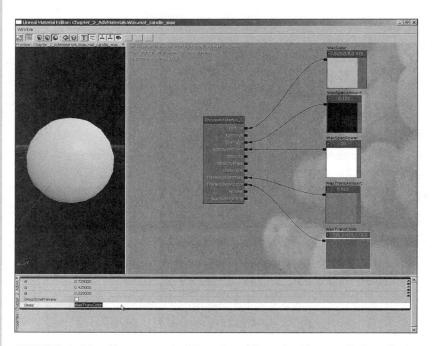

FIGURE 2.40   You now control the color of the subsurface scattering effect.

13. Open the advanced_materials_candle map and apply the material to the candle mesh in the map. You should see the candle appear to be glowing toward the top and fade out as it approaches the bottom. This is because the light hitting the top of the candle is being passed on to the unlit portions based on the values passed to the TransmissionMask and TransmissionColor channels.

END TUTORIAL 2.6

In **TUTORIAL 2.7**, you re-create the effects of using the TransmissionMask and TransmissionColor channels of the material using the CustomLighting channel and MLM_Custom lighting model. This serves to give you a greater understanding of what is going on behind the scenes. Note that this is not necessarily an exact reproduction of the calculations of the standard material channels but rather a way to create the same effect.

TUTORIAL 2.7: Candle Wax Material, Part II: Custom Diffuse Lighting

1. Right-click the mat_candle_wax material in the Generic Browser and choose Duplicate. If you have not completed **TUTORIAL 2.6**, you may duplicate the mat_candle_wax_Finish material instead. Enter the following information in the dialog that appears and click OK:

  ▸ **Package**: Chapter_2_AdvMaterials

  ▸ **Group**: Wax

  ▸ **Name**: mat_candle_wax_custom

2. Double-click the new material to open it in the Material Editor and break all the links from the expressions to the material node's channels (see **FIGURE 2.41**).

  We begin by setting up the basic network needed to calculate lighting. The first step is to determine where the light is hitting and where it isn't. To do this, the dot product of the light's direction vector and the surface's normal needs to be calculated.

3. Off to the right of the existing expressions, create a LightVector expression by dragging it from the Material Expressions list or selecting it from the context menu. Name the expression **LightVector**.

4. Below the LightVector expression, create a Constant3 expression by holding down the 3 key and left-clicking. Name the expression **NormalVector** and set the following values (see **FIGURE 2.42**):

  ▸ **R**: 0.0

  ▸ **G**: 0.0

  ▸ **B**: 1.0

  The vector (0,0,1) is being used in place of a normal map here for simplicity. This causes the mesh's normals to be used in the calculation. If a normal map is desired, a TextureSample expression would be used here instead.

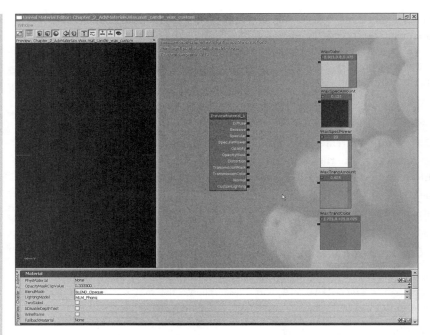

FIGURE 2.41 Disconnect all existing links.

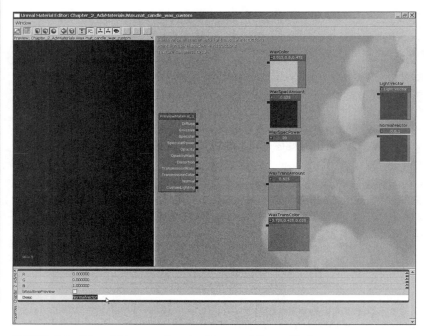

FIGURE 2.42 Add a new Constant3 named NormalVector.

5. To the left of the LightVector and NormalVector expressions, create a DotProduct expression. Name the expression **DiffuseDotProduct**.

6. Connect the Output of the LightVector expression to the A input of the DiffuseDotProduct expression. Then, connect the Output of the NormalVector expression to the B input of the DiffuseDotProduct expression (see **FIGURE 2.43**).

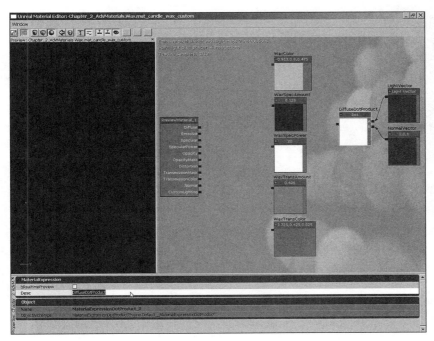

FIGURE 2.43   Connect the LightVector and NormalVector into the DiffuseDotProduct.

This calculation produces a value of 1.0, where the current light being calculated is hitting the surface dead on, and interpolates to a value of 0.0 where the light is hitting the surface perpendicularly.

To keep any values outside the range of 0.0 to 1.0 from being used in this calculation, we will now clamp the output of this calculation to that range.

7. Below the DiffuseDotProduct expression, create a Constant expression. Name the expression **DiffuseClampConst0** and leave it set to a value of 0.0.

8. Duplicate the DiffuseClampConst0 expression and position the new expression below the original. Name the new expression DiffuseClampConst1 and set its value to 1.0 (see **FIGURE 2.44**).

9. To the left of the DiffuseDotProduct expression, create a Clamp expression. Name the expression **DiffuseClamp**.

2

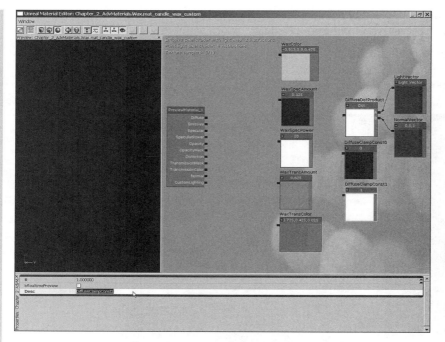

FIGURE 2.44 You now have two constants to use as a clamp.

10. Make the following connections:

- ▶ DiffuseDotProduct-Output → Clamp-Input(unlabeled)

- ▶ DiffuseClampConst0-Output → Clamp-Min

- ▶ DiffuseClampConst1-Output → Clamp-Max

At this point, the result of this calculation can be multiplied by the diffuse color to produce the basic lighting of the Lambert lighting model.

11. Move the WaxColor expression above and slightly to the left of the DiffuseClamp expression.

12. To the left of the WaxColor and DiffuseClamp expressions, create a Multiply expression. Name this expression **DiffuseMult**.

13. Make the following connections (see **FIGURE 2.45**):

- ▶ WaxColor-Output → DiffuseMult-A

- ▶ DiffuseClamp-Output → DiffuseMult-B

- ▶ DiffuseMult-Output → Material-CustomLighting

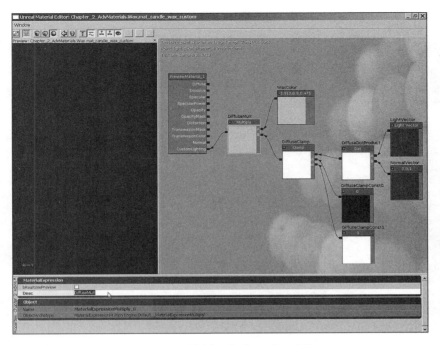

FIGURE 2.45   You are now multiplying in the color of the wax.

14. Select the material node and set the LightingModel property to MLM_Custom. The material in the preview should now appear to be lit using the diffuse color. It is still missing the specular highlights of the standard lighting model, though. We add these in **TUTORIAL 2.8**. Commit the changes to the material and save the package to preserve your work.

END TUTORIAL 2.7

Specularity uses the same basic principle employed in **TUTORIAL 2.7** to create the diffuse lighting, but it uses the reflection vector (or the direction of the camera reflected across the surface's normals) in the dot product with the light's direction vector.

TUTORIAL 2.8: Candle Wax Material, Part III: Custom Specular Highlights

1. Open the mat_candle_wax_custom material in the Material Editor. If you have not completed **TUTORIAL 2.7**, you may open the mat_candle_wax_custom_01 material instead.

2. Select the DiffuseDotProduct, DiffuseClampConst0, DiffuseClampConst1, and DiffuseClamp expressions and duplicate them by pressing Ctrl+C and Ctrl+V. Move the new set of expressions above the originals and replace any occurrences of "Diffuse" in the names of the new expressions with "Spec" (see **FIGURE 2.46**).

2

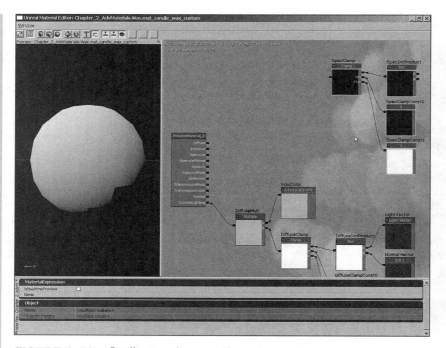

FIGURE 2.46   Duplicate and rename the nodes as shown.

3. To the right of the SpecDotProduct expression, create a ReflectionVector expression. Name the expression **ReflectVector**.

4. Connect the Output of the ReflectVector expression to the A input of the SpecDotProduct expression. Then, connect the Output of the LightVector expression to the B input of the SpecDotProduct expression (see **FIGURE 2.47**).

Essentially, this calculation will output a value of 1.0 when light reflects off the surface of the mesh and hits the camera dead on, and interpolates to a value of 0.0 as that reflection of light gets farther from the camera.

5. Position the WaxSpecPower expression below the SpecClamp expression.

6. To the left of the SpecClamp expression, create a Power expression. Name the expression **SpecPowerMult**.

7. Connect the Output of the SpecClamp expression to the Base input of the SpecPowerMult expression. Then, connect the Output of the WaxSpecPower expression to the Exp input of the SpecPowerMult expression (see **FIGURE 2.48**).

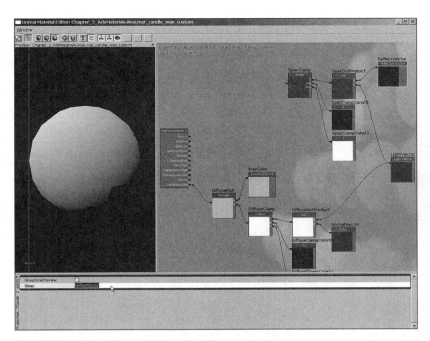

FIGURE 2.47   Connect the nodes like so.

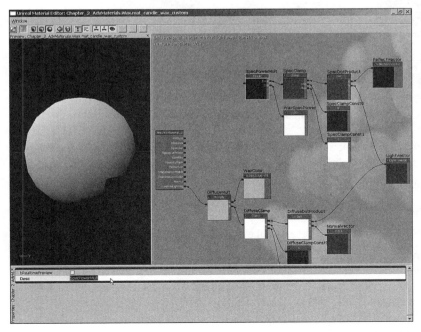

FIGURE 2.48   You now raise the value of SpecClamp by the power of the WaxSpecPower value.

8. Position the WaxSpecAmount expression below the SpecPowerMult expression.

9. To the left of the SpecPowerMult expression, create a Multiply expression. Name the expression **SpecMult**.

10. Connect the Output of the SpecPowerMult expression to the A input of the SpecMult expression. Then, connect the Output of the WaxSpecAmount expression to the B input of the SpecMult expression (see **FIGURE 2.49**).

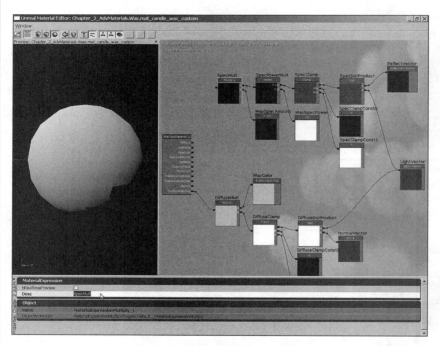

FIGURE 2.49   You now multiply the SpecPowerMult by the WaxSpecAmount.

11. To the left of the DiffuseMult and SpecMult expressions, create an Add expression. Name the expression **DiffuseAdd**. Then, make the following connections (see **FIGURE 2.50**):

  ▶ SpecMult-Output → DiffuseAdd-A

  ▶ DiffuseMult-Output → DiffuseAdd-B

  ▶ DiffuseAdd-Output → Material-CustomLighting

12. There should now be a specular highlight on the material in the preview, just as with the standard lighting model. The only thing left to create is the network that re-creates the Transmission effect. Commit the changes to the material and save the package to preserve your progress.

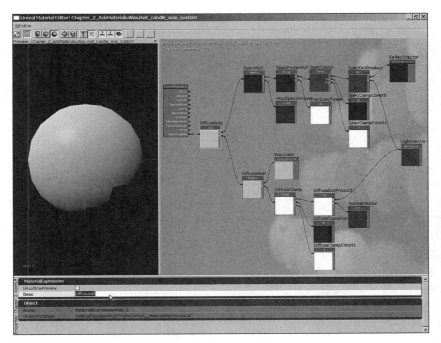

FIGURE 2.50 Make the shown connections.

END TUTORIAL 2.8

In order to create a transmission effect, you need to understand what it does on a fundamental level. Transmission takes the light that strikes the surface on one side of the mesh and transfers it to the other side. This means we can take the opposite of the diffuse lighting calculation we created earlier and we should get lighting on the opposite side of the mesh to where the light is actually striking, which is exactly what we want.

TUTORIAL 2.9: Candle Wax Material, Part IV: Custom Transmission

1. Open the mat_candle_wax_custom material in the Material Editor. If you have not completed **TUTORIAL 2.8**, you may open the mat_candle_wax_custom_02 material instead.

2. To the left of the DiffuseClamp expression, create a OneMinus expression. Name the expression **TransmissionOneMinus**.

3. Connect the Output of the DiffuseClamp expression to the input of the TransmissionOneMinus expression (see **FIGURE 2.51**).

2

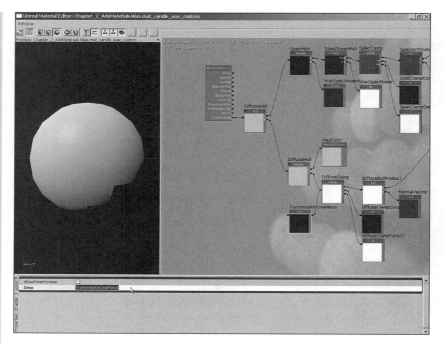

FIGURE 2.51   Connect DiffuseClamp to TransmissionOneMinus.

4. Slight adjustments will need to be made to the transmission color and amount values in order to attain an exact reproduction of the standard material. Select the WaxTransAmount expression and set its value to 0.2. Then, select the WaxTransColor expression and set the following values:

  ▶ **R**: 0.6875

  ▶ **G**: 0.17

  ▶ **B**: 0.0

5. To the left of the WaxTransAmount and WaxTransColor expression, create a Multiply expression. Name the expression **TransmissionMult1**.

6. Connect the Output of the WaxTransAmount expression to the A input of the TransmissionMult1 expression. Then, connect the Output of the WaxTransColor expression to the B input of the TransmissionMult1 expression (see **FIGURE 2.52**).

7. To the left of the TransmissionMult1 expression, create a new Multiply expression. Name the expression TransmissionMult2.

8. Connect the Output of the TransmissionMult1 expression to the A input of the TransmissionMult2 expression. Then, connect the Output of the TransmissionOneMinus expression to the B input of the TransmissionMult2 expression (see **FIGURE 2.53**).

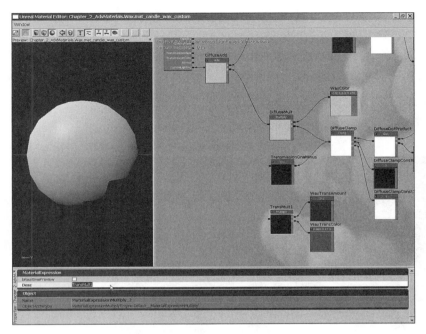

FIGURE 2.52 Connect the new nodes together.

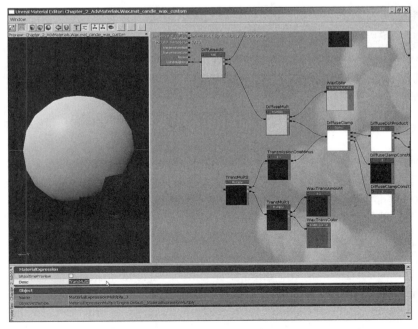

FIGURE 2.53 This multiplies the first transmission multiplier by OneMinus.

9. To the left of the DiffuseAdd and TransmissionMult2 expressions, create a new Add expression. Name the expression **FinalAdd**.

10. Make the following connections (see **FIGURE 2.54**):

   ▸ DiffuseAdd-Output → FinalAdd-A

   ▸ TransmissionMult2-Output → FinalAdd-B

   ▸ FinalAdd-Output → Material-CustomLighting

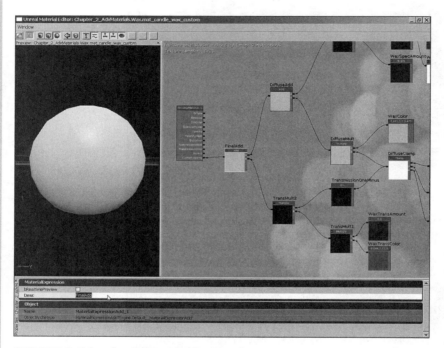

FIGURE 2.54   Create these final connections.

11. Commit the changes to the material and save the package to preserve your work.

12. Apply the new material to the candle mesh in the advanced_materials_candle map. The appearance should not seem to change, or at most very slightly. However, you now have a much greater level of control over how lighting affects the surface.

END TUTORIAL 2.9

TUTORIALS 2.10 through **2.19** walk you through creating a base fur material as well as instancing the base material to create two entirely different results. Typically, a fur material would employ the use of the BumpOffset expression to create the basic fur effect. In order to make the fur more customizable, the math behind the BumpOffset is used to create a network that performs the same function, but allows for parameters to be used in place of the properties of the BumpOffset expression. Similarly, we create a network, again using parameters, that performs the same function as the Fresnel expression to further enhance the material by adding the ability to create highlights around the edges. You begin by setting up the diffuse texture, normal map, and specular expressions for the material.

> **NOTE**
>
> All expressions are named by setting their Desc properties and are referred to by those names throughout these tutorials. When dealing with naming parameter expressions, it is assumed that naming refers to setting both the ParameterName and Desc properties.

TUTORIAL 2.10: Fur Material, Part I: Basic Setup

1. Open the Generic Browser and right-click the background. Choose New Material, enter the following information in the dialog that appears, and then click OK:

   ▶ **Package**: Chapter_2_AdvMaterials

   ▶ **Group**: Fur

   ▶ **Name**: mat_fur

2. Select the fur_height texture in the Chapter_2_AdvMaterials package and create a TextureSampleParameter2D by dragging it from the Material Expression List or selecting it from the context menu. Enter **DiffuseTex_Base** in the ParameterName and Desc properties of this expression.

3. Connect the RGB output of the DiffuseTex_Base expression to the Diffuse channel of the material (see **FIGURE 2.55**).

4. Select the fur_normal texture in the Chapter_2_AdvMaterials package and create a TextureSampleParameter2D expression using it. Name the expression **NormalTex_Base**.

5. Connect the RGB output of the NormalTex_Base expression to the Normal channel of the material (see **FIGURE 2.56**).

6. Create a ScalarParameter expression. Name the expression **Specular** and set its DefaultValue to 1.5.

7. Create a new Multiply expression by holding down the M key and left-clicking to the left of the Specular expression. Name the expression **SpecMult**.

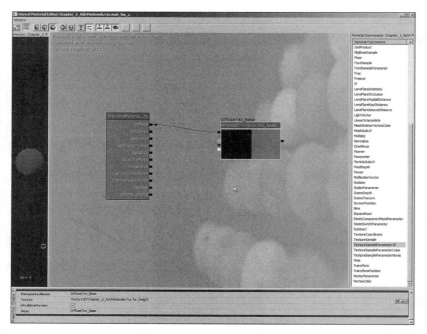

FIGURE 2.55   Create and connect TextureSampleParameter2D for the DiffuseTex_Base texture.

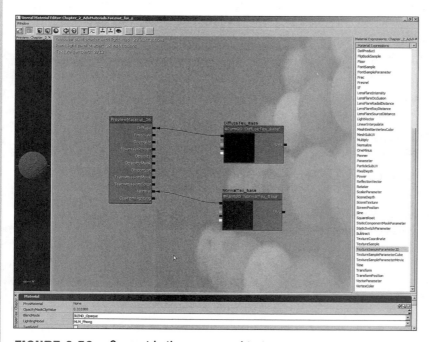

FIGURE 2.56   Connect in the new normal texture.

8. Make the following connections (see **FIGURE 2.57**):

▶ DiffuseTex_Base-RGB → SpecMult-A

▶ Specular-Output → SpecMult-B

▶ SpecMult-Output → Material Specular

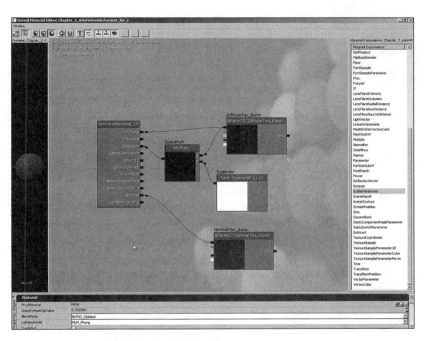

FIGURE 2.57   Multiply the objects like so.

9. Select the Specular and SpecMult expressions and duplicate them by pressing Ctrl+C and Ctrl+V. Move the new expressions below the originals.

10. Change the names of the new expressions as follows (see **FIGURE 2.58**):

▶ New ScalarParameter Expression → SpecPower

▶ New Multiply Expression → SpecPowerMult

11. Set the DefaultValue of SpecPower to 20.

12. Make the following connections (see **FIGURE 2.59**):

▶ DiffuseTex_Base-RGB → SpecPowerMult-A

▶ SpecPower-Output → SpecPowerMult-B

▶ SpecPowerMult-Output → Material SpecularPower

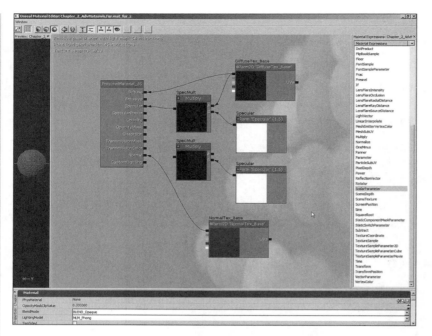

FIGURE 2.58   The nodes have been duplicated and renamed.

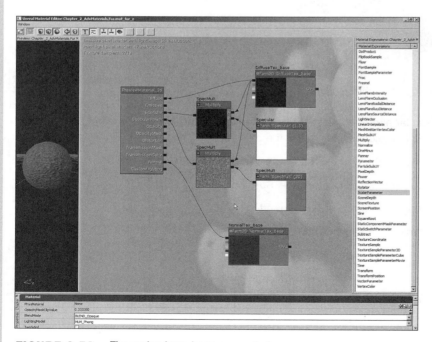

FIGURE 2.59   The nodes have been connected.

At this point, you should have a simple material showing the diffuse texture (which is nothing more than some grayscale noise) with the normal map and some specularity, but nothing that really resembles fur. Cheap carpet, maybe. In **TUTORIAL 2.11**, however, our effect starts to take shape.

13. Commit the changes to the material and save the package to preserve your work.

END TUTORIAL 2.10

Continue from **TUTORIAL 2.10**, or open the mat_fur_01 material from within the Chapter_2_AdvMaterials package included in the files for this chapter. In **TUTORIAL 2.11**, you set up the network responsible for handling the tiling of the texture coordinates of the material.

TUTORIAL 2.11: Fur Material, Part II: Texture Coordinate Tiling Control

1. Create a TextureCoordinate expression by dragging it from the Material Expressions list or selecting it from the context menu. Name the expression **FurTexCoord**. This node simply gives us some base texture coordinates to build upon (see **FIGURE 2.60**).

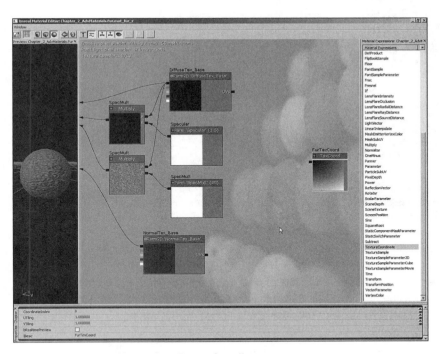

FIGURE 2.60   Create a new TextureCoordinate.

2

2. Below the FurTexCoord expression, create a ScalarParameter expression by dragging it from the Material Expressions list or selecting it from the context menu. Name this expression **UVTiling**. Set the DefaultValue to 4.0. The value of this expression is multiplied by the FurTexCoord and determines the number of times the fur textures tile across the surface.

3. To the left of the FurTexCoord and UVTiling expressions, create a Multiply expression. Name this expression **UVMult**.

4. Connect the output of the FurTexCoord expression to the A input of the UVMult expression. Then, connect the output of the UVTiling expression to the B input of the UVMult expression (see **FIGURE 2.61**).

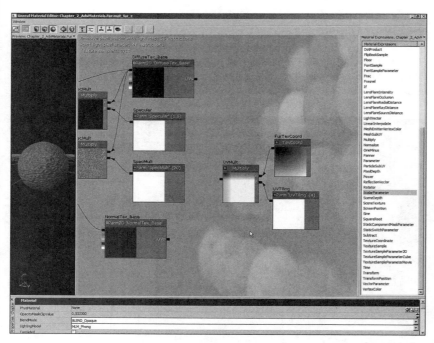

FIGURE 2.61   Connect the new multiply.

5. This gives us basic control over the tiling of the texture coordinates. In **TUTORIAL 2.12**, we begin creating the network responsible for producing the fur effect. Commit the changes to the material and save the package to preserve your work.

END TUTORIAL 2.11

Continue from **TUTORIAL 2.11**, or open the mat_fur_02 material from within the Chapter_2_AdvMaterials package included in the files for this chapter.

TUTORIAL 2.12: Fur Material, Part III: Recreating Bump Offset

1. In this tutorial, we begin re-creating the BumpOffset expression using a network that creates the basic fur effect. For your reference, here is the equation used by the BumpOffset expression:

   BumpOffset = TexCoords + CamaeraVector.RG * (Height * HeightRatio + HeightRatio * -RefPlane)

   With the texture coordinates already built in **TUTORIAL 2.11**, the order in which the network is built from this point on will follow the equation from right to left.

2. Below the UVTiling expression, create a Constant expression. Name the expression **BumpConst** and set its value to –1.0.

3. Below the BumpConst expression, create a ScalarParameter expression. Name the expression **RefPlane** and set its value to 0.5 as a default (see **FIGURE 2.62**). The value of this expression is the equivalent to the RefPlane property of the BumpOffset expression.

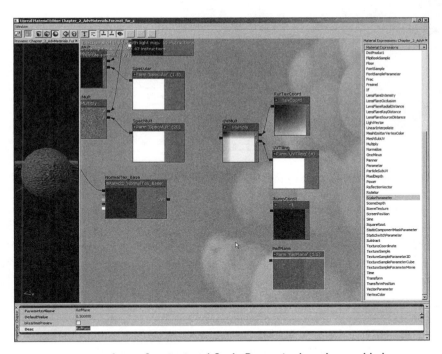

FIGURE 2.62   A new Constant and ScalarParameter have been added.

4. To the left of the BumpConst and RefPlane expressions, create a Multiply expression. Name the expression **BumpMult1**.

5. Connect the output of the BumpConst expression to the A input of the BumpMult1 expression. Then, connect the output of the RefPlane expression to the B input of the BumpMult1 expression (see **FIGURE 2.63**). This will simply reverse the sign of the value of the RefPlane expression.

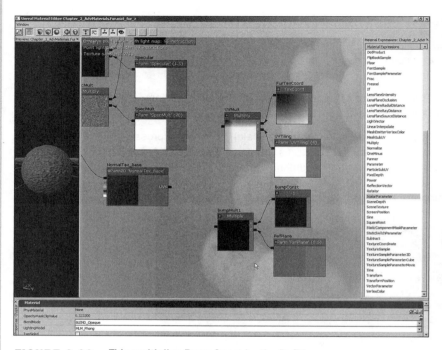

FIGURE 2.63   This multiplies BumpConst by the RefPlane.

6. Below the RefPlane expression, create a ScalarParameter expression. Name the expression **HeightRatio** and set its value to 0.025 as a default. The value of this expression is equivalent to that of the HeightRatio property of the BumpOffset expression.

7. To the left of the BumpMult1 expression, create another Multiply expression. Name this expression **BumpMult2**.

8. Connect the output of the BumpMult1 expression to the A input of the BumpMult2 expression. Then, connect the output of the HeightRatio expression to the B input of the BumpMult2 expression (see **FIGURE 2.64**). This multiplies the HeightRatio by the opposite of the RefPlane, just as is done in the BumpOffset expression behind the scenes.

9. Below the HeightRatio expression, create a TextureSampleParameter2D expression using the fur_height texture. Name the expression **BumpHeightTex_Alpha**. This is the texture that holds the height information normally connected to the Height input of a BumpOffset expression. We will assume that the height data is stored in the Alpha channel of this texture, hence the "_Alpha" suffix in the name.

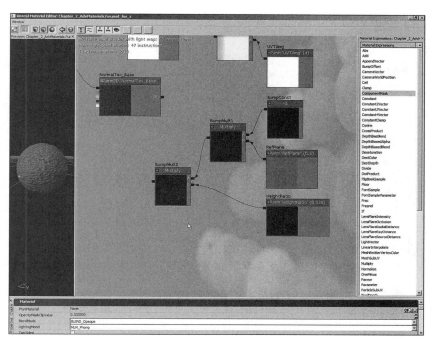

FIGURE 2.64   Connect in the new nodes as shown.

10. To the right of the BumpHeightTex_Alpha expression, create a new Multiply expression. Name the expression **BumpMult3**.

11. Connect the output of the HeightRatio expression to the A input of the BumpMult3 expression. Then, connect the Alpha output of the BumpHeightTex_Alpha expression to the B input of the BumpMult3 expression (see **FIGURE 2.65**).

12. To the left of the BumpMult2 expression, create an Add expression. Name the expression **BumpAdd1**.

13. Connect the output of the BumpMult2 expression to the A input of the BumpAdd1 expression. Then, connect the output of the BumpMult3 expression to the B input of the BumpAdd1 expression (see **FIGURE 2.66**).

14. So far we have followed the equation for the bump offset effect exactly. In **TUTORIAL 2.13**, we alter it slightly in order to make it more customizable. Commit the changes to the material and save the package to preserve your progress.

2

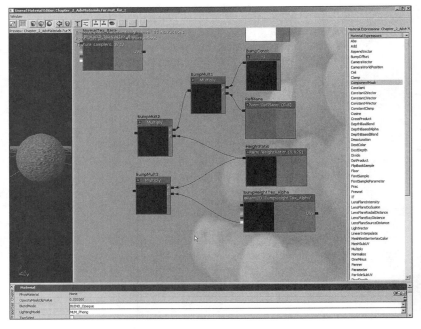

FIGURE 2.65
Multiply the
HeightRatio by the
BumpHeightTex_
Alpha.

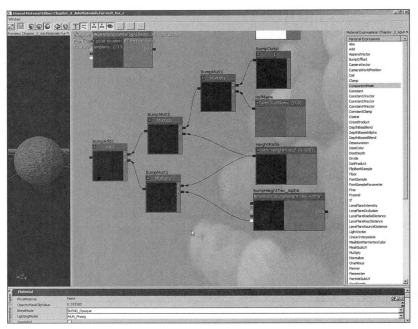

FIGURE 2.66
We are now adding
the results together.

END TUTORIAL 2.12

Continue from **TUTORIAL 2.12**, or open the mat_fur_03 material from within the Chapter_2_AdvMaterials package included in the files for this chapter.

TUTORIAL 2.13: Fur Material, Part IV: Extending Bump Offset

1. This is the point where our network diverges from the equation of the BumpOffset expression in that instead of using the CameraVector's R and G components by themselves, we add the R and G components of a VectorParameter expression to the CameraVector. This allows the fur to appear to flow in a specified direction. If the desired effect in an instanced material does not require this functionality, the values of each component of the extra vector can be set to 0.0 and its effects are nullified.

2. Below the BumpHeightTex_Alpha expression, create a CameraVector expression by dragging it from the Material Expressions list or selecting it from the context menu. Name the expression **CamVector**.

3. Below the CamVector expression, add a VectorParameter expression. Name the expression **FurDirection**. Leave the values of its components at 0.0 as the default (see **FIGURE 2.67**).

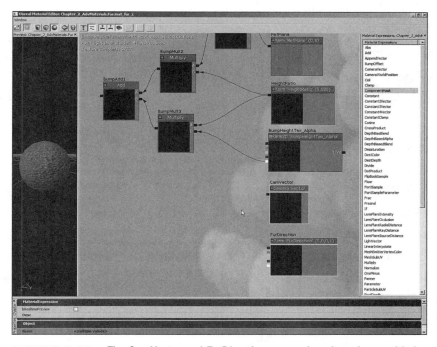

FIGURE 2.67 The CamVector and FurDirection expressions have been added.

4. To the left of the CamVector and FurDirection expressions, create an Add expression. Name the expression **VecAdd**.

5. To the left of the VecAdd expression, create a new ComponentMask expression. Name the expression **VecMask** and select the R and G check boxes (see **FIGURE 2.68**).

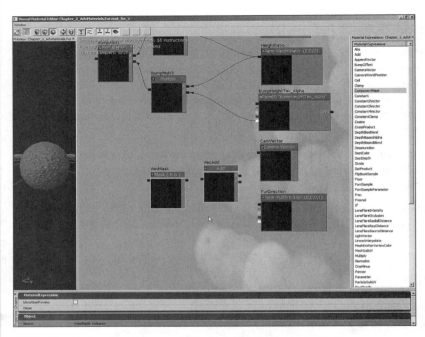

FIGURE 2.68   Create a new Add and a new Component Mask.

6. To the left of the BumpAdd1 expression, create a Multiply expression. Name the expression **BumpMult4**.

7. To the left of the UVMult and BumpMult4 expressions, create an Add expression. Name the expression **BumpAdd2**.

8. Make the following connections (see **FIGURE 2.69**):

- ▸ CamVector-Output → VecAdd-A
- ▸ FurDirection-RGB → VecAdd-B
- ▸ VecAdd-Output → VecMask-Input
- ▸ BumpAdd1-Output → BumpMult4-A
- ▸ VecMask-Output → BumpMult4-B
- ▸ UVMult-Output → BumpAdd2-A
- ▸ BumpMult4-Output → BumpAdd2-B
- ▸ BumpAdd2-Output → DiffuseTex_Base-UVs
- ▸ BumpAdd2-Output → NormalTex_Base-UVs

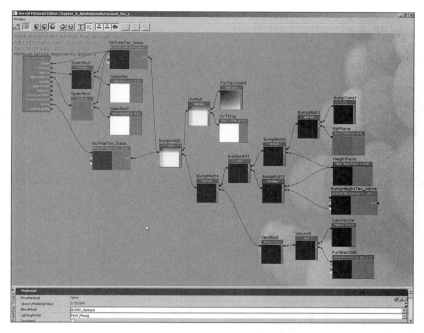

FIGURE 2.69 Connect your nodes like so. The nodes have been shifted a bit for better placement.

9. You should see the basic fur effect in the preview at this point, but there are still some details that can be added to enhance the effect. Commit the changes to the material and save the package to preserve your progress.

END TUTORIAL 2.13

Continue from **TUTORIAL 2.13**, or open the mat_fur_04 material from within the Chapter_2_AdvMaterials package included in the files for this chapter.

TUTORIAL 2.14: Fur Material, Part V: Re-creating Fresnel

1. Now that the basic fur effect is in place, we add the ability to color the fur. We want to be able to add highlights to the edges of the material to simulate the translucency of hair or to give the fur the appearance of changing color from the roots to the tips. This is achieved by creating a network that performs the function of a Fresnel expression while making it customizable within any instances of the material. For your reference, here is the equation used to calculate the Fresnel expression's result:

Fresnel = (1 – Max(Normal dot Camera, 0)) ^ Exponent

2. Begin by moving all your nodes to the right, away from the Material node. Off to the left of the DiffuseTex_Base expression, create a CameraVector expression. Name the expression **EdgeCamVector**.

3. To the left of the EdgeCamVector expression, create a DotProduct expression. Name the expression **EdgeDotProduct** (see **FIGURE 2.70**).

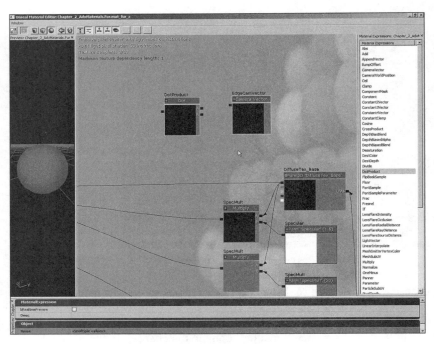

FIGURE 2.70   The EdgeCamVector and EdgeDotProduct have now been created.

4. Connect the Output of the EdgeCamVector expression to the A input of the EdgeDotProduct. Then, connect the RGB output of the NormalTex_Base expression to the B input of the EdgeDotProduct expression.

   This calculation outputs a value of 1.0 when the normal of the surface is parallel to the direction the camera is pointing and a value of 0.0 when the normal of the surface is perpendicular to the direction the camera is facing, with an interpolation between the two.

5. Below the EdgeDotProduct expression, create a Constant expression. Name the expression **EdgeMinConst** and leave its value set to 0.0.

6. Below the EdgeMinConst expression, create a second Constant expression. Name the expression **EdgeMaxConst** and set its value to 1.0.

7. To the left of the EdgeDotProduct expression, create a Clamp expression by dragging it from the Material Expressions list or selecting it in the context menu. Name the expression **EdgeClamp**.

8. Connect the output of the EdgeDotProduct expression to the top, unlabeled input of the EdgeClamp expression. Then, connect the Output of the EdgeMinConst expression to the

Min input of the EdgeClamp expression, and connect the Output of EdgeMaxConst to the Max input of the EdgeClamp expression (see **FIGURE 2.71**).

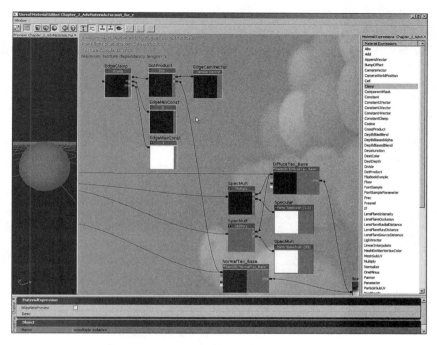

FIGURE 2.71   Connect your nodes together like so.

This ensures that the value passed on is between 0.0 and 1.0.

9. To the left of the EdgeClamp expression, create a OneMinus expression. Name the expression **EdgeOneMinus**.

10. Connect the Output of the EdgeClamp expression to the Input of the EdgeOneMinus expression (see **FIGURE 2.72**).

This is done because the expected behavior for the Fresnel expression is to output a value of 0.0 when the normal of the surface is parallel to the direction the camera is facing and a value of 1.0 when the normal of the surface is perpendicular to the direction the camera is facing. This, as you may have noted, is the opposite of how the dot product works, hence the inversion.

11. Below the EdgeOneMinus expression, create a ScalarParameter expression. Name the expression **BaseColorExtent**. Set its default value to 3.0.

12. To the left of the EdgeOneMinus expression, create a Power expression. Name the expression **EdgePower**.

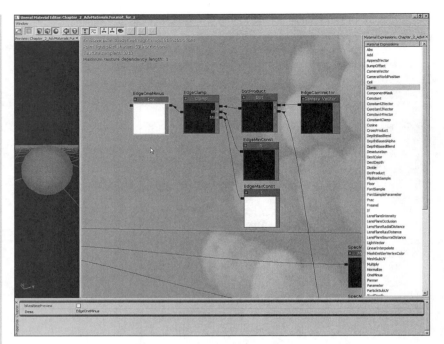

FIGURE 2.72   Connect the EdgeClamp to the EdgeOneMinus.

13. Connect the Output of the EdgeOneMinus expression to the Base input of the EdgePower expression. Then, connect the Output of the BaseColorExtent expression to the Exp input of the EdgePower expression (see **FIGURE 2.73**).

This calculation determines how quickly the output value falls off from 1.0 to 0.0 (or white to black, as the case may be), as the normal goes from perpendicular to parallel. A higher value for the BaseColorExtent expression means a quicker falloff and, as a result, there is much less white and much more black. Our intended use of the result of this network is to blend between a base color and a highlight color. The quicker the falloff, the farther out the base color will reach, hence the name for the parameter being BaseColorExtent.

14. Connect the Output of the EdgePower expression to the Diffuse channel of the material. You should see the fade from black to white in the preview (see **FIGURE 2.74**). The basis for the edge highlight is in place, but we still need to create the network that adds the colors to the material. Commit the changes to the material and save the package to preserve your progress.

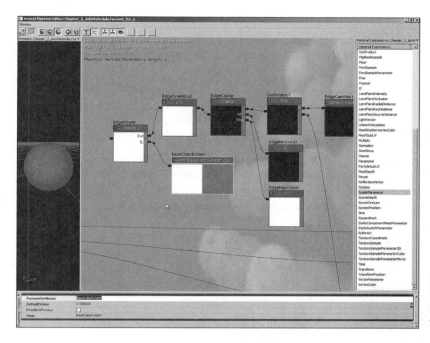

FIGURE 2.73
Connect the
EdgeOneMinus to
the EdgePower.

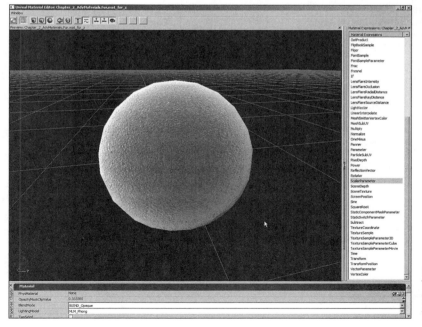

FIGURE 2.74
Your result should
look something like
this.

END TUTORIAL 2.14

Continue from **TUTORIAL 2.14**, or open the mat_fur_05 material from within the Chapter_2_ AdvMaterials package included in the files for this chapter.

TUTORIAL 2.15: Fur Material, Part VI: Base Color

1. With the Fresnel network finished, we can focus on adding in the diffuse colors for the material. This relies on the use of parameters in order to maintain the ability to customize on a per-instance basis.

2. Above the Fresnel network, create a ScalarParameter expression. Name the expression **BaseColorAmount** and set its value to 2.5 as a default (see **FIGURE 2.75**).

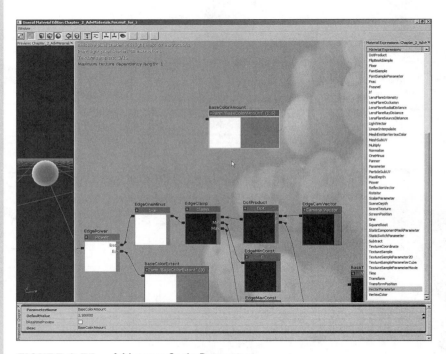

FIGURE 2.75   Add a new ScalarParameter.

3. Below the BaseColorAmount expression, create a VectorParameter expression. Name the expression **BaseColor**. Set the following values as defaults:

   ▸ **R**: 0.6

   ▸ **G**: 0.2

   ▸ **B**: 0.14

   ▸ **A**: 1.0

4. To the left of the BaseColor and BaseColorAmount expressions, create a Multiply expression. Name the expression **BaseColorMult**.

5. Connect the Output of the BaseColorAmount expression to the A input of the BaseColorMult expression. Then, connect the RGB output of the BaseColor expression to the B input of the BaseColorMult expression (see **FIGURE 2.76**).

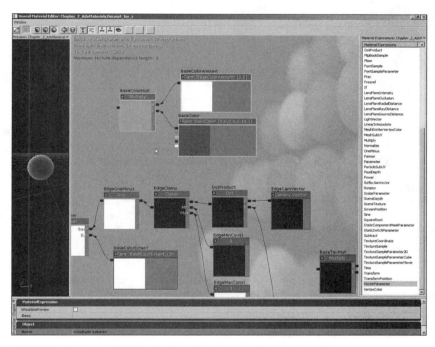

FIGURE 2.76   Multiply the BaseColorAmount by the BaseColor.

Of course, it would perfectly fine to simply use the VectorParameter expression by itself, but using a color and a multiplier here allows the color components to be set within the normal 0.0-to-1.0 range and then use the amount multiplier to overdrive them if necessary. This means the color is easily identifiable from the preview of the VectorParameter. When you're overdriving the values of a color directly, the expression's preview becomes white, even though the actual color may be a super-bright red.

6. To the left of the BaseColorMult expression, create a new Multiply expression. Name the expression **BaseTexMult**.

7. Connect the Output of the BaseColorMult expression to the A input of the BaseTexMult expression. Then, connect the RGB output of the DiffuseTex_Base expression to the B input of the BaseTexMult expression (see **FIGURE 2.77**).

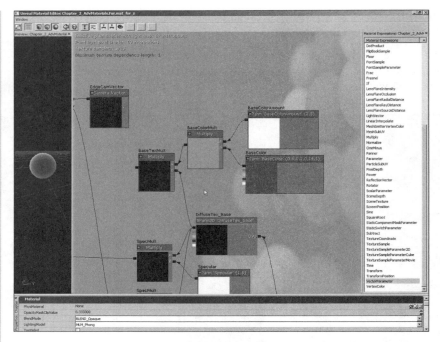

FIGURE 2.77   This multiplies the BaseColorMult result by the DiffuseTex_Base.

8. Below the BaseTexMult expression, create a OneMinus expression. Name the expression **BaseOneMinus**. Connect the EdgePower expression into its input.

9. To the left of the BaseTexMult and BaseOneMinus expressions, create a Multiply expression. Name the expression **BaseFinalMult**.

10. Connect the Output of the BaseTexMult expression to the A input of the BaseFinalMult expression. Then, connect the Output of the BaseOneMinus expression to the B input of the BaseFinalMult expression (see **FIGURE 2.78**).

    Using the OneMinus expression here causes the inner area to become white and the outer area to become black. This allows us to color this area with the base color.

11. If you want to test the effects of this portion of the network, connect the output of the BaseFinalMult expression to the Diffuse channel of the material. This completes the network for the base color of the fur (see **FIGURE 2.79**). In **TUTORIAL 2.16**, we construct the network for the highlight color and add them together to produce the diffuse coloring. Commit the changes to the material and save the package to preserve your progress.

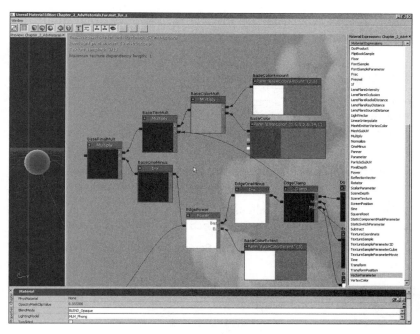

FIGURE 2.78
Multiply the
BaseTexMult by the
BaseOneMinus.

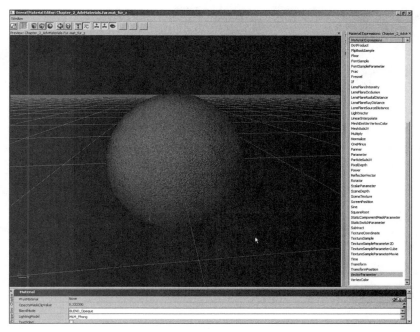

FIGURE 2.79
At this point, your
material appears
very dark.

END TUTORIAL 2.15

Continue from **TUTORIAL 2.15**, or open the mat_fur_06 material from within the Chapter_2_AdvMaterials package included in the files for this chapter.

TUTORIAL 2.16: Fur Material, Part VII: Highlight Color

1. The network for the highlight color is essentially the same as the base color network with the exception of the removal of the OneMinus expression. As such, we simply duplicate the base color network minus the OneMinus expression and rename the duplicated expressions.

2. Select the BaseColor, BaseColorAmount, BaseColorMult, BaseTexMult, and BaseFinalMult expressions by holding down Ctrl+Alt and dragging a marquee around them.

3. Press Ctrl+C and Ctrl+V to duplicate the expressions and move them above the Fresnel network but below the BaseColor network. You may need to reorganize your nodes.

4. Replace any occurrences of "Base" in the Desc and ParameterName properties of the new expression with "Tip" (see **FIGURE 2.80**).

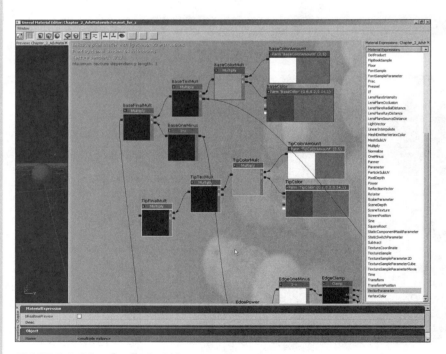

FIGURE 2.80   Duplicate and rename the nodes.

5. Set the value of the TipColorAmount expression to 15.0 as the default. Then, set the following values as defaults for the TipColor expression:

> ▸ **R**: 0.5

> ▸ **G**: 0.35

> ▸ **B**: 0.2

> ▸ **A**: 1.0

6. Connect the RGB output of the DiffuseTex_Base expression to the empty input of the TipTexMult expression (see **FIGURE 2.81**).

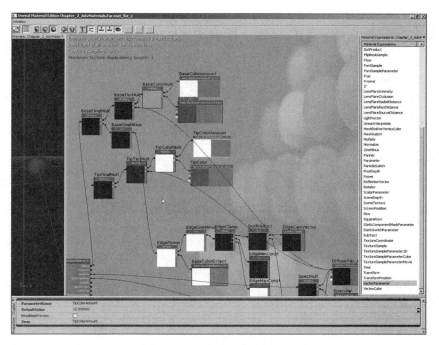

FIGURE 2.81   Connect the DiffuseTex_Base to the TipTexMult.

7. Connect the Output of the EdgePower expression to the empty input of the TipFinalMult expression.

8. To the left of the BaseFinalMult and TipFinalMult expressions, create an Add expression. Name the expression **ColorAdd**.

9. Connect the Output of the BaseFinalMult expression to the A input of the ColorAdd expression. Then, connect the Output of the TipFinalMult expression to the B input of the ColorAdd expression (see **FIGURE 2.82**).

2

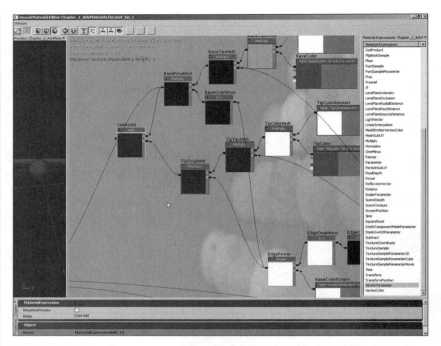

FIGURE 2.82   You are now adding the BaseFinalMult to the TipFinalMult.

10. Because there may be situations where the use of two colors is simply not needed, we are going to provide the ability to disable the highlight color and simply use the base color. This is done through the use of a StaticSwitchParameter. To the left of the ColorAdd expression, create a StaticSwitchParameter expression. Name the expression **DiffuseMultiColor**.

11. Connect the Output of the ColorAdd expression to the A input of the DiffuseMultiColor expression. Then, connect the Output of the BaseTexMult expression to the B input of the DiffuseMultiColor expression. The output of the BaseTexMult expression is used to bypass the effects of the Fresnel network, allowing the base color to cover the entire surface.

12. Connect the Output of the DiffuseMultiColor expression to the Diffuse channel of the material. You should see the base color fading into the highlight color in the preview. If you do not, make sure that the DefaultValue property for the DifuseMultiColor node is set to True (checked).

13. At this point, you material is only moderately convincing as a fur shader (see **FIGURE 2.83**). There is still one more feature to add in **TUTORIAL 2.17** to the diffuse network. This allows the fur effect to be masked to appear only in certain areas. Commit the changes to the material and save the package to preserve your work.

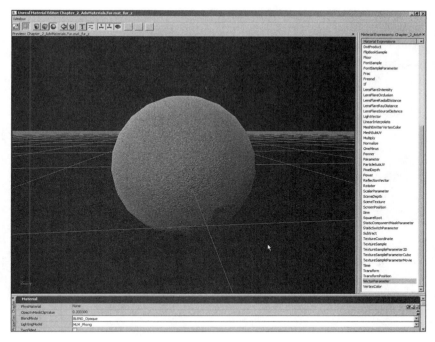

FIGURE 2.83   Your result should look like so.

END TUTORIAL 2.16

Continue from **TUTORIAL 2.16**, or open the mat_fur_07 material from within the Chapter_2_ AdvMaterials package included in the files for this chapter.

In **TUTORIAL 2.17**, we provide the ability to mask the color network set up previously, limiting it to a specific area of the material, while providing a texture that is used in the masked area in place of the color network. This is assuming the mask texture is only black and white with no in-between shades of gray. Any gray areas cause the texture and color network to blend together.

TUTORIAL 2.17: Fur Material, Part VIII: Diffuse Mask

1. Below the DiffuseMultiColor expression, create a new TextureSampleParameter2D expression using the fur_height texture as the default texture. Name the expression **DiffuseTex_Overlay**.

2. Below the DiffuseTex_Overlay expression, create a TextureSampleParameter2D expression using the mask_all_color texture from the Chapter_2_AdvMaterials package as the default texture. Name the expression **DiffuseTex_Mask** (see **FIGURE 2.84**).

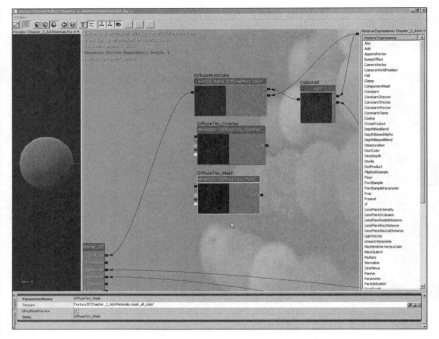

FIGURE 2.84   The DiffuseTex_Overlay and DiffuseTex_Mask have now been added.

3. To the left of the DiffuseMultiColor, DiffuseTex_Mask, and DiffuseTex_Overlay expressions, create a LinearInterpolate expression. Name the expression **DiffuseInterp**.

4. Make the following connections (see **FIGURE 2.85**):

    ▶ DiffuseMultiColor-Output → DiffuseInterp-A

    ▶ DiffuseTex_Overlay-RGB → DiffuseInterp-B

    ▶ DiffuseTex_Mask-Alpha → DiffuseInterp-Alpha

    ▶ DiffuseInterp-Output → Material-Diffuse

    ▶ DiffuseInterp-Output → SpecMult-A

    ▶ DiffuseInterp-Output → SpecPowerMult-A

5. The effect in the preview does not change because the mask texture is meant only to display the output of the color network. Commit the changes to the material and save the package to preserve your work.

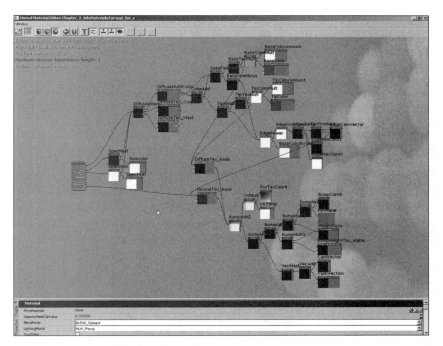

FIGURE 2.85   Connect the network as shown. The nodes have been rearranged.

END TUTORIAL 2.17

Continue from **TUTORIAL 2.17**, or open the mat_fur_08 material from within the Chapter_2_ AdvMaterials package included in the files for this chapter.

Now that the diffuse portion of the material has masking in place, it stands to reason that the same principle should be implemented on the normal map because having the fur normal map applied to a part of the surface that has no fur on it would look out of place. In **TUTORIAL 2.18**, we do just that.

TUTORIAL 2.18: Fur Material, Part IX: Normal Mask

1. Below the NormalTex_Base expression, create a new TextureSampleParameter2D expression using the fur_normal texture as its default texture. Name the expression **NormalTex_Overlay**.

2. Below the NormalTex_Overlay expression, create another TextureSampleParameters2D expression using the mask_all_color texture as its default. Name the expression **NormalTex_Mask**.

3. To the left of the NormalTex_Base, NormalTex_Mask, and NormalTex_Overlay expressions, create a LinearInterpolate expression. Name the expression **NormalInterp** (see **FIGURE 2.86**).

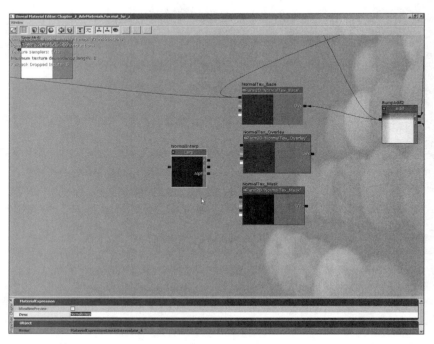

FIGURE 2.86   Three new nodes have been added.

4. Make the following connections:

▶ NormalTex_Base-RGB → NormalInterp-A

▶ NormalTex_Overlay-RGB → NormalInterp-B

▶ NormalTex_Mask-Alpha → NormalInterp-Alpha

5. Below the NormalInterp expression, create a VectorParameter expression. Name the expression **NormalMapAmount**. Give it the following default values:

▶ **R**: 1.0

▶ **G**: 1.0

▶ **B**: 1.0

▶ **A**: 1.0

6. To the left of the NormalInterp and NormalMapAmount expressions, create a Multiply expression. Name the expression **NormalMult**.

7. Make the following connections (see **FIGURE 2.87**):

- ▶ NormalInterp-Output → NormalMult-A
- ▶ NormalMapAmount-RGB → NormaMult-B
- ▶ NormalMult-Output → EdgeDotProduct-B
- ▶ NormalMult-Output → Material-Normal

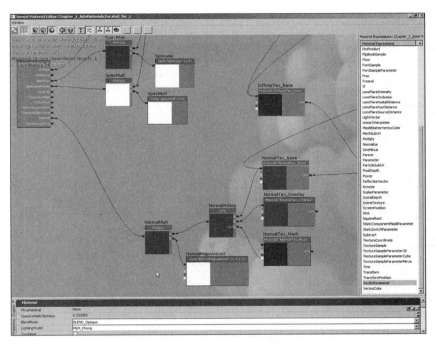

FIGURE 2.87   Make the connections shown.

8. Again, the changes made are not apparent in the preview because of the texture being used in the mask expression as the default. Commit the changes to the material and save the package to preserve your progress.

END TUTORIAL 2.18

Continue from **TUTORIAL 2.18**, or open the mat_fur_09 material from within the Chapter_2_ AdvMaterials package included in the files for this chapter.

To finish off the fur effect, we add the ability to make the edges of the fur appear fuzzy in **TUTORIAL 2.19**. A very convincing effect can be achieved, albeit limited to curved surfaces (which creates possible problems with complex surfaces). For this reason, the option to use this effect is provided to the artist.

TUTORIAL 2.19: Fur Material, Part X: Fuzzy Edges

1. Select the Fresnel network from the earlier diffuse color tutorials. This network includes CamEdgeVector, EdgeDotProduct, EdgeMinConst, EdgeMaxConst, EdgeClamp, EdgeOneMinus, and EdgePower. Duplicate the network by pressing Ctrl+C and Ctrl+V. Then, position the new network below the rest of the material's network.

2. Replace all occurrences of "Edge" in the Desc properties of these new expressions with "Fuzzy." Also, change the name of the duplicate BaseColorExtent expression to **Fuzziness** (see **FIGURE 2.88**).

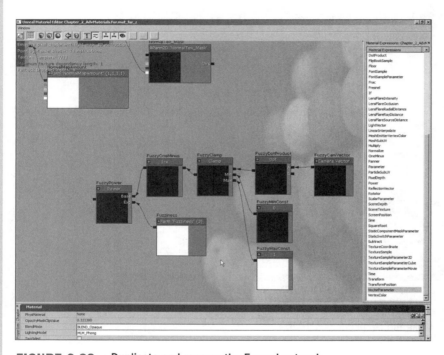

FIGURE 2.88 Duplicate and rename the Fresnel network.

3. Below the FuzzyCamVector expression, create a new TextureSampleParameter2D expression using the tangent_normal texture. Name the expression **FuzzyNormalTex**.

   This allows a completely separate normal map to be used for the transparency effect because sometimes the normal map can cause anomalies when used in this effect. For that reason, the default texture is simply a true blue (0,0,1) color that causes the tangent normals, or the normals of the mesh itself, to be used (see **FIGURE 2.89**).

4. Connect the RGB output of the FuzzyNormalTex expression to the B input of the FuzzyDotProduct expression.

5. Below the Fuzziness expression, create a TextureSampleParameter2D expression using the fur_height texture as the default. Name the expression FuzzyTransparencyTex_Alpha.

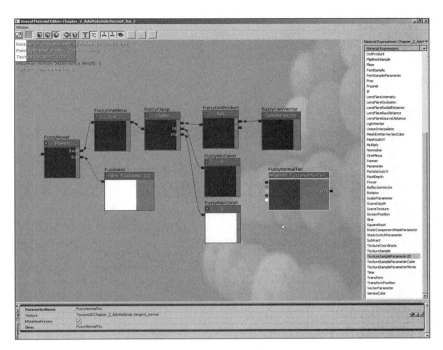

FIGURE 2.89   The new normal is used for Fuzziness.

6. Connect the Output of BumpAdd2 to the UVs input of FuzzyTransparencyTex_Alpha.

7. To the left of the FuzzyPower expression, create a Multiply expression. Name the expression **FuzzyMult**.

8. Connect the Output of the FuzzyPower expression to the A input of the FuzzyMult expression. Then, connect the Alpha output of the FuzzyTransparencyTex_Alpha expression to the B input of the FuzzyMult expression (see **FIGURE 2.90**).

9. To the left of the FuzzyMult expression, create a OneMinus expression. Name the expression **FuzzyOneMinus2**.

10. Below the FuzzyOneMinus2 expression, create a Constant expression. Name the expression **NoFuzzValue** and set its value to 1.0.

11. Below the NoFuzzValue expression, create a TextureSampleParameter2D expression using the mask_all_color texture as its default. Name the expression **FuzzyMaskTex**.

12. To the left of the FuzzyOneMinus2, NoFuzzValue, and FuzzyMaskTex expressions, create a LinearInterpolate expression. Name the expression **FuzzyInterp**.

13. Below the FuzzyInterp expression, create a Constant expression with a default value of 0.925. Name this expression **FuzzyCutoffValue**.

2

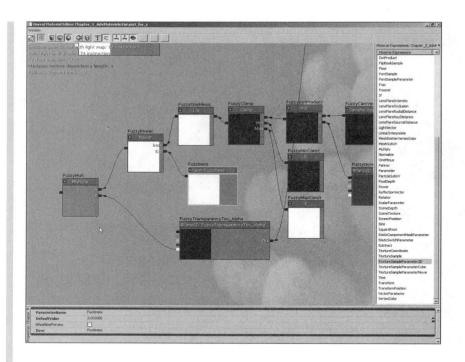

FIGURE 2.90   Multiply the FuzzyPower expression by the Alpha of FuzzyTransparencyTex_Alpha.

14. Below the FuzzyCutoffValue expression, create another Constant expression with a default value of 0. Name this expression **FuzzyZero**.

15. To the left of the FuzzyInterp expression, create an If expression named **FuzzyCondition**.

16. To the left of the FuzzyCondition expression, create a StaticSwitchParameter expression. Name the expression **Fuzzy** and check the DefaultValue box as the default.

17. Make the following connections (see **FIGURE 2.91**):

- ▶ FuzzyMult-Output → FuzzyOneMinus2-Input
- ▶ FuzzyOneMinus2-Output → FuzzyInterp-A
- ▶ NoFuzzValue-Output → FuzzyInterp-B
- ▶ FuzzyMaskTex-Alpha → FuzzyInterp-Alpha
- ▶ FuzzyInterp-Output → FuzzCondition-A
- ▶ FuzzyCutoffValue-Output → FuzzyCondition-B
- ▶ NoFuzzValue-Output → FuzzyCondition-A>B
- ▶ NoFuzzValue-Output → Fuzzy-A=B

▶ FuzzyZero-Output → FuzzyCondition-A<B

▶ FuzzyCondition-Output → Fuzzy-A

▶ NoFuzzValue-Output → Fuzzy-B

▶ Fuzzy-Output → Material-Opacity

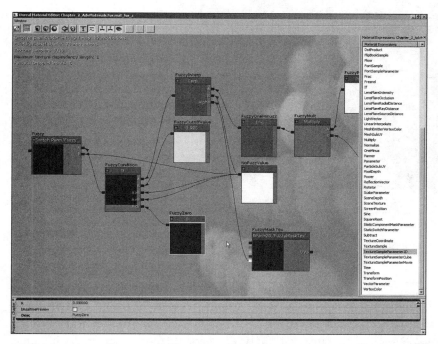

FIGURE 2.91   Here are all the nodes connected. (Nodes have been arranged for wire readability.)

18. Of course, nothing has changed in the preview at this point because the material is still using the BLEND_Opaque blend mode. Select the material node and set the following:

▶ **OpacityMaskClipValue**: 0.925

▶ **BlendMode**: BLEND_Masked

19. You should now see the fuzzy edges of the material in the preview (see **FIGURE 2.92**). Adjusting the Fuzziness expressions value determines the extent of the fuzzy effect. Commit the changes to the material and save the package to preserve your work.

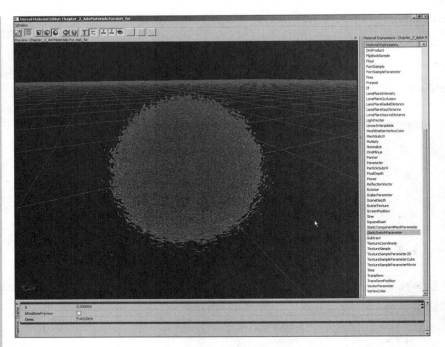

FIGURE 2.92   Your fur material is complete.

END TUTORIAL 2.19

To show the power of material instancing, we create two instances of the mat_fur material and use their parameters to create two entirely different materials over the course of the next two tutorials. In **TUTORIAL 2.20**, we create a material that is very similar to the base material, with some slight changes and different colors.

TUTORIAL 2.20: Fur Material Blonde Instance

1. Right-click the mat_fur_final material in the Generic Browser and choose Create New Material Instance Constant from the context menu. Enter the following information in the dialog that appears and then click OK:

   ▶ **Package**: Chapter_2_AdvMaterials

   ▶ **Group**: Fur

   ▶ **Name**: mat_fur_final_blonde

2. Expand the ScalarParameterValues section. Check the boxes next to the following properties in the Material Instance Editor to cause the values of the instance to override the base material's values and then set the corresponding values for each (see **FIGURE 2.93**).

- ▶ **BaseColorExtent**: 2.5

- ▶ **TipColorAmount**: 25.0

- ▶ **RefPlane**: 5.0

- ▶ **HeightRatio**: 0.05

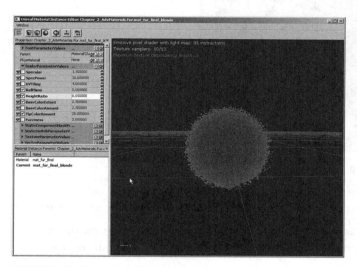

FIGURE 2.93 Apply the new values to the instance.

3. Expand the VectorParameterValues section. Check the boxes next to the following properties and set the corresponding values for each:

- ▶ **BaseColor**:

  - ▶ **R**: 0.035

  - ▶ **G**: 0.03

  - ▶ **B**: 0.015

  - ▶ **A**: 1.0

- ▶ **TipColor**:

  - ▶ **R**: 0.75

  - ▶ **G**: 0.55

  - ▶ **B**: 0.3

  - ▶ **A**: 1.0

4. The material should now appear to be a slightly longer-haired, blonde version of the base material (see **FIGURE 2.94**). Close the Material Instance Editor and save the package to preserve your progress.

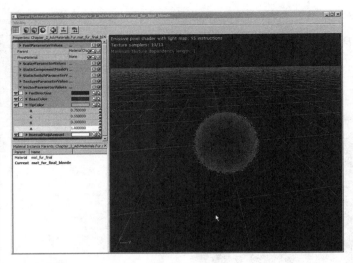

FIGURE 2.94   The look of the fur changes slightly.

In **TUTORIAL 2.21**, we create another instance of the fur material, but this time the result is something entirely different, a tennis ball. This requires changing values and using alternate textures in order to complete the effect.

TUTORIAL 2.21: Fur Material Tennis Ball Instance

1. Right-click the mat_fur_final material in the Generic Browser and choose Create New Material Instance Constant. Enter the following values in the dialog that appears and then click OK:

   ▸ **Package**: Chapter_2_AdvMaterials

   ▸ **Group**: Fur

   ▸ **Name**: mat_tennis_ball

2. Expand the ScalarParameterValues section. Check the boxes next to the following properties and set the corresponding values for each (see **FIGURE 2.95**):

   ▸ **BaseColorAmount**: 6.0

   ▸ **Fuzziness**: 8.0

   ▸ **HeightRatio**: 0.05

   ▸ **Specular**: 0.05

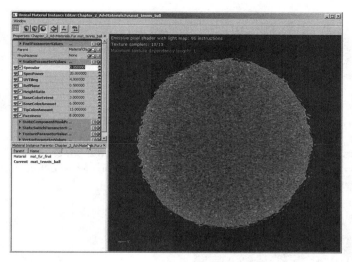

FIGURE 2.95   Change the parameters as shown.

3. Expand the TextureParameterValues section. Check the boxes next to the following properties and set the corresponding texture for each:

- ▶ **DiffuseTex_Base**: tennis_ball_base

- ▶ **BumpHeightTex_Alpha**: tennis_ball_base

- ▶ **DiffuseTex_Overlay**: tennis_ball_diffuse

- ▶ **NormalTex_Overlay**: tennis_ball_normal

- ▶ **NormalTex_Base**: tennis_ball_normal_base

- ▶ **NormalTex_Mask**: tennis_ball_mask

- ▶ **DiffuseTex_Mask**: tennis_ball_mask

4. Expand the StaticSwitchParameterValues section. Set the value of DiffuseMultiColor to False (unchecked).

5. Expand the VectorParameterValues section. Check the boxes next to each of the following properties and set the corresponding values:

- ▶ **BaseColor**:

    - ▶ **R**: 0.525

    - ▶ **G**: 0.8

    - ▶ **B**: 0.2

    - ▶ **A**: 1.0

2

- ▶ **FurDirection**:

  - ▶ **R**: 3.5

  - ▶ **G**: 7.5

  - ▶ **B**: 0.0

  - ▶ **A**: 1.0

- ▶ **NormalMapAmount**:

  - ▶ **R**: 1.0

  - ▶ **G**: 1.0

  - ▶ **B**: 3.0

  - ▶ **A**: 1.0

6. You should now see a tennis ball in the preview window, assuming you have the sphere primitive selected as the preview mesh (see **FIGURE 2.96**). This shows the power of instancing materials. By changing just a few properties and textures, a completely different material can be created. Save the package to preserve your progress.

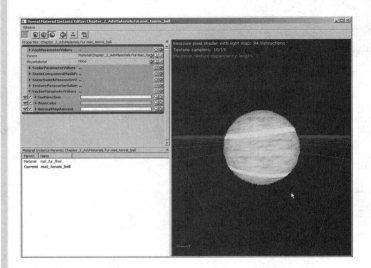

FIGURE 2.96   Your material now looks like a tennis ball.

END TUTORIAL 2.21

Throughout **TUTORIALS 2.22** through **2.29**, you create a customizable water surface material. This material is rather complex and requires a good deal of shader instructions as it's constructed. The object of **TUTORIAL 2.22** is to show you many different techniques that can be used when creating a water material without putting too much emphasis on performance. If performance becomes an issue when creating a material such as this (which will most likely cover a good deal of the screen), certain parts of the material may have to be omitted as a compromise.

> **NOTE**
>
> All expressions are named by setting their Desc properties and are referred to by those names throughout these tutorials. When dealing with naming parameter expressions, it is assumed that naming refers to setting both the ParameterName and Desc properties.

TUTORIAL 2.22: Configurable Water Material, Part I: Setup and Texture Coordinates

1. Right-click in the Generic Browser and choose New Material. Enter the following information in the dialog that appears and then click OK:

   ▶ **Package**: Chapter_2_AdvMaterials

   ▶ **Group**: Water

   ▶ **Name**: mat_water

2. In order to get transparency in this material, along with an accurate specular highlight, we are going to use the MLM_Unlit lighting model and create the specular highlight manually within the material. In the material node's properties, set the following:

   ▶ **BlendMode**: BLEND_Translucent

   ▶ **LightingModel**: MLM_Unlit

   We work our way through the material's expression network, from right to left for the most part. As such, we begin by setting up the texture coordinate network for the material. In this material, the texture coordinates are going to control the size (as in frequency, not amplitude) of the ripples of the water. The goal is to make the texture coordinates customizable without racking up too many instructions.

   You can always rearrange the expressions as you go, but give yourself a good deal of room to work and create a TextureCoordinate expression off to the right of the workspace. Name the expression **TexCoords** and leave the UTiling and VTiling properties set to 1.0 (see **FIGURE 2.97**).

3. Below the TexCoords expression, create a ScalarParameter expression. Name the expression **UVTiling** and set its value to 36.0 as the default.

4. To the left of the TexCoords and UVTiling expressions, create a Multiply expression. Name the expression **TexCoordsMult**.

5. Connect the Output of the TexCoords expression to the A input of the TexCoordsMult expression. Then, connect the Output of the UVTiling expression to the B input of the TexCoordsMult expression (see **FIGURE 2.98**).

   This gives us control over the tiling of the material from any instances of the material. One benefit of this, besides the customizability of the material, is that material instances provide much faster feedback for changes to the material.

6. Above the TexCoords expression, create a Time expression. Name the expression **PannerTime**.

7. Above the PannerTime expression, create a ScalarParameter expression. Name the expression **RippleSpeed** and set its value to 1.0 as the default.

8. To the left of the PannerTime and RippleSpeed expressions, create a Multiply expression. Name the expression **RippleMult**.

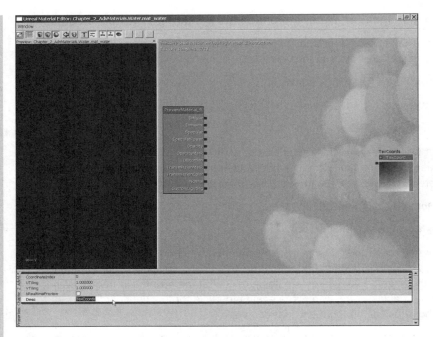

FIGURE 2.97   The TexCoords node has been created.

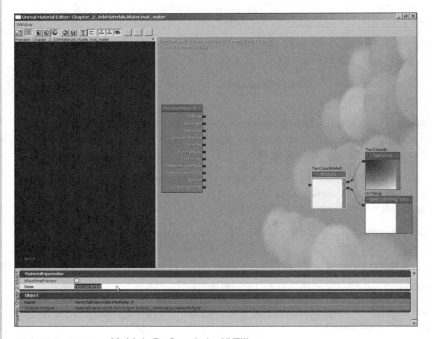

FIGURE 2.98   Multiply TexCoords by UVTiling.

9. Connect the Output of the RippleSpeed expression to the A input of the RippleMult expression. Then, connect the Output of the PannerTime expression to the B input of the RippleMult expression (see **FIGURE 2.99**).

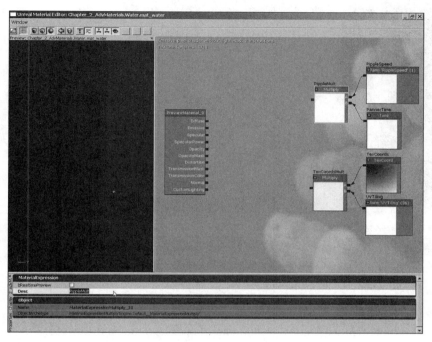

FIGURE 2.99   Connect the nodes together as shown.

As you will see, this gives us control over the speed at which any Panner expressions move.

10. Commit the changes to the material and save the package to preserve your progress.

END TUTORIAL 2.22

TUTORIAL 2.23: Configurable Water Material, Part II: Panning Texture Coordinates

1. Open the mat_water material in the Material Editor. If you have not completed **TUTORIAL 2.22**, you may open the mat_water_01 material instead.

2. To the left of the existing networks, create a Panner expression. Name the expression **Ripple1PannerY** and set the following values (see **FIGURE 2.100**):

   ▶ **SpeedX**: 0.0

   ▶ **SpeedY**: 0.1

2

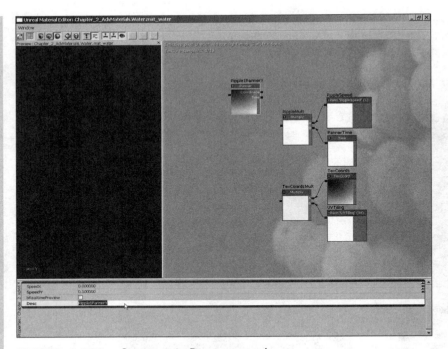

FIGURE 2.100   Create a new Panner expression.

3. To the left of the Ripple1PannerY expression, create a TextureSample expression using the colored_clouds texture from the Chapter_2_AdvMaterials package. Name the expression **CloudTex1**.

4. Connect the Output of the Ripple1PannerY expression to the UVs input of the CloudTex1 expression (see **FIGURE 2.101**).

5. To the left of the CloudTex1 expression, create a ComponentMask expression. Name the expression **CloudMask1** and check the R and G boxes.

6. Connect the RGB Output of the CloudTex1 expression to the input of the CloudMask1 expression (see **FIGURE 2.102**).

7. Below the CloudMask1 expression, create a Panner expression. Name the expression **Ripple1PannerX** and set the following values:

   ▸ **SpeedX**: –0.1975

   ▸ **SpeedY**: 0.0

8. To the left of the CloudMask1 and Ripple1PannerX expressions, create an Add expression. Name the expression **Ripple1Add**.

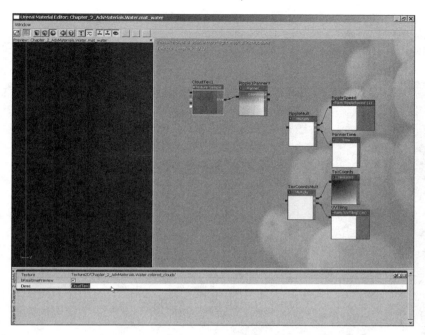

FIGURE 2.101 Connect the Ripple1PannerY to the UVs of CloudTex1.

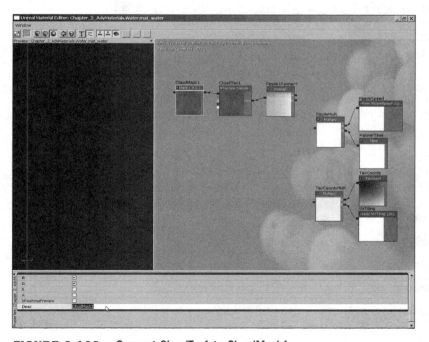

FIGURE 2.102 Connect CloudTex1 to CloudMask1.

9. Connect the Output of the CloudMask1 expression to the A input of the Ripple1Add expression. Then, connect the Output of the Ripple1PannerX expression to the B input of the Ripple1Add expression (see **FIGURE 2.103**).

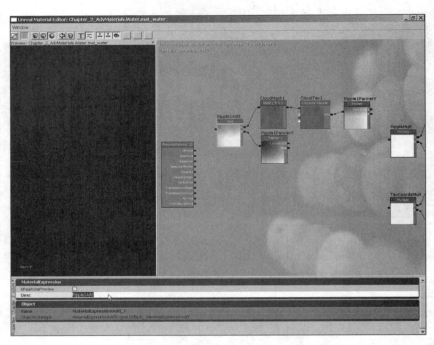

FIGURE 2.103   Add CloudMask1 and Ripple1PannerX.

Essentially, this network is distorting the texture coordinates by using the red and green channels of the texture as texture coordinates and adding them to the texture coordinates produced by the second Panner expression. This effect is extremely versatile and it has many potential uses.

10. Select the five expressions that make up the Ripple1 network and duplicate them by pressing Ctrl+C and Ctrl+V. Move the new expression below the originals. Replace any occurrences of "Ripple1" in the names of the new expressions with "Ripple2". Change the names of the CloudTex1 and CloudMask1 expressions to CloudTex2 and CloudMask2 (see **FIGURE 2.104**).

11. Change the values of the new Panner expressions as follows:

▶ **Ripple2PannerY**

    ▶ **SpeedX**: 0.0

    ▶ **SpeedY**: −0.125

▶ **Ripple2PannerX**

    ▶ **SpeedX**: 0.145

    ▶ **SpeedY**: 0.0

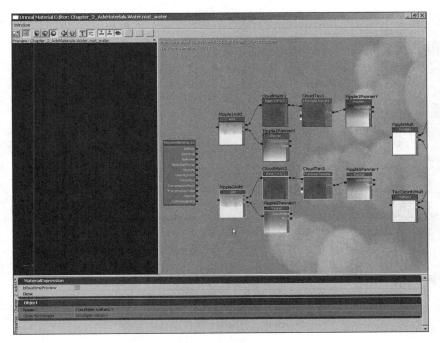

FIGURE 2.104   Duplicate and rename the network.

12. Make the following connections (see **FIGURE 2.105**):

- ▶ RippleMult-Output → Ripple1PannerY-Time
- ▶ RippleMult-Output → Ripple1PannerX-Time
- ▶ RippleMult-Output → Ripple2PannerY-Time
- ▶ RippleMult-Output → Ripple2PannerX-Time
- ▶ TexCoordsMult-Output → Ripple1PannerY-Coordinates
- ▶ TexCoordsMult-Output → Ripple1PannerX-Coordinates
- ▶ TexCoordsMult-Output → Ripple2PannerY-Coordinates
- ▶ TexCoordsMult-Output → Ripple2PannerX-Coordinates

13. Select all the expressions present in the material and press the C key to place a comment box around these expressions. Name it **Ripples**. This will make it easier to move large groups of expressions around later on. Commit the changes to the material and save the package to preserve your work.

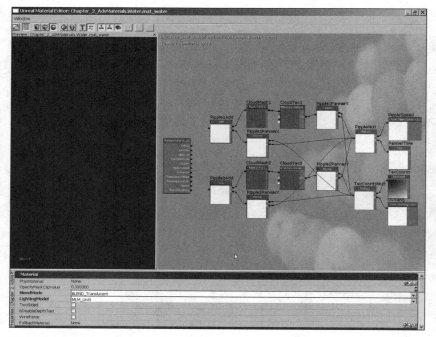

FIGURE 2.105   Make the connections shown.

END TUTORIAL 2.23

TUTORIAL 2.24: Configurable Water Material, Part III: Normals

1. Open the mat_water material in the Material Editor. If you have not completed **TUTORIAL 2.23**, you may open the mat_water_02 material instead.

   With the texture coordinates out of the way, we can now set up the network that controls the normals for the material. This network blends two normal maps and their alpha channels together. This helps to prevent any patterns from forming when tiling the material across the surface. We also provide a mechanism for controlling the amplitude of the ripples by modifying the normal maps.

2. To the left of the Ripples section, create a TextureSampleParameter2D expression using the water_normal_1 texture as its default. Name the expression **NormalTex1** (see **FIGURE 2.106**). Using a parameter here allows the material to be used potentially for various types of fluids other than water or simply to create different types of water, such as oceans versus lakes.

> **NOTE**
>
> You may need to move your Ripples section off to the right. Click Ripples to select the comment block and move it like any other expression.

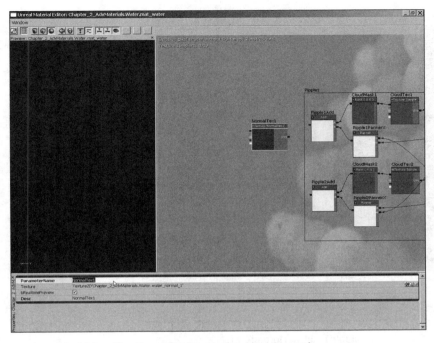

FIGURE 2.106   The NormalTex1 node has been created.

3. Below the NormalTex1 expression, create another TextureSampleParamter2D expression using the water_normal_2 texture as its default. Name the expression **NormalTex2**.

4. Connect the Output of the Ripple1Add expression to the UVs input of the NormalTex1 expression (see **FIGURE 2.107**). Then, connect the Output of the Ripple2Add expression to the UVs input of the NormalTex2 expression.

5. To the left of the NormalTex2 expression, create an Add expression. Name the expression **NormalAdd**.

6. Connect the RGB output of the NormalTex1 expression to the A input of the NormalAdd expression. Then, connect the RGB output of the NormalTex2 expression to the B input of the NormalAdd expression.

7. To the left of the NormalTex1 expression, create another Add expression. Name the expression **NormalAlphaAdd**.

8. Connect the Alpha output of the NormalTex1 expression to the A input of the NormalAlphaAdd expression. Then, connect the Alpha output of the NormalTex2 expression to the B input of the NormalAlphaAdd expression (see **FIGURE 2.108**).

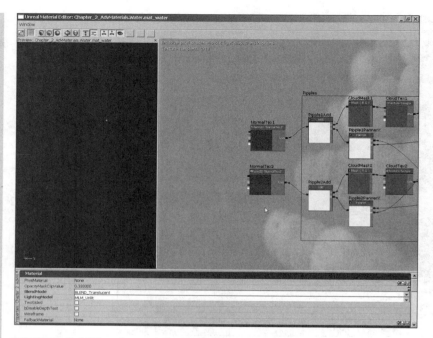

FIGURE 2.107   Connect the Ripple1Add to NormalTex1.

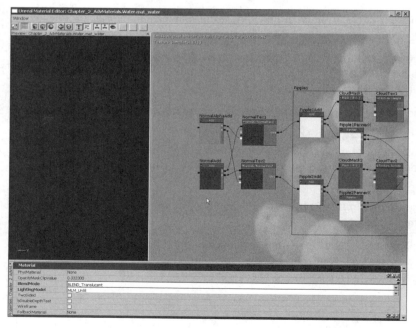

FIGURE 2.108   Add the alpha of NormalTex1 to the alpha of NormalTex2.

The Alpha channels are assumed to hold grayscale caustic maps matching the normal maps.

9. Below the NormalAdd expression, create a VectorParameter expression. Name the expression **WaterChopVector** and set the following values:

- ▶ **R**: 1.0
- ▶ **G**: 1.0
- ▶ **B**: 1.0
- ▶ **A**: 1.0

This vector is multiplied by the combined normal maps. By adjusting the B component of the vector, you cause the normal map to be either amplified (by lowering the value) or softened (by increasing the value).

10. To the left of the WaterChopVector expression, create a Multiply expression. Name the expression **ChopMult**.

11. Connect the Output of the NormalAdd expression to the A input of the ChopMult expression (see **FIGURE 2.109**). Then, connect the RGB output of the WaterChopVector expression to the B input of the ChopMult expression.

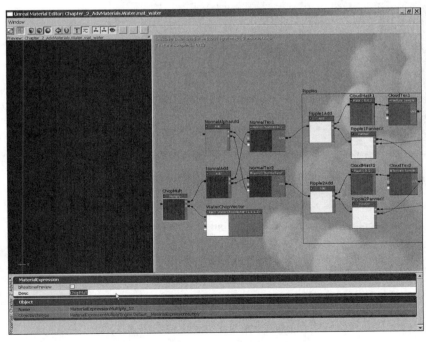

FIGURE 2.109   Multiply WaterChopVector by NormalAdd.

The output of the ChopMult expression is the final modified normal map. This is what will be connected to any expression that requires normals as inputs.

12. Connect the Output of the ChopMult expression to the material node's Normal channel.

13. Above the NormalAlphaAdd expression, create a Constant expression. Name the expression **ChopInvertConst** and set its value to 1.0.

14. To the left of the ChopInvertConst expression, create a Divide expression. Name the expression **ChopInvert**.

15. Connect the Output of the ChopInvertConst expression to the A input of the ChopInvert expression. Then, connect the Blue output of the WaterChopVector expression to the B input of the ChopInvert expression (see **FIGURE 2.110**).

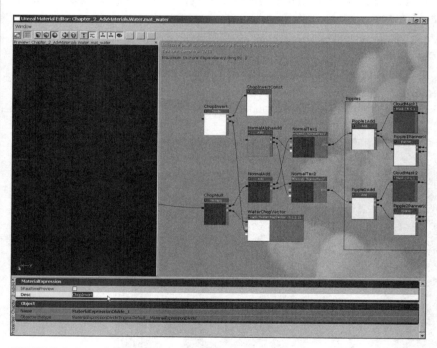

FIGURE 2.110　Divide ChopInvertConst by the Blue output of WaterChopVector.

16. To the left of the ChopInvert expression, create a Power expression. Name the expression **DiffuseColorContrast**.

17. Connect the Output of the NormalAlphaAdd expression to the Base input of the DiffuseColorContrast expression. Then, connect the Output of the ChopInvert expression to the Exp input of the DiffuseColorContrast expression (see **FIGURE 2.111**).

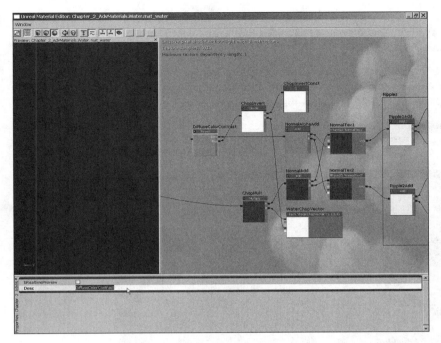

FIGURE 2.111   You are now raising the value of NormalAlphaAdd to the power of ChopInvert.

By using the power expression here, we are essentially increasing or decreasing the contrast of the combined alpha channels of the normal maps. This is then multiplied by the diffuse color to increase the caustic look of the water when the choppiness is increased.

18. The output of the DiffuseColorContrast expression will not be connected to anything at this point, because we have not yet created the network it feeds into. Select the expressions created in this tutorial and press the C key to create a comment block around them. Name the comment block **Normals**. Commit the changes to the material and save the package to preserve your progress.

END TUTORIAL 2.24

TUTORIAL 2.25: Configurable Water Material, Part IV: Reflection

1. Open the mat_water material in the Material Editor. If you have not completed **TUTORIAL 2.24**, you may open the mat_water_03 material instead.

Because water is a reflective surface, we need to add the ability to place a reflection in the material. However, in order to make this material general enough to be used for different types of fluid surfaces, the ability to kill out the reflection is provided as well.

2

2. To the left of the Normals section, create a ReflectionVector expression. Name the expression **ReflectVector**. This expression provides the texture coordinates for the cubemap used as the reflection map.

3. To the left of the ReflectVector expression, create a Transform expression. Name the expression **ReflectTransform** and make sure the TransformType property is set to TRANSFORM_World. This expression ensures the reflection is oriented correctly.

4. Connect the Output of the ReflectVector expression to the Input of the ReflectTransform expression (see **FIGURE 2.112**).

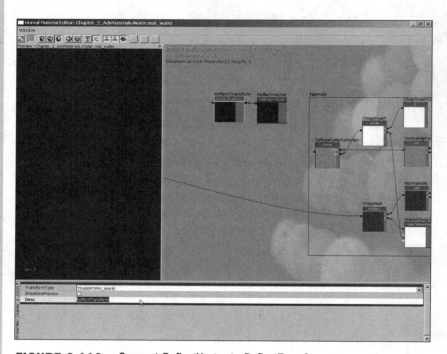

FIGURE 2.112   Connect ReflectVector to ReflectTransform.

5. To the left of the ReflectTransform expression, create a TextureSampleParameterCube expression using the cube_water_terrain cubemap as its default texture. Name the expression **ReflectionCubeMap**.

6. Connect the Output of the ReflectTransform expression to the UVs input of the ReflectionCubeMap (see **FIGURE 2.113**).

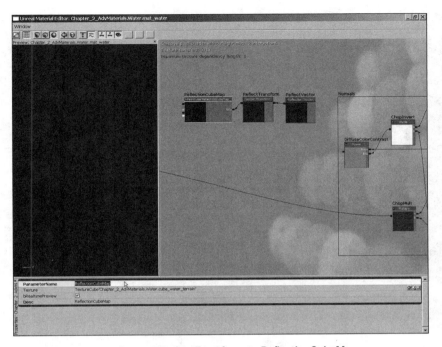

FIGURE 2.113   Connect ReflectTransform to ReflectionCubeMap.

7. Below the ReflectionCubeMap expression, create a ScalarParameter expression. Name the expression **ReflectionStrength** and set its value to 1.0 as a default.

8. To the left of the ReflectionCubeMap and ReflectionStrength expressions, create a Multiply expression. Name the expression **ReflectMult**.

9. Connect the RGB output of the ReflectionCubeMap expression to the A input of the ReflectMult expression. Then, connect the Output of the ReflectionStrength expression to the B input of the ReflectMult expression (see **FIGURE 2.114**).

10. Connect the Output of the ReflectMult expression to the material node's Emissive channel in order to preview the reflection and normals.

11. Select the expressions created in this tutorial and press the C key to create a comment block. Name the comment block **Reflection**. Commit the changes to the material and save the package to preserve your work.

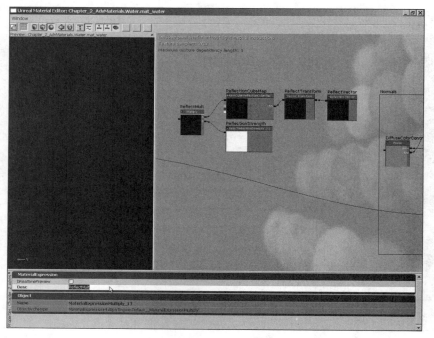

FIGURE 2.114   Multiply ReflectionCubeMap by ReflectionStrength.

END TUTORIAL 2.25

TUTORIAL 2.26: Configurable Water Material, Part V: Diffuse Color

1. Open the mat_water material in the Material Editor. If you have not completed **TUTORIAL 2.25**, you may open the mat_water_04 material instead.

    With the reflection network in place, we can add the network that controls the diffuse color of the material. This can be used to color the water or create entirely different types of fluids.

2. Above the Reflection section, create a VectorParameter expression. Name the expression **WaterColor** and set the following values as the defaults:

    ▸ **R**: 0.075

    ▸ **G**: 0.0825

    ▸ **B**: 0.12

    ▸ **A**: 1.0

3. To the left of the WaterColor expression, create a Multiply expression. Name the expression **ColorMult**.

4. Connect the RGB output of the WaterColor expression to the A input of the ColorMult expression. Then, connect the Output of the DiffuseColorContrast expression to the B input of the ColorMult expression (see **FIGURE 2.115**). This adjusts the color based on the choppiness of the water.

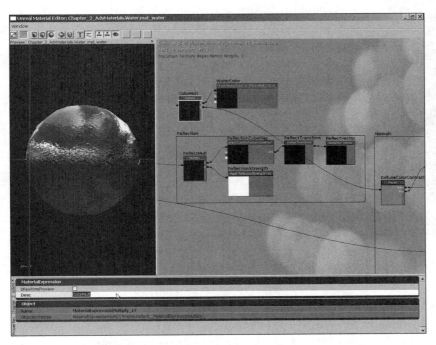

FIGURE 2.115   Your nodes should connect like so.

5. To the left of the ColorMult expression, create an Add expression. Name the expression **DiffuseAdd**.

6. Connect the Output of the ColorMult expression to the A input of the DiffuseAdd expression. Then, connect the Output of the ReflectMult expression to the B input of the DiffuseAdd expression. This calculation adds the reflection to the color (see **FIGURE 2.116**).

7. Connect the Output of the DiffuseAdd expression to the material node's Emissive input in place of the connection presently there to preview the addition of the color to the water.

8. Select the expressions created in this tutorial and press the C key to create a comment block. Name the comment block **DiffuseColor**. Commit the changes to the material and save the package to preserve your work.

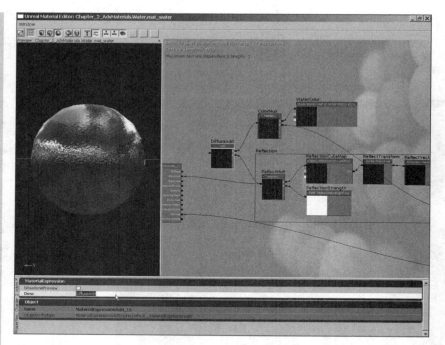

FIGURE 2.116   Add the ColorMult node to the ReflectMult node.

END TUTORIAL 2.26

TUTORIAL 2.27: Configurable Water Material, Part VI: Specular Highlight

1. Open the mat_water material in the Material Editor. If you have not completed **TUTORIAL 2.26**, you may open the mat_water_05 material instead.

   To finish off the diffuse portion of the material, we need to add a specular highlight. The reflection gives it that shiny feel, but adding the specular highlight allows it to look even more believable. You have seen this previously in the Candle Wax Material tutorials, so it should be familiar.

2. Above the DiffuseColor section, create a VectorParameter expression. Name the expression **LightVector** and set the following values (see **FIGURE 2.117**):

   ▸ **R**: 0.5

   ▸ **G**: 0.5

   ▸ **B**: 1.0

   ▸ **A**: 1.0

   This allows us to specify a direction for the light, most likely the sun, in the map in which the material is being used.

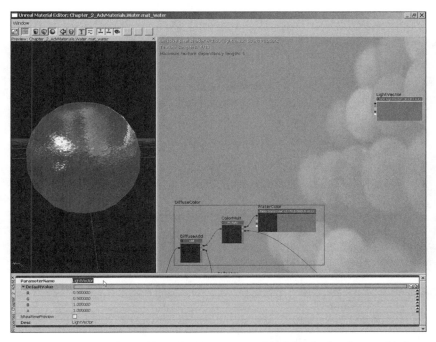

FIGURE 2.117 A new VectorParameter named LightVector has been added.

3. To the left of the LightVector expression, create a Normalize expression. Name the expression **LightNorm**. This is used to ensure that the vector used in the next calculation is a unit vector, meaning its length is 1.0.

4. Connect the RGB output of the LightVector expression to the input of the LightNorm expression (see **FIGURE 2.118**).

5. Above the LightNorm expression, create a ReflectionVector expression. Name the expression **SpecReflectVector**.

6. To the left of the SpecReflectVector and LightNorm expressions, create a DotProduct expression. Name the expression **SpecDotProduct**.

7. Connect the Output of the SpecReflectVector to the A input of the SpecDotProduct expression. Then, connect the Output of the LightNorm expression to the B input of the SpecDotProduct expression (see **FIGURE 2.119**).

8. Below the SpecDotProduct expression, create a Constant expression. Name the expression **SpecClampConst0** and leave its value set to 0.0.

9. Below the SpecClampConst0 expression, create another Constant expression. Name the expression **SpecClampConst1** and set its value to 1.0.

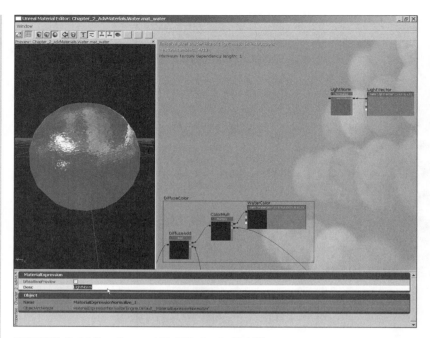

FIGURE 2.118   Connect LightVector to LightNorm.

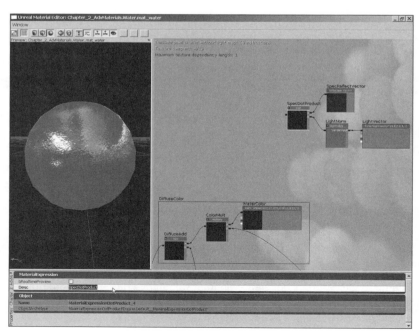

FIGURE 2.119   You are now taking the dot product of SpecReflectVector and LightNorm.

10. To the left of the SpecDotProduct expression, create a Clamp expression. Name the expression **SpecClamp**.

11. Make the following connections (see **FIGURE 2.120**):

 ▶ SpecDotProduct-Output → SpecClamp-Input(unlabeled)

 ▶ SpecClampConst0-Output → SpecClamp-Min

 ▶ SpecCalmpConst1-Output → SpecClamp-Max

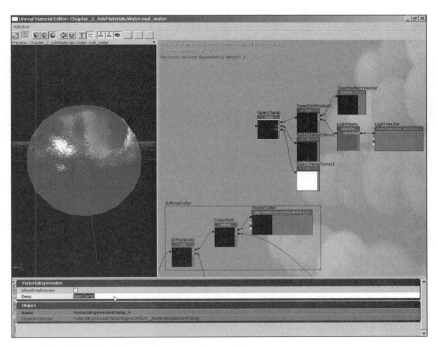

FIGURE 2.120   Connect your nodes as shown.

12. Below the SpecClamp expression, create a ScalarParameter expression. Name the expression **SpecularPower** and set its value to 200.0 as the default.

13. To the left of the SpecClamp expression, create a Power expression. Name the expression **SpecPowerExp**.

14. Connect the Output of the SpecClamp expression to the Base input of the SpecPowerExp expression. Then connect the Output of the SpecularPower expression to the Exp input of the SpecPowerExp expression (see **FIGURE 2.121**).

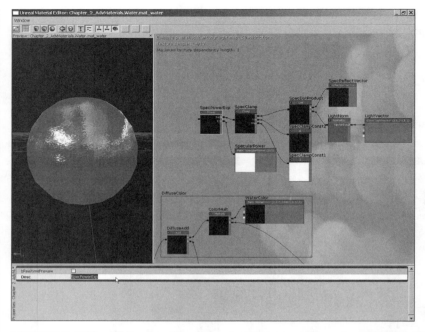

FIGURE 2.121   This raises SpecClamp by the power of the value of SpecularPower.

15. Below the SpecPowerExp expression, create a VectorParameter expression. Name the expression **SpecularColor** and set the following values:

> ▸ **R**: 1.5

> ▸ **G**: 1.35

> ▸ **B**: 0.8

> ▸ **A**: 1.0

16. To the left of the SpecPowerExp expression, create a Multiply expression. Name the expression **SpecAmountMult**.

17. Connect the Output of the SpecPowerExp expression to the A input of the SpecAmountMult expression. Then, connect the RGB output of the SpecularColor expression to the B input of the SpecAmountMult expression (see **FIGURE 2.122**).

18. To the left of the SpecAmountMult expression, create an Add expression. Name the expression **DiffuseFinalAdd**.

19. Make the following connections (see **FIGURE 2.123**):

> ▸ SpecAmountMult-Output → DiffuseFinalAdd-A

> ▸ DiffuseAdd-Output → DiffuseFinalAdd-B

> ▸ DiffuseFinalAdd-Output → Material-Emissive

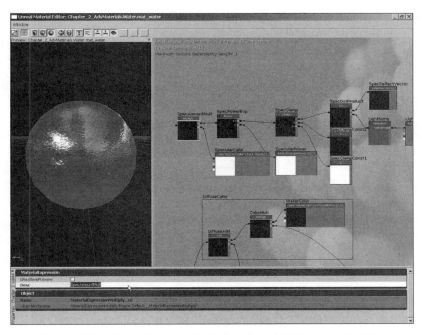

FIGURE 2.122 You will now multiply SpecPowerMult by SpecularColor.

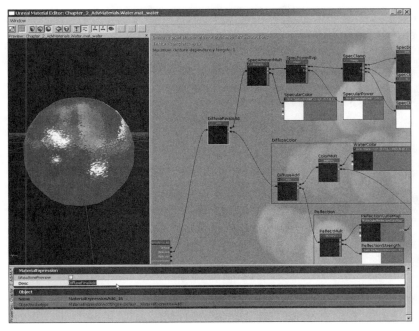

FIGURE 2.123 Connect your nodes like so.

2

20. The specular highlight should now be visible on the material in the preview. Place a comment box around all the nodes created in this tutorial and then name the box **Specular**. Commit the changes to the material and save the package to preserve your work.

END TUTORIAL 2.27

TUTORIAL 2.28: Configurable Water Material, Part VII: Transparency

1. Open the mat_water material in the Material Editor. If you have not completed **TUTORIAL 2.27**, you may open the mat_water_06 material instead.

   The next section in the water material we need to create is for the transparency. We are going to use a depth-based system that determines the transparency (or opacity, depending on how you look at it) based on the distance from the water surface to whatever is behind it or under it. The basic idea is to sample the depth of the pixel being rendered and sample the depth of the pixel behind it. The difference between those is equivalent to the depth of the water. Then, we can set up a network to blend between levels of transparency based on that depth.

2. Below the Reflection section, create a DestDepth expression by dragging it from the Material Expressions list or selecting it from the context menu. Name the expression **BottomDepth** (see **FIGURE 2.124**).

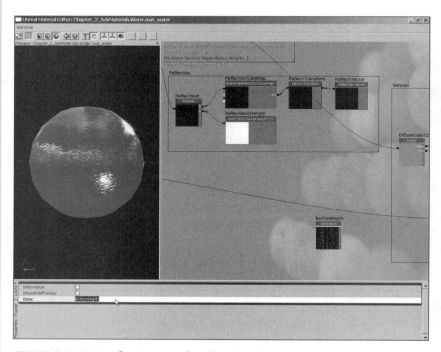

FIGURE 2.124   Create a new DestDepth node.

3. Below the BottomDepth expression, create a PixelDepth expression by dragging it from the Material Expressions list or selecting it from the context menu. Name the expression **TopDepth**.

4. To the left of the BottomDepth and TopDepth expressions, create a Subtract expression by holding down the S key and left-clicking. Name the expression **DepthDiff**.

5. Connect the Output of the BottomDepth expression to the A input of the DepthDiff expression. Then, connect the Output of the TopDepth expression to the B input of the DepthDiff expression (see **FIGURE 2.125**).

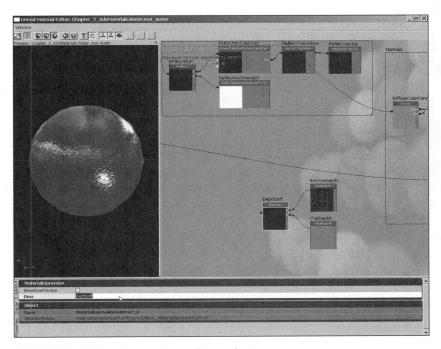

FIGURE 2.125   Connect the nodes as shown.

The result of this calculation is the depth of the water surface above the ground. In order to use this, we need to normalize this value to a range of 0.0 to 1.0 so that it can be used as the Alpha value for a LinearInterpolate expression. To do this, we divide by some value that represents the depth at which the water's surface will become completely opaque. Then, we clamp the result between 0.0 and 1.0 and plug it into a LinearInterpolate expression that blends between a minimum and maximum opacity value.

6. To the left of the DepthDiff expression, create a Divide expression. Name the expression **DepthNormalize**.

7. Below the DepthDiff expression, create a ScalarParameter expression. Name the expression **ExtinctionDepth** and set its value to 1024 as the default.

8. Connect the Output of the DepthDiff expression to the A input of the DepthNormalize expression. Then, connect the Output of the ExtinctionDepth expression to the B input of the DepthNormalize expression (see **FIGURE 2.126**).

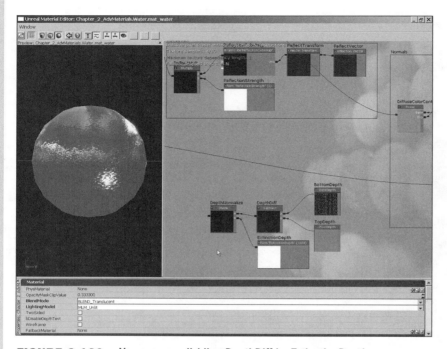

FIGURE 2.126   You are now dividing DepthDiff by ExtinctionDepth.

9. To the left of the DepthNormalize expression, create a Clamp expression. Name the expression **DepthClamp**.

10. Below the DepthNormalize expression, create a Constant expression. Name the expression **DepthClampMin** and leave its value set to 0.0.

11. Below the DepthClampMin expression, create another Constant expression. Name the expression **DepthClampMax** and set its value to 1.0.

12. Make the following connections (see **FIGURE 2.127**):

▶ DepthNormalize-Output → DepthClamp-Input(unlabeled)

▶ DepthClampMin-Output → DepthClamp-Min

▶ DepthClampMax-Output → DepthClamp-Max

13. Above the DepthClamp expression, create a ScalarParameter expression. Name the expression **MaxOpacity** and set its value to 0.75 as the default.

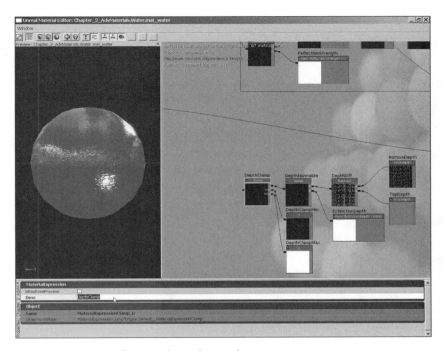

FIGURE 2.127   Connect the nodes as shown.

14. Above the MaxOpacity expression, create another ScalarParameter expression. Name the expression **MinOpacity** and set its value to 0.25 as the default.

15. To the left of the MaxOpacity expression, create a LinearInterpolate expression. Name the expression **DepthInterp**.

16. Make the following connections (see **FIGURE 2.128**):

   ▶ MinOpacity-Output → DepthInterp-A

   ▶ MaxOpacity-Output → DepthInterp-B

   ▶ DepthClamp-Output → DepthInterp-Alpha

17. To the left of the DepthInterp expression, create a DepthBiasedAlpha expression. Name the expression **DepthBlend** and set its BiasScale property to 25.0.

18. Connect the Output of the DepthInterp expression to the Alpha input of the DepthBlend expression. Then, connect the Output of the DepthBlend expression to the material node's Opacity channel.

19. Select all the expressions created in this tutorial and press the C key to create a comment block. Name the comment block **Transparency** (see **FIGURE 2.129**).

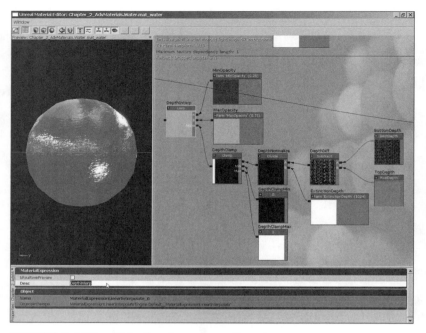

FIGURE 2.128   Make the shown connections.

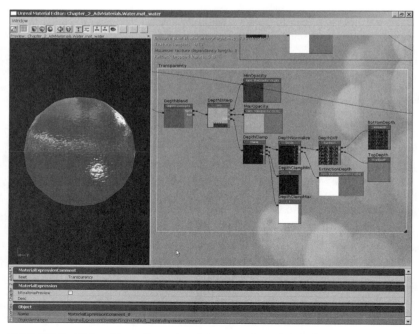

FIGURE 2.129   The entire network has now been labeled.

20. The only effect of this that's immediately apparent in the preview is that the material turns semitransparent. The depth blend only functions correctly in an actual map. Commit the changes to the material and save the package to preserve your work.

END TUTORIAL 2.28

TUTORIAL 2.29: Configurable Water Material, Part VIII: Refraction

1. Open the mat_water material in the Material Editor. If you have not completed **TUTORIAL 2.28**, you may open the mat_water_07 material instead.

The final step in creating the water material is to set up some refraction. In the case of Unreal materials, the term *distortion* may be more accurate because that is truly what is happening. The network we set up will attempt to mimic true refraction, but it's merely an approximation created through trial and error to get a satisfactory result.

2. Below the Transparency section, create a ScalarParameter expression. Name the expression **IndexOfRefraction** and set its value to 1.33, or the index of refraction of water (see **FIGURE 2.130**).

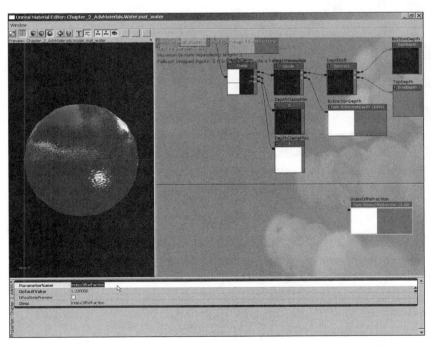

FIGURE 2.130   Create a new ScalarParameter named IndexOfRefraction.

3. Below the IndexOfRefraction expression, create a Constant expression. Name the expression **IndexCorrectionConst** and set its value to 1.0.

4. To the left of the IndexOfRefraction expression, create a Subtract expression. Name the expression **IndexCorrection**.

5. Connect the Output of the IndexOfRefraction expression to the A input of the IndexCorrection expression. Then, connect the Output of the IndexCorrectionConst expression to the B input of the IndexCorrection expression (see **FIGURE 2.131**).

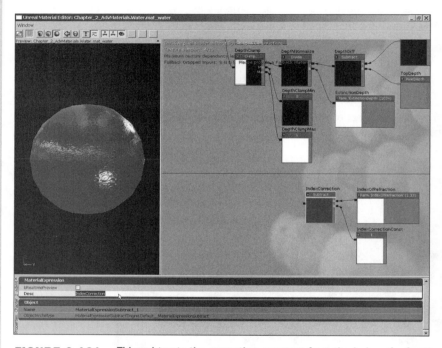

FIGURE 2.131   This subtracts the correction constant from the index of refraction.

This is simply a small correction to the value of the parameter arrived at by testing to see what value worked the best.

6. Below the IndexCorrection expression, create a Constant expression. Name the expression **IndexClampMin** and leave its value set to 0.0.

7. To the left of the IndexCorrection expression, create a Clamp expression. Name the expression **IndexClamp**.

8. Connect the Output of the IndexCorrection expression to the Input (which is unlabeled) of the IndexClamp expression. Then, connect the Output of the IndexClampMin expression to the Min input of the IndexClamp expression (see **FIGURE 2.132**).

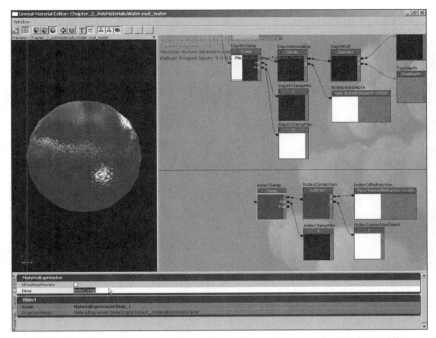

FIGURE 2.132   Clamp IndexCorrection with a minimum of IndexClampMin.

9. Below the IndexClamp expression, create a Constant expression. Name the expression **RGMultiplier** and set its value to 12.0.

10. Below the RGMultiplier expression, create another Constant expression. Name the expression **Bmultiplier** and set its value to 0.133.

11. To the right of the IndexClamp expression, create a Multiply expression. Name the expression **RGMult**.

12. Below the RGMult expression, create another Multiply expression. Name the expression **BMult**.

13. Make the following connections (see **FIGURE 2.133**):

  ▶ IndexClamp-Output → RGMult-A

  ▶ RGMultiplier-Output → RGMult-B

  ▶ IndexClamp-Output → BMult-A

  ▶ Bmultiplier-Output → BMult-B

14. To the left of the RGMult expression, create an AppendVector expression. Name the expression **RGAppend**.

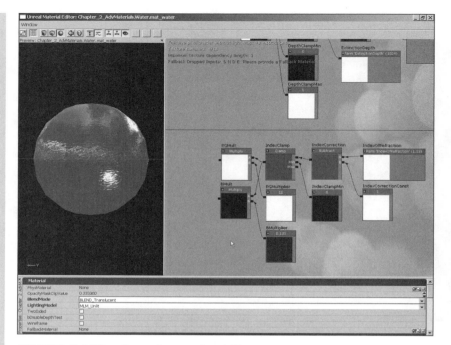

FIGURE 2.133   Connect your network like so.

15. Connect the Output of the RGMult expression to both the A and B inputs of the RGAppend expression.

This creates a two-component vector with both components having the same value, which is determined by multiplying the corrected index of refraction by 12.0, a value arrived at by testing to find the one that worked best.

16. To the left of the RGAppend expression, create another Append expression. Name the expression **BAppend**.

17. Connect the Output of the RGAppend expression to the A input of the BAppend expression. Then, connect the Output of the BMult expression to the B input of the BAppend expression (see **FIGURE 2.134**).

This adds a third component to the previous vector that has a much lower value than the other two components. This vector is multiplied by the normals of the material and then applied to the Distortion channel to create the final effect.

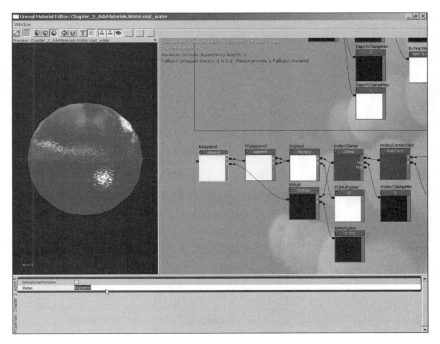

FIGURE 2.134   This appends RGAppend to BMult.

18. To the left of the BAppend expression, create a Multiply expression. Name the expression **RefractMult**.

19. Connect the RGB output of the ChopMult expression from the Normals section to the A input of the RefractMult expression. Then, connect the Output of the BAppend expression to the B input of the RefractMult expression.

20. Connect the Output of the RefractMult expression to the materials Distortion channel. Select the expressions created in this tutorial and press the C key to create a comment block. Name the comment block **Refraction**. Commit the changes to the material and save the package to preserve your progress (see **FIGURE 2.135**).

    If you would like to test this material out in a real situation, feel free to create a material instance using this material as its parent. Then, open the DM-CH_02_Water map and apply the instanced material to the plane in the map. After that, you should be able to adjust the parameter values of the instanced material and see their effects in the viewport (see **FIGURE 2.136**).

2

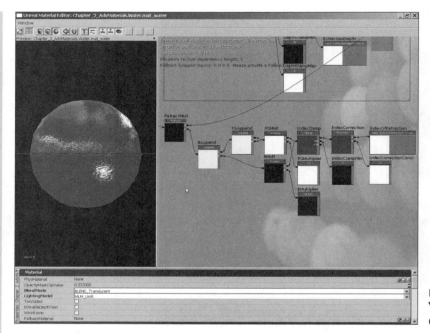

FIGURE 2.135
Your network is
complete.

FIGURE 2.136
The final water
material in action.

END TUTORIAL 2.29

Over the course of **TUTORIALS 2.30** through **2.34**, you create a toon material, or *cel shader* as it is often called. This material attempts to reproduce the look of hand-drawn graphics by limiting the number of color levels available and outlining the object. We use the CustomLighting channel of the material to achieve the desired result.

> **NOTE**
>
> All expressions are named by setting their Desc properties and are referred to by those names throughout these tutorials. When dealing with naming parameter expressions, it is assumed that naming refers to setting both the ParameterName and Desc properties.

TUTORIAL 2.30: Configurable Toon Material, Part I: Setup, TextureCoordinates, and Normals

1. Right-click in the Generic Browser and choose New Material. Enter the following information in the dialog that appears and then click OK:

   - **Package**: Chapter_2_AdvMaterials
   - **Group**: Toon
   - **Name**: mat_toon

2. Select the material node and set the LightingModel property to MLM_Custom. This allows us to use the CustomLighting channel for the material.

3. Give yourself some room to work and create a TextureCoordinate expression off to the right. Name the expression **TexCoords** and leave its UTiling and VTiling values set to 1.0 because this is just a base to work from (see **FIGURE 2.137**).

4. Below the TexCoords expression, create a ScalarParameter expression. Name the expression **UVTiling** and set its value to 1.0 as the default.

5. To the left of the TexCoords and UVTiling expressions, create a Multiply expression. Name the expression **UVMult**.

6. Connect the Output of the TexCoords expression to the A input of the UVMult expression. Then, connect the Output of the UVTiling expression to the B input of the UVMult expression (see **FIGURE 2.138**).

   This calculation provides control over the tiling of the texture coordinates within any instance of this material.

7. Select the expressions created so far and press the C key to create a comment block. Name the comment block **TextureCoordinates**.

8. To the left of the TextureCoordinates section, create a TextureSampleParameter2D expression using the tangent_normal texture as its default texture. Name the expression **NormalTex**.

9. Duplicate the NormalTex expression and position the new version below the original. Change the name of the new expression to OutlineNormalTex.

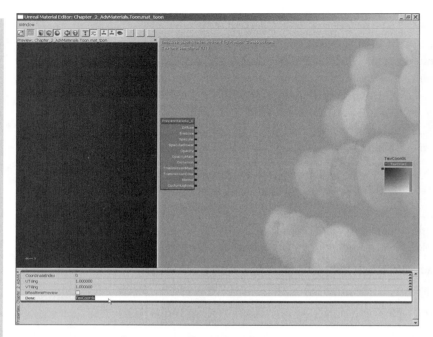

FIGURE 2.137   Create a new TextureCoordinate node.

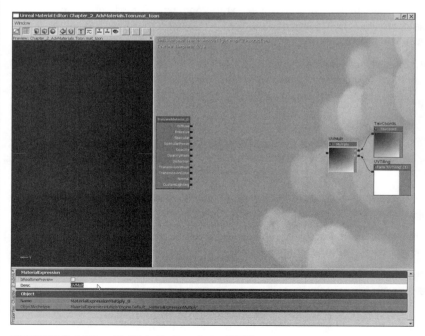

FIGURE 2.138   Multiply TexCoords by UVTiling.

10. Connect the Output of the UVMult expression to the UVs input of the NormalTex expression. Then, connect the Output of the UVMult expression to the UVs input of the OutlineNormalTex expression (see **FIGURE 2.139**).

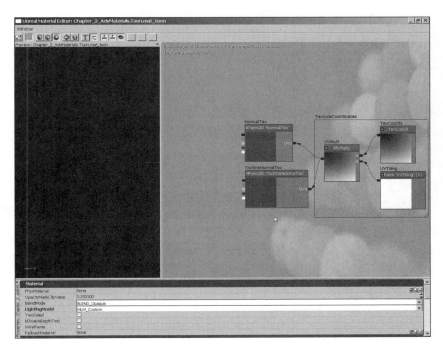

FIGURE 2.139 Connect the nodes as shown.

11. Select the two new expressions and press the C key to create a new comment block. Name the comment block **Normals** (see **FIGURE 2.140**).

12. Commit the changes to the material and save the package to preserve your progress.

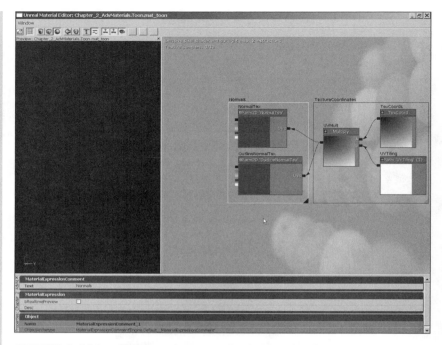

FIGURE 2.140   Make sure to comment out your network.

END TUTORIAL 2.30

TUTORIAL 2.31: Configurable Toon Material, Part II: Diffuse Color

1. Open the mat_toon material in the Material Editor. If you have not completed **TUTORIAL 2.30**, you may open the mat_toon_01 material instead.

   Because we are using the custom lighting model, we need to calculate our own lighting. This requires calculating the dot product of the light's direction vector and the normals of the surface. This is the same process used in the wax material previously, so it should be familiar.

2. To the left of the Normals section, create a LightVector expression. Name the expression **DiffuseLightVector** (see **FIGURE 2.141**).

3. To the left of the DiffuseLightVector expression, create a DotProduct expression. Name the expression **DiffuseDotProduct**.

4. Connect the output of the DiffuseLightVector expression to the A input of the DiffuseDotProduct expression. Then, connect the RBG output of the NormalTex expression to the B input of the DiffuseDotProduct expression (see **FIGURE 2.142**).

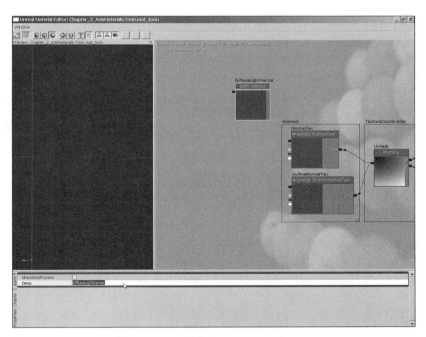

FIGURE 2.141   Create a new LightVector expression.

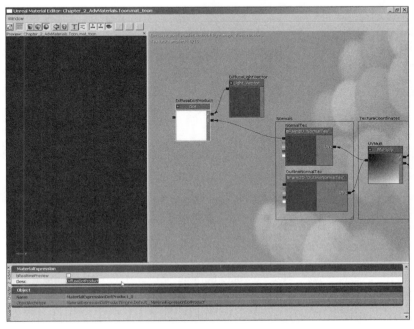

FIGURE 2.142   This calculates the dot product of the light vector and the surface normal.

Now, we need to clamp the result of this calculation to make sure no unexpected values get through.

5. Below the DiffuseDotProduct expression, create a Constant expression. Name the expression **DiffuseClampMin** and leave its value set to 0.0.

6. Below the DiffuseClampMax expression, create another Constant expression. Name the expression **DiffuseClampMax** and set its value to 1.0.

7. To the left of the DiffuseClampMin expression, create a Clamp expression. Name the expression **DiffuseClamp**.

8. Make the following connections (see **FIGURE 2.143**):

   ▸ DiffuseDotProduct-Output → DifuseClamp-Input(unlabeled)

   ▸ DiffuseClampMin-Output → DiffuseClamp-Min

   ▸ DiffuseClampMax-Output → DiffuseClamp-Max

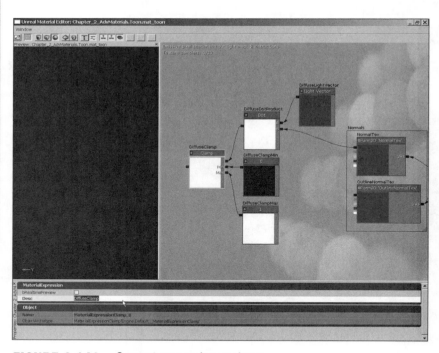

FIGURE 2.143   Connect your nodes as shown.

9. Above the DiffuseClamp expression, create a VectorParameter expression. Name the expression **DiffuseColor** and set the following values:

- ▶ **R**: 1.0

- ▶ **G**: 0.0

- ▶ **B**: 0.0

- ▶ **A**: 1.0

10. To the left of the DiffuseColor expression, create a Multiply expression. Name the expression **DiffuseMult**.

11. Make the following connections (see **FIGURE 2.144**):

- ▶ DiffuseColor-RGB → DiffuseMult-A

- ▶ DiffuseClamp-Output → DiffuseMult-B

- ▶ DiffuseMult-Output → Material-CustomLighting

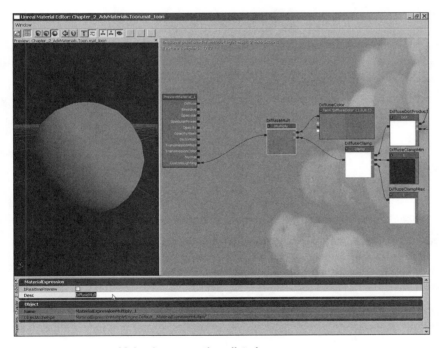

FIGURE 2.144   Make the connections listed.

12. Select the expression created in this tutorial and press the C key to create a comment block. Name the comment block **Diffuse** (see **FIGURE 2.145**).

13. You should see the material shaded, meaning it is lit (red in the preview). Commit the changes to the material and save the package to preserve your progress.

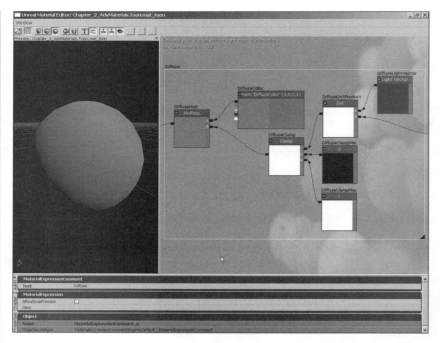

FIGURE 2.145   Place a comment around this section of the network.

END TUTORIAL 2.31

TUTORIAL 2.32: Configurable Toon Material, Part III: Specular Highlight

1. Open the mat_toon material in the Material Editor.

   Adding specularity to a toon material is not absolutely necessary but is more a matter of personal preference and the desired end result. We are going to add in the functionality and allow the artist to decide whether it is needed on a per-instance basis by adjusting parameter values.

2. Above the Diffuse section, create a new LightVector expression. Name the expression **SpecLightVector**. We are using a separate LightVector expression for the specular calculation purely for ease of readability (see **FIGURE 2.146**).

3. Above the SpecLightVector expression, create a ReflectionVector expression. Name the expression **ReflectVector**.

4. To the left of the ReflectVector and SpecLightVector expressions, create a DotProduct expression. Name the expression **SpecDotProduct**.

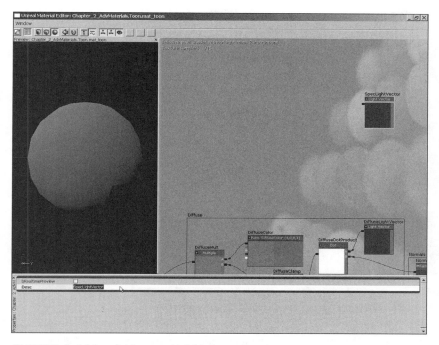

FIGURE 2.146   Add a new LightVector expression.

5. Connect the Output of the ReflectVector expression to the A input of the SpecDotProduct expression. Then, connect the Output of the SpecLightVector expression to the B input of the SpecDotProduct expression (see **FIGURE 2.147**).

6. Below the SpecDotProduct expression, create a Constant expression. Name the expression **SpecClampMin** and leave its value set to 0.0.

7. Below the SpecClampMin expression, create another Constant expression. Name the expression **SpecClampMax** and set its value to 1.0.

8. To the left of the SpecClampMin expression, create a Clamp expression. Name the expression **SpecClamp**.

9. Make the following connections (see **FIGURE 2.148**):

- ▶ SpecDotProduct-Output → SpecClamp-Input(unlabeled)
- ▶ SpecClampMin-Output → SpecClamp-Min
- ▶ SpecClampMax-Output → SpecClamp-Max

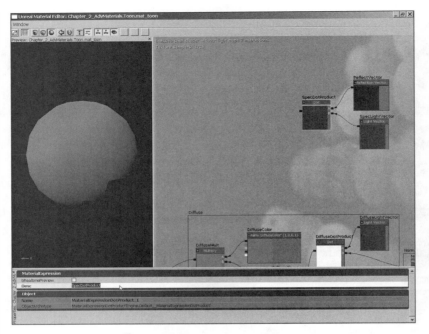

FIGURE 2.147   You now get the dot product of the reflection vector and the specular light vector.

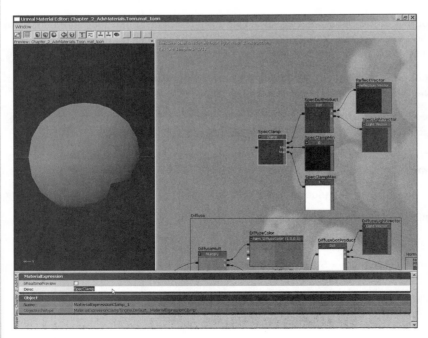

FIGURE 2.148   Connect your nodes as shown here.

In order to make the specular highlight respect the normals of the surface, we need to do another dot product calculation of the result so far and the normals.

10. To the left of the SpecClamp expression, create a new DotProduct expression. Name the expression **SpecNormalDotProduct**.

11. Connect the Output of the SpecClamp expression to the A input of the SpecNormalDotProduct expression. Then, connect the RGB output of the NormalTex expression from the Normals section to the B input of the SpecNormalDotProduct expression (see **FIGURE 2.149**).

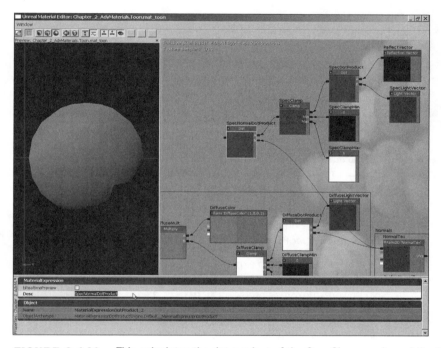

FIGURE 2.149 This calculates the dot product of the SpecClamp node and the NormalTex.

12. To the left of the SpecNormalDotProduct expression, create a new Clamp expression. Name the expression **SpecNormalClamp**.

13. Make the following connections (see **FIGURE 2.150**):

  ▶ SpecNormalDotProduct-Output → SpecNormalClamp-Input(unlabeled)

  ▶ SpecClampMin-Output → SpecNormalClamp-Min

  ▶ SpecClampMax-Output → SpecNormalClamp-Max

14. Below the SpecNormalClamp expression, create a ScalarParameter expression. Name the expression **SpecPower** and set its value to 25.0 as the default.

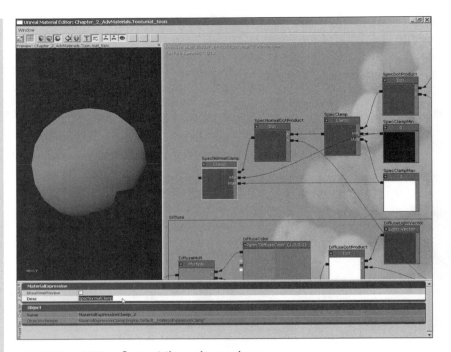

FIGURE 2.150   Connect the nodes as shown.

15. To the left of the SpecNormalClamp and SpecularPowerExp expressions, create a Power expression. Name the expression **SpecPowerExp**.

16. Connect the Output of the SpecNormalClamp expression to the Base input of the SpecPowerExp expression. Then, connect the Output of the SpecularPower expression to the Exp input of the SpecPowerExp expression (see **FIGURE 2.151**).

This calculation determines the tightness of the specular highlight. It can also be thought of as determining how glossy the material is.

17. Below the SpecPowerExp expression, create a VectorParameter expression. Name the expression **SpecularColor** and set the following values:

> ▶ **R**: 0.5
>
> ▶ **G**: 0.0
>
> ▶ **B**: 0.0
>
> ▶ **A**: 1.0

18. To the left of the SpecPowerExp expression, create a Multiply expression. Name the expression **SpecMult**.

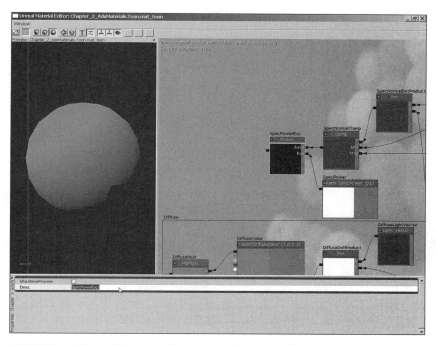

FIGURE 2.151   This raises the value of SpecNormalClamp to the power of the value of SpecularPowerExp.

19. Connect the Output of the SpecPowerExp expression to the A input of the SpecMult expression. Then, connect the RGB output of the SpecularColor expression to the B input of the SpecMult expression (see **FIGURE 2.152**).

This calculation determines how bright and what color the specular highlight will be. We could have made the brightness and color two separate expressions and multiplied them to get this effect, which may be friendlier to the artist, but this would have added extra expressions. This decision is more personal preference than anything because the two extra expressions would most likely not noticeably harm performance.

20. To the left of the SpecMult expression, create an Add expression. Name the expression **SpecAdd**.

21. Make the following connections (see **FIGURE 2.153**):

- ▸ SpecMult-Output → SpecAdd-A

- ▸ DiffuseMult-Output → SpecAdd-B

- ▸ SpecAdd-Output → Material-CustomLighting

2

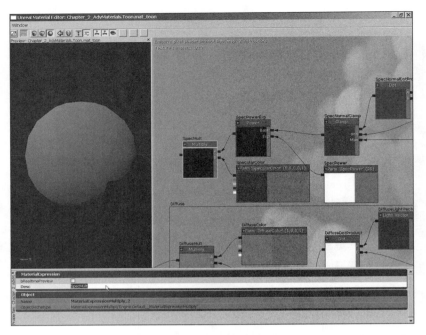

FIGURE 2.152   Multiply the SpecPowerExp node by the SpecularColor node.

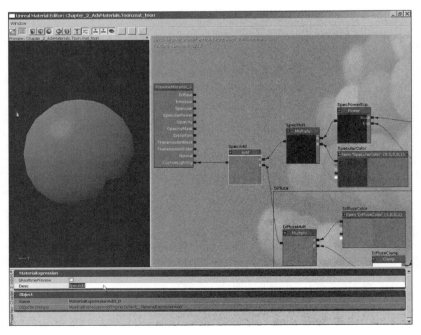

FIGURE 2.153   Connect the nodes as shown.

This calculation adds the specular highlight to the diffuse color to produce the final color information that will eventually be passed to the network creating the toon effect. At this point, however, it is simply passed to the material to preview the results.

22. Select the expressions created in this tutorial and press the C key to create a new comment block. Name the comment block **SpecularHighlight**. Commit the changes to the material and save the package to preserve your work (see **FIGURE 2.154**).

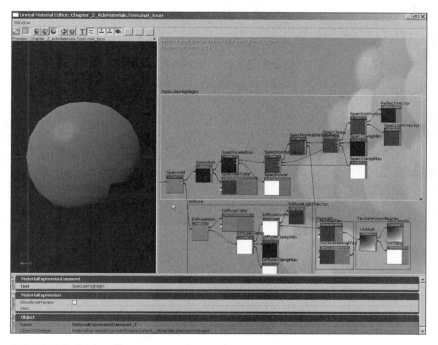

FIGURE 2.154   Comment out the section.

END TUTORIAL 2.32

TUTORIAL 2.33: Configurable Toon Material, Part IV: Cel Shading

1. Open the mat_toon material in the Material Editor. If you have not completed **TUTORIAL 2.32**, you may open the mat_toon_03 material instead.

The toon network essentially takes the color information from the Diffuse and Specular sections and converts the smooth shading to a stepped shading. The math behind this function is fairly simple. The color passed from the Specular section is multiplied by the number of color levels desired. Then, the Floor expression is used to remove any fractions, leaving the color information with only whole number values. Finally, those values are divided by the number of color levels. The number of levels is configurable, and an ambient color is added as well.

2. To the left of the SpecularHighlight and Diffuse sections, create a ScalarParameter expression. Name the expression **ColorLevels** and set its value to 3.0 as the default (see **FIGURE 2.155**).

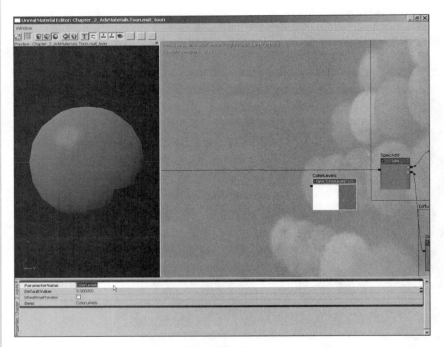

FIGURE 2.155   Create a new ScalarParameter.

3. To the left of the ColorLevels expression, create a Multiply expression. Name the expression **CelMult**.

4. Connect the Output of the SpecAdd expression to the A input of the CelMult expression. Then, connect the Output of the ColorLevels expression to the B input of the CelMult expression (see **FIGURE 2.156**).

5. To the left of the CelMult expression, create a Floor expression. Name the expression **CelFloor**.

6. Connect the Output of the CelMult expression to the Input of the CelFloor expression.

7. To the left of the CelFloor expression, create a Divide expression. Name the expression **CelDivide**.

8. Connect the Output of the CelFloor expression to the A input of the CelDivide expression. Then, connect the Output of the ColorLevels expression to the B input of the CelDivide expression (see **FIGURE 2.157**).

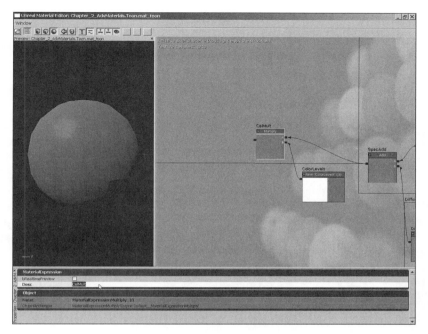

FIGURE 2.156 Multiply the SpecAdd by the ColorLevels.

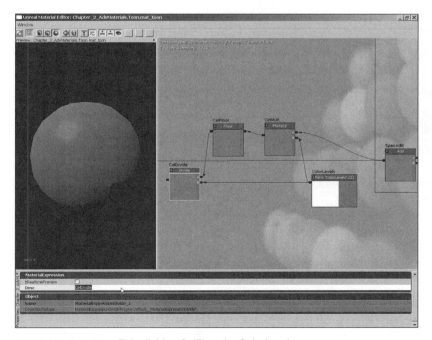

FIGURE 2.157 This divides CelFloor by ColorLevels.

2

9. Below the CelDivide expression, create a VectorParameter expression. Name the expression **AmbientColor** and set the following values:

   ▸ **R**: 0.2

   ▸ **G**: 0.0

   ▸ **B**: 0.0

   ▸ **A**: 1.0

10. To the left of the CelDivide and AmbientColor expression, create an Add expression. Name the expression **AmbientAdd**.

11. Connect the Output of the CelDivide expression to the A input of the AmbientAdd expression. Then, connect the RGB output of the AmbientColor expression to the B input of the AmbientAdd expression (see **FIGURE 2.158**).

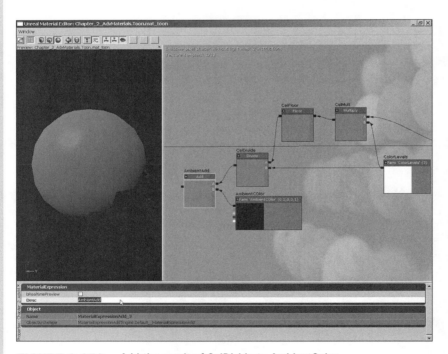

FIGURE 2.158   Add the result of CelDivide to AmbientColor.

12. Select the expression created in this tutorial and press the C key to create a new comment block. Name the comment block **CelShading**.

13. Connect the Output of the AmbientAdd expression to the CustomLighting channel of the material node. You should see the stepped color effect in the preview (see **FIGURE 2.159**). Commit the changes to the material and save the package to preserve your progress.

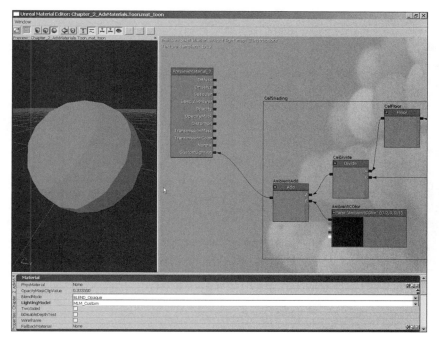

FIGURE 2.159 Your network should give this result.

END TUTORIAL 2.33

TUTORIAL 2.34: Configurable Toon Material, Part V: Outlines

1. Open the mat_toon material in the Material Editor. If you have not completed **TUTORIAL 2.33**, you may open the mat_toon_04 material instead.

   The last part of the toon material is to add the outline. This is accomplished using a network containing a Fresnel expression and a Power expression. This allows us to adjust the width of the lines from within any instances of the material.

2. Below the CelShading section, create a Fresnel expression. Name the expression **LineFresnel** (see **FIGURE 2.160**).

3. Connect the RGB output of the OutlineNormalTex expression to the Normal input of the LineFresnel expression.

   This allows a normal map to be specified and used in determining where the lines appear. One benefit of this is that it makes the material more usable on flat surfaces because the Fresnel expression can cause a fairly undesirable effect based solely on the normals of a flat mesh.

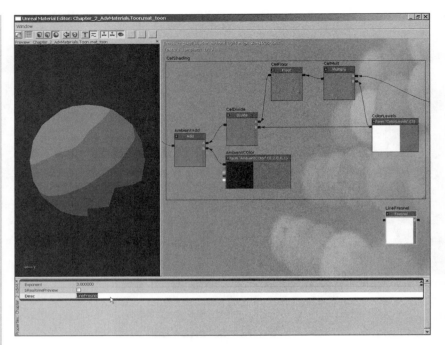

FIGURE 2.160   Add a new Fresnel node.

4. To the left of the LineFresnel expression, create a OneMinus expression. Name the expression **LineInvert**.

5. Connect the Output of the LineFresnel expression to the Input of the LineInvert expression (see **FIGURE 2.161**).

6. Below the LineFresnel expression, create a ScalarParameter expression. Name the expression **LineWidth** and set its value to 1.0 as the default.

7. Below the LineWidth expression, create a Constant expression. Name the expression **LineConst** and set its value to 5.0.

8. To the left of the LineWidth expression, create a Multiply expression. Name the expression **LineWidthMult**.

9. Connect the Output of the LineWidth expression to the A input of the LineWidthMult expression. Then, connect the Output of the LineConst expression to the B input of the LineWidthMult expression (see **FIGURE 2.162**).

10. To the left of the LineInvert and LineWidthMult expressions, create a Power expression. Name the expression **LineWidthPower**.

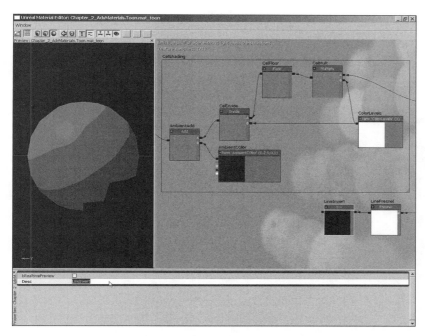

FIGURE 2.161   Connect LineFresnel into LineInvert.

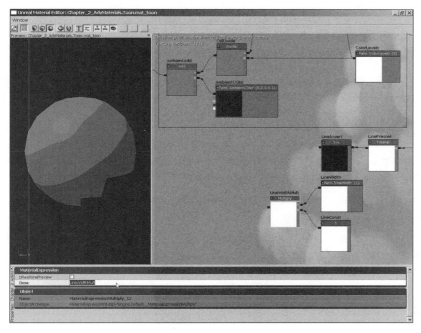

FIGURE 2.162   This multiplies LineWidth by LineConst.

11. Connect the Output of the LineInvert expression to the Base input of the LineWidthPower expression. Then, connect the LineWidthMult expression to the Exp input of the LineWidthPower expression (see **FIGURE 2.163**).

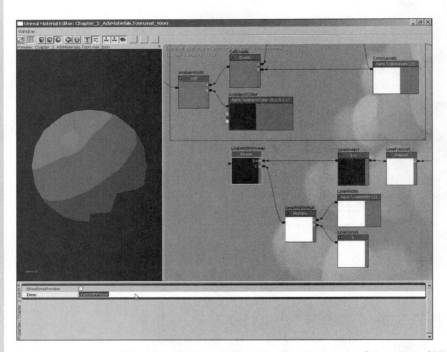

FIGURE 2.163   This raises the value of LineInvert by the power of the value of LineWidthMult.

12. To the left of the LineWidthPower expression, create another OneMinus expression. Name the expression **LineRevert**.

13. Connect the Output of the LineWidthPower expression to the Input of the LineRevert expression.

14. Below the LineRevert expression, create a VectorParameter expression. Name the expression **LineColor** and leave the values of its components set to 0.0 as the defaults.

15. To the left of the LineColor expression, create a Multiply expression. Name the expression **LineColorMult**.

16. Connect the RGB output of the LineRevert expression to the A input of the LineColorMult expression. Then, connect the Output of the LineColor expression to the B input of the LineColorMult expression (see **FIGURE 2.164**).

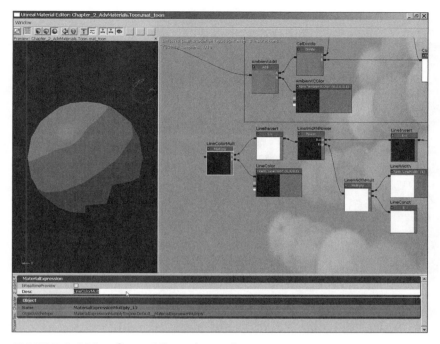

FIGURE 2.164   Connect the nodes as shown.

17. To the left of the CelShading section, create a Multiply expression. Name the expression **FinalMult**.

18. Connect the Output of the AmbientAdd expression to the A input of the FinalMult expression. Then, connect the LineWidthPower expression to the B input of the FinalMult expression.

19. To the left of the FinalMult and LineColorMult expressions, create an Add expression. Name the expression **FinalAdd**.

20. Make the following connections (see **FIGURE 2.165**):

  ▶ FinalMult-Output → FinalAdd-A

  ▶ LineColorMult-Output → FinalAdd-B

  ▶ FinalAdd-Output → Material-CustomLighting

2

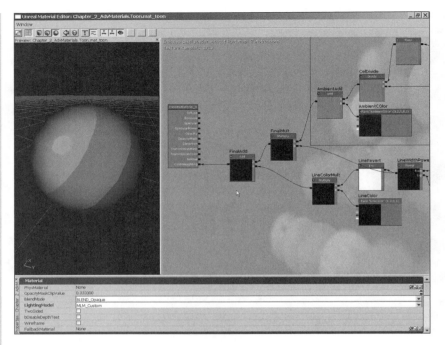

FIGURE 2.165   Make these final connections.

21. You should see the final effect in the preview at this point, including the stepped color and the outline (see **FIGURE 2.166**). The outline may be difficult to see because it is black by default, but you can adjust the color of the line to see that it is working. Commit the changes to the material and save the package to preserve your work.

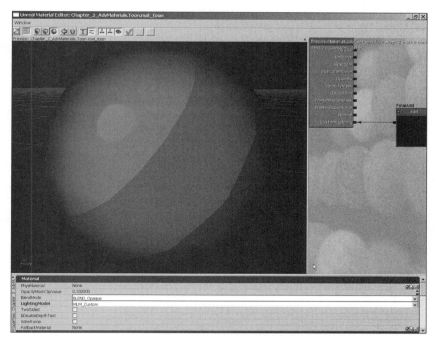

FIGURE 2.166   Your result will look like this.

END TUTORIAL 2.34

Summary

This chapter has covered the creation of several high-end and practical materials. We hope you use the tutorials included here as a guide to help you stretch both your skill set and your imagination in terms of what you can conceive of when working with the Material Editor. In the grand scheme of things, we've really only scratched the surface of what you can do, and from here you should have a good idea of the many different types of materials that can easily be created in Unreal Engine 3!

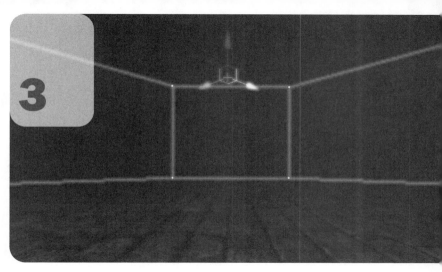

Chapter 3

Working with Volumes

Volumes are three-dimensional spaces programmed to be aware of when an object (such as a player) has entered them. They can then enact a variety of possible effects on that object. They have a wide variety of possible uses in your levels. You can use volumes to simply designate certain parts of the level, affect sounds or post-processes, or to alter the standard laws of physics that exist within Unreal. Volumes can also provide a simple means to handle level streaming, which allows them to replace the older concept of *zoning* that was used for level optimization in versions of the Unreal Engine prior to 3.

Volumes are always present in your levels in some manner. By default, a single volume encompasses the entire level called the *DefaultPhysicsVolume* (see **FIGURE 3.1**). We discuss PhysicsVolumes in greater detail later in this chapter.

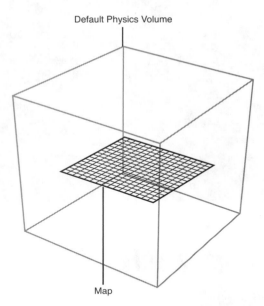

FIGURE 3.1   This diagram illustrates the concept of the DefaultPhysicsVolume.

If you need any sort of physics variation in your level—be it from water, force fields, or just a reduced sense of gravity—you need to place other volumes in your level. This is done by simply specifying an area with the Red Builder Brush and choosing a particular volume by right-clicking the Add Volume icon 🛡 to select the type of volume you want to create.

Keep in mind that due to the advent of Geometry Mode and its ability to model the Red Builder Brush, it is possible to form a volume in virtually any shape from within UnrealEd. However, as with all Binary Space Partition (BSP) brushes, the simpler your shape, the better your performance. By having volumes with too many faces, having faces that are not aligned to the grid, or having faces that do not meet at 90-degree angles, you are increasing the possibility of errors, although you are certainly not guaranteeing that you will have problems. Within those guidelines, however, any shape is theoretically possible.

Available Volume Types

Here is a list of the available volumes, along with a very brief description of what each one does. These volumes are covered in richer detail as you progress through this chapter:

BlockingVolume—Creates collisions with actors

ColorScaleVolume—Affects the overall coloring of a level

DynamicBlockingVolume—A BlockingVolume that can move

DynamicTriggerVolume—A TriggerVolume that can move

GravityVolume—A volume that can alter gravity

LadderVolume—Enables the ability to climb ladders

LevelStreamingVolume—Assists with level visibility when streaming levels

LightVolume—Controls which objects are affected by a light

PhysicsVolume—Provides a variety of effects to the physical properties of a level

PostProcessVolume—Can alter the post-process effects of a level

ReverbVolume—Changes the playback of sound effects

TriggerVolume—Can trigger Kismet events upon entry or exit

These volumes all derive from the base Volume class, and some of them derive from each other. In **FIGURE 3.2**, you can see the inheritance relationship from the base Volume class.

> **NOTE**
>
> At the time of this writing, LadderVolumes are not entirely functional. Also, for games similar in play style to Unreal Tournament 3, it is generally understood that ladders are not a good gameplay element. For these reasons, LadderVolumes should be avoided in most cases.

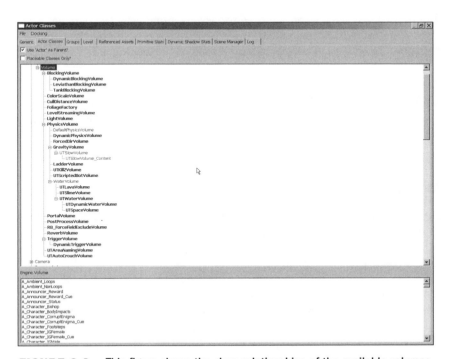

FIGURE 3.2   This figure shows the class relationships of the available volumes.

Basic Volume Properties

A few properties are inherent to volumes in general and are always accessible on any volume, except where excess functionality has been explicitly hidden. Here is a list of each of these properties, as well as a brief description of each one.

> **AssociatedActor**—This is a slightly dated variable that was used to create VolumeTrigger-style reactions between volumes and an actual actor, such as a Trigger Actor. In general, you do not need to use it because you can activate a Touch event using any volume.
>
> **bForcePawnWalk**—This disables the ability to run within the area of the volume.
>
> **bProcessAllActors**—This forces the volume to process all actors that pass within it. In general, you can leave this property at its default value (False).
>
> **LocationName**—This interesting property allows you to associate a name with a volume, which can be useful to keep track of a player's location. For instance, you could have a volume that encompasses the control room of a battleship and set the LocationName to Control Room. You could then retrieve this information and put it in the UI system, or use it anywhere it would be handy to have a named location for the player.
>
> **LocationPriority**—This is used when you have two volumes that have two different location names but are overlapping each other. The volume with the higher priority is the one your player is considered to be within, for the sake of LocationName.

It should be noted that the ColorScale, LevelStreaming, PostProcess, and Reverb Volumes do not seem to have the properties listed here. Because all the volume types are derived from the basic volume class, the properties are indeed there, but have been hidden within the editor because they are not really necessary for those volumes.

BlockingVolumes

The BlockingVolume is the simplest type of volume available, because all volumes have the ability to block actors inherently. This volume acts as a collision object for your level and is not visible by default. This volume can affect players and/or weapons in the level, based on the CollisionType property, located under the Collisions tab.

An interesting question that might arise is whether it is more efficient to use a BlockingVolume over a static mesh that uses collisions. Both objects use the same code for collisions, so there is no processing benefit one way or the other. However, because static meshes are instanced throughout the scene, only one copy of the collision model for a static mesh exists in the scene. This means you can save memory by using collision-based static meshes, especially if you need to block many different locations.

DynamicBlockingVolume

The BlockingVolume is also available in a dynamic form, the DynamicBlockingVolume. This is essentially the same as a standard BlockingVolume, except that the location and rotation of the dynamic version is capable of being animated throughout the level.

TUTORIAL 3.1: Adding Collision to a Force Field

1. Launch UnrealEd and open the DM-CH_03_Volumes_Begin map included on the DVD in the files for this chapter. This level shows a room with a force field at the door followed by a room full of water (see **FIGURE 3.3**). We use volumes to complete these effects.

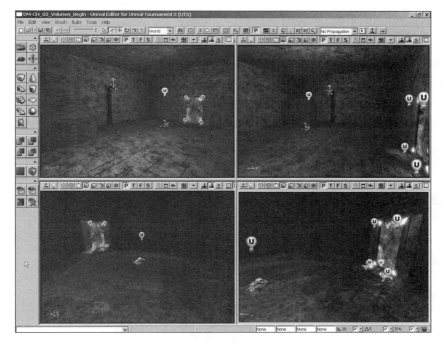

FIGURE 3.3   The DM-CH_03_Begin map.

2. Set your Drag Grid value to 16.

3. Create a new Cube with the following settings:

   ▶ **X**: 256

   ▶ **Y**: 16

   ▶ **Z**: 256

Click Build and Close when finished (see **FIGURE 3.4**).

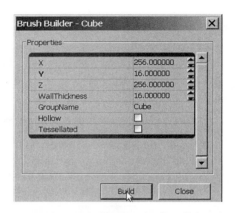

4. Position the Red Builder Brush in the Front and Side viewports so that it is centered in all axes on the doorway between the two rooms (see **FIGURE 3.5**).

5. Right-click the Add Volume button and choose DynamicBlockingVolume from the context menu that appears (see **FIGURE 3.6**). We are using a DynamicBlockingVolume rather than a normal BlockingVolume because we are going to move it out of the way later on.

FIGURE 3.4   The appropriate Cube builder settings.

6. The volume you just created blocks everything but weapon fire by default. Select the volume and press F4 to open its properties. In the Collision tab, set the CollisionType property to COLLIDE_BlockAll. This causes weapon fire to be blocked by the volume as well.

7. Rebuild the map and test it out. The force field now prevents you from entering the next room. Save your progress because we use the same map in subsequent tutorials.

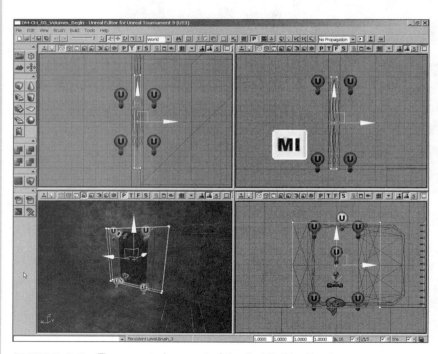

FIGURE 3.5   The correct placement of the Red Builder Brush.

BlockingVolume
ColorScaleVolume
CullDistanceVolume
DynamicBlockingVolume
DynamicPhysicsVolume
DynamicTriggerVolume
FoliageFactory
ForcedDirVolume
GravityVolume
LadderVolume
LevelStreamingVolume
LeviathanBlockingVolume
LightVolume
PhysicsVolume
PortalVolume
PostProcessVolume
RB_ForceFieldExcludeVolume
ReverbVolume
TankBlockingVolume
TriggerVolume
UTAreaNamingVolume
UTAutoCrouchVolume
UTDynamicWaterVolume
UTKillZVolume
UTLavaVolume
UTScriptedBotVolume
UTSlimeVolume
UTSpaceVolume
UTWaterVolume

FIGURE 3.6   Choose DynamicBlockingVolume from the context menu.

END TUTORIAL 3.1

LeviathanBlockingVolume

This volume is a BlockingVolume meant to only block the Leviathan vehicle. It lets all other actors, including players, pass.

TankBlockingVolume

This volume is a BlockingVolume meant only to block tank vehicles (for example, the Goliath). It lets all other actors, including players, pass.

PhysicsVolumes

A PhysicsVolume exhibits some change in the standard physics of the level whenever the player enters it. You can use it to control such things as velocity, friction, and how much damage a player takes while in a given area. Several other volumes extend from the base PhysicsVolume, each of which is discussed in this section.

This volume controls the standard physics within your level. This volume is given a very low Priority value in its properties, meaning that if you pass into any other volume in your level, the effects of the DefaultPhysicsVolume are overridden.

To access the DefaultPhysicsVolume, open the Level Browser and click your current level to select it. Then, right-click and choose Show Selected in Scene Manager. This brings up the Scene Manager window. Make sure the Show Brushes option at the top of the browser is checked, and you will see an entry for the DefaultPhysicsVolume object. On the right side of the browser, you will see all the available properties for the volume.

Here are some of the more commonly used properties that control the physics in your level:

> **bPainCausing and DamagePerSec**—These two properties work hand-in-hand to cause your volume to damage a player as long as the player is within it. The bPainCausing property activates the ability to cause damage, and DamagePerSecond is exactly that. You can set DamagePerSecond to a negative value and the volume will have a regenerative effect.

> **GroundFriction**—This property allows you to control the amount of friction as a player moves across the ground while within the volume. This can be used to simulate slippery surfaces such as ice and oil.

> **ZoneVelocity**—This property is a bit like gravity, although it can be used to apply force in any direction using the three axes. Objects within the volume are accelerated up to the designated velocity while taking friction values into effect.

> **bPhysicsOnContact**—This property causes the volume to exert its physical forces on objects once they break the plane of contact with the volume, rather than when their pivot enters the volume.

> **bBounceVelocity**—When combined with positive Z ZoneVelocity, this property allows objects entering the volume from above to bounce rather than simply land.

> **bNeutralZone**—This property prevents all objects within the volume from taking damage.

> **RigidBodyDamping**—This property provides a loss of energy (damping) effect on all rigid bodies that enter the volume. Raising the value beyond 0 slows down all rigid bodies that move through the volume.

Continue from **TUTORIAL 3.1**. If you have not completed **TUTORIAL 3.1**, you may open the DM-CH_03_Volumes_01 map provided with the files for this chapter. In the previous tutorial, we added collision to the force field in our map. Now, we want to make running into the force field cause damage to the player.

TUTORIAL 3.2: Causing Damage

1. Right-click the Cube primitive builder button and create a new Cube brush using the following values (see **FIGURE 3.7**):

▸ **X**: 256

▸ **Y**: 32

▸ **Z**: 256

Click Build and Close when finished.

2. Position the builder brush centered in all axes on the doorway between the two rooms (see **FIGURE 3.8**). Note that the thickness of this brush is greater than that of the original BlockingVolume. The reason for this is that the player can actually enter this PhysicsVolume before coming in contact with the BlockingVolume.

FIGURE 3.7   The appropriate Cube builder settings.

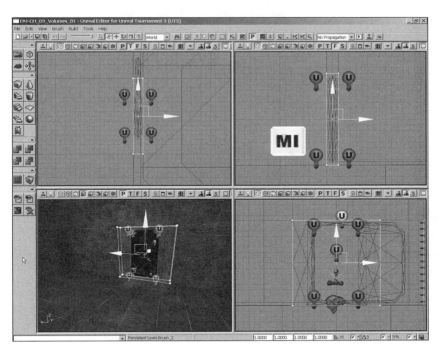

FIGURE 3.8   The proper placement for the Red Builder Brush.

3. Right-click the Add Volume button and choose PhysicsVolume from the list of available volumes (see **FIGURE 3.9**).

4. Select the physics volume and press F4 to open its properties. In the PhysicsVolume section, set the following properties (see **FIGURE 3.10**):

  ▸ **bPainCausing**: True (Selected)

  ▸ **DamagePerSec**: 10.0

  ▸ **DamageType**: UTDmgType_LinkPlasma

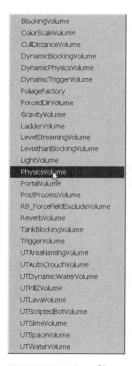

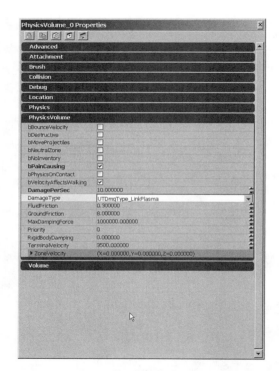

FIGURE 3.9   Choose PhysicsVolume from the context menu.

FIGURE 3.10   The PhysicsVolume Properties window.

5. Save and test your map. We now have a force field that not only blocks players and weapon fire, but also causes damage to players who run into it. To see the effects of the DamageType, enter **behindview 1** in the console while playing the game to view the player in third-person view.

6. Save the map to preserve your progress.

END TUTORIAL 3.2

DynamicPhysicsVolume

The DynamicPhysicsVolume is identical to the standard PhysicsVolume with the exception that its location and rotation can be animated through the use of Matinee.

ForcedDirVolume

The ForcedDirVolume allows the designer to force UTVehicles (or any individual subclass thereof) to go in a particular direction. This volume is somewhat similar to a BlockingVolume, only instead of simply stopping the vehicle, ForcedDirVolume ushers it along in a specified direction to keep it, and thus the gameplay, moving. This volume has some properties of its own that are explained next:

> **Arrow**—This component determines the direction in which vehicles are forced. The direction can be modified by adjusting the Rotation property of the Arrow component.
>
> **bAllowBackwards**—When this property is true, negative forces are allowed to be imparted on the vehicles.
>
> **bBlockPawns**—When this property is true, the ForcedDirVolume also blocks pawns.
>
> **bBlockSpectators**—When this property is true, the ForcedDirVolume also blocks spectators.
>
> **bDenyExit**—When true, this property keeps the player from exiting the vehicle while affected by the ForcedDirVolume.
>
> **bIgnoreHoverboards**—When this property is true, hoverboards are not affected by the ForcedDirVolume.
>
> **TypeToForce**—This property determines whether all, or a subclass of, UTVehicles are affected by the ForcedDirVolume. When this property is set to None, all UTVehicles are affected.

GravityVolume

The GravityVolume is based on the PhysicsVolume. This volume allows you to adjust gravity levels for all actors within the volume. Its default value is –520. If you set this to a positive value, gravity within the volume is reversed. However, this does not mean the player simply floats off the ground. The player needs some sort of initial hop to get off the ground, and then the GravityVolume takes over.

UTKillZVolume

This volume very simply kills any pawns that enter it. It is usually used to kill players at a certain depth when falling, such as falling into a pit or falling out of the world. The UTKillZVolume has one property:

> **KillZDamageType**—This property determines the type of damage used when killing the pawn.

UTScriptedBotVolume

This volume destroys any bots created through Kismet when they exit the volume. This can be useful if you want to limit scripted bots to a specific area of the map.

WaterVolume

The purpose of the WaterVolume is to make the player feel as if he is within a watery environment. This is achieved by having a default FluidFriction value of 2.4 and extending the original PhysicsVolume to provide the ability to play sound effects as a player enters and exits the water, as well as to spawn actors upon entry or exit. These actors could be a variety of different things, but a good example would be particle-based bubbles or splash effects. This volume cannot be placed within a map itself, but provides the basis for several other volumes which are placeable. Some of the prominent properties of the WaterVolume are listed here:

> **FluidFriction**—This controls the amount of friction applied by the water as the player swims through it. The higher this value, the harder it "feels" to move through the water.

> **EntrySound and ExitSound**—These properties take SoundCues that can be used for splash sound effects when entering and exiting the volume.

> **EntryActor and ExitActor**—These properties determine the actor that is spawned when the player enters and exits the volume. Typically, these would contain splash effects, often in the form of particle emitters.

> **PawnEntryActor**—This property allows you to specify an actor to be spawned when a pawn enters the volume.

UTWaterVolume

The UTWaterVolume extends the WaterVolume by handling the spawning of different effects when a pawn, projectile, or vehicle enters the volume. This volume also causes damage to pawns whose heads are contained within the volume after a certain amount of time to simulate drowning. When creating standard water within UT3, this would be the volume you would use.

Continue from **TUTORIAL 3.2**. If you have not completed **TUTORIAL 3.2**, you may open the DM-CH_03_Volumes_02 map provided with the files for this chapter. You can see water in one of the rooms in the map. This water is purely visual at this point. If you were to play the map and jump into the water, you would fall to the bottom just as if it were not there. We need to add a UTWaterVolume in order to make the player behave as if he were in actual water.

TUTORIAL 3.3: Adding Water

1. Right-click the Cylinder primitive builder button
   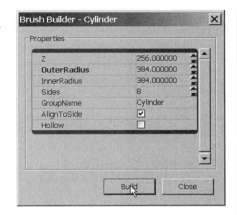 to open the Cylinder building properties.
   Enter the following values (see **FIGURE 3.11**):

   ▸ **Z**: 256

   ▸ **OuterRadius**: 384

   ▸ **Sides**: 8

   Click Build and Close when finished.

2. Use the Top and Side viewports to position the
   Red Builder Brush to fit in the carved-out area
   for the water in the large cylinder room (see
   FIGURE 3.12). It should be aligned in all axes
   with the carved-out brush.

FIGURE 3.11   The appropriate
Cylinder builder settings.

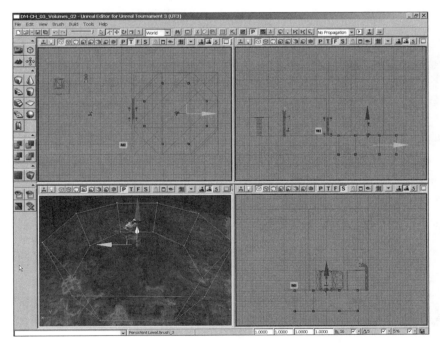

FIGURE 3.12   Place the cylinder brush as shown.

3. Right-click the Add Volume button and choose UTWaterVolume from the list of available
   volumes (see **FIGURE 3.13**).

3

4. Go ahead and rebuild the map and then test it out. However, remember to start in the room with the water because you cannot pass through the doorway between the rooms yet. Right-click the floor of the water room and choose Play from Here.

5. We could stop at this point and have fully functional water. However, the player currently sinks in the water. By setting the ZoneVelocity property, we can cause the player to slowly rise to the surface when not moving.

6. Set your ZoneVelocity's Z parameter to 3, which makes the player seem to barely float (see **FIGURE 3.14**). However, feel free to experiment with other values as well.

7. Save the map to preserve your progress.

FIGURE 3.13   Select UTWaterVolume from the context menu.

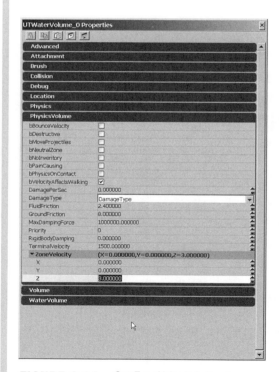

FIGURE 3.14   Set ZoneVelocity's Z value as you see fit.

END TUTORIAL 3.3

UTLavaVolume

The UTLavaVolume is identical to the WaterVolume, other than a few default values of properties. FluidFriction has been bumped up to 8.0 to slow the player down greatly within this volume. Also, a very high damage of 20.0 per second has been implemented to hurt any players caught within this volume.

UTSlimeVolume

This volume is also identical to a WaterVolume, with the exception of the default values of a few properties. It has a higher FluidFriction value (5.0) and is set to cause damage of 7.0 per second. As identified by its name, this volume is used to simulate pools of slime within a map.

UTSpaceVolume

This volume is meant to simulate being in the vacuum of space. It is essentially a UTWaterVolume, which plays no splash effects or sounds. It has no special properties, and no specific setup is required.

LadderVolume

The LadderVolume is a special version of the PhysicsVolume that allows your character to climb a surface as if it was a ladder. Typically, this ladder is placed against a climbable surface, such as a ladder static mesh.

Each LadderVolume has a specified direction, indicated by a pink arrow that is visible within the volume. This arrow must point toward the surface that should be climbed. When a pawn (player) that has its bCanClimbLadders property set to True enters a LadderVolume and faces a direction within 45 degrees of the specified direction, that pawn enters the Phys_Ladder physics state and then starts climbing the ladder (see **FIGURE 3.15**).

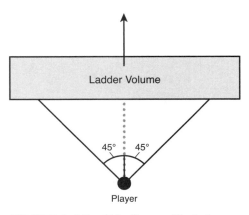

FIGURE 3.15   This diagram illustrates how LadderVolume direction works.

Here are three important properties for LadderVolumes:

> **bAutoPath**—When set to True, this property automatically creates Ladder actors at the top and bottom of the volume that are used in

NOTE

At the time of this writing, LadderVolumes are not entirely functional. Also, for games similar in play style to Unreal Tournament 3, it is generally understood that ladders are not a good gameplay element. For these reasons, LadderVolumes should be avoided in most cases.

path building and AI. Otherwise, these actors must be placed manually by the level designer. The default value for this property is True.

bAllowLadderStrafing—When set to True, this property allows the player to shimmy side-to-side on the ladder while climbing. Otherwise, only vertical motion is allowed. The default value is True.

bNoPhysicalLadder—When this property is set to True, the player starts climbing as soon as he enters the volume, regardless of whether there is any climbable surface or static mesh. The default value is False.

3

Continue from **TUTORIAL 3.3**. If you have not completed **TUTORIAL 3.3**, you may open the DM-CH_03_Volumes_03 map provided with the files for this chapter. In the large cube-shaped room is a raised area in one corner with a ladder up one side. This ladder, like the water before, is only visual at this point. If the player runs up to the ladder, nothing happens. We need to add a LadderVolume to allow the player to climb the ladder.

TUTORIAL 3.4: Adding Ladders

1. Right-click the Cube primitive builder button to open the Cube building properties. Enter the following values (see **FIGURE 3.16**):

   ▸ **X**: 64

   ▸ **Y**: 96

   ▸ **Z**: 256

   Click Build and Close when finished.

FIGURE 3.16   The appropriate Cube builder settings.

2. Position the builder brush flush up against the raised area brush in the Y axis, centered on the ladder in the X axis, and even with the floor in the Z axis (see **FIGURE 3.17**).

3. Right-click the Add Volume button and choose LadderVolume from the list of available volumes (see **FIGURE 3.18**).

4. Leave all the settings at their defaults because those work fine. Rebuild the map and then test out the ladder.

5. Save the map to preserve your progress.

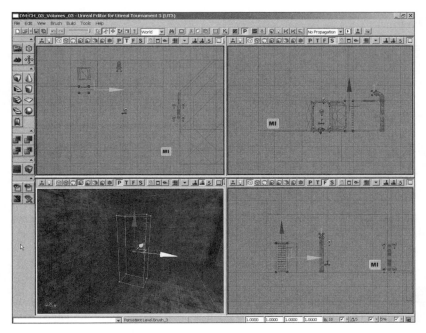

FIGURE 3.17
Place the Cube
brush as shown.

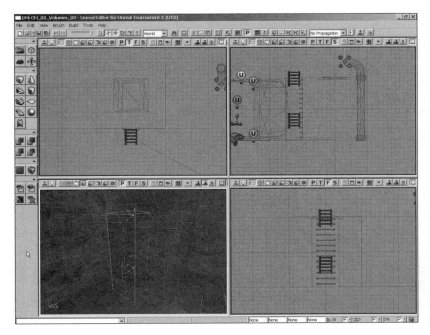

FIGURE 3.18
The LadderVolume
and its associated
actors.

END TUTORIAL 3.4

TriggerVolume

A TriggerVolume is a simplified volume used to trigger Touch Events in Kismet. It is true that any volume can in fact do this; however, the TriggerVolume has had all other functionality stripped away, meaning that it is perfect when all you want to do is trigger a Kismet sequence, but don't want to have to worry about any other settings. This volume is unique in that it has a green wireframe instead of the standard pink.

DynamicTriggerVolume

The DynamicTriggerVolume is identical to the standard TriggerVolume, except the dynamic version can have its location and rotation animated through Matinee.

Continue from **TUTORIAL 3.4**. If you have not completed **TUTORIAL 3.4**, you may open the DM-CH_03_Volumes_04 map provided with the files for this chapter. We add a series of functionalities over the next five tutorials by using TriggerVolumes, Kismet, and Matinee.

TUTORIAL 3.5: Triggering Events, Part I: Adding the TriggerVolume

1. Select the static mesh positioned on top of the raised area in the corner of the large cube-shaped room (see **FIGURE 3.19**). This allows us to have the builder brush positioned here after building the Cube brush in the next step.

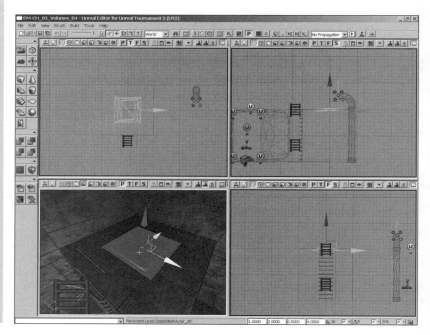

FIGURE 3.19
Select the static mesh shown.

2. Right-click the Cube primitive builder button 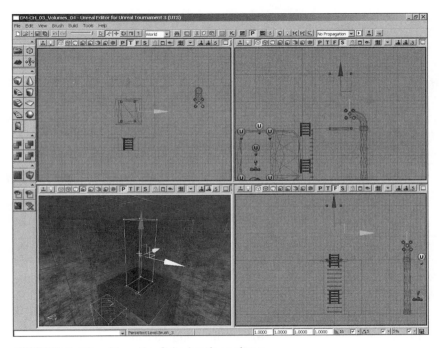 to open the Cube building properties. Enter the following values:

  ▸ **X**: 96

  ▸ **Y**: 64

  ▸ **Z**: 256

Click Build and Close when finished.

3. In the Side viewport, move the builder brush 136 units up, or in the positive Z direction (see **FIGURE 3.20**).

FIGURE 3.20   Place the Cube brush as shown.

4. Right-click the Add Volume button and choose TriggerVolume from the list of available volumes.

5. Select the newly created TriggerVolume and open the Kismet Editor by clicking the Kismet icon **K** in the Toolbar.

6. Right-click in Kismet and choose New Event Using TriggerVolume_0 > Touch to add a new Touch event for the TriggerVolume. This is the basis for the following tutorials (see **FIGURE 3.21**).

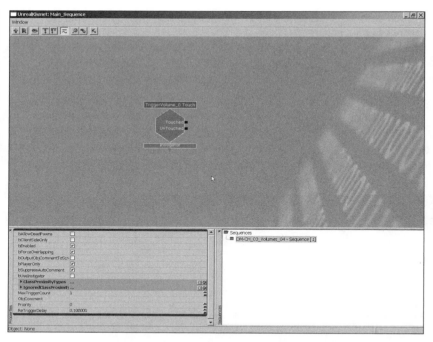

FIGURE 3.21   The Kismet Touch event has been created.

7. Save the map to preserve your progress.

END TUTORIAL 3.5

Make sure you have completed **TUTORIAL 3.5** before attempting this tutorial. If you have not completed **TUTORIAL 3.5**, you may open the DM-CH_03_Volumes_05 map provided with the files for this chapter.

TUTORIAL 3.6: Triggering Events, Part II: Moving the DynamicBlockingVolume

1. Select the DynamicBlockingVolume for the force field and open Kismet. Use the Search for Actors button if necessary ![icon]. Create a new Matinee sequence by right-clicking in Kismet and choosing New Matinee. Then double-click the new Matinee sequence to open the Matinee Editor (see **FIGURE 3.22**).

2. Right-click in the empty Track List on the left and choose Add New Empty Group. Enter **ForceField** for the name and click OK (see **FIGURE 3.23**).

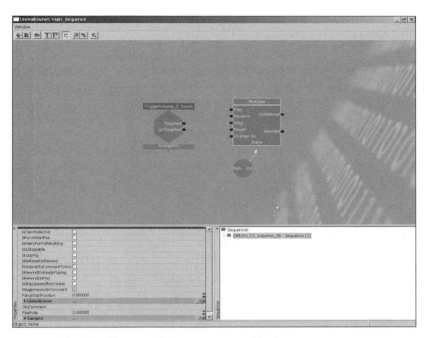

FIGURE 3.22 The new Matinee sequence object.

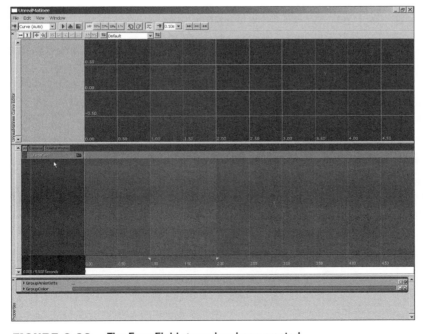

FIGURE 3.23 The ForceField group has been created.

3. Make sure the ForceField group is selected, right-click it, and choose Add New Movement Track (see **FIGURE 3.24**).

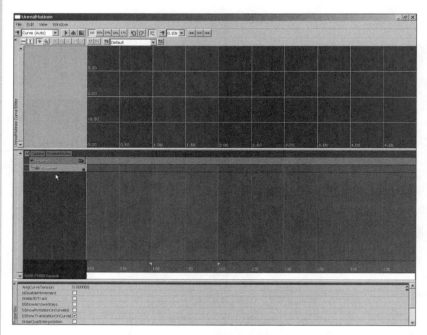

FIGURE 3.24   The ForceField group now has a new Movement track.

4. An initial key is already set at Time=0.0. Set the time slider to 1.0 and click the Add Key button ![button]. This creates a new key that is selected and ready to be adjusted in the viewport.

5. Move the DynamicBlockingVolume down 256 units to set the position for the key (see **FIGURE 3.25**).

6. Scrub through the timeline in the Matinee Editor to make sure the volume moves in the viewport. Close the Matinee Editor when finished.

7. Right-click in Kismet and choose Action > Misc > Delay to add a Delay sequence object (see **FIGURE 3.26**). The Duration property of this sequence object can be adjusted later to tweak the timing of the force field's shutdown sequence.

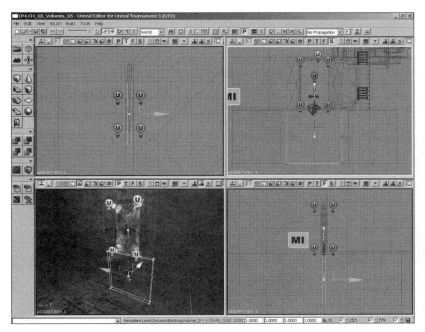

FIGURE 3.25 The DynamicBlockingVolume has now been moved down.

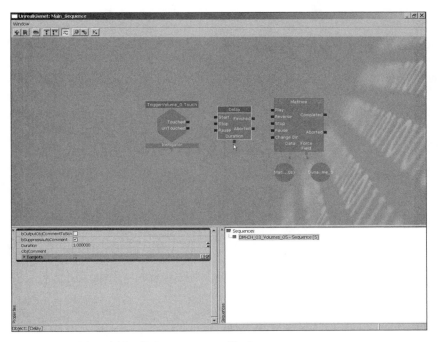

FIGURE 3.26 Add a Delay sequence object.

8. Click the Touch output from the TriggerVolume's Touch event and drag to the Start input of the Delay sequence object to create a link between them (see **FIGURE 3.27**).

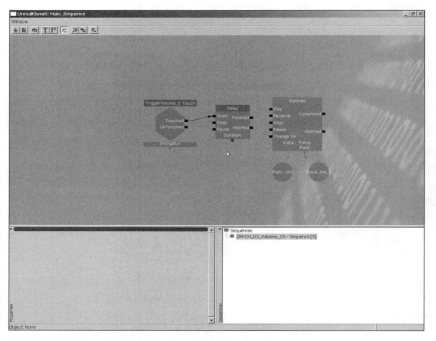

FIGURE 3.27   Link the Touch to the Delay as shown.

9. Click the Finished output from the Delay sequence object and drag to the Play input on the Matinee sequence to create a link between them (see **FIGURE 3.28**).

10. Save the map to preserve your progress.

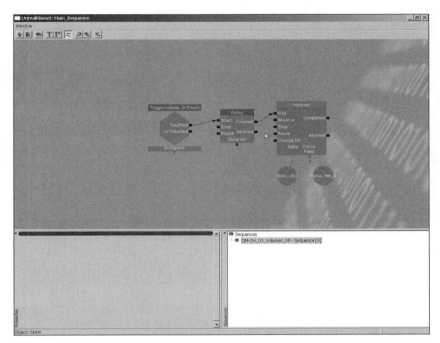

FIGURE 3.28   The Delay connects to the Matinee object.

END TUTORIAL 3.6

Continue from **TUTORIAL 3.6**. If you have not completed **TUTORIAL 3.6**, you may open the DM-CH_03_Volumes_06 map provided with the files for this chapter. We must now deactivate the effects of the PhysicsVolume so that the player is not harmed by passing through the door.

TUTORIAL 3.7: Triggering Events, Part III: Toggling the PhysicsVolume

1. Select the PhysicsVolume that currently causes damage for the force field (use the Search for Actors button 🔍 if necessary) and open Kismet.

2. Right-click in Kismet and choose Action > Toggle > Toggle (see **FIGURE 3.29**).

3. Right-click the Target variable link of the Toggle sequence object and choose New Object Var Using PhysicsVolume_0 to create an object variable for the physics volume and link it to the Target input (see **FIGURE 3.30**).

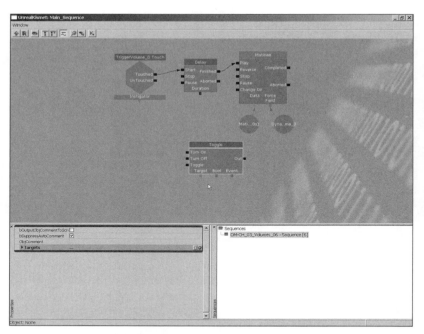

FIGURE 3.29   Add a Toggle sequence object.

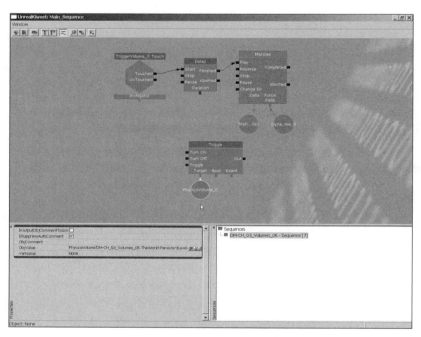

FIGURE 3.30   The Object Variable designates the damaging PhysicsVolume for the Toggle object.

4. Click the Finished output from the Delay sequence object and drag to the Toggle input on the Toggle sequence object to create a link between them (see **FIGURE 3.31**).

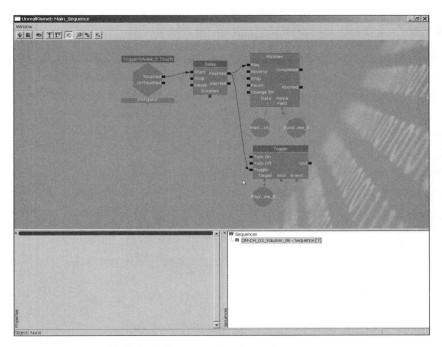

FIGURE 3.31   Link the Delay to the Toggle as shown.

5. Save the map to preserve your progress.

END TUTORIAL 3.7

Continue from **TUTORIAL 3.7**. If you have not completed **TUTORIAL 3.7**, you may open the DM-CH_03_Volumes_07 map provided with the files for this chapter. We now adjust the material of the force field so that it appears to have been shut off.

TUTORIAL 3.8: Triggering Events, Part IV: Turning Off the Force Field Material

1. Select the MaterialInstanceActor (this actor simply holds a reference to a MaterialInstanceConstant so it can be altered in Matinee) in one of the viewports (see **FIGURE 3.32**).

2. Open Kismet and double-click the Matinee sequence to open the Matinee Editor (see **FIGURE 3.33**).

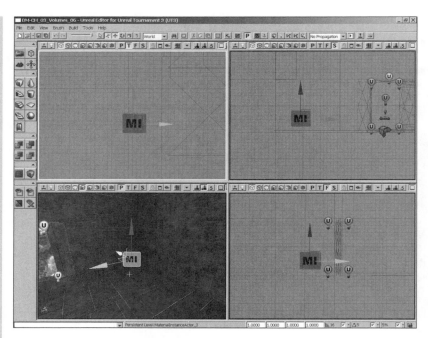

FIGURE 3.32   The Material Instance actor appears like so.

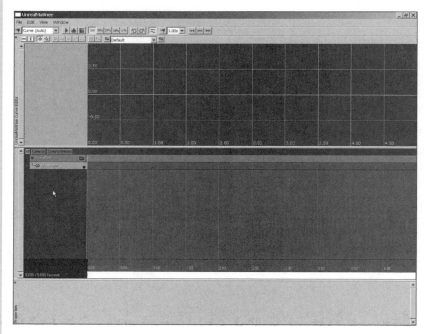

FIGURE 3.33   The Matinee Editor

3. Right-click in the Track List and choose Add Empty New Group. Enter **ForceColor** for the name and click OK (see **FIGURE 3.34**).

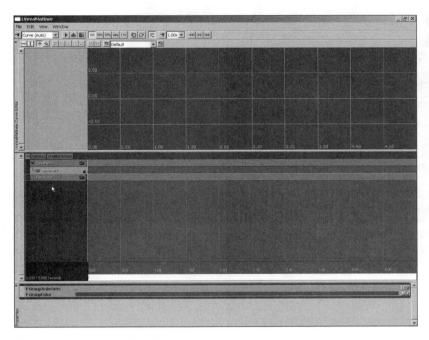

FIGURE 3.34   Add the ForceColor group.

4. Right-click the ForceColor group and choose Add New Vector Material Param Track. Once this is created, select the track and set its ParamName property to ForceFieldColor. This name corresponds to the Vector Parameter currently attached to the material instance constant (see **FIGURE 3.35**).

5. With the time slider at 0.0, click the Add Key button to add an initial key. Then move the time slider to 1.0 and click the Add Key button again to add the final key.

6. If the Curve Editor is not already open, click the Toggle Curve Editor button. Click the small square button in the lower-right corner of the track to make the track visible in the Curve Editor (see **FIGURE 3.36**).

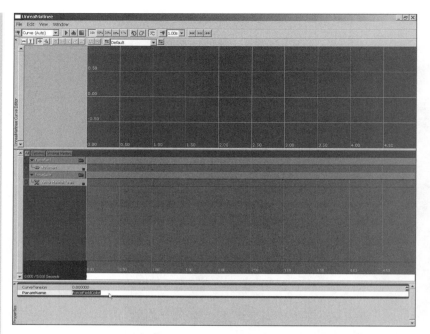

FIGURE 3.35   The ForceColor group now has a new Vector Material Param Track.

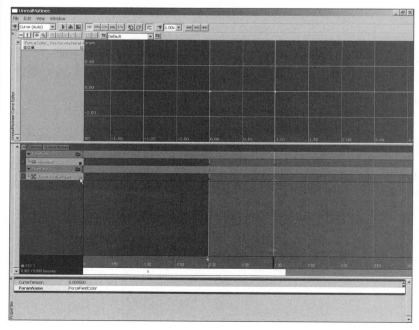

FIGURE 3.36   Click this button to show the selected curve in the Curve Editor.

7. Because this is a vector, each key actually has three keys in the Curve Editor (one for R, G, and B). They currently appear as one because they are directly on top of each other. Select each one of the individual keys, right-click it, and choose Set Value. Enter **1.0** for the value and click OK. Repeat this process for the remaining individual keys at Time=0.0. You should end up with a curve going from 1.0 at Time=0.0 to 0.0 at Time=1.0 (see **FIGURE 3.37**).

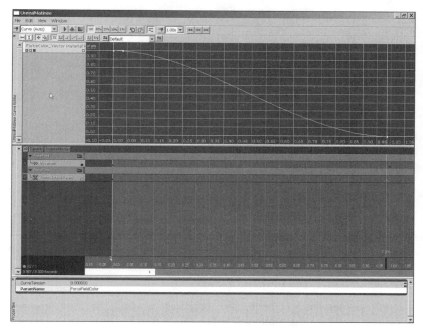

FIGURE 3.37   The resulting curve after modifying the initial key's values.

8. Scrub the time slider in Matinee to make sure that the material is disappearing in the main editor's viewports. Save your progress.

9. Save the map to preserve your progress.

END TUTORIAL 3.8

Continue from **TUTORIAL 3.8**. If you have not completed **TUTORIAL 3.8**, you may open the DM-CH_03_Volumes_08 map provided with the files for this chapter. We now adjust the material of the activation button so that it appears to have been switched on.

TUTORIAL 3.9: Triggering Events, Part V: Turning On the Activation Button Material

1. Select the matInst_floor_button material in the Generic Browser within the Volumes_Demo package and then open Kismet (see **FIGURE 3.38**).

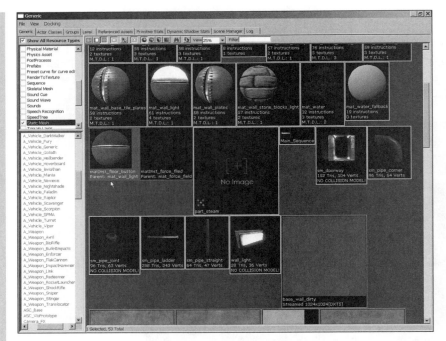

FIGURE 3.38   The matInst_floor_button material instance, as seen in the Generic Browser.

2. Right-click in Kismet and choose Action > Material Instance > Set VectorParam to add a Set VectorParam sequence object (see **FIGURE 3.39**).

3. Select the Set VectorParam sequence object to view its properties. Click the Use Current Selection In Browser button ◄ for the MatInst property to set it to the select material in the Generic Browser.

4. Set the ParamName property to LightColor.

5. Set the VectorValue property's components to the following values:

   ▶ **B**: 2.4

   ▶ **G**: 4.0

   ▶ **R**: 4.0

6. Click the Touch output from the TriggerVolume's Touch event and drag to the Set VectorParam sequence object's In input to create a link between them (see **FIGURE 3.40**).

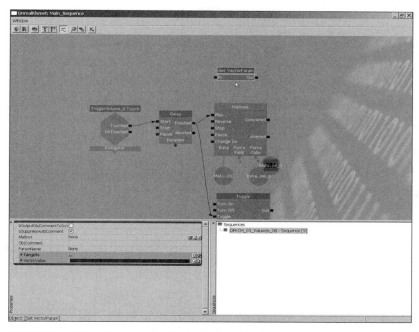

FIGURE 3.39 The new Set VectorParam object

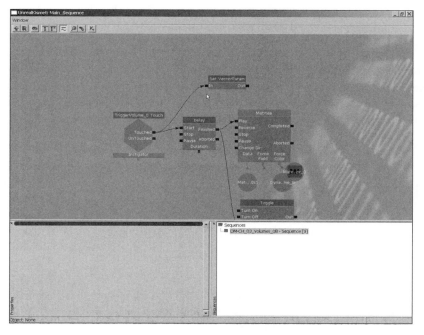

FIGURE 3.40 Link the Touch event to the new Vector Material Param Track.

7. Rebuild the map and test out the sequence.

You should now have a functional sequence that performs the following actions when the player climbs the ladder and stands on the button:

- ▸ The button lights up.
- ▸ The force field becomes invisible.
- ▸ The force field stops blocking the player and weapon fire.
- ▸ The force field stops causing damage.

8. Save your progress. Feel free to adjust the timing of the sequence using the Duration property of the Delay sequence object.

END TUTORIAL 3.9

PostProcessVolume

The PostProcessVolume allows you to modify the current post-process being used in specific areas of the map. It does not allow you to apply a new post-process; to do this, one would use a Kismet sequence. The bEnable properties for Bloom, Depth of Field (DOF), Motion Blur, and Scene Effect determine whether the volume affects each of those aspects of a post-process. The bUseDefaults property forces the original settings of the post-process, meaning that the volume has no effect. For more information on post-processing, see Chapter 8, "Post-Process Effects."

Continue from **TUTORIAL 3.9**. If you have not completed **TUTORIAL 3.9**, you may open the DM-CH_03_Volumes_09 map provided with the files for this chapter. The water at this point looks pretty good and functions very well. To add to the water effect, though, we are going to make the camera blur when the player is underwater. To do this, we use a PostProcessVolume and the DOF (Depth of Field) effect.

TUTORIAL 3.10: Adding a Blur Effect

1. We could build a new brush for this volume, but we already have one in the exact shape and size we need, so why not just use that one? To do this, select the UTWaterVolume created previously. Then, right-click it and choose Polygons > To Brush. This makes a builder brush in the shape and location of the selected brush (see **FIGURE 3.41**).

2. Right-click the Add Volume button 🛡 and choose PostProcessVolume from the list of available volumes.

3. Select the new PostProcessVolume and open its properties. Use the Search for Actors tool if necessary, because there are multiple brushes directly on top of each other.

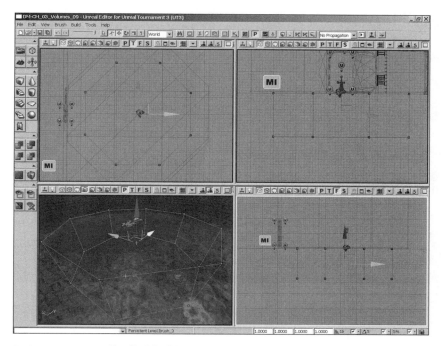

FIGURE 3.41   The Red Builder Brush should now be in the same location as the WaterVolume.

4. In the PostProcessVolume section, deselect bEnableBloom and bEnableSceneEffect and select bEnableDOF.

5. Now, set the following properties to these values:

   ▶ **DOF_BlurKernelSize**: 2.0

   ▶ **DOF_FalloffExponent**: 2.0

   ▶ **DOF_FocusInnerRadius**: 100.0

   ▶ **DOF_InterpolationDuration**: 0.1

   ▶ **DOF_MaxNearBlurAmount**: 0.0

6. Rebuild the map and test out the effects of the new volume (see **FIGURE 3.42**).

7. Save your progress.

> **TIP**
>
> You can view the effects of this and other PostProcessVolumes in the editor viewports by toggling on the Post Process Volume Previs button ![icon] for that viewport.

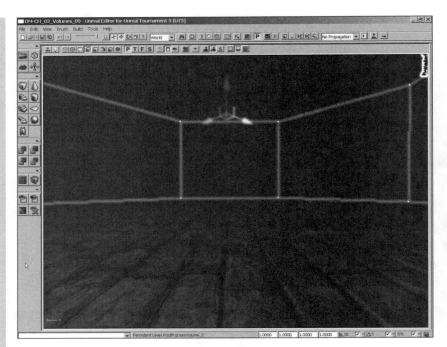

FIGURE 3.42   The view becomes blurry when underwater.

END TUTORIAL 3.10

LevelStreamingVolume

These volumes assist with level streaming by automatically loading the level corresponding with each volume whenever the player enters it. Because level streaming is not covered in this text, the use of this volume falls outside the scope of this chapter.

LightVolume

Lighting volumes are another method of determining what objects a light affects, aside from lighting channels. They work by enabling you to designate a list of volumes: inclusion volumes or exclusion volumes. Simply put, objects that are within any of the volumes listed in the InclusionVolumes list are illuminated, whereas any objects that are within volumes listed in the ExclusionVolumes list are not (see **FIGURE 3.43**).

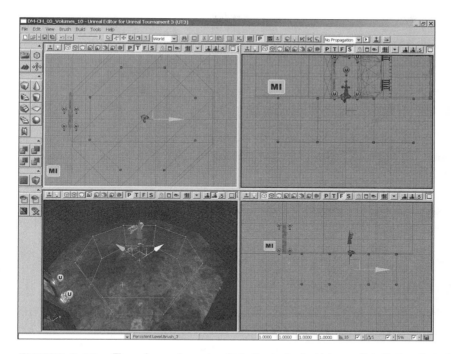

FIGURE 3.43   The volume shown is within the InclusionVolumes list. Notice that objects outside of the volume are unlit.

Lighting volumes are activated through the bUseVolumes property. Typically, you then add volumes to one of the arrays for InclusionVolumes or ExclusionVolumes. You can use both if you like; however, keep in mind that in such cases, any objects that fall into both an inclusion and exclusion volume are unlit, and so are any objects that are not within any volumes.

ColorScaleVolume

This volume tints the overall color of your level by the color specified in the ColorScale property. Note when editing this property that X, Y, and Z are analogous to R, G, and B, respectively. Therefore, setting the X value to 1 and Y and Z to 0 tints your scene with 100% red. The InterpTime volume controls the time period over which the tint reaches its maximum value.

ReverbVolume

A ReverbVolume affects all sounds that play while the player is within it. The volume's purpose is to replicate the way sounds reverberate in a variety of environments, including mountains, forests, stone hallways, and many more. Presets for each type of environment can be found in the

3

volume's ReverbType property. Also available are properties to control sound volume while within the volume's area, as well as the FadeTime, which controls how long it takes to fade from the normal sound to the associated reverb type.

RB_ForceFieldExcludeVolume

This volume acts as a boundary to force field effects caused by force field actors, such as the RB_CylindricalForceActor. Force fields have no effect on actors within this volume. The RB_ForceFieldExcludeVolume has one property:

> **ForceFieldChannel**—This property determines which force fields to exclude. Any force field actors using the same channel specified here are excluded. All other force fields still continue to have effect.

UTAreaNamingVolume

This volume's only use is to name specific areas of the map. This is used mainly for displaying locations on the scoreboard, but could be used for other purposes with a little imagination. This volume uses the LocationName property previously described to name the area enclosed by the volume.

UTAutoCrouchVolume

This volume forces players on console versions of UT3 to automatically crouch. This is important because there is no control for manually crouching on consoles. This volume has no properties specific to itself.

FoliageFactory

The FoliageFactory is used to randomly place static meshes throughout a specified area. This is similar to the foliage system available within the Terrain system, only it makes use of volumes to determine the placement instead of painting on the terrain. The static meshes can be directed to be created on BSP, other static meshes, and/or terrain actors within the volume. Like the terrain system's foliage, the instanced static meshes created by the FoliageFactory are only rendered when the camera is within a certain distance as a performance optimization. The properties of the FoliageFactory are explained in the following list:

FacingFalloffExponent—This is an exponent that the density factor for facing foliage is raised to before it is multiplied by the value of the SurfaceAreaPerInstance property. Facing foliage includes foliage created as a result of the SurfaceDensityDownFacing, SurfaceDensityUpFacing, and SurfaceDensitySideFacing properties.

MaxInstanceCount—This specifies the maximum number of static meshes that can be created by this FoliageFactory.

Meshes—This is an array that allows for several different static meshes, each with its own set of properties to be spawned with the same FoliageFactory:

InstanceStaticMesh—This is the static mesh to be used for this item in the Meshes array.

Material—The material assigned here overrides the default material of the static mesh assigned to the InstanceStaticMesh property. This only overrides the first material if the static mesh uses multiple materials.

MaxDrawRadius—This is the maximum distance from the camera at which instances of this static mesh are rendered.

MinTransitionRadius—This is the distance from the camera at which instances of this static mesh begin to fade out.

MinScale X/Y/Z—This property allows you to set a minimum scale in each axis for this static mesh.

MaxScale X/Y/Z—This property specifies the maximum scale for this static mesh in each axis. The actual scale of any instance is a random value between the MinScale and MaxScale for each axis.

SwayScale—This property determines the extent to which instances of this static mesh are affected by any WindDirectionalSource actors in the map.

Seed—This allows the random placement to be adjusted so that you get the distribution that suits you.

SurfaceAreaPerInstance—This property controls the total amount of surface area within each instance of the volume that has foliage applied to it, or the "base density" of the foliage. Lower values yield higher density of foliage and vice-versa.

bCreateInstancesOnBSP—When this property is true, instances of this static mesh are spawned on BSP surfaces within the FoliageFactory.

bCreateInstancesOnStaticMeshes—When this property is true, instances of this static mesh are spawned on static meshes within the FoliageFactory.

bCreateInstancesOnTerrain—When this property is true, instances of this static mesh are spawned on terrain within the FoliageFactory.

SurfaceDensityDownFacing—This determines the density of the instanced static meshes on surfaces facing downward within the FoliageFactory.

SurfaceDensitySideFacing—This determines the density of the instanced static meshes on vertical surfaces within the FoliageFactory.

3

SurfaceDensityUpFacing—This determines the density of the instanced static meshes on surfaces facing upward within the FoliageFactory.

VolumeFalloffExponent—This is an exponent that the density factor for volume foliage is raised to before it is multiplied by the value of the SurfaceAreaPerInstance property. Volume foliage includes foliage created as a result of the VolumeFalloffRadius property.

VolumeFalloffRadius—This property represents the distance from the volume's surface that foliage may be spawned. The density of foliage decreases smoothly between the number of units defined in this property inside the volume and the same number of units outside the volume. For instance, a value of 5 means that foliage density drops off 5 units outwards from the surface of the volume as well as 5 units inward, reaching its peak at the locations of the surface.

Summary

Volumes provide you with a way to create a wide variety of gameplay effects and afford the designer with incredible power in controlling the flow of a level—whether simply blocking a player from entering an area or controlling how the player sees or moves through a level. In *Unreal Tournament 3*, volumes play a key role in post-processing, object blocking, and level labeling. Be sure to think of creative ways you can implement the use of volumes in your own levels!

Chapter 4

Physics Objects

Physics objects are actors that can move, collide, and otherwise behave according to a physically accurate simulation, which is performed by the PhysX physics engine. This engine is integrated into Unreal Engine 3 and is responsible for all physical simulations—often called *dynamic simulations*—that take place during gameplay. Physics objects in Unreal are typically rigid bodies, or a series of rigid bodies attached to one another through the use of constraints. In this chapter, we explain what rigid bodies and constraints are as well as how they are used.

Types of Physics Objects

When working with physics simulations in Unreal, it is important to remember that you have four main types of physics objects available: KActors, KAssets, Constraints, and Impulse and Force Actors. Every physics object you create will be one of these types.

In very general terms, here are the differences between these four types of objects: A KActor is just a single rigid physics object, such as a billiard ball. A KAsset is a skeletal mesh that is animated through the use of a collection of physics objects attached to one another through constraints (for example, a ragdoll). A Constraint is a force that can hold two or more KActors together, or affect them in some way. Impulse and Force Actors exhibit some sort of force on physics objects, pushing them around in some way. Each of these types of objects is explored in more depth in its own respective section.

TUTORIAL 4.1: Creating a Basic Physics Simulation

1. Launch UnrealEd and open the DM-CH_04_KActor map and the Chapter_04_Physics package, both included on the DVD in the files for this chapter.

2. Open the Generic Browser. In the Chapter_04_Physics package, double-click the sm_crate static mesh to open the Static Mesh Editor. From the Collision menu, choose Simplified 6-DOP collision and click Yes if you are prompted to overwrite the current collision. Adding a collision mesh is necessary to create a dynamic object (see **FIGURE 4.1**).

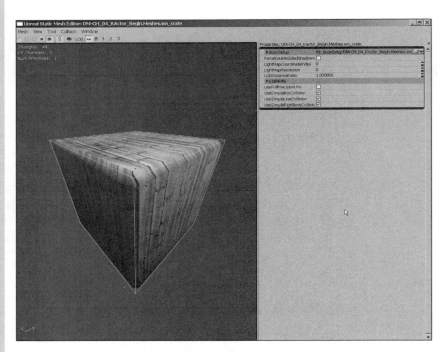

FIGURE 4.1   The collision mesh appears as a wireframe around the object.

3. Expand the BodySetup area of the static mesh's properties and then set the MassScale property to 0.5. This lessens the mass by half, making the box easier to push around (see **FIGURE 4.2**).

4. Close the Static Mesh Editor and make sure that the sm_crate is selected in your Generic Browser.

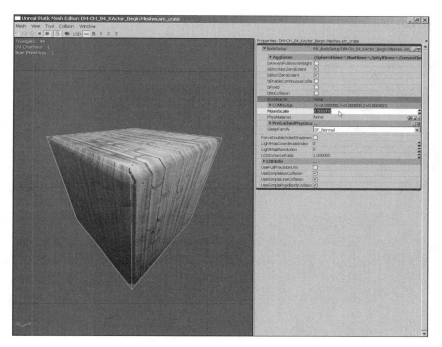

FIGURE 4.2   The MassScale property controls the amount of mass the object has.

5. Right-click the floor of the level and choose Add Actor > Add RigidBody: StaticMesh Chapter_04_Physics.sm_crate (see **FIGURE 4.3**). This creates a KActor using the selected static mesh.

6. With the mesh selected in the viewport, press F4 to open the Properties window. Expand the KActor section and check the bWakeOnLevelStart property (see **FIGURE 4.4**). This causes the KActor to be active as soon as the level starts.

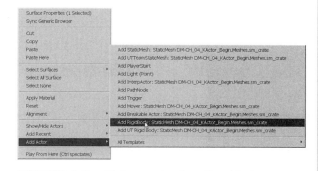

FIGURE 4.3   Make sure to place the object as a RigidBody instead of a StaticMesh.

7. Rebuild the map, save it, and then test it out. While testing the map, enter **physicsgun** into the console to use the physics gun weapon. You can now interact with the object and move it around in the scene. Left-clicking the box pushes it with a slight impulse away from you, and right-dragging allows you to pick up the object and hurl it about.

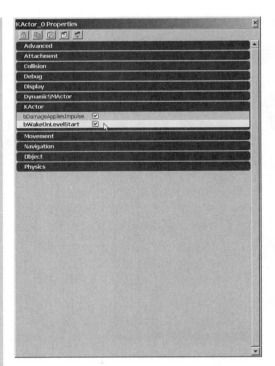

4

FIGURE 4.4   The bWakeOnLevelStart property causes a KActor to begin the level in motion.

END TUTORIAL 4.1

The Concept of Rigid Bodies

Before we get too far into the actual types of physics objects you will use in Unreal Engine 3, you need a general understanding of rigid bodies. Conceptually, a rigid body is an object that behaves as a perfectly solid object, and does not deform in any way regardless of how much force is applied to it. As such, rigid bodies cannot exist in the real world, because every object eventually deforms—at least slightly—once a strong enough force is applied to it. Rigid bodies are commonly used in computer physics simulations because they can be calculated very quickly. Despite the fact that they do not perfectly represent real-world behavior, they can be used to very closely approximate physical behavior in a realistic manner.

Rigid bodies represent the primary method of physics object calculation in Unreal Engine 3. KActors make rigid body calculations by using a static mesh as the basis. Even KAssets, which are skeletal meshes that deform and therefore cannot be calculated like rigid bodies in and of themselves, use invisible rigid body collision objects to calculate how the skeleton animates, and the skeleton then drives the deformation of the mesh.

It can be a little confusing to know the difference between rigid bodies and KActors, because creating a KActor in the UnrealEd viewport requires that you choose Add RigidBody from the Add Actor context menu. For the purposes of this text, however, we differentiate a rigid body as a more conceptual object, and a KActor as a physics object that uses rigid body calculations for simulation.

Working with Rigid Bodies in Unreal

Because KActors and KAssets use rigid bodies for their calculations, several properties within both types of actors pertain to rigid body behavior. The properties are divided into two separate groups: one handling collisions and the other handling the nature of the rigid body itself.

Collision Properties

For starters, we look at the collision-based properties of rigid bodies, which can be found in the physics object's Properties window. You can access these by expanding the following (see **FIGURE 4.5**):

▶ Collision tab

▶ CollisionComponent

▶ Collision

Here is a breakdown of the important properties found within the Collision area:

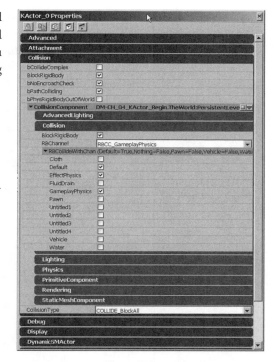

FIGURE 4.5 The collision properties expanded.

> **BlockRigidBody**—This property tells the rigid body whether or not to collide with other rigid bodies. If this is false, the RBCollideWithChannel property has no effect.
>
> **RBChannel**—This property is the channel this rigid body belongs to. Other actors use this to determine whether or not to collide with this rigid body.
>
> **RBCollideWithChannel**—This property allows you to choose the RBChannels with which the rigid body may collide. Any other rigid body that shares the same channel collides with the rigid body. This property is only functional if BlockRigidBody is True.

It should be noted that duplicates of these properties can be found in the StaticMeshComponent of KActors as well as in the SkeletalMeshComponent of KAsset. It does not matter which area you use to access the properties, because changes in one propagate to the other.

RB_BodySetup

The second section of properties, which governs the physical nature of the rigid bodies themselves, is part of the RB_BodySetup class. These properties cannot be accessed through the actor's Properties window. However, the location varies depending on whether you're looking at a KActor or KAsset. For KActors, the properties can be found under the Static Mesh Editor (see **FIGURE 4.6**). For KAssets, they are located in the PhAT Editor, which we cover in more depth later in this chapter (see **FIGURE 4.7**). In either case, you can find the properties under the BodySetup area.

It should also be noted that a KActor only has one RB_BodySetup. A KAsset, on the other hand, has a different RB_BodySetup for each of the separate rigid bodies it contains. Also, if a static mesh has no collision model set up for it, the BodySetup area is empty.

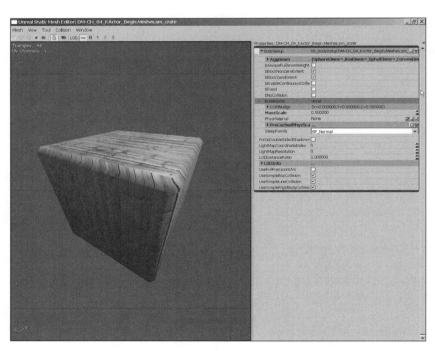

FIGURE 4.6   The BodySetup properties under the Static Mesh Editor.

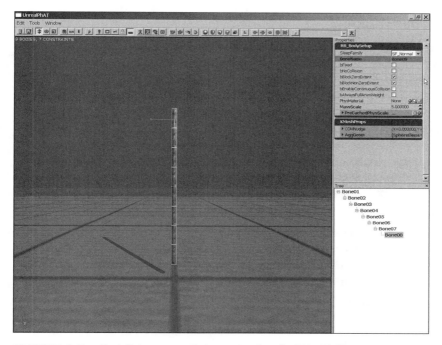

FIGURE 4.7   BodySetup properties are also found within PhAT.

Here are the pertinent properties that can be found in this section. It should be noted that some of these properties only pertain to KAsset, and have no effect on KActors. Such properties are designated in their descriptions.

> **PhysicalMaterial**—This property allows you to associate a PhysicalMaterial with the rigid body. When the property is set in the Static Mesh Editor's BodySetup, it applies to all KActor instances using that static mesh.
>
> To control properties on a per-instance basis, you can override the PhysicalMaterial using the PhysicalMaterialOverride property, located in the particular mesh's Properties window, by expanding DynamicSMActor > StaticMeshComponent > Physics. Physical materials are explained in detail later in this chapter.
>
> **MassScale**—This can be used as a multiplier to scale the automatic mass calculation. This automatic mass is calculated as being the volume of the body multiplied by the Density value of the PhysicalMaterial applied to the body. The MassScale is then multiplied on top of that.
>
> **BoneName**—This property associates a rigid body with a bone of a skeletal mesh and is only applicable to KAssets.

bFixed—This causes the body to be static, or fixed in space. Although it can be used on either KActors or KAssets, you will generally not use it on a KActor because you would use a static mesh if you wanted it to be static. It is, however, very useful for having parts of a KAsset be static while other parts continue to be dynamic. For instance, if you had created a KAsset of a hanging light fixture, you could use the bFixed property on the rigid body at the base of the chain, thereby affixing that body in space so that the light doesn't simply fall to the ground.

bBlockZeroExtent and bBlockNonZeroExtent—These two properties tell the body whether to return hits on traces made with the given extent type, which is a very technical way of saying whether the rigid body can block weapons or geometry collisions, respectively. In the case of these properties, *zero extent* usually refers to weapon fire and *non-zero extent* to collisions with geometry.

bNoCollisions—This property causes the rigid body not to collide with anything.

bEnableContinuousCollisionDetection—This property is an enhancement to the normal collision detection of the body to keep it from passing through objects when traveling at a high speed. Although this may sound advantageous, it should generally be avoided on any rigid bodies that are not accelerated to high speeds.

bAlwaysFullAnimWeight—This forces the physics of the body to be blended into the skeletal meshes' animations, regardless of the PhysicsWeighting of the skeletal mesh, assuming the skeletal mesh actor has bEnableFullAnimWeightBones set to True as well. Because this only affects skeletal meshes, it would have no effect on a KActor.

SleepFamily—This property allows you to choose between presets used to determine when physics actors go to sleep. The SF_Sensitive preset is useful for physics objects that are meant to move at slower speeds and would normally be put to sleep.

KActors

Now that you have a general understanding of rigid bodies and the ways they can be controlled, we can talk about the physics objects that use them. The first of these is the KActor, which is a static mesh that uses rigid body calculations for a physics simulation. To be more precise, a KActor is a single static mesh that uses the PHYS_RigidBody physics type to determine its position, rotation, and linear and angular velocities (see **FIGURE 4.8**). This differs from a KAsset, which is a skeletal mesh whose animation is driven by a series of physics objects constrained to one another.

In order for a static mesh to be used as a KActor, it must have a simplified collision model (see **FIGURE 4.9**). Without a collision model, the BodySetup property is nonfunctional, and the object cannot be added to the map as a KActor.

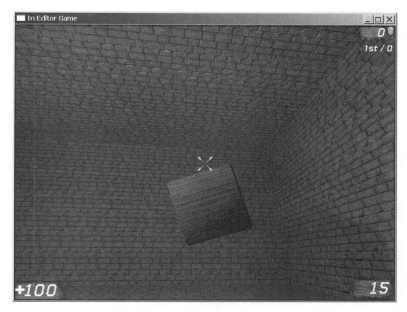

FIGURE 4.8   KActors look just like static meshes, but can be interacted with inside the game.

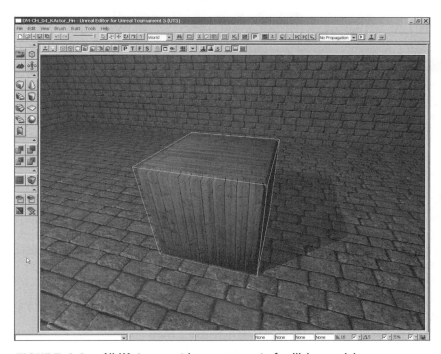

FIGURE 4.9   All KActors must have some sort of collision model.

Because they are derived from static meshes, KActors can be non-uniformly scaled. When this is done, the mesh still behaves appropriately, and the scaling does not hinder the simulation. This is because the mass of the object is automatically calculated from the volume of the mesh (see **FIGURE 4.10**).

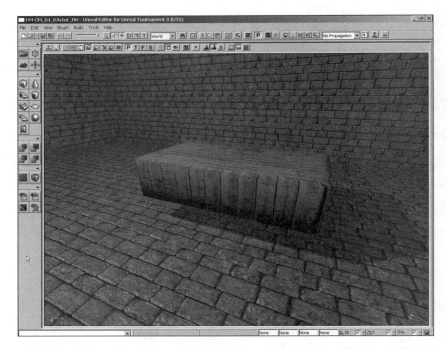

FIGURE 4.10   You can nonuniformly scale a KActor, and it still behaves properly.

Although many of the properties governing the behavior of KActors are actually handled through the BodySetup properties within the Static Mesh Editor, as described in the previous section, KActors do have some of their own properties, located in their Properties window.

The following properties are located under the KActor tab of the Properties window:

bWakeOnLevelStart—With this property set to True, the KActor is active and in motion as soon as the level begins. When this property is set to False, the KActor is "asleep," meaning that it is frozen in space and not being calculated as a rigid body. The KActor stays in this state until something comes along to "wake it up," such as a weapon projectile or a collision with another object. The default for bWakeOnLevelStart is False.

bDamageAppliesImpulse—In general, this property allows you to knock KActors around by shooting them with a weapon, or to knock them around with the force of an explosion, such as with a grenade. If set to True, this property allows damage applied to a KActor to in turn apply a physical force, or impulse, to the KActor. If this property is set to False, damage applied to the KActor has no affect on its physical behavior.

When damage is applied to an object, it is done so using a specific DamageType. Each available DamageType has a KDamageImpulse property that controls the magnitude of the impulse to be applied along the momentum vector.

The following properties are located under the SMDynamicActor tab of the Properties window:

bPawnsCanBaseOn—This property allows players to be able to stand on a KActor while it is active. The default value for this property is False.

bSafeBaseIfAsleep—This property works in tandem with bPawnsCanBaseOn. If this property is set to True, a KActor immediately goes to sleep if a player stands on it. If this property is set to False, the KActor continues using its physics simulation. Because pawns (the actors that the players typically control during gameplay) use a "soft attachment" when standing on an object, they are still free to move around on the KActor while it is simulating. This can lead to problems with the camera becoming jittery.

TUTORIAL 4.2: Placing KActors for a Race Game

1. Open the DM-CH_04_PhysGame_Begin map and the Chapter_04_Physics package, both included on the DVD in the files for this chapter.

2. Open the Generic Browser and select the sm_platform static mesh, located within the Chapter_04_Physics package. Place this mesh in your level as a KActor by right-clicking in the Perspective viewport and choosing Add Actor >RigidBody: StaticMesh Chapter_04_Physics.sm_platform.

3. Move the mesh into the cylindrically shaped room just above the cube-shaped room in the Top viewport and then rotate it –90 degrees around the X-axis. Set the DrawScale3D Y and Z to 4.0 to make the platform larger (see **FIGURE 4.11**).

4. Duplicate this new KActor four times (for a total of five) using Ctrl+C, Ctrl+V. Position the KActors so that one is aligned with each door to the room and the other two fill in the spaces between them. Ignore any overlapping because we move them vertically in the Z-axis shortly.

5. In the Top viewport, select the KActor in front of the door at the south end of the room. In the Side viewport, align the top of the KActor with the bottom of the doorway (see **FIGURE 4.12**).

6. In the Top viewport, select the KActor in front of the door to the right of the room and align the top of the platform with the bottom of the northwest doorway.

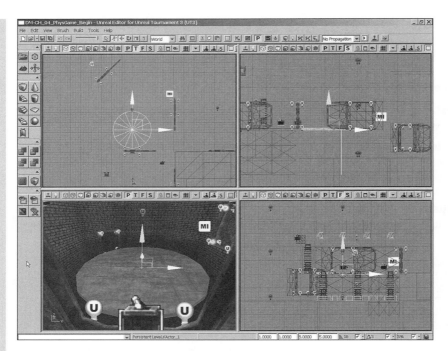

FIGURE 4.11   Position the KActor like so in your level.

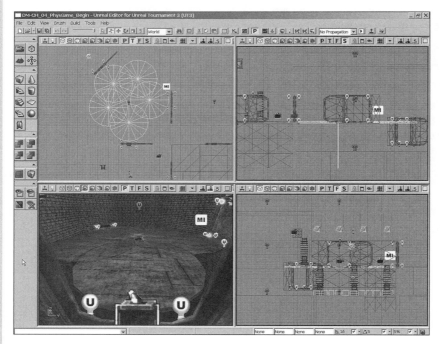

FIGURE 4.12   The platform is aligned like so.

The remaining KActors should be spaced out evenly in the Z-axis to fill in the space between the top and bottom platforms (see **FIGURE 4.13**). The idea is that the player has to move these platforms around in order to get to the lower doorway and then slide them around again to get back up to the doorway on the right. The order of the platforms in the Z-axis is not important.

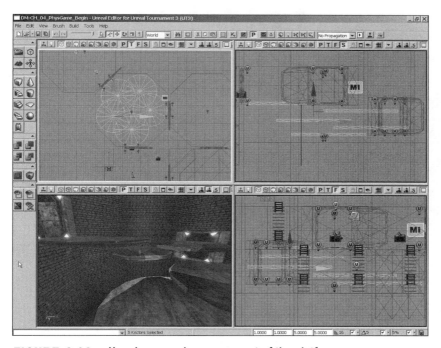

FIGURE 4.13   Here is a sample arrangement of the platforms.

7. Select the bottommost of the platforms and duplicate it. Move it upward in Z 752 units from the floor and then move it into the cylindrically shaped room to the west of the room where the platforms were originally placed. Set the DrawScale3D Y and Z to 4.0 for this platform.

8. Press F4 to open the Properties window for this KActor and set the following properties:

> ▸ **bPawnCanBaseOn**: True

> ▸ **bSafeBaseIfAsleep**: False

9. Duplicate this new platform and position it to the left of the original. These platforms are driven with a pulley system, allowing the player to reach the upper areas (see **FIGURE 4.14**).

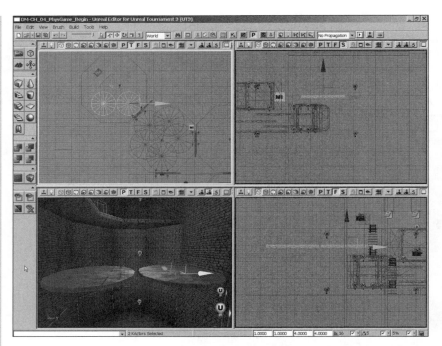

FIGURE 4.14   These two new copies are used later for a pulley demonstration.

10. Save your map.

END TUTORIAL 4.2

Continue from **TUTORIAL 4.2**, or open the DM-CH_04_PhysGame_01 map included on the DVD in the files for this chapter.

TUTORIAL 4.3: Puck Game KActor Spawn

1. Select the sm_plinko_chip static mesh from the Chapter_04_Physics package in the Generic Browser. Once this is selected, open the Kismet Editor and find the green-shaded section labeled Spawn Module.

2. Add a new Actor Factory by right-clicking and choosing New Action > Actor > Actor Factory. Select the Actor Factory sequence object to view its properties. Deselect the CheckSpawnCollision property to force the spawned actors to disregard any collision when spawning. Click to the right of the Factory property and then click the Create a New Object button ▼. Choose ActorFactoryRigidBody (see **FIGURE 4.15**).

3. Expand the properties of this newly created factory. Click the Use Selection in Browser button  for the StaticMesh property to use the sm_plinko_chip mesh selected earlier.

4. Expand the DrawScale3D property and set the following values to determine the scale for the spawned rigid bodies:

    ▸ **X:** 1.75

    ▸ **Y:** 0.5

    ▸ **Z:** 0.5

5. Expand the InitialVelocity property and set the following values:

    ▸ **X:** 0.0

    ▸ **Y:** 0.0

    ▸ **Z:** -50.0

FIGURE 4.15 Choose ActorFactoryRigidBody from the window that appears.

6. Deselect the bEncroachCheck property. This tells the rigid body to cause Touch events when it collides with objects.

7. Check bNotifyRigidBodyCollision, which causes collision events for the rigid body to be triggered. This allows us to later add sound effects to the spawned pucks.

8. Select the four Note actors in the map, above the wall of pegs, that act as the locations to spawn the chips from. Right-click the Spawn Point variable link of the Actor Factory sequence object and choose New Object Vars Using Note_3... from the context menu to add Object Variables for each of the Note actors.

9. Set the PointSelection property of the Actor Factory to PS_Random to choose one of the Note actors to spawn from at random.

10. Drag a link from the A <= B output of the Float Counter to the left of the Actor Factory to the Spawn Actor input of the Actor Factory. Then, drag a link from the Finished output of the Actor Factory to the In input of the Change Collision action to the right of the Actor Factory. Finally, drag a link from the Spawned variable link of the Actor Factory to the Object Variable named SpawnedChip, which is also linked to the Change Collision sequence action.

11. Save your level.

END TUTORIAL 4.3

KAssets

A KAsset is a system in which a skeletal mesh is animated using rigid body simulations. To be precise, a KAsset is a skeletal mesh, such as a character, in which each bone of the skeleton is associated with an invisible physical body (see **FIGURE 4.16**). These physical bodies are then attached to one another through constraints, which work similarly to joints. Wherever the physical bodies move, they in turn move the bones of the skeleton, which then animates the skeletal mesh. An easy example would be a character that is being used as a ragdoll. KAssets can be scaled uniformly, thereby simply making them larger or smaller. However, they cannot be non-uniformly scaled and still function properly.

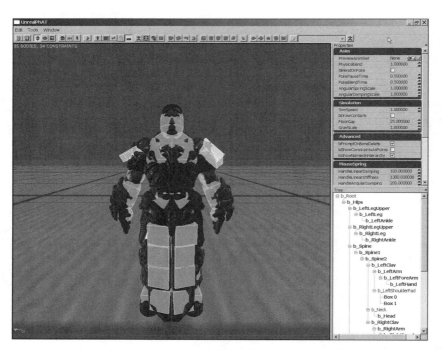

FIGURE 4.16   Here you can see a skeletal mesh character and the physical objects that drive the KAsset.

Physical bodies used in KAssets come in three shapes: boxes, spheres, and capsuloid shapes known as *sphyls* (see **FIGURE 4.17**). For character KAssets, or ragdolls, sphyls are the most commonly used shape.

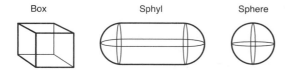

FIGURE 4.17   These images represent the three physical body types available.

Each physical object in a KAsset is attached to another physical object using some form of constraint. These constraints can act like hinges, ball and socket joints, pulleys, or sliding rails, depending on the type of constraint employed. We cover constraints in more detail later in this chapter.

The physical objects that comprise a KAsset have their own RB_BodySetup containing the properties for that body, which are exactly like the BodySetup properties available to KActors. To access these BodySetups, you must go into the Physics Asset Tool (or PhAT), which we cover later in this chapter. The KAsset itself also has a separate set of collision properties available within its Properties window. These are similar to the properties found in KActors:

bBlockPawns—This property determines whether the KAsset blocks pawns (typically players) that collide with it.

bWakeOnLevelStart—With this property set to True, the KAsset is active and in motion as soon as the level begins. When this property set to False, the KAsset is "asleep," meaning that it is frozen in space and not being calculated as a rigid body. The KAsset stays in this state until something comes along to "wake it up," such as a weapon projectile or a collision with another object. The default for bWakeOnLevelStart is False.

bDamageAppliesImpulse—In general, this property allows you to knock KAssets around by shooting them with a weapon, or to knock them around with the force of an explosion, such as with a grenade. If set to True, this property allows damage that is applied to a KAsset to in turn apply a physical force, or impulse, to the KAsset. If this property is set to False, damage applied to the KAsset has no affect on its physical behavior.

When damage is applied to an object, it is done so using a specific DamageType. Each available DamageType has a KDamageImpulse property that controls the magnitude of the impulse to be applied along the momentum vector.

Continue from **TUTORIAL 4.3**, or open the DM-CH_04_PhysGame_02 map included on the DVD in the files for this chapter.

TUTORIAL 4.4: Placing a Ragdoll KAsset

1. Select the SK_CH_BaseMale_Physics PhysicsAsset, located in the Generic Browser under the HC_AnimHuman package. Right-click in the Perspective viewport and choose Add Actor > PhysicsAsset: SK_CH_BaseMale_Physics to add a physics asset to the map (see **FIGURE 4.18**).

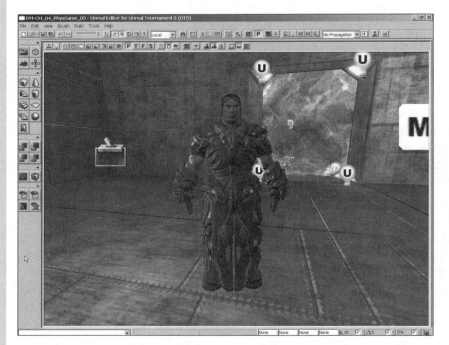

FIGURE 4.18   The KAsset looks like a character with its arms at a 45-degree angle.

2. Position the KAsset in the cube-shaped room and then press F4 to open the Properties window.

3. Check the bWakeOnLevelStart property, which causes the KAsset to become physically active once the level starts.

4. Rebuild the map and then test it out. Enter **gravitygun** in the console to equip the gravity gun. You can fling the KAsset around like a ragdoll by right-dragging it, and you can apply an impulse to it by clicking it (see **FIGURE 4.19**).

5. Save your level.

FIGURE 4.19   Feel free to play with your new KAsset!

END TUTORIAL 4.4

Constraints

Constraints are actors that join two rigid bodies together in a particular manner. They can have a variety of different behaviors depending on their type and settings, such as joints, hinges, and pulleys. Constraints have six degrees of freedom to which they can apply limits or forces, if desired. For the purposes of this text, we refer to these degrees of freedom as *DOFs* (see **FIGURE 4.20**).

By adjusting these degrees of freedom, a designer can control the behavior of the joint. For instance, allowing for only rotation in a single axis provides hinge-like behavior, whereas allowing rotation in all three axes functions like a ball-and-socket joint.

The DOFs divide into two types: linear and angular. Linear constraints pertain to motion in 3D space,

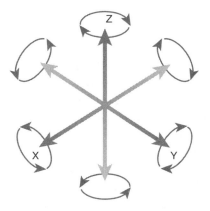

FIGURE 4.20   This diagram illustrates the six degrees of freedom.

whereas angular constraints affect rotation. As an example, you could consider the movement of a dresser drawer to be constrained to linear motion in a single axis, allowing for a sliding motion. This could be replicated in Unreal using a Prismatic Constraint.

Constraints can be placed between any two rigid bodies, and they are set up very easily. Simply create a constraint actor, place it appropriately in the scene (such as between the two bodies being constrained), and then designate the constrained bodies within the constraint's properties. As you designate the bodies, a red bounding box surrounds the first body and a blue box surrounds the second, allowing for easy identification of the constrained bodies.

There is a fundamental difference between the ways Unreal designates the axes for linear and angular motion. Linear axes are fairly easy because they coincide with the world axes (X, Y, and Z). However, when you look at the angular axes on a constraint, you find Swing1, Swing2, and Twist. To visualize these axes, extend your arm straight out from your side. Swinging your arm forward from the shoulder toward your chest and backward toward your back would exhibit rotation about the Swing1 axis. Rotating your shoulder up and down would exhibit rotation about Swing2. Finally, rotating your shoulder as if turning an invisible doorknob would exhibit rotation about the Twist axis.

Both linear and angular DOFs can be limited to prevent some or all motion in a given axis. However, some ground rules should be established about how this works because limits for linear and angular movement behave differently than one might expect. Linear limits are spherical in nature, meaning that you essentially limit the maximum distance one constrained object can be from its counterpart in 3D space. However, because the limit must be a perfect sphere, you cannot limit different axes with different values. Think about it: A sphere's width and depth must always be the same. In practical terms, this means that if you limit your X, Y, and Z values with different nonzero numbers, Unreal only uses the largest value, and with that value it constructs a theoretical sphere to control the maximum distance one object can travel from another.

Angular limits, on the other hand, can use different values for the three given axes. You can visualize limits on the two swing axes as an elliptical cone that is centered on the Twist axis. If that's a bit technical then consider this: Let's go back to sticking your arm out to the side again. Now, pretend that you can only swing your arm forward and back about 10 degrees in either direction. Let's now say that you can swing your arm up and down about 45 degrees in either direction. With those limits in place, if you were to pinwheel your arm around, you would be tracing a very tall but thin elliptical cone with your arm. Limits on the Twist axis simply control how far your shoulder can twist about, which you should have no problem visualizing; simply twist your arm forward as far as it possibly goes, and then try to twist it just a little more. That slight pain you feel is your own angular limit kicking in.

Types of Constraint Actors

Although four different types of constraints are available for placement in your levels, it should be known that they are all the same type of actor, differing only in their applied settings. In fact, by adjusting the settings of any one of the constraint actors, you can effectively change it into any of the others. The four types are RB_BSJointActor, RB_HingeActor, RB_PrismaticActor, and RB_Pulley-JointActor. Before we discuss each of these types individually, it is important for us to take a look at the base class from which each of these types derive: the RB_ConstraintActor.

RB_ConstraintActor

This actor is not placeable in your level. It is, however, the basis from which the four placeable constraints are created. Any properties that this actor has are passed down to each of the other constraint actors listed within it in the Actor Classes Browser. It also contains the RB_ConstraintSetup and RB_Constraint Instance categories, which contain most of the properties for constraining rigid bodies. However, the RB_ConstraintActor also has some properties of its own, listed next (see **FIGURE 4.21**):

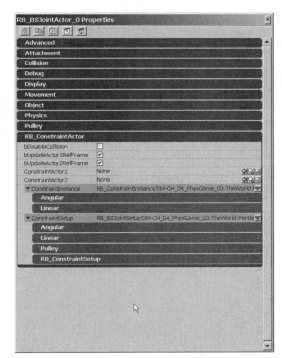

FIGURE 4.21   The RB_ConstraintActor properties.

> **bDisableCollision**—A value of True disables all collisions between the two actors bound to the constraint.
>
> **bUpdateActor1RefFrame/ bUpdateActor2RefFrame**—When either of these properties is checked, the location of the constraint actor is used as the reference point for the respective constrained actor. For example, if you were to check only bUpdateActor1RefFrame and then

move the constraint actor, then the point of reference (or the point about which the constraint pivots Actor 1) changes location along with the constraint. If you then check only bUpdateActor2RefFrame and move the constraint actor, the reference point for Actor 1 is left behind and you update the reference point for Actor 2. These reference points are connected to the bounding box that surrounds the constrained actors by a wire.

This process is used when setting up a Pulley constraint or to offset various DOF limits.

ConstraintActor1/ConstraintActor2—These properties contain the actors constrained together through the constraint actor. Adding actors into these fields may appear confusing at first, especially with the Use Generic Browser button located on the right side when you select the property. You simply need to type the name of the actor into the field.

If you select the actor you would like to constrain, you will see its name appear near the bottom of the UnrealEd interface in the Status Bar. You do not need to type the full extents of the name; you only need to enter the last section, typically starting with *kactor_* and ending with some number. For instance, if the actor in question has an extended name of PersistentLevel.Kactor_1, you would only need to type **kactor_1** into the ConstraintActor property field.

If a user wanted to constrain a particular KActor to the world (if it were chained to the ceiling, for instance), then you would simply leave ConstraintActor1 set to None and place the actor to be constrained into ConstraintActor2.

Pulley

The Pulley category contains the properties you need in order to create a functional pulley-style constraint (see **FIGURE 4.22**).

> **TIP**
>
> Try using Note actors for your pulley pivot objects. You can give them a text message so that you and other level designers on your team can see what they're used for!

PulleyPivotActor1/ PulleyPivotActor2—These properties hold the actors used for the two pivots of a pulley constraint. These would be placed very much like the pulleys would in a dual-pulley system, typically directly above the two objects being constrained.

RB_ConstraintSetup

The RB_ConstraintSetup category contains a variety of properties that mostly pertain to setting up limits to how the constraint can behave. These properties are listed next (see **FIGURE 4.23**):

JointName—This property is mainly used for identification purposes within the Physics Asset Tool (PhAT) and is usually the name of the bone with which the constraint has been associated.

ConstraintBone1—This property holds the name of the first (child) bone or body to which the constraint has been connected.

ConstraintBone2—This property holds the name of the second (parent) bone or body to which the constraint has been connected.

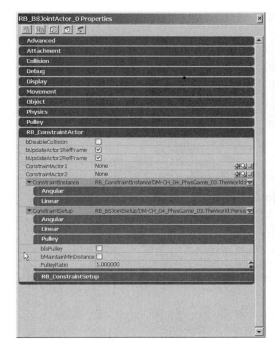

FIGURE 4.22   The Pulley category contains properties that allow you to create pulley constraints.

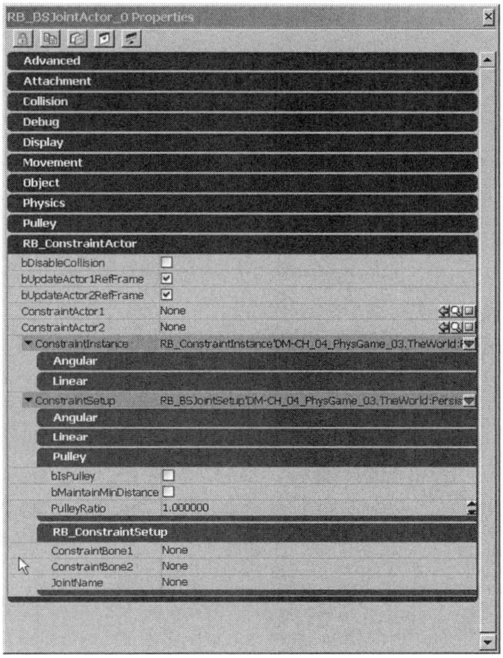

FIGURE 4.23   The RB_ConstraintSetup properties.

Linear

Linear X/Y/Z Setups—These properties allow you to establish limits on linear movement in the three axes.

> **bLimited**—This property controls whether or not the constraint should limit linear movement along a given axis.

> **LimitSize**—Effective only if bLimited is set to True. This property controls how many units in both the positive and negative direction the constrained body is allowed to move along the given axis. Remember, as mentioned earlier in the chapter, that linear limits are spherical, meaning that if you place different nonzero numbers into the LimitSize for different axes, Unreal uses only the largest value to create the theoretical sphere in which to constrain your object.

bLinearLimitSoft—This property determines whether the limit employed is "hard" or "soft," such that a value of True uses a soft limit and False uses hard. A hard limit can be thought of as a limit that is completely rigid, as if striking a wall. Hard limits have no give; you strike their extents and can go no further.

Soft limits, on the other hand, allow for stretching of the constraint according to the linearLimitStiffness value. The effect is a bit like a rubber band in that once you reach the extent of the limit, you can drive the constrained object a bit further. However, the further beyond the limit you go, the more strongly the constraint tries to pull the object back within the range of its limits. The effect is like a snapping spring-loaded object.

> **NOTE**
>
> The LinearLimitStiffness property requires very high values to have a noticeable effect. Even values around 500 result in very little tension on the constrained object.

LinearLimitStiffness—This property is only valid if bLinearLimitSoft is set to True. It controls how much force the constraint applies to prevent the body from receiving linear motion beyond the extents of the soft limit. Higher values result in less stretching.

LinearLimitDamping—This property controls the amount of dissipated energy—in this case, linear velocity—that occurs when a constrained object strikes the extents of a soft limit.

bLinearBreakable—This property allows you to control whether the constraint can be broken if enough linear force is applied to one or both of the objects. A broken constraint releases its hold on the two constrained objects, meaning in practical terms that the constraint no longer has an effect.

LinearBreakThreshold—This value dictates the amount of linear force necessary to break a given constraint. The higher the value, the harder it is to break the constraint.

Angular

bSwingLimited—This property determines whether the Swing axes have any rotational limits applied to them.

Swing1LimitAngle—Valid only if bSwingLimited is checked. This property controls, in degrees, the extents of rotation for the given constraint in the positive and negative direction about the Swing1 axis.

Swing2LimitAngle—Valid only if bSwingLimited is checked. This property controls, in degrees, the extents of rotation for the given constraint in the positive and negative direction about the Swing2 axis.

bTwistLimited—This property controls whether the Twist axis is limited.

TwistLimitAngle—Valid only if bSwingLimited is checked. This property controls, in degrees, the extents of rotation for the given constraint in the positive and negative direction about the Twist axis.

bSwingLimitSoft—Like bLinearLimitSoft, this property controls whether the Swing axes are using soft limits. This means that rotation can be pushed beyond the extents of the limit, after which the constraint attempts to snap the object back within the limits based on the value of the SwingLimitStiffness property.

SwingLimitStiffness—This property controls how stiff the soft limit is, or how much force the constraint exerts to prevent the body from being rotated beyond the limit. Higher values result in more force to keep the object within the extents.

SwingLimitDamping—This value controls how much of the angular force of the constrained body dissipates upon striking the extents of the soft limit.

bTwistLimitSoft—This property determines whether the Twist axis exhibits soft limits rather than hard.

TwistLimitStiffness—As with other limit stiffness properties, this one controls how much force the constraint exerts to prevent the body from rotating beyond the limit.

TwistLimitDamping—This property controls the amount of rotational force that is lost as the body rotates into the soft limit.

bAngularBreakable—Setting this property to False allows the constraint to be broken if an amount of rotation force is applied to it that is greater than or equal to the value of the AngularBreakThreshold property.

AngularBreakThreshold—This value controls the amount of angular force required to break the constraint. The property is only valid if bAngularBreakable is set to True.

Pulley

bIsPulley—This Boolean property controls whether the constraint acts as a pulley.

bMaintainMinDistance—This property forces the constraint to maintain the initial distance between all the bodies involved in the pulley constraint. In effect, this causes the "virtual ropes" that form the pulley to remain taut, thus eliminating any slack.

PulleyRatio—This property allows you to control how much relative motion is translated from one object to the next. For instance, a complex pulley system in the real world might require that the user pull four meters of cable to lift a weight only a few inches into the air. By adjusting the pulley ratio, you could achieve this effect. A value of 1 results in equal motion between the two objects. Values less than 1 result in less motion on the opposite side of the pulley, whereas values greater than 1 result in more motion on the opposite side of the pulley.

RB_ConstraintInstance

The RB_ConstraintInstance category contains a variety of properties that control forces that the constraint can apply to the constrained body (see **FIGURE 4.24**). These forces are known as *drives*. Two types of drives are available on constraints. The first is the position drive, which attempts to keep the constrained object either in a given location or at a given rotation. The other type of drive is the velocity drive, which attempts to force the constrained object to maintain a linear or angular velocity.

Linear

Linear Position Drives (X/Y/Z)—These properties allow you to activate a linear position drive along any of the three primary axes. These drives force the constrained bodies to try to achieve and maintain the position set in the LinearPositionTarget property for that particular axis.

Linear Velocity Drives (X/Y/Z)—
These properties allow you to set a
linear velocity drive for a given axis,
which causes the constrained body
to try to achieve and maintain
the velocity set in the
LinearVelocityTarget property for
that particular axis.

LinearDriveSpring—This property
controls how hard the constraint
attempts to achieve and maintain
its position target. The property is
only used for linear position drives.

LinearDriveDamping—This property
determines how much linear velocity is dissipated while the constraint
is trying to achieve and maintain
the position target. Low
LinearDriveDamping values combined with high LinearDriveSpring
result in a springy wobble. This
property is only used for linear
position drives.

LinearDriveForceLimit—This is the
maximum amount of force that the

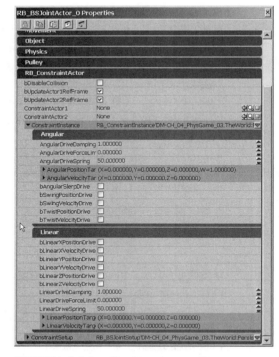

FIGURE 4.24   Here you can see the
RB_ConstraintInstance properties expanded.

linear velocity drive applies when trying to achieve and maintain its velocity target.
As such, the property is only used with linear velocity drives.

Angular

Swing/Twist Position Drives—Setting these properties allows you to activate an angular position drive on either of the Swing axes or the Twist axis. When these properties
are active, the constraint tries to achieve and maintain the angular position specified in
the AngularPositionTarget property.

Swing/Twist Velocity Drives—Setting an angular velocity drive on a constraint causes
the constrained object to attempt to achieve and maintain the angular velocity specified
in the AngularVelocityTarget property. This is perfect for objects that need to continuously spin, such as a fan propeller.

bAngularSlerpDrive—Enabling this property causes your angular drives—both position
and velocity—to use a spherical linear interpolation, or *slerp*, for their calculation rather
than the standard calculation.

AngularDriveSpring—This property determines the amount of force the constraint
applies to try to achieve and maintain its angular position target. The property is only
used with angular position drives.

AngularDriveDamping—This controls the dissipation of angular velocity while the drive is trying to achieve and maintain its angular position target. This is only used with position drives.

AngularDriveForceLimit—This sets the maximum amount of force applied to the object in order to attempt to achieve and maintain its velocity target. The property is only used by angular velocity drives.

Placeable Constraint Types

The following actors are simply constraints to which certain presets have been applied to give them a specific type of behavior. As mentioned earlier, you can change any of these constraints into any of the other types by modifying their properties:

RB_BSJointActor—This constraint has all its linear DOFs limited to 0, but all angular DOFs nonlimited. This means that the constraint behaves like a ball-and-socket joint, allowing for rotation in all three directions. It does not, however, allow for linear movement.

RB_HingeActor—This constraint has all its linear and swing DOFs limited to 0, and its Twist DOF is nonlimited. This allows the constraint to function like the hinges on a door or a trunk lid.

RB_PrismaticActor—The Prismatic constraint has all of its angular DOFs and the Y and Z linear DOFs limited to 0. It's X linear DOF, however, is nonlimited, allowing it to function as if sliding on a rail. This can be used to create carts that travel on straight tracks, or drawers in a dresser.

RB_PullyJointActor—This constraint type has its bIsPulley property set to True, which causes many of the remaining properties, such as limits, to no longer have an effect.

Continue from **TUTORIAL 4.4**, or open the DM-CH_04_PhysGame_03 map included on the DVD in the files for this chapter.

TUTORIAL 4.5: Gravity Platform Constraints

1. In the Actor Classes Browser, select RB_ConstraintActor > RB_PrismaticActor.

2. Right-click one of the five platform KActors placed in the cylindrically shaped room that lies directly above the cube-shaped room. Choose Add RB_PrismaticActor Here from the context menu to place the constraint (see **FIGURE 4.25**).

3. Position the constraint in the center of the KActor. Press F4 to open the constraint's properties.

4. We need to specify which actor the constraint is going to affect. Click the Lock Selected Actors button located in the upper-left corner of the Properties window. This allows you to select another actor without losing your current properties.

5. Once the button has been clicked, select the KActor that the constraint is centered over.

4

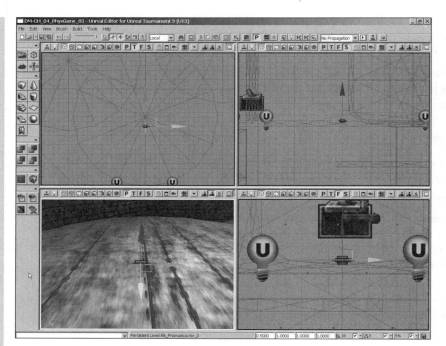

FIGURE 4.25   The RB_PrismaticActor appears on the platform.

6. In the Properties window, locate the ConstraintActor2 property, found under RB_ConstraintActor, and click the Use Current Selection in Browser button .

7. Under RB_ConstraintActor, locate Linear and set the LinearYSetup > bLimited property to 0. This allows the actor to move only along the XY plane (see **FIGURE 4.26**).

8. Duplicate the constraint actor so that there is a separate constraint for each of the platforms in the room. Position each duplicate over one of the platforms, and use the ConstraintActor2 property to assign each respective platform to each constraint, as shown in Step 6 (see **FIGURE 4.27**).

9. Save your level.

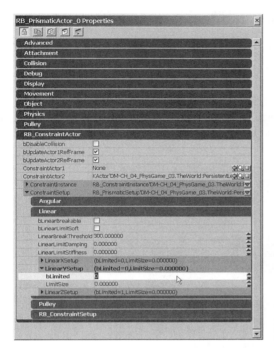

FIGURE 4.26   By deactivating limitation in the Y-axis, you allow the object to move freely in X and Y.

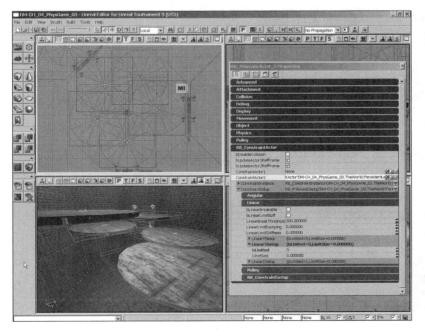

FIGURE 4.27
Assign each of your platforms to its newly duplicated respective actor. This constrains each platform to the XY plane.

END TUTORIAL 4.5

Continue from **TUTORIAL 4.5**, or open the DM-CH_04_PhysGame_04 map included on the DVD in the files for this chapter.

TUTORIAL 4.6: Pulley Platform Constraints, Part I: Prismatic Joints

1. In the Actor Classes Browser, select RB_ConstraintActor > RB_PrismaticActor. Place one of these actors on one of the two platform KActors located within the northeast cylindrically shaped room (see **FIGURE 4.28**). Check in the Top viewport if you're unsure.

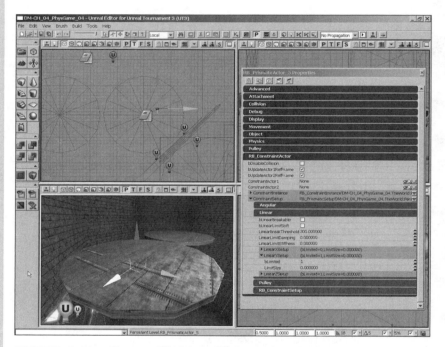

FIGURE 4.28   Place an RB_PrismaticActor on one of the two platforms.

2. Position the constraint in the center of the KActor, and press F4 to open the Properties window. Click the Lock Selected Actors button located in the upper-left corner of the Properties window. This allows you to select another actor without losing your current properties.

3. Once the button is checked, select the KActor that the constraint is centered over.

4. In the Properties window, locate the ConstraintActor2 property, found under RB_ConstraintActor, and click the Use Current Selection in Browser button ⧉ (see **FIGURE 4.29**).

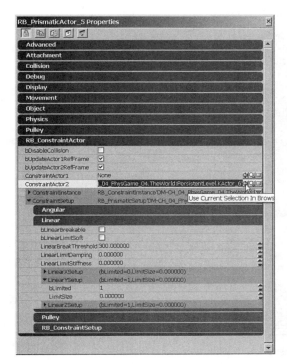

FIGURE 4.29   The platform has now been added to the ConstraintActor2 property.

5. Under RB_ConstraintActor, locate Linear, set the LinearXSetup > bLimited property to 1, and set the LinearZSetup > bLimited property to 0. This allows the actor to only move along the Z-axis.

6. Duplicate the constraint actor and position the duplicate over the other platform. Use the ConstraintActor2 property to assign the opposite platform to the newly duplicated constraint, as shown in Step 5 (see **FIGURE 4.30**).

7. Save your level.

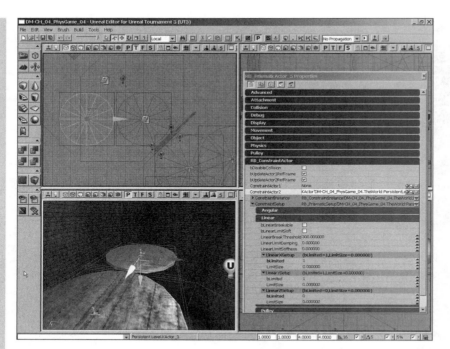

FIGURE 4.30   Duplicate the constraint and associate it with the second platform.

END TUTORIAL 4.6

Continue from **TUTORIAL 4.6**, or open the DM-CH_04_PhysGame_05 map included on the DVD in the files for this chapter.

TUTORIAL 4.7: Pulley Platform Constraints, Part II: Pulley Joint

1. In the Actor Classes Browser, select RB_ConstraintActor > RB_PulleyJointActor. Place one of these actors on one of the two platform KActors placed in the northwest cylindrically shaped room (see **FIGURE 4.31**). Check the Top viewport if you're not sure.

2. Select the RB_PulleyJointActor and press F4 to open the Properties window. As you did in the previous tutorials, click the Lock Selected Actors button 🔒 in the upper-left corner of the window. Select the platform closest to the door. Then, in the Properties window, locate the ConstraintActor1 property under RB_ConstraintActor and click the Use Current Selection in Browser button ◄.

3. Select the opposite platform and click the Use Current Selection in Browser button ◄ .next to the ConstraintActor2 property (see **FIGURE 4.32**).

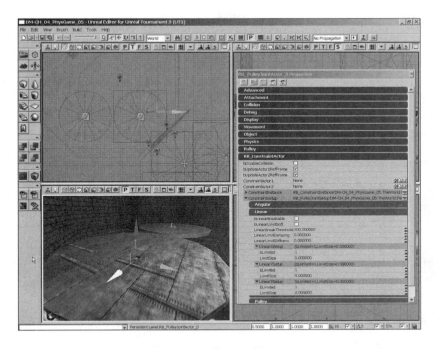

FIGURE 4.31   Place a PulleyJointActor on one of the two platforms.

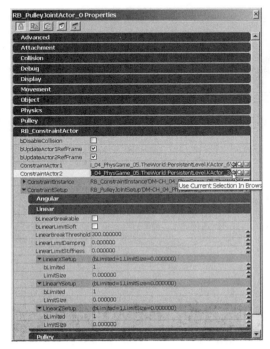

FIGURE 4.32   Assign the two platforms to ConstraintActor1 and ConstraintActor2.

4. We now need to set up the position of the pulley constraint for each actor. Follow these steps to do this:

    a. In the Properties window, deselect the bUpdateActor2RefFrame property. This means that when you next move the constraint, you only adjust its position relative to ConstraintActor1.

    b. Move the constraint to the center of the first KActor, which is the one nearest the door (see **FIGURE 4.33**).

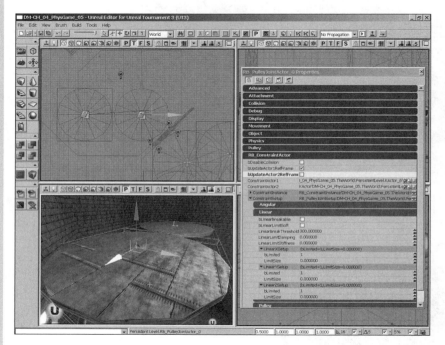

FIGURE 4.33   The constraint is now positioned relative to Constraint Actor 1.

    c. Select bUpdateActor2RefFrame and deselect bUpdateActor1RefFrame (see **FIGURE 4.34**).

    d. Position the RB_PulleyJointActor in the center of the second platform KActor.

    e. Deselect bUpdateActor2RefFrame (both should now be deselected) and move the constraint in between the two platforms (see **FIGURE 4.35**). This does not affect the constraint, but does make it easier to select in the future.

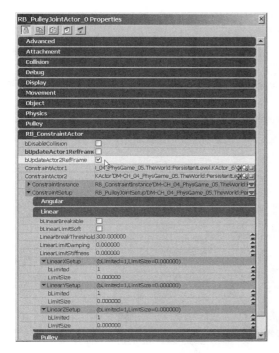

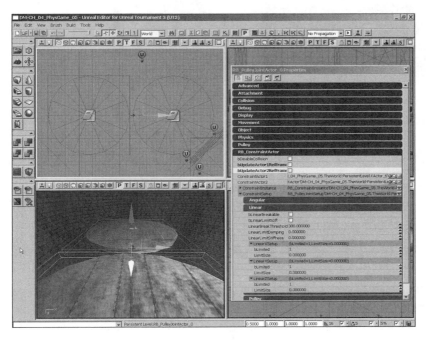

FIGURE 4.34 Swapping the property values now means you are adjusting the constraint's position relative to Constraint Actor 2.

FIGURE 4.35 With both UpdateActorRefFrame properties deselected, move the constraint in between the two platforms.

5. We now need to place the pivots for the pulleys, which requires separate actors to be designated as the pivots. Follow these steps:

a. In the Actor Classes Browser, select the Note actor. Place this actor in the center of the platform KActor nearest the door, which is the same actor used as ConstraintActor1 for the pulley (see **FIGURE 4.36**).

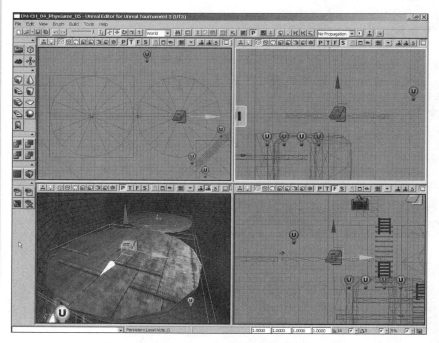

FIGURE 4.36   The Note actor is used as a pulley pivot.

b. Duplicate the Note actor and then place the duplicate in the center of the opposite platform.

c. Select both Note actors and, in the Side viewport, move them upward so that they are both 128 units from the ceiling (see **FIGURE 4.37**).

d. Select the RB_PulleyJointActor and open the Properties window. Click the Lock Selected Actors button 🔒 to lock the window.

e. Select the Note actor in the center of the platform nearest the door and then click the Use button next to the PulleyPivot1 property.

f. Repeat the previous step to place the other Note actor into the PulleyPivot2 property.

6. Save and test your map. You can now pull downward on one of the platforms, and the other rises into the air.

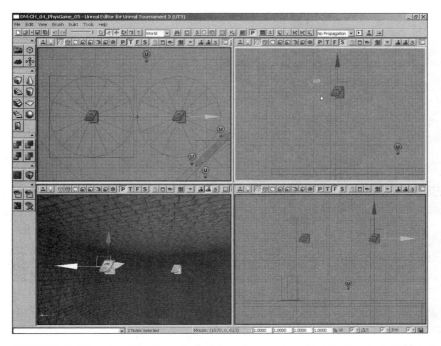

FIGURE 4.37 Just like the actual pulleys in a real-world pulley system, the pivots are placed above the load-bearing objects.

END TUTORIAL 4.7

The Physics Asset Tool (PhAT)

So far we have discussed KActors, KAssets, and Constraints. We now take a slight detour from level-placeable objects and take a look at how these three elements come together with the Physics Asset Tool, also known as PhAT. Using PhAT, you can create Physics Assets that can later be used to generate KAssets in your levels (see **FIGURE 4.38**). This is done by bringing in a skeletal mesh, applying rigid bodies to the bones, and constraining them together with the available constraints.

When creating a Physics Asset using PhAT, you can choose to have the system automatically create bodies for the bones of the skeletal mesh. Doing so requires that you have only a single root bone and that this root bone have some vertices weighted to it. Only then can it create all the necessary bodies correctly. If the root does not have any vertices weighted to it, the automatic rigid body generation only creates bodies for one of the root's children bones, along with all its descendents. This is fine if the root only has one child bone, but if there are any others, they need to be created manually.

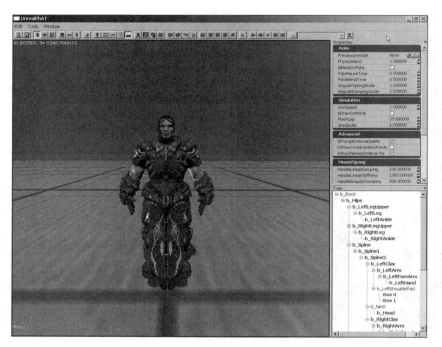

FIGURE 4.38   The Physics Asset Tool (PhAT).

Fortunately, PhAT also allows you to create and manipulate your own set of rigid bodies to be associated with each of the bones of the skeleton. This is necessary in any case where the automatically generated set of bodies is either incomplete or unsatisfactory.

Best of all, PhAT allows you the ability to test your work and see how your new Physics Asset behaves in a level as a KAsset. Once you have created your Physics Asset, you can test it within PhAT, flinging it around to see if it reacts appropriately.

Interface Components

Like many of the tools integrated into Unreal Editor, PhAT has its own unique user interface. **FIGURE 4.39** breaks down each individual area, and the corresponding list describes each one.

> **Toolbar**—The toolbar provides you with access to different editing modes, simulation playback controls, and rigid body editing tools.
>
> **Viewport**—The PhAT viewport allows for visual feedback and editing capabilities. It is a lit and shadowed view of the Physics Asset, and offers a grid and a plane to provide collision for the asset during simulation.

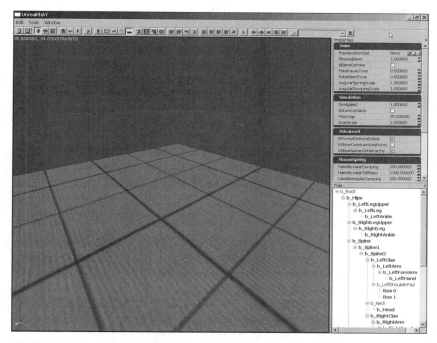

FIGURE 4.39   The PhAT interface breaks down into four key components.

Properties panel—The contents of this panel update dynamically based on what is selected and the current editing mode in which PhAT currently resides. When nothing is selected in the viewport, the Properties panel displays the simulation's properties. If PhAT is in Body Editing Mode and one of the skeleton's rigid bodies is selected, the panel shows the RB_BodySetup properties. If PhAT is in Constraint Editing Mode and one of the asset's constraints is selected, the panel shows the constraint's properties.

Tree—The Tree shows a hierarchy of the bones and the bodies associated with them in Body Editing Mode. When in Constraint Editing Mode, the Tree shows a hierarchy of bones and the constraints associated with them. If there are no rigid bodies, such as when you're creating a new Physics Asset, the Tree panel only shows the hierarchy of bones in the skeleton.

Continue from **TUTORIAL 4.7**.

TUTORIAL 4.8: Creating a Rope Physics Asset

1. Select the skelMesh_rope skeletal mesh from the Chapter_04_Physics package in the Generic Browser. Right-click it and choose Create New Physics Asset from the context menu. Enter the name **PA_rope** for the new Physics Asset and click OK (see **FIGURE 4.40**).

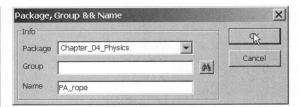

FIGURE 4.40   Enter the name into the field that appears.

2. The New Physics Asset dialog appears. This allows you to establish the properties used to automatically generate the bodies that are attached to each bone in the skeletal mesh. For now, leave all settings at their default values and click OK.

The Physics Asset Tool (PhAT) now opens with the new Physics Asset loaded. You will see the skeletal mesh along with the newly created rigid bodies, which appear as purple boxes.

3. In the Tree list to the right, select Bone01 (see **FIGURE 4.41**). This currently refers to the rigid body associated with Bone01, not the actual skeletal mesh bone itself. The properties for this rigid body appear in the properties area.

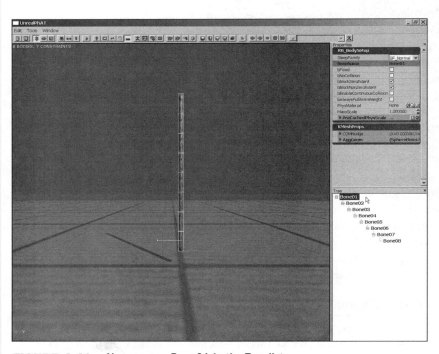

FIGURE 4.41   You can see Bone01 in the Tree list.

4. Set the MassScale property to 5.0. We now set this property for each of the other bodies. Select each body in the Tree and set its MassScale property to 5.0.

5. Click the Editing Mode button [B] in the Toolbar to enter Constraint mode. From the Tree list, select Bone02, which now refers to the constraint bound to the rigid body. Set the following properties:

   ▸ **bTwistLimited**: True

   ▸ **TwistLimitAngle**: 22.5

6. Click the Instance Properties button [i] (or press the I key) to view the constraint's instance properties. Set the following (see **FIGURE 4.42**):

   ▸ **bTwistPositionDrive**: True

   ▸ **AngularDriveSpring**: 250.0

This causes the joints of the rope to have a drive, which attempts to keep the rope from bending. For our purposes, this is excellent, considering that the rope hangs from the ceiling at all times. If the rope had the potential to ever fall to the ground, this would not work so well, because the rope would appear to magically straighten itself out if bent.

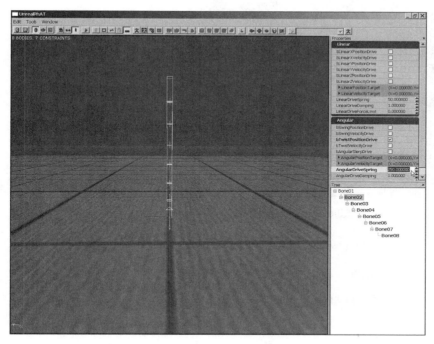

FIGURE 4.42   Set the instance properties as shown.

7. We now copy these properties to the other constraints in the tree. You can do this using the COPY PROPERTIES TO... button 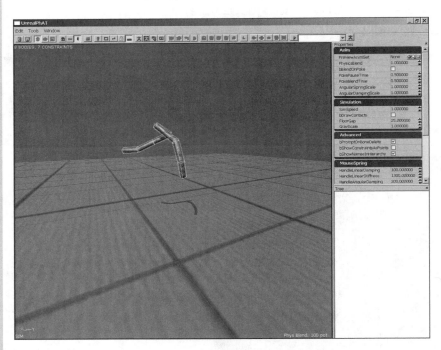 or by simply pressing Ctrl+C and then selecting the constraint to which you want to copy the properties. Do this for each of the remaining constraints.

8. You can now test the Physics Asset within PhAT by clicking the Toggle Simulation button in the Toolbar. During the simulation, holding down Ctrl and left-clicking the Physics Asset applies an impulse, whereas holding down Ctrl and right-clicking the Physics Asset allows you to manipulate it very much like manipulating physics objects in the In-Editor Game (see **FIGURE 4.43**).

FIGURE 4.43   You can now test the rope in your levels.

9. You want to make sure the Physics Asset is behaving like a rope. Feel free to make any adjustments to the Physics Asset at this time, or simply experiment with values to see what sort of behavior you can generate.

10. Save the Chapter_04_Physics package.

END TUTORIAL 4.8

Continue from **TUTORIAL 4.8**, or open the DM-CH_04_PhysGame_06 map included on the DVD in the files for this chapter.

TUTORIAL 4.9: Placing Rope KAssets

1. In the Generic Browser, select the PA_rope asset from the Chapter_04_Physics package. Place this actor in the map by right-clicking and choosing Add Actor > Add PhysicsAsset: PA_rope. Then position it so that it is hanging from the ceiling of the cylindrical room that is just to the east of the cube-shaped room, as seen from the Top viewport.

2. Press F4 to open the Properties window for the KAsset. Set the bWakeOnLevelStart property to True so that the rope is active when the level starts.

3. Duplicate the KAsset and move the duplicate down so that the duplicate is placed right at the end of the original.

4. Repeat the previous step one more time to create three total copies of the rope mesh, each hanging end-to-end from the ceiling (see **FIGURE 4.44**).

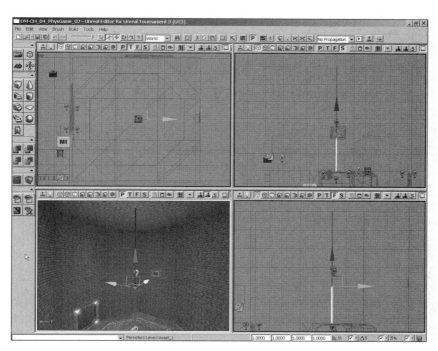

FIGURE 4.44   You now have a series of rope actors.

5. Select the Ragdoll KAsset that has been placed in the level and position it so that its left hand is aligned with the bottom of the lowest rope KAsset. All four of these KAssets are joined together in the next tutorial with constraints so that they can be combined as if the ragdoll were chained to the ceiling by its arm.

6. Save your level. There is nothing to test at this point.

END TUTORIAL 4.9

Continue from **TUTORIAL 4.9**, or open the DM-CH_04_PhysGame_07 map included on the DVD in the files for this chapter.

TUTORIAL 4.10: Ragdoll Swing Constraints

1. In the Actor Classes Browser, select RB_ConstraintActor > RB_BSJointActor. Place this actor in the cylindrically shaped room to the east of the cube-shaped room, where you can see the three rope KAssets and the ragdoll (see **FIGURE 4.45**).

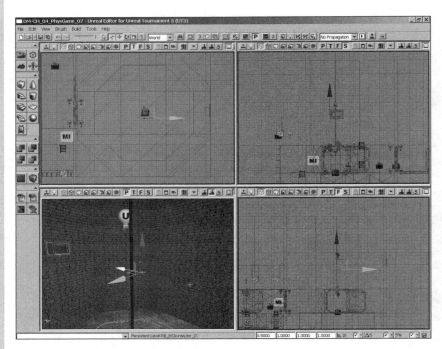

FIGURE 4.45   Place the RB_BSJointActor inside the room.

2. Position the new BSJointActor so that it is in the center of the topmost rope KAsset in the X and Y axes, and right against the ceiling. This should be precisely the point where the KAsset needs to attach to the ceiling (see **FIGURE 4.46**). Press F4 to open the properties for the constraint, and click the Lock Selected Actors button 🔒.

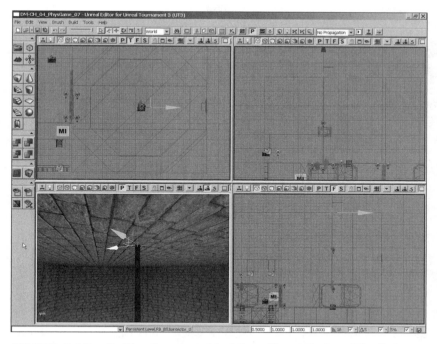

FIGURE 4.46   Position the actor against the ceiling at the top of the first rope.

   3. Select the topmost rope KAsset and, in the Properties window, click the Use button next
      to the ConstraintActor2 property under RB_ConstraintActor. Next, expand
      RB_ConstraintActor > ConstraintSetup > RB_ConstraintSetup, and set the
      ConstraintBone2 property to Bone01.

   4. Duplicate the constraint actor and position the new duplicate where the topmost rope
      KAsset meets the next KAsset. Press F4 to open the Properties window and click the Lock
      Selected Actors button 🔒 (see **FIGURE 4.47**).

   5. Select the topmost rope KAsset and, in the Properties window, click the Use Current
      Selection in Browser button 🔧 next to ConstraintActor1. Select the middle rope KAsset
      and use the same method to assign it to ConstraintActor2. Locate the ConstraintBone1
      property and set it to Bone08.

   6. Duplicate the constraint again, and position the duplicate where the middle and bottom-
      most rope KAssets meet. Use the skills you've gained so far to assign the middle KAsset
      to ConstraintActor1 and the bottom KAsset to ConstraintActor2.

   7. Duplicate the constraint one more time, and position the duplicate so that it sits at the
      point where the bottom rope KAsset meets the ragdoll's left hand (see **FIGURE 4.48**).
      Use the skills you have gained so far to assign the bottommost rope KAsset to
      ConstraintActor1 and the ragdoll KAsset to ConstraintActor2. Finally, locate the
      ConstraintBone1 property and set it to LftHand.

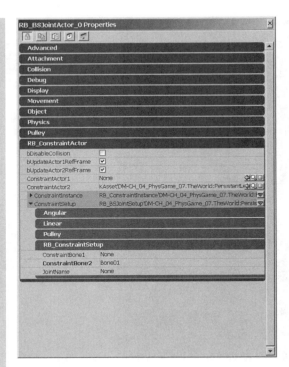

FIGURE 4.47   Duplicate the constraint and assign the first two ropes to it.

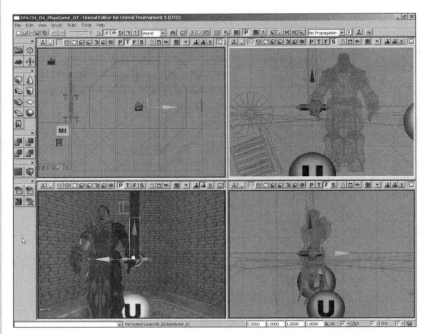

FIGURE 4.48   The last constraint attaches the ragdoll to the ropes.

8. Save your map and test the system. The ragdoll should now be hanging from the ceiling by its arm.

END TUTORIAL 4.10

Continue from **TUTORIAL 4.10**.

TUTORIAL 4.11: Creating a Bridge Physics Asset

1. Select the skelMesh_bridge skeletal mesh from the Chapter_04_Physics package in the Generic Browser. Right-click it and choose Create New Physics Asset. Enter the name **PA_Bridge** and click OK (see **FIGURE 4.49**).

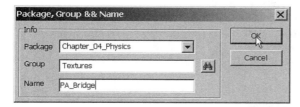

FIGURE 4.49   Enter a name into the field and click OK.

2. In the New Physics Asset dialog, click OK and use the default settings. The PhAT editor now opens.

3. Click the Editing Mode button [B] to switch to Constraint Mode. From the Tree list, select Bone02, which in this case refers to the constraint bound to Bone02. In the Properties window, set the following properties (see **FIGURE 4.50**):

   ▶ **bSwingLimited**: True

   ▶ **bTwistLimited**: True

4. Click the COPY PROPERTIES TO... button [=] and select the next constraint. Repeat this process to copy the properties to all constraints.

5. Click the Toggle Simulation button [▶] to test your new Physics Asset. When finished, close PhAT and save the package.

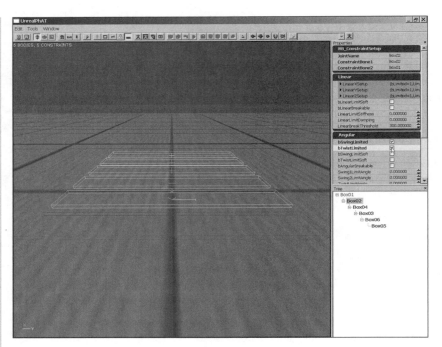

FIGURE 4.50   Set the limited properties like so.

Continue from **TUTORIAL 4.11**, or open the DM-CH_04_PhysGame_08 map included on the DVD in the files for this chapter.

TUTORIAL 4.12: Placing Bridge KAssets

1. Select the PA_Bridge Physics Asset from the Chapter_04_Physics package in the Generic Browser. Place this actor in your level by right-clicking and choosing Add Actor > Add PhysicsAsset: PA_Bridge. Then position it in the northeast cylindrically shaped room, so that it is even with the door that faces along the X-axis (see **FIGURE 4.51**).

2. Open the Properties window for the bridge and then check the bWakeOnLevelStart property to cause the bridge to go active once the level starts.

3. Duplicate the bridge and position it in the Top viewport so that it sits at the end of the original copy. Repeat this two more times to create four total bridges that span across the room (see **FIGURE 4.52**).

4. Save your level. If you tested the level now, all the bridges would fall to the ground because they have not yet been constrained.

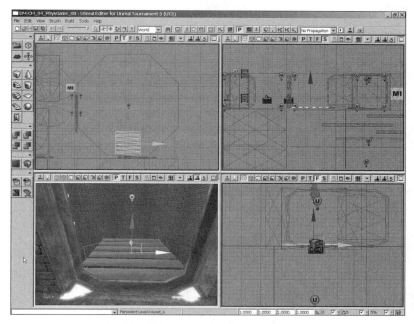

FIGURE 4.51   Position the bridge actor as shown.

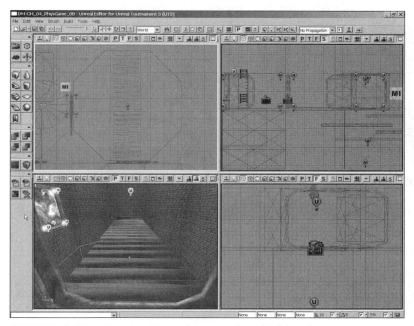

FIGURE 4.52   You should now have a series of bridge pieces.

END TUTORIAL 4.12

Continue from **TUTORIAL 4.12**, or open the DM-CH_04_PhysGame_09 map included on the DVD in the files for this chapter.

TUTORIAL 4.13: Bridge Constraints

1. In the Actor Classes Browser, select RB_Constraint > RB_HingeActor. Add this actor to the level, and position it so that it rests in the center of the bottommost bridge KAsset in the Y and Z axes (as seen from the Top viewport), but positioned in X so that it rests right against the wall. This constraint is used to anchor the first bridge to the wall (see **FIGURE 4.53**).

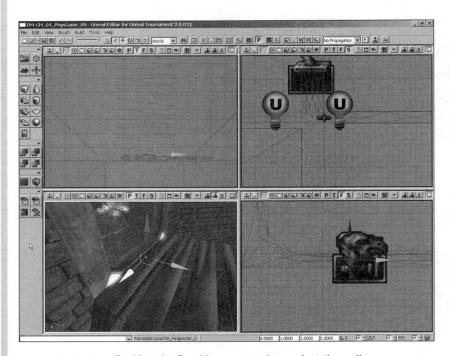

FIGURE 4.53   Position the first hinge constraint against the wall.

2. Open the Properties window for the constraint, and set the following properties in the Collision and ConstraintSetup section:

   ▸ **Collision**:

      ▸ **CollisionType**: COLLIDE_BlockAll

   KAssets do not collide with players by default. It is necessary to set this property to make sure the player can walk on the bridge.

   ▸ **ConstraintSetup**:

      ▸ **bTwistLimited**: True

> ▶ **SwingLimit2Angle**: 45.0

> ▶ **TwistLimitAngle**: 0.0

This keeps the bridge pieces from rotating around the X and Z axes, which gives the bridge a coherent appearance.

3. Click the Lock Selected Actors button 🔒. Select the first bridge KAsset and click the Use Current Selection in Browser button ◀ for ConstraintActor2. Next, under ConstraintSetup > RB_ConstraintSetup, set the ConstraintBone2 property to Box01. If the wood plank nearest the wall does not appear with a blue wireframe outline, rotate each of the bridge Physics Assets 180 degrees around the Z-axis so they are oriented correctly.

4. Duplicate the constraint and position it between the first and second bridge KAssets. Open its Properties window and click the Lock Selected Actors button 🔒. Assign the first bridge KAsset to ConstraintActor1 and the second bridge KAsset to ConstraintActor2. Finally, set the ConstraintBone1 property to Box05 (see **FIGURE 4.54**).

5. Duplicate the constraint actor again, this time positioning it between the second and third bridge KAssets. Use the skills you've gained so far to set ConstraintActor1 to the second bridge KAsset and to set ConstraintActor2 to the third bridge KAsset (see **FIGURE 4.55**).

6. Repeat the previous step to create a new constraint that rests between the third and fourth bridge KAsset, with its ConstraintActor1 property set to the third bridge KAsset, and ConstraintActor2 to the fourth bridge KAsset.

7. Duplicate the constraint one final time and place the duplicated constraint where the fourth bridge KAsset meets the wall. Set both ConstraintActor1 and ConstraintBone1 to None. Then, set the ConstraintBone2 property to Box05 (see **FIGURE 4.56**).

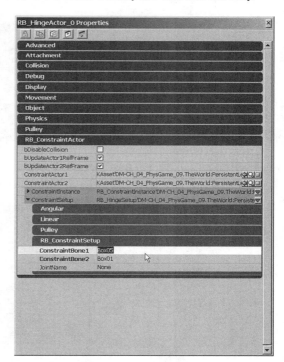

FIGURE 4.54   The new constraint attaches the first and second spans of the bridge.

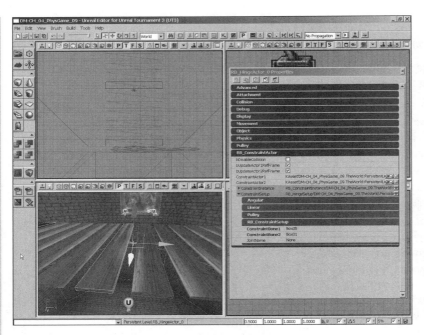

FIGURE 4.55   This new duplicate constrains the second and third bridge pieces.

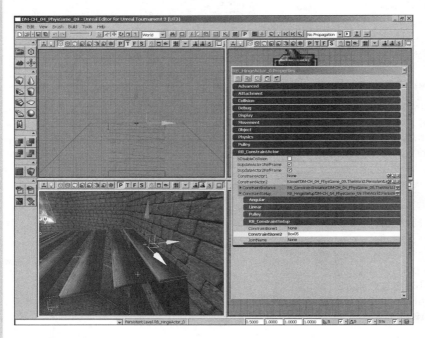

FIGURE 4.56   The final constraint attaches the last bridge piece to the wall.

8. Save your level and test it. Your bridge should now be suspended between the two walls.

END TUTORIAL 4.13

Cloth

Rigid bodies are not the only kind of physical object one can create in Unreal Engine 3. You can also create soft bodies in the form of cloth objects, which generally simulate how cloth works in the real world. However, it should be noted that these types of physics calculations are very complex and use a great deal of processing power. The cloth system works by creating a set of virtual springs between the vertices of a skeletal mesh. A set of properties controls the behavior of these springs, and thus the nature of the cloth.

When opening a skeletal mesh in the AnimSet Editor, you will see under the Mesh tab a Cloth section. This section allows you to establish which parts of the mesh are actually considered to be cloth objects, as well as how to set up the properties to control how the cloth behaves (see **FIGURE 4.57**).

FIGURE 4.57   Cloth objects can add a nice amount of realism to your level.

Controlling which part of the mesh is treated as a cloth is actually very simple in practice, although it does take some forethought when creating your character in your 3D package, as well as some knowledge of skinning in 3D animation packages. The cloth system allows you to designate certain bones that are considered "cloth bones." Any vertices that are receiving any weighting from these bones are considered part of the cloth. This means that if you want a skeletal mesh to appear to have some sort of cloth hanging off of it, you need to create an extra bone just for that purpose and weight all of the mesh vertices intended to be part of the cloth to that bone.

Metal Cloth

Metal cloth is the name given to the ability of the cloth simulation to cause the surface of the mesh to behave as if it were made of metal. This allows meshes to retain their original shape until contacted by other objects, at which time they dent. This makes the cloth system much more flexible and provides another element for level designers to use in creating believable, realistic levels.

Cloth Properties

Once you have established which parts of the mesh are controlled via the cloth system, you merely need to establish a few properties to control the behavior, and you're ready to have some cloth in your levels. Here are the properties used to control cloth:

bForceNoWelding—Enabling this option causes the feature that welds the seams of the mesh together to be disregarded.

ClothBones—This property is an array of names of all the bones to be included in the cloth simulation. Any vertices that are at all weighted to the bones contained in this array are considered part of the cloth.

bEnableClothBendConstraints—This property controls whether the ClothBendStiffness properties have any effect.

bEnableClothDamping—This property determines whether the ClothDamping property has any effect.

bUseClothCOMDamping—This property reduces the effect of stretching on damped cloth objects that are attached to something, such as a flag attached to a flagpole.

ClothStretchStiffness—This property controls the stiffness of the cloth springs when they are stretched along their length. Higher values result in less elasticity in the cloth.

ClothBendStiffness—This property controls how much the springs resist being bent. Higher values result in a firmer cloth that resists bending. This property is only valid if bEnableClothBendConstraints is set to True.

ClothDensity—This value is multiplied by the size of the triangles surrounding each vertex to determine the mass of the cloth.

ClothThickness—This property controls the theoretical thickness of the cloth that is used for collision detection.

ClothDamping—This controls the amount of resistance to movement exhibited by each vertex of the cloth object. This property is only valid if bEnableClothDamping is set to True.

ClothIterations—This is the number of calculations run during each frame to simulate the cloth's behavior. Higher numbers result in a more accurate simulation at the cost of computation time. Setting this too high could result in performance issues.

ClothFriction—This controls the amount of resistance to movement exhibited by each vertex of the cloth when in contact with other bodies.

ClothRelativeGridSpacing—This property is intended for optimization and controls how the first pass of collision detection takes place on the cloth object. Lowering this value decreases the number of detailed collision calculations while increasing the overhead of the first pass of collision detection. Higher values use a finer-grain detailed collision calculation. The default value is 0.25.

ClothPressure—This property sets the air pressure of the cloth when dealing with a closed mesh. You can imagine an inner tube filled with air. The more air it is filled with, the more pressure inside it. ClothPressure works the same way. This property is only valid when bEnableClothPressure is set to True.

ClothCollisionResponseCoefficient—This property determines how much influence collisions with rigid bodies have on the cloth.

ClothAttachmentResponseCoefficient—This property determines how much influence attachments to rigid bodies have on the cloth.

ClothAttachmentTearFactor—This property determines how much force can be applied to an attachment before the cloth tears.

ClothSleepLinearVelocity—This property determines the minimum velocity at which the cloth can move and have its simulation still remain active. If this value is negative, the engine's default value is used.

bEnableClothOrthoBendConstraints—Similar to bEnableClothBendConstraints, this property institutes resistance to minimize the bending or folding of cloth objects. This method uses angular springs as opposed to the distance springs used by the bEnableClothBendConstraints property. This method is also slightly more processor intensive.

bEnableClothSelfCollision—This property determines whether cloth objects collide with themselves to keep the cloth for interpenetrating.

bEnableClothPressure—This property causes the cloth to use the ClothPressure property, which allows for the simulation of inflatable objects.

bEnableClothTwoWayCollision—Typically, rigid bodies can affect cloth objects but not vice-versa. With this property active, cloth can affect a rigid body. Consider a sheet of fabric pulled across a large ball, causing the ball to roll.

ClothSpecialBones—This property contains skeletal mesh bones to which the cloth object is attached. The benefit of attaching cloth in this way is that the bone can have its BoneType property set to CLOTHBONE_BreakableAttachment, which allows the cloth to be torn off the bone if enough force is applied to it.

bEnableClothLineChecks—This property is necessary if you want to shoot cloth or have Pawns (nonplayer characters) interact with the cloth object.

bClothMetal—This property determines whether the regular cloth simulation or metal cloth simulation is to be used with this cloth object.

ClothMetalImpulseThreshold—This is the minimum amount of force that must be applied to the metal cloth object in order to cause deformation.

ClothMetalPenetrationDepth—Used only with metal cloth, higher values of this property allow for greater deformation when the metal cloth object is struck by a rigid body.

ClothMetalDeformationDistance—This is the maximum distance that any vertex of the metal cloth is allowed to deform from its original location relative to the cloth object.

bEnableClothTearing—This property determines whether the cloth is allowed to tear along its seams. For tearing to be used, vertices must be reserved using the ClothTearReserve property.

ClothTearFactor—This property determines the maximum amount of stretching that can occur before the cloth tears.

ClothTearReserve—This is the amount of vertices to be reserved for the tearing functionality. As cloth is torn, extra vertices are created to accommodate the tear. If the number of vertices reaches the value of this property, the cloth cannot be torn any further.

Continue from **TUTORIAL 4.13**.

TUTORIAL 4.14: Creating a Flag Cloth

1. Double-click the skelMesh_flag_cloth skeletal mesh located in the Chapter_04_Physics package in the Generic Browser to open it in the AnimSet Editor. This skeletal mesh has the flag vertices weighted to a special bone named "Flag" (see **FIGURE 4.58**).

2. In the Properties panel, make sure the Mesh tab is selected. Scroll down to the Cloth section. In the ClothBones array, click the Add Item button 🔘. Type the value **Flag** into this new entry.

3. Set the following properties:

   ▸ **bEnableBendConstraints**: True   ▸ **ClothThickness**: 5.0

   ▸ **bEnableClothDamping**: True   ▸ **ClothDamping**: 0.25

   ▸ **ClothStretchStiffness**: 0.75   ▸ **ClothIterations**: 10

   ▸ **ClothBendStiffness**: 0.5   ▸ **ClothFriction**: 0.0

   ▸ **ClothDensity**: 0.5

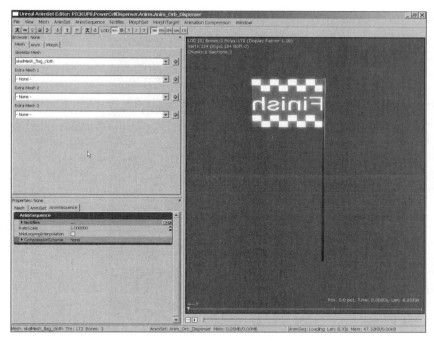

FIGURE 4.58   The flag cloth object appears in the AnimSet Editor.

4. In the Toolbar, click the Toggle Cloth button 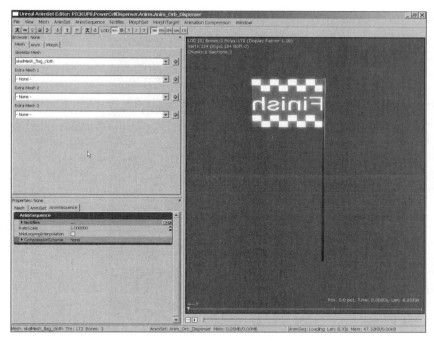 to begin the cloth simulation. You'll notice that the flag isn't doing anything. We have one more property to activate. Under the SkeletalMesh section in the Mesh tab of the Properties panel, set bForceCPUSkinning to True (see **FIGURE 4.59**).

The flag is now moving slightly, although a little more motion would be nice. The yellow directional pointer in the viewport, with the label "Wind: 10" just beneath it, represents the strength and direction of the wind.

5. Hold down the W key and the left mouse button. By dragging the mouse, you can change the direction of the wind. Hold down W and right-drag to change the wind's strength.

6. Set the wind's strength to around 100.0 and change the direction. You should notice much more realistic behavior from the flag.

7. Save your package.

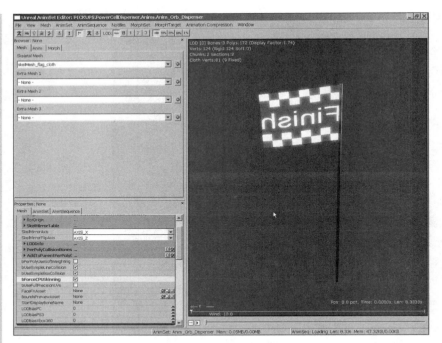

FIGURE 4.59   As soon as you set bForceCPUSkinnning, the flag comes to life.

END TUTORIAL 4.14

Continue from **TUTORIAL 4.14**, or open the DM-CH_04_PhysGame_10 map included on the DVD in the files for this chapter.

TUTORIAL 4.15: Placing Flags

1. Select the skelMesh_flag_cloth skeletal mesh in the Generic Browser. Place a copy of this mesh in the cube-shaped room by right-clicking and choosing Add Actor > Add SkeletalMesh: SkeletalMesh Chapter_04_Physics.skelMesh_flag_cloth (see **FIGURE 4.60**). If you have not completed the previous tutorials, you may use the skelMesh_flag_cloth_01 asset provided in the Chapter_04_Physics package instead.

2. Set the DrawScale of the mesh to 0.5. Uniformly scaling does not damage the simulation.

3. Position the mesh in the Top viewport so that it is even in the X-axis with the trigger that lies in the upper-right corner of the room and just inside the wall on the right side of the room, as shown.

4. Rotate the skeletal mesh in the Top viewport so that the flag is pointing to the left.

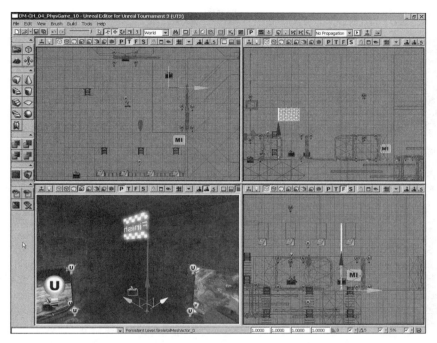

FIGURE 4.60   A copy of the mesh has been placed into the room.

5. With the skeletal mesh selected, press F4 to open the Properties window. Under SkeletalMeshActor > SkeletalMeshComponent > Cloth, set the bEnableClothSimulation property to True (see **FIGURE 4.61**). Without this property set, the cloth simulation does not run in the game. Also, set the ClothWind X and Y properties to –100.0. This property controls the force affecting the cloth within the game.

6. Duplicate the flag and position it so that it sits on the other side of the trigger, just inside the short wall that rises from the floor. Then select both of the flags and duplicate the pair (for a total of four) and move the two new duplicates to the other side of the trigger in the doorway to the room containing the gravity platforms.

7. With the two new flags selected, open the Properties window and expand SkeletalMeshActor > SkeletalMeshComponent > Rendering. Locate the Materials property and click the Add New Item button 🔲 twice.

8. Using the Generic Browser, assign the mat_start_icon material (located within the PhysicsContent package) into the Materials1 slot (see **FIGURE 4.62**).

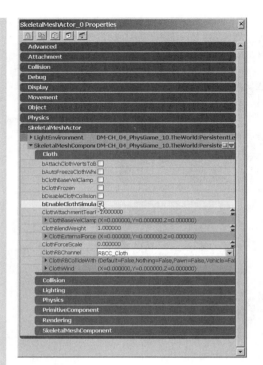

FIGURE 4.61   Make sure to set the bEnableClothSimulation property.

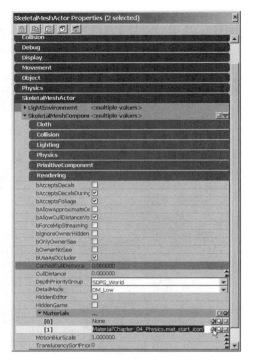

FIGURE 4.62   The material is now applied to the flag.

9. In the Generic Browser, select the skelMesh_flag_cloth_Physics Physics Asset in the Chapter_04_Physics package. Then, select all four of the flags and click the Use Current Selection in Browser button for the PhysicsAsset property of the actors, located in the SkeletalMeshComponent section. Finally, set the CollisionType property to COLLIDE_BlockAll. This causes the flag pole to have collision.

10. Save, rebuild, and test your level. You should now have flags that dynamically blow in the wind.

END TUTORIAL 4.15

Impulse and Force Actors

Another pair of actors that can be extremely useful for dynamic simulations in Unreal Engine 3 is Impulse and Force actors. These actors apply a specific type of force to your dynamic objects, thereby moving them in some way. An example would be to create an explosion that sends your objects flying out from a center point in a radial manner, or perhaps you could blow down a series of standing objects with a strong wind. All the actors that are available to help you achieve these effects are fairly simple in nature. The Impulse actors apply a one-time burst of energy that can be triggered via Kismet. The Force actors apply constant force over time, which causes the objects to continuously accelerate. These actors can be activated and deactivated in Kismet.

RB_LineImpulseActor

The LineImpuseActor allows you to create a one-time force that is applied along a single vector, designated by a red arrow in the editor viewports. Here are the properties available to control its behavior:

> **ImpulseStrength**—This property controls the amount of force applied to rigid body objects.

> **ImpulseRange**—This setting controls the distance from the Impulse actor, along the vector that a rigid body must be within to be affected by the impulse.

> **bStopAtFirstHit**—Setting this property to True causes the Impulse actor to only affect the first object it comes across along its vector and no other object.

> **bVelChange**—If set to True, this property causes the ImpulseStrength to be treated like a direct change in velocity, meaning that the mass of the object is ignored. If this property is set to False, the ImpulseStrength acts like a traditional impulse, applying a certain amount of force and taking the mass of the object into the equation.

RB_RadialImpulseActor

The RadialImpulseActor applies a one-time force that extends outward in a spherical radius from the location of the actor. This radius is denoted by red orthogonal circles within the editor's viewports. Here are the pertinent properties to control the behavior of this actor:

> **ImpulseStrength**—This property controls the amount of force applied to rigid body objects receiving 100% of the force.

> **ImpulseRadius**—This is the radial distance in all directions from the Impulse actor within which all dynamic objects must be located to be affected by the impulse.

> **ImpulseFalloff**—This property allows you to designate the type of falloff used in the application of the impulse's force.

>> **RIF_Constant**—Constant falloff results in the impulse being applied in equal amounts to all objects that fall within the radius.

>> **RIF_Linear**—This setting causes the amount of energy applied by the Impulse actor to fall off linearly from the location of the Impulse actor to the extent of its radius.

> **bVelChange**—If set to True, this property causes the ImpulseStrength to be treated like a direct change in velocity, meaning that the mass of the object is ignored. If this property is set to False, the ImpulseStrength acts like a traditional impulse, applying a certain amount of force and taking the mass of the object into the equation.

RB_Thruster

A Thruster is a Force actor that applies constant force along its local X-axis, which is denoted by a yellow arrow in the editor's viewports. This actor needs to be attached to a dynamic object in order to have any effect. The benefit of using a Thruster is that you apply the force in a *local* direction rather than a global one. This means that if the orientation of the object changes, so does the direction of the force. A good example would be a rocket that begins to spin out of control. Here are the properties that control this actor:

> **ThrustStrength**—This property controls the amount of force applied to the dynamic object to which the Thruster has been attached.

> **bThrustEnabled**—This property toggles the Thruster's force on and off. The property is best controlled via Kismet using a Toggle sequence object, allowing you to turn the Thruster actor on and off during gameplay.

RB_RadialForceActor

This actor is very similar to the RadialImpulseActor, except that instead of its force being applied in a one-time-only fashion, the force can be applied constantly to all objects that fall within the actor's radius as long as the RadialForceActor is active. Here are the properties needed to control this actor:

> **ForceStrength**—This is the amount of force applied to all bodies within the radius of the actor that are receiving 100% of the force.

> **ForceRadius**—This property sets the distance from the Force actor in all directions within which rigid bodies must be placed to be affected by the actor.

> **ForceFieldChannel**—This is simply an identifier specifying which channel this force actor is in for use with RB_ForceFieldExcludeVolumes.

> **SpinTorque**—This property determines the force with which actors affected by this Force actor spin around their local Z-axis.

> **SwirlStrength**—This determines the amount of rotational force applied around the Z-axis of the Force actor.

> **ForceFalloff**—This property allows you to designate the type of falloff used in the application of the actor's force.

> > **RIF_Constant**—Constant falloff results in the impulse being applied in equal amounts to all objects that fall within the radius.

> > **RIF_Linear**—This setting causes the amount of energy applied by the Force actor to fall off linearly from the location of the Force actor to the extent of its radius.

> **RadialForceMode**—This property allows you to designate the type of force to be used by this Force actor.

> > **RFT_Force**—Force mode applies a constant force to all actors being affected.

RFT_Impulse—Impulse mode applies a one-time force to all actors being affected.

bForceActive—This property simply toggles the Force actor on and off, and is most commonly activated within Kismet using a Toggle sequence object.

RB_CylindricalForceActor

This actor applies a constant force in a similar fashion to the RB_RadialForceActor, but it can apply the force emanating out from the center of a cylinder as well as in a circular manner around the circumference of the cylinder. Here are the major properties of this actor:

EscapeVelocity—This sets the velocity at which physics objects within the influence of this actor stop being affected by the radial force.

ForceFieldChannel—This is simply an identifier specifying which channel this Force actor is in for use with RB_ForceFieldExcludeVolumes.

ForceHeight—This sets the height of the cylinder that determines the extent of this actor's influence.

ForceRadius—This sets the radius at the bottom of the cylinder.

ForceTopRadius—This property sets the radius at the top of the cylinder.

HeightOffset—This allows the cylinder to be offset vertically from the position of the Force actor.

LiftFalloffHeight—This property determines the relative location vertically where the force applied by this actor begins to fall off linearly. A value of 0 causes the falloff to begin at the bottom of the cylinder, whereas a value of 1 causes the falloff to begin at the top, resulting in no falloff.

LiftStrength—This is the amount of force applied along the length of the cylinder.

RadialStrength—This is the amount of force applied from the center of the cylinder outward.

RotationalStrength—This is the amount of force applied around the circumference of the cylinder.

bForceActive—This property simply toggles the Force actor on and off, and is most commonly activated within Kismet using a Toggle sequence object.

Continue from **TUTORIAL 4.15**, or open the DM-CH_04_PhysGame_11 map included on the DVD in the files for this chapter.

TUTORIAL 4.16: Ragdoll Swing Radial Impulse

1. In the Actor Classes Browser, select the RB_RadialImpulseActor. Place this actor in the center of the water surface static mesh in the cylindrically shaped room that is just to the right of the cube-shaped room when viewed from the Top viewport (see **FIGURE 4.63**).

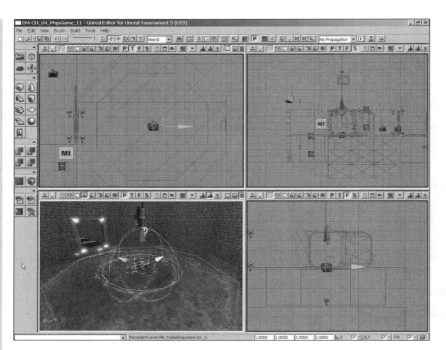

FIGURE 4.63   Place the RadialImpulseActor like so.

2. Position the Impulse actor so that it is aligned in the same XY plane as the water surface mesh, and directly in the center of it as seen from the Top viewport.

3. With the Impulse actor selected, press F4 to open the Properties window. Under RB_RadialImpulseActor > ImpulseComponent, set the following values:

> ▶ **ImpulseRadius**: 384.0

> ▶ **ImpulseStrength**: 128.0

4. Open the Kismet Editor and find the red section labeled "Ragdoll Impulse Loop." In this section, add a new Level Startup event by right-clicking and choosing New Event > Level Startup from the context menu.

5. Create a Delay action by right-clicking and choosing New Action > Misc > Delay. Select this new Delay object and set its Duration property to 3.0 (see **FIGURE 4.64**).

6. Create a new Toggle action by right-clicking and choosing New Action > Toggle > Toggle from the context menu.

7. Make the following connections (see **FIGURE 4.65**):

> ▶ Level Startup: Out → Delay: Start

> ▶ Delay: Finished → Toggle: Turn On

> ▶ Toggle: Out → Delay: Start

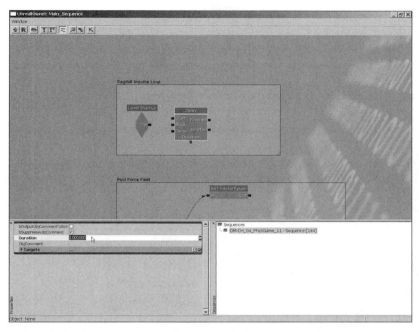

FIGURE 4.64   Create a new Delay object with a 3-second duration.

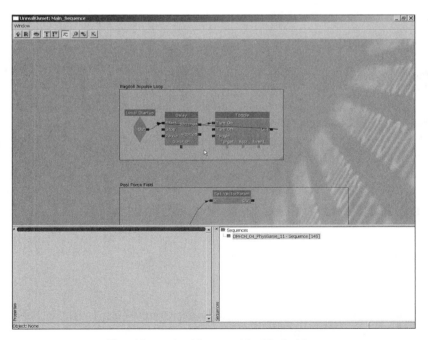

FIGURE 4.65   The objects should connect in this fashion.

8. Select the RB_RadialImpulseActor in the viewport and then in the Kismet Editor. Right-click the Target input of the Toggle object and choose New Object Var Using... to place a new Object Variable containing the RadialImpulseActor and automatically connect it to the toggle (see **FIGURE 4.66**).

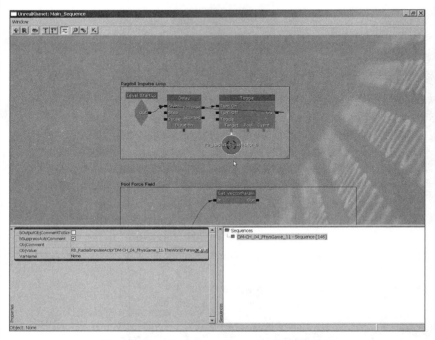

FIGURE 4.66   The Toggle object now affects the RadialImpulseActor.

9. Save and test your level. The ragdoll above the pool of water should get thrown around by the impulse for the RB_RadialImpulseActor every 3 seconds.

END TUTORIAL 4.16

Physics-Specific Kismet Sequence Objects

Several sequence objects are available within Kismet that pertain specifically to various dynamic simulation situations. In this section, we describe each of these objects.

Physics Events

The following is a list of the Kismet events that relate to physics simulations. These can cause various actions to be triggered when they occur.

Constraint Broken—This event is activated when the associated constraint actor is broken. A good example of its use would be to turn off a dynamic light when the cable attaching it to the wall via a constraint is broken free of the electrical fixture.

Projectile Landed—This event is activated when any projectile has landed. It outputs the pawn who originally shot the projectile, as well as the projectile that just landed. The event also outputs any witnesses to the landing.

Rigid Body Collision—This event is activated when a rigid body collides with another object. You need to attach the rigid body to this event through the use of an Attach to Event action, which itself must be fed input by another action, such as Level Startup. The Rigid Body Collision event also requires that the bNoEncroachCheck property on the rigid body is set to False in order to work properly.

Touch—This event is called when an object touches the associated rigid body. This event requires that the associated rigid body has its bNoEncroachCheck property set to False and its CollisionType property set to COLLIDE_TouchAll, COLLIDE_TouchWeapons, or COLLIDE_TouchAllButWeapons.

Physics Actions

The following is a list of Kismet actions that prove useful for physics simulations:

Set BlockRigidBody—This action allows you to set the BlockRigidBody property for actors such as static meshes, skeletal meshes, KActors, KAssets, and so on.

Set Physics—This action allows you to set the Physics property for any actor. This can be used to deactivate or reactivate a rigid body.

Set RigidBodyIgnoreVehicles—At the time of this writing, this sequence object is not completely implemented and is nonfunctional.

Continue from **TUTORIAL 4.16**, or open the DM-CH_04_PhysGame_12 map included on the DVD in the files for this chapter.

TUTORIAL 4.17: Rigid Body Collision Kismet Event

1. Open the Kismet Editor and find the blue section labeled "Collision Sound Modulation." In this section, add a Rigid Body Collision event (New Event > Physics > Rigid Body Collision). With the object selected, set the following values in the properties area (see **FIGURE 4.67**):

   ▶ **MaxTriggerCount**: 0

   ▶ **MinCollisionVelocity**: 1.0

2. Add a new Play Sound action (New Action > Sound > Play Sound) and set the following properties for it:

   ▶ **PlaySound**: SoundCue'Chapter_04_Physics.bangCue'

   ▶ **VolumeMultiplier**: 0.5

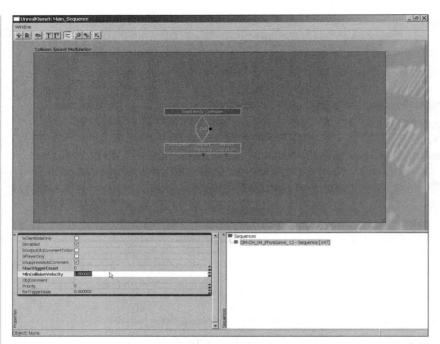

FIGURE 4.67   Add a Rigid Body Collision event.

3. Position the new Play Sound action directly to the right of the Rigid Body Collision event; then create a link from the Out output of the Rigid Body Collision event to the Play input of the Play Sound action (see **FIGURE 4.68**).

4. Add an Attach to Event action (New Action > Event > Attach to Event). Position it above and to the left of the Rigid Body Collision event. Drag a link from the Event output at the bottom of the object onto the Rigid Body Collision event, connecting the two (see **FIGURE 4.69**).

5. Create a link from the Finished output of the existing Actor Factory action in the Spawn Module section to the In input of the Attach to Event action.

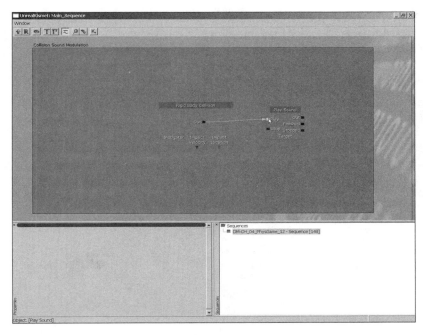

FIGURE 4.68   Link the two objects together as shown.

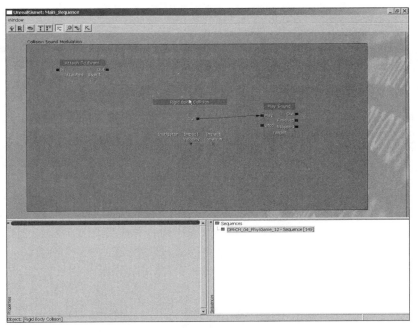

FIGURE 4.69   The Attach to Event action actually triggers the event when a collision from our KActor occurs.

6. Create a new Named Variable (New Variable > Named Variable). In the Properties area, enter **SpawnedChp** for the FindVarName property. Position this variable just below the Attach to Event action, and connect it to the Attachee input (see **FIGURE 4.70**).

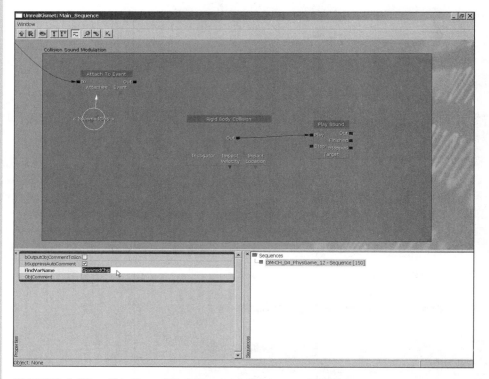

FIGURE 4.70   This Named Variable stores the spawned KActor.

7. Duplicate the Named Variable created in the previous step. Position the duplicate below the Play Sound action created earlier in this tutorial, and connect the Target input to the newly duplicated Named Variable (see **FIGURE 4.71**).

8. Save and test your level. You should now hear a sound played when the chips are spawned.

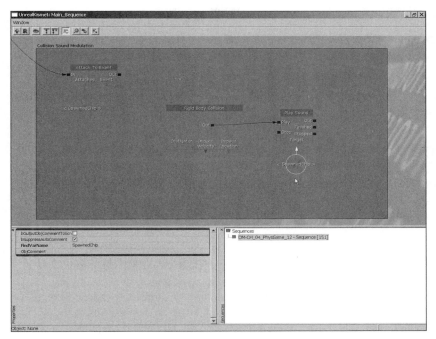

FIGURE 4.71   The Play Sound now targets the KActor object to spatialize the sound effect.

END TUTORIAL 4.17

Physical Materials

A Physical Material is an asset that contains a variety of physical properties for how a particular rigid body should behave in a simulation. Things such as friction, density, and impact sound can all be stored within a Physical Material. This material can then be applied to KActors or the rigid bodies within a KAsset in a variety of ways. First, it can be associated with a static mesh within the Static Mesh Editor under the BodySetup category. Second, it can be associated with a specific KActor within its PhysMaterialOverride property, located under StaticMeshComponent > Physics. Physical Materials are applied to KAssets—or technically, the rigid bodies that make up the KAssets—through PhAT.

You can also apply a Physical Material directly to a standard material, which allows you to specify the types of sound effects played when a dynamic object strikes any surface to which the standard material has been applied. However, setting this up completely requires a bit of programming and is therefore not explored in this book.

Here are the properties that can be controlled via Physical Materials:

AngularDamping—This property controls a rigid body's resistance to rotation. Higher values result in less rotation.

Density—This value is multiplied by the volume of a body to calculate its mass.

Friction—This controls the amount of resistance to movement when the object to which the material has been applied is sliding against another surface. Higher values result in higher resistance.

LinearDamping—This property controls a body's resistance to linear movement. Higher values result in less movement.

Restitution—Simply put, this property controls the percentage of energy retained after a body experiences a collision. A value of 0 results in complete loss of motion upon impact, whereas a value of 1 causes the body to exit a collision with the same amount of force it had before the impact. Values greater than 1 results in the body having more energy after it bounces than it had prior to the collision. This means that—provided damping is not a factor—the object gets progressively faster each time it bounces.

Impact and Slide Events—Impact and Slide events allow a level designer to play sounds and spawn particle systems to help accentuate a variety of dynamic effects in a simulation. For example, one could cause a sheet of particle-based sparks to fly out and a horrific screech fills the air when a piece of metal scrapes across the ground.

ImpactEffect—This property holds the particle system used when the body collides with a surface.

ImpactSound—This contains the SoundCue played when the body collides with a surface.

ImpactReFireDelay—This setting controls the amount of time (in seconds) to wait before an impact effect or impact sound can be retriggered.

ImpactThreshold—This is the minimum velocity with which the body must collide to trigger the specified impact effect and impact sound.

SlideEffect—This property holds the particle system to use when the body slides along a surface.

SlideSound—This property contains the SoundCue played when the body slides along a surface.

SlideReFireDelay—This setting controls the amount of time (in seconds) to wait before a slide effect or slide sound can be retriggered.

SlideThreshold—This is the minimum velocity with which the body must slide to trigger the specified slide effect and slide sound.

Parent/PhysicalMaterialProperty—These two properties work in conjunction to allow you to use inheritance to create a base Physical Material that contains default settings and then apply this base Physical Material to all objects in a scene, after which you can adjust the default properties of the base Physical Material through the use of other

Physical Materials. However, doing so requires the use of coding and is therefore beyond the scope of this book.

UT3 does provide its own PhysicalMaterialProperty object, called UTPhysicalMaterialProperty, that allows a MaterialType to be set for the Physical Material. This is used in conjunction with standard materials and the Pawn class to determine which footstep sounds to play. Because this technically is not related to physics, we do not focus on its use in this chapter.

Continue from **TUTORIAL 4.17**.

TUTORIAL 4.18: Creating a Physical Material for a Puck

1. In the Generic Browser, select the Chapter_04_Physics package. Right-click in a blank area of the browser and choose New Physical Material. Enter the name **physMat_puck** and click OK. The properties for the new Physical Material open (see **FIGURE 4.72**).

2. Set the following properties to the designated values:

   ▶ **AngularDamping**: 50.0

   ▶ **Density**: 10.0

   ▶ **Friction**: 0.0

   ▶ **Restitution**: 0.55

3. Back in the Generic Browser, double-click the sm_plinko_chip static mesh to open the Static Mesh Editor. Expand the BodySetup section and click the Show Generic Browser button ![button] next to the PhysMaterial property.

4. Select the newly created Physical Material and then click the Use Current Selection in Browser button ![button] in the Static Mesh Editor. The Physical Material has now been assigned to the puck (see **FIGURE 4.73**).

5. Save your package.

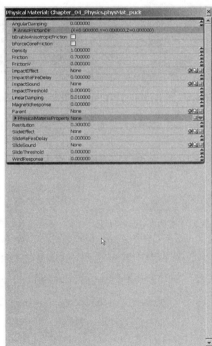

FIGURE 4.72   The Physical Materials Properties window.

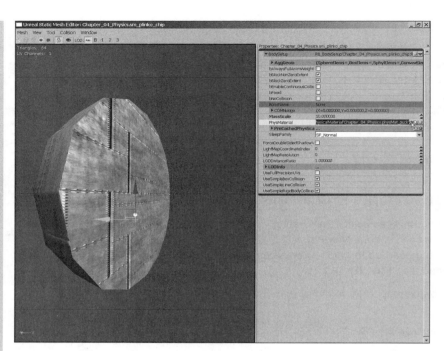

FIGURE 4.73   The new Physical Material has now been applied to the plinko chip.

END TUTORIAL 4.18

Continue from **TUTORIAL 4.18**.

TUTORIAL 4.19: Creating a Physical Material for Gravity Platforms

1. In the Generic Browser, open the Chapter_04_Physics package. Right-click in a blank area of the browser and choose New Physics Material. Enter the name **physMat_ GravityPlatform** and click OK (see **FIGURE 4.74**).

2. In the Properties window that appears, enter the following values:

   - ▶ **AngularDamping**: 100000.0
   - ▶ **Density**: 10.0
   - ▶ **Friction**: 0.2
   - ▶ **ImpactRefireDelay**: 0.1
   - ▶ **LinearDamping**: 2.0
   - ▶ **Restitution**: 0.55

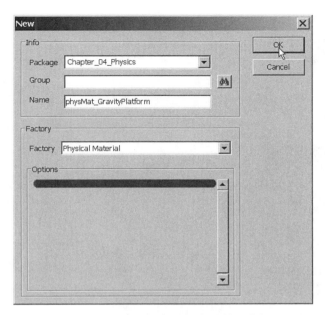

FIGURE 4.74   Create a new Physical Material.

3. Locate the ImpactSound property and click the Show Generic Browser button 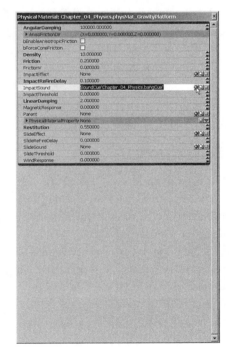. Locate and select the bangCue from within the PhysicsGame package and close the Generic Browser if it is in your way. Click the Use Current Selection in Browser button for the ImpactSound property (see **FIGURE 4.75**).

The selected SoundCue now plays when the platforms experience a collision.

4. Double-click the sm_platform static mesh in the Generic Browser to open it in the Static Mesh Editor. Expand the BodySetup section in the static mesh's properties and click the Show Generic Browser button for the PhysMaterial property. Select the physMat_GravityPlatform Physical Material you just created.

5. Back in the Static Mesh Editor, click the Use Current Selection in Browser button next to the PhysMaterial property (see **FIGURE 4.76**).

FIGURE 4.75   Add the "bangCue" SoundCue into the ImpactSound property.

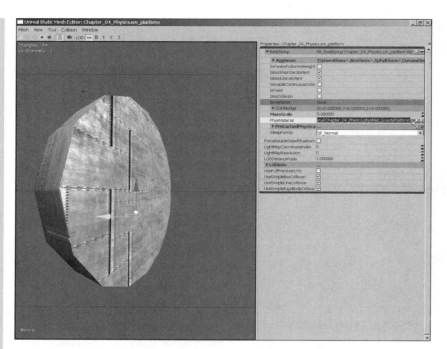

FIGURE 4.76   This new Physical Material now affects the platforms.

   6. Save your package.

END TUTORIAL 4.19

Summary

Physics simulation is a technically demanding subject, both in terms of development and how such simulations calculate during gameplay. Although Unreal Engine 3 has been designed to optimize the use of physics calculations, there is still some responsibility on the part of the level designer to make sure things remain smooth during gameplay. Remember that heavy physics-using levels aren't typically best suited for Internet-based gameplay. Still, now that you have completed this chapter, you should have a much stronger understanding of how you can make use of physics objects in your levels, and how dynamic interactivity can influence and enhance the feel of your Unreal worlds!

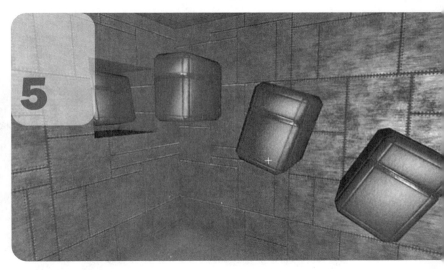

Chapter 5

Creating Special Effects with Particle Systems

At its most basic level, a particle can be defined simply as a point in space. In game engines such as Unreal, these points are animated within the scene to create behaviors such the motion of dust, flames, rising smoke, or a near infinite variety of other effects. The particles are then rendered in-game in a variety of ways, usually by placing a small piece of geometry at the location of the point, such as a plane. This plane faces the camera and displays a particular texture, allowing designers to create the visual aspect of effects such as smoke, dust, and fire (see **FIGURE 5.1**). However, these are only a very small example of the different roles that particles play in in-game special effects. We expand upon what can be accomplished with particles as you progress through this chapter.

In Unreal, particles are sent forth into the scene by emitters. An *emitter* is simply a point in space from which particles may spawn. How particles are spawned by and exit the emitter will control the overall behavior of the effect.

FIGURE 5.1   The flame effect you see here has been created with particles.

5

Emitters are held within particle systems. A *particle system* is a collection of one or more emitters, each of which with a particular arrangement of rules, allowing for easy creation of a wide variety of visual effects that require complex, repetitive, and/or predictable behavior.

Each emitter within a particle system can behave completely independently of any other emitters within the same system. This means that within a single particle system, you can have many different emitters, each creating different aspects of a single total effect. For example, a torch that is mounted to a wall requires much more than just flames alone. It needs flames, smoke, heat shimmer distortion, and perhaps even falling sparks. Within one particle system, you can create a separate emitter to handle each of these effects.

Particle systems are added to a level through the creation of Emitter actors, not to be confused with the emitters that exist within a particle system (see **FIGURE 5.2**). These actors provide the level designer with a placeable location from which to spawn the particle effect. This actor can be animated or controlled through Matinee and Kismet.

From the level designer's standpoint, the heart of the particle special effects creation system in Unreal Editor is the intuitive Cascade editing system, which is the primary tool used throughout this chapter. This special window allows you to create the various emitters found within each particle system, as well as provides the ability to add and control a variety of behavioral and visual aspects of your particles, all while seeing real-time feedback in a Preview window.

As a side note, it is important for you to remember that although you can add multiple emitters into a single particle system, the particles themselves are rendered in the order in which their respective emitters were added into the system. For example, if you had three different emitters, the second emitter's particles would render in front of the first emitter's, and the third emitter's particles would render in front of the second's.

Anatomy of a Particle System

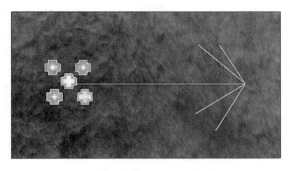

FIGURE 5.2   The Emitter actor allows you to place a particle system in your level.

Although a particle system itself is an actor with its own set of properties, in order for that system to be a part of a successful special effect, it needs to contain several other components. These components include a ParticleSpriteEmitter, the particles themselves, a TypeDataModule, and any combination of other modules, each of which can be used to define a particular aspect of the particle behavior. In this section, you are introduced to each of these components, as well as the relevant properties for each one (see **FIGURE 5.3**).

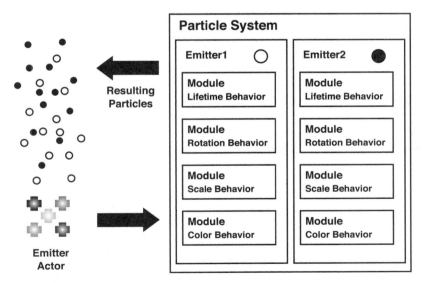

FIGURE 5.3   This diagram illustrates the relationship of the various components of a particle system.

First, let's start with the particle system itself. Think of a particle system as a container that holds all the other components for a complete particle effect. A particle system is created within the Generic Browser by right-clicking within a blank area of the browser and choosing New Particle

System. When you do this, the Cascade Particle System Editor appears, which we discuss later in this chapter. However, the particle system itself has a variety of properties that control how the particle system will work with the particles produced from it. These properties are covered next.

Particle System Properties

The particle system, as created in the Generic browser, has some fundamental properties of its own:

SystemUpdateMode—This property determines how the emitters of this particle system are updated. It has the following settings:

EPSUM_RealTime—With this setting, the emitters will be updated once at every frame of gameplay. This means that if the game is playing back at 60 frames per second, your particle system is updating 60 times per second as well.

EPSUM_FixedTime—With this setting, the emitters will be updated according to the rate specified in the UpdateTime_FPS property. This allows you to specify a rate of update for the particle system that differs from the game's frame rate.

UpdateTime_FPS—This is the number of times per second to update the emitters of this particle system, but only if they are using the EPSUM_FixedTime setting in their SystemUpdateMode property.

WarmupTime—This is the number of seconds to play the emitters before rendering the particle system. This means the engine will calculate the status of the emitters after they have been playing for this many seconds and use that as their beginning states.

For example, consider a flame coming from a torch. You wouldn't want the player to see the initial spawning of the first particles from the torch body; it would look like the torch spontaneously ignited. Instead, this setting allows you to "play" the animation of the system for a certain number of seconds, so that when rendering begins, the torch already appears to be burning.

SecondsBeforeInactive—This is the amount of seconds a particle system must go without being rendered before it will stop being updated, or go inactive. A value of 0 causes the particle system to always be active.

LOD Properties

LODMethod—This determines how levels of detail (LODs) for the emitters of this particle system will be determined. LODs allow you to change various properties of the particle system based on the player's distance from it. We cover LODs in greater depth later in this chapter. The LODMethod property contains the following settings:

Automatic—This means the engine will decide which LOD to use based on the values set in the LODDistances property.

DirectSet—This means the game will set the LOD to use directly. This property is controlled through scripting.

LODDistanceCheckTime—This property controls the number of seconds between LOD distance checks performed by the engine when LODMethod is set to Automatic. For example, a setting of 2 will cause the engine to check LOD distances every 2 seconds.

LODDistances—This is an array of distances to use for automatic LOD determination. The slot number in the array represents the LOD to use, and the value is the minimum distance at which to use that LOD.

Thumbnail

ThumbnailWarmup—This is the number of seconds to play the emitters before rendering the thumbnail of the particle system in the Generic Browser.

bUseRealtimeThumbnail—This determines whether the particle system thumbnail in the Generic Browser will be a real-time animated preview or an image determined by the user.

Bounds

bUseFixedRelativeBoundingBox—This determines whether the engine should calculate the bounding box based on the location of all the particles of all the emitters of the particle system or use the FixedRelativeBoundingBox.

FixedRelativeBoundingBox—This is the size of the bounding box used if bUseFixedRelativeBoundingBox is set to true.

> **NOTE**
>
> Setting this property to true allows you to save processing time, but could cause a particle system to not be rendered or updated when particles are or should still be in view.

TUTORIAL 5.1: Your First Particle System, Part I: Basic Setup

1. Launch Unreal Editor and open the Chapter_05_Particles package in the Generic Browser. Right-click the background and chose New ParticleSystem. Enter the following in the dialog that appears:

   - **Package**: Chapter_05_Particles
   - **Group**: Particles
   - **Name**: part_sparks

2. Click OK. A new dialog will appear. This is the Cascade particle system editor, and it's your primary tool for working with particle systems (see **FIGURE 5.4**).

5

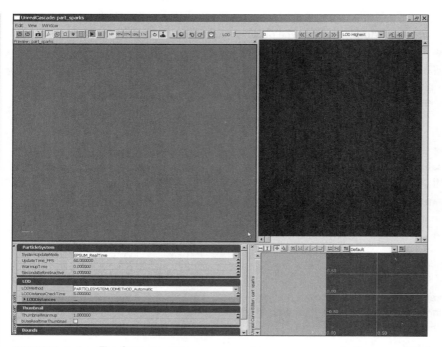

FIGURE 5.4   The Cascade editor appears as soon as you create the new particle system.

3. Select the mat_demo_flare material, located in the Chapter_05_Particles package in the Generic Browser. Once the material is selected, navigate back to Cascade. Right-click in the black empty panel in the upper-right corner of Cascade (this is known as the Emitter List) and choose NewParticleSpriteEmitter from the context menu (see **FIGURE 5.5**).

FIGURE 5.5   By having the material selected before you create a new sprite emitter, that material is automatically applied to the emitter.

4. This creates a new emitter in the particle system with the selected material applied to it. This emitter will also have three modules applied to it by default: Lifetime, Initial Size, and Initial Velocity.

5. You may notice that this emitter's particles are not visible initially. This is because the material applied to the emitter relies on a color that must be sent from the emitter into the material. Not being able to see the particles as we edit the emitter will make it very difficult and is not a good workflow.

6. Before we go any further, right-click below the Initial Velocity module and choose Color > Initial Color from the context menu. This will add an Initial Color module to the emitter, which will be responsible for passing color information to the material (see **FIGURE 5.6**).

The default values are just fine for now because we are just beginning our initial editing. Later on, we will be adjusting the color through the use of another color module.

7. Select the emitter module (this is the block at the top of the Emitter List) to display the emitter's properties in the Properties panel. Set the EmitterName property to Sparks (see **FIGURE 5.7**). For our purposes, this is simply for identification inside of Cascade.

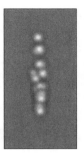

FIGURE 5.6   Once you add the Initial Color, the particles will appear.

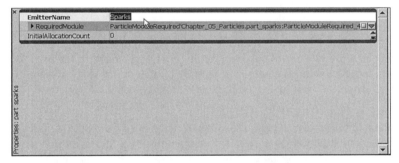

FIGURE 5.7   Changing the emitter's name makes the emitter easier to identify later.

8. Expand the RequiredModule to see the majority of the emitter module's properties. One of them is the ScreenAlignment, which determines how the particles are oriented with respect to the camera and how they handle their size. By default, this is set to PSA_Square, which means the emitter has square particles that are directly facing the camera at all times. Change this to PSA_Velocity so that the particles of this emitter are allowed to have nonuniform dimensions with the local Y-axis always facing the direction of their velocity (see **FIGURE 5.8**).

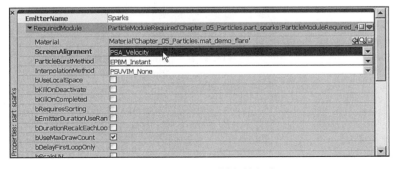

FIGURE 5.8   Set ScreenAlignment to PSA_Velocity.

9. Scroll down, if necessary, to the SpawnRate property. This controls the number of particles emitted every second. Set this to 25.0 (see **FIGURE 5.9**).

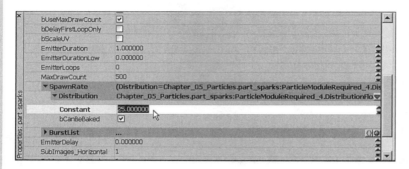

FIGURE 5.9   SpawnRate controls how quickly particles are emitted from the system.

10. Now that we have specified the number of particles for our emitter, we need to tell them how long to live. Each particle has a predetermined amount of time during which it will be updated and drawn. When the time is up, the particle dies and is deleted from the system.

11. Select the Lifetime module to display its properties. This module has one property—also called Lifetime—that by default allows us to specify a range between a Min value and a Max value. From this range, a random value will be picked for each particle. Set the following values:

- ▶ **Min**: 0.5

- ▶ **Max**: 1.0

This causes each particle to have a lifetime of some number between 0.5 and 1.0 seconds (see **FIGURE 5.10**).

12. Select the Initial Size module to view its properties. This module has a single property, called StartSize, that allows us to specify a range of values by default, but the Min and Max in this case are vectors (one number for each of the three axes: X, Y, and Z) so there are three values to set for each one. Set the following values:

FIGURE 5.10   You must select the Lifetime module to see the Lifetime property.

- ▶ **Max**:

  - ▶ **X**: 1.0

  - ▶ **Y**: 4.0

  - ▶ **Z**: 1.0

▶ **Min**:

  ▶ **X**: 0.5

  ▶ **Y**: 2.0

  ▶ **Z**: 0.5

13. The size in the Y-axis is set higher because that is the direction of velocity. This gives the particles a slight appearance of streaking. In **TUTORIAL 5.2**, this effect will be exaggerated through the use of another type of size module. You'll also notice that the particles are much smaller. Zoom in the camera with the right mouse button to see them up close (see **FIGURE 5.11**).

14. Select the Initial Velocity module to view its properties. Just like the StartSize property in the Initial Size module, the StartVelocity property provides us with Min and Max vectors by default. Set the following values:

  ▶ **Max**:

    ▶ **X**: 50.0

    ▶ **Y**: 50.0

    ▶ **Z**: 100.0

  ▶ **Min**:

    ▶ **X**: –50.0

    ▶ **Y**: –50.0

    ▶ **Z**: 50.0

FIGURE 5.11   The particles are now stretched a bit, although you have to zoom in to see them.

15. These values cause the particles to travel in random directions in the XY plane while traveling upward (see **FIGURE 5.12**).

16. Save the Chapter_05_Particles package so you don't lose your work.

5

FIGURE 5.12   Your sparks are now shooting upward, kind of like a sprinkler.

END TUTORIAL 5.1

Particle Sprite Emitters

A particle sprite emitter is the object responsible for spawning (or *emitting*) particles into the level. All particles emitted from a single emitter use the same material and are subject to the same series of behavioral rules, as specified by the modules contained within that emitter. We will cover the various modules later in this chapter.

By default, all emitters are considered to be "sprite" emitters. The word *sprite* refers to the type of particle the emitter is producing. A sprite is a four-sided polygonal plane that always faces the camera and has a material. For example, a sprite can have an image of a single puff of smoke, but when you emit many particles with similar smoke puff pictures on them, they start to form the illusion of a volume of smoke (see **FIGURE 5.13**).

A separate sprite emitter is required for each aspect of a special effect. For example, if you're creating a fire effect, including flames, smoke, and sparks, then each of those elements would require its own emitter (see **FIGURE 5.14**). One emitter would produce sprites that look like flames, each of those particles using the same set of behavioral rules; another emitter would produce the smoke, using a separate set of rules; and a third emitter would produce the sparks. If any other elements need to be added to the effect, such as larger puffs of flame that have different behavior than the original flame, you would need to add a new emitter for this new element.

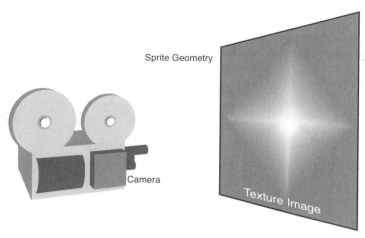

FIGURE 5.13   This diagram illustrates the concept of a sprite.

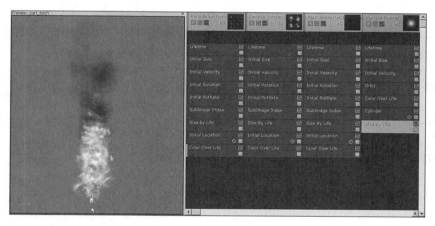

FIGURE 5.14   The flame, smoke, and sparks in this effect are all being created by separate emitters within the particle system.

Particle emitters are created and added to the particle system from within Cascade, Unreal's particle system editor. Each of these emitters contains a series of modules used to define specific aspects of the behavior of the particles produced by that emitter. We discuss the concept of modules later in this section.

Sprite Emitter Properties

Sprite emitters come with a set of properties independent of any additional modules. These control rudimentary aspects of the emitter, such as the name and the number of particles from the emitter that are allowed to exist at any given time:

EmitterName—This is simply a name for identifying this particle emitter.

InitialAllocationCount—This is the number of particles that should have memory allocated at the time of initialization. If this is 0, the peak amount of particles will be calculated and used as the value. It is possible that this calculation will be higher than the amount actually needed. In such a case, setting this property allows for better memory management.

RequiredModule

The RequiredModule is a basic set of properties inherent to all emitters. It contains the following properties:

Material—This is the material applied to the sprite particles produced by this emitter.

ScreenAlignment—This determines how the particles of this emitter are aligned with respect to the camera as well as how they handle size. This property has the following settings:

PSA_Square—This setting causes sprite particles to be facing the camera at all times and only allows uniform sizes of sprite particles. The X value of size vectors will control the size of both dimensions of a sprite particle.

PSA_Rectangle—This setting causes sprite particles to be facing the camera, but allows for nonuniform scaling of sprite particles. The X and Y values of size vectors control the size of sprite particles.

PSA_Velocity—This setting causes sprite particles to have their Y-axis aligned to the direction of their velocity and allows each particle to be scaled nonuniformly. The X and Y values of size vectors will control the size of the sprite particles.

PSA_TypeSpecific—This setting allows the TypeData module, specifically the Mesh TypeData module, to control the alignment of the particles for this emitter.

ParticleBurstMethod—At the time of this writing, this property is nonfunctional.

InterpolationMethod—This is the method of switching between sub-images of the emitter's material. It contains the following settings:

PSUVIM_None—This disables all SubUV functionality of the emitter.

PSUVIM_Linear—This cycles through the sub-images of the material in order, starting from the upper-left corner and going horizontally across each row, starting at the top and progressively moving downward.

PSUVIM_Linear_Blend—This setting cycles through the sub-images of the material in the same order as PSUVIM_Linear, but differs in that it adds blending between each sub-image.

PSUVIM_Random—This cycles through the sub-images of the material randomly.

PSUVIM_Random_Blend—This cycles through the sub-images of the material randomly while blending between each sub-image.

bUseLocalSpace—When this property is true, all calculations for the emitter and particles will be done in local space. When this property is false, calculations are done using the world transform of the parent of the emitter.

The result of this property is most evident when rotating an emitter actor. Say you have a particle system consisting of one emitter that is emitting particles with a positive Z velocity, or upward. Using either setting, the particles will be emitted traveling in the local Z-axis of the emitter actor no matter what its rotation is. The difference is visible as you actually rotate the emitter actor.

When you use local space, all the existing particles are rotated with the emitter actor so they continue traveling in the emitter's local positive Z-axis. When you use the world transform of the parent, the existing particles continue traveling in the direction they were already going. Only the newly emitted particles are affected by the rotation (see **FIGURE 5.15**).

FIGURE 5.15   Both of these emitters have been rotated. The one on the left is using world space, the other is using local space.

bKillOnDeactivate—When this property is true, all existing particles will be destroyed when the particle emitter becomes inactive. When this property is false, all existing particles will be allowed to continue through their lifetimes regardless of whether the particle system becomes inactive or not.

bKillOnComplete—When this property is true, the particle system will destroy this particle emitter after it has completed. *Completed* means it has run for its duration (determined by EmitterDuration, EmitterDurationLow, and bEmitterDurationUseRange) the number of times specified in EmitterLoops. If EmitterLoops is 0, the particle emitter never completes and will never be destroyed.

bRequiresSorting—When this property is true, the particles of this emitter will be sorted against each other based on depth. If this property is false, no depth sorting will occur within this emitter.

bEmitterDurationUseRange—When this property is true, the emitter's duration is calculated by selecting a random value between the values of the EmitterDurationLow and EmitterDuration properties. If this property is false, the emitter's duration is precisely the value of the EmitterDuration property.

bDurationRecalcEachLoop—When this property is true and bEmitterDurationUse Random is also true, the random duration will be calculated before each loop. If this property is false and bEmitterDurationUseRandom is true, the random duration for the emitter will only be calculated the first loop and the same duration will be used from then on.

bUseMaxDrawCount—When this property is true, the emitter will clamp the amount of particles it can draw at one time. The rest of the particles will still exist and be updated, but only the first X number of particles will be drawn to the screen, where X is the value of the MaxDrawCount property.

When this property is false, all particles of the emitter will be drawn to the screen.

bDelayFirstLoopOnly—When this property is true, the delay specified in the EmitterDelay property will only be applied to the emitter the first time through. All subsequent loops will have no delay. When this property is false, all loops of the emitter will be delayed.

bScaleUV—When this property is true and if the emitter is a mesh emitter, the UVs of the mesh will be scaled to fit the sub-image's size. When this property is false, the UVs will be unaffected.

EmitterDuration—This sets the number of seconds to run the emitter before looping.

EmitterDurationLow—This is the lower bound of the range to use for calculating a random duration for the emitter. Only used if the bEmitterDurationUseRange property is set to true.

EmitterLoops—This is the number of times the emitter will play for its duration before stopping and being considered completed. If this value is 0, the emitter will never be considered "completed" and will loop continuously.

MaxDrawCount—This is the number of particles to draw to the screen at one time when bUseMaxDrawCount is true.

SpawnRate—This is the number of particles that this emitter will emit per second (see **FIGURE 5.16**). This property uses a distribution. Distributions are explained in Appendix A, "Distributions."

BurstList—This property is an array used to determine when and how many particles to spawn in bursts. Each element in the array consists of the following:

   Time—This is the relative time over the life of the emitter to emit the burst. For example, a value of 3 will result in a 3-second burst.

   Count—If CountLow is 0, this is the amount of particles to burst. If CountLow is not 0, this is the upper bound for the range to use in determining a random amount of particles to burst.

   CountLow—This is the lower bound for the range to use in determining a random amount of particles to burst. If it's set to 0, only the Count property is used and no range is calculated.

FIGURE 5.16   Increasing the spawn rate creates more particles.

EmitterDelay—This is the number of seconds to wait before the emitter actually starts spawning particles into the scene.

SubImagesHorizontal—This is the amount of sub-images of the material in the horizontal direction.

SubImagesVertical—This is the amount of sub-images in the vertical direction.

RandomChanges—This is the amount of changes from one sub-image to the next when using PSUVIM_Random or PSUVIM_Random_Blend.

Particles

Particles are the actual produced object from a particle system. When you're working in Unreal Editor, each particle is some sort of geometry that is created by the emitter and behaves according to the rules specified in an emitter's properties and modules. Typically, this geometry is in the form of a sprite, which, as mentioned previously, is simply a four-sided plane that always faces the camera and contains a material. Each of these particles is created with a lifetime, which is the number of seconds it will continue to be updated and drawn. Once a particle is spawned, the number of its lifetime begins to count down. When that countdown reaches zero, the particle is destroyed.

Particles themselves do not have properties. Their settings are instead specified by the addition and control of emitter modules, discussed next.

TypeData Modules

In essence, TypeData modules allow you to change the type of particle you will be creating with your emitter. That is to say, they change the behavior of the particle on a fundamental level. By default, an emitter contains a Sprite TypeData module, which allows the emitter to create sprites as described earlier. However, you also have the option of creating Beam, Mesh, and Trail TypeData modules to change your current particles to that particular type. These TypeData modules are added to the particle system using Cascade. This section describes the different kinds of TypeData modules available. Note that Beam, Mesh, and Trail emitters are discussed in greater depth in their own respective sections of this chapter.

Beam

The Beam TypeData module causes the emitter to create beams of connected particles, spanning between two designated points (see **FIGURE 5.17**). The segments of a beam are created by a series of planes all rotated about a single axis. These beams can have noise applied to them, allowing them to have an irregular shape such as that of a lighting bolt.

For more information on beams, see the "Beam Emitters" section, later in this chapter.

FIGURE 5.17   The beams in this image are the result of a beam emitter.

Mesh

The Mesh TypeData module causes an emitter to spawn static meshes rather than sprites (see **FIGURE 5.18**). Aside from this singular fact, such an emitter behaves very similarly to a sprite emitter.

For more information on mesh emitters, see the "Mesh Emitters" section, later in this chapter.

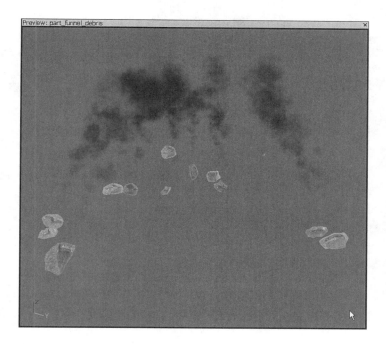

FIGURE 5.18   Mesh emitters allow you to emit static meshes rather than sprites.

Trail

The Trail TypeData modules cause the emitter to create trails of connected particles that are left behind as the emitter moves (see **FIGURE 5.19**). An example would be a streak left behind while an emitter is animated across a scene.

For more information on trail emitters, see the "Trail Emitters" section, later in this chapter.

Fluid

The Fluid and Mesh Fluid TypeData modules (listed as ParticleModuleTypeDataMeshNxFluid and ParticleModuleTypeDataNxFluid) cause the emitter to use the PhysX physics engine's fluid solver for calculating the position, velocity, and lifetime of the emitter's particles.

For more information on fluid emitters, see the "Fluid Emitters" section, later in this chapter.

5

FIGURE 5.19   The streaking trail left behind by this object is the result of a trail emitter.

Modules

Modules are the heart of every emitter because they are used to create a specific set of rules for the emitter—or its particles—to follow. Each module serves a different purpose. One type of module controls the initial velocity of a particle at the time of its creation, whereas another controls the size of the particle throughout its lifetime.

Modules are placed within an emitter inside the Cascade editor, and are seen as a vertical list of orange boxes. These boxes are processed from top to bottom, meaning that if you place two modules of the same type within an emitter, the lower of the pair will override the values of the first (see **FIGURE 5.20**).

In order to help you gauge the changes in behavior created by the addition of each module, you can enable or disable the effects of each one in the list. For example, if you've just added a module to make the particles get larger over time, but are having a hard time seeing the effect due to the particles' current motion, you can deactivate the module causing that motion.

More information on modules can be found later in this chapter in the "Types of Particle Modules" section.

Complete **TUTORIAL 5.1** before attempting **TUTORIAL 5.2**. If you have not completed it, you may use the part_sparks_01 ParticleSystem instead.

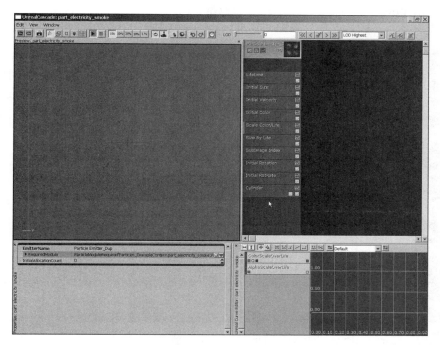

FIGURE 5.20   Modules begin to stack up as you add them to your emitters.

TUTORIAL 5.2: Your First Particle System, Part I: Extended Setup

1. If you have not already, open the part_sparks particle system in Cascade by double-clicking it in the Generic Browser (see **FIGURE 5.21**).

2. With the basic setup completed, the behavior and appearance of the emitter can be refined and extended through the use of additional modules.

3. The first adjustment we are going to make is to the color of the particles. The Initial Color module added in **TUTORIAL 5.1** causes the particles to be plain white with a constant alpha of 1.0, or completely opaque. Because these are sparks, they should have some sort of color and fade away as they grow older.

4. Right-click below the Initial Color module and choose Color > Scale Color/Life from the context menu. This module allows us to scale the color set in the Initial Color module over the lifetime of the particle. Because that color happens to be white (1.0, 1.0, 1.0, 1.0), the color of the particles will be whatever we set in this module (see **FIGURE 5.22**).

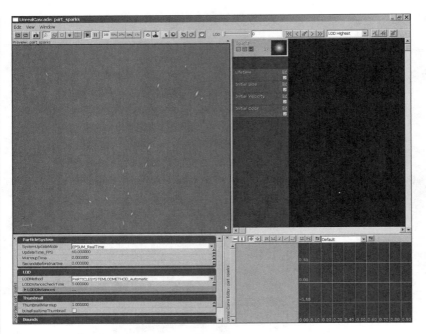

FIGURE 5.21   Open your Sparks particle system in Cascade.

5. Select the new Scale Color/Life module to view its properties. The ColorOverLife property defaults to a curve with two points present. The purpose of curves is to change the value of a property over time. For more information on how these curves work, please see Appendix A, "Distributions."

6. We are not going to need the second point because the color will be constant over the life of the particle. Click the Delete Item button of the 1 slot to delete that point from the curve. Now, set the following values (see **FIGURE 5.23**):

▶ **0**:

    ▶ **InVal**: 0.0

    ▶ **OutVal**:

        ▶ **X**: 20.0

        ▶ **Y**: 10.0

        ▶ **Z**: 5.0

FIGURE 5.22   Add a new Scale Color/Life module.

This gives the particles a nice glowing orange color.

7. With the color set, it is time to set the Alpha so the particles will fade out as they die, rather than just pop out of existence instantaneously. The AlphaOverLife property defaults to a single constant value. We need a curve so the alpha can change over time. Click the right side of the Distribution under AlphaOverLife. Then, click the Create a New Object button . From the flyout list that appears, choose DistributionFloatConstantCurve (see **FIGURE 5.24**).

8. Now we have a curve, but as you can see if you expand the ConstantCurve and then try to expand the Points array, it has no points in it. Click the right side of the Points array and then click the Add Item button ⚙ twice to add two points to the curve. Set the following values:

   - **0**:
     - **InVal**: 0.0
     - **OutVal**: 1.0
   - **1**:
     - **InVal**: 1.0
     - **OutVal**: 0.0

This should cause the Alpha of the particles to fade from full opacity when the particle is spawned to completely transparent when the particle dies.

Because this emitter is supposed to be creating sparks, it will look a little odd if the sparks simply travel in a straight line up into space, as they are currently. To fix this, we can add some acceleration to simulate the effects of gravity on the particles.

FIGURE 5.23 Your particles now turn orange across their lifetime.

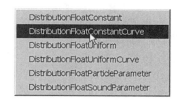

FIGURE 5.24 Switching to a FloatConstantCurve Distribution allows your alpha to be animated over time.

9. Right-click the Scale Color/Life module and choose Acceleration > Acceleration. Again we see Min and Max vectors, but in this case, we really only need one vector because gravity is constant on all objects (see **FIGURE 5.25**).

10. Click the right side of the Distribution under Acceleration and then click the Create a New Object button ![icon]. From the flyout list that appears, choose DistributionVectorConstant. Now we have a single vector to work with. Set the following values:

  ▸ **Constant**:

    ▸ **X**: 0.0

    ▸ **Y**: 0.0

    ▸ **Z**: –325.0

The particles should begin moving up and then arc downward because of the acceleration.

11. In order to exaggerate the streaking of the particles in the direction of their movement, we will use a Size By Velocity module. Right-click below the Acceleration module and choose Size > Size By Velocity. This allows for the scaling of the particles in any of the three axes based on their velocities.

12. VelocityMultiplier is multiplied by the velocity of the particle before it is multiplied by the particle's size. This is necessary because the velocity can be quite large. Set the following values (see **FIGURE 5.26**):

  ▸ **Constant**:

    ▸ **X**: 0.025

    ▸ **Y**: 0.025

    ▸ **Z**: 0.025

FIGURE 5.25   A new Acceleration module has been added.

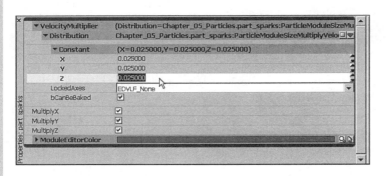

FIGURE 5.26   Set your constant vector for VelocityMultiplier, like so.

13. The three check boxes below VelocityMultiplier determine whether the size in the specified axis will be affected by the module. We only want to scale the size in the Y-axis, so set the following:

- ▶ **MultiplyX**: False

- ▶ **MultiplyY**: True

- ▶ **MultiplyZ**: False

14. This completes the spark effect. Now, let's place it in a level and see how it looks. Open the DM-CH_05_Electricity_Begin map (see **FIGURE 5.27**).

FIGURE 5.27   The DM-CH_05_Electricity_Begin map has some lights to which we can add the effect.

15. Select the part_sparks particle system in the Generic Browser. Then, right-click one of the lights on the wall and choose Add Actor > Add Emitter: part_sparks from the context menu (see **FIGURE 5.28**).

16. Using the translation widget, place the emitter near one of the corners of the light so it appears the light is producing sparks. If you like, you can also use the rotation widget to rotate the emitter (see **FIGURE 5.29**).

17. Save the Chapter_05_Particles package so you don't lose your work. You may also save the map if you wish.

5

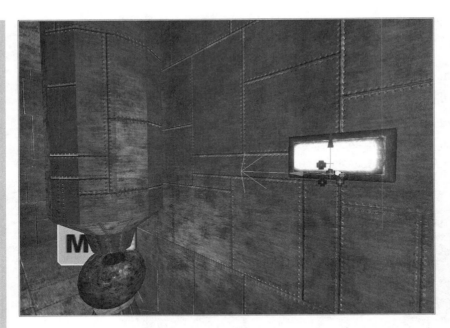

FIGURE 5.28   An Emitter actor is placed in your level.

FIGURE 5.29   Position the emitter so that it looks like the light is sparking.

END TUTORIAL 5.2

Cascade Particle System Editor

The Cascade editor is the central part of particle system setup for level designers. The editor provides complete control over every aspect of particle modification and fine-tuning, including emitter creation, the addition of modules, the tweaking of properties, and visual evaluation.

Cascade Interface

At the top of the Cascade window, you will see the menu bar, which is similar to many of the menu bars found throughout Unreal Editor. The menu bar of the Cascade interface includes the ability to toggle certain rendering options, control the visibility of the

> **NOTE**
>
> The different panels of the Cascade editor can be docked in different locations, including outside the editor itself, by dragging on each panel's individual title bar.

editor's main panels, generate levels of detail (LODs), and save the package in which the particle system currently resides (see **FIGURE 5.30**).

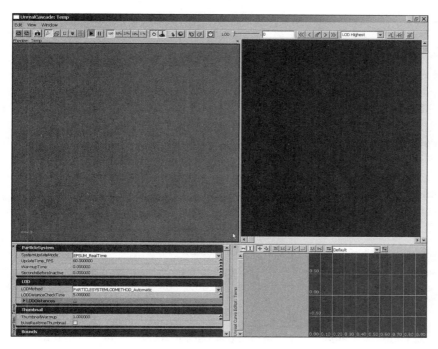

FIGURE 5.30   The Cascade editor has a simple interface that allows for a deep level of control.

Toolbar

The Cascade toolbar contains several buttons that provide access to common functions (see **FIGURE 5.31**). Each of these is described in the following list:

FIGURE 5.31   The Cascade editor toolbar

Restart Sim —This button will restart the playback of the particle system in the preview panel.

Restart in Level —This will restart the playback of the particle system in the editor's level viewports.

> **NOTE**
>
> Much of the functionality of the toolbar is only available when you have created at least one emitter in your particle system.

Save Thumbnail Image —Clicking this button will take a snapshot of the particle system to be used as the thumbnail in the Generic Browser.

Toggle Orbit Mode —This activates and deactivates orbiting of the preview window camera.

Toggle Wireframe —This displays the Preview window in a wireframe mode.

Toggle Bounds —This button displays a sphere that encloses the extents of all particles in the system. This sphere automatically expands to account for changes, such as an increase in lifetime. To reset the sphere back to its defaults—say, if you lowered the particle lifetime—you can simply click the Restart Sim button.

Toggle PostProcess —This allows you to toggle certain post-processing effects within the Preview window, including Bloom, DOF, Motion Blur, and the PPVolume Material.

Toggle Grid —This button toggles the visibility of an XY grid, which you can use as a collision-free ground reference.

Play —This starts the playback of the particle system.

Pause —This pauses the playback of the particle system.

Speed Buttons —These buttons allow you to change the playback speed of the Preview window. They range from Full Speed (100%) down through 50%, 25%, 10%, and 1%.

Toggle Loop System —This button toggles playback looping for the particle system. Without this button activated, the system will play back to its "completed" state only once.

Toggle Realtime —This sets the Preview window to update during every frame.

Background Color —By clicking this button, you can set the background color for the Preview window.

Toggle Wireframe Sphere —This button shows a wireframe sphere in the Preview window of the specified radius.

Undo/Redo —These buttons work like standard undo/redo buttons, allowing you to take back a previous action or to replace an undone action.

Performance Check —At the time of this writing, this button is nonfunctional.

LOD Slider —This slider allows you to choose any number between 0 and 100 to create a level of detail (LOD). Remember that LODs are simply various distances beyond which the particle effect is simplified to save processing power. Basically, the effect should get simpler the farther the player moves away from it.

Think of the value as the percentage of the distance set for the lowest level of detail. Zero signifies the highest LOD setting (or 0% of the distance to the lowest LOD), whereas 100 is the lowest setting, corresponding to 100% of the distance to the lowest LOD. For example, if your lowest LOD had a distance of 4000 units, then setting the slider to 50 would correspond to half of that distance, or 2000 units. By setting the slider to this value, you have the ability to create a new LOD at that 50% mark.

To add a new level of detail, simply move the slider to any number a certain percentage along the slider and click the Add LOD button. For instance, if you wanted four total levels of detail, you could move the

> **NOTE**
>
> The range values for each LOD are designated within the particle system's properties and can be edited there.

slider one-third of the way along its length and click Add LOD, then move it to two-thirds and click Add LOD again. Combined with the Lowest and Highest LODs, which are there by default, you now have four total LODs.

LOD Field —This number will update between 0 and 100 as you move the slider, but you can also enter a value into it manually.

Jump to LOD buttons —These buttons are very similar to the "jump to keyframe" buttons found in most 3D animation packages.

The buttons on the far left and far right jump to the highest and lowest LODs, respectively. The second buttons in from the ends jump to the next highest and next lowest LODs along the percentage, respectively.

The center button creates a new LOD based on the percentage setting of the slider/text field.

LOD dropdown —This is a dropdown list that contains all the LODs you've created so far. Using this dropdown, you can easily select one of the LODs without having to use the slider or try to remember its specific value.

Regenerate Lowest LOD —This button will reset the lowest level of detail so that its spawn rate is one-tenth the spawn rate of the highest LOD. The button also clears out any intermediate levels of detail between the lowest and the highest.

Regenerate Lowest LOD Duplicating Highest LOD —This button regenerates the lowest LOD using the same values present in the highest LOD.

Delete LOD —This button deletes the LOD currently selected.

Preview Panel

The Preview panel is a 3D Perspective viewport that provides real-time visual feedback of each of the emitters belonging to the particle system. This allows you to instantly see the results of any changes made to the emitter's modules or properties, without needing an actual copy of the particle system placed in the level (see **FIGURE 5.32**).

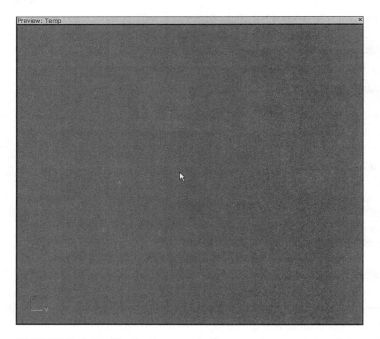

FIGURE 5.32   The Preview panel allows you to see your particle system while you work.

The Preview panel can be navigated as follows:

- ▶ Holding down the left mouse button while dragging causes the viewport to rotate, or orbit, around the origin.

- ▶ Holding down the right mouse button while dragging causes the viewport to zoom in or out.

- ▶ Holding down the middle mouse button while dragging pans the viewport left, right, up, or down.

Emitter List Panel

This panel, as its name suggests, shows a list of all of the emitters found within the particle system. Each emitter is displayed as a vertical column consisting of the various modules that make up that emitter. These columns are listed horizontally across the panel, allowing you access to any module of any emitter very quickly (see **FIGURE 5.33**).

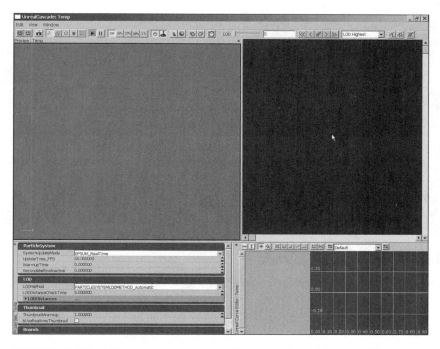

FIGURE 5.33 All your emitters and modules are placed within the Emitter List.

If no emitters have been created, this area will appear blank. New emitters and modules can be added to the area by right-clicking.

- ▶ Right-clicking on a blank area will provide the option of creating a new ParticleSpriteEmitter.

- ▶ Right-clicking on the emitter module or in a blank area below an emitter will provide options to add modules, TypeData modules, or perform operations on the emitter such as duplication or deletion.

- ▶ Right-clicking on a module or TypeData module provides options to delete the module or reset it to its default state (Note that the Reset option is nonfunctional at the time of this writing).

Modules within the Emitter List can be reordered or even transferred to different emitters by left-dragging them in the panel. By holding Ctrl as you left-drag, you can copy the module to another emitter rather than moving it (see **FIGURE 5.34**).

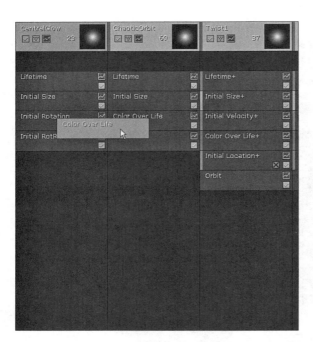

FIGURE 5.34   Dragging an existing module allows you to reorder it or transfer it to another emitter.

Modules can also be instanced between two emitters, meaning that the module is being "shared." Changing the properties of either instance automatically changes the properties of the other. Instancing is done by holding Shift and left-dragging the module. Shared modules are designated by a "+" next to their names.

Properties Panel

The Properties panel is where you will do most of the tweaking and adjustment for your particle system. The properties for the currently selected emitter, module, or particle system will be displayed within this panel. Visually and functionally speaking, it is no different from any other properties window found in Unreal Editor (see **FIGURE 5.35**).

Curve Editor Panel

The Curve Editor allows you to adjust any distribution curves that are being used by the properties of your emitters or modules (see **FIGURE 5.36**). Each module in the Emitter List contains a small button ▦ that is used to send that module's relevant properties to the curve editor for adjustment. The Curve Editor's functions are essentially no different from any other curve editor found within Unreal. For more information on using a curve editor within Unreal Editor, see Appendix B, "The Curve Editor."

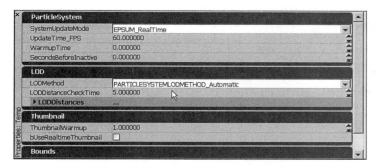

FIGURE 5.35   The Properties panel is where most of the work for the emitter takes place.

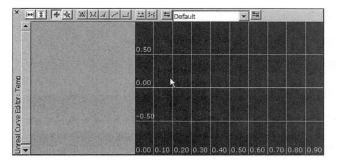

FIGURE 5.36   The Curve Editor allows you to edit distribution curves.

Throughout **TUTORIAL 5.3** and the remainder of the chapter, we create a series of very specific effects for a sample level. It begins with a fairly complex plasma generator that sits in the center of the room. This plasma generator fires massive electrical beams at four other pillars around the room. Each of these pillars has its own electrical beam system surrounding it. When the main electrical beams are striking each pillar, splash bolts from the lighting appear, and the sphere at the center of each column heats up. If the sphere overheats, it starts to smoke and eventually explodes, leaving smoking shrapnel behind.

We begin this series of effects by creating the plasma generator at the center of the room. This is going to be an intricate effect, composed of many different emitters.

TUTORIAL 5.3: Plasma Generator, Part I: Initial Setup

1. Launch Unreal Editor. If necessary, open the Chapter_05_Particles package in the Generic Browser. Right-click the background and choose New ParticleSystem. Enter the following settings in the dialog that appears (see **FIGURE 5.37**):

    ▸ **Package**: Chapter_05_Particles

    ▸ **Group**: Particles

    ▸ **Name**: part_plasma_generator

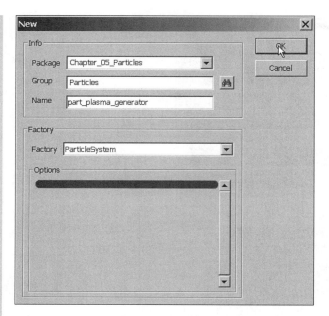

FIGURE 5.37   Enter the information as shown.

2. Press OK. The Cascade particle editor should open.

3. This particle system is going to be limited to a specific area, so there is no need for the bounds to be recalculated during play. This would simply be a waste of resources. To keep the bounds from being calculated, check the bUseFixedRelativeBounds box in the Bounds section. Then set the following values to define the extents of the bounding box for the particle system (see **FIGURE 5.38**):

- ▶ **FixedRelativeBoundingBox**:
    - ▶ **Min**:
        - ▶ **X**: −35.0
        - ▶ **Y**: −35.0
        - ▶ **Z**: −35.0
    - ▶ **Max**
        - ▶ **X**: 35.0
        - ▶ **Y**: 35.0
        - ▶ **Z**: 35.0

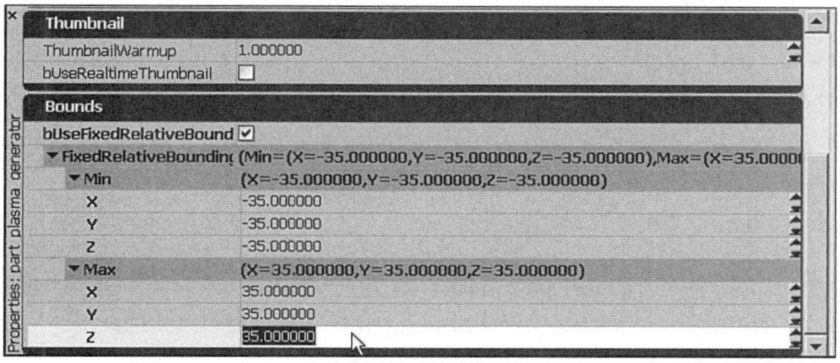

FIGURE 5.38   Set the size of your bounding box as shown.

4. That completes the initial creation and setup of the plasma generator particle system. Save the Chapter_05_Particles package.

END TUTORIAL 5.3

Particle-Specific Material Expressions

The Material Editor contains two material expressions that are designed specifically for use with the particle systems: Vertex Color and SubUV. Although both of these expressions are covered in Chapter 2, "Advanced Material Construction," this section covers their use in terms of particle systems on a deeper level.

Vertex Color

Controlling the color of your particles is a two-stage process. The first stage involves adding one of the various color modules—such as Initial Color or Color Over Life—to the emitter. This alone, however, is not enough to actually apply color to your materials. Particles, like virtually every renderable actor in Unreal, require a material for their final look. The color produced by your color module must be transferred to the material that is placed on the particles themselves.

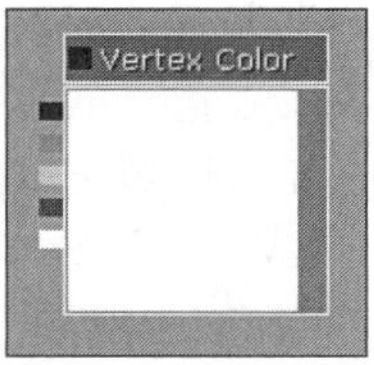

This is where the second stage comes in, which is the application of the Vertex Color material expression (see **FIGURE 5.39**). This expression receives the color from the color modules that are bound to the particle system to which the material is applied. The expression uses the color from the module and applies it to your material however you choose.

FIGURE 5.39   The Vertex Color material expression

An interesting aspect of the Vertex Color material expression is that you do not have to use it strictly for color. It has four channels (RGBA), each of which can be used separately to transfer any kind of data you like into your material. For instance, let's say you take a Color Over Life module and use it to animate the color of the particle from full red to full blue. You now have two channels that are animated over the life of the particle, one moving up and the other down, which you can connect to things such as the speed of a Panner or perhaps drive the Alpha of a Linear Interpolate. The data can be used in a great number of ways, so don't limit yourself to thinking of it strictly as a color system.

In **FIGURE 5.40**, you can see a more conventional use of the Vertex Color material expression, in which it is being used to drive a multiplier of color and opacity for an existing texture.

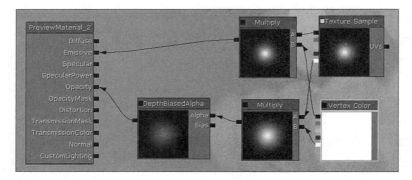

FIGURE 5.40   This image shows a typical material setup for a Vertex Color–based material.

ParticleSubUV

Emitters provide for the use of textures that are composed of multiple sub-images in order to create variation or animation. Just as when controlling the color of particles, using sub-images requires that the material be set up in a special manner to handle those sub-images. This setup requires the ParticleSubUV material expression.

FIGURE 5.41 shows an example of a typical ParticleSubUV-style texture. Notice that the different images are divided into an equally spaced grid. The purpose of the ParticleSubUV material expression is to take these images and place them one at a time onto the actual particle.

FIGURE 5.42 shows the network for a sample material setup. In this case, the RGB value of the ParticleSubUV is being multiplied by a VertexColor, which is also receiving data from the particle system. The Alpha of the ParticleSubUV is multiplied by the Alpha of the Vertex Color and is being used to drive the material's Opacity value.

> **NOTE**
>
> The material shown in these figures would use the MLM_Unlit lighting model and one of the blend modes that provides for transparency, such as Translucent, Additive, or Modulate.

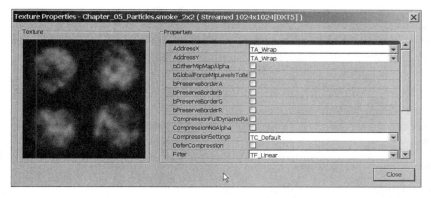

FIGURE 5.41   Here is an example of a texture that would be used by a ParticleSubUV material expression.

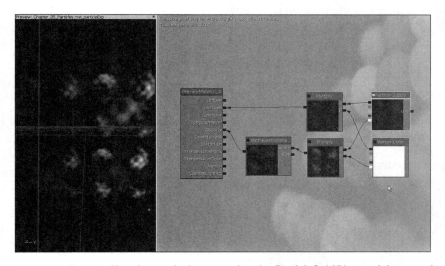

FIGURE 5.42   Here is a typical setup using the ParticleSubUV material expression.

MeshSubUV

The MeshSubUV expression is essentially the same as the ParticleSubUV expression in that it allows sub-images of a larger image to be used on particles. However, this expression is specifically meant to be used with materials applied to static meshes used with mesh emitters. Its use and setup within a material is identical to that of the ParticleSubUV expression.

TUTORIAL 5.4 continues from **TUTORIAL 5.3**, so be sure to complete it before proceeding.

TUTORIAL 5.4: Plasma Generator, Part II: Flare Material Creation

1. Before we go any further with the particle system, we are going to need a material to apply to our particles. In order to allow this material to be used in multiple emitters while having different colors, we are going to use the VertexColor expression to allow the emitters themselves to control the color.

2. Navigate to the Chapter_05_Particles package in the Generic Browser, right-click the background, and choose New Material. Enter the following in the dialog that appears (see **FIGURE 5.43**):

   ▶ **Package**: Chapter_05_Particles

   ▶ **Group**: Materials

   ▶ **Name**: mat_flare

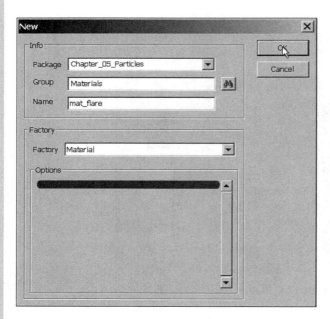

FIGURE 5.43   Create a new material named mat_flare.

3. Click OK. The Material Editor should open with the new material in it.

4. In the material node's properties, change the LightingModel to MLM_Unlit. Then, change the BlendMode to BLEND_Translucent.

5. Back in the Generic Browser, select the flare texture, which can be found in the Chapter_05_Particles package. Then, in the Material Editor, add a TextureSample expression (see **FIGURE 5.44**). It should have the flare texture assigned to its Texture property. If not, assign it by clicking the Use Current Selection in Browser button 🔁.

6. Add a VertexColor expression directly under the TextureSample expression (see **FIG-URE 5.45**).

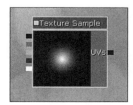

FIGURE 5.44   Your flare texture should appear in your Texture Sample.

FIGURE 5.45   Add a new VertexColor material expression.

7. Add a Multiply expression to the left of the TextureSample. Connect the RGB output of the TextureSample expression to the A input of the Multiply expression. Then connect the RGB output of the VertexColor to the B input of the Multiply expression (see **FIGURE 5.46**).

8. Add another Multiply expression to the left of the VertexColor expression. Connect the Alpha output of the TextureSample to the A input of the new Multiply expression. Connect the Alpha output of the VertexColor expression to the B input of the new Multiply expression (see **FIGURE 5.47**).

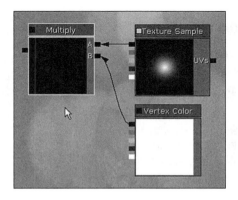

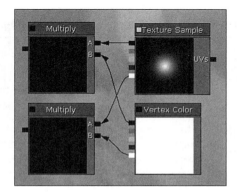

FIGURE 5.46   The VertexColor now modifies the TextureSample.

FIGURE 5.47   The Alpha from the VertexColor can now be used to fade the material.

9. Connect the top Multiply expression's output to the Emissive channel of the material node. Then, connect the output of the bottom Multiply expression to the Opacity channel of the material node (see **FIGURE 5.48**).

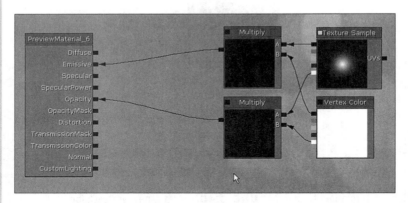

FIGURE 5.48   Connect the Multiply expressions into the material like this.

10. Finally, click the Apply Changes button ▦ and close the Material Editor.

11. Save the Chapter_05_Particles package.

END TUTORIAL 5.4

TUTORIAL 5.5 continues from **TUTORIAL 5.4**, so be sure to complete it before proceeding. You need to have the Chapter_05_Particles package open in the Generic Browser. If you have not completed **TUTORIAL 5.4**, you may use the mat_flare_01 material in place of the mat_flare material.

TUTORIAL 5.5: Plasma Generator, Part III: Central Glow

1. The first emitter we are going to set up is the central glow because it should be drawn behind the others. This is basically made up of stationary, rotating particles.

2. If it is not already open, double-click the part_plasma_generator particle system in the Generic Browser to open it in Cascade.

3. In the Generic Browser, select the mat_flare material located within the Chapter_05_Particles package. Right-click in the Emitter List and choose New ParticleSpriteEmitter to add an emitter to the system (see **FIGURE 5.49**).

4. Select the emitter module to view its properties in the Properties panel. Set the EmitterName to CentralGlow. Then, expand the RequiredModule and scroll down to SpawnRate if it is not visible. Set the Constant property of the SpawnRate distribution to 10.0 (see **FIGURE 5.50**).

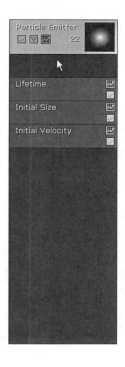

FIGURE 5.49   Add a new sprite emitter to the Emitter List.

FIGURE 5.50   Changing the name helps with identification later.

5. Select the Lifetime module to view its proper-ties. A variance in the lifetimes of these parti-cles would simply not be noticeable in the final effect, so the uniform distribution is not necessary. Click to the right of the Distribution and then click the Create a New Object button . In the flyout list that appears, choose DistributionFloatConstant (see **FIGURE 5.51**).

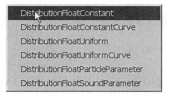

FIGURE 5.51   Set the Lifetime property to a float constant.

5

6. In the new distribution you've created, set the following (see **FIGURE 5.52**):

   ▶ **Constant**: 2.0

7. Now select the Initial Size module and set the following values (see **FIGURE 5.53**):

   ▶ **StartSize**:

      ▶ **Max**:

         ▶ **X**: 100.0

         ▶ **Y**: 1.0

         ▶ **Z**: 1.0

      ▶ **Min**:

         ▶ **X**: 75.0

         ▶ **Y**: 1.0

         ▶ **Z**: 1.0

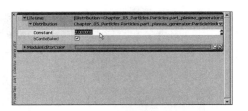

FIGURE 5.52   Each particle now lives for 2 seconds.

> **NOTE**
>
> The Y and Z values are actually meaningless because we are using sprites, which only use the X value when determining size.

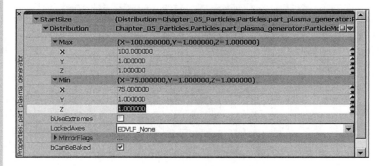

FIGURE 5.53   These settings cause the particles to be born with a size between 75 and 100.

8. Save your package.

END TUTORIAL 5.5

TUTORIAL 5.6 continues from **TUTORIAL 5.5**, so be sure to complete it before proceeding. You need to have the Chapter_05_Particles package open in the Generic Browser. If you have not completed **TUTORIAL 5.5**, you may open the part_plasma_generator_02 particle system and use it.

TUTORIAL 5.6: Plasma Generator, Part IV: Central Glow, Continued

1. The CentralGlow emitter's particles do not need any velocity, so it makes no sense to have an Initial Velocity module. Right-click the Initial Velocity module and choose Delete Module from the context menu (see **FIGURE 5.54**).

2. We need some type of color module because our material is using the VertexColor expression. The color of these particles does not need to change over the lives of the particles. However, we do want the Alpha to fade in and out, so right-click below the Initial Size module and choose Color > Color Over Life from the context menu and then select the module to view its properties (see **FIGURE 5.55**).

3. You'll notice that the ColorOverLife property defaults to a constant curve distribution. Because we are just using a single color for these particles, a curve really isn't necessary. Click the right side of the Distribution and click the Create a New Object button . From the flyout list that appears, choose DistributionVectorConstant. Then, set the following values (see **FIGURE 5.56**):

   ▶ **Constant**

      ▶ **X**: 2.0

      ▶ **Y**: 2.0

      ▶ **Z**: 4.0

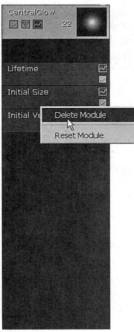

FIGURE 5.54
Delete the Initial
Velocity module.

FIGURE 5.55   Create
a new Color Over Life
module.

NOTE

The use of a curve with only one point does not incur a performance penalty as opposed to using a constant distribution as long as bCanBeBaked is checked. The use of a constant distribution here is merely for clarity. If there is a chance that modifying the color over the life of the particle may be desired, leaving this as a curve with a single point is perfectly acceptable.

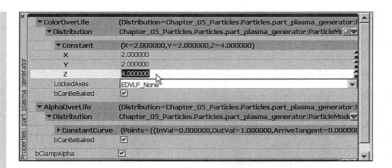

FIGURE 5.56   Set the ColorOverLife property to a vector constant with the shown settings.

4. Scroll down to the AlphaOverLife property. We do want a curve here, but we need some more points in order to fade the alpha in and out. Click the right of the Points array and then click the Add New Item button 🔲 twice to add two new points to the array, for a total of four points. Now, set the following values for the points (see **FIGURE 5.57**):

> ▸ **0**:
>
>> ▸ **InVal**: 0.0
>>
>> ▸ **OutVal**: 0.0
>
> ▸ **1**:
>
>> ▸ **InVal**: 0.25
>>
>> ▸ **OutVal**: 0.05

> ▸ **2**:
>
>> ▸ **InVal**: 0.75
>>
>> ▸ **OutVal**: 0.05
>
> ▸ **3**:
>
>> ▸ **InVal**: 1.0
>>
>> ▸ **OutVal**: 0.0

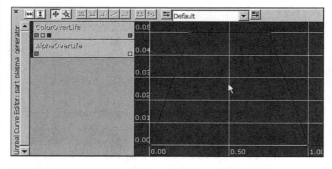

FIGURE 5.57   The points created graph out like so.

5. You'll notice that the alpha values we used are really low. This is because there are several particles drawing over each other at any given time and the color is overdriven.

6. Now we need to add some rotation to the particles. Right-click below the Color Over Life module and choose RotationRate > Initial RotRate from the context menu. By default, this will give the particles a rotation rate between 0 and 1, which is one full rotation per second. We want the particles to have an equal chance of rotating in either direction, though not quite so fast, so set the following values (see **FIGURE 5.58**):

> **NOTE**
>
> You may find that you have a certain curve—such as one that fades in and out—that is used quite often. In such cases, it can be much more efficient to set it up once and create a CurveEdUserPreset for the curve that can easily be reused and adjusted as needed. This saves a great deal of time and effort. For more information on using curve presets, see Appendix B.

- ► **StartRotationRate**:
    - ► **Min**: –0.5
    - ► **Max**: 0.5

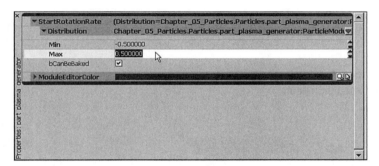

FIGURE 5.58   Add a new Initial RotRate module and set the StartRotationRate property.

7. By itself the rotation rate module does a good job, but a little more randomness in the rotation of each particle would be nice. To accomplish this, right-click below the Initial RotRate module and choose Rotation > Initial Rotation from the context menu. By setting the initial rotation of the particles, you can give the particles a more random appearance. Because the default gives the particles a rotation between 0 and 1 and that suits our needs, we leave the values of this module alone (see **FIGURE 5.59**).

5

FIGURE 5.59   Add an Initial Rotation module.

8. Make sure to save your package so your work is not lost.

END TUTORIAL 5.6

Types of Particle Modules

This section discusses the different particle modules you may use to control the behavior of your particle systems. It should be noted that many of the properties outlined within these modules make use of distributions. For more information on how these curves work, please see Appendix A, "Distributions."

While you read the definitions for each of these modules, you will come across two terms you need to be familiar with: RelativeLife and EmitterTime. Their definitions are provided here:

> **RelativeLife**—This term pertains to the life of the individual particle and is equivalent to TimeSinceBirth / Lifetime.
>
> **EmitterTime**—This pertains to the emitter and is equivalent to TimeActive / EmitterDuration.

Acceleration Modules

Acceleration modules allow you to change the velocity of a particle over time. For instance, you can apply downward acceleration to simulate the effect of gravity (see **FIGURE 5.60**). There are two acceleration modules available: Acceleration and Acceleration/Life.

Acceleration

This module sets the acceleration in each axis for each particle at its birth. This acceleration is taken directly from the vector specified in the acceleration property if a constant distribution is being used. If the distribution is uniform, the acceleration is randomly selected from between the Min and Max vectors. This acceleration is applied to every particle at every frame.

FIGURE 5.60   The downward arc of these particles is created by negative Z acceleration.

> **Acceleration**—This property is a vector distribution used to set the acceleration of the particle. This distribution should not be a curve.

Acceleration/Life

This module sets the acceleration in each axis for each particle over the lifetime of the particle (see **FIGURE 5.61**). The acceleration is calculated by finding the value of the vector distribution curve specified in the AccelOverLife property for the particle's current RelativeLife and is then applied to the particle.

> **AccelOverLife**—This is a vector distribution used to set the acceleration. This distribution should be a curve.

Attraction Modules

Attraction modules provide the ability to change the velocity of particles by drawing them toward a specific location or source. You can attract your particles to lines through space, to other particles, and to individual points in space (see **FIGURE 5.62**).

FIGURE 5.61   The AccelerationOverLife property causes this smoke to be pulled in the X direction after the particles are halfway through their lifetime.

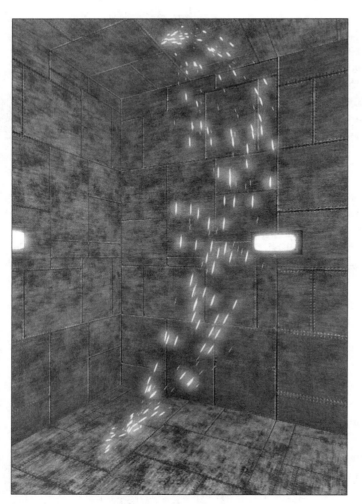

FIGURE 5.62   These particles are being drawn toward a designated point.

Line Attractor

This module causes the particles of this emitter to be attracted to, or drawn toward, a line (see **FIGURE 5.63**). This line is defined using the EndPoint properties within the module. Any time the particles overshoot their target, they will reverse direction, provided the strength for the attractor is strong enough to pull them back.

> **EndPoint0**—This is a vector specifying the location of one end of the line. The coordinates are relative to the location of the emitter.
>
> **EndPoint1**—This is a vector specifying the location of the other end of the line. The coordinates are relative to the location of the emitter.

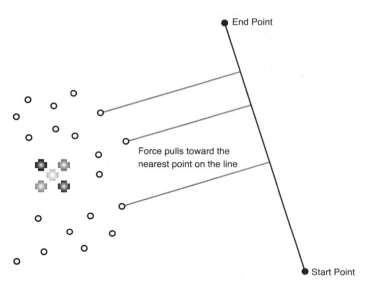

FIGURE 5.63 This diagram shows how a line attractor pulls particles toward the line.

Range—This is a float distribution (can be a curve) determining the maximum distance from the line where attraction should occur.

When a curve is being used, this is calculated by finding the value of the distribution for the current EmitterTime.

Strength—This is a float distribution (can be a curve) determining the amount of attraction.

When a curve is being used, this is calculated by finding the value of the distribution for the current EmitterTime.

Particle Attractor

This module causes the particles of this emitter to be attracted to, or drawn toward, the particles of another emitter in the same particle system (see **FIGURE 5.64**). Any time the particles over-shoot their target, they will reverse direction, provided the strength for the attractor is strong enough to pull them back.

EmitterName—This is the name of the emitter to which the particles of this emitter should be attracted.

Range—This is a float distribution (can be a curve) determining the maximum distance from the other emitter's particle where attraction should occur.

When a curve is being used, this is calculated by finding the value of the distribution for the current EmitterTime.

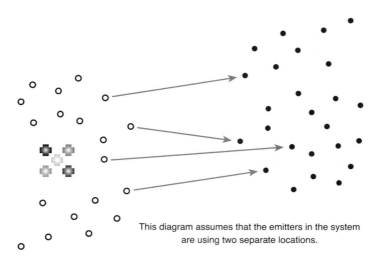

This diagram assumes that the emitters in the system
are using two separate locations.

FIGURE 5.64   This diagram shows how particles from one emitter can be attracted to particles
from another emitter.

bStrengthByDistance—When this property is true, the amount of attraction is determined by using the following equation:

(Range – Distance) / Range

When this property is false, the amount of attraction is determined by calculating the
value of the Strength property for the RelativeLife of the other emitter's particle.

Strength—This is a float distribution (can be a curve) determining the amount of
attraction.

When a curve is being used, this is calculated by finding the value of the distribution
for the current EmitterTime.

bAffectBaseVelocity—When this property is true, the affect of the attraction on the particle's velocity will be added to its base velocity, which is the particle's velocity at the
beginning of each frame.

When this property is false, the effect of the attraction on the particle's velocity will be
taken into account during the current frame, but the particle will revert to its base
velocity at the end of the frame.

SelectionMethod—This is the method for determining which particle from the other
emitter the particle from this emitter is attracted to. This property contains the following settings:

Random—This method causes the particle to be attracted to a random particle from
the other emitter.

Sequential—This method causes the particle to be attracted to the matching particle in sequential order.

This means that the first particle from this emitter will be attracted to the first particle from the other emitter, the second particle from this emitter will be attracted to the second particle from the other emitter, and so on.

bRenewSource—When this property is true, the particle will be assigned a new particle to be attracted to when the current attracting particle is destroyed.

When this property is false, the particle will cease to be attracted to anything and continue on its own until it is destroyed.

bInheritSourceVelocity—When this property is true, the particle will inherit the velocity of the attracting particle if it is destroyed.

When this property is false, no velocity will be transferred from the attracting particle when it is destroyed.

Point Attractor

This module causes the particles of this emitter to be attracted to, or drawn toward, a point designated in world space (see **FIGURE 5.65**). This line is defined using the EndPoint properties within the module. Any time the particles overshoot their target, they will reverse direction, provided the strength for the attractor is strong enough to pull them back.

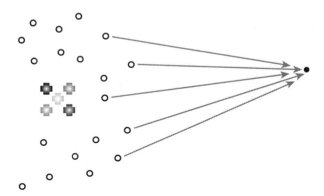

FIGURE 5.65   This diagram shows how particles can be attracted to a single point.

Position—This is a vector distribution (can be a curve) that specifies a point in space relative to the emitter.

When a curve is being used, this is calculated by finding the value of the distribution for the current EmitterTime.

Range—This is a float distribution (can be a curve) specifying the maximum distance from the point that particles will become attracted.

When a curve is being used, this is calculated by finding the value of the distribution for the current EmitterTime.

Strength—This is a float distribution (can be a curve) specifying the amount of attraction exerted by the point.

When a curve is being used, this is calculated by finding the value of the distribution for the current EmitterTime.

StrengthByDistance—When this property is true, the amount of attraction is determined by using the following equation:

(Range—Distance) / Range

When this property is false, the amount of attraction is determined by calculating the value of the Strength property for the current EmitterTime.

bAffectBaseVelocity—When this property is true, the affect of the attraction on the particle's velocity will be added to its base velocity, which is the particle's velocity at the beginning at each frame.

When this property is false, the effect of the attraction on the particle's velocity will be taken into account during the current frame, but the particle will revert to its base velocity at the end of the frame.

bOverrideVelocity—At the time of this writing, this property is nonfunctional.

Beam Modules

See the section "Beam Emitters" for descriptions of these modules.

Collision Module

The collision module enables you to cause particles to bounce off or collide with surfaces in the level (see **FIGURE 5.66**).

Collision

This module causes the particles of this emitter to collide with world geometry and any mesh that is set to collide with other objects through its Collision component properties:

DampingFactor—This is a vector distribution (can be a curve) specifying how much of the particle's velocity it loses upon each collision. A value of 0.0 means the particle retains all of its velocity, and a value of 1.0 means the particle will lose all of its velocity, which essentially stops the particle.

When a curve is being used, this is calculated by finding the value of the distribution for the current EmitterTime when the particle is spawned.

DampingFactorRotation—This is a vector distribution (can be a curve) specifying how much of the particle's rotation it loses upon each collision. A value of 0.0 means the particle retains all of its rotation, and a value of 1.0 means the particle will lose all of its rotation.

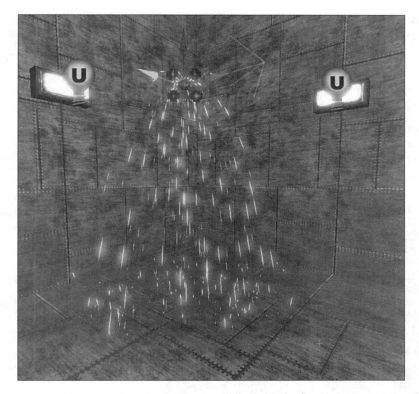

FIGURE 5.66   These particles are colliding with the floor geometry as they fall.

When a curve is being used, this is calculated by finding the value of the distribution for the current EmitterTime when the particle is spawned.

MaxCollisions—This is a float distribution (can be a curve) that specifies the maximum number of times a particle can collide with other objects before the CollisionCompletionOption is performed.

When a curve is being used, this is calculated by finding the value of the distribution for the current EmitterTime when the particle is spawned.

CollisionCompletionOption—This property determines how the particle should behave once it has reached the number of collisions specified by the MaxCollisions property. This property contains the following options:

> **Kill**—This option causes the particle to be destroyed.
>
> **Freeze**—This option causes the particle to be frozen at the point of the collision. To be *frozen* means that the particle will not move or rotate. Also, any other modules such as size and color will no longer update.
>
> **HaltCollisions**—This causes collision checks concerning this particle to cease.

FreezeTranslation—This option causes the particle to cease translation. Everything else will continue to be updated.

FreezeRotation—This option causes the particle to cease rotation. Everything else will continue to be updated.

FreezeMovement—This option causes the particle to cease translation and rotation. Everything else, such as color, size, and so on, will continue to be updated.

bApplyPhysics—When this property is true, the particles will impart an impulse on the objects they collide with according to the velocity at impact and the ParticleMass (see **FIGURE 5.67**).

When this property is false, no impulses are applied.

FIGURE 5.67   The rigid body in this image is propelled by the particles striking it.

ParticleMass—This is a float distribution (can be a curve) that specifies the mass of the particle used in the physics calculation if bApplyPhysics is true.

DirScaler—This value is multiplied by the bounds of each particle when doing collision checks.

bPawnsDoNotDecrementCount— When this property is true, particles that collide with pawns will not have those collisions counted in their number of collisions, but otherwise collide as they would with any other surface.

> **TIP**
>
> Scaling the particle bounds can be useful in avoiding apparent interpenetrations or gaps due to transparency or other factors.

When this property is false, particles count collisions with pawns that could possibly result in the particle being left frozen in mid air.

bOnlyVerticalNormalsDecrementCount—When this property is true, particle collisions will only be counted in the number of collisions if the normal of the surface the particle collided with is considered vertical after taking into account the VerticalFudgeFactor.

When this property is false, all collisions regardless of the surface's normal will be counted in the number of collisions.

VerticalFudgeFactor—This value determines how close a normal must be to vertical to be considered vertical when bOnlyVerticalNormalsDecrementCount is set to true.

A perfectly vertical normal has a Z value of 1.0. The range used to determine verticality is 1.0—VerticalFudgeFactor to 1.0.

Color Modules

Color modules provide the ability to set the color of a particle at the time of its birth or to change or adjust the color of the particle based on its age. You can also set colors for particles independently on an instance-by-instance basis.

> **NOTE**
>
> The color modules require the material applied to the particles to contain the Vertex Color material expression!

Initial Color

This module determines the color of the particles of the emitter when they are spawned. The color of each particle remains constant throughout the life of that particle:

StartColor—This is a vector distribution (can be a curve) that specifies the color of the particles. X, Y, and Z correspond to R, G, and B.

When a curve is being used, this is calculated by finding the value of the distribution for the current EmitterTime when the particle is spawned.

StartAlpha—This is a float distribution (can be a curve) that specifies the Alpha of the particles.

When a curve is being used, this is calculated by finding the value of the distribution for the current EmitterTime when the particle is spawned.

bClampAlpha—When this property is true, the value of StartAlpha will be clamped between 0.0 and 1.0.

When this property is false, no clamping will take place.

Parameter Color

This module allows each instance of the particle system containing this emitter in the level to set the color for this emitter independently of the other instances by applying a material instance constant to the emitter's Material property and referencing a parameter in that material instance constant.

> **NOTE**
>
> The effect of this module can also be achieved by using a VectorParticleParameterDistribution in a Color module.

ColorParam—This is the name of the parameter in the material instance constant.

DefaultColor—This is the color to use if the parameter is not set in the emitter actor's properties.

Color Over Life

This module allows the color of this emitter's particles to be changed over the life of the particle:

ColorOverLife—This is a vector distribution (should be a curve) that specifies the colors to set the particles to.

This is calculated by finding the value of the distribution for the current RelativeLife of the particle.

AlphaOverLife

This is a float distribution (should be a curve) specifying the alpha values to use for the particles. This is calculated by finding the value of the distribution for the current RelativeLife of the particle.

bClampAlpha—When this property is true, the value from AlphaOverLife will be clamped between 0.0 and 1.0.

When this property is false, no clamping will take place.

Scale Color/Life

This module allows the color of this emitter's particles to be scaled over the life of the particle (or over the duration of the emitter):

ColorScaleOverLife—This is a vector distribution (should be a curve) that specifies the color to multiply by the particle's initial color.

This is calculated by finding the value of the distribution for the current RelativeLife of the particle when bEmitterTime is false or for the current EmitterTime if bEmitterTime is true.

AlphaScaleOverLife—This is a float distribution (should be a curve) that specifies the value to multiply by the particle's initial Alpha value.

This is calculated by finding the value of the distribution for the current RelativeLife of the particle when bEmitterTime is false or for the current EmitterTime if bEmitterTime is true.

bEmitterTime—When this property is true, the distributions of this module will use the EmitterTime to calculate their values.

When this property is false, the distributions of this module will use the RelativeLife of the particle to calculate their values.

Kill Modules

Kill modules allow you to delete or "kill" a particle based on certain conditions, such as when it enters or exits a particular volume or when it passes beyond a certain elevation. Removing particles in this way helps to maintain level efficiency by preventing the calculation of particles that cannot be seen by the player.

Kill Box

This module causes this emitter's articles to be destroyed when leaving or entering an area specified by a box. The box can be previewed in Cascade's viewport by enabling the 3D preview (see **FIGURE 5.68**).

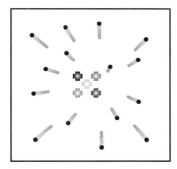

Particles die as soon as they exit the box.

FIGURE 5.68   This diagram illustrates the theoretical box used to kill your particles. This box is adjustable.

LowerLeftCorner—This is a vector distribution (should not be a curve) specifying the lower corner of the box. This is the lowest value of the X, Y, and Z axes for the box.

UpperRightCorner—This is a vector distribution (should not be a curve) that specifies the location of the upper corner of the box. This is the highest value of the X, Y, and Z axes for the box.

> **NOTE**
>
> As you may already know, in a standard 3-dimensional environment, you can define a box with a single line running from, say, the upper northwest corner to the lower southeast corner, assuming that the sides of the box are orthogonal to the three primary axes. In this case, we define the line with two points and that line in turn defines the box.

bAbsolute—When this property is true, the location specified for the box will be considered to be using world space coordinates.

When this property is false, the location of the box will be considered to be using the local space of the emitter.

bKillInside—When this property is true, the particles will be destroyed when they enter the box.

When this property is false, the particles will be destroyed when the leave the box.

Kill Height

This module causes this emitter's particles to be destroyed when they are located above or below a certain height. The plane representing the height can be previewed in the viewport by enabling the 3D preview:

Height—This is a float distribution (should not be a curve) that specifies the height above or below which the particles will be destroyed.

bAbsolute—When this property is true, the location specified for the plane will be considered to be using world space coordinates.

When this property is false, the location of the plane will be considered to be using the local space of the emitter.

bFloor—When this property is true, this emitter's particles will be destroyed when they are located below the height.

When this property is false, this emitter's particles are destroyed when they are located above the height.

Lifetime Module

This module sets the number of seconds that each particle lasts before it is destroyed (see **FIG-URE 5.69**).

Lifetime—This is a float distribution (can be a curve) that specifies the number of seconds the particle should live for.

When a curve is being used, this is calculated by finding the value of the distribution for the current EmitterTime when the particle is spawned.

Location Modules

Location modules allow you to define emitter position, where particles are placed at the instant of their birth and their position throughout their lifetime. This position can be defined via direct coordinates or through random locations within volumes of different shapes and sizes.

FIGURE 5.69   The particles on the left are set to live longer lifetimes than the ones on the right.

Initial Location

This module sets the location of this emitter's particles when they are spawned.

StartLocation—This is a vector distribution (can be a curve) specifying the spawn location of the particle relative to the emitter.

When a curve is being used, this is calculated by finding the value of the distribution for the current EmitterTime when the particle is spawned.

Direct Location

This module sets the location of this emitter's particles over their lifetime:

Location—This is a vector distribution (should be a curve) that specifies the location of the particle.

When a curve is being used, this is calculated by finding the value of the distribution for the current RelativeLife of the particle.

LocationOffset—This is a vector distribution (can be a curve) specifying the offset from the value of Location for each emitter.

When a curve is being used, this is calculated by finding the value of the distribution for the current EmitterTime when the particle is spawned and remains constant over the life of the particle.

ScaleFactor—This is a vector distribution (can be a curve) that specifies values to multiply by the particle's velocity.

When a curve is being used, this is calculated by finding the value of the distribution for the current RelativeLife of the particle.

Direction—At the time of this writing, this property is nonfunctional.

Emitter InitLoc

This module sets the spawn location of the particles emitted from this emitter to the current location of particles belonging to another emitter, the source emitter, in the same particle system.

EmitterName—This is the name of the source emitter whose particles' locations will be used as the initial locations for this emitter's particles.

SelectionMethod—This determines which particles from the source emitter will be associated with the particles of this emitter. This property contains the following settings:

Random—This method causes this emitter's particles to be associated with a randomly chosen particle from the source emitter.

Sequential—This method causes this emitter's particles to be associated with the matching particle from the source emitter. This means that the first particle from this emitter will be associated with the first particle from the source emitter, the second particle from this emitter will be associated with the second particle from the source emitter, and so on.

InheritSourceVelocity—When this property is true, the particle of this emitter will inherit the velocity of its associated particle from the source emitter.

When this property is false, the velocity of the associated particle is ignored.

InheritSourceVelocityScale—This is a value to multiply by the associated particle's velocity.

bInheritSourceRotation—When this property is true, the particle of this emitter will inherit the rotation of its associated particle from the source emitter.

When this property is false, the rotation of the associated particle will be ignored.

InheritSourceRotationScale—This is a value to multiply by the associated particle's rotation.

Emitter DirectLoc

This module sets the particles from this emitter to the location of the matching particles from another emitter, the source emitter, in the same particle system.

This means that the first particle from this emitter is associated with the first particle from the source emitter, the second particle from this emitter is associated with the second particle from the source emitter, and so on.

> **EmitterName**—This is the name of the source emitter whose particles' locations are used as the initial locations for this emitter's particles.

Cylinder

This module sets the location of the particles of this emitter when they are spawned using a theoretical cylinder shape (see **FIGURE 5.70**).

> **RadialVelocity**—When this property is true, the particle's velocity component of the axis specified in HeightAxis is ignored.
>
> **StartRadius**—This is a float distribution (can be a curve) specifying the radius of the cylinder shape.
>
> When a curve is being used, this is calculated by finding the value of the distribution for the current EmitterTime when the particle is spawned.

FIGURE 5.70   When the cylinder module is used, particles are emitted from the volume of a theoretical cylinder.

> **StartHeight**—This is a float distribution (can be a curve) that specifies the height of the cylinder shape.
>
> When a curve is being used, this is calculated by finding the value of the distribution for the current EmitterTime when the particle is spawned.
>
> **HeightAxis**—This determines the axis along which the cylinder's height should be aligned. This property contains the following settings:
>
> > **HEIGHTAXIS_X**—This aligns the height axis of the cylinder along the X-axis.
> >
> > **HEIGHTAXIS_Y**—This aligns the height axis of the cylinder along the Y-axis.
> >
> > **HEIGHTAXIS_Z**—This aligns the height axis of the cylinder along the Z-axis.
>
> **Positive_X**—If this property is true, particles are emitted from positive X side of the shape.
>
> **Positive_Y**—If this property is true, particles are emitted from positive Y side of the shape.
>
> **Positive_Z**—If this property is true, particles are emitted from positive Z side of the shape.
>
> **Negative_X**—If this property is true, particles are emitted from negative X side of the shape.

Negative_Y—If this property is true, particles are emitted from negative Y side of the shape.

Negative_Z—If this property is true, particles are emitted from negative Z side of the shape.

SurfaceOnly—If this property is true, particles are only emitted from the surface of the shape and not the volume that the shape defines.

If this property is false, particles are emitted from the entire volume the shape defines, including the surface.

Velocity—If this property is true, particles use any radial velocity defined in the velocity module for the emitter.

VelocityScale—This is a float distribution (can be a curve) specifying the amount to multiply by the radial velocity defined in the velocity module.

When a curve is being used, this is calculated by finding the value of the distribution for the current EmitterTime.

StartLocation—This is a vector distribution (can be a curve) specifying the origin for the location shape in the X, Y, and Z axes.

When a curve is being used, this is calculated by finding the value of the distribution for the current EmitterTime.

Sphere

This module sets the location of the particles of this emitter when they are spawned within the volume of a theoretical sphere shape (see **FIGURE 5.71**).

StartRadius—This is a float distribution (can be a curve) that specifies the radius of the sphere shape.

When a curve is being used, this is calculated by finding the value of the distribution for the current EmitterTime when the particle is spawned.

Positive_X—If this property is true, particles are emitted from positive X side of the shape.

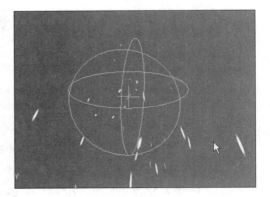

FIGURE 5.71   When the sphere module is used, particles are emitted from the volume of a theoretical sphere.

Positive_Y—If this property is true, particles are emitted from positive Y side of the shape.

Positive_Z—If this property is true, particles are emitted from positive Z side of the shape.

Negative_X—If this property is true, particles are emitted from negative X side of the shape.

Negative_Y—If this property is true, particles are emitted from negative Y side of the shape.

Negative_Z—If this property is true, particles are emitted from negative Z side of the shape.

SurfaceOnly—If this property is true, particles are only emitted from the surface of the shape and not the volume that the shape defines.

If this property is false, particles are emitted from the entire volume the shape defines, including the surface.

Velocity—If this property is true, particles use any radial velocity defined in the velocity module for the emitter.

VelocityScale—This is a float distribution (can be a curve) specifying the amount to multiply by the radial velocity defined in the velocity module.

When a curve is being used, this is calculated by finding the value of the distribution for the current EmitterTime.

StartLocation—This is a vector distribution (can be a curve) specifying the origin for the location shape in the X, Y, and Z axes.

When a curve is being used, this is calculated by finding the value of the distribution for the current EmitterTime.

Orbit Module

The orbit module allows you to give the illusion that particles are revolving around a specific position.

Orbit

This module sets an offset for each particle from its actual location and a rotation and rotation rate around that location for each axis. This would be considered more of a revolution as opposed to the rotation of the Rotation and RotationRate modules (see **FIGURE 5.72**).

Each component of this module can be set to only affect the particle at spawn time or during each update of the particle. Also, multiple modules can be used together to create unique effects.

It should be noted that Orbit is essentially a rendering trick. The particles themselves are located at the emitter and do not

FIGURE 5.72   These particles are orbiting their emitter.

technically "move." However, the rendering engine displays them in various locations to give the illusion that they are orbiting. This is an important factor to keep in mind if you try to make other particle emitters send particles to the location of the orbiting particles. They simply move toward the center of the emitter and appear to ignore the orbiting particles.

Chaining

ChainMode—This property controls how the Orbit module is combined with any previous Orbit modules in the list. It contains the following settings:

EOChainMode_Add—This adds the current Orbit module's result to the previous module.

EOChainMode_Scale—This setting multiplies the current module's result by the previous module.

EOChainMode_Link—This setting allows you to combine the results of multiple Orbit modules in a unique way, allowing for suborbital systems. This setting will behave a bit differently depending on whether or not the module in question is the first Orbit module in the list, and whether the Orbit module placed directly above the current Orbit module is also set to Link.

If there is an Orbit module just above the current Orbit module, and both of them are set to Link, then the offset of the second Orbit begins from the location of the particle after the first Orbit is calculated. If this sounds confusing, consider the Earth and Moon's relation to the Sun. The Earth revolves around the Sun, which would represent the result of our first Orbit module, but the Moon also revolves around the Earth, which would be the result of the second module. Now, mentally hide the Sun and Earth so that all you can see is the behavior of the Moon. This spirographic pattern is the kind of relationship we're describing (see **FIGURE 5.73**).

If there is another Orbit above the current Orbit that is not set to Link, then the results of the previous Orbit are discarded, and only the results of the current Orbit are used.

Offset

OffsetAmount—This is a vector distribution (can be a curve) specifying the distance in each axis to offset the rendered particle from the actual particle's location.

When a curve is being used, this is calculated by finding the value of the distribution for the RelativeLife of the particle or the current EmitterTime, depending on the bUseEmitterTime property in the OffsetOptions.

OffsetOptions—See the "Options" description later in the list.

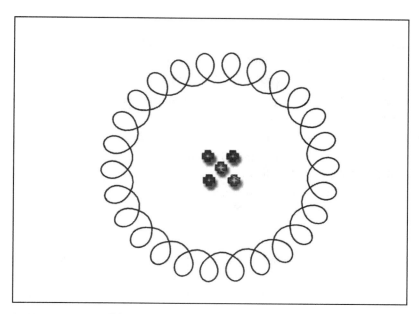

FIGURE 5.73 This diagram shows the pattern created when two linked Orbit modules are applied.

Rotation

RotationAmount—This is a vector distribution (can be a curve) specifying the rotation about each axis of the offset and rendered particle with respect to the actual particle's location.

When a curve is being used, this is calculated by finding the value of the distribution for the RelativeLife of the particle or the current EmitterTime, depending on the bUseEmitterTime property in the RotationOptions.

Using a constant curve here in association with having bProcessDuringUpdate set to true would allow you to control the rotation over time, similar to how RotationRate works, but with much more precision.

RotationOptions—See the "Options" description later in this list.

RotationRate

RotationRateAmount—This is a vector distribution (can be a curve) specifying the rate at which the offset and rendered particle will be rotated about each axis with respect to the actual particle's location.

When a curve is being used, this is calculated by finding the value of the distribution for the RelativeLife of the particle or the current EmitterTime, depending on the bUseEmitterTime property in the RotationRateOptions.

RotationRateOptions—See the "Options" description later in this list.

Options

bProcessDuringSpawn—If this property is true, the corresponding property is calculated and applied when the particle is spawned.

If this property is false, the property is not applied during spawning.

bProcessDuringUpdate—If this property is true, the corresponding property will be calculated and applied when the particle is updated.

If this property is false, the property is not applied during the update process.

bUseEmitterTime—If this property is true, the corresponding property uses the current EmitterTime when evaluating its distribution.

If this property is false, the property uses the RelativeLife of the particle.

Orientation Modules

By default, sprite particles face the camera automatically. No matter where the viewpoint moves, a sprite adjusts its orientation so that it always remains perpendicular to the camera. With this orientation module, such behavior can be overridden to cause the particle to face a certain direction.

Lock Axis

This module forces the particles of this emitter to face a certain axis. This only works with sprite particles.

LockAxisFlags—This determines which axis the particles of this emitter will face. This property contains the following settings:

EPAL_X—This setting forces the particles to face the positive X direction.

EPAL_Y—This setting forces the particles to face the positive Y direction.

EPAL_Z—This setting forces the particles to face the positive Z direction.

EPAL_NEGATIVE_X—This setting forces the particles to face the negative X direction.

EPAL_NEGATIVE_Y—This setting forces the particles to face the negative Y direction.

EPAL_NEGATIVE_Z—This setting forces the particles to face the negative Z direction.

Rotation Modules

In certain circumstances, you may find yourself needing to establish certain rotational behavior for your particles. For instance, you could have sprite particles that used an image texture, and you always want the image to be rotated in a certain fashion. Using the rotation emitters, you can define a particular rotation at the time of a particle's birth, or change the rotation throughout the life of the particle.

Init Mesh Rotation

This module is described in the section "Mesh Emitters."

Initial Rotation

This module sets the rotation of the particles of this emitter when they are spawned. This only works with sprite particles (see **FIGURE 5.74**).

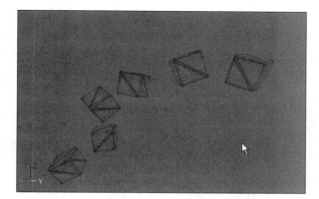

FIGURE 5.74   Each of these particles has a different rotation at birth.

Although there is a module specifically for mesh particle rotation, this module will also affect meshes. Because it has only a single float value, this value is applied to all axes of the mesh. The same behavior could be created using the Init Mesh Rotation module if the EDVLF_XYZ LockedAxes setting is used.

> **StartRotation**—This is a vector distribution (can be a curve) specifying the rotation about the axis the particle is facing. A value of 0.0 is equal to 0 degrees and a value of 1.0 is equal to 360 degrees.
>
> When a curve is being used, this is calculated by finding the value of the distribution for the current EmitterTime when the particle is spawned.

Rotation/Life

This module sets the rotation of the particles of this emitter throughout their lifetime. This only works with sprite particles.

Although there is a module specifically for mesh particle rotation, this module affects meshes. Because it has only a single float value, this value is applied to all axes of the mesh.

> **RotationOverLife**—This is a float distribution (should be a curve) specifying the rotation of the particles about their facing axis.
>
> When a curve is being used, this is calculated by finding the value of the distribution for the current RelativeLife of the particle.
>
> **Scale**—When this property is true, the value of RotationOverLife is multiplied by the particle's initial rotation.
>
> When this property is false, the value of RotationOverLife is added to the particle's initial rotation.

Rotation Rate Modules

In cases where you need particles that are constantly rotating, the rotation rate modules allow you to define an initial rate of rotation, or to establish how the rate of rotation changes over time.

Init Mesh RotRate

This module is described in the section "Mesh Emitters."

Initial RotRate

This module sets the rate in rotations per second at which a particle continually rotates. This only works for sprite particles.

Although there is a module specifically for mesh particle rotation rate, this module affects meshes. Because it has only a single float value, this value is applied to all axes of the mesh.

> **StartRotationRate**—This is a float distribution (can be a curve) that specifies the rate at which a particle continually rotates about its facing axis.
>
> When a curve is being used, this is calculated by finding the value of the distribution for the current EmitterTime when the particle is spawned.

RotRate/Life

This module scales the rate at which a particle is continually rotated throughout its lifetime.

Although there is a module specifically for mesh particle rotation rate, this module affects meshes. Because it has only a single float value, this value is applied to all axes of the mesh.

> **LifeMultiplier**—This is a float distribution (should be a curve) specifying the value to multiply by the particle's initial rotation rate.
>
> When a curve is being used, this is calculated by finding the value of the distribution for the current RelativeLife of the particle.

Size Modules

With the size modules, you can define the size of a particle at the time of its birth, as well as set or modify that size based on such conditions as particle age or velocity.

Initial Size

This module sets the size of the particles of this emitter when they are spawned:

> **StartSize**—This is a Vector distribution (can be a curve) that specifies the size of the particle. For sprite particles, only the X value is used and represents the dimensions of the square plane of the sprite. For mesh particles, X, Y, and Z are the DrawScale3D values for the mesh.
>
> When a curve is being used, this is calculated by finding the value of the distribution for the current EmitterTime when the particle is spawned.

Size By Life

This module sets the size of this emitter's particles over their lifetime by scaling the particle's current size (see **FIGURE 5.75**). This module does not override other size modules above it in the stack.

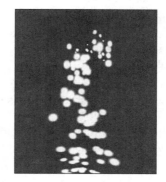

FIGURE 5.75 Notice how the particles appear to grow over their lifetimes.

> **LifeMultiplier**—This is a vector distribution (should be a curve) that specifies the values by which the particle's size are multiplied.
>
> When a curve is being used, this is calculated by finding the value of the distribution for the current RelativeLife of the particle.
>
> **MultiplyX**—When this property is true, the X component of the particle's size is affected by this module.
>
> When this property is false, the X component of the particle's size is unaffected.
>
> **MultiplyY**—When this property is true, the Y component of the particle's size is affected by this module.
>
> When this property is false, the Y component of the particle's size is unaffected.
>
> This only has an effect on mesh particles.

NOTE

When you're using sprite particles, unchecking MultiplyX causes this module to have no effect.

MultiplyZ—When this property is true, the Z component of the particle's size is affected by this module.

When this property is false, the Z component of the particle's size is unaffected.

This only has an effect on mesh particles.

Size By Velocity

This module sets the size of this emitter's particles based on their current speed, where speed is the magnitude of the particles' velocity vector:

VelocityMultiplier—This is a vector distribution (should be a curve) specifying values to multiply by the particle's velocity in order to scale the velocity before using it to set the size.

When a curve is being used, this is calculated by finding the value of the distribution for the current RelativeLife of the particle.

MultiplyX—When this property is true, the X component of the particle's size is affected by this module.

When this property is false, the X component of the particle's size is unaffected.

> **NOTE**
>
> When you're using sprite particles, unchecking MultiplyX causes this module to have no effect.

MultiplyY—When this property is true, the Y component of the particle's size is affected by this module.

When this property is false, the Y component of the particle's size is unaffected.

This only has an effect on mesh particles.

MultiplyZ—When this property is true, the Z component of the particle's size is affected by this module.

When this property is false, the Z component of the particle's size is unaffected.

This only has an effect on mesh particles.

Size Scale

This module sets the size of this emitter's particles over their lifetime by scaling the particles' initial size. This module overrides other Size By Life, Size By Velocity, and Size Scale modules above it in the stack.

SizeScale—This is a vector distribution (should be a curve) that specifies the values by which the particle's size is multiplied.

When a curve is being used, this is calculated by finding the value of the distribution for the current RelativeLife of the particle.

EnableX—At the time of this writing, this property is nonfunctional.

EnableY—At the time of this writing, this property is nonfunctional.

EnableZ—At the time of this writing, this property is nonfunctional.

Spawn Module

The spawn module is used when you need a particle to basically become an emitter unto itself, releasing other particles as it travels. The overall effect is similar to a trail.

Spawn PerUnit

This module causes this emitter to spawn particles based on its rate of movement:

bProcessSpawnRate—When this property is true, the SpawnRate property in this emitter's RequiredModule contributes to the particle spawning. This causes particles to be spawned even when the emitter is not moving.

When this property is false, the SpawnRate is ignored, meaning that no particles will be spawned when the emitter is not moving.

SpawnPerUnit—This is a float distribution (can be a curve) specifying the number of particles to spawn for each unit the emitter moves.

UnitScalar—This is a value that the SpawnPerUnit value is divided by in order to get the final number of particles to spawn for each unit the emitter has moved.

bIgnoreSpawnRateWhenMoving—When this property is true, the SpawnRate property of the emitter will not contribute to particle spawning when the emitter is moving.

When this property is false, the contribution of the SpawnRate property is determined by bProcessSpawnRate.

MovementTolerance—This value allows for some leeway when deciding whether or not the emitter is moving. If the distance the emitter has moved is less than this value multiplied by the UnitScalar, then the emitter is not considered to be moving.

SubUV Modules

In cases where you do not want every sprite article to have the same texture, you can create subUV textures in which the texture is divided up into a grid of different images. Using subUV modules, you can then define how each individual image portion is applied to each particle, or how the image changes over time. In effect, this allows you to play an animation across the surface of a sprite particle, rather than being limited to a static texture.

SubImage Index

This module tells the particles of this emitter which sub-image they should use by index. This only works for emitters using a material with sub-images and an InterpolationMethod *not* set to PSUVIM_None (see **FIGURE 5.76**).

FIGURE 5.76   The different textures used in this effect are the result of a SubImage Index.

SubImageIndex—This is a float distribution (can be a curve) specifying the index of the sub-image that this emitter's particles should display.

Remember that the index of sub-images is zero based, so the first texture will be equal to index 0. Also, you should use a value that is slightly higher than the index you wish to use. For instance, if you want to cycle through each sub-image of a 2×2 material (meaning indices 0 through 3) during each particle's lifetime, you would create a constant curve distribution with two slots. Slot 0 would have an InVal of 0.0 and an OutVal of 0.0. Slot 1 would have an InVal of 1.0 and an OutVal of 3.01.

This is because the bound will not have an equal chance of being used as the random value, so you use a value slightly higher so that the upper bound has an equal chance of being used.

When a curve is being used, this is calculated by finding the value of the distribution for the current RelativeLife of the particle.

SubUV Direct

This module tells the particles of this emitter which sub-image they should use by coordinates. This only works for an emitter using a material with sub-images and an InterpolationMethod *not* set to PSUVIM_None.

SubUVPosition—This is a vector distribution (can be a curve) that specifies the texture coordinates from which to begin sampling the material. The X component is the number of texels from the left edge, and the Y component is the number of texels from the top edge. The Z component is ignored.

When a curve is used, this is calculated by finding the value of the distribution for the current RelativeLife of the particle.

SubUVSize—This is a vector distribution (can be a curve) specifying the dimensions of the area to be sampled. The X component is the number of texels across, and the Y component is the number of texels down. The Z component is ignored.

When a curve is being used, this is calculated by finding the value of the distribution for the current RelativeLife of the particle.

SubUV Select

This module tells the particles of this emitter which sub-image they should use by row and column. This only works for an emitter using a material with sub-images and an InterpolationMethod *not* set to PSUVIM_None.

> **SubImageSelect**—This is a vector distribution (can be a curve) specifying the row and column of the sub-image to use. The X component is the column, and the Y component is the row. The Z component is ignored.
>
> When a curve is being used, this is calculated by finding the value of the distribution for the current RelativeLife of the particle.

Trail Modules

Trail modules are discussed in the section "Trail Emitters."

Velocity Modules

As the name suggests, velocity modules allow you to control the velocity of a particle. This velocity can be defined at birth, controlled via particle age, or simply set to be inherited as a percentage from the parent emitter.

Initial Velocity

This module sets the velocity for this emitter's particles when they are spawned (see **FIGURE 5.77**).

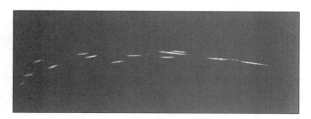

FIGURE 5.77   Initial velocity sets the speed at which these particles are leaving the emitter.

> **StartVelocity**—This is a vector distribution (can be a curve) specifying the velocity direction and magnitude.
>
> When a curve is being used, this is calculated by finding the value of the distribution for the current EmitterTime.
>
> **StartVelocityRadial**—This is a float distribution (can be a curve) that specifies the magnitude of the velocity along the vector calculated by subtracting the emitter's location from the particle's spawn location.
>
> When a curve is being used, this is calculated by finding the value of the distribution for the current EmitterTime.

Inherit Parent Velocity

This module passes the velocity (or a portion of the velocity) of the emitter on to the particle when it is spawned.

Scale—This is a vector distribution (can be a curve) specifying the portion of the velocity in each axis to pass along to the particle.

When a curve is being used, this is calculated by finding the value of the distribution for the current EmitterTime.

Velocity/Life

This module sets the velocity of this emitter's particles throughout their lifetimes.

VelOverLife—This is a vector distribution (should be a curve) specifying either the velocity of the particle or values to multiply by the particle's current velocity, depending on the Absolute property.

Absolute—When this property is true, the value of VelOverLife sets the particle's velocity directly. This overrides any previous velocity modules in the stack.

When this property is false, the values of VelOverLife are multiplied by the current velocity of the particle.

TUTORIAL 5.7 continues from **TUTORIAL 5.6**, so be sure to complete it before proceeding. You need to have the Chapter_05_Particles package open in the Generic Browser. If you have not completed **TUTORIAL 5.6**, you may use the part_plasma_generator_03 particle system to complete this tutorial.

TUTORIAL 5.7: Plasma Generator, Part IV: Chaotic Orbiting Particles

1. The next emitter to add to this system creates small, randomly orbiting particles. If it is not already, open the part_plasma_generator particle system in Cascade by double-clicking it in the Generic Browser. With the mat_flare material selected in the Generic Browser, right-click in the empty space of the Emitter List to the right of the CentralGlow emitter and choose New ParticleSpriteEmitter (see **FIGURE 5.78**).

2. Select the emitter module to view its properties in the Properties panel and set the EmitterName to ChaoticOrbit.

3. Select the Lifetime module to view its properties. As in the previous emitter, a variance in the lifetimes of these particles would simply not be noticeable. Click on the right of the Distribution and then click the Create a New Object button ⬇. In the flyout list that appears, choose DistributionFloatConstant. Set the following value (see **FIGURE 5.79**):

   ▶ **Constant**: 3.0

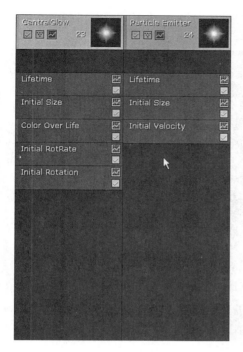

FIGURE 5.78   Create another emitter within the particle system.

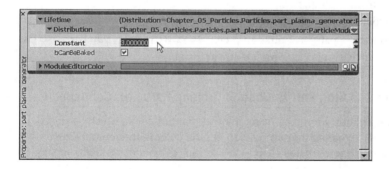

FIGURE 5.79   All the particles from this emitter have a 3-second lifetime.

4. Select the Initial Size module to view its properties. These particles need to be relatively small with some variation, so enter these values:

- ▸ **StartSize:**
  - ▸ **Max:**
    - ▸ **X:** 5.0
    - ▸ **Y:** 1.0
    - ▸ **Z:** 1.0
  - ▸ **Min:**
    - ▸ **X:** 1.0
    - ▸ **Y:** 1.0
    - ▸ **Z:** 1.0

5. While these particles will be moving, the movement is the result of an Orbit module, so the Initial Velocity module is not needed. Right-click the Initial Velocity module and choose Delete Module (see **FIGURE 5.80**).

6. Save your package.

END TUTORIAL 5.7

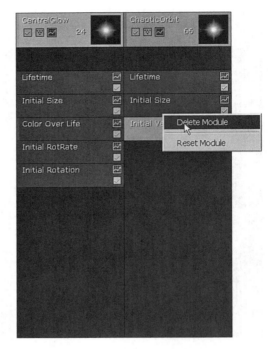

FIGURE 5.80   Delete the Initial Velocity module.

TUTORIAL 5.8 continues from **TUTORIAL 5.7**, so be sure to complete it before proceeding. You need to have the Chapter_05_Particles package open in the Generic Browser. If you have not completed **TUTORIAL 5.7**, you may use the part_plasma_generator_04 particle system to complete this tutorial.

TUTORIAL 5.8: Plasma Generator, Part V: Chaotic Orbiting Particles, Continued

1. As with the CentralGlow emitter, we will be using the mat_flare material, which uses a VertexColor expression. This means that we have to set the color in the emitter itself. Again, as before, we want these particles to fade in and out to avoid any visual popping. Right-click below the Initial Size module and choose Color > Color Over Life from the context menu (see **FIGURE 5.81**).

2. Select the new module to view its properties. Click on the right side of the Distribution for ColorOverLife and click the Create a New Object button ▼. From the flyout list that appears, choose DistributionVectorConstant. Then, set the following values:

- ▸ **Constant**
  - ▸ **X:** 4.0
  - ▸ **Y:** 4.0
  - ▸ **Z:** 1.0

3. Scroll down to the AlphaOverLife property. We want to fade in and out, so we need a curve here, but we need some more points in order to fade the alpha in and then out. Click on the right of the Points array and then click the Add New Item button 🔲 twice to add two new points to the array. Now, set the following values for the points (see **FIGURE 5.82**):

- ▶ **0**:
  - ▶ **InVal**: 0.0
  - ▶ **OutVal**: 0.0
- ▶ **1**:
  - ▶ **InVal**: 0.25
  - ▶ **OutVal**: 1.0
- ▶ **2**:
  - ▶ **InVal**: 0.75
  - ▶ **OutVal**: 1.0
- ▶ **3**:
  - ▶ **InVal**: 1.0
  - ▶ **OutVal**: 0.0

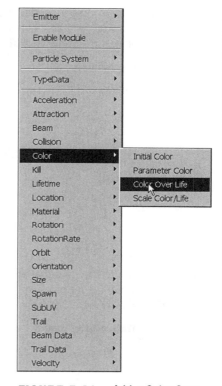

FIGURE 5.81   Add a Color Over Life module.

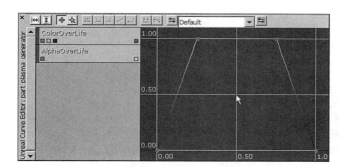

FIGURE 5.82   You need a total of four points to create the appropriate curve.

4. As mentioned previously, in order to get the movement of the particles for this emitter, we are going to use an Orbit module. Right-click below the Color Over Life module and choose Orbit > Orbit. Select the new module to view its properties. The first section is Chaining, which contains the ChainMode property that defaults to EOCHainMode_Link. This is the setting we want, so leave this property as it is. We do want to set the OffsetAmount property in the Offset section, although we can keep the uniform distribution. Set the following values (see **FIGURE 5.83**):

- ▸ **OffsetAmount**:
    - ▸ **Max**:
        - ▸ **X**: 18.0
        - ▸ **Y**: 18.0
        - ▸ **Z**: 18.0
    - ▸ **Min**:
        - ▸ **X**: 12.0
        - ▸ **Y**: 12.0
        - ▸ **Z**: 12.0

5. Scroll down to the RotationRate section. The RotationRateAmount property defaults to a uniform distribution. Set the following values:

- ▸ **RotationRateAmount**:
    - ▸ **Max**:
        - ▸ **X**: 0.5
        - ▸ **Y**: 0.5
        - ▸ **Z**: 0.5
    - ▸ **Min**:
        - ▸ **X**: 0.25
        - ▸ **Y**: 0.25
        - ▸ **Z**: 0.25

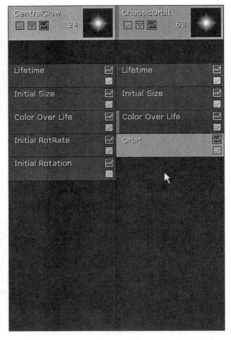

FIGURE 5.83   The new Orbit module has been added.

This gives us variation, but all the particles will be orbiting in the same general direction (although it will hardly be noticeable because they are rotating around each axis). It would be nice to have the particles orbit randomly in all directions, but using negative values for the minimum will cause some of the particles to have no rotation at all, which is more of a problem visually then having them all rotating in the same direction.

However, if you were determined to have some particles rotating in the opposite direction, you could optionally right-click next to the emitter and duplicate it. You could take the duplicate of this emitter, as well as the original, and cut their spawn rate properties by half, and then invert the RotationRateAmount property values for the second emitter. This would give you particles moving in the opposite direction. It should be noted, though, that we chose not to go this route because the effect would not be significantly noticeable.

6. Save the Chapter_05_Particles package so you don't lose your progress.

END TUTORIAL 5.8

TUTORIAL 5.9 continues from **TUTORIAL 5.8**, so be sure to complete it before proceeding. You need to have the Chapter_05_Particles package open in the Generic Browser. If you have not completed **TUTORIAL 5.8**, you may use the part_plasma_generator_05 particle system to complete this tutorial.

TUTORIAL 5.9: Plasma Generator, Part VI: Twist Orbiting Particles Shared Setup, Continued

1. We create the twist orbiting particles that corkscrew their way up from the bottom to the top. This effect actually requires two emitters to complete, but these two emitters are virtually identical except for one module. In order to make things more efficient, we utilize the sharing capability of modules. This way, we can quickly make changes to one of the emitter's modules, and those changes are propagated to the other automatically.

2. We need to create a new emitter. If the part_plasma_generator particle system is not open in Cascade, open it now by double-clicking it in the Generic Browser. Then, with the mat_flare material selected in the Generic Browser, right-click to the right of the current emitters in the empty space of the Emitter List and choose New ParticleSpriteEmitter (see **FIGURE 5.84**).

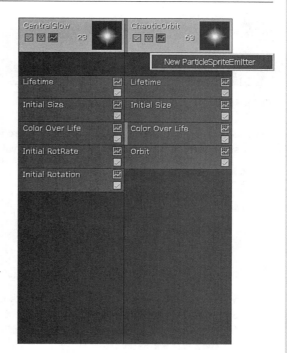

FIGURE 5.84   Add a new sprite emitter to the particle system.

3. Select the emitter module and set the EmitterName to Twist1. Expand the RequiredModule and set the following properties:

   ▶ **EmitterDuration**: 0.25

   ▶ **EmitterDelay**: 0.5

This causes the emitter to emit particles for 0.25 seconds, pause for 0.5 seconds, and then repeat the process, giving the effect of short bursts of particles.

4. Select the Lifetime module to view its properties. As in the previous emitter, a variance in the lifetimes of these particles would simply not be noticeable. Click on the right of the Lifetime distribution and then click the Create a New Object button 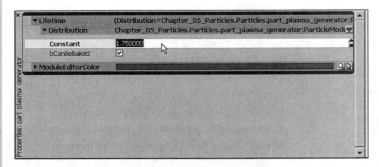. In the flyout list that appears, choose DistributionFloatConstant and set the following value (see **FIGURE 5.85**):

   ▸ **Constant**: 1.75

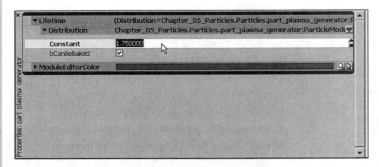

FIGURE 5.85   Add a constant set to 1.75.

5. Select the Initial Size module to view its properties. These particles need to be relatively small with some variation, so enter these values:

   ▸ **StartSize**:

▸ **Max**:	▸ **Min**:
▸ **X**: 10.0	▸ **X**: 1.0
▸ **Y**: 1.0	▸ **Y**: 1.0
▸ **Z**: 1.0	▸ **Z**: 1.0

6. Select the Initial Velocity module to view its properties. Click on the right of the StartVelocity distribution and then click the Create a New Object button 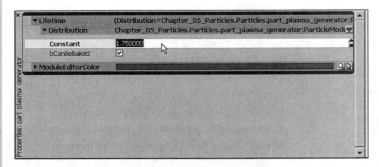. In the flyout list that appears, choose DistributionVectorConstant and set the following values (see **FIGURE 5.86**):

   ▸ **Constant**:

       ▸ **X**: 0.0

       ▸ **Y**: 0.0

       ▸ **Z**: 40.0

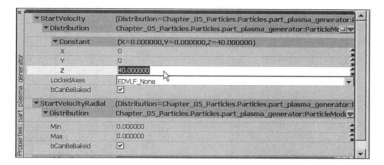

FIGURE 5.86   This gives the particles a constant upward motion.

7. As with the previous emitter, we are using the mat_flare material, which uses a VertexColor expression, so we have to set the color in the emitter itself. Again, as before, we want these particles to fade in and out to avoid any visual popping. Right-click below the Initial Size module and choose Color > Color Over Life (see **FIGURE 5.87**).

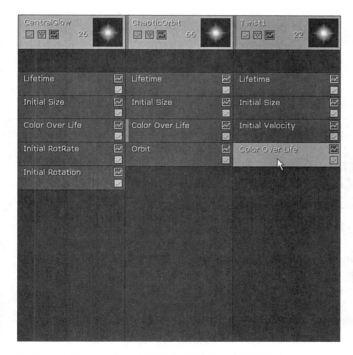

FIGURE 5.87   Add a new Color Over Life module.

8. Select the module to view its properties. Click on the right side of the Distribution for ColorOverLife and click the Create a New Object button ▼. From the flyout list that appears, choose DistributionVectorConstant. Then, set the following values:

- ▶ **Constant**

  - ▶ **X**: 4.0

  - ▶ **Y**: 2.0

  - ▶ **Z**: 1.0

9. Scroll down to the AlphaOverLife property. We want to fade in and out, so we need a curve here, but we need some more points in order to fade the alpha in and out. Click on the right of the Points array and then click the Add New Item button 🔲 twice to add two new points to the array. Now, set the following values for the points (see **FIGURE 5.88**):

- ▶ **0**:

  - ▶ **InVal**: 0.0

  - ▶ **OutVal**: 0.0

- ▶ **1**:

  - ▶ **InVal**: 0.25

  - ▶ **OutVal**: 1.0

- ▶ **2**:

  - ▶ **InVal**: 0.75

  - ▶ **OutVal**: 1.0

- ▶ **3**:

  - ▶ **InVal**: 1.0

  - ▶ **OutVal**: 0.0

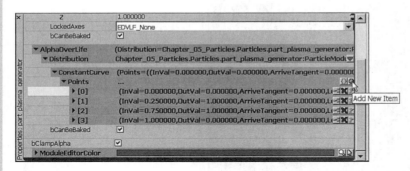

FIGURE 5.88   Create four points for the curve.

10. We need to specify a location at which these particles begin. Right-click below the Color Over Life module and choose Location > Initial Location from the context menu. Select the Initial Location module to view its properties. Click on the right of the StartLocation distribution and then click the Create a New Object button 🔽. In the flyout list that appears, choose DistributionVectorConstant. Set the following values (see **FIGURE 5.89**):

- ▶ **Constant**:

  - ▶ **X**: 0.0

  - ▶ **Y**: 0.0

  - ▶ **Z**: –35.0

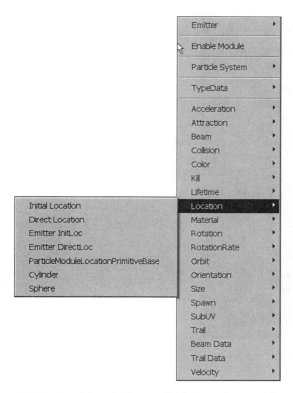

FIGURE 5.89   Add a new Initial Location module.

11. Right-click the emitter module and choose Emitter > Duplicate + Share Emitter from the context menu. This creates a new emitter with all its modules linked to the Twist 1 emitter's

> **NOTE**
>
> You can distinguish modules that are linked to other modules by the "+" after their name.

modules. Select the new emitter's emitter module and set the EmitterName to Twist2 (see **FIGURE 5.90**).

12. Save the Chapter_05_Particles package so you do not lose your work.

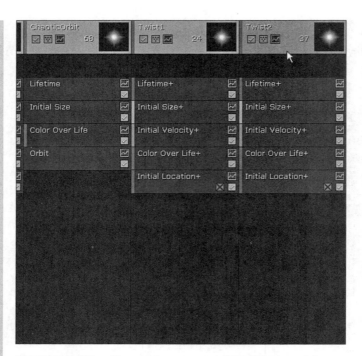

FIGURE 5.90   You now have a copy of the Twist1 module.

END TUTORIAL 5.9

TUTORIAL 5.10 continues from **TUTORIAL 5.9**, so be sure to complete it before proceeding. You need to have the Chapter_05_Particles package open in the Generic Browser. If you have not completed **TUTORIAL 5.9**, you may use the part_plasma_generator_06 particle system to complete this tutorial.

TUTORIAL 5.10: Plasma Generator, Part VII: Twist Orbiting Particles Orbit Configuration

1. Continuing from where **TUTORIAL 5.9** left off, right-click below the Initial Location module of the Twist1 emitter and choose Orbit > Orbit. Select the Orbit module to view its properties (see **FIGURE 5.91**).

2. We are going to make these particles appear to follow the surface of a sphere from one pole to the other. In order to so this, we need to control the OffsetAmount over the life of the particle, which requires a curve distribution. Click on the right side of the Distribution of OffsetAmount and click the Create a New Object button. From the flyout list that appears, select DistributionVectorConstantCurve. Because we are using a curve to control the offset over the life of the particle, we need to tell the emitter to process the offset during each update. To do this, set the following property:

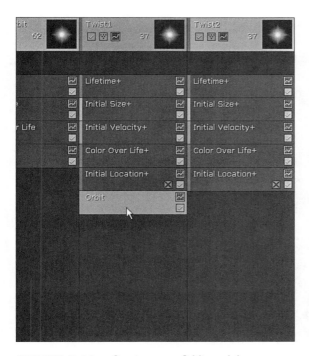

FIGURE 5.91   Create a new Orbit module.

- ▸ **OffsetOptions**:
    - ▸ **bProcessDuringupdate**: True

3. We now have a curve distribution, but the Points array is currently empty. In order to get the particles to behave as desired, we need three points. Click on the right side of the Points array and click the Add New Item button 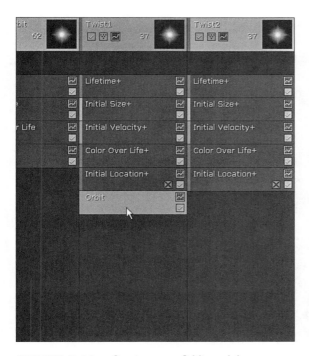 three times. Set the following values for the three points of the curve (see **FIGURE 5.92**):

- ▸ **0**:
    - ▸ **InVal**: 0.0
    - ▸ **OutVal**:
        - ▸ **X**: 0.0
        - ▸ **Y**: 0.0
        - ▸ **Z**: 0.0
- ▸ **1**:
    - ▸ **InVal**: 0.5
    - ▸ **OutVal**:

- ▸ **X**: 0.0
- ▸ **Y**: 30.0
- ▸ **Z**: 0.0
- ▸ **2**:
    - ▸ **InVal**: 1.0
    - ▸ **OutVal**:
        - ▸ **X**: 0.0
        - ▸ **Y**: 0.0
        - ▸ **Z**: 0.0

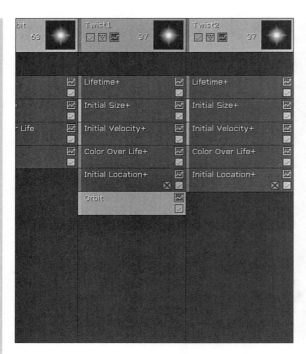

FIGURE 5.92   The curve needs a total of three points.

4. Now we have the points in the right location on the curve, but if you view the curve in the Curve Editor, you will see that the shape of the curve is not quite what we want.

5. To view the curve in the Curve Editor, click the button on the Orbit module that looks like a little wavy curve ▦. The Curve Editor should be populated with all the curves of the Orbit module. The only one we care about is the Y curve of the OffsetAmount, so the others can be disabled. Click the yellow box in the bottom-right corner of the RotationAmount and RotationRateAmount curves to turn them off. Then, click the red and blue boxes of the OffsetAmount curve to turn the X and Z curves off as well.

6. To frame up the curve in the editor, click the first two buttons in the Curve Editor's toolbar ⟷ ↕. Now, you can see that the curve we have is simply linear between each point. It should be obvious that there is no way this is going to follow the surface of a sphere. What we want is a curve that starts out fast, slows as it reaches the middle point, and speeds up again as it reaches the final point, much like a parabola facing downward for the math-inclined (see **FIGURE 5.93**). Of course, ideally what we want is the shape of the curve to be a perfect half-circle, but that is not possible so we will get as close to that shape as we can.

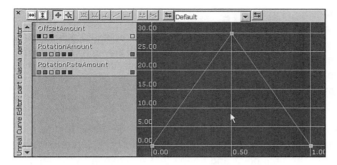

FIGURE 5.93   You can now see the curve in the Curve Editor.

7. To get this curve shape, we need to adjust the tangents of the points. This can be done in the Curve Editor directly or by adjusting the values in the Property panel. We are going to stick to the Property panel because this allows you to be much more precise. However, keep the Curve Editor open so you can view the results of the values entered.

8. We start by adjusting the first point. In the Points array, set the following values (see **FIGURE 5.94**):

   ▸ **0**:

      ▸ **LeaveTangent**:

         ▸ **X**: 0.0

         ▸ **Y**: 180.0

         ▸ **Z**: 0.0

      ▸ **InterpMode**: CIM_CurveUser

9. You should be able to see the shape of the curve update in the Curve Editor as soon as the InterpMode is changed.

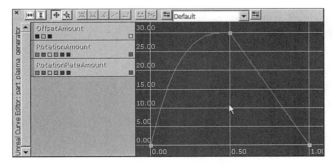

FIGURE 5.94   The curve is now shaped like so.

It might initially seem that in order to adjust the shape of the other half of the curve, the same process done to the first point would need to be done to the last point, but with an opposite tangent value. However, this would only be half correct.

In order to get a smooth curve arriving at the final point, the InterpMode of the middle point needs to be changed, rather than the InterpMode of the final point. You can confirm this by changing the InterpMode of the final point and noting that no change to the shape of the curve takes place.

10. Knowing this, set the following for the second point:

  ► **1**:

    ► **InterpMode**: CIM_CurveUser

The shape should have changed to a smooth curve between the two points (see **FIGURE 5.95**).

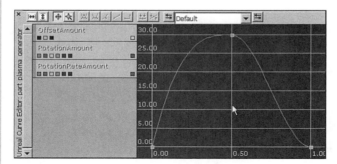

FIGURE 5.95   Notice the new shape of the curve.

11. We are ready to set the tangent values of the final point to complete the shape of the curve. Set the following:

  ► **2**:

    ► **ArriveTangent**:

      ► **X**: 0.0

      ► **Y**: –180.0

      ► **Z**: 0.0

That should do it for setting up the OffsetAmount curve.

12. Scroll down to the Rotation section in the Orbit module. The RotationAmount defaults to a uniform distribution, but we only need a constant. Click on the right side of the Distribution and then click the Create a New Object button 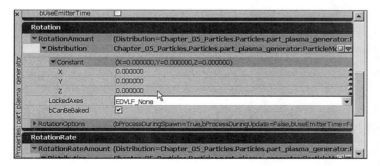. In the flyout list that appears, choose DistributionVectorConstant. The values of the distribution default to 0.0, which is just what we want in this case (see **FIGURE 5.96**).

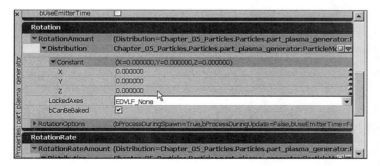

FIGURE 5.96   Leave the values at 0.0.

13. Scroll down to the RotationRate section in the Orbit module. Again, the RotationRateAmount defaults to a uniform distribution, but we only need a constant. Click on the right side of the Distribution and then click the Create a New Object button. In the flyout list that appears, choose DistributionVectorConstant. Enter the following values:

- ▶ **Constant**:
  - ▶ **X**: 0.0
  - ▶ **Y**: 0.0
  - ▶ **Z**: 0.5

14. Hold down Ctrl and then click and drag the Orbit module from the Twist1 emitter to the Twist2 emitter. This creates a copy of this emitter in the second emitter. Select the Orbit module, scroll down to the Rotation section, and enter the following values (see **FIGURE 5.97**):

- ▶ **Constant**:
  - ▶ **X**: 0.0
  - ▶ **Y**: 0.0
  - ▶ **Z**: 0.5

15. Save the Chapter_05_Particles package so you won't lose your work.

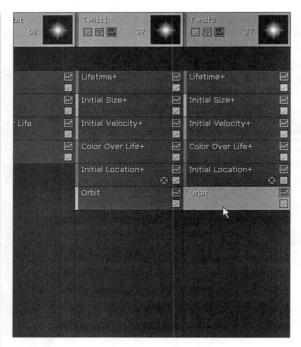

FIGURE 5.97   Copy the Orbit module to the Twist2 emitter.

END TUTORIAL 5.10

Beam Emitters

Adding a Beam TypeData module to your SpriteEmitter turns it into a beam emitter. Simply put, a beam emitter produces a single particle from a location designated as the *source*. This particle travels toward an endpoint known as the *target*. A single sprite is drawn between the source and the particle as it travels, creating the illusion of a beam. This sprite always faces the camera. In order to give the beam the appearance of volume, multiple sprites are rotated about the length of the beam. These sprites are known as "sheets" (see **FIGURE 5.98**).

> **NOTE**
>
> The sheets added to a beam increase the number of vertices in the beam. The vertex count gets higher if a great deal of noise is added to the beam. You should be aware that a single beam emitter cannot have more than 5000 vertices. Failure to heed this limitation causes the engine to crash. Therefore, be very careful when employing many sheets with lots of noise!

This would represent a single segment of the beam.

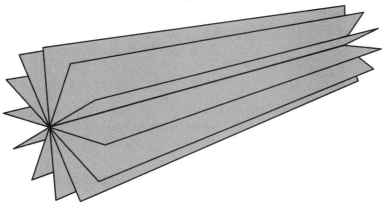

FIGURE 5.98   This diagram illustrates how sheets work on a beam.

To make the beam appear more visually interesting, noise can be added to it as it is created. When this is done, the beam actually consists of a series of segments, between which points are used to create the jagged noisy effect. A series of sprites is applied, each bridging between the intermediate points along the path where noise is applied.

In-game weapons will often make use of beam emitters to produce their visual effect. Other examples of phenomena that are good candidates for using beam emitters are lighting bolts and lasers, or any type of imaginary effect that shares the same behavioral characteristics as these phenomena.

Beam TypeData Module

This module makes an emitter act as a beam emitter by overriding and extending the basic emitter behavior, properties, and functionality. This module comes with its own set of properties that controls the basic beam emitting functionality. These properties are listed by category.

Beam

> **BeamMethod**—This property sets the method the beam emitter uses to generate the beam. It contains the following settings:
>
>> **Distance**—This causes the beams of the emitter to extend to a specified distance along the local X-axis of the emitter.
>>
>> **Target**—This setting causes the beams of the emitter to extend toward a location specified by a target module.
>>
>> **Branch**—At the time of this writing, this method has not been implemented.
>
> **TextureTile**—At the time of this writing, this property has not been implemented.

TextureTileDistance—This is the length, in Unreal units, of each tile of the texture along the length of the beam particles. At the time of this writing, this property is used to control the tiling of the texture, rather than TextureTile.

> **NOTE**
>
> Texture tiling is disabled when a Noise module is added that has its bLowFreq_Enabled property set to true. In other words, enabling noise disables texture tiling.

Sheets—This is the number of sheets to use for each beam particle. These are evenly rotated about the length of the beam to give the appearance of volume.

It should be noted that any value less than 3 causes only one sheet to be used. A value of 3 or higher will cause that many sheets to be used.

Users should also be aware that if the number for this property is set higher than 2, then the value effectively becomes a multiplier for the number of vertices in the beam. For this reason, it is important to try to achieve the desired effect in as few sheets as possible.

MaxBeamCount—This is the number of beams this emitter should have. You can think of this as the equivalent to the SpawnRate property of sprite emitters.

Users should be aware that this value is effectively a multiplier for the number of vertices in the beam. For this reason, it is important to try to achieve the desired effect in as few sheets as possible.

Speed—This sets the rate at which the endpoint of the beam particle will travel from the source to the target. If this property is set to 0.0, the beam particles will be spawned with the endpoint already at the target, resulting in an instantaneous beam.

InterpolationPoints—This is the number of points along the length of the beam to use for determining the shape of the beam. InterpolationPoints can be thought of as the detail factor for the beam. When this number is less than or equal to 0, the beam will be straight. When this value is greater than 0, the tangents of the source and target will be used and the beam is shaped accordingly using the number of points specified here.

bAlwaysOn—When set to true, this causes at least one particle beam to remain on at all times.

Taper

TaperMethod—This sets the method used to taper the beam, or change its size over the length of the beam particles. This property contains the following settings:

None—This setting causes no tapering to be performed to the beam particles of the beam emitter.

Full—This setting causes the calculation of the TaperFactor distribution to be performed over the range of the source (designated with a value of 0) to the target (designated 1) whether the beam has reached the target or not.

Partial—This setting causes the calculation of the TaperFactor distribution to be performed over the range of the source being 0 to the current location of the beam particle being 1.

TaperFactor—This is a float distribution (can be a curve) that, in conjunction with the TaperScale, represents a scaling factor for the width of the beam particles over their length.

When a curve is being used, the value of the distribution is calculated depending on the TaperMethod.

TaperScale—This is a float distribution (can be a curve) that is multiplied by the value of TaperFactor to determine the final taper amount.

When a curve is being used, the value of the distribution is calculated depending on the TaperMethod.

Rendering

At the time of this writing, the properties in the Rendering category no longer have any effect. The sections that follow describe their theoretical functions should they be implemented.

RenderGeometry—At the time of this writing, this has no effect, checked or not. The geometry is always rendered.

RenderDirectLine—If this property is true, in addition to the actual geometry, a straight yellow line from the source to the particle's current location will be drawn regardless of beam noise or tangents, with the source indicated by a green cross and the target indicated by a red cross (see **FIGURE 5.99**).

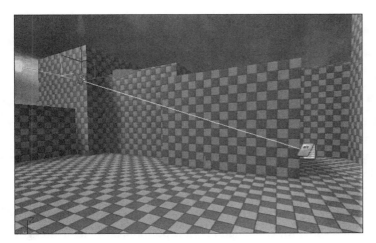

FIGURE 5.99   RenderDirectLine gives this result.

RenderLines—If this property is true, in addition to the actual geometry, one yellow line is drawn from the source (indicated by a green cross) to the target (indicated by a white cross). This line is straight if no noise is currently being applied. If noise is being applied, the line passes through each noise point, indicated by blue crosses. If noise tessellation is used as well, noise tessellation points are drawn on the line, which appear as a smooth curve because of the tessellation, and are indicated by yellow and purple crosses (see **FIGURE 5.100**).

Another line is also drawn if the beam is being interpolated, meaning that InterpolationPoints is greater than 1. This line takes into account the tangents of the source and target, and interpolation points are drawn along the curve indicated by red crosses.

RenderTessellation—At the time of this writing, this is identical to the RenderLines property.

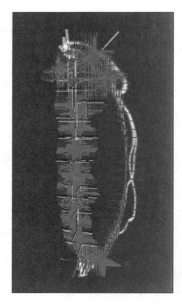

FIGURE 5.100   RenderLines show any noise applied to the beam.

Branching

BranchParentName—At the time of this writing, this does nothing because beam branching has not been implemented.

Distance

Distance—This is the length of the beam when the Distance BeamMethod is used.

Beam Emitter Modules

Although beam emitters use many of the same modules as other emitters—such as Lifetime, Color, and Size—there are also modules that perform specialized functions solely for beam emitters. These modules are listed under the "Beam" heading in the right-click menu and are colored a light purple color in Cascade.

Beam Modifier

This module alters, by adding to or scaling, any combination of the position, tangent, or strength of either the source or target of the beam emitter.

Modifier

ModifierType—This property controls whether the module modifies the source or the target of the beam emitter.

Source—This setting causes the module to modify the source of the beam emitter.

Target—This setting causes the module to modify the target of the beam emitter.

Position

PositionOptions—See the "Options" section.

Position—This is a vector distribution (can be a curve) specifying the amount to add to or multiply by the source or target location in each axis.

When a curve is being used, this is calculated by finding the value of the distribution for the current EmitterTime.

Tangent

TangentOptions—See the "Options" section.

Tangent—This is a vector distribution (can be a curve) specifying the amount to add to or multiply by the source or target tangent direction in each axis.

When a curve is being used, this is calculated by finding the value of the distribution for the current EmitterTime.

Strength

StrengthOptions—See the "Options" section.

Strength—This is a float distribution (can be a curve) specifying the amount to add to or multiply by the source or target strength.

When a curve is being used, this is calculated by finding the value of the distribution for the current EmitterTime.

Options

bModify—If this property is true, this section of the module affects the beam emitter.

If this property is false, this section of the module is ignored.

bScale—If this property is true, the value of this section's distribution is multiplied by the beam emitter's value.

If this property is false, the value of this section's distribution is added to the beam emitter's value.

bLock—If this property is true, this value is locked for the life of the particle, meaning the value assigned when the particle is spawned will be its value throughout its lifetime.

If this property is false, this value is updated throughout the particle's lifetime.

Noise

This module adds noise along the length of the beam particles of the beam emitter. Previous noise modules within the emitter's module stack is overridden (see **FIGURE 5.101**).

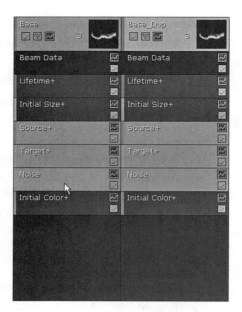

FIGURE 5.101   The Noise module is responsible for making your beam appear jagged.

bLowFreq_Enabled—If this property is true, noise from this module is applied to the beam emitter.

If this property is false, no noise from this module is applied.

bNRScaleEmitterTime—If this property is true, the value of NoiseRangeScale is determined according to the current EmitterTime.

If this property is false, the value of NoiseRangeScale is determined according to the RelativeLife of the beam particle. However, it should be noted that at the time of this writing, the use of RelativeLife to determine NoiseRangeScale is not yet implemented. This means that this property should always be set to true.

bSmooth—If this property is true, the points along the beam to which the noise is applied smoothly interpolate to their next locations. This causes the beam to animate smoothly rather than "flicker."

If this property is false, the points along the beam to which the noise is applied snap to their next locations.

bOscillate—If this property is true, and using a uniform distribution for NoiseRange and bUseExtremes is true for that distribution, the value of the distribution alternates between the Min and Max of the distribution instead of randomly switching between the two.

If this property is false, the NoiseRange distribution acts as a normal distribution in all cases.

bUseNoiseTangents—At the time of this writing, this property is not implemented.

bTangentNoise—If this property is true, the noise from this module is applied to the endpoint, or target, which will cause the target to deviate from its specified location.

If this property is false, the noise from this module is only applied to the noise points between the source and target.

bApplyNoiseScale—If this property is true, the NoiseScale is used to scale the noise applied to the beam particles.

If this property is false, the NoiseRange is used with no modification from the NoiseScale.

Frequency—This is the maximum amount of noise points that can be used for applying the noise of this module. Note that this also increases vertex count (see **FIGURE 5.102**).

Frequency_LowRange—If not 0, this is a lower bound (used in conjunction with Frequency as the upper bound) for selecting a random amount of noise points to use as the maximum amount of noise points to use for this module.

NoiseRange—This is a vector distribution (can be a curve) specifying the distance to offset the noise points when applying the noise of this module.

When a curve is being used, this is calculated by finding the value of the distribution for the ratio of the index of the current noise point (zero-based counting from the source to the target) to the maximum number of noise points allowed as specified by the Frequency property.

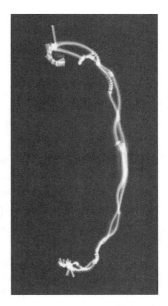

FIGURE 5.102   Higher frequency values will increase the amount of noise in the beam.

NoiseRangeScale—This is a float distribution (can be a curve) specifying a value to multiply by the value of NoiseRange, effectively scaling it. This allows the amount of noise applied to a beam particle to easily be altered over time.

When a curve is being used, this is calculated by finding the value of the distribution for either the current EmitterTime or RelativeLife of the beam particle, depending on the bNRScaleEmitterTime property. However, it should be noted that at the time of this writing, the use of RelativeLife to determine NoiseRangeScale is not yet implemented.

NoiseSpeed—This is a vector distribution (can be a curve) specifying the speed in each axis with which each noise point moves to its next location. This should only have an effect when bSmooth is true because the points snap from location to location when it is false.

When a curve is being used, this is calculated by finding the value of the distribution for the current EmitterTime.

NoiseLockRadius—This is the maximum distance from the current location of the noise point from its next location, where it will be snapped to that location. This only has an effect when bSmooth is true because the points automatically snap when it is false.

NoiseLockTime—This value controls the locking of noise points to their locations.

If it's equal to 0.0, the noise points of this beam particle are not locked to their locations at all.

If it's less than 0.0, the noise points are locked to their location for the life of the beam particle.

If it's greater than 0.0, the noise points are locked to their locations for this amount of time, up to the life of the particle.

NoiseTension—This value controls the direction of the tangents at each noise point and, thus, the apparent tension of the beam particle.

This property should be set between 0.0 and 1.0. Values outside that range can have undesirable results.

NoiseTangentStrength—This value controls the strength of, or how hard the beam tries to follow, the tangent entering and leaving each noise point.

NoiseTessellation—This value represents how many segments the beam particle has between each noise point, providing the ability to have smooth, curvy beams (see **FIGURE 5.103**).

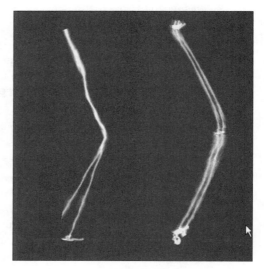

FIGURE 5.103   Increasing the tessellation can help smooth the curve.

More tessellations equals more vertices rendered, so only use as many as are needed to get the desired result. Always keep the 5,000 vertex limit in mind!

FrequencyDistance—This is the distance between each noise point along the beam. The maximum number of noise points the beam particle will have is calculated by taking the smaller value between the Frequency and the result of dividing the beam's length by this number.

NoiseScale—This is a float distribution (can be a curve) specifying the amount to scale the value of the NoiseRange when applying noise to the beam particles.

When a curve or uniform distribution is being used, this is calculated by finding the value of the distribution for the ratio of actual noise points present, taking the FrequencyDistance into account, to the maximum number allowed as specified by the Frequency property.

In essence, this property allows you to adjust the strength of the noise based on how many noise points are being used. This could be useful when dealing with LODs. There could be far fewer noise points used at greater distances, but with more noise to still have the noise visible at those distances.

Source

This module sets the point of origin and tangent from that point for the beam particles of a beam emitter. Previous source modules within the emitter's module stack will be overridden (see **FIGURE 5.104**).

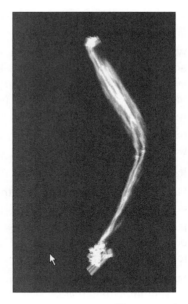

FIGURE 5.104   The source is the point where the beam starts.

SourceMethod—This sets the method used to determine the source of the beam particles for the beam emitter. This property contains the following settings:

Default—This, as its name suggests, is the default method. It is used as a fallback when other methods fail for some reason, such as when the emitter or actor pointed to by the SourceName property does not exist. With this method, the Source property determines the origin for the beam particles of the beam emitter.

UserSet—This method uses an array of points (which are specified in code) as the origin for the beam particles of the beam emitter.

Emitter—This method uses the emitter's location as the origin for the beam particles of the beam emitter.

Particle—This method uses the particles of another emitter within the same particle system as the origin for the beam particles of the beam emitter.

Actor—This method uses an Actor in the game as the origin for the beam particles of the beam emitter.

SourceTangentMethod—This sets the method used to determine the tangent of the beam particles leaving from the origin. This property contains the following settings:

Direct—This method uses a straight line from the source to the target as the tangent.

UserSet—This method uses an array of tangents (which are specified in code) as the tangent.

Distribution—This method uses the value of the SourceTangent property as the tangent.

Emitter—This method uses the direction the emitter is facing along its local X-axis as the tangent.

SourceName—When the Particle source method is used, this is the name of the Emitter to use as the source.

When the Actor source method is used, this is the name of a parameter used to reference the Actor in the world to use as the source for the beams. A name is placed here, such as BeamSource. Then, in the emitter actor's InstancedParameters array, a parameter is created with a matching name, and the Actor to use as the source is assigned to the parameter in there.

bSourceAbsolute—If this property is true, the value of Source is considered to be in world space coordinates.

If this property is false, the value of Source is considered to be relative to the emitter.

bLockSource—If this property is true, each beam particle has the same source for its entire life.

If this property is false, the source for an individual beam particle is allowed to change during its lifetime, which could be the desired result if the Source property uses a uniform or curve distribution.

bLockSourceTangent—If this property is true, each beam particle has the same source tangent for its entire life.

If this property is false, the source tangent for an individual beam particle is allowed to change during its lifetime, which could be the desired result if the SourceTangent property uses a uniform or curve distribution.

bLockSourceStrength—If this property is true, each beam particle has the same source strength for its entire life.

If this property is false, the source strength for an individual beam particle is allowed to change during its lifetime, which could be the desired result if the SourceStrength property uses a uniform or curve distribution.

Source—This is a vector distribution (can be a curve) specifying the location of the origin of the beam particles for this emitter.

When a curve is being used, this is calculated by finding the value of the distribution for the current EmitterTime.

SourceTangent—This is a vector distribution (can be a curve) specifying the tangent, or direction, of the beam particles as they leave the source.

When a curve is being used, this is calculated by finding the value of the distribution for the RelativeLife of the beam particle.

SourceStrength—This is a vector distribution (can be a curve) specifying the strength of, or how hard the beam tries to follow, the tangent leaving the source.

When a curve is being used, this is calculated by finding the value of the distribution for the RelativeLife of the beam particle.

Target

This module sets the endpoint and tangent leading into that point for the beam particles of a beam emitter. Previous target modules within the emitter's module stack will be overridden (see **FIGURE 5.105**).

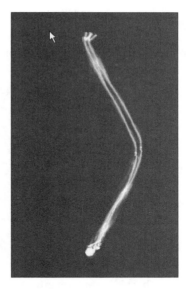

FIGURE 5.105   The target is the point where the beam ends.

TargetMethod—This sets the method used to determine the target of the beam particles for the beam emitter. This property contains the following settings:

Default—This, as its name suggests, is the default method. It is used as a fallback when other methods fail for some reason, such as when the emitter or actor pointed to by the TargetName property does not exist. With this method, the Target property determines the endpoint for the beam particles of the beam emitter.

UserSet—This method uses an array of points (which are specified in code) as the endpoint for the beam particles of the beam emitter.

Emitter—This method uses the emitter's location as the endpoint for the beam particles of the beam emitter.

Particle—This method uses the particles of another emitter within the same particle system as the endpoint for the beam particles of the beam emitter.

Actor—This method uses an Actor in the game as the endpoint for the beam particles of the beam emitter.

TargetTangentMethod—This sets the method used to determine the tangent of the beam particles leaving from the origin. This property contains the following settings:

Direct—This method uses a straight line from the source to the target as the tangent.

UserSet—This method uses an array of tangents (which are specified in code) as the tangent.

Distribution—This method uses the value of the TargetTangent property as the tangent.

Emitter—This method uses the direction the emitter is facing as the tangent.

TargetName—When the Particle target method is used, this is the name of the Emitter whose particles are used as the target.

When the Actor target method is used, a name is placed here, such as BeamTarget. Then, in the emitter actor's InstancedParameters array, a parameter is created with a matching name, and the actor to use as the target is assigned to the parameter in there.

bTargetAbsolute—If this property is true, the value of Target is considered to be in world space coordinates.

If this property is false, the value of Target is considered to be relative to the emitter.

bLockTarget—If this property is true, each beam particle has the same target for its entire life.

If this property is false, the target for an individual beam particle is allowed to change during its lifetime, which could be the desired result if the Target property uses a uniform or curve distribution.

bLockTargetTangent—If this property is true, each beam particle has the same target tangent for its entire life.

If this property is false, the target tangent for an individual beam particle is allowed to change during its lifetime, which could be the desired result if the TargetTangent property uses a uniform or curve distribution.

bLockTargetStrength—If this property is true, each beam particle has the same target strength for its entire life.

If this property is false, the target strength for an individual beam particle is allowed to change during its lifetime, which could be the desired result if the TargetStrength property uses a uniform or curve distribution.

Target—This is a vector distribution (can be a curve) specifying the location of the endpoint of the beam particles for this emitter.

When a curve is being used, this is calculated by finding the value of the distribution for the current EmitterTime.

TargetTangent—This is a vector distribution (can be a curve) specifying the tangent, or direction, of the beam particles as they approach the target.

When a curve is being used, this is calculated by finding the value of the distribution for the RelativeLife of the beam particle.

TargetStrength—This is a vector distribution (can be a curve) specifying the strength of, or how hard the beam tries to follow, the tangent leaving the target.

When a curve is being used, this is calculated by finding the value of the distribution for the RelativeLife of the beam particle.

LockRadius—This is the maximum distance from the current endpoint of the beam particle to the target location where the endpoint will be snapped to the target location when using target locking. This is only used if the Speed of the Beam TypeData module is *not* set to 0.0.

TUTORIAL 5.11 continues from **TUTORIAL 5.10**. If you have not completed **TUTORIAL 5.10**, you may use the part_plasma_generator_07 particle system for this tutorial. You need to have the Chapter_05_Particles package open in the Generic Browser.

TUTORIAL 5.11: Plasma Generator, Part VIII: Plasma Beams

1. We are going to create the actual plasma. This effect is the same as those clear glass spheres that have bolts of electricity shooting from the center to the surface of the sphere. To achieve this effect, we will use a beam emitter. If it is not already, open the part_pasma_generator particle system in Cascade by double-clicking it in the Generic Browser (see **FIGURE 5.106**).

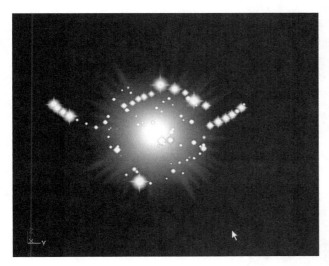

FIGURE 5.106   Currently, your effect looks like this.

2. Select the mat_electricity material in the Generic Browser. Then, right-click in the empty space of the Emitter List just to the right of the Twist2 emitter and choose New ParticleSpriteEmitter from the context menu.

3. Select the emitter module of the new emitter and set the EmitterName to **PlasmaBeams** (see **FIGURE 5.107**).

4. Right-click the empty space below the emitter module and choose TypeData > New Beam Data. Select the Beam TypeData module to view its properties. Set the following values (see **FIGURE 5.108**):

    ▶ **MaxBeamCount**: 20

    ▶ **Speed**: 50.0

5

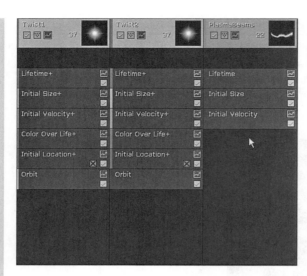

FIGURE 5.107   Create a new emitter named PlasmaBeams.

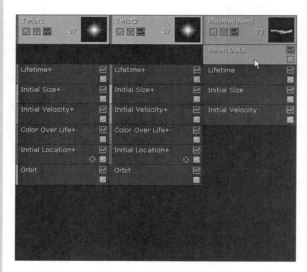

FIGURE 5.108   By adding the Beam TypeData module, you have created a beam emitter.

5. These particles' lifetimes should have some variation to keep the beams from spawning at predictable intervals. Select the Lifetime module to view its properties and set these values:

   ▶ **Lifetime**:

      ▶ **Min**: 2.0

      ▶ **Max**: 3.0

6. Select the Initial Size module to view its properties. The uniform distribution here helps give the beams a random appearance. Set the following values:

   ▸ **StartSize**:
      ▸ **Max**:
         ▸ **X**: 6.0
         ▸ **Y**: 1.0
         ▸ **Z**: 1.0
      ▸ **Min**:
         ▸ **X**: 1.0
         ▸ **Y**: 1.0
         ▸ **Z**: 1.0

7. Again, we have no need for velocity with this emitter, so right-click the Initial Velocity module and choose Delete (see **FIGURE 5.109**).

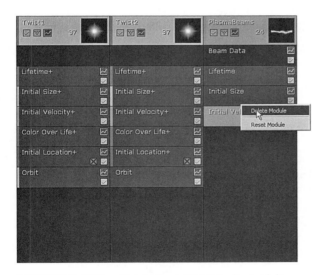

FIGURE 5.109   Delete the Initial Velocity module.

8. The mat_electricity material uses a VertexColor expression, meaning that we need to set the color in the emitter. Once again, we are going to fade the particles in and out, so we need a module that can alter the color over the life of the particle. Right-click below the Initial Size module and choose Color > Color Over Life from the context menu (see **FIGURE 5.110**).

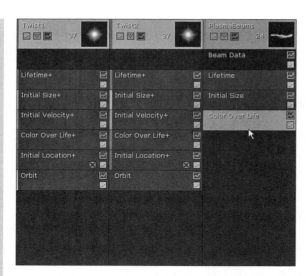

FIGURE 5.110   Apply a new Color Over Life module to the emitter.

9. Click on the right side of the Distribution for ColorOverLife and click the Create a New Object button . From the flyout list that appears, choose DistributionVectorConstant. Then, set the following values:

  ▶ **Constant**

    ▶ **X**: 1.0

    ▶ **Y**: 1.0

    ▶ **Z**: 4.0

10. Scroll down to the AlphaOverLife property. We want to fade in and out, meaning that we will need a curve. However, we need some more points in order to fade the Alpha in and then fade it back out. Click on the right of the Points array and then click the Add New Item button twice to add two new points to the array. Now, set the following values for the points (see **FIGURE 5.111**):

  ▶ **0**:

    ▶ **InVal**: 0.0

    ▶ **OutVal**: 0.0

  ▶ **1**:

    ▶ **InVal**: 0.25

    ▶ **OutVal**: 1.0

  ▶ **2**:

    ▶ **InVal**: 0.75

    ▶ **OutVal**: 1.0

  ▶ **3**:

    ▶ **InVal**: 1.0

    ▶ **OutVal**: 0.0

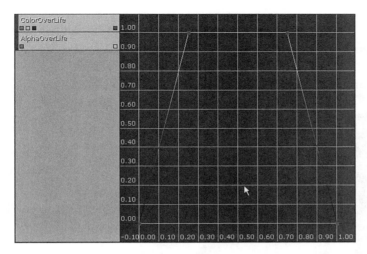

FIGURE 5.111   The points create a curve that appears like so.

11. The beam particles need a source to designate the location from which to spawn. Right-click below the Color Over Life module and choose Beam > Source from the context menu. Select the new module to view its properties and set the following:

   ▸ **Source**:
      ▸ **Constant**:
         ▸ **X**: 0.0
         ▸ **Y**: 0.0
         ▸ **Z**: 0.0

12. The beams also need a target to tell them where to end. Right-click below the Source module and choose Beam > Target. Select the new module to view its properties.

13. We want to set a range so the beams go to random locations, but the default is a constant distribution. Click on the right side of the Distribution for Target and then click the Create a New Object button 🔽. From the flyout list that appears, choose DistributionVectorUniform and then set the following:

   ▸ **Target**:
      ▸ **Max**:
         ▸ **X**: 27.5
         ▸ **Y**: 27.5
         ▸ **Z**: 27.5
      ▸ **Min**:
         ▸ **X**: –27.5
         ▸ **Y**: –27.5
         ▸ **Z**: –27.5
      ▸ **bLockTarget**: True (Checked)

14. Save the Chapter_05_Particles package so you don't lose your work.

END TUTORIAL 5.11

Mesh Emitters

When you add a Mesh TypeData module to an emitter, it becomes a mesh emitter. This type of emitter behaves almost identically to a standard sprite emitter, except that instead of each particle being a single sprite, each particle is a static mesh (see **FIGURE 5.112**).

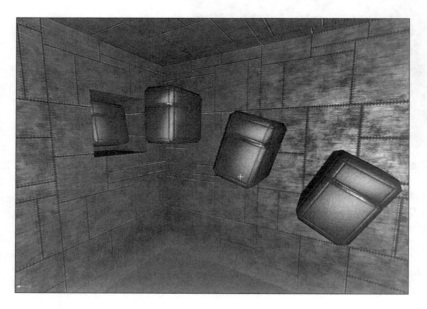

FIGURE 5.112   These static meshes are being "dumped" into the scene with a mesh emitter.

Good candidates for the use of mesh emitters would be effects such as muzzle flash for weapons, where a mesh could be used to create the exact shape of the flare and then combined with other particle effects. Other candidates would be globule particles or debris from an explosion.

It should be noted that some of the emitter's properties have different effects on mesh emitters than they do on sprite emitters. These properties and their effects are outlined here:

> **Material**—This is the material to apply to the mesh particles of this emitter, depending on the Mesh TypeData module's bOverrideMaterial property.
>
> **ScreenAlignment**—This determines how the particles of this emitter are aligned with respect to the camera. This property contains the following settings:
>
>> **PSA_Square**—This setting has no apparent effect.
>>
>> **PSA_Rectangle**—This setting has no apparent effect.
>>
>> **PSA_Velocity**—The X-axis of the mesh will be aligned with its velocity.
>>
>> **PSA_TypeSpecific**—This setting allows the Mesh TypeData module to control the alignment of the particles for this emitter.

Mesh TypeData Module

This module is what turns a standard emitter into a mesh emitter by overriding and extending the basic emitter behavior, properties, and functionality. This module comes with its own set of properties that control the basic mesh emission functionality.

Mesh—This is a reference to the static mesh to use for the particles of this emitter.

CastShadows—If this property is true, the meshes emitted from this emitter will cast shadows. Note that at the time of this writing, this property is nonfunctional.

If this property is false, the meshes emitted from this emitter will not cast shadows.

Because particles are dynamic in nature, casting shadows for them is a very processing intensive action. This option should be used with great care.

DoCollisions—At the time of this writing, this property is nonfunctional. It is likely that its functionality was replaced with the Collision module.

bOverrideMaterial—If this property is true, the material applied to the emitter will override the first material of the static mesh. This should only be used with meshes that use a single material. For meshes with more than one material, use the Mesh Material module instead.

MeshAlignment—This determines the alignment of the mesh particles emitted from this emitter when the base emitter's ScreenAlignment is set to PSA_TypeSpecific. This property contains the following settings:

MeshFaceCameraWithRoll—This setting forces the mesh's local X-axis to face the camera and allows the mesh to rotate only about that axis.

The rotation appears to only work when used with the standard rotation or rotation rate modules and not with the mesh rotation and rotation rate modules.

> **NOTE**
>
> Mesh emitters use many of the standard modules because they are so very similar to sprite emitters. These modules appear just like any other module, unlike Beam and Trail modules, which have their own special color to designate them.

MeshFaceCameraWithSpin—This forces the mesh's local X-axis to face the camera and allows the mesh to rotate about the mesh's local Y-axis.

The rotation appears to only work when used with the standard rotation or rotation rate modules and not with the mesh rotation and rotation rate modules.

MeshFaceCameraWithLockedAxis—This setting forces the mesh's local Z-axis to face up and then rotate about that axis to keep the local X-axis facing the camera. At the time of this writing, this setting can yield unpredictable results.

Mesh Material Module

Unlike sprite emitters, the meshes that come from a mesh emitter require actual materials rather than just a texture. With this module, the material can be overridden.

Mesh Material

This module contains an array of materials that is used to override the default materials of the static mesh used by the mesh emitter.

> **MeshMaterials**—This is the array of materials that directly corresponds to the materials of the static mesh of the mesh emitter.

Mesh Rotation Modules

Whereas sprites face the camera by default and therefore can typically only rotate around a single axis, mesh particles can rotate around all three axes. With the mesh rotation modules, this rotation can be defined at birth and controlled throughout the life of the particle.

Init Mesh Rotation

This module sets the rotation at the time of spawning of the particles of an emitter that has a Mesh TypeData module applied to it (see **FIGURE 5.113**).

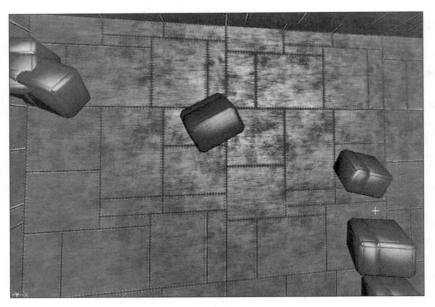

FIGURE 5.113   Note that each of these meshes has a different rotation.

> **StartRotation**—This is a vector distribution (can be a curve) specifying the rotation in each axis. A value of 0.0 is equal to 0 degrees, and a value of 1.0 is equal to 360 degrees.

When a curve is being used, this is calculated by finding the value of the distribution for the current EmitterTime when the particle is spawned.

bInherentParent—When this property is true, the rotation will be considered to be in the local space of the emitter.

When this property is false, the rotation will be considered to be in world space.

Mesh Rotation Rate Modules

When you need a mesh to spin in some way, it's time to employ mesh rotation rate modules. These modules allow you to set the rate of rotation at the time of birth or to change it over the life of the particle.

Init Mesh RotRate

This module sets the rate in rotations per second at which the particles of an emitter with a Mesh TypeData module continually rotate.

StartRotationRate—This is a vector distribution (can be a curve) that specifies the rate at which a mesh particle will rotate about all its axes.

When a curve is being used, this is calculated by finding the value of the distribution for the current EmitterTime when the particle is spawned.

TUTORIAL 5.12 continues from **TUTORIAL 5.11**. If you have not completed **TUTORIAL 5.11** yet, you may use the part_plasma_generator_08 particle system to complete this tutorial. You need to have the Chapter_05_Particles package open in the Generic Browser.

The center of the plasma generator effect consists of a glob of liquid metal that is created using a mesh emitter.

TUTORIAL 5.12: Plasma Generator, Part IX: Morphing Molten Metal Glob

1. If it isn't already, open the part_plasma_generator particle system in Cascade by double-clicking it in the Generic Browser. With the mat_center_ball material selected in the Generic Browser, right-click to the right of the PlasmaBeams emitter and choose New ParticleSpriteEmitter (see **FIGURE 5.114**).

2. Select the emitter module and set the EmitterName to **MoltenGlob**. Expand the RequiredModule and set the following:

   ▶ **SpawnRate**:

     ▶ **Constant**: 4.0

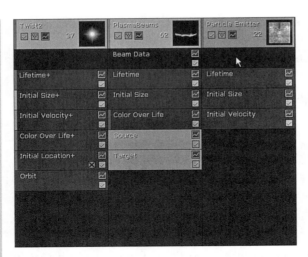

FIGURE 5.114   Create a new emitter for the Plasma Generator.

3. To make this emitter a mesh emitter, we need to add a Mesh TypeData module. Right-click in the empty space just below the emitter module and choose TypeData > New Mesh Data. Select the Mesh TypeData module and set the following (see **FIGURE 5.115**):

   ▶ **Mesh**: WP_Redeemer.Mesh.S_FX_DeemerSphere (as the name suggests, this mesh is located in the WP_Redeemer package)

   ▶ **bOverrideMaterial**: True

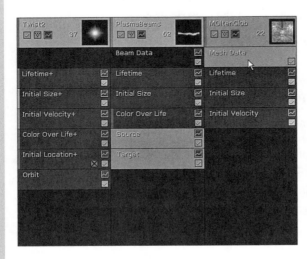

FIGURE 5.115   Add a Mesh TypeData to create a mesh emitter.

4. Select the Lifetime module to view its properties. Set the following values:

   ▶ **Lifetime**:

      ▶ **Min**: 2.0

      ▶ **Max**: 3.0

5. Select the Initial Size module to view its properties in the Properties panel. You may have noticed that there doesn't seem to be any mesh particles in the preview. The mesh we are using is quite large, so it needs to be scaled down a great deal. First, though, we don't need a uniform distribution, which is the default. Click on the right side of the Distribution and then click the Create a New Object button . From the flyout list that appears, choose DistributionVectorConstant. Then, enter the following values:

   ▶ **StartSize**:

      ▶ **Constant**:

         ▶ **X**: 0.0875

         ▶ **Y**: 0.1

         ▶ **Z**: 0.0875

6. This is another case where velocity is not needed. Right-click the Initial Velocity module and choose Delete (see **FIGURE 5.116**).

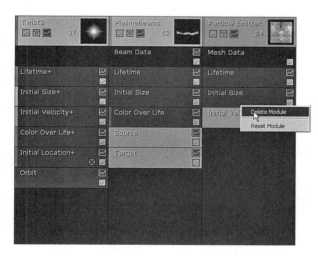

FIGURE 5.116   Delete the Initial Velocity module.

7. To avoid any visual popping, we are going to scale the size of the meshes up and down at the beginning and end of their lives. To do this, right-click below the Initial Size module and choose Size > Size Scale (see **FIGURE 5.117**).

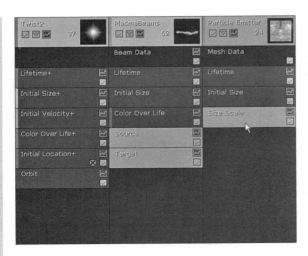

FIGURE 5.117   Add a Size Scale module.

8. This gives us a constant distribution by default, which won't allow us to alter the scale over time. Click on the right side of the Distribution and then click the Create a New Object button ⬇. From the flyout list that appears, choose DistributionVectorConstantCurve.

9. We are going to use four points in much the same way as we handled fading Alphas previously. Click on the right side of the Points array and click the Add New Item button 🖥 four times to add four points to the array. Now, set the following values for the points (see **FIGURE 5.118**):

- **0**:
  - **InVal**: 0.0
  - **OutVal**:
    - **X**: 0.0
    - **Y**: 0.0
    - **Z**: 0.0
- **1**:
  - **InVal**: 0.33
  - **OutVal**:
    - **X**: 1.0
    - **Y**: 1.0
    - **Z**: 1.0

- **2**:
  - **InVal**: 0.67
  - **OutVal**:
    - **X**: 1.0
    - **Y**: 1.0
    - **Z**: 1.0
- **3**:
  - **InVal**: 1.0
  - **OutVal**:
    - **X**: 0.0
    - **Y**: 0.0
    - **Z**: 0.0

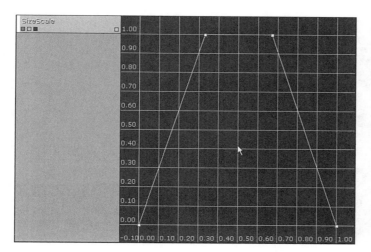

FIGURE 5.118   Your new curve appears like so if viewed in the Curve Editor.

10. To get the molten, blobby look, we need to add some rotation to the particles. Because this is a mesh emitter, we should use the mesh-specific rotation rate module. Right-click below the Size Scale module and choose RotationRate > Init Mesh RotRate from the context menu.

11. This will default to a uniform distribution, but we only need a constant distribution. Click on the right side of the Distribution and then click the Create a New Object button ▼. From the flyout list that appears, choose DistributionVectorConstant. Then, set the following values:

> ▶ **StartRotationRate**:
>
> > ▶ **Constant**:
> >
> > > ▶ **X**: 0.5
> > >
> > > ▶ **Y**: 0.5
> > >
> > > ▶ **Z**: 0.5

12. Like we did before, we are going to use a rotation module to give a little more randomness to the particles' rotations. Right-click below the Init Mesh RotRate and choose Rotation > Init Mesh Rotation. This defaults to a uniform distribution, which is just what we want. Set the following values (see **FIGURE 5.119**):

> ▶ **StartRotation**:
>
> > ▶ **Max**:   ▶ **Min**:
> >
> > > ▶ **X**: 1.0   ▶ **X**: 0.0
> > >
> > > ▶ **Y**: 1.0   ▶ **Y**: 0.0
> > >
> > > ▶ **Z**: 1.0   ▶ **Z**: 0.0

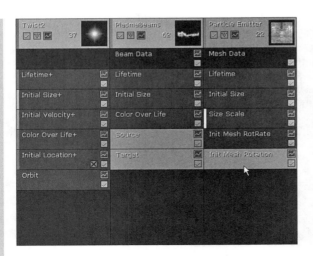

FIGURE 5.119 Add a new Init Mesh Rotation module.

13. Save the Chapter_05_Particles package so you don't lose your work.

END TUTORIAL 5.12

Trail Emitters

By adding a Trail TypeData module to an emitter, you change it into what is known as a *trail emitter*. A trail emitter does essentially what its name says: It leaves a trail. This is done by emitting a series of particles as the emitter moves. Between these particles, sprites are drawn and are connected end to end to form the trail. Projectiles and flying vehicles often use trail emitters to create the effect of flying at high speed through the air.

It should be noted that at the time of this writing, only one trail can be emitted from a trail emitter at a time (see **FIGURE 5.120**).

Trail TypeData Module

This is the module responsible for making a standard emitter into a trail emitter by overriding and extending the basic emitter behavior, properties, and functionality. The module comes with its own set of properties that control the basic trail-emitting functionality.

> **TessellationFactor**—This is the number of intermediate points between each particle used to give the trail more detail, resulting in a smoother appearance.

FIGURE 5.120   Trail emitters leave a streak of sprite particles behind them.

TessellationStrength—This is the tangent strength used to interpolate between the interpolation points. The tangent direction is the direction the source was traveling when the particle was spawned.

TextureTile—At the time of this writing, this property is nonfunctional.

MaxTrailCount—This is the maximum number of trails this emitter can have.

At the time of this writing, this is locked to 1 because having multiple trails per emitter is not yet implemented.

MaxParticleInTrailCount—This is the maximum number of particles that will be emitted as part of the trail.

If this number of particles is emitted and alive at the same time, no more particles will be emitted until some particles die. In this situation, a sprite will be drawn between the last particle emitted and the source, which can be visually displeasing. Therefore, it is important to balance the lifetimes, spawning rate, and max number of particles to make sure there are always enough particles to keep enough detail in the trail.

RenderGeometry—At the time of this writing, this has no effect, checked or not.

RenderDirectLine—At the time of this writing, this has no effect, checked or not.

RenderLines—At the time of this writing, this has no effect, checked or not.

RenderTessellation—At the time of this writing, this has no effect, checked or not.

Trail Emitter Modules

Controlling the behavior of particle trails is fairly simple, and only requires the use of two modules: Source and Taper. Technically, a trail emitter works without these modules, but you will need them if you want total control over the shape of the trail itself.

Source

This module sets the source or origin for the trail particles of the trail emitter.

SourceMethod—This determines how the source is specified. It contains the following settings:

Default—This setting causes the location of the emitter to be used as the source location for the trail.

Particle—This setting causes the trail to use the location of particles from another emitter within the same particle system to be used as the source location for the trail. At the time of this writing, this method is not fully implemented.

Actor—This setting causes the location of an Actor in the world to be used as the source location for the trail.

SelectionMethod—This determines the particle used as the source location chosen when using the Particle SourceMethod. It contains the following settings:

Random—This setting causes a random particle from the other emitter to be chosen as the source.

Sequential—This setting causes the particle with the corresponding index to be chosen as the source. This should always be the particle that was spawned first out of all the active particles because only one trail is allowed.

SourceName—If the Particle SourceMethod is being used, this is the name of the other emitter within the same particle system whose particles should be used as the source for the trail.

If the Actor SourceMethod is being used, this is the name of a parameter that will be used to reference the Actor in the world to use as the source for the trail. A name is placed here, such as TrailSource. Then, in the emitter actor's InstancedParameters array, a parameter is created with a matching name, and the actor to use as the source is assigned to the parameter in there.

SourceStrength—This determines the strength of, or how hard the trail tries to stick to, the tangent leaving from the source.

bLockSourceStrength—If this property is true, the SourceStrength value assigned at the spawning of the trail and will remain constant over the life of the trail.

bInheritRotation—This causes the trail to take on the rotation of the particle used as the source when using the Particle SourceMethod. At the time of this writing, this property is nonfunctional.

SourceOffsetCount—This is the number of slots to have in the SourceOffsetDefaults. Changing this value will add slots to or delete slots from the SourceOffsetDefaults array. The array will not update automatically upon changing this value.

SourceOffsetDefaults—This is an array of vectors specifying relative locations to the actual source to use as the origin of the trail. The length of this array is determined by the SourceOffsetCount property. To see the effects of changing the SourceOffsetCount, the array must be collapsed and then expanded again. The index of the array directly corresponds to the index of the trail, so the first slot is used for the first trail, the second slot will be used for the second trail, and so on. At the time of this writing, there is no reason to have more than one slot in the array because only one trail is allowed at a time.

Spawn

This module sets rules for the spawning of the trail particles of the trail emitter.

SpawnDistanceMap—This is (and must always be) a float particle parameter distribution that specifies a mapping of the moved distance to the amount of particles to spawn for the trail.

Here are the only properties of the parameter distribution that are required to be set:

Min/MaxInput and Min/MaxOutput—Min/MaxInput represent the lower and upper bounds of the range for the distance the source has moved. No particles will be spawned until the source's cumulative movement is greater than or equal to the distance specified by MinInput.

Min/MaxOutput represent the lower and upper bounds of the range for the amount of particles to spawn. They directly correspond to the MinInput and MaxInput.

The amount of particles spawned is equal to the number of times the MaxInput distance was traveled, multiplied by the MaxOutput added to the mapped value of the leftover distance. Here it is in math equation terms:

The result of Floor(DistanceTraveled / MaxInput) * MaxOutput added to the mapped value of Floor(DistanceTraveled / MaxInput) minus MinInput.

MinSpawnVelocity—This determines the minimum speed the source must be moving in order to spawn any particles. This can be used to keep a slow-moving object from leaving a trail no matter how far it moves.

Taper

In **TUTORIAL 5.13**, we step away from the plasma generator and create some trail emitters to move around a central cylinder in our demo room.

> **NOTE**
>
> At the time of this writing, the taper module is nonfunctional. To change the size of the trail over its length, simply use a curve distribution on the Initial Size module for the emitter.

TUTORIAL 5.13: Trail Creation

1. Create a new particle system with the following information (see **FIGURE 5.121**):

   ▶ **Package**: Chapter_05_Particles

   ▶ **Group**: Emitters

   ▶ **Name**: part_trail

2. With the mat_trail material selected in the Generic Browser (this material can be found in the Chapter_05_Particles package), create a new emitter in the particle system by right-clicking and choosing New ParticleSpriteEmitter from the context menu (see **FIGURE 5.122**).

FIGURE 5.121   Create a new particle system with this information.

FIGURE 5.122   This new sprite emitter has the mat_trail material applied.

3. Add a Trail TypeData module (right-click and choose TypeData > New Trail Data from the context menu) to the emitter and set the following (see **FIGURE 5.123**):

   ▶ **MaxParticleInTrailCount**: 25

4. Select the Lifetime module. Click on the right side of the Distribution and then click the Create a New Object button ▼. From the flyout list that appears, choose DistributionFloatConstant. Then, set the value to 0.5 (see **FIGURE 5.124**).

5. Select the Initial Size module. Go to the StartSize property. Click on the right side of the Distribution and then click the Create a New Object button ▼. From the flyout list that appears, choose DistributionVectorConstant. Then, set the value of X to 15.0. The values for Y and Z are irrelevant (see **FIGURE 5.125**).

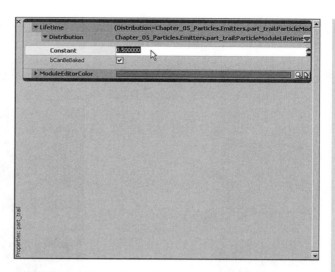

FIGURE 5.124 This setting causes all trails to have a half-second lifetime.

FIGURE 5.123 Adding the Trail TypeData makes the emitter into a trail emitter.

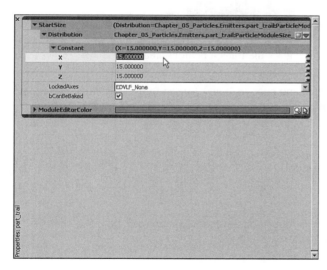

FIGURE 5.125 Make sure that the Initial Size's X value is set to 15.

6. Delete the Initial Velocity module by right-clicking it and choosing Delete Module (see **FIGURE 5.126**).

7. Add a Trail Source module (right-click and choose Trail > Source from the context menu). All the default values will work fine (see **FIGURE 5.127**).

FIGURE 5.126   The Initial Velocity module is unnecessary.

FIGURE 5.127   The Source module gives the trails a point of creation.

8. Add a Trail Spawn module (right-click and choose Trail > Spawn from the context menu). Expand the SpawnDistanceMap property and set these values (see **FIGURE 5.128**):

   ▶ **MinInput**: 10.0

   ▶ **MaxInput**: 192.0

   ▶ **MinOutput**: 1.0

   ▶ **MaxOutput**: 25.0

9. Add an Initial Color module (right-click and choose Color > Initial Color from the context menu) and set the following (see **FIGURE 5.129**):

   ▶ **StartColor**:

      ▶ **X**: 0.75

      ▶ **Y**: 0.75

      ▶ **Z**: 2.0

   ▶ **StartAlpha**: 0.5

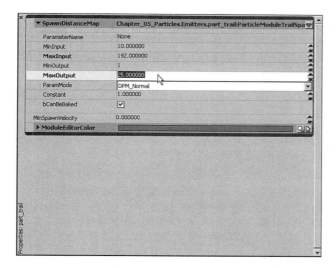

FIGURE 5.128   The Spawn module is what actually creates the trails.

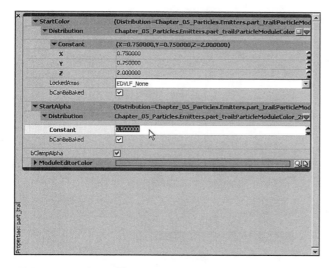

FIGURE 5.129   These settings result in a bluish trail. Feel free to experiment with your own color values later.

10. Save the package.

END TUTORIAL 5.13

We now add our trails into our level. If you have not completed **TUTORIAL 5.13**, you may use the part_trail_01 particle system in place of the part_trail particle system when instructed. Make sure that you have the DM-CH_05_Electricity_Beginmap (included on the DVD in the files for this chapter) and the Chapter_05_Particles package open.

TUTORIAL 5.14: Trail Placement

1. Select the part_trail particle system in the Generic Browser and right-click in the level on one of the spheres surrounding the center pillar near the top. Choose Add Actor > Add Emitter: part_trail from the context menu (see **FIGURE 5.130**).

2. For fun, activate Real Time feedback in the Perspective viewport and move the emitter around. You should see the trail as you move. Center the emitter on one of the spheres that surround the central column near the ceiling (adjust the Grid Snap settings accordingly). Press F4 to open its properties when you are finished (see **FIGURE 5.131**).

3. Click the Lock Selected Actors button 🔒 (located in the upper-right corner of the Properties window) and select the sphere. Expand the Attachment section of the properties and click the Use Current Selection in Browser button ◀ for the Base property. This will attach the emitter to the sphere as if they were one object.

4. When finished, click the Lock Selected Actors button 🔒 again to deactivate it (see **FIGURE 5.132**).

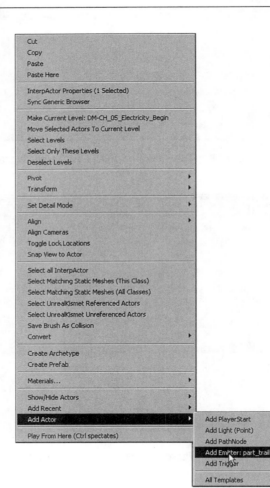

FIGURE 5.130   Add an emitter actor for the part_trail particle system.

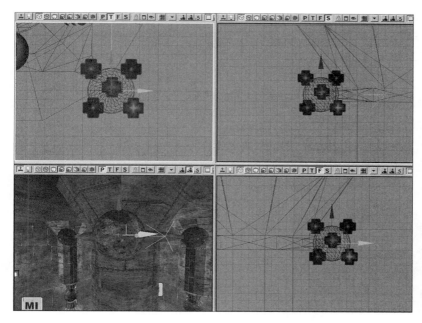

FIGURE 5.131
The emitter actor
should be at the
center of the sphere.

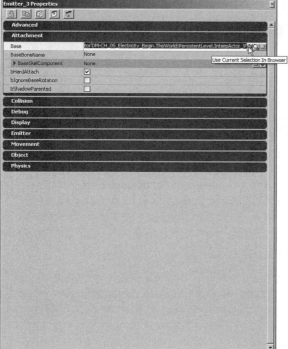

FIGURE 5.132   Attach the emitter actor
to the sphere.

5. Duplicate the first emitter and move it to the center of the next sphere around the pillar. Click the Lock Selected Actors button and select the sphere. Again, expand the Attachment section of the properties and click the Use Current Selection in Browser button for the Base property.

6. When finished, click the Lock Selected Actors button again to deactivate it (see **FIGURE 5.133**).

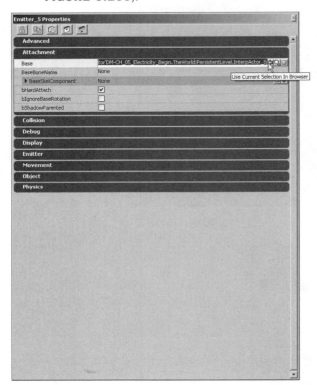

FIGURE 5.133   Duplicate the emitter and attach it to the next sphere.

7. Duplicate the second emitter and move it to the center of the next sphere around the pillar. Click the Lock Selected Actors button and select the sphere. Expand the Attachment section of the properties and click the Use Current Selection in Browser button for the Base property.

8. When finished, click the Lock Selected Actors button again to deactivate it.

9. Duplicate the third emitter and move it to the center of the next sphere around the pillar. Click the Lock Selected Actors button and select the sphere. Expand the Attachment section of the properties and click the Use Current Selection in Browser button for the Base property.

10. When finished, click the Lock Selected Actors button 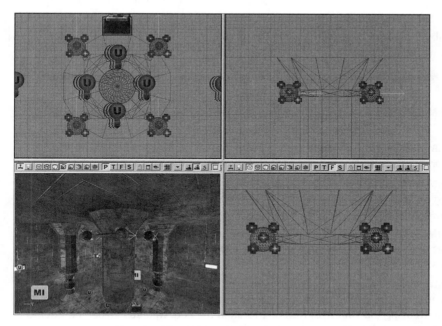 again to deactivate it (see **FIGURE 5.134**).

FIGURE 5.134   You should now have four emitters, one attached to each sphere.

11. Save your progress. You now have four trail emitters attached to the spheres at the top of the level. Feel free to test them out by trying the level.

END TUTORIAL 5.14

Fluid Emitters

When you add a Fluid or Mesh Fluid TypeData module to an emitter, it becomes a fluid emitter. This type of emitter behaves somewhat different from a standard sprite emitter, in that each particle's position, velocity, and lifetime are controlled by the PhysX physics engine's fluid solver.

Good candidates for use of fluid emitters would be effects such as debris from structures being shot at and objects crumbling. The solving capability of the PhysX engine makes it possible to have many particles all interacting with the environment dynamically to create interesting effects not possible with other emitter types.

The Fluid and Mesh Fluid TypeData modules both contain a set of the same basic properties that control how the emitter's particles behave. Some of these properties are very technical and only control optimizing the efficiency of the emitter. As such, we will be focusing on those properties that directly affect the look and behavior of the particles. In addition, the Mesh Fluid TypeData module has a subset of properties dealing with setting the mesh to be used. Descriptions of all these properties are provided here:

> **FluidRotationMethod**—This property determines how fluid particles are rotated and oriented.
>
> > **FMRM_SPHERICAL**—This method is a good candidate for round objects such as rocks or anything that can roll around on the ground.
> >
> > **FMRM_BOX**—This method is a good candidate for box-like shapes where you want the object to come to rest on any one of the sides of mesh.
> >
> > **FMRM_LONG_BOX**—This method is a good candidate for a box-like shape where you only want it to come to rest on two of its local axes (these would be the Y- and Z-axes).
> >
> > **FMRM_FLAT_BOX**—This method is a good candidate for a flat object, such as a sheet of paper, a leaf, or a feather. It only allows the particle to come to rest on its Z-axis.
>
> **FluidRotationCoefficient**—This property is used by the FluidRotationMethod property to determine the amount of rotation allowed. Values between 1 and 5 are usually suitable for emitters using the FMRM_SPHERICAL rotation method, whereas values between 0.5 and 2 are suitable for emitters using the other rotation methods.
>
> **FluidRotationCoefficient**—This property is used by the FluidRotationMethod property to determine the amount of rotation allowed. Values between 1 and 5 are usually suitable for emitters using the FMRM_SPHERICAL rotation method, whereas values between 0.5 and 2 are suitable for emitters using the other rotation methods.
>
> **Mesh**—This is a reference to the static mesh to use for the particles of this emitter.
>
> **CastShadows**—If this property is true, the meshes emitted from this emitter will cast shadows. Note that at the time of this writing, this property is nonfunctional.
>
> If this property is false, the meshes emitted from this emitter do not cast shadows.
>
> Because particles are dynamic in nature, casting shadows for them is a very processing-intensive action. This option should be used with great care.
>
> **DoCollisions**—At the time of this writing, this property is nonfunctional. It is likely that its functionality was replaced with the Collision module.
>
> **bOverrideMaterial**—If this property is true, the material applied to the emitter will override the first material of the static mesh. This should only be used with meshes that use a single material. For meshes with more than one material, use the Mesh Material module instead.
>
> **MeshAlignment**—This determines the alignment of the mesh particles emitted from this emitter when the base emitter's ScreenAlignment is set to PSA_TypeSpecific. This property contains the following settings:

MeshFaceCameraWithRoll—This setting forces the mesh's local X-axis to face the camera and allows the mesh to rotate only about that axis.

The rotation appears to only work when used with the standard rotation or rotation rate modules and not with the mesh rotation and rotation rate modules.

MeshFaceCameraWithSpin—This forces the mesh's local X-axis to face the camera and allows the mesh to rotate about the mesh's local Y-axis.

The rotation appears to only work when used with the standard rotation or rotation rate modules and not with the mesh rotation and rotation rate modules.

MeshFaceCameraWithLockedAxis—This setting forces the mesh's local Z-axis to face up and then rotate about that axis to keep the local X-axis facing the camera. At the time of this writing, this setting can yield unpredictable results.

FluidMaxParticles—This property represents the maximum number of particles that this specific TypeData module can simulate in any single frame. You need to keep in mind that this TypeData module is shared between any instances of this particle system within a level, meaning this value is split among those instances.

FluidRestParticlesPerMeter/FluidKernelRadiusMultiplier—These properties are used to calculate the radius of a fluid particle. FluidRestParticlesPerMeter actually represents the stable rest density of the fluid. The radius of a fluid particle is calculated by dividing the FluidKernelRadiusMultiplier by the FluidRestParticlesPerMeter. Here's the formula:

Radius = FluidKernelRadiusMultiplier / FluidRestParticlesPerMeter

FluidRestDensity—This property represents the target density of the fluid. This can usually be left at its default value; however, when you're using bFluidTwoWayCollision, this value is used in determining the mass of fluid particles that impacts the repulsion effect between the particles and any rigid bodies they come into contact with.

FluidMotionLimitMultiplier—This is the maximum distance a fluid particle is allowed to traverse in a single timestep.

FluidCollisionDistanceMultiplier—This property determines the distance that must be maintained between the fluid particles and any geometry they collide with during the simulation. This value must be positive.

FluidPacketSizeMultiplier—In order to make use of parallelization in the fluid simulation, the space is broken up into smaller packets. This property determines the size of those packets.

FluidStiffness—This property represents the force with which particles closer than the rest density allows for are pushed apart. Values that are too high cause the simulation to become unstable.

FluidViscosity—This value determines the thickness of the fluid, or its viscosity. Higher values for this property cause the fluid to appear more like some sort of goo.

FluidDamping—This is simply a damping factor applied to the velocity of the fluid particles that reduce the velocity of the particles in the simulation.

FluidExternalAcceleration—This property allows you to simulate wind or buoyancy by setting the acceleration.

FluidStaticCollisionRestitution—This property determines the amount of velocity retained by the fluid particles after colliding with a static surface. A value of 0 causes the particles not to bounce at all. A value of 1 causes the particles to bounce with the same velocity with which they hit the surface.

FluidStaticCollisionAdhesion—This property determines the amount of velocity retained by the fluid particles along the static surface they are colliding against. A value of 0 causes the particles not to slide along the surface at all. A value of 1 causes the particles to slide along the surface with the same velocity with which they hit the surface.

FluidStaticCollisionAttraction—This property determines the amount of attraction between the fluid particles and the static surface they collide against.

FluidDynamicCollisionRestitution—This property determines the amount of velocity retained by the fluid particles after colliding with a dynamic surface. A value of 0 causes the particles not to bounce at all. A value of 1 causes the particles to bounce with the same velocity with which they hit the surface.

FluidDynamicCollisionAdhesion—This property determines the amount of velocity retained by the fluid particles along the dynamic surface they are colliding against. A value of 0 causes the particles not to slide along the surface at all. A value of 1 causes the particles to slide along the surface with the same velocity with which they hit the surface.

FluidDynamicCollisionAttraction—This property determines the amount of attraction between the fluid particles and the dynamic surface they collide against.

FluidCollisionResponseCoefficient—This value determines the amount of impulse transferred from the fluid particles to rigid bodies when bFluidTwoWayCollision is enabled.

FluidSimulationMethod—This property determines whether particles interact with each other.

> **FMSM_NO_PARTICLE_INTERACTION**—This method means that particles will not interact with each other at all.

> **FMSM_SPH**—This method causes all particles to use Smoothed Particle Hydrodynamics when interacting with each other.

> **FMSM_MIXED_MODE**—This method causes half the particles every other frame to use Smoother Particle Hydrodynamics, but all other particles will have interaction disabled. This method can cause strange behavior at times.

FluidEmitterType—This property determines how the fluid particles are emitted.

> **FMET_CONSTANT_FLOW**—This type uses the FluidEmitterRate property to determine how many particles are emitted per second.

> **FMET_CONSTANT_PRESSURE**—This type uses the FluidRestParticlesPerMeter property to ensure that a stable rest density is attained when the particles are emitted.

FluidEmitterShape—This property defines the shape from which the particles will be emitted.

> **FMES_RECTANGLE**—This causes the particles to be emitted from a rectangular shape determined by the FluidEmitterDimensionX and FluidEmitterDimensionY properties.

> **FMES_ELLIPSE**—This causes the particles to be emitted from an elliptical shape determined by the FluidEmitterDimensionX and FluidEmitterDimensionY properties.

bFluidStaticCollision—When this property is enabled, the particles collide with the surfaces of static objects.

bFluidDynamicCollision—When this property is enabled, the particles collide with the surfaces of dynamic objects.

bFluidTwoWayCollision—When this property is enabled, the particles pass their forces on to any colliding rigid bodies that also have this property enabled.

FluidForceScale—This scales the amount of force applied to the particles of this emitter from force fields.

FluidEmitterMaxParticles—This is the maximum number of particles that can be emitted from a single instance of this emitter within a level.

FluidEmitterRandomPos—This property determines a range from which a random vector is chosen, which is then added to the position of each particle. If any of the values of this property are 0, then nothing is added to the particle's position for that axis.

FluidEmitterRandomAngle—This property specifies a range from which a random angle is chosen. This is then added to the velocity of each particle.

FluidEmitterFluidVelocityMagnitude—This is the magnitude of the velocity of the particles of this emitter when emitted.

FluidEmitterRate—This property determines the number of particles to emit each second when the FMET_CONSTANT_FLOW emitter type is selected.

FluidEmitterParticleLifetime—This is the number of seconds that each particle will live after being emitted.

FluidEmitterRepulsionCoefficient—This value determines the transfer of impulse from an emitter to any rigid bodies it is attached to.

Levels of Detail

The term *levels of detail*, typically referred to simply as *LOD*, may already be familiar to you, as it has already been used in the discussion of static meshes. It generally refers to the use of less detail for objects as the camera moves away from them. This is important because the farther away something is in-game, the smaller it is on the screen. By making it functionally simpler in some way, you can have an effect that looks very similar—if not identical—when viewed at a distance, but is created with much less processing overhead.

Particle systems use levels of detail in this way. Levels of detail can be established by the user, and set to correspond with various distances from the camera. The particle system will cycle through its various levels of detail as it gets farther from the camera. In particle systems, however, tremendous control has been provided to allow the user to change virtually any aspect of the particle effect based on the camera's distance. For example, you can change the spawn rate, particle size, speed, or even color, if that's necessary.

A practical example would be an effect such as steam rising from a grate in the floor. When the player is close to the steam, you want a lot of particles of various sizes so that the effect remains convincing. However, if viewed from a considerable distance away, those extra particles are hardly visible anyway, and are simply adding processing overhead that is not necessary. By establishing levels of detail, you can have the particle system become very simple at long range, and get more complex as the player approaches, finally reaching its full effect once the player is close to the grate (see **FIGURE 5.135**).

FIGURE 5.135   This particle system becomes much simpler as the camera moves away from it.

There are some things you should be aware of, however, when using LODs. The first is that Cascade will automatically create the lowest level of detail for your particle system based on the emitter's settings when you use the Regenerate Lowest LOD command from the Edit menu of Cascade (or its button ⌐ᴸ on the Cascade toolbar). However, doing this will wipe out any intermediate levels of detail between the lowest and the highest, so it's best to have your highest level finalized before going on to generate lower levels. By default, the lowest level of detail will be automatically created simply by taking the SpawnRate property for each emitter and dividing it by 10.

By default, you cannot edit the properties of particle system modules at lower levels of detail. When you step down into these lower levels of detail—using the slider or combo box at the top of the Cascade window—you will notice your modules become covered in a noisy texture and cannot be changed. In order to make them editable, you will need to enable them at these lower levels by right-clicking them and choosing Enable Module from the context menu. However, note that you cannot again disable a module in a lower level of detail without simply wiping out your LODs using the Regenerate Lowest LOD command.

Also be aware that just because you have enabled a module at one particular LOD, that does not mean it is automatically enabled for any other LODs. It will need to be enabled in any LODs where you wish to edit the properties of that module.

LODs do not respect module sharing (instancing), meaning that only at the highest level of detail is any sharing taking place. In any other LOD, the modules must be enabled and edited separately.

LODs can change automatically based on distance from the camera, which is the typical behavior. They can also be edited using code. However, such editing is beyond the scope of this book.

At the time of this writing, beams and trails do not respect LODs.

We are going to jump away from working with the plasma generator emitter for a moment to take a look at using LODs. The reason for this is that at the time of this writing, enabling modules in lower LODs when an Orbit module is present in the particle system causes Unreal Editor to crash. Another particle system has been provided for you to use for **TUTORIAL 5.15**. You need to have the Chapter_05_Particles package open in the Generic Browser.

TUTORIAL 5.15: Using LODs, Part I: Lowest LOD Setup

1. Double-click the part_fire particle system located in the Chapter_05_Particles package to open it in Cascade. You will see this is just a fire and smoke effect composed of three emitters. Right-click the Flame emitter's main module and choose Particle System > Select ParticleSystem. In the Properties panel of Cascade, you should see the properties for the particle system. The LODMethod is set to Automatic, so levels of detail switching will be handled by the engine, but a few changes to the other properties need to be made.

2. In the LOD section, set the following:

   ▶ **LODDistanceCheckTime**: 0.25

   ▶ **LODDistances**:

      ▶ **1**: 750.0

   This causes the engine to check the camera's distance from the particle system every 0.25 seconds and will switch to the lower level of detail when the particle system is 750 units away or more.

   Now, we need to tell the emitters how to look and act at that low level of detail.

3. The first thing we need to do is have Cascade generate the lowest level of detail based on the emitters we have created thus far. Go to the Edit menu and choose Regenerate Lowest LOD (see **FIGURE 5.136**).

4. Once the lowest LOD has been generated, we need to switch to it so it can be previewed and edited. This can be done several ways through the toolbar. One method is to drag the LOD slider all the way to the right until the text box to its right reads 100. Another method would be to simply enter **100** into the text box. A third method is to click the Jump to Lowest LOD Level button ⏩. The final method is to select LOD Lowest from the dropdown list. Use one of these methods to select the lowest LOD level.

FIGURE 5.136   Clicking the Regenerate Lowest LOD button performs the same function.

You know you have been successful in switching levels of detail because all the modules should now appear "dirty" (covered in a noise texture). They are marked as noneditable at the lower levels of detail by default (see **FIGURE 5.137**).

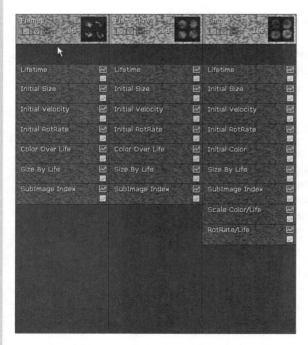

FIGURE 5.137   At lower levels of detail, disabled modules appear with a noisy texture on them.

Regenerating the lowest LOD has lowered the SpawnRate properties of each emitter, but these values need to be adjusted further to give us the exact results we are looking for.

5. First, we look at the Flames emitter. In order to actually adjust the properties of any module, we need to enable it. Right-click the main emitter module of the Flames emitter and choose Enable Module. The noisy overlay should disappear and the properties should now be editable.

6. Expand the RequiredModule and make note of the value of SpawnRate, which should be 7.5. As you can see, there are gaps between the flames, especially at a distance. Upping the number of particles a little should help to fix this (see **FIGURE 5.138**). Set the following:

▶ **SpawnRate**: 10.0

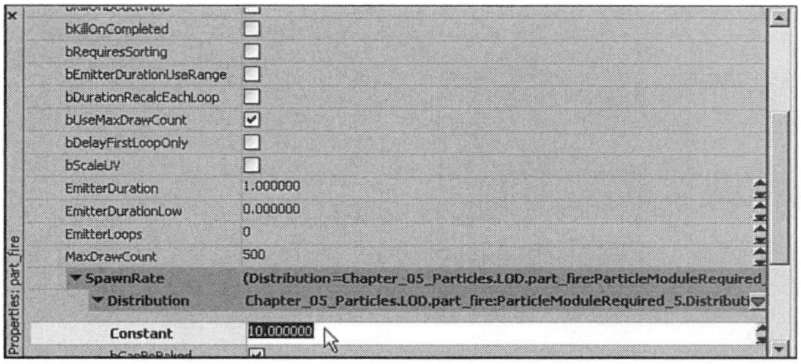

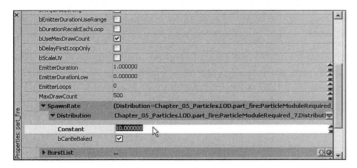

FIGURE 5.138   Enable the Flames emitter and set its SpawnRate to 10.0.

We have increased the number of particles, but there are still some gaps between the flames. Of course, we could always increase the number of particles more, but we are trying to optimize. Therefore, keeping the number of particles low is essential.

7. Instead of using more particles, we are going to increase the size of the particles, giving the illusion of more particles when viewed at a distance. Right-click the Initial Size module and choose Enable Module. As with the emitter module, the noisy overlay should disappear and its properties should become editable (see **FIGURE 5.139**).

FIGURE 5.139   Enable the Initial Size module.

8. Expand the StartSize property and set the following values:

▶ **Min**:

▶ **X**: 20.0

The rest of the values can be left at their current settings. That should give the flames enough size to fill the gaps between them at a distance without using many particles.

9. Next is the FlameGlow emitter. We are essentially going to perform the exact same process on this emitter because its settings are identical to the Flames emitter's settings. Begin by enabling the main module of the FlameGlow emitter. Then, expand the RequiredModule and set the SpawnRate property to 10.0, just as we did with the Flames emitter (see **FIGURE 5.140**).

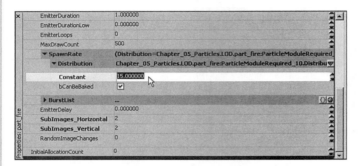

FIGURE 5.140   Enable the FlameGlow emitter at this LOD and then set the SpawnRate property.

10. Enable the Initial Size module of the FlameGlow emitter and set the following value:

   ▶ **StartSize**:

      ▶ **Min**:

         ▶ **X**: 20.0

We make one other adjustment to the FlameGlow emitter. We are going to change the Color Over Life module slightly to allow the blue color to show a little longer. This is mainly because it tends to disappear when viewed at a distance with the current settings.

11. Right-click the Color Over Life module and choose Enable Module. Then expand the Points array of the ColorOverLife property. We are only going to be adjusting the InVal settings of the two points because this determines the relative time when the colors are displayed. Set the following values:

   ▶ **0**:

      ▶ **InVal**: 0.15

   ▶ **1**:

      ▶ **InVal**: 0.33

12. The final emitter is the Smoke emitter. The same basic adjustments are made to this emitter, but the values used will be slightly different. First off, we need to increase the number of particles being emitted.

13. Right-click the Smoke emitter module and choose Enable Module to make it editable. Then, select the emitter module if it isn't selected automatically, expand the RequiredModule, and set the following value (see **FIGURE 5.141**):

   ▸ **SpawnRate**: 15.0

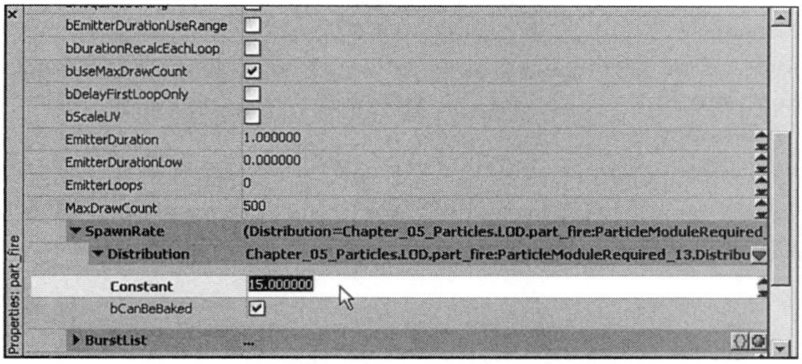

FIGURE 5.141   Set the SpawnRate for the Smoke emitter to 15.0.

A value of 15.0 here helps to close up the gaps between puffs of smoke.

Now that we have the number of particles set to an acceptable level, the size of the particles needs to be adjusted. We are going to increase both the minimum and the maximum size of these particles this time.

14. Right-click the Initial Size module of Smoke and choose Enable Module. Then, select the Initial Size module and set the following values:

   ▸ **StartSize**:

      ▸ **Max**:

         ▸ **X**: 35.0

      ▸ **Min**:

         ▸ **X**: 25.0

This should fairly well eliminate any gaps between puffs of smoke.

15. Save the Chapter_05_Particles package so you don't lose your work.

END TUTORIAL 5.15

TUTORIAL 5.16 continues from **TUTORIAL 5.15**, so be sure to complete it before proceeding. You need to have the Chapter_05_Particles package open in the Generic Browser, and make sure you are viewing the part_fire particle system in Cascade. If you have not completed **TUTORIAL 5.15** yet, you may use the part_fire_01 particle system instead.

TUTORIAL 5.16: Using LODs, Part II: Intermediate LOD Setup

1. We now have a highest and lowest level of detail all set up. To keep the emitter from going through a sudden drop from the highest to the lowest level of detail, we are going to add an intermediate level of detail as well.

2. To create a new LOD, enter **50** in the text box to the right of the LOD slider. Then, click the Add LOD button ⬛ in the toolbar. This creates a new LOD halfway between the highest and lowest levels of detail in terms of distance, but it will have the values of the highest level of detail by default so we need to go through and set up the values as we did in **TUTORIAL 5.15** (see **FIGURE 5.142**).

FIGURE 5.142　Make sure to move the slider to 50 before clicking the Add LOD button.

3. Right-click the emitter module of the Flames emitter and choose Enable Module. The noisy overlay should disappear and the properties should now be editable.

4. Expand the RequiredModule and make note of the value of SpawnRate, which should be 75, because that was the value used in the highest level of detail. Because this LOD is halfway between the highest and lowest, we are going to use values that are halfway between the highest and lowest levels' settings (see **FIGURE 5.143**). Set the following:

   ▶ **SpawnRate**: 42.5

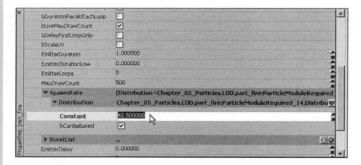

FIGURE 5.143　Enabling the Flames module and setting the SpawnRate to 42.5 decreases the glow a bit.

5. As with the lowest LOD, we also set the Initial Size in this LOD. Right-click the Initial Size module of the Flames emitter and choose Enable Module. Then, select the Initial Size module and set the following value:

   ▶ **StartSize**:

       ▶ **Min**:

           ▶ **X**: 12.5

This value should be halfway between the highest and lowest LOD values for this property.

6. Next is the FlameGlow emitter. Right-click its emitter module and choose Enable Module to make it editable. Then select the emitter module if it isn't automatically selected. Expand the RequiredModule and set the following:

   ▶ **SpawnRate**: 42.5

7. Right-click the Initial Size module and choose Enable Module to make it editable. Then, select the Initial Size module and set the following value:

   ▶ **StartSize**:

     ▶ **Min**:

       ▶ **X**: 12.5

8. Right-click the Color Over Life module of the FlameGlow emitter and choose Enable Module. Then, expand the Points array of the ColorOverLife property and set the following values:

   ▶ **0**:

     ▶ **InVal**: 0.1125

   ▶ **1**:

     ▶ **InVal**: 0.2667

Again, this simply makes the blue color of the flames more visible at greater distances.

9. The final emitter is the Smoke emitter. Right-click the Smoke emitter module and choose Enable Module to make it editable. Then, select the emitter module if it isn't automatically selected, expand the RequiredModule, and set the following value:

   ▶ **SpawnRate**: 45.0

Now that we have the number of particles set to an acceptable level, the size of the particles needs to be adjusted. We increased both the minimum and the maximum size of these particles in the lowest LOD, so we must do the same here.

10. Right-click the Initial Size module of Smoke and choose Enable Module. Then, select the Initial Size module and set the following values:

   ▶ **StartSize**:

     ▶ **Max**:   ▶ **Min**:

       ▶ **X**: 30.0   ▶**X**: 15.0

11. Save the Chapter_05_Particles package so you don't lose your work.

END TUTORIAL 5.16

Emitter Actor

The Emitter actor is the placeable actor used to position a particle system in a map. It holds a reference to the particle system and provides access to a few properties that can control individual instances of the particle system, allowing for variation in different locations, all while using the same system. In this section, we cover those properties that are specific to particle behavior (see **FIGURE 5.144**).

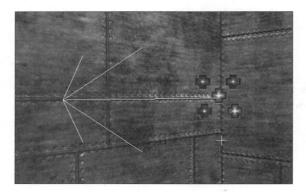

FIGURE 5.144   The emitter actor is the key to placing particle systems in your level.

LOD

The Level of Detail (LOD) section contains properties that allow you to control the way levels of detail are handled as the view moves toward and away from the particle system.

> **bOverrideLODMethod**—If this property is true, the LODMethod of the particle system is disregarded in favor of the LODMethod of the emitter actor.
>
> If this property is false, the LODMethod of the particle system is used.
>
> **LODMethod**—This is the method of determining the current level of detail to use for the emitter if bOverrideLODMethod is true.
>
> These methods are explained previously in this chapter in the "Particle System Properties" section.

ParticleSystemComponent

The Particle System Component section contains important properties for controlling the particle system at the level of the placeable actor. This allows for individual differentiation of each placed instance of the particle system.

bAutoActivate—If this property is true, the emitter begins running when the level begins.

If this property is false, the emitter is turned off when the level begins.

bResetOnDetach—If this property is true, the emitter is reset when it is detached from the scene.

InstanceParameters—This is a list of parameters and their values that provide the ability to customize individual instances of a particle system in the level. This is used by such properties as a trail emitter's SourceName in order to specify which emitter will be creating the trail.

SecondsBeforeInactive—This is the number of seconds that the emitter must go without being rendered in order to be deactivated, meaning it will stop being updated until it is rendered again.

Template—This is the reference to the particle system to use for this emitter actor.

Modifying Particle Systems In-Game

Creating impressive visuals is really only half the battle when working with in-game special effects. The heart of the gaming experience lies in interaction, and there's no better way to push this onto the player than by having your stellar special effects be able to be changed in-game through some type of player action. In Unreal Engine 3, there are several ways in which this can be accomplished. One can use Kismet, Matinee, or even code. Because scripting is technically beyond the scope of this book, we will focus on the first two options.

Kismet Modifications

Toggle—The Toggle sequence object can be used to turn an emitter actor (and therefore a single instance of a particle system) on or off when that emitter actor is connected to the Toggle's Target variable input (see **FIGURE 5.145**).

Set Particle Param—Kismet provides a Set Particle Param action that can be used to set the value of any particle parameter present in a particle system. This includes setting scalar (float) values, vectors, colors, and actors.

Variable Inputs

Target—This is a reference to the emitter actor that you wish to modify.

Scalar Value—This is a float value to use for any scalar parameters specified in the InstanceParameters array of this sequence object when bOverrideScalar is true.

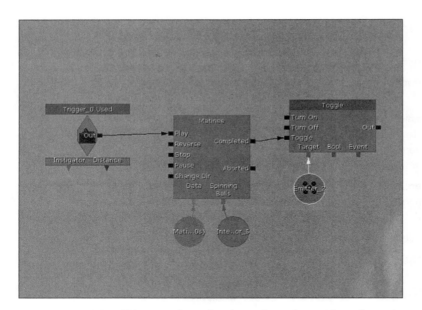

FIGURE 5.145   This network toggles the emitter when a trigger is used.

Properties

bOverrideScalar—If this property is true, the value of the Scalar Value input or the Scalar Value property will be used as the value for any scalar parameters in the InstanceParameters array.

InstanceParameters—This is an array of parameters that references the parameters that should be set by this sequence object.

ScalarValue—This value will be used to override the scalar values of the scalar parameters in the InstanceParameters array if no variable is attached to the Scalar Value input (see **FIGURE 5.146**).

Matinee Modifications

Movement—Like certain other actors, emitters can be moved using a Movement track in Matinee. It should be noted that the Movement > Physics property must be set to PHYS_Interpolating (which is not the default setting) in order for the emitter to be moved by this track.

Float Particle Param Track—The float particle param track allows the value of a float parameter distribution belonging to a particular instance of a particle system by means of the attached emitter actor to be animated over time.

It has one property, ParamName, which is the name of the parameter to control with the track.

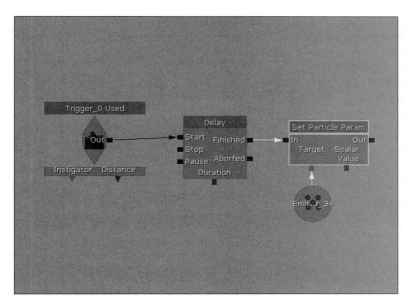

FIGURE 5.146   This network changes the color of the particles.

Particle Toggle Track—The toggle track allows the turning on and off of an instance of a particle system at any point during the Matinee sequence. It has one property, bFireEventsWhenJumpingForward, which causes the keys of this track to be triggered even if the sequence is skipped.

TUTORIAL 5.17 begins the process of creating the remaining effects for our sample level. It should be noted that we now begin generalizing some of the steps you have completed many times now. For example, we assume you know how to add various modules and change Distribution types. We shorten the steps to show essentially what it is you need to set and then move on.

If you have not yet completed the previous tutorials in this chapter, this may prove confusing. It will be best if you have completed all other tutorials in this chapter before starting **TUTORIAL 5.17** and all the remaining tutorials in this chapter.

TUTORIAL 5.17: Primary Lightning Beams

1. In the Generic Browser, right-click in the background and choose New Particle System from the context menu. Enter the following information and then click OK (see **FIGURE 5.147**).

    ▶ **Package**: Chapter_05_Particles

    ▶ **Group**: Emitters

    ▶ **Name**: part_central_beams

2. Cascade appears. Jump back to the Generic Browser and select the mat_ electricity material from the Chapter_05_Particles package. In Cascade, right-click in the Emitter List and choose New Particle Sprite Emitter. Set the name of this new emitter to **CentralBeams** (see **FIGURE 5.148**).

3. Add a new Beam TypeData module to the emitter and set the following values (see **FIGURE 5.149**):

   ▶ **MaxBeamCount**: 1

   ▶ **Speed**: 0.0

4. Select the Lifetime module. Using the skills you have acquired so far, change the Distribution type to a FloatConstant. Set the new value to **0.5** (see **FIGURE 5.150**).

FIGURE 5.147   Create a new particle system for the central beams.

FIGURE 5.148   Create a new Sprite emitter named CentralBeams.

FIGURE 5.149   The Beam TypeData turns the emitter into a Beam emitter.

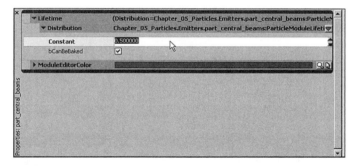

FIGURE 5.150   Set the Lifetime property to 0.05.

5. Select the Initial Size module. Change the Distribution type to VectorConstant. Set the following (see **FIGURE 5.151**):

   ▸ **X**: 35.0

   ▸ Leave Y and Z at their default values; they are irrelevant.

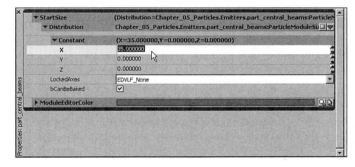

FIGURE 5.151   Set the Initial Size module to 35 for X.

6. Delete the Initial Velocity module and then add a new Initial Color module. Select it and set the following values (see **FIGURE 5.152**):

   ▸ **X**: 0.75

   ▸ **Y**: 0.75

   ▸ **Z**: 2.0

7. Add a Beam Source module from the Beam section of the context menu. Select it and then set the following values (see **FIGURE 5.153**):

   ▸ **SourceMethod**: PEB2STM_Actor

   ▸ **SourceName**: BeamSource

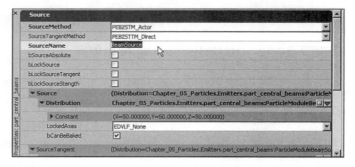

FIGURE 5.153   This method allows the beam to start at a particular actor.

FIGURE 5.152   The Initial Color module makes the beams electric blue.

5

8. Add a Beam Target module. Select it and then set the following values:

- ▶ **TargetMethod**: PEB2STM_Actor
- ▶ **TargetName**: BeamTarget

9. By doing this, you are setting the beam up to follow an actor. However, you will not be able to see a preview of the effect in Cascade. To remedy this, set the Target property's distribution values to the following (see **FIGURE 5.154**):

- ▶ **X**: 0.0
- ▶ **Y**: 0.0
- ▶ **Z**: 200.0

10. Add a Beam Noise module. Select it and set the following properties:

- ▶ **bLowFreq_Enabled**: True
- ▶ **bSmooth**: True
- ▶ **Frequency**: 3

- ▶ **NoiseRange**: Change this property's distribution over to a VectorUniform and set the following:

  - ▶ **Max**:

    - ▶ **X**: 35.0

    - ▶ **Y**: 5.0

    - ▶ **Z**: 5.0

  - ▶ **Min**:

    - ▶ **X**: 25.0

    - ▶ **Y**: −5.0

    - ▶ **Z**: −5.0

- ▶ **NoiseLockTime**: 0.2

- ▶ **NoiseTension**: 0.25

These properties define the type of noise we will be creating. Turning on bLowFreq_Enabled allows us to use noise. The bSmooth property causes the animation to be smooth rather than

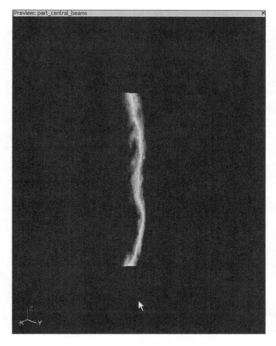

FIGURE 5.154   You should now see the effect in the Cascade preview.

jerky. The low frequency gives us distinct jagged points in the beam. The NoiseRange property controls how far the noise can move in each direction. The NoiseLockTime constrains the noise points to a specific location for 0.2 seconds. NoiseTension is controlling the tangents of each noise point and thus the shape of the curve as it enters and exits each point (see **FIGURE 5.155**).

11. Right-click the CentralBeams emitter and choose Emitter > Duplicate + Share Emitter from the context menu. In the copy of the emitter that appears, delete the existing Noise module. Then, hold down the Ctrl key and drag the Noise module from the first emitter over to the second. This allows you to have an unshared copy of the module so that they can have different values. With the new Noise module selected, set the following (see **FIGURE 5.156**):

  - ▶ **NoiseRange**:

    - ▶ **Max**:

      - ▶ **X**: −25.0

      - ▶ **Y**: 5.0

      - ▶ **Z**: 5.0

    - ▶ **Min**:

      - ▶ **X**: −35.0

      - ▶ **Y**: −5.0

      - ▶ **Z**: −5.0

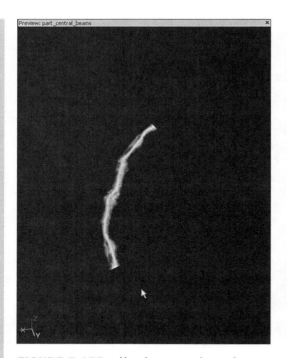

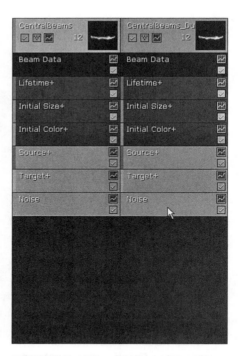

FIGURE 5.155   Your beam now has noise applied.

FIGURE 5.156   Duplicate the emitter and copy over a new Noise module.

12. Save your package so that you do not lose your work.

END TUTORIAL 5.17

In **TUTORIAL 5.18**, we now place our new electrical beam effect into our level. This requires the placement of an emitter actor, as well as the establishment of some particle parameters to set up the source and target for the beams.

TUTORIAL 5.18: Placing Central Beams

1. Open the DM-CH_05_Plasma_Begin map included on the DVD in the files for this chapter. In the Generic Browser, select the part_central_beams particle system. In the level, right-click some point in the room and choose Add Actor > Emitter: part_central_beams from the context menu. Position this emitter in the Top viewport so that it is between the plasma generator sphere and the column to the right of the room (see **FIGURE 5.157**).

2. Open the properties of the emitter (F4). Uncheck the bAutoActivate property so that the emitter will not be running when the level starts (see **FIGURE 5.158**).

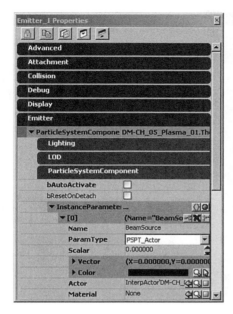

FIGURE 5.157   Place the new emitter in the level.

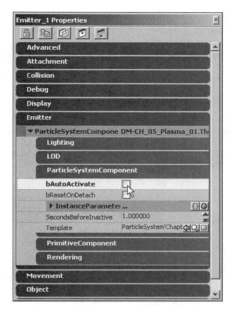

FIGURE 5.158   Unchecking bAutoActivate is critical to having the effect be triggered through Kismet.

3. Click the right side of the InstanceParameters area to expose the Add New Item button , and click it twice to create two new slots. Expand slot 0 and set the following (see **FIGURE 5.159**):

   ▶ **Name**: BeamSource

   ▶ **ParamType**: PSPT_Actor

4. Click the Lock Selected Actors button in the upper-left corner of the Properties window. Select the transparent sphere static mesh at the center of the plasma generator. Back in the Properties window, click the Use Current Selection in Browser button of the Actor property for slot 0.

5. Deselect the Lock Selected Actors button when finished.

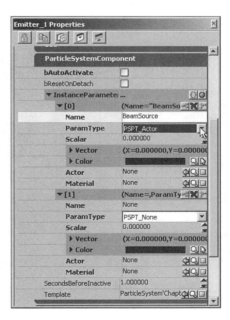

FIGURE 5.159   Add two slots and set slot 0 to BeamSource.

5

6. Expand slot 1 and set the following (see **FIGURE 5.160**):

   ▸ **Name**: BeamTarget

   ▸ **ParamType**: PSPT_Actor

7. Again, use the Lock Selected Actors button to constrain focus to the emitter. Select the metallic sphere that is on the right side of the room as seen from the Top viewport. Click the Use Current Selection in Browser button next to the Actor property for slot 1.

8. Deselect the Lock Selected Actors button when finished (see **FIGURE 5.161**).

9. Duplicate the emitter by selecting it and pressing Ctrl+C, Ctrl+V. Move this duplicate so that it is between the central column and the bottommost sphere, when seen from the Top viewport. For this new duplicate, use the skills gained in step 6 to set the Actor property for slot 1 to the name of the sphere at the bottom of the room, as seen from the Top viewport (see **FIGURE 5.162**).

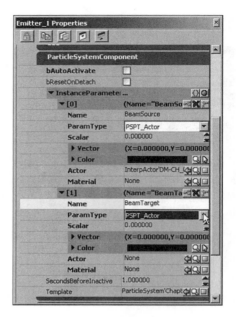

FIGURE 5.160   The BeamTarget property is now looking for an actor.

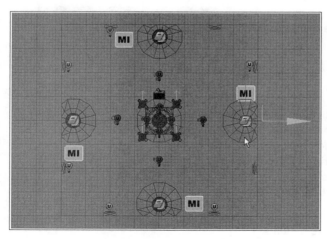

FIGURE 5.161   Make sure to select the rightmost sphere as seen from the Top viewport.

10. Repeat this process two more times, creating two more duplicates of the emitter and associating their slot 1 Actor properties with the left and top spheres, respectively, as seen from the Top viewport. This allows the beams to strike all four of the spheres (see **FIGURE 5.163**).

11. Save your map so that you do not lose your progress. You will not be able to see your results until we finish the final Kismet sequence.

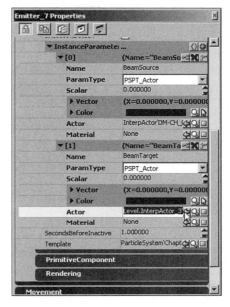

FIGURE 5.162   Duplicate the emitter and set slot 1 to the bottom sphere, as seen from the Top viewport.

FIGURE 5.163   You should now have four emitters, one linked to each of the four spheres.

END TUTORIAL 5.18

Our next effect is to place static electrical arcs that span from the top to the bottom of the four perimeter columns in **TUTORIAL 5.19**. Once again, this relies on beam emitters, although they will be slightly different than those created for the central beams.

TUTORIAL 5.19: Column Beams, Part I

1. In the Generic Browser, right-click the background and create a new ParticleSystem using the following values (see **FIGURE 5.164**):

   ▶ **Package**: Chapter_05_Particles

   ▶ **Group**: Emitters

   ▶ **Name**: part_column_beams

2. Again, Cascade appears. In the Generic Browser, make sure the mat_electricity material is selected and then create a new emitter in the Emitter List of the Kismet window. Set the name of this emitter to **ColumnBolt** (see **FIGURE 5.165**).

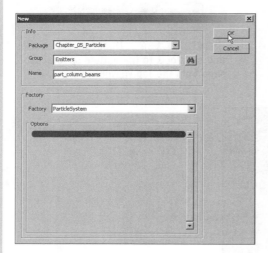

FIGURE 5.164 This new particle system creates beams that arc along the exterior columns.

FIGURE 5.165 Create a new emitter in the particle system.

3. Add a Beam TypeData module to the emitter and set the following values (see **FIGURE 5.166**):

   ▶ **MaxBeamCount**: 1

   ▶ **Speed**: 0.0

   ▶ **InterpolationPoints**: 40

4. Select the Lifetime module. Change the Distribution type to FloatConstant and set the value to 0.5 (see **FIGURE 5.167**).

5. Select the Initial Size module. Change the Distribution type to a VectorConstant and set the value of X to 25.0. Leave the other values at 0.0 (see **FIGURE 5.168**).

FIGURE 5.166
Add a Beam TypeData module to create a beam emitter.

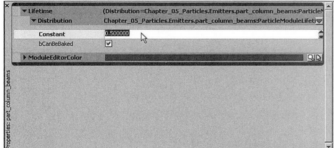

FIGURE 5.167   The lifetime should be a constant 0.5 seconds.

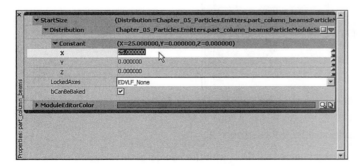

FIGURE 5.168   Set the Initial Size to a constant with an X value of 25.

6. Delete the Initial Velocity module. Add an Initial Color module and set the color values to the following (see **FIGURE 5.169**):

▸ **X**: 0.75

▸ **Y**: 0.75

▸ **Z**: 2.0

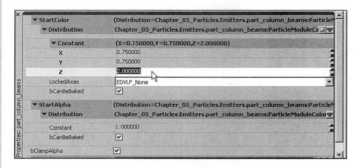

FIGURE 5.169   Again, we use an electric blue for the beams.

7. Add a Beam Source module. Select it and then set the following (see **FIGURE 5.170**):

▸ **SourceTangentMethod**: PEB2STTM_UserSet

▸ **Source**:

▸ **X**: 0.0

▸ **Y**: 0.0

▸ **Z**: 0.0

▸ **SourceStrength**: 175.0

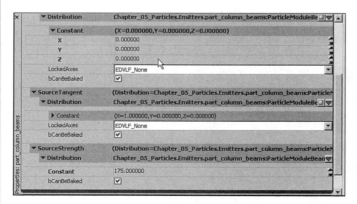

FIGURE 5.170   We use a locally based source this time, with the source at the location of the emitter.

8. Add a Beam Target module. Select it and then set the following (see **FIGURE 5.171**):

- ▸ **TargetTangentMethod**: PEB2STTM_UserSet
- ▸ **Target**:
    - ▸ **X**: 0.0
    - ▸ **Y**: 0.0
    - ▸ **Z**: 132.0
- ▸ **TargetStrength**: –175.0

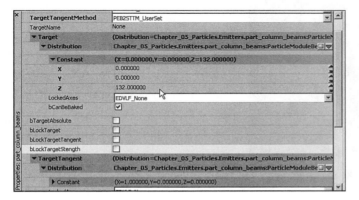

FIGURE 5.171   The Target is 132 units higher than the emitter.

9. Add a Beam Noise module. Select it and then set the following (see **FIGURE 5.172**):

- ▸ **bLowFreq_Enabled**: True
- ▸ **bSmooth**: True
- ▸ **Frequency**: 15
- ▸ **NoiseRange**: Change to a VectorUniform distribution and set the following:

▸ **Max**:	▸ **Min**:
▸ **X**: 5.0	▸ **X**: –5.0
▸ **Y**: 5.0	▸ **Y**: –5.0
▸ **Z**: 5.0	▸ **Z**: –5.0

- ▸ **NoiseTangentStrength**: 25.0
- ▸ **NoiseTessellation**: 22
- ▸ **FrequencyDistance**: 20.0

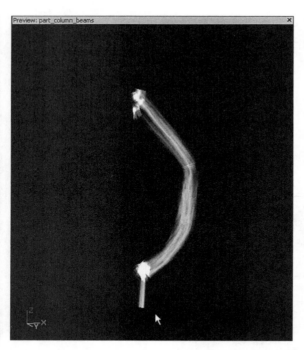

Preview: part_column_beams

FIGURE 5.172   This should make the beam noisy and give it an arced shape.

10. Save the package.

END TUTORIAL 5.19

In **TUTORIAL 5.20**, we continue with the construction of the emitters for the column beams. This involves duplicating the emitter within the particle system and using this new duplicate to cause the new copy of the beam to shoot in three other directions. You need to have the part_column_beams particle system from **TUTORIAL 5.19** open in Cascade. If you have not completed it, you may use the part_column_beams_01 particle system instead.

TUTORIAL 5.20: Column Beams, Part II

1. Duplicate and share the emitter by right-clicking it and choosing Duplicate+Share Emitter. Delete the Source module from the new emitter. Hold down Ctrl and drag the Source module from the first emitter to the new emitter, making a copy of it. Change the following value (see **FIGURE 5.173**):

  ▸ **SourceStrength**: −175.0

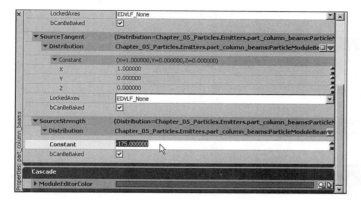

FIGURE 5.173 Duplicate and share the emitter; then replace the Source module with a non-shared duplicate of the original, but with different settings.

2. Delete the Target module from the new emitter. Hold down Ctrl and drag the Target module from the first emitter to the new emitter, making a copy of it. Change the following values (see **FIGURE 5.174**):

▶ **TargetStrength**: 175.0

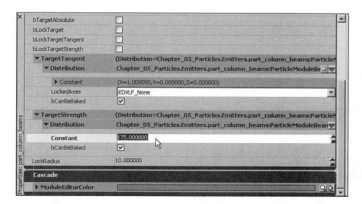

FIGURE 5.174 Also replace the Target module with a shared duplicate with new settings.

3. Duplicate+Share the second emitter to create a third copy. Delete the Source module from this new emitter. Hold down Ctrl and drag the Source module from the second emitter to the new emitter, making a copy of it. Change the following values (see **FIGURE 5.175**):

▶ **SourceTangent**:

   ▶ **X**: 0.0

   ▶ **Y**: 1.0

   ▶ **Z**: 0.0

▶ **SourceStrength**: −175.0

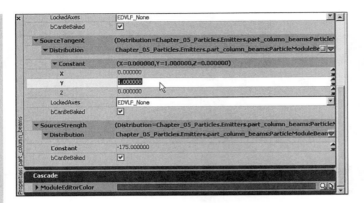

FIGURE 5.175   Once again, duplicate the emitter and replace the Source module with a nonshared version.

4. Delete the Target module from the third emitter. Hold down Ctrl and drag the Target module from the first emitter to the third emitter, making a copy of it. Change the following values (see **FIGURE 5.176**):

   ▶ **TargetTangent**:

       ▶ **X**: 0.0

       ▶ **Y**: 1.0

       ▶ **Z**: 0.0

   ▶ **TargetStrength**: 175.0

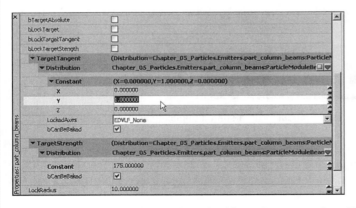

FIGURE 5.176   The third emitter should now have a nonshared Target module.

5. Duplicate+Share the third emitter, creating a fourth. Delete the Source module from the new emitter. Hold down Ctrl and drag the Source module from the third emitter to the new emitter, once again making a copy of it. Change the following value:

   ▸ **SourceStrength**: 175.0

6. Delete the Target module from the new emitter. Hold down Ctrl and drag the Target module from the first emitter to the new emitter, making a copy of it.

7. Save the package. Your emitter should now be creating four separate beams of electricity (see **FIGURE 5.177**).

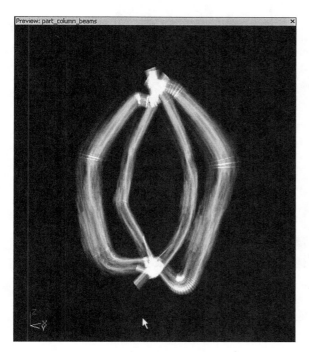

FIGURE 5.177   The final effect of the four separate beams of electricity.

END TUTORIAL 5.20

In **TUTORIAL 5.21**, we place the part_column_beams particle system into our level. Make sure that you have the Chapter_05_Particles package open and that the map used in the previous tutorials to place the central beam emitters is open as well.

TUTORIAL 5.21: Placing Column Beams

1. Select the part_column_beams particle system in the browser.

2. Add it to the level by right-clicking on the floor of the level and choosing Add Actor > Emitter: part_column_beams. Move it to the center of the rightmost column as seen from the Top viewport, about 90 units above the floor (see **FIGURE 5.178**).

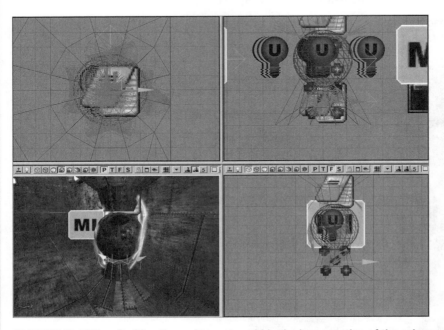

FIGURE 5.178   Position the emitter actor within the lower portion of the column.

3. In the Top viewport, Alt-drag the emitter (to duplicate it) and move it to the center of the column at the bottom of the room.

4. Duplicate the emitter and move it to the center of the column at the left of the room.

5. Duplicate the emitter and move it to the center of the column at the top of the room.

6. Save the map. You now have electrical arcs surrounding the spheres at each column (see **FIGURE 5.179)**.

FIGURE 5.179   All four columns should now have electrical arcs.

END TUTORIAL 5.21

As a secondary effect of the primary electrical beam that comes from the center of the room, we also create "splash bolts" of lighting that arc away to seemingly random locations. This requires another beam emitter. Make sure you have the Chapter_05_Particles package used in the previous tutorials open before beginning **TUTORIAL 5.22**.

TUTORIAL 5.22: Splash Beams

1. Create a new ParticleSystem using the following values (see **FIGURE 5.180**):

   ▸ **Package**: Chapter_05_Particles

   ▸ **Group**: Emitters

   ▸ **Name**: part_splash_beams

2. With the mat_electricity material selected in the Generic Browser, create a new emitter in the particle system. Set the name of this emitter to SplashBolts (see **FIGURE 5.181**).

FIGURE 5.180   Create a new emitter with this information.

5

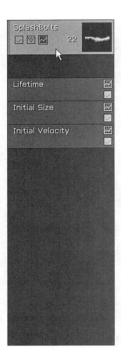

FIGURE 5.181   Create a new emitter within the particle system.

3. Add a Beam TypeData module and set the following values (see **FIGURE 5.182**):

   ▸ **MaxBeamCount**: 10

   ▸ **Speed**: 0.0

4. Select the Lifetime module. Change the Distribution type to a FloatConstant and set the value to 0.425.

5. Select the Initial Size module. Change the Distribution type to a VectorConstant and set the value for X to 35.0. Leave the remaining values at 0.0.

6. Delete the Initial Velocity module. Add an Initial Color module and set the color values as follows (see **FIGURE 5.183**):

   ▸ **X**: 0.75

   ▸ **Y**: 0.75

   ▸ **Z**: 2.0

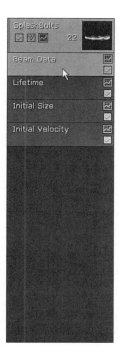

FIGURE 5.182   Add the Beam TypeData module to create another beam emitter.

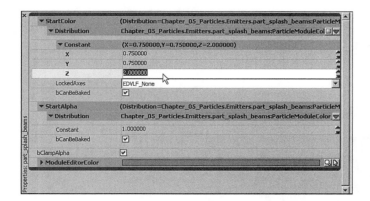

FIGURE 5.183   Since we're still creating electricity, we use the same electric blue value.

7. Add a Beam Source module. Set the following values:

  ▶ **SourceMethod**: PEB2STM_Actor

  ▶ **SourceName**: BeamSource

8. You should also set the Source distribution values to 0.0 for X, Y, and Z. This is for preview purposes within Cascade only because we are using the Actor source method in-game (see **FIGURE 5.184**).

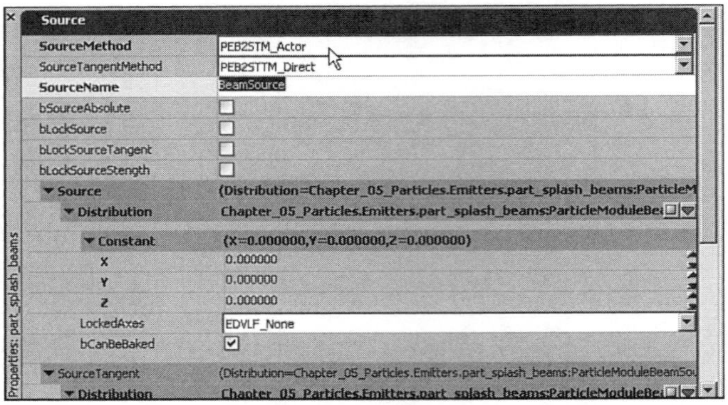

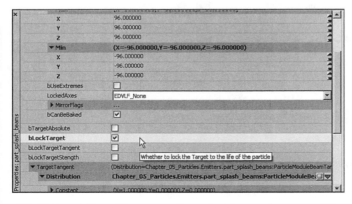

FIGURE 5.184   As with the Central Beams, we use an actor for the source.

9. Add a Beam Target module. Change the Target distribution to a VectorUniform and set the following values (see **FIGURE 5.185**):

> ▸ **TargetMethod**: PEB2STM_UserSet

> ▸ **Target**:

>> ▸ **Max**:

>>> ▸ **X**: 96.0

>>> ▸ **Y**: 96.0

>>> ▸ **Z**: 96.0

>> ▸ **Min**:

>>> ▸ **X**: –96.0

>>> ▸ **Y**: –96.0

>>> ▸ **Z**: –96.0

>> ▸ **bLockTarget**: True (Checked)

FIGURE 5.185   This causes the splash beams to surround the source.

10. Add a Beam Noise module. Set the following values (see **FIGURE 5.186**):

- ▸ **bLowFreq_Enabled**: True
- ▸ **bSmooth**: True
- ▸ **Frequency**: 3
- ▸ **NoiseRange**: Change to a VectorUniform distribution and set the following:

▸ **Max**:	▸ **Min**:
▸ **X**: 5.0	▸ **X**: –5.0
▸ **Y**: 5.0	▸ **Y**: –5.0
▸ **Z**: 5.0	▸ **Z**: –5.0

- ▸ **NoiseLockTime**: 0.2
- ▸ **NoiseTension**: 0.25

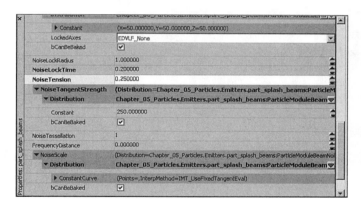

FIGURE 5.186   The beams are now noisy.

11. Save the package. The splash beam effect is ready for placement.

END TUTORIAL 5.22

We are now ready to start placing the splash beam effects throughout the level. These will not actually be visible unless the central beam is striking one of the columns. We control the toggling behavior later through Kismet. Make sure that you have the Chapter_05_Particles package open and that the ParticleElectricity map used in the previous tutorials is open as well.

TUTORIAL 5.23: Placing Splash Beams

1. Select the part_splash_beams particle system in the browser. Add a new Emitter actor to the level and move it just underneath the metallic sphere to the right of the room, as seen from the Top viewport. This is a temporary location. It is eventually inside the sphere, but putting it outside for now makes it easier to select (see **FIGURE 5.187**).

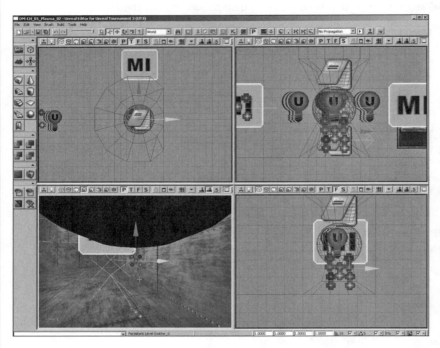

FIGURE 5.187   Center the splash beam's Emitter actor on the rightmost column's sphere, as seen in the Top viewport.

2. Open the Emitter actor's properties. Uncheck bAutoActivate. This prevents the particle system from being active when the level starts (see **FIGURE 5.188**).

3. Click on the InstanceParameters array to expose the Add Item button ⬛. Click it once to add one item. Expand the newly created slot 0 and set the following (see **FIGURE 5.189**):

   ▸ **Name**: BeamSource

   ▸ **ParamType**: PSPT_Actor

4. Click the Lock Selected Actors button 🔒. Select the metallic sphere the emitter is closest to and click the Use Current Selection in Browser button 🔄 of the Actor property for slot 0 (see **FIGURE 5.190**).

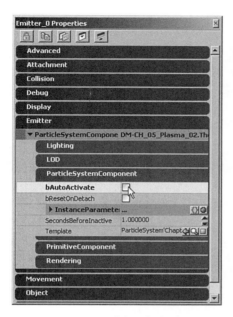

FIGURE 5.188   bAutoActivate must be unchecked for the effect to be timed correctly.

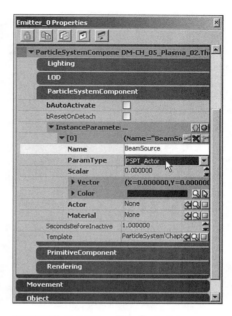

FIGURE 5.189   This first slot causes the beam source to be assigned to an actor.

5. Turn off the Lock Selected Actors feature. Duplicate the emitter and place the new emitter just next to the metallic sphere at the bottom of the room, as seen from the Top viewport. Click the Lock Selected Actors button 🔒 again. Select the metallic sphere and click the Use Current Selection in Browser button 🔷 of the Actor property for slot 0.

6. Repeat the previous step to create a duplicate of the emitter that is located just above the leftmost sphere, as seen from the Top viewport. Also, as before, associate the Actor property for slot 0 with the respective sphere.

7. Repeat the previous step one more time to create a duplicate of the emitter that will be located inside the topmost sphere as seen from the Top viewport. Once again, associate the Actor property for slot 0 with the respective sphere (see **FIGURE 5.191**).

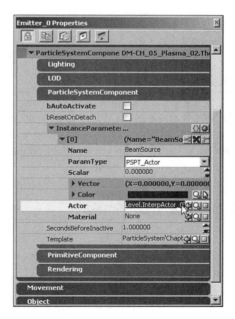

FIGURE 5.190   Make sure the Actor line shows the name of the nearest sphere.

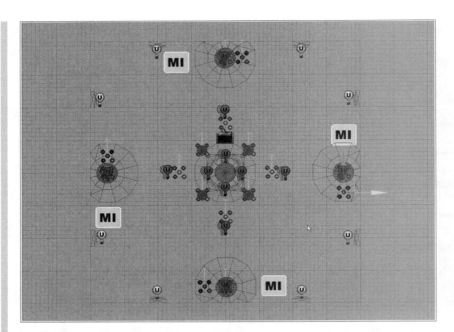

FIGURE 5.191   You should now have four separate emitter actors, each associated with its respective sphere through slot 0's Actor property.

8. When finished, position all the emitters inside their respective spheres.

9. Save the map. The splash beams are now ready to be activated, but they won't really be visible until we're done setting up the necessary Kismet sequence.

END TUTORIAL 5.23

It's time to move on to another aspect of our effects. As each sphere is being struck by the central beam, that sphere heats up and starts emitting black smoke. In **TUTORIAL 5.24**, we start the process of creating the smoke effect. Make sure you have the Chapter_05_Particles package used in the previous tutorials open.

TUTORIAL 5.24: Smoke

1. Create a new particle system using the following values (see **FIGURE 5.192**):

   ▶ **Package**: Chapter_05_Particles

   ▶ **Group**: Emitters

   ▶ **Name**: part_smoke

2. With the mat_smoke material selected in the Generic Browser, create a new emitter in the particle system (see **FIGURE 5.193**).

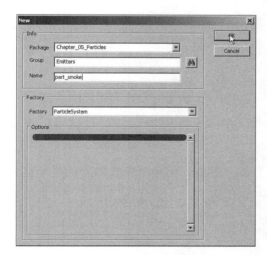

FIGURE 5.192 Create a new particle system for the smoke.

3. Expand the RequiredModule and set the following:

- ▶ **SpawnRate**: 50.0
- ▶ **InterpolationMethod**: PSUVIM_Random
- ▶ **SubImages_Horizontal**: 2
- ▶ **SubImages_Vertical**: 2

FIGURE 5.193 The new emitter produces our smoke particles.

The SubImages properties allow the particle system to take advantage of the texture used in the material. Feel free to open up the material in the Material Editor to see how it was created (see **FIGURE 5.194**).

4. Select the Lifetime module and set a range of 2.0 to 3.0.

5. Select the Initial Size module and set a range of 25.0 to 45.0 for X. The values for Y and Z do not matter.

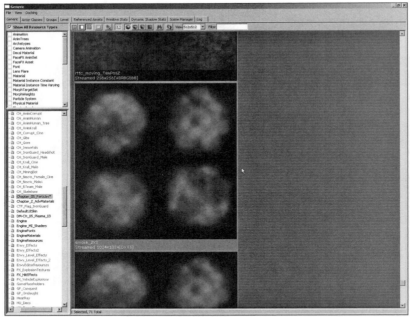

FIGURE 5.194   This is the texture used for the smoke effect. The 2×2 design is the reason we must use the SubImages properties.

6. Select the Initial Velocity module and set the following values (see **FIGURE 5.195**):

▶ **StartVelocity**

   ▶ **Max**:

      ▶ **X**: 0.0

      ▶ **Y**: 0.0

      ▶ **Z**: 100.0

   ▶ **Min**:

      ▶ **X**: 0.0

      ▶ **Y**: 0.0

      ▶ **Z**: 75.0

▶ **StartRadialVelocity**

   ▶ **Min**: 25.0

   ▶ **Max**: 50.0

FIGURE 5.195   This causes the smoke to rise as it is emitted.

7. Save your package. The basis for the smoke effect is now complete. However, you cannot yet see it because we need a color module. In **TUTORIAL 5.25**, we establish the remaining aspects of the effect.

END TUTORIAL 5.24

We now set up the control for the color of our smoke, as well as some more of its behavior. Make sure you have the Chapter_05_Particles package used in the previous tutorials open and that you are looking at the part_smoke particle system within Cascade. If you have not completed **TUTORIAL 5.24**, you may use the part_smoke_01 particle system instead.

TUTORIAL 5.25: Smoke, Continued

1. Add an Initial Color module to the emitter. Change the StartColor Distribution type to a FloatConstantCurve. Add seven points to the curve and set these values for them (see **FIGURE 5.196**):

- ▶ **0**:
  - ▶ **InVal**: 0.0
  - ▶ **OutVal**:
    - ▶ **X**: 0.0
    - ▶ **Y**: 0.0
    - ▶ **Z**: 0.0
- ▶ **1**:
  - ▶ **InVal**: 0.167
  - ▶ **OutVal**:
    - ▶ **X**: 0.167
    - ▶ **Y**: 0.167
    - ▶ **Z**: 0.167
- ▶ **2**:
  - ▶ **InVal**: 0.33
  - ▶ **OutVal**:
    - ▶ **X**: 0.33
    - ▶ **Y**: 0.33
    - ▶ **Z**: 0.33

- ▶ **3**:
  - ▶ **InVal**: 0.5
  - ▶ **OutVal**:
    - ▶ **X**: 0.5
    - ▶ **Y**: 0.5
    - ▶ **Z**: 0.5
- ▶ **4**:
  - ▶ **InVal**: 0.67
  - ▶ **OutVal**:
    - ▶ **X**: 0.33
    - ▶ **Y**: 0.33
    - ▶ **Z**: 0.33
- ▶ **5**:
  - ▶ **InVal**: 0.83
  - ▶ **OutVal**:
    - ▶ **X**: 0.167
    - ▶ **Y**: 0.167
    - ▶ **Z**: 0.167

5

▸ **6**:

  ▸ **InVal**: 1.0

  ▸ **OutVal**:

    ▸ **X**: 0.0

    ▸ **Y**: 0.0

    ▸ **Z**: 0.0

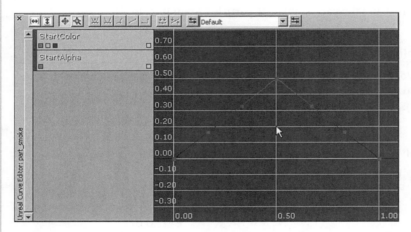

FIGURE 5.196   If viewed in the Curve Editor, your new curve appears like so.

This causes the particles to be spawned in different shades of gray, depending on the current EmitterTime when they are spawned.

2. Add a Scale Color/Life module. The ColorScaleOverLife distribution should have two points. Set the following values (see **FIGURE 5.197**):

▸ **0**:

  ▸ **InVal**: 0.2

  ▸ **OutVal**:

    ▸ **X**: 1.0

    ▸ **Y**: 1.0

    ▸ **Z**: 1.0

▸ **1**:

  ▸ **InVal**: 0.5

  ▸ **OutVal**:

    ▸ **X**: 0.0

    ▸ **Y**: 0.0

    ▸ **Z**: 0.0

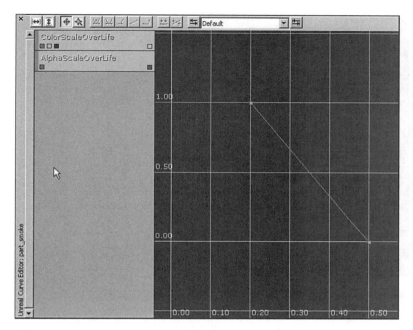

FIGURE 5.197   This causes the smoke to fade to black.

3. Set the AlphaScaleOverLife property's distribution to a FloatConstantCurve.

4. Send the curves of the Scale Color/Life module to the Curve Editor by clicking the little curve button 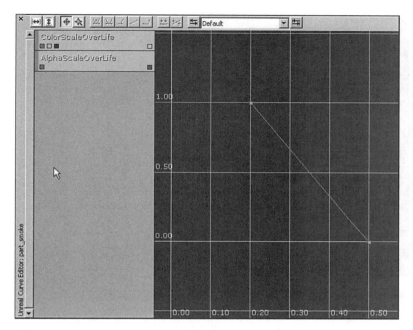 on the module. Right-click the AlphaScaleOverLife curve block and choose Preset Curve. The CurveEd Preset window opens. Select User-Set from the dropdown list in the X/Red/X-Max section (it is the only dropdown enabled).

5. Click the UserCurve property and then click the Show Generic Browser button 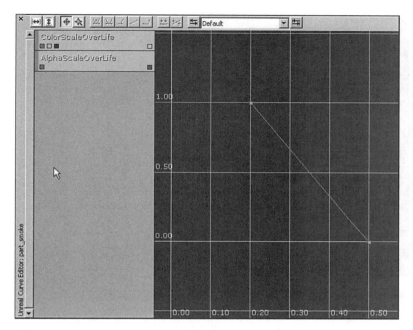. Select the curve_fade_in_out preset curve in the Chapter_05_Particles package and then click the Use Current Selection in Browser button 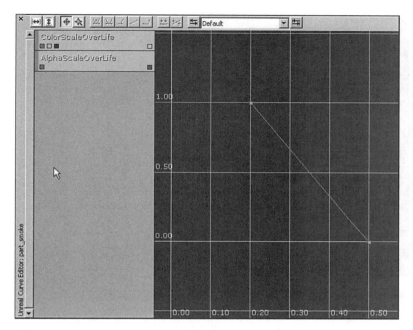 of the UserCurve property. Click OK at the bottom of the window. You should have a nice curve that fades the Alpha from 0 to 1 and then from 1 back to 0 over the life of the particle. This curve was created using specific settings and then saved as a preset (see **FIGURE 5.198**). Remember that you can do this as well; feel free to make curve types that you might commonly run into, and then save them as presets. For more information on how to save curves, see Appendix B.

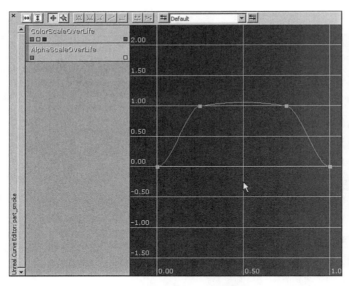

FIGURE 5.198   The imported curve appears like so.

6. Add a Size By Life module. Add a point to the LifeMultiplier distribution for a total of three points in the curve and then set the following values (see **FIGURE 5.199**):

- ▶ **0**:
  - ▶ **InVal**: 0.0
  - ▶ **OutVal**:
    - ▶ **X**: 0.25
    - ▶ **Y**: 0.25
    - ▶ **Z**: 0.25
- ▶ **1**:
  - ▶ **InVal**: 0.33
  - ▶ **OutVal**:
    - ▶ **X**: 2.0
    - ▶ **Y**: 2.0
    - ▶ **Z**: 2.0
- ▶ **2**:
  - ▶ **InVal**: 1.0
  - ▶ **OutVal**:
    - ▶ **X**: 6.0
    - ▶ **Y**: 6.0
    - ▶ **Z**: 6.0

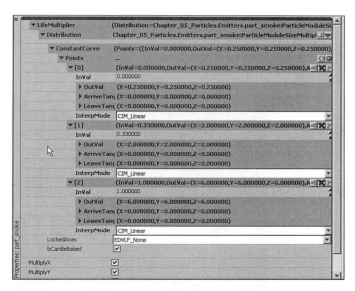

FIGURE 5.199 The three points cause the particles to grow throughout their lifetimes.

7. Add a SubImage Index module. Change the distribution to a FloatUniform and set the following (see **FIGURE 5.200**):

   ▶ **Min**: 0.0

   ▶ **Max**: 3.01

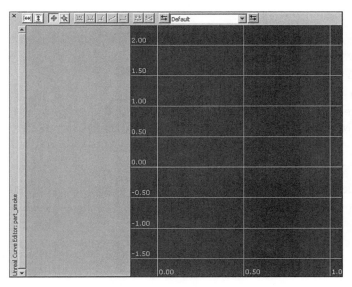

FIGURE 5.200 Remember to set Max to just a little more than the number of the highest index value.

8. Add an Initial Rotation module; the default values work fine.

9. Add an Initial RotRate module and set the following values:

▸ **Min**: −0.2

▸ **Max**: 0.2

10. Add a Cylinder location module and set the following (see **FIGURE 5.201**):

▸ **StartRadius**: 45.0

▸ **StartHeight**: 1.0

▸ **SurfaceOnly**: True

▸ **Velocity**: True

11. Return to the emitter's RequiredModule. Change the SpawnRate property's distribution to ParticleParameter and set the following values:

▸ **ParameterName**: SmokeParticles

▸ **MinInput**: 0.0

▸ **MaxInput**: 6.0

▸ **MinOutput**: 0.0

▸ **MaxOutput**: 50.0

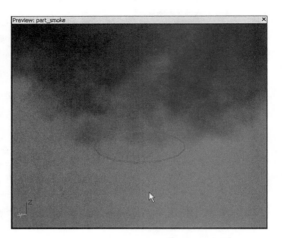

FIGURE 5.201   The Cylinder location module causes the particles to be emitted from a theoretical volume.

12. Right-click the emitter module and choose Particle System > Select ParticleSystem. In the Properties window, set the SecondsBeforeInactive property to 1000. This keeps the smoke emitters from being set to inactive and not rendering the smoke.

13. Save the package. You will not currently be able to see any smoke. This is because the ParticleParameter has currently removed the SpawnRate. However, this also means that we will be able to later activate the smoke through Kismet by ramping up the SpawnRate.

END TUTORIAL 5.25

Now that our smoke mesh has been designed, it's time to place the appropriate emitter actors into the level in **TUTORIAL 5.26**. However, these will not be functional until the Kismet sequence is finalized. Make sure that you have the Chapter_05_Particles package open and that the DM-CH_05_Plasma map in which you placed the beam emitters in the previous tutorials is open as well.

TUTORIAL 5.26: Placing Smoke

1. Select the part_smoke particle system in the Generic Browser. Add a new Emitter actor to the level and move it to the center of the metallic sphere to the right of the room, as seen in the Top viewport (see **FIGURE 5.202**).

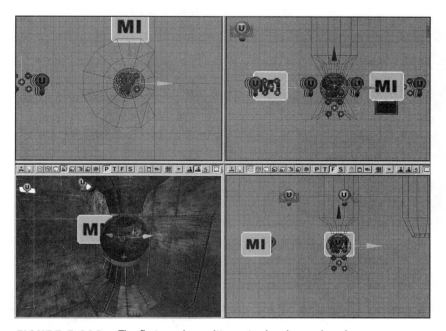

FIGURE 5.202   The first smoke emitter actor has been placed.

2. In the Top viewport, duplicate the emitter and place the new emitter inside of the metallic sphere at the bottom of the room.

3. Still in the Top viewport, duplicate the emitter and place the new emitter inside of the metallic sphere to the left of the room.

4. Duplicate the emitter one more time and place the new emitter inside of the metallic sphere at the top of the room, as seen in the Top viewport.

5. Save the map (see **FIGURE 5.203**).

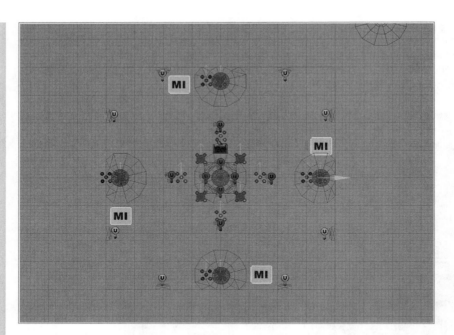

FIGURE 5.203   Each of the four spheres should now have its own smoke emitter.

END TUTORIAL 5.26

In **TUTORIAL 5.27**, we create a mesh emitter system that simulates chunks of exploding spheres flying apart as they overheat and disintegrate. We break this tutorial into four smaller "bite-sized" pieces so that it's easier to follow along. Make sure you have the Chapter_05_Particles package used in the previous tutorials open.

TUTORIAL 5.27: Debris Chunks with Smoke, Part I

1. Create a new ParticleSystem and using the following values (see **FIGURE 5.204**):

    ▶ **Package**: Chapter_05_Particles

    ▶ **Group**: Emitters

    ▶ **Name**: part_debris

2. Create a new emitter in the particle system and name it **Chunks**.

3. Expand the RequiredModule and set the SpawnRate to 0.0. Also, set bKillOnCompleted to True as well as EmitterLoops to 1. We will be using the BurstList to spawn the particles for this emitter. Add an item to the BurstList array and set the following value:

    ▶ **Count**: 12

4. Add a Mesh TypeData module and set the Mesh property to point to the sphere_chunk static mesh, which can be found in the Chapter_05_Particles package (see **FIGURE 5.205**).

5. Select the Lifetime module and set the following values:

   ▶ **Min**: 5.0

   ▶ **Max**: 8.0

6. Select the Initial Size module and set the following values:

   ▶ **Min**:

      ▶ **X**: 1.0

      ▶ **Y**: 1.0

      ▶ **Z**: 1.0

   ▶ **Max**:

      ▶ **X**: 0.5

      ▶ **Y**: 0.5

      ▶ **Z**: 0.5

7. Select the Initial Velocity module and set the following values:

   ▶ **Min**:

      ▶ **X**: 150.0

      ▶ **Y**: 150.0

      ▶ **Z**: 150.0

   ▶ **Max**:

      ▶ **X**: –150.0

      ▶ **Y**: –150.0

      ▶ **Z**: 100.0

8. We now set up the system that fades the color of the particles from glowing orange to black. Add a Color Over Life module and select the ColorOverLife property (particles will suddenly appear). Add one point (for a total of three points) and then set the following values (see **FIGURE 5.206**):

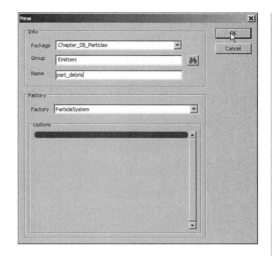

FIGURE 5.204   Create a new particle system with the shown information.

FIGURE 5.205   The Mesh TypeData module turns the emitter into a mesh emitter.

- **0**:
  - **InVal**: 0.0
  - **OutVal X**: 6.0
  - **InterpMode**: CIM_CurveAuto
- **1**:
  - **InVal**: 0.5
  - **OutVal X**: 0.375
  - **InterpMode**: CIM_CurveAuto
- **2**:
  - **InVal**: 0.925
  - **OutVal X**: 0.0

9. Using the Color Over Life module, we also cause the emitted mesh particles to fade away, rather than simply pop out of existence. Change the AlphaOverLife distribution to a FloatConstantCurve and add two points to the curve. Set the following values (see **FIGURE 5.207**):

- **0**:
  - **InVal**: 0.65
  - **OutVal**: 1.0
- **1**:
  - **InVal**: 1.0
  - **OutVal**: 0.0

10. Save the package.

> **NOTE**
>
> We only change the X (red) values. The Y and Z values are irrelevant.

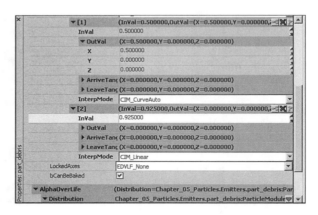

FIGURE 5.206　These points cause the color to fade from its glowing orange to a dull black.

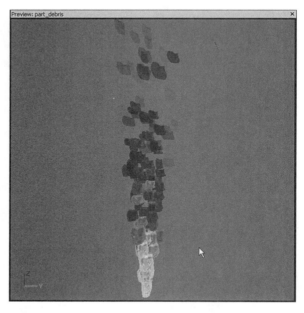

FIGURE 5.207　The chunks now fade away at the end of their lifetimes.

END TUTORIAL 5.27

In **TUTORIAL 5.28**, we continue with the debris effect by tweaking the rotation and collision of the chunks when they are emitted. Make sure that you have the Chapter_05_Particles package used in the previous tutorials open and that you're looking at the part_debris particle system within Cascade. If you have not completed **TUTORIAL 5.27**, you may use the part_debris_01 particle system instead.

TUTORIAL 5.28: Debris Chunks with Smoke, Part II

1. Add an Initial Rotation module and leave it at its default settings (see **FIGURE 5.208**).

> **NOTE**
>
> You could use an Init Mesh Rotation module, but because we're not changing much, it makes little difference.

2. Add an Initial RotRate module and set the following:

   ▶ **Min**: –1.0

   ▶ **Max**: 1.0

3. Add a RotRate/Life module and add one point to its LifeMultiplier curve, for a total of three points in the curve. Set the following values (see **FIGURE 5.209**):

   ▶ **0**:

      ▶ **InVal**: 0.0

      ▶ **OutVal**: 1.0

      ▶ **InterpMode**: CIM_CurveUser

   ▶ **1**:

      ▶ **InVal**: 0.5

      ▶ **OutVal**: 0.5

      ▶ **ArriveTangent**: –3.25

      ▶ **LeaveTangent**: –3.25

      ▶ **InterpMode**: CIM_CurveUser

   ▶ **2**:

      ▶ **InVal**: 0.75

      ▶ **OutVal**: 0.0

FIGURE 5.208   Add an Initial Rotation module.

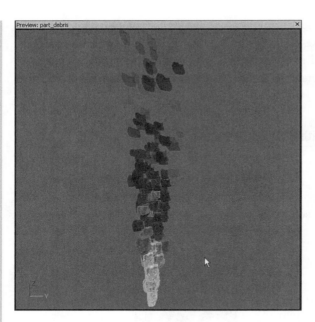

FIGURE 5.209   These points slow the rate of rotation over the life of the particle.

4. Add an Acceleration module and change the Acceleration distribution to a VectorConstant with the following values (see **FIGURE 5.210**):

   ▶ **X**: 0.0

   ▶ **Y**: 0.0

   ▶ **Z**: −200.0

5. Add a Collision module and set the following values:

   ▶ **DampingFactor**: Change to a VectorConstant distribution and set these values:

      ▶ **X**: 0.5

      ▶ **Y**: 0.5

      ▶ **Z**: 0.5

   ▶ **MaxCollisions**:

      ▶ **Min**: 5.0

      ▶ **Max**: 8.0

   ▶ **CollisionCompletionOption**: EPCC_FreezeMovement

6. Save the package.

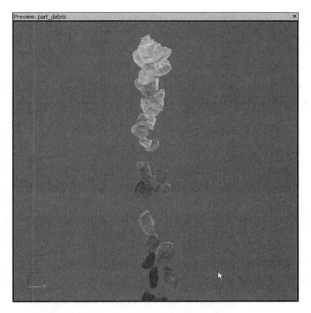

FIGURE 5.210   The particles now fall when created.

END TUTORIAL 5.28

In this part of the setup for the debris emitter, we begin the setup in **TUTORIAL 5.29** for the smoke that comes from each chunk as it is emitted. Make sure that you have the Chapter_05_Particles package used in the previous tutorials open and that you're looking at the part_debris particle system within Cascade. If you have not completed **TUTORIAL 5.28**, you may use the part_debris_02 particle system instead.

TUTORIAL 5.29: Debris Chunks with Smoke, Part III

1. With the mat_smoke material selected in the browser, create a new emitter in the particle system (see **FIGURE 5.211**).

2. Expand the RequiredModule and set the following values:

   ▸ **bKillOnCompleted**: True

   ▸ **EmitterDuration**: 5.0

   ▸ **EmitterLoops**: 1

   ▸ **SpawnRate**: Change to a FloatParticleParameter distribution

      ▸ **ParameterName**: SmokeParticles

      ▸ **MinInput**: 0.0

- ▶ **MaxInput**: 6.0

- ▶ **MinOutput**: 0.0

- ▶ **MaxOutput**: 50.0

- ▶ **Constant**: 30.0

- ▶ **InterpolationMethod**: PSUVIM_Random

- ▶ **SubImages_Horizontal**: 2

- ▶ **SubImages_Vertical**: 2

3. Select the Lifetime module and set a range of 2.5 to 4.0.

4. Select the Initial Size module and set a range of 10.0 to 20.0 for X. Again, Y and Z do not matter.

5. Select the Initial Velocity module and set the following values (see **FIGURE 5.212**):

- ▶ **StartVelocity**

  - ▶ **Max**:

    - ▶ **X**: 10.0

    - ▶ **Y**: 10.0

    - ▶ **Z**: 100.0

  - ▶ **Min**:

    - ▶ **X**: –10.0

    - ▶ **Y**: –10.0

    - ▶ **Z**: 75.0

- ▶ **StartRadialVelocity**

  - ▶ **Min**: 25.0

  - ▶ **Max**: 50.0

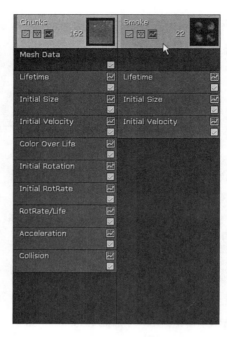

FIGURE 5.211   This new emitter will be used to create smoke trails for the chunks.

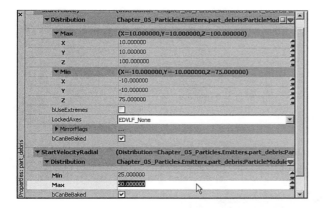

FIGURE 5.212   These settings cause the smoke to rise as it is born and spread out radially.

6. Add an Initial Color module. Change the StartColor distribution to a VectorConstantCurve. Add seven points to the curve and set these values for them:

- **0**:
  - **InVal**: 0.0
  - **OutVal**:
    - **X**: 0.0
    - **Y**: 0.0
    - **Z**: 0.0
- **1**:
  - **InVal**: 0.167
  - **OutVal**:
    - **X**: 0.167
    - **Y**: 0.167
    - **Z**: 0.167
- **2**:
  - **InVal**: 0.33
  - **OutVal**:
    - **X**: 0.33
    - **Y**: 0.33
    - **Z**: 0.33
- **3**:
  - **InVal**: 0.5
  - **OutVal**:
    - **X**: 0.5
    - **Y**: 0.5
    - **Z**: 0.5
- **4**:
  - **InVal**: 0.67
  - **OutVal**:
    - **X**: 0.33
    - **Y**: 0.33
    - **Z**: 0.33
- **5**:
  - **InVal**: 0.83
  - **OutVal**:
    - **X**: 0.167
    - **Y**: 0.167
    - **Z**: 0.167

▶ **6**:

> ▶ **InVal**: 1.0
>
> ▶ **OutVal**:
>
> > ▶ **X**: 0.0
> >
> > ▶ **Y**: 0.0
> >
> > ▶ **Z**: 0.0

This causes the particles to be spawned in different shades of gray, depending on what the EmitterTime is when they are spawned (see **FIGURE 5.213**).

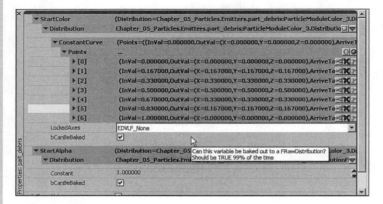

FIGURE 5.213   This is the same setup we used for the smoke effects earlier.

7. Add a Scale Color/Life module. The ColorScaleOverLife distribution has two points in the curve. Set the following values (see **FIGURE 5.214**):

▶ **0**:

> ▶ **InVal**: 0.2
>
> ▶ **OutVal**:
>
> > ▶ **X**: 1.0
> >
> > ▶ **Y**: 1.0
> >
> > ▶ **Z**: 1.0

▶ **1**:

> ▶ **InVal**: 0.5
>
> ▶ **OutVal**:
>
> > ▶ **X**: 0.0
> >
> > ▶ **Y**: 0.0
> >
> > ▶ **Z**: 0.0

8. In the ScaleColor/Life module, set the AlphaScaleOverLife property's distribution to FloatConstantCurve.

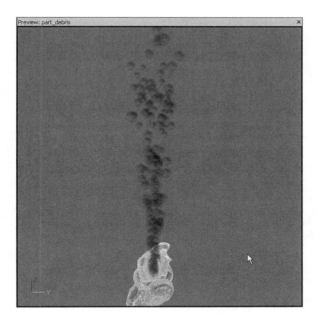

FIGURE 5.214   The smoke now turns black through its lifetime.

9. Send the curves of the Scale Color/Life module to the Curve Editor by clicking the little curve button ![icon] on the module. Right-click the AlphaScaleOverLife curve block and choose Preset Curve. The CurveEd Preset window opens. Select User-Set from the dropdown list in the X/Red/X-Max section (it is the only dropdown enabled).

10. Click the UserCurve property and then click the Show Generic Browser button ![icon]. Select the curve_fade_in_out preset curve in the Chapter_05_Particles package and click the Use Current Selection in Browser button ![icon] of the UserCurve property. Click OK at the bottom of the window (see **FIGURE 5.215**). You should have a nice curve that fades the Alpha from 0 to 1 and then from 1 back to 0 over the life of the particle.

11. Save your package.

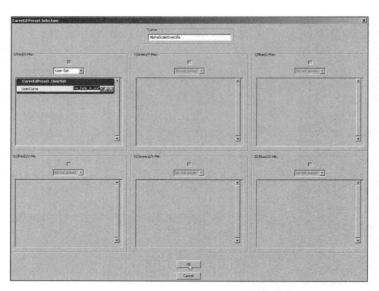

FIGURE 5.215   The CurveEd Preset Selection dialog

END TUTORIAL 5.29

In **TUTORIAL 5.30**, we set the size of each smoke particle and control the manner in which it is emitted from the debris mesh particles. Make sure that you have the Chapter_05_Particles package used in the previous tutorials open and that you're looking at the part_debris particle system within Cascade. If you have not completed **TUTORIAL 5.29**, you may use the part_debris_03 particle system instead.

TUTORIAL 5.30: Debris Chunks with Smoke, Part IV

1. Add a Size By Life module to the smoke emitter. Add a point to the LifeMultiplier distribution for a total of three points in the curve and then set the following values (see **FIGURE 5.216**):

    ▸ **0**:

        ▸ **InVal**: 0.0

        ▸ **OutVal**:

            ▸ **X**: 0.25

            ▸ **Y**: 0.25

            ▸ **Z**: 0.25

    ▸ **1**:

        ▸ **InVal**: 0.33

        ▸ **OutVal**:

            ▸ **X**: 2.0

            ▸ **Y**: 2.0

            ▸ **Z**: 2.0

- ▶ **2**:
    - ▶ **InVal**: 1.0
    - ▶ **OutVal**:
        - ▶ **X**: 6.0
        - ▶ **Y**: 6.0
        - ▶ **Z**: 6.0

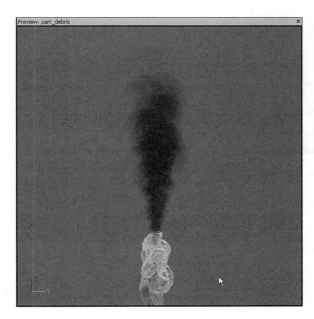

FIGURE 5.216   This causes the smoke to grow as it lives.

2. Add a SubImage Index module. Change the distribution to a FloatUniform and set the following values:

- ▶ **Min**: 0.0
- ▶ **Max**: 3.01

3. Add an Initial Rotation module and leave the values at their defaults (see **FIGURE 5.217**).

4. Add an Initial RotRate module and set the following values:

- ▶ **Min**: –0.2
- ▶ **Max**: 0.2

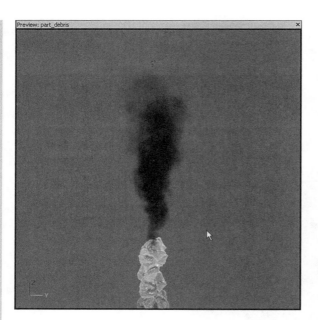

FIGURE 5.217   The Initial Rotation module adds some variation to the smoke.

5. Add an Emitter InitLoc location module and set the following (see **FIGURE 5.218**):

- ▶ **EmitterName**: Chunks
- ▶ **SelectionMethod**: ELESM_Sequential
- ▶ **InheritSourceVelocity**: True
- ▶ **bInheritSourceRotation**: True
- ▶ **InheritSourceVelocityScale**: 0.25

6. Save the package. We will not be placing these emitters into the level; this will be handled through Kismet.

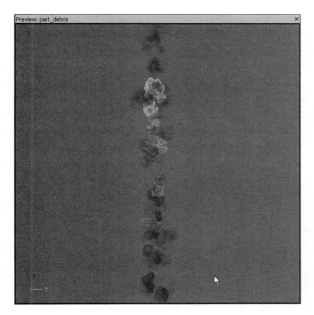

FIGURE 5.218   This causes the smoke to be born at the location of the chunk particles.

END TUTORIAL 5.30

In **TUTORIAL 5.31**, we begin establishing our Kismet sequence. Note that this chapter assumes that you are relatively familiar with placing and connecting Kismet sequence objects.

If you would like to start these tutorials with the earlier parts of the setup completed, simply open the DM-CH_05_Kismet_Begin map included on the DVD in the files for this chapter.

NOTE

Depending on how you have set up your scene, the number values Unreal Editor places in your actor names will likely be different than those you see here in the book. You need to know where you have placed the emitters in your level, and what effect each emitter is producing. Be sure to check the emitter's Template property if you get confused!

TUTORIAL 5.31: Kismet Initial Setup

1. Start by selecting the part_plasma_generator particle system in the Generic Browser and placing an emitter for it in the scene. Position this emitter in the center of the room, within the pale blue sphere. Open its properties and set its bAutoActivate property to False (unchecked).

2. Select the trigger in the map and open Kismet. Right-click and choose New Event Using Trigger_0 > Used from the context menu (see **FIGURE 5.219**).

3. Place a Toggle action next to the event. In the scene, select the emitter actor for the plasma generator (it should be located at the center of the central sphere). Then, back in Kismet, right-click the Target link and create a new object variable from that emitter. Set this Toggle's ObjComment to Plasma Toggle. This is how this action will be referred to when making connections (see **FIGURE 5.220**).

FIGURE 5.219   The Trigger's Used event will begin the entire sequence.

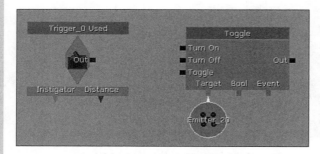

FIGURE 5.220   The plasma generator emitter connects to the Toggle.

4. Connect the Out of the trigger's Used event to the Turn On input of the Plasma Toggle (see **FIGURE 5.221**).

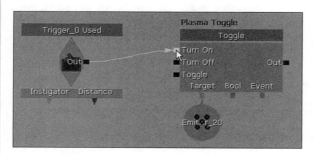

FIGURE 5.221   The Trigger now activates the plasma generator.

5. Place a Delay action and connect the Out of the Toggle to the Start of the Delay (see **FIGURE 5.222**).

6. Place a Random Switch action and connect the Finished of the Delay to the In of the Random Switch. Set the LinkCount of the Random Switch to 4 (see **FIGURE 5.223**).

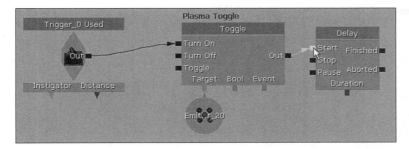

FIGURE 5.222   Connect a new Delay sequence object.

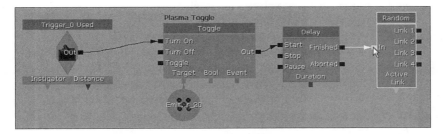

FIGURE 5.223   The Random Switch is used to decide which beam will fire.

7. Place another Toggle action and connect the object variables holding the central beam emitter, the splash beam emitter, and the light that resides precisely in between the cen-

tral column and the metallic sphere to the right of the room when viewing from the Top viewport to the Target link. Make sure to only include those objects that are on the right side of the room, as seen from above, and none of the others. The idea is that you are activating the right side's beam effects.

8. Set this Toggle's ObjComment to Toggle1On. This is how this action is referred to when making connections (see **FIGURE 5.224**).

9. Connect the Link 1 output of the Random Switch to the Turn On input of the Toggle1On (see **FIGURE 5.225**).

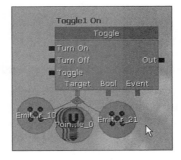

FIGURE 5.224   Connect all three objects to the Toggle's target. Be careful as to which emitter you choose! Check the Template property if you're unsure.

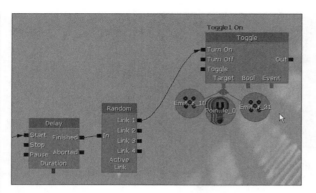

FIGURE 5.225   If Link 1 is chosen, then these objects are toggled on.

10. Save your progress.

END TUTORIAL 5.31

TUTORIAL 5.32 shows how to animate the material for the four spheres, as well as the SpawnRate of our smoke, by way of Matinee. This allows the spheres to appear to get "hotter" through changing the material, and for

> **NOTE**
>
> **TUTORIAL 5.32** assumes a basic knowledge of Matinee.

the amount of smoke emitted by each sphere to increase with the temperature. Make sure that you have the level you saved at the end of **TUTORIAL 5.31** open and that you are looking at the Kismet sequence. If you have not completed the previous tutorial, you may open the DM-Ch_05_Kismet_01 map instead.

TUTORIAL 5.32: Kismet Material and Particle Animation

1. Add a Delay action to the right of the last Toggle action. Connect the Out of the Toggle to the Start of this new Delay. Set the ObjComment of the Delay to Random Delay. This is how we will be referring to this action when making connections (see **FIGURE 5.226**).

2. Place a Random Float variable and connect it to the Duration link of the Random Delay. Set the Min and Max of the Random Float to 1.0 and 4.0, respectively.

> **NOTE**
>
> Because this chapter does not focus directly on animating materials, the MaterialInstanceActors have already been placed in the level. They are used to alter the material for the spheres, which is why there is one actor set aside for each sphere.

3. Create a new Matinee sequence and double-click it to open it (see **FIGURE 5.227**).

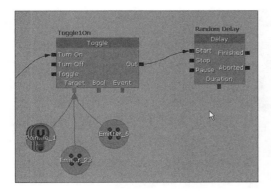

FIGURE 5.226 Create a new Delay action. This is used to set up a random duration for the beams.

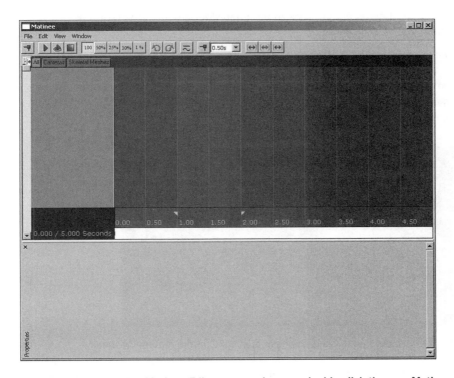

FIGURE 5.227 The Matinee Editor opens when you double-click the new Matinee sequence.

4. Select the MaterialInstanceActor next to the sphere to the right of the room when viewed from the Top viewport. Add a new group to the Matinee sequence and name it **EnergyMat** (see **FIGURE 5.228**).

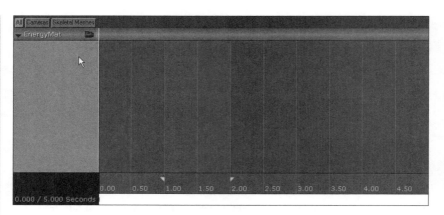

FIGURE 5.228   This new group is associated with the MaterialInstanceActor.

5. Create a new Float Material Param Track to the EnergyMat group and set its ParameterName property to **Energy**.

6. Set a key with a value of 0.0 at Time=0.0 and a key with value 6.0 at Time=6.0 (see **FIGURE 5.229**). This will require that you move the Duration flag to accommodate the extended time. As a reminder, you can add the key by clicking the Add Key button ⊣ on the toolbar, and you can change the value of a key by right-clicking it and choosing Set Value from the context menu that appears.

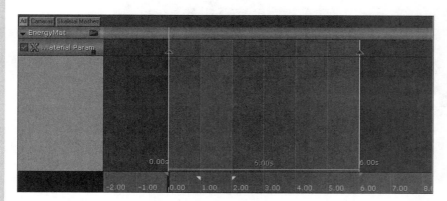

FIGURE 5.229   The two keys are used to increase the "heat" of the material instance.

7. Select the smoke particles emitter placed inside the sphere to the right of the room when viewed from the top viewport. Add a new group to the Matinee sequence and name it **SmokeParticles**.

8. Create a new Float Particle Param Track to the SmokeParticles group and set its ParameterName property to **SmokeParticles** (see **FIGURE 5.230**).

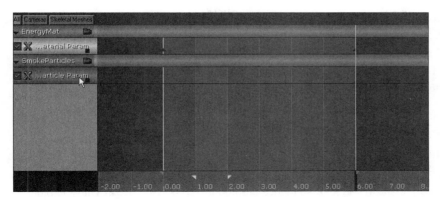

FIGURE 5.230 The Float Particle Param Track drives the amount of smoke particles being emitted by the sphere as it heats up.

9. Set a key with a value of 0.0 at Time=0.0 and a key with value 6.0 at Time=6.0.

10. Make these connections (see **FIGURE 5.231**):

> ▶ Toggle1On-Out → Matinee-Play
>
> ▶ Random Delay-Finished → Matinee-Reverse
>
> ▶ Random Delay-Finished → Random Switch-In

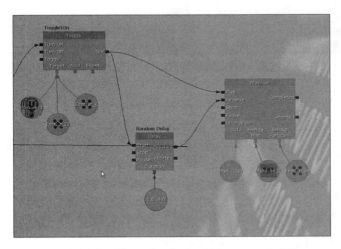

FIGURE 5.231 The network should be connected like so.

11. Save your level so that you do not lose your progress.

END TUTORIAL 5.32

If you have not completed **TUTORIAL 5.32**, you may open the DM-Ch_05_Kismet_02 map to begin **TUTORIAL 5.33**. To add to the effect of our spheres' glow, we animate a series of orange lights in the level to get brighter while the spheres get hot. Because the initial Matinee system is already set up and the lights we need are already in place, this will be very easy to do. Even though this has little to do with particles, it is a very important way to accentuate your final effect.

TUTORIAL 5.33: Animating Lights with Matinee

1. In the rightmost sphere—as seen from the Top viewport—select the blue light that resides within the sphere. You may need to click the Show All Actors button ![icon] to make it visible.

2. Back in Kismet, open the Matinee sequence created in **TUTORIAL 5.32**. With the blue light selected, add a new group to the Matinee named **GlowLight** (see **FIGURE 5.232**).

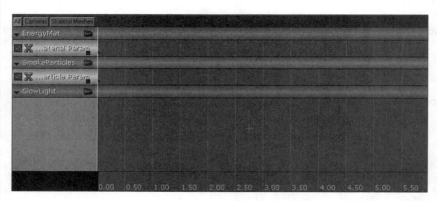

FIGURE 5.232   This new group is connected to the light at the center of the sphere.

3. Add a new Color Property Track to the group and click OK in the dialog that appears.

4. Add a key at frame 0.0. Right-click the key you just created and choose Set Color. You should set this color to the same color the light was initially set to. Add a second key at 6.0 and right-click it to change the color. Set the color for this second key to bright orange-red.

5. We now need to adjust the curves of this transition. If you scrub the Matinee timeline and watch the viewport, you'll probably see why. The blue-to-orange shift results in a primarily purple look to our light for a pretty good chunk of the time. Click the small black box in the lower-right corner of the LightColor track and then click the Toggle Curve Editor button ![icon] located at the top of the Matinee window. This opens up the curves for this track in the Curve Editor (see **FIGURE 5.233**).

6. The green channel does not change much, so we can leave that alone. Click the small green box in the OrangeLight_LightColor track on the left side of the Curve Editor to hide the green curve.

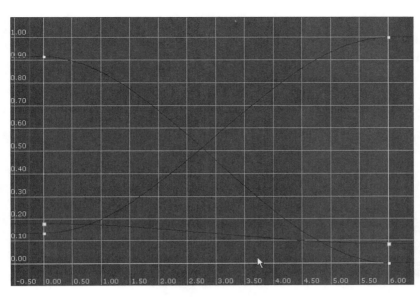

FIGURE 5.233
The curves look like so in the Curve Editor when first opened.

7. Select the first key of the blue curve and move the tangent handle down so that the curve quickly swoops down to 0 without actually crossing it. Then, move the tangent handle of the first key of the red curve upward so that the curve arcs up very quickly without crossing 1.0 (see **FIGURE 5.234**).

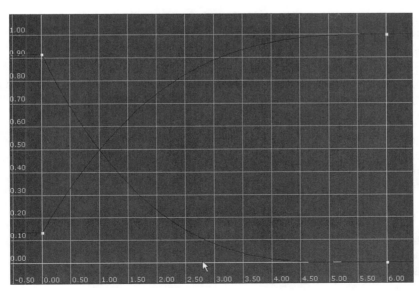

FIGURE 5.234
Your newly edited curves appear like so.

8. Close Matinee and save your progress.

END TUTORIAL 5.33

In **TUTORIAL 5.34**, we now add the component to our sequence that destroys a sphere once its explosion threshold has been reached. The component will also spawn the debris particles. If you have not completed **TUTORIAL 5.33**, you may open the DM-Ch_05_Kismet_03 map to begin here.

TUTORIAL 5.34: Kismet Spawn and Destroy

1. Place an Actor Factory action and set its ObjComment to Spawn Debris (see **FIGURE 5.235**).

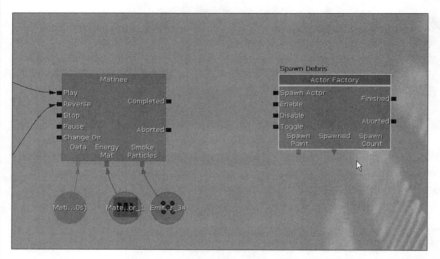

FIGURE 5.235   This new action creates our debris during gameplay.

2. Connect the Completed output of the Matinee to the Spawn Actor input of the Spawn Debris action.

3. With the Actor Factory selected, click the right side of the Factory property and create an ActorFactoryEmitter. Set the ParticleSystem property of the factory to point to the part_debris particle system in the Chapter_05_Particles package (see **FIGURE 5.236**).

4. Select the metallic sphere to the right of the room when viewed from the top viewport and right-click the Spawn Point link of the Spawn Debris action; choose Create New Object Var Using... (see **FIGURE 5.237**).

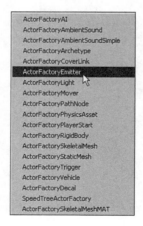

FIGURE 5.236   You can find the ActorFactoryEmitter in the dropdown on the right side of the Factory property.

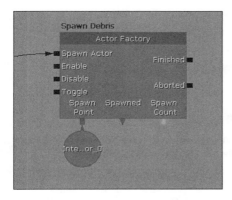

FIGURE 5.237   You should now have a new Object Variable that is associated with the rightmost sphere, as seen from the Top viewport.

5. Place a Destroy action (under Actor) and set its ObjComment to Kill Ball.

6. Connect the object variable just created to the Target link of the Kill Ball action.

7. Connect the Finished output of the Spawn Debris to the In of the Kill Ball (see **FIGURE 5.238**).

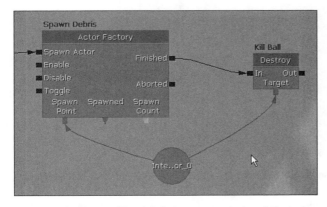

FIGURE 5.238   The debris is now created and the sphere is destroyed once the Matinee sequence completes.

8. Save your progress.

END TUTORIAL 5.34

The next step is to set up the initial conditions for the beams in **TUTORIAL 5.35**. We check to see if the beams are on and if the sphere has been destroyed before actually activating the system.

This keeps us from turning on beams that point toward destroyed spheres. If you have not completed **TUTORIAL 5.34**, you may open the DM-Ch_05_Kismet_04 map to begin here.

TUTORIAL 5.35: Kismet Initial Conditions

1. In between the Random Switch and the Toggle1On action, place a Compare Bool condition and set its ObjComment to **Check Ball Killed**. This will be used to bypass the network if the sphere has already been destroyed.

> **NOTE**
>
> Fitting this new action in place may require that you move the rest of the network to the right.

2. Right-click the Bool link and choose Create New Bool Variable. Set the VarName of the variable to **bBall1Destroyed** (see **FIGURE 5.239**).

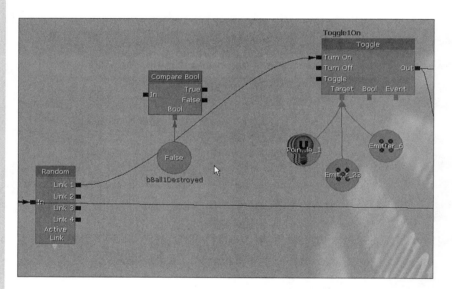

FIGURE 5.239   Create a new Boolean variable to hold the value of whether the ball is destroyed.

3. Place another Compare Bool condition and set its ObjComment to **Check Beam On**. This will be used to bypass the Toggle1On action if the beams are already on. The emitters don't like to be turned on when they are already on, and at times will actually turn off instead.

4. Right-click the Bool link and choose Create New Bool Variable. Set the VarName of the variable to **bBeam1On** (see **FIGURE 5.240**).

5. Connect the False of Check Ball Killed to the In of Check Beam On.

6. Place a Bool action (under Set variable) and set its ObjComment to **Set Beam On**.

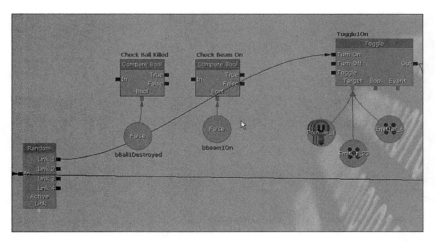

FIGURE 5.240   The new Compare Bool and Boolean variable have been created.

7. Connect its Target link to the bBeam1On variable (see **FIGURE 5.241**).

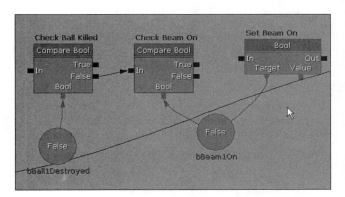

FIGURE 5.241   The new Bool action is setting the value of the bBeam1On variable.

8. Right-click the Value link and choose Create New Bool variable. Set the bValue property to 1.

9. Connect the False link of Check Beam On to the In of Set Beam On (see **FIGURE 5.242**).

10. Right-click the Turn On link of the Toggle1On action and choose Cut Connections. Then, right-click the In of Check Ball Killed and choose Paste Connections (see **FIGURE 5.243**).

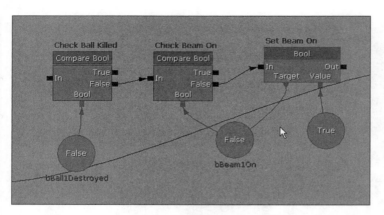

FIGURE 5.242   Connect Check Beam On and Set Beam On like so.

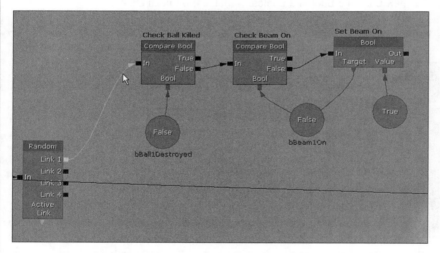

FIGURE 5.243   Using Paste Connections connects the Random's Link 1 to the Check Ball Killed action's input.

11. Make the following connections:

> ▶ Check Ball Killed-True → Random Switch-In
>
> ▶ Check Beam On-True → Random Delay-Start
>
> ▶ Check Beam On-True → Matinee-Play
>
> ▶ Set Beam On-Out → Toggle1On-Turn On

12. Save your progress.

END TUTORIAL 5.35

TUTORIAL 5.36 sets up a system that eliminates this network from being triggered again by the Random Switch later on. Effectively, this means that the link connecting to this network will be dead, which makes sense; once the sphere in this end of the room is destroyed, you don't want the beam to come back on. If you have not completed **TUTORIAL 5.35**, you may open the DM-Ch_05_Kismet_05 map to begin here.

TUTORIAL 5.36: Kismet Kill Link

1. Place a Set Particle Param action to the right of the Kill Ball action and set its ObjComment to **Kill Smoke** (see **FIGURE 5.244**).

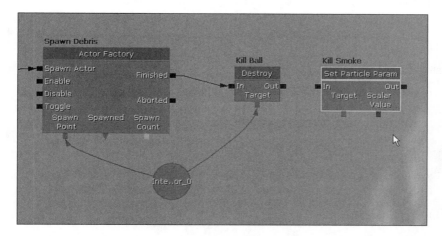

FIGURE 5.244   This new action is used to turn off our smoke emitter.

2. Add an item to the InstanceParameters array and set the following:

    ▸ **Name**: SmokeParticles

    ▸ **ParamType**: PSPT_Scalar

3. Select the smoke emitter for the metallic ball to the right of the room when viewed from the Top viewport. Right-click the Target link of the Update Particles action and choose New Object Var Using... to create a variable connected to the link.

4. Place a Set Bool action (under Set variable) and set its ObjComment to **Set Ball Killed** (see **FIGURE 5.245**).

5. Create a Named Variable and set its FindVarName property to **bBall1Destroyed**. Connect it to the Target link of the Set Ball Killed action.

6. Right-click the Value link of the Set Ball Killed action and choose Create New Bool Variable. Set its value to 1 (True).

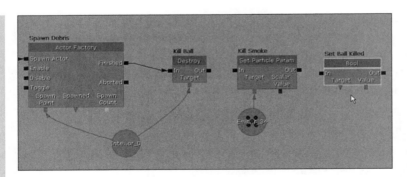

FIGURE 5.245 This new Set Bool action designates the sphere on this side of the room as destroyed.

7. Make the following connections (see **FIGURE 5.246**):

   ▶ Kill Ball-Out → Kill Smoke-In

   ▶ Kill Smoke-Out → Set ball Killed-In

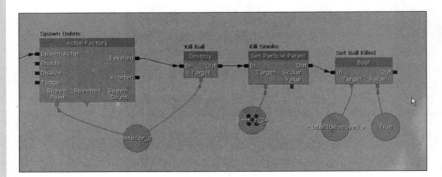

FIGURE 5.246 Your new network connects like this.

8. Create a new Toggle action, set the ObjComment property to **Turn Off Light and Arcs**, and connect the Out of Set Ball Killed to the Turn Off of the new Toggle.

9. Select the light at the center of the rightmost sphere (as viewed from the Top viewport) as well as the emitter that is in the base of the column creating the upward electrical arcs. Back in Kismet, right-click the Target input of the new Toggle and choose New Object Var Using... from the context menu. This will connect these two object variables to the target (see **FIGURE 5.247**).

10. Save your progress.

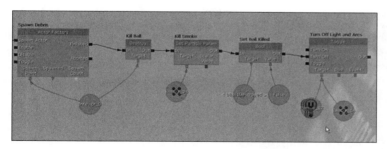

FIGURE 5.247   Your new network connects like this.

END TUTORIAL 5.36

In **TUTORIAL 5.37**, we now establish the system that turns off our beam when the sphere is destroyed. If you have not completed **TUTORIAL 5.36**, you may open the DM-Ch_05_Kismet_06 map to begin here.

TUTORIAL 5.37: Kismet Toggle Off

1. Place a Toggle action to the right of all the other actions and set its ObjComment to **Toggle1Off**.

2. Locate the three object variables connected to Toggle1On. Duplicate them and connect the duplicates to Toggle1Off (see **FIGURE 5.248**).

3. Connect the Out of Turn Off Light and Arcs to the Turn Off of Toggle1Off.

4. Place a Bool action (under Set variable) and set its ObjComment to **Set Beam Off**.

5. Create a Named Variable and set its FindVarName property to **bBeam1On**. Connect it to the Target link of the Set Beam Off action (see **FIGURE 5.249**).

6. Right-click the Value link and choose Create New Bool Variable. The default value (False) is what we want, so don't change that.

7. Connect the Out of Toggle1Off to the In of Set Beam Off (see **FIGURE 5.250**).

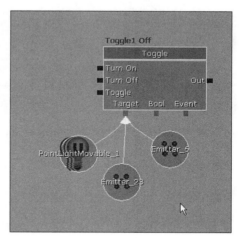

FIGURE 5.248   Here you can see the new Toggle and its variables.

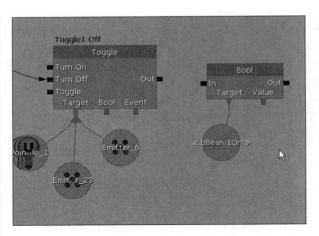

FIGURE 5.249   The new Bool and its Named Variable are now in place.

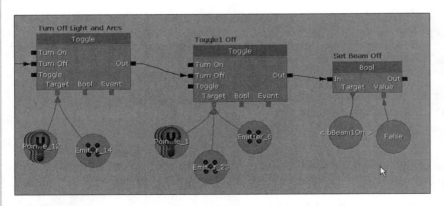

FIGURE 5.250   The new action is now integrated into the network.

8. Save your progress.

END TUTORIAL 5.37

In **TUTORIAL 5.38**, we now take the massive network we've created and duplicated it to create the beams that will connect to the remaining spheres in the room. This requires adjusting some of the variables in the network. Take your time; this is easy to mess up! If you have not completed **TUTORIAL 5.37**, you may open the DM-Ch_05_Kismet_07 map to begin here.

TUTORIAL 5.38: Kismet Links 2, 3, and 4

1. Select the entire network to the right of the Random Switch action and duplicate it. Move the new network below the original (see **FIGURE 5.251**).

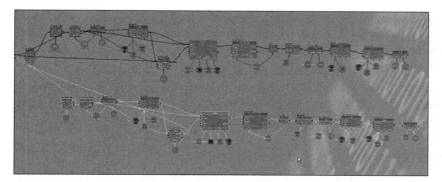

FIGURE 5.251   The entire network has now been duplicated and moved down.

2. Go through and rename all the variables that have a "1" in their names, replacing the 1 with 2.

3. Update the object variables to point to the correct light and emitters in the level. These should be the light and emitters (central beams, splash beams, smoke) associated with the metallic sphere at the bottom of the room when viewed from the Top viewport.

The following is a reminder list as to what to change on the second copy of the network:

- ▶ **Check Ball Killed (Compare Bool)**: Change the varname of bBall1Destroyed to bBall2Destroyed.

- ▶ **Check Beam On (Compare Bool)**: Change the varname of bBeam1On to bBall2On.

- ▶ **Toggle1 On**: Change the ObjComment to Toggle2Off. Get object variables for the bottom sphere's Central Beam emitter, Splash Beam emitter, and the light that is centered in between the central column and the bottom sphere.

- ▶ **Matinee**: Replace the object variable connected to EnergyMat with a new object variable from the materialinstanceactor next to the bottom sphere. Replace the object variable connected to Smoke Particles with a new object variable from the smoke emitter from the center of the bottom sphere. Replace the object variable connected to Glow Light with a new object variable from the blue light at the center of the bottom sphere.

- ▶ **Spawn Debris (Actor Factory)**: Replace the object variable connected to the Point input with a new object variable created from the InterpActor for the bottommost sphere. Remember to also connect this new object variable to the Target of the Kill Ball (Destroy) action.

- **Kill Smoke**: Duplicate the object variable connected to the Smoke Particles input on the Matinee sequence object, and connect the duplicate to the Target input.

- **Set Ball Killed**: Change the findvarname for the Target input's Boolean variable to bball2destroyed.

- **Turn Off Light and Arcs**: Replace the two object variables with new object variables referencing the light at the center of the bottom sphere and the emitter for the electrical arcs, which is within the base of the bottommost column, as seen from the Top viewport.

- **Toggle1Off**: Change objcomment to Toggle2Off. Get object variables for the bottom sphere's Central Beam emitter, Splash Beam emitter, and the light that is at the center of the sphere. These can be duplicated from Toggle2Off if you have already acquired these variables.

- **Set Beam Off**: Change Target's Boolean variable findvarname to bball2on.

4. Connect the Link2 output of the Random Switch to the In of the Check Ball Killed action of the new network (see **FIGURE 5.252**).

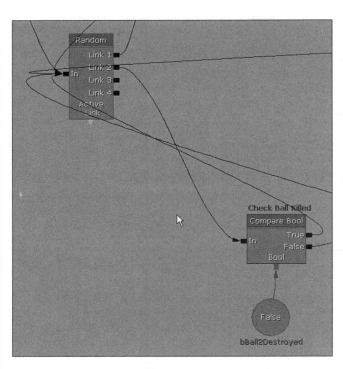

FIGURE 5.252   The second network is now activated by Link 2.

5. Repeat this process two more times, replacing the numbered variables with the correct numbers (3 and 4) and updating the object variables to point to the correct light and emitters for the metallic spheres to the left and at the top of the room when viewed from the top.

6. Connect the Link 3 and Link 4 outputs of the Random Switch action to the In links of the Check Ball Killed actions for the respective new networks (see **FIGURE 5.253**).

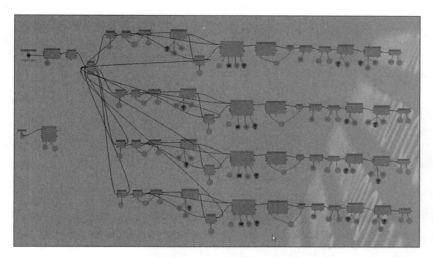

FIGURE 5.253   The remaining two networks are now using links 3 and 4.

7. Connect the False link of the Check Ball Killed action of each network to the Turn Off input of the Toggle*Off actions of each of the other three networks. This means the False output of each Check Ball Killed action will be connected to three Toggle actions. A fast way to do this is to right-click the False output of the Check Ball Killed action and choose Copy Connections from the context menu, and then right-click the Turn Off input of each of the three Toggle*Off actions and choose Paste Connections.

8. Save your progress. Don't run your level without completing **TUTORIAL 5.39**!

END TUTORIAL 5.38

At this point, you should have four total copies of the network, each with its own set of variables that distinguish a particular beam emitter, splash beam emitter, smoke emitter, debris emitter, and lights. However, we still have a problem. At this time, once all the spheres are destroyed, the game gets caught in an infinite loop in which it checks to see if a random sphere is destroyed, discovers that it is, and checks to see if another random sphere is destroyed, and repeats forever. This locks up the game rather quickly once all four of the spheres are gone.

We can fix this problem by putting in a series of checks. These checks will see if any of the spheres are still remaining. If they have all been destroyed, the Random Switch will not be activated again, which will prevent us from accidentally killing the game. To begin **TUTORIAL 5.39**, you may open the DM-Ch_05_Kismet_08 map if you have not completed **TUTORIAL 5.38**.

TUTORIAL 5.39: Kismet End Conditions

1. Back in the original (first) network, place a Compare Bool condition above and to the right of the Set Ball Killed action and set its ObjComment to **Check Ball2 Killed**.

2. Create a Named variable and set its FindVarName property to **bBall2Destroyed**. Connect the variable to the Bool link of the Check Ball2 Killed condition (see **FIGURE 5.254**).

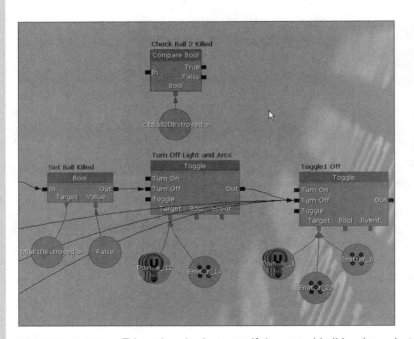

FIGURE 5.254   This action checks to see if the second ball has been destroyed.

3. Connect the Out of the Set Ball Killed action to the In of the Check Ball2 Killed action.

4. Duplicate the Check Ball2 Killed action along with its variable. Move the copy slightly to the right of the original, and change the references to Ball2 to Ball3.

5. Connect the True of the Check Ball2 Killed action to the In of the Check Ball3 Killed action (see **FIGURE 5.255**).

6. Repeat steps 4 and 5 to create a third Compare Bool to check the status of Ball4 (see **FIGURE 5.256**).

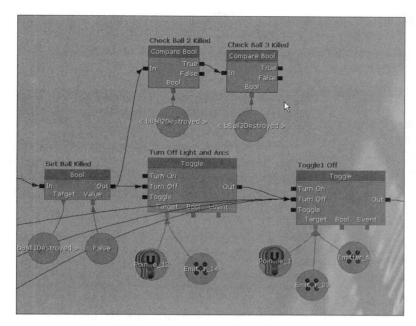

FIGURE 5.255   There is now a second Compare Bool checking the status of Ball3.

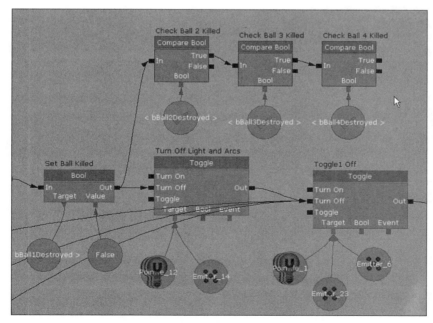

FIGURE 5.256   You are now checking the status of all remaining spheres.

7. Connect the False links of each of the Bool conditions to the In of the Random Switch action. Once again, a fast way to do this is to copy the connections from the In of the Random Switch and then paste them onto the False outputs of each of the Compare Bools.

8. Select all three of the Compare Bool actions along with their variables. Duplicate these sequence objects for each of the three remaining networks, and connect them to their respective Set Ball Killed actions. Change the references of the ObjComments and FindVarNames to reflect the following criteria:

   ▶ Network 2: Checks Ball1, Ball3, and Ball4

   ▶ Network 3: Checks Ball1, Ball2, and Ball4

   ▶ Network 4: Checks Ball1, Ball2, and Ball3

9. Save your progress and rebuild your lighting (if necessary). You should now (finally) be ready to test out your level (see **FIGURE 5.257**)!

FIGURE 5.257   Each of your spheres should now detonate after the beam has been focused on them for a few seconds.

END TUTORIAL 5.39

Troubleshooting the Effect

Here is a list of likely places where your effect could have problems. Be sure to check these if you have any difficulties:

▶ The Trail emitters around the top of the room can sometimes lose their Template value when doing attachments. If you don't see trails, make sure to reassign their template to part_trails.

▶ Make sure your Beam Spray emitters are associated with the proper InterpActor through their Instanced Parameters.

▶ Make sure your object variables are chosen carefully. Double-check the Template property to make sure you have the right one selected.

- ▶ Check all your Named Variables, and make sure that they are referencing the proper variables. Also, make sure that any duplicated variables being referenced by a Named Variable have had their names changed appropriately.

- ▶ If you notice that your smoke isn't switching off, you can try adding a Float Variable to the Scalar input of your Kill Smoke actions.

Summary

Unreal Editor's particle system runs deep. It provides you with a degree of power over your particle systems similar to that of today's high-end special-effects software. Now that you have completed this chapter, we encourage you to test your skills and develop your own custom particle systems. By combining multiple emitters, making the most of your modules, and employing Kismet to help control how the particles change throughout your gameplay, you will find that special effects in Unreal give you vast amounts of creative power and can enable you to create some truly unique and exciting gaming experiences!

Chapter 6

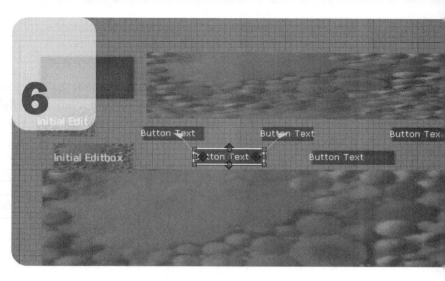

Creating User Interfaces

User interfaces are a common feature in many games, allowing the designer to display a variety of information to the user, and providing the user with access to certain options. In Unreal Engine 3, user interfaces (*UIs* for short) also provide a way to create a head-up display (HUD) for the player to view important information during gameplay. In this chapter, you learn about the UnrealUI System and how it can be used to create a variety of UIs, ranging from a selection of options to a constantly updating UI serving as an in-game HUD.

UI Components

A UI in Unreal is composed of three primary components: the UIScene, a collection of widgets, and some series of Kismet sequences. Knowing the purpose and function of each of these components is necessary to create your user interfaces.

The basic foundation of a user interface is a UIScene. When designing a UI, the very first step is to create your initial UIScene and construct the UI upon it. A UIScene is simply a collection of various functional parts, known as *widgets*. Widgets include such things as buttons, sliders, progress bars, and other components that create the finalized UI. It may help to think of the relationship of UIScenes to widgets as being the same as the relationship of a level to its included actors (see **FIGURE 6.1**).

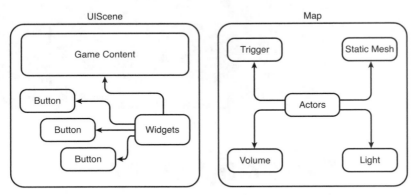

FIGURE 6.1   This diagram illustrates the relationship between widgets and UIScenes.

Functionality for a UI comes from Kismet. When working with user interfaces, you have access to a specialized version of the Kismet Editor that contains a variety of UI-relevant events. Each of these events is divided up into a series of states, which we will discuss later.

UIs Versus HUDs

An interesting and almost philosophical concept to consider when working on UIs is the decision whether to create a conventional user interface, which would take over all gameplay until the player completes whatever task is required within the UI, or a head-up display, which simply outputs and updates information to the screen during gameplay. Traditionally, UIs are reserved for the very beginning of a game, allowing the user to change certain game options (such as resolution and difficulty), to load a saved game, or to simply start a new game. UIs can also become a gameplay element, allowing players to interact with certain game elements. In some cases they can even become a game unto themselves. For example, you could theoretically use a UI to control conversations with other characters in your game, or perhaps use it to control a computer that exists in the game's world.

A HUD, on the other hand, has an entirely different function. Its purpose is to deliver pertinent information throughout gameplay, and to do it in a nondistractive manner. HUD elements could include crosshairs for a weapon, a number or indicator for how much health the player has, a radar screen for tracking enemy movements, or even just a simple timer and score display. The tricky part to keep in mind is that both traditional user interfaces and HUDs are developed as a part of the UI system and require similar techniques to create, although they use different options.

UI Design Workflow Overview

Creating UIs for use in your games can be a daunting task. You need to know what sort of functionality you're going to need, whether you're going to need multiple UIs to get the job done, and a variety of other considerations. However, when boiled down, UI creation can be simplified into three basic steps: layout, functionality, and implementation.

Layout

This phase of UI design involves the actual creation of the look and feel of the UI. Are you creating a traditional UI or a HUD? Will you use images? Sliders? Buttons? What sort of information are you going to convey to the user, and what is it you need him or her to do? It's always a good idea to start this phase of creation with a pen and paper. Jot down some notes about exactly what it is you need to accomplish, and start your design from there.

You will then create your UIScene inside of the UIScene Editor. This is where you actually get to lay out all the buttons, switches, and dials that make up your UI. Again, make sure you have a plan of attack; don't jump into a UI thinking you can just slap something together.

Functionality

This is where you make the UI you've just created actually do something. This involves the use of Kismet. As you work with UIs, you'll discover that an entire collection of Kismet sequence objects is solely dedicated to working with UIs. Using Kismet, you'll cause each aspect of your UI to have some sort of effect on your game.

Implementation

By the time you reach the implementation stage, you have a functioning UI. Even though the process can be described fairly quickly, you shouldn't get the idea that reaching this stage is easy. Getting to this part of your workflow can take considerable time, depending on the level of complexity in getting your UI to be functional. Now all you need to worry about is how the user is going to come across your UI in the first place. Does the UI appear when the game begins or when the character uses a particular object? This last part of the UI workflow involves making your UI into a seamless gaming element, rather than just a theoretical design.

In **TUTORIAL 6.1**, we create the basic widget layout for our first user interface. However, keep in mind that because we are currently using only the default skin, our first few UIs will not have a very exciting appearance. Later in the chapter, we discuss the process of skinning and adjusting styles, at which point you will be able to change the look of your UIs to suit your tastes.

TUTORIAL 6.1: Your First UI, Part I: Creating the Basic Layout

1. Launch Unreal Editor and open the DM-CH_06_Goodbye_Start map included on the DVD in the files for this chapter.

2. Your first step is to create a new User Interface Scene. In the Generic Browser, right-click and choose New UIScene from the context menu. Enter the following information (see **FIGURE 6.2**):

    Package: Chapter_06_UI

    Group: UIScenes

    Name: UI_Goodbye_World

3. The UIScene Editor automatically appears once you have created the new UIScene. We discuss this editor in depth later in this chapter. For now, we need to create the various control objects (widgets) that will comprise our simple UI.

FIGURE 6.2   This package will be reused throughout the chapter.

    a. In the UIScene Editor's toolbar, click the Label Button icon ![ABC]. Then, in the main viewport of the UIScene Editor, drag out a new Label Button onto the grid. Note that you can resize the button by dragging the handles at the corners (see **FIGURE 6.3**).

    b. In the Label Button's properties, expand the Data tab and the Caption Data Source category. Inside you find the MarkupString property, which controls what text appears in the button.

    c. Set the MarkupString property to **Goodbye World** (see **FIGURE 6.4**).

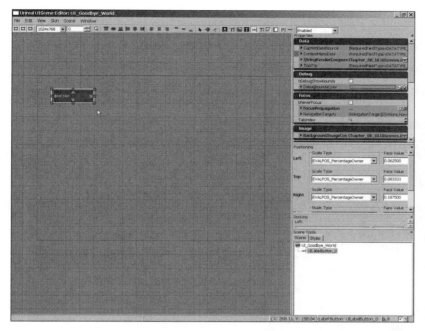

FIGURE 6.3 The Label Button has been placed.

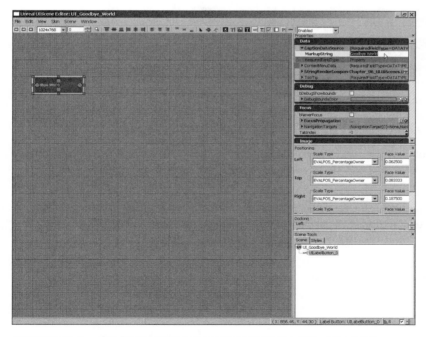

FIGURE 6.4 The MarkupString property controls the text of the label.

d. Also under the Data category, expand the StringRenderComponent property and locate the StyleOverride category. Check TextAlignment and set the following properties underneath the TextAlignment property (see **FIGURE 6.5**):

UIORIENT_Horizontal: Center

UIORIENT_Vertical: Center

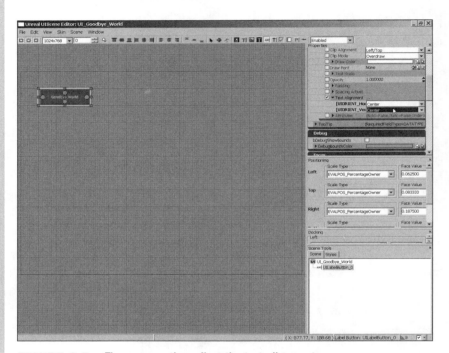

FIGURE 6.5   These properties adjust the text alignment.

e. Close the UIScene Editor and save your package when finished.

For the sake of example, we're going to implement this UI into our level before we add our functionality so that you can see the layout as it would appear in an actual UI. We do this using Kismet.

4. Open the Kismet Editor for your level by clicking the Kismet button **K** at the top of the Unreal Editor user interface. Right-click in the Sequence view and choose New Event > Level Beginning (see **FIGURE 6.6**).

5. Right-click and choose New Action > UI > Open Scene. Connect a wire from the Out output of the Level Beginning event to the In input of the Open Scene sequence object (see **FIGURE 6.7**).

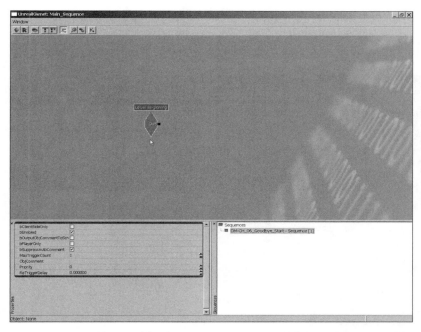

FIGURE 6.6   The Level Beginning event opens our UIScene when the level starts.

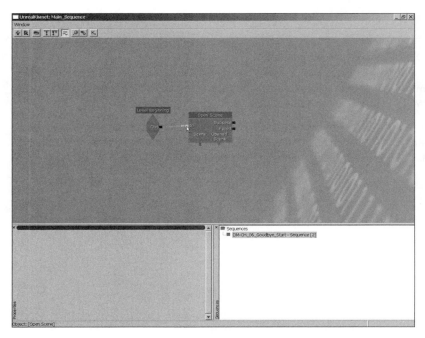

FIGURE 6.7   The new Open Scene object launches our UI.

6. Right-click the small pink input box underneath the Scene label on the Open Scene sequence object and choose Create New Object Variable from the context menu (see **FIGURE 6.8**).

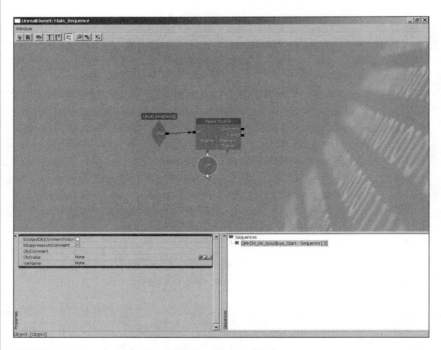

FIGURE 6.8 An object variable has been added.

7. Select the new object variable. Using the Generic Browser, set the ObjValue property to the UI_Goodbye_World UIScene (see **FIGURE 6.9**).

8. Save and test your map by right-clicking the floor and choosing Play From Here. When you launch the map, you will notice the UI appear (see **FIGURE 6.10**). Currently the button is nonfunctional. If you press the Esc key, the UI will disappear.

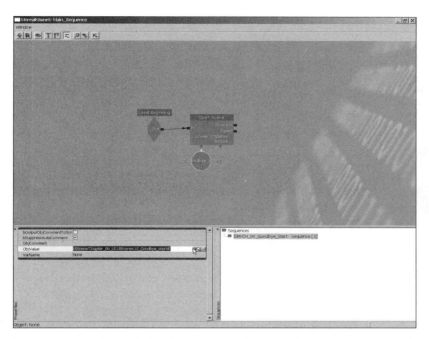

FIGURE 6.9   The object variable now specifies our UI.

FIGURE 6.10   The UI now appears when you launch the game.

END TUTORIAL 6.1

The UI Scene Editor

The UI Scene Editor is your primary tool for designing user interfaces. It provides a visual interface within which you can lay out all your widgets, establish their properties, and access Kismet to insert your functionality. The Scene Editor is broken up into six primary parts, as shown in **FIGURE 6.11**.

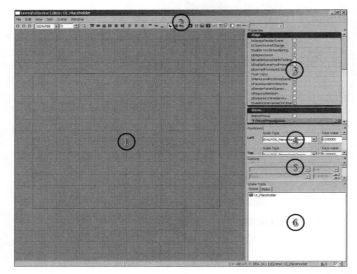

1. Scene viewport
2. Scene toolbar
3. Scene Properties panel
4. Scene Positioning panel
5. Scene Docking panel
6. Scene Tools panel

FIGURE 6.11   The UI Scene Editor

The Scene Viewport

This is the large area that dominates the left side of the UIScene Editor. Here, you create the layout for your UI by placing a variety of widgets. This viewport can be navigated very similarly to Unreal Editor's standard orthogonal viewports, in that you can left-click-drag in an empty area to move about, and zoom in and out by dragging with the left and right mouse buttons. If you need to reset your view to eliminate the effects of zooming, you may choose View > Reset View from the main menu bar.

> **NOTE**
>
> As with many of the editor windows within Unreal Editor, each of the panels can be moved, undocked, closed, and opened, allowing for a highly customizable editor interface!

The Scene Toolbar

This area holds a series of icons that pertain to commonly performed tasks in the Editor. Here, you find commands to show or hide guide outlines, resize the UIScene, align widgets and text, create a variety of widgets, and preview enabled and disabled states on selected widgets.

The Scene Properties Panel

The Scene Properties panel is where you set up the pertinent properties for each of the widgets in your scene. It is very similar to the Properties windows scattered throughout other areas of Unreal Editor.

The Scene Positioning Panel

The Scene Positioning panel contains the settings used to control the selected widget's location and scale based on the size of the game window. This keeps the UIScene looking proper no matter what the size of the window on which the game is being played.

The Scene Docking Panel

The Scene Docking panel allows the docking of the selected widget to be set through Properties windows instead of visually in the viewport.

The Scene Tools Panel

This panel provides a hierarchical list of all the widgets in your UIScene. You will also find a list of all the styles available for the

> **TIP**
>
> Each of the panels for the UIScene Editor can be shown and hidden using the editor's Window menu.

multiple aspects of your UI. You can change each of these styles and then save them to a new skin. Working with skins and styles is discussed later in this chapter.

Complete **TUTORIAL 6.1** before attempting **TUTORIAL 6.2**. If you have not done so, you may use the UI_Goodbye_World_01 UIScene and DM-CH_06_Goodbye_01 map to complete this tutorial.

TUTORIAL 6.2: Your First UI, Part II: Adding Functionality

1. In the Generic Browser, locate the Chapter_06_UI package and double-click the UI_Goodbye_World UIScene to open the UIScene Editor.

2. In the Scene viewport, right-click the button and choose Kismet Editor from the context menu (see **FIGURE 6.12**).

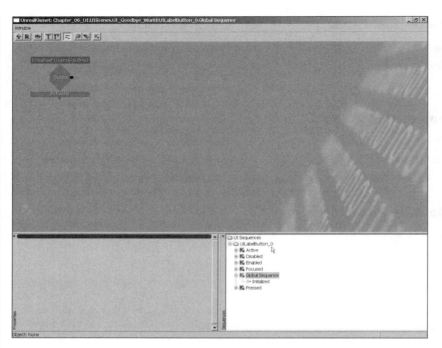

FIGURE 6.12   This Kismet Editor is unique to the button widget.

6

3. In the Kismet Editor, select the Focused Sequence in the Sequences panel. You will see that there is an On Click event present in this sequence already. This event is triggered whenever the user clicks the button (see **FIGURE 6.13**).

4. Right-click in the Kismet workspace just to the right of the On Click event and choose New Action > Misc > Console Command. Create a wire from the Out output of the On Click event to the In input of the Console Command (see **FIGURE 6.14**).

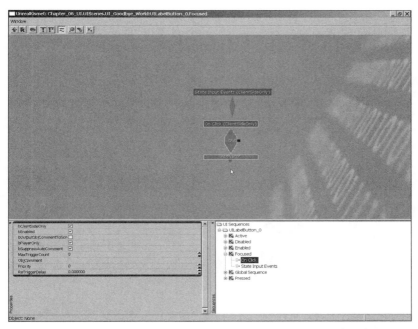

FIGURE 6.13   An On Click event triggers actions when the mouse button is pressed.

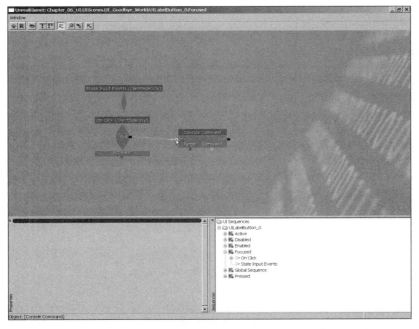

FIGURE 6.14   Connect the On Click event to the Console Command.

5. Select this new Console Command, and in its Properties window, set the Command property to exit. This means that whenever the user clicks the button, the console command exit will be triggered, thus exiting the game (see **FIGURE 6.15**).

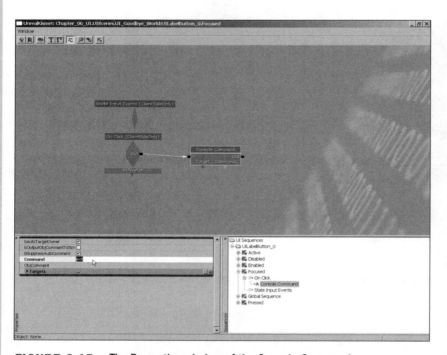

FIGURE 6.15   The Properties window of the Console Command

6. Open the map from the **TUTORIAL 6.1** and test the level. When you click the button, the In Editor Game should exit.

7. Save your package to preserve your work.

END TUTORIAL 6.2

The UI Widgets

A *widget* is simply an element of the UI that performs some specific task. These include buttons, text-entry fields, progress bars, and virtually anything else that either provides information to and/or receives input from the user. It helps to understand which widgets are currently available to you. This section details all the available UI widgets as of the time of this writing. You will also notice that each description includes the available states for each widget. These are here merely for your reference; we discuss the importance of states later in this chapter.

Button

A Button widget is simply a click interface component. It provides access to a Kismet On Click event, meaning you can cause actions to occur when this widget is clicked. This widget does not have a textual label.

Available States: Active, Disabled, Enabled, Focused, Pressed

> **NOTE**
>
> The widgets detailed here are those available in the Toolbar. Many others can only be created from the right-click context menu by clicking in the viewport or the Scene list. Most of those are specific to gameplay within *UT3* and require some sort of scripting to accompany them in order to properly function. As such, we focus on the basic widgets that can be used as standalone components within a UIScene.

Checkbox

The Checkbox widget holds a Boolean value displayed as either a "checked" or "unchecked" status on the widget. The value is toggled via clicking on the widget. This widget has a special event in Kismet called the Checkbox Value event; it can be used to trigger actions based on the status of the check box.

Available States: Active, Disabled, Enabled, Focused, Pressed

Editbox T

The Editbox widget allows users to enter text into a visible field on the UI. The text can be used in Kismet through the Editbox Value event. For example, this widget could be used in areas where you need the player to input his or her name.

Available States: Active, Disabled, Enabled, Focused, Pressed

Image

The Image widget is noninteractive, meaning that it does not receive input of any kind. It is simply used to display a texture. It can also display a material, should you need an animated effect.

Available States: Disabled, Enabled

Label T

This Label widget is simply used to display text on your UI layout.

Available States: Disabled, Enabled

Label Button

The Label Button widget performs exactly like the Button widget, with the added benefit of having a textual label on top of it.

Available States: Active, Disabled, Enabled, Focused, Pressed

List

The List widget displays information onto the screen in a row-and-column format. It gathers this information from a linked data store. We discuss data stores later in this chapter.

Available States: Active, Disabled, Enabled, Focused, Pressed

Numeric EditBox (Context Menu)

The Numeric EditBox widget is simply a numeric entry field that has incremental and decremental buttons. These buttons are very similar to the "spinners" found in 3ds Max.

Available States: Active, Disabled, Enabled, Focused, Pressed

Panel

The Panel widget is essentially a container. It can have other widgets within it, allowing you to easily group a collection of other widgets together.

Available States: Disabled, Enabled, Focused

Progressbar (Context Menu)

The Progressbar widget provides visual feedback of a numeric value. You can commonly find these on loading screens and other operations that take significant amounts of time. However, you could also use one to track a player's progress through a level or as a health bar.

Available States: Active, Disabled, Enabled, Focused, Pressed

Slider

The Slider widget allows you to set a numeric value by dragging a track bar.

Available States: Active, Disabled, Enabled, Focused, Pressed

ToggleButton

The ToggleButton widget is identical to the Button widget, with one exception: pressing the ToggleButton switches it to the Pressed state until it is pressed again.

Available States: Active, Disabled, Enabled, Focused, Pressed

Working with Widgets

Knowing what the widgets are isn't enough to really get started in creating a UI for your game. You also have to know what abilities are available to you for laying widgets out in your UIScene.

The most common functions for laying out widgets are creating, parenting, moving, and resizing them.

Widget Creation

Creating widgets is easy and can be accomplished in one of three ways. The first is to use the icons located in the Toolbar. Simply click the icon for the appropriate widget and then drag the new widget onto the Scene viewport. Just remember to click the Selection tool icon when you're finished; otherwise, you will find yourself creating another copy of that particular widget the next time you click the mouse. The advantage of using this method is the speed and simplicity of widget selection, but it also has the drawback of only having only a few widget types available (see **FIGURE 6.16**).

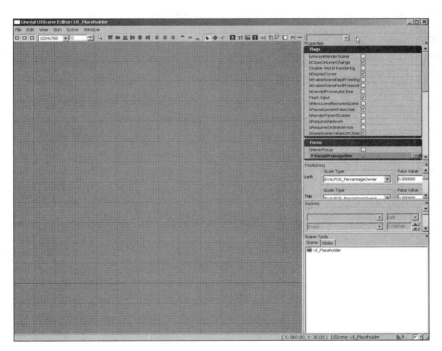

FIGURE 6.16   The Toolbar contains several of the default widgets.

Another method of widget creation is to right-click in the Scene viewport and choose Place Widget from the context menu (see **FIGURE 6.17**). This has three distinct advantages: First, it allows you access to all the available widget types. Second, it allows you to create a tag for the widget at the time of its creation. Third, it provides you an easy method to choose a parent object for your new widget. We'll talk more about parenting and widget hierarchies next.

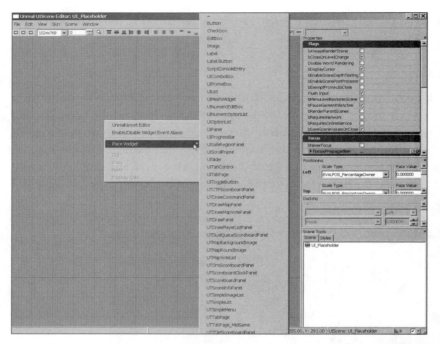

FIGURE 6.17   The right-click context menu shows many widgets not displayed in the Toolbar.

The third and final method of widget creation is similar to the second, but rather than right-clicking in the Scene viewport, you instead right-click in the Scene hierarchy list in the Scene Tools window. If you right-click there, you see a context menu exactly like the one that appears in the viewport. By right-clicking directly on one of the widgets listed, you can choose the parent for the newly created widget.

Parenting Hierarchies

Widgets can form hierarchies inside your UIScene, allowing you to treat a certain collection of widgets as a single entity. The relationship is fairly simple and will be quickly recognized by those who have any experience in programming interfaces in MEL (Maya Embedded Language) or Delphi.

A child object can be moved, rotated, or scaled independently of the parent. However, any transformation performed on the parent propagates down to the children. A real-world analogy would be to look at the relationship between you and the Earth. You can walk around wherever you want upon its surface, but wherever the planet goes, you go along for the ride. This means that if you have made Button a child of a Panel widget, you can move the button wherever you like, regardless of the position of the panel. However, as soon as you move the panel, you'll notice that the button moves right along with it.

You can create parenting relationships in the UIScene Editor in a few ways. The first is during the creation of a widget. If you right-click the top of an existing widget in the scene and choose Place Widget from the context menu, the new widget will be created as the child of the original (see **FIGURE 6.18**).

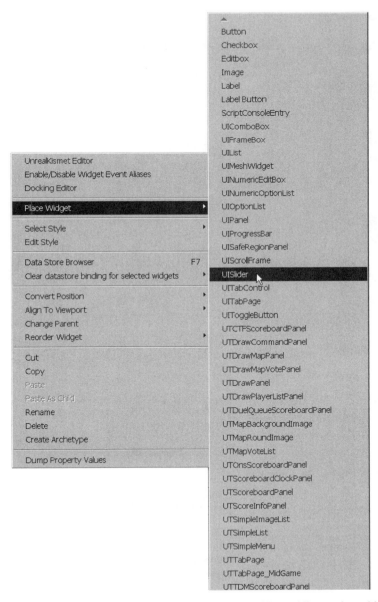

FIGURE 6.18   If you right-click and place a widget while another widget is selected, the new widget will be a child of the original.

The second method is to use the Scene Tools window's Scene panel. The list displayed in this window reflects the hierarchy of all the widgets in your scene. You can change this hierarchy, making a selected widget a child of another widget, by simply dragging any listed widget on top of any other widget. The widget that was dragged becomes the child (see **FIGURE 6.19**).

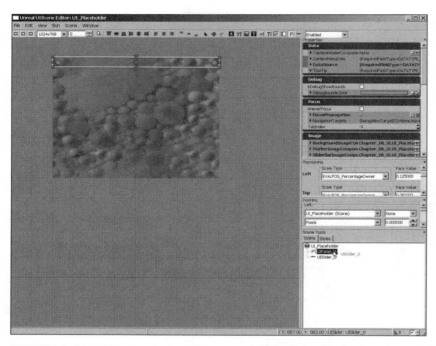

FIGURE 6.19   You can also create a parent/child relationship by dragging widgets on top of one another in the Scene list.

The third way to create a parent/child relationship is to select a widget, right-click it, and choose Change Parent from the context menu. This displays a list of all the widgets in the scene, and you can select which one will become the parent of your chosen widget (see **FIGURE 6.20**).

FIGURE 6.20   The Change Parent command opens a window from which you can choose the new parent of the selected widget.

Moving Widgets

One of the first skills you'll need to master is moving widgets within your UIScene. This can be done by simply selecting a widget and dragging the blue bar that surrounds it. Make sure to click in between the resizing handles on the widget. When your mouse is in the proper position, the cursor will change to a crosshairs icon (see **FIGURE 6.21**).

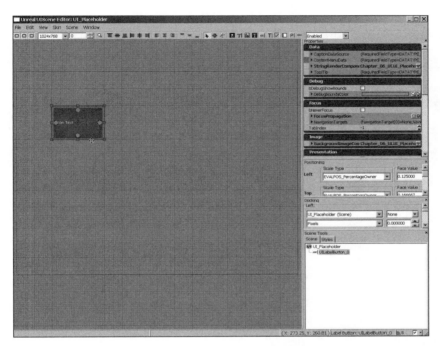

FIGURE 6.21 When you mouse over the blue lines of a selected widget, the moving crosshairs become visible.

Another method of moving widgets around the scene is to place your cursor over the selected widget, hold down the Ctrl key, and left-mouse-drag. This essentially does the same thing as the previous method, but doesn't require the accuracy of placing the cursor over the blue outline of the widget, thus making it easier to quickly move widgets.

Rotating Widgets

Widget rotation is a little more technical than moving widgets; it requires two parts. First, you need the pivot of rotation, known as the *rotation anchor*. This appears as a small orange circle containing a crosshairs, located by default at the center of a widget (see **FIGURE 6.22**). The properties controlling the location for the rotation anchor can be found in a widget's properties under the Presentation tab. There, you will see the Rotation category, and under that you will find AnchorPosition and AnchorType. By changing the AnchorType property's value to RA_Absolute, you can relocate the anchor to any position on the viewport using the AnchorPosition's Value property. Contrary to what you might expect, when you use the RA_Absolute AnchorType, the value of the AnchorPosition's Value property is actually relative to the upper-left corner of the widget and not truly absolute. The other AnchorType values place the rotation anchor at various locations relative to the widget.

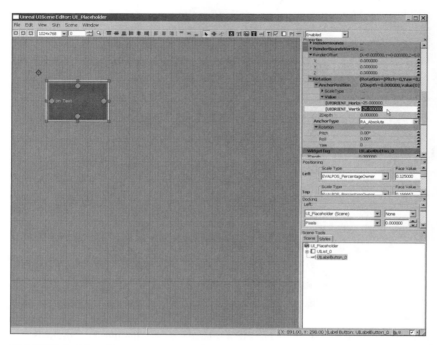

FIGURE 6.22   Here, you can see the rotation anchor moved to the left and slightly above the widget.

The second thing you need to rotate a widget is the rotation amount. This can also be found in a widget's properties under the Presentation tab. Again, you will see the Rotation category, and under that you will find the Rotation property. This property is a rotator in type, and it gives you access to three-dimensional rotations of the widget. This can create interesting effects because it allows the normally two-dimensional widget to appear to be in 3D if animated (although that requires some sort of script support). More to the point, this allows widgets to be skewed to create more interesting shapes (see **FIGURE 6.23**).

> **NOTE**
>
> Widget rotations are discussed here simply as a measure of inclusion. However, it should be noted that rotating widgets can cause problems when using multiple resolutions and when positioning widgets later in the design process. It is generally advised that you avoid rotating your widgets if at all possible.

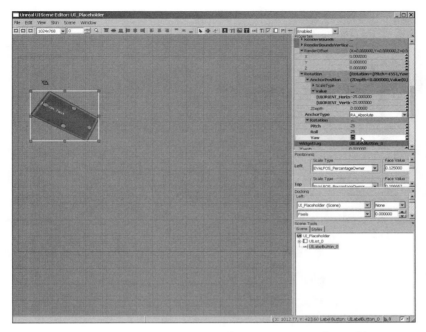

FIGURE 6.23   The Rotation property affects the rotation of the widget.

It is also possible to interactively rotate widgets right in the viewport by placing the cursor over the selected widget, holding down the Shift key, and left-mouse-dragging. This is a less accurate means of rotation because it snaps in increments and only affects the Yaw rotation, but it can be good for making quick rotations.

Resizing Widgets

Resizing widgets is almost as easy as moving them. When you select a widget, you will notice a series of reddish handles placed about its edges. Each of these is a resizing handle that you can use to change the size of the selected widget. Handles placed at the corners resize the widget in two dimensions at once, whereas handles placed on the sides only resize the widget in a single direction (see **FIGURE 6.24**).

The Positioning Editor

Having precise position controls for your widgets can be important, especially on more complex UIs. At some point, alignment will become an important factor, and when that happens, you'll need a precise way to handle the placement and scaling of your widgets, rather than simply moving them and scaling them by hand. To help you out with this, the UIScene Editor contains the Positioning panel, which allows you to position and scale your widgets based on numeric values (see **FIGURE 6.25**).

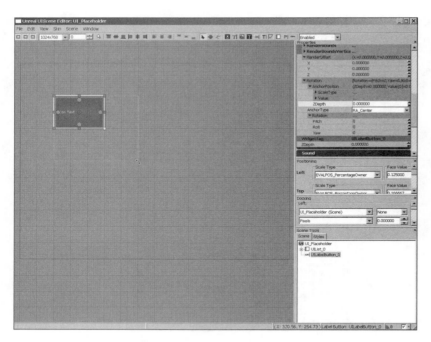

FIGURE 6.24   You can resize a widget by dragging one of the handles.

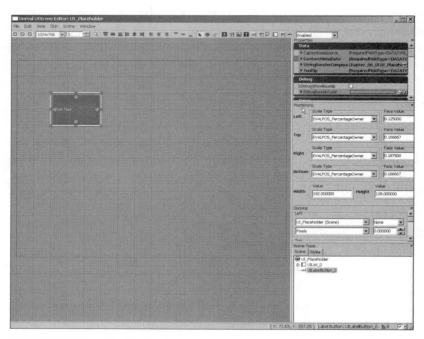

FIGURE 6.25   The Positioning panel

To fully understand the Positioning panel, you have to understand the concept of widget faces. Each widget can be thought of as a two-dimensional object with a top, a bottom, a left side, and a right side. Each of these sides is considered to be a face. You can move each face of a widget around individually, thereby precisely positioning the widget as well as precisely scaling it. Top and bottom faces can be moved vertically, whereas the left and right faces can be moved horizontally.

Faces are repositioned using two inputs. The first is the Scale Type. This tells the Positioning panel how to interpret the second input,

> **NOTE**
>
> All the available Scale Types have the EVALPOS prefix.

the Face Value. The six separate Scale Types are described next. You should be aware that each face of a widget can use a different Scale Type if required.

PixelViewport

This Scale Type interprets the Face Value of all four faces in terms of the absolute number of pixels from the viewport's origin, which has 2D coordinates of (0,0) and is placed in the upper-left corner of the viewport. For instance, if you set the Top face of a widget to PixelViewport and set its Face Value to 36, then the Top face would be 36 pixels down from the top of the viewport.

PixelScene

PixelScene works similarly to PixelViewport, but with two major distinctions. First, the origin coordinates (0,0) are no longer positioned at the upper-left corner of the viewport, but are instead calculated from the upper-left corner of the actual UI scene. This can be extremely useful if you find yourself navigating the viewport frequently. The second major difference is in how the Face Value properties are calculated. Instead of all four faces being calculated in absolute pixel values from the origin, only the Top and Left faces are calculated in such a manner. The Bottom and Right Face Values represent the distance in pixels from the opposite face, meaning they should reflect the height and width of the actual widget.

PixelOwner

This Scale Type behaves in a similar method to PixelScene, but rather than pixel values being calculated from the origin (upper-left corner) of the UIScene, calculations are instead based on the origin (again, the upper-left corner) of the parent widget. This means that if a selected widget is a child of another widget, you can place the child within precise pixel values within its parent. If a widget has no parent, these values will be the same as if you were calculating them using the PixelScene Scale Type.

PercentageViewport

The PercentageViewport Scale Type calculates from the origin of the viewport, just as the PixelViewport setting. However, instead of using absolute pixel values, the Face Value parameter instead uses a value between 0 and 1 that reflects the percentage of the entire viewport. For example, if you wanted the Left face of a widget to be positioned precisely at the center of the viewport, but did not necessarily know the width of the viewport, you could use PercentageViewport as your Scale Type and set the Face Value to 0.5.

PercentageScene

This Scale Type behaves in the same manner as PercentageViewport, in that it uses a percentage value between 0 and 1 for the Face Value parameter. However, this Scale Type calculates its percentage based on the width and height of the scene, rather than the viewport.

PercentageOwner

The PercentageOwner Scale Type functions similarly to the PercentageViewport and Percentage Scene Scale Types, using a percentage value between 0 and 1 for the Face Value. This value, however, represents the percentage of the parent rather than the scene. If an object has no parent, this Scale Type behaves the same way as PercentageScene.

Docking

An important ability for keeping your widgets aligned is docking. Docking allows you to create relationships between the faces of different widgets so that they always move in a synchronized fashion. In a way, it is very much like creating parent/child relationships between the faces of different widgets.

Docking requires at least two separate widgets. To dock the face of a widget, first select the widget. You will notice that four orange circles appear next to the center of each face. These are the docking handles. Simply drag one of them to another widget, and the docking handles for that widget will appear in red. Drag on top of one of the neighboring widget's handles to complete the dock. A curved line appears when the dock is complete, pointing out the face to which you have docked the widget (see **FIGURE 6.26**). You will also notices that the orange docking handle now has a black X at its center.

Once a face is docked, you can no longer manipulate that face through either direct dragging or the Positioning Editor. However, if you move the face to which the other original face is docked, the docked face will move in tandem with it. This means that you could dock all the left faces in a long list of buttons to the left face of the topmost button, and then simply adjust the width of the top button, thereby adjusting the width of all the faces docked to it.

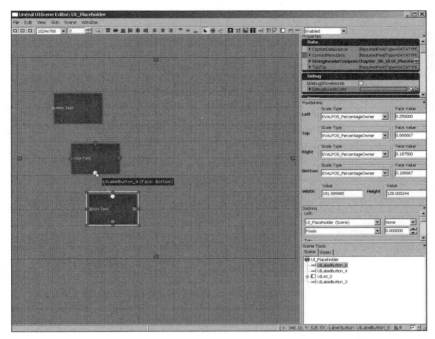

FIGURE 6.26   To dock, simply drag from one of the orange handles on a selected widget to a docking handle on another widget.

In general, it is a good idea to dock like faces with one another. For instance, you would *not* typically want to dock the left face of one widget with the top face of another. Doing so will often have impractical results.

Docking can be removed in two ways. The first is simply by right-clicking a docked handle and choosing either Break Dock Link or Break ALL Dock Links. The second way is through the Docking panel (see **FIGURE 6.27**). The Docking panel shows which object each face of a selected widget is docked to, as well as the face to which the dock is attached. You can also use the Docking panel to establish an offset in pixels from the dock target. This means, for example, that you could dock the top of two buttons together, but you could offset the docked button by 50 pixels from the docked target.

As a demonstration of UI interactivity, **TUTORIAL 6.3** details the creation of a very simple game that takes place entirely within a UI. The game entails a Progressbar that continuously gets smaller unless the player keeps clicking the button. If the player clicks the button fast enough, the Progressbar will max out and the player wins. Otherwise, the bar will shrink to nothing and the player loses.

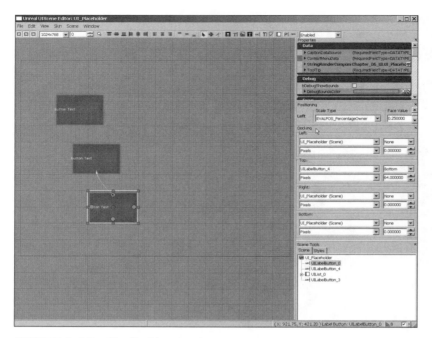

FIGURE 6.27   The Docking panel

6

TUTORIAL 6.3: Building a Game Within a UI, Part I: Basic Layout

1. Launch Unreal Editor. In the Generic Browser, right-click and choose New UIScene from the context menu. Enter the following information:

   ▸ **Package**: Chapter_06_UI

   ▸ **Group**: UIScenes

   ▸ **Name**: UI_MiniGame

   When the UIScene Editor appears, our first step is to establish the size of the UI scene. From the UIScene Editor's toolbar, set the Scene size to 640×480 (see **FIGURE 6.28**). It will be set to 1024×768 by default.

2. Click the Label Button icon ▥ and create a new Label Button in the center of the scene, near the bottom. Be sure to navigate the Scene viewport to gauge the extents of the scene. In the Properties area, expand the CaptionDataSource located under the Data tab and set the MarkupString property to Start.

3. Expand the StringRenderComponent section, expand the StyleOverride category, and finally expand TextStyleCustomization. Check the box to the left of Text Alignment and set both the UIORIENT_Horizontal and UIORIENT_Vertical properties to Center (see **FIGURE 6.29**).

   Make sure you select the Selection tool when finished.

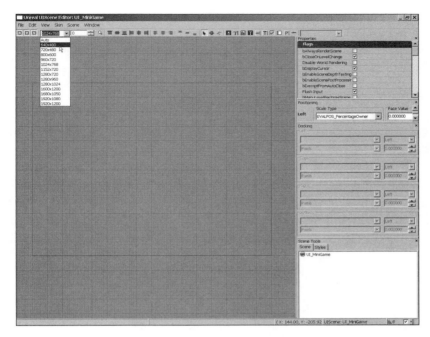

FIGURE 6.28 Set the Scene Size to 640×480.

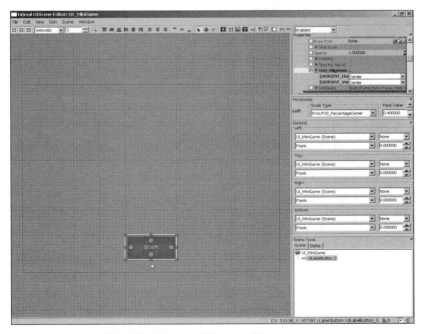

FIGURE 6.29 The Label Button will appear like so.

4. Deselect the Label Button and then right-click in the Scene viewport and create a new UIProgressbar. Leave it's UI Tag set to its default value and then click OK. Position the new widget near the top of the scene, running from the left side to the right side, but leaving a little room near the top (see **FIGURE 6.30**).

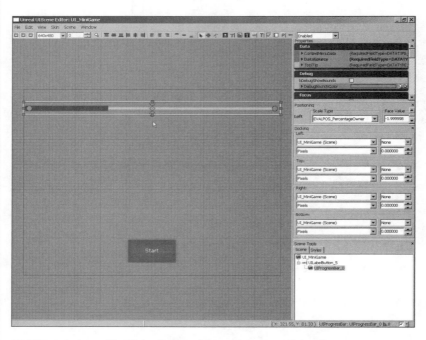

FIGURE 6.30   Place the Progressbar near the top of the UI.

5. Click the Label icon ![T] and place it in the center of the UI between the Progressbar and the Label Button (see **FIGURE 6.31**). Expand DataSource in the Properties panel and set its MarkupString property to Click Start to Play!

6. Expand the StringRenderComponent section, expand the StyleOverride category, and finally expand TextStyleCustomization. Check the box to the left of Text Alignment and set both the UIORIENT_Horizontal and UIORIENT_Vertical properties to Center.

7. In the Positioning panel, set both the Right and Bottom ScaleType properties to EVAL-POS_PercentageOwner so the Label will scale with the scene.

8. Save your package.

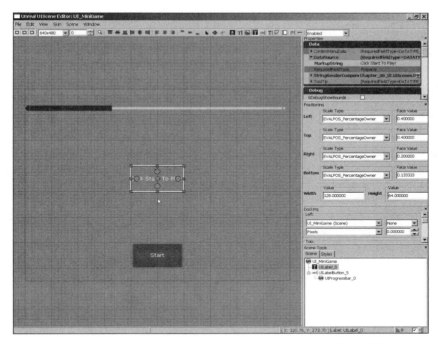

FIGURE 6.31   The new Label has been placed in the center of the UI.

END TUTORIAL 6.3

Widgets States

Every widget can exist in a variety of states. These states define what a user can and cannot do with a widget at that particular time. They also control the style of the widget. Various Kismet events can be triggered based on the current state of a UI widget. The following list details the available states. Note that not every widget can exist in all the states.

Active—This state is entered whenever a user hovers the mouse over a particular widget. For instance, you could use this state to produce rollover effects on a particular widget.

Disabled—Put simply, a widget that is in the Disabled state cannot be used. It cannot be placed into the Focused state, meaning that it cannot receive input from the user. A widget in the Disabled state cannot change its own state. Essentially, a Disabled widget will remain nonfunctional until some other event places it into the Enabled state.

Enabled—The Enabled state allows a widget to receive focus, or to be placed in the Focused state.

Focused—A widget in the Focused state can receive user input. Widgets can be placed into this state either through the Focus Chain or through the NextControl and PreviousControl input event aliases, both of which we discuss later in this chapter.

Pressed—This essentially means that a user has clicked the widget. To be more precise, a widget can enter this state when it is already in the Focused state and receives any user input that is bound to the "Clicked" input event alias. By default, this is bound to the left mouse button.

Global Sequence—In your sequence list, you will see the Global Sequence listed among all the available states. The Global Sequence is not really a state in and of itself; it is instead a means for you to attach events and styles to the widget regardless of the state it is currently in.

Continue from **TUTORIAL 6.3**. If you have not yet completed it, you may open the UI_MiniGame_01 UIScene to complete **TUTORIAL 6.4**.

Our functionality for this game follows the simple flow chart shown in **FIGURE 6.32**.

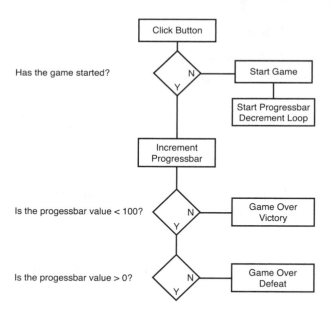

FIGURE 6.32   Tug of War game functionality flow chart

TUTORIAL 6.4: Building a Game Within a UI, Part II: Creating Initial Functionality

1. Open the UIScene Editor for the UI_MiniGame UIScene. Select the Label Button at the bottom of the UI, right-click it, and choose Kismet Editor from the context menu (see **FIGURE 6.33**).

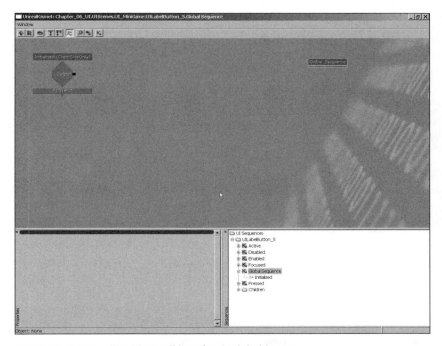

FIGURE 6.33   The Kismet Editor for the label button.

2. We want the Progressbar to update when the button is clicked. The Focused state has an On Click event by default, so this is a good place to start. Select the Focused sequence in the Sequence list (see **FIGURE 6.34**).

3. We now need to create the first part of our functionality, which is to check to see if the game should start playing. We will be building this network off to the right of the On Click event. This event is triggered whenever the button is clicked (see **FIGURE 6.35**).

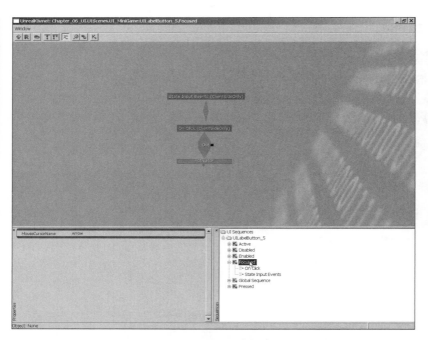

FIGURE 6.34   Select the Focused sequence state in the Sequence list.

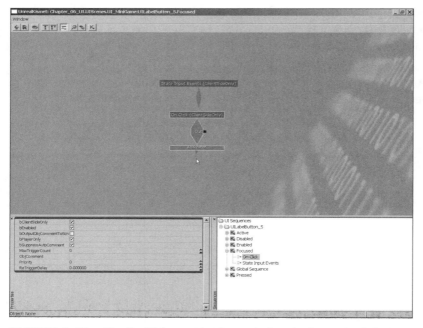

FIGURE 6.35   The On Click event is triggered when the button is clicked.

a. Right-click and choose New Condition > Comparison > Compare Bool. Use a wire to link this to the On Click event (see **FIGURE 6.36**).

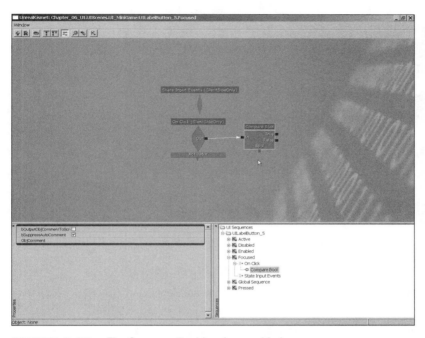

FIGURE 6.36   The Compare Bool has been added.

b. Right-click the Bool input and choose Create New Bool Variable. Set the bValue property to 1 (see **FIGURE 6.37**).

c. Create a Set Bool sequence object (New Action > Set Variable > Bool) and wire it to the True output of the Compare Bool (see **FIGURE 6.38**).

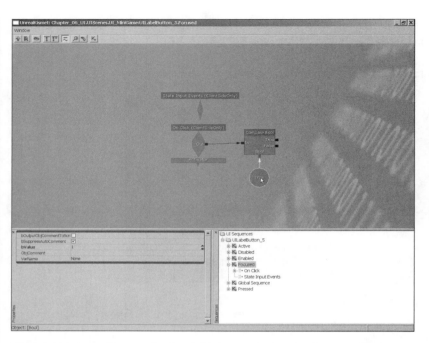

FIGURE 6.37   The new Bool variable is attached to the Compare Bool.

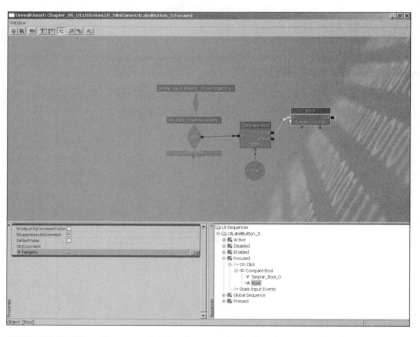

FIGURE 6.38   The new Set Bool connects to the Compare Bool.

d. Right-click the Value input and choose Create New Bool Variable. Verify that the bValue property is set to 0 (see **FIGURE 6.39**).

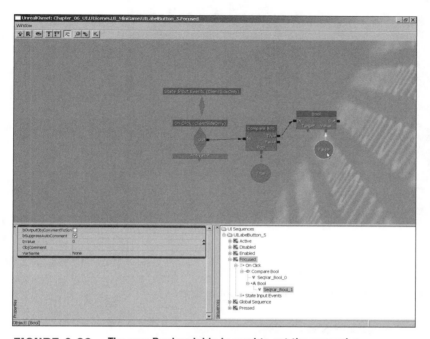

FIGURE 6.39   The new Bool variable is used to set the new value.

e. Drag a wire from the Target output of the Set Bool to the Bool variable currently connected to the Compare Bool object (see **FIGURE 6.40**).

4. We will now set up the basis to begin our game by adding the functionality of the Label Button.

a. Create a new Get ProgressBar Value sequence (New Action > Get Value > Get ProgressBar Value) and attach it to the Compare Bool's False output (see **FIGURE 6.41**).

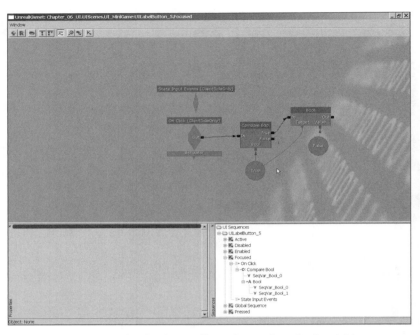

FIGURE 6.40   The Set Bool now affects the previous Bool variable.

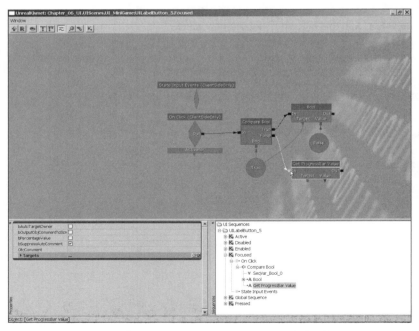

FIGURE 6.41   The Get ProgressBar sequence object is in place.

b. In the UIScene Editor, select the Progressbar. Then, back in the Kismet Editor, right-click and choose Create New Object Variable using Progressbar_0 from the context menu. Wire this new object variable to the Get ProgressBar Value Target input (see **FIGURE 6.42**).

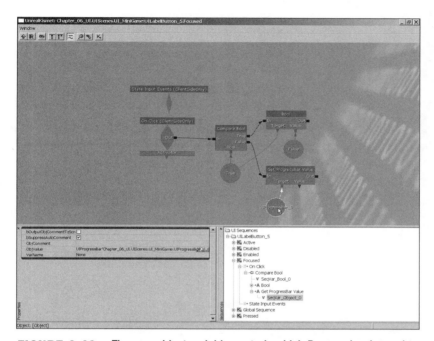

FIGURE 6.42   The new object variable controls which Progressbar is used to acquire the value.

c. Right-click the Get Progressbar Value's Value Output and choose Create New Float Variable (see **FIGURE 6.43**).

d. Right-click and choose New Action > Math > Add Float to create a new sequence object. Connect this new sequence object to the Get ProgressBar Value (see **FIGURE 6.44**).

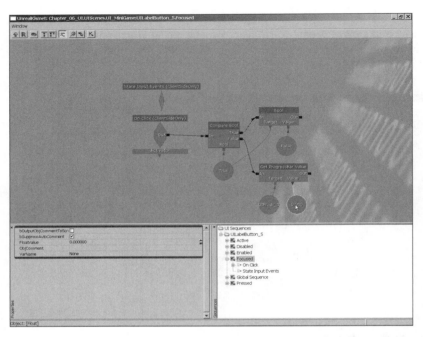

FIGURE 6.43   This float variable stores the current value of the Progressbar.

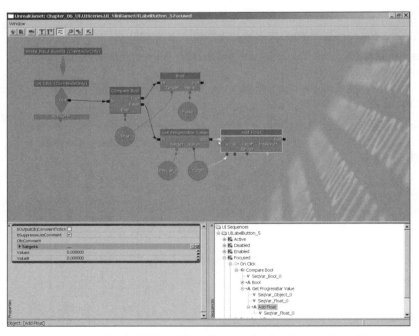

FIGURE 6.44   The Add Float object links to the Get ProgressBar object.

e. Connect the existing Float Variable to the A input of the Add Float object. Then, right-click the B input and create a new Float variable, setting its FloatValue property to 10.0 (see **FIGURE 6.45**).

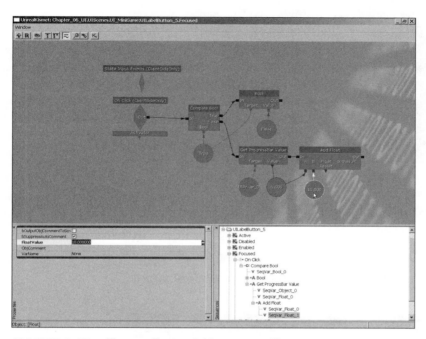

FIGURE 6.45   The new Float variable connects like so.

f. Create a new Float variable and connect it to the Add Float object's Float Result output (see **FIGURE 6.46**).

g. Create a Set ProgressBar Value (New Action > Set Value > Set ProgressBar Value) and connect it to the Add Float object. Wire the object variable currently connected to the Get ProgressBar Value to the Target and then connect the Result Float variable to the New Value input (see **FIGURE 6.47**).

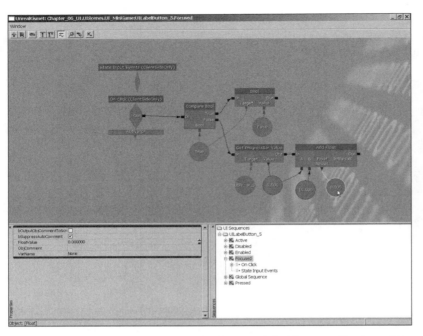

FIGURE 6.46   You're now storing the final result inside a new Float variable.

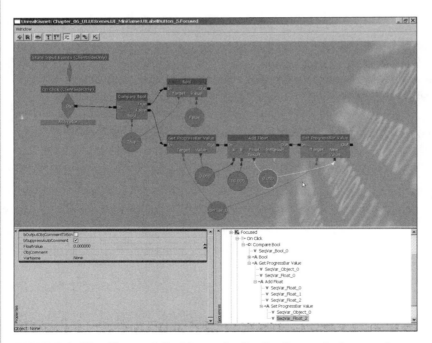

FIGURE 6.47   The result float is now feeding the Progressbar's new value.

5. The next step is to set the Progressbar's value to 50 to start the game.

  a. Create a new Set ProgressBar Value (New Action > Set Value > Set ProgressBar
  Value) and connect it to the True output of the Compare Bool (see
  FIGURE 6.48).

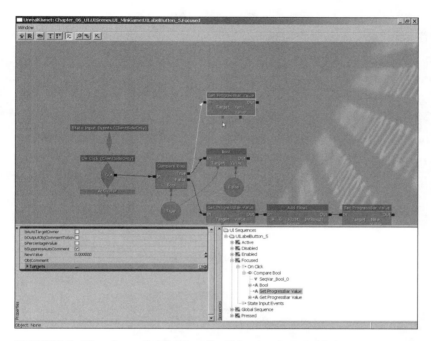

FIGURE 6.48   A new Set ProgressBar Value has been added.

  b. Locate the object variable you created in the previous step that refers to the
  Progressbar and then duplicate it with Ctrl+C, Ctrl+V. Connect the new duplicate
  to the Target of the new Set ProgressBar Value (see **FIGURE 6.49**).

  c. Right-click the New Value input and choose Create New Float Variable. Set the
  FloatValue of this new variable to 50 (see **FIGURE 6.50**).

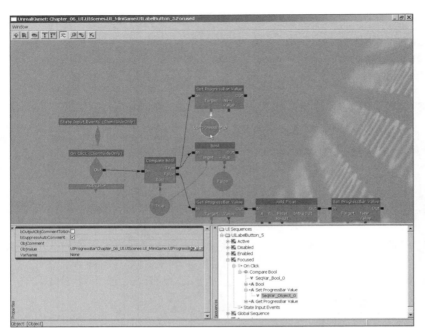

FIGURE 6.49   The new object variable controls which Progressbar gets set.

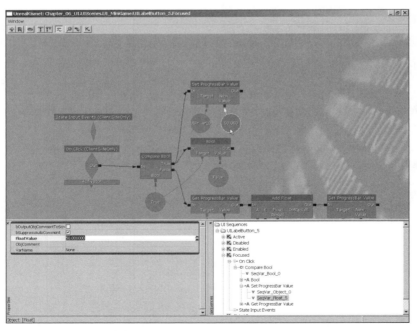

FIGURE 6.50   We set the Progressbar's value to 50 when the game starts.

6. The last step in this tutorial is to set the label text of the Label Button to reflect that the player should be clicking.

   a. Create a new Set Text Value object (New Action > Set Value > Set Text Value) and connect it to the True output of the Compare Bool (see **FIGURE 6.51**).

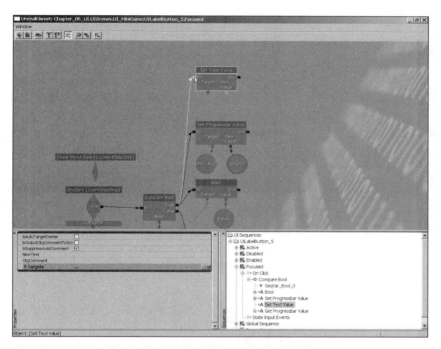

FIGURE 6.51   Create the Set Text Value and attach it like so.

   b. In the UIScene Editor, select the Label Button. Then, in the Kismet Editor, right-click and choose Create New Object Variable using LabelButton_0. Connect this new object variable to the Target of the new Set Label Text object (see **FIGURE 6.52**).

   c. Right-click the New Value input of the Set Label Text object and choose Create New String Variable (see **FIGURE 6.53**). Set the StrValue of this new variable to Click!

7. Save your package. At this time, you do not really need to test anything.

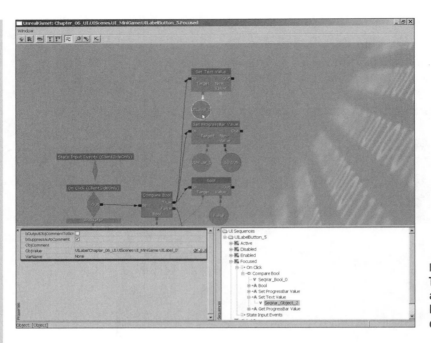

FIGURE 6.52
The new object variable controls which label is being changed.

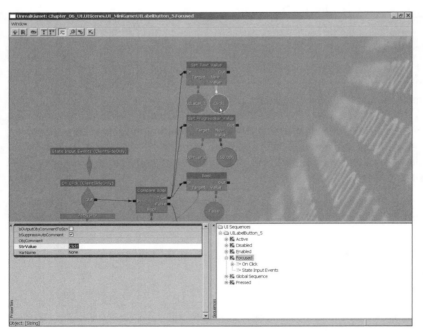

FIGURE 6.53
You're now telling the player to click the button during gameplay.

END TUTORIAL 6.4

Continue from **TUTORIAL 6.4**. If you have not yet completed it, you may use the UI_MiniGame_02 UIScene to complete **TUTORIAL 6.5**.

The first part of our game loop requires a delay. This prevents the loop from trying to run every single frame of gameplay, which would result in a significant performance hit, the locking up of the game, or the game crashing altogether.

TUTORIAL 6.5: Building a Game Within a UI, Part III: Creating a Simple Game Loop in Kismet

1. Open the UI_MiniGame UIScene in the UIScene editor by double-clicking it. Select the Label Button in the viewport, right-click it, and choose UnrealKismet Editor.

2. Select the Focused state in the Sequences list. Create a new Delay sequence object (New Action > Misc > Delay) and connect its Start input to the Out of the Set Bool object (see **FIGURE 6.54**). Set the Duration property to 0.5.

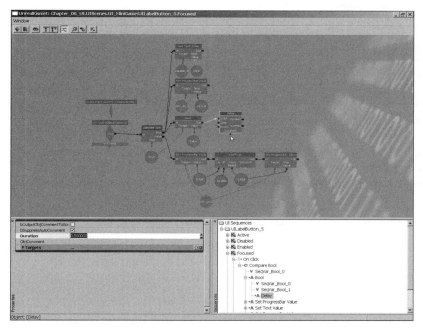

FIGURE 6.54   The Delay object keeps the game loop from over-iterating.

3. We will now set up the behavior for the Progressbar in our loop. Fortunately, all the sequence objects we need have already been created.

   a. Select the Get ProgressBar Value, Add Float, and Set ProgressBar Value sequence objects that are currently connected to the False output of the

Compare Bool. Select all the variables attached to them as well (see
FIGURE 6.55).

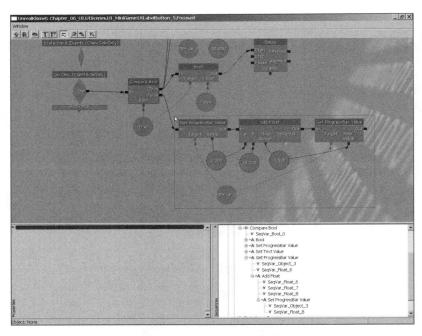

FIGURE 6.55   Select all the objects shown within the box.

b. Duplicate all these objects with Ctrl+C, Ctrl+V. Place the new duplicates near the
Delay sequence object and then wire the Finished output of the Delay into the In
input of the new Get ProgressBar Value (see **FIGURE 6.56**).

c. Select the Float variable that is currently plugged into the new Add Float object's
B value and set its FloatValue property to −1 (see **FIGURE 6.57**).

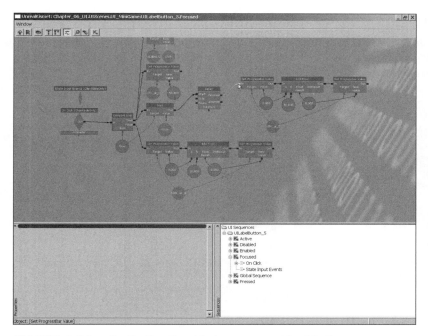

FIGURE 6.56   Duplicating the objects saves considerable time.

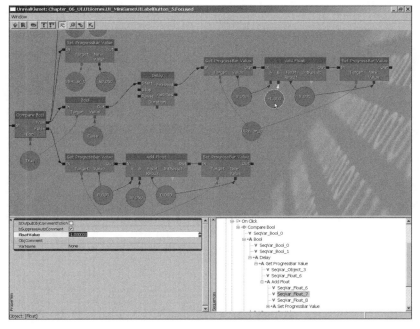

FIGURE 6.57   Reset the new Float variable to –1.

4. We now need to check our system to see whether the player has won or lost the game.

    a. Create a new Compare Float object (New Condition > Comparison > Compare Float) and attach it to the Out of the Set ProgressBar Value. Set the ObjComment property to Check for Win (see **FIGURE 6.58**).

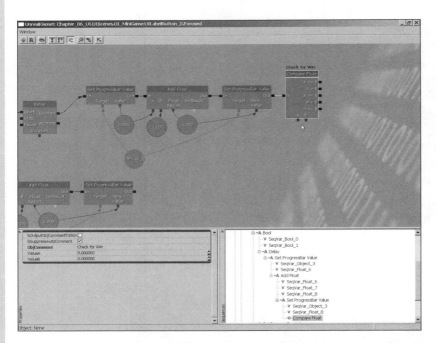

FIGURE 6.58   The first condition checks to see if the player has won the game.

    b. Connect the A value to the Float Variable that is currently connected to the New Value of the Set ProgressBar Value (see **FIGURE 6.59**).

    c. Right-click the B input and choose Create New Float Variable. Set its Float Value to 99.0 (see **FIGURE 6.60**).

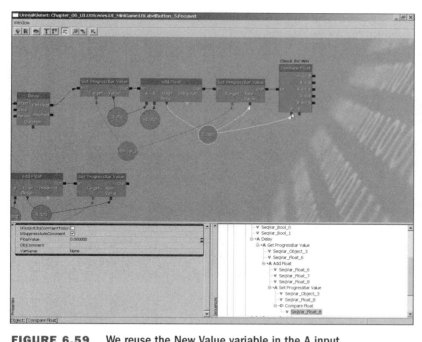

FIGURE 6.59   We reuse the New Value variable in the A input.

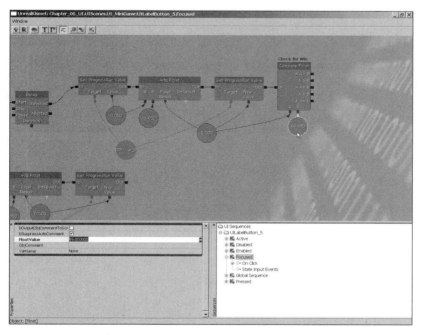

FIGURE 6.60   We're now checking the Progressbar's value against a value of 99.0.

d. Select the Compare Float object as well as the Float Variable connected to the B input and then duplicate them with Ctrl+C, Ctrl+V. Notice that the connection to Input A is maintained. Move the new duplicate to the right and then plug the A<B output into the In input of the new Compare Float (see **FIGURE 6.61**).

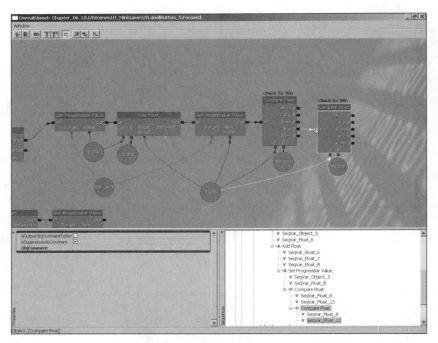

FIGURE 6.61   If the Progressbar is not greater than 99.0, we check to see if the player has lost the game.

e. Set the ObjComment of the duplicated Compare Float to Check for Loss. Then set the FloatValue of the duplicated Float Variable to 0.0 (see **FIGURE 6.62**).

5. We now need to create the behavior that happens when the game ends. For a win, we'll change the Label to read "You Win" and for a loss to "You Lose."

a. Create a new Set Text Value (New Action > Set Value > Set Text Value). Set the ObjComment for this object to Win (see **FIGURE 6.63**).

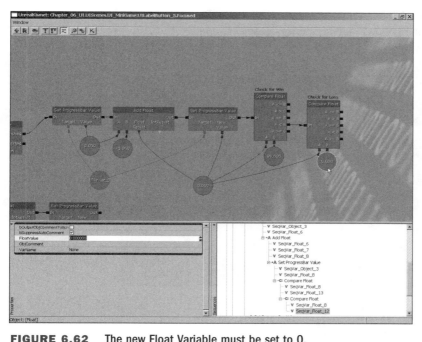

FIGURE 6.62   The new Float Variable must be set to 0.

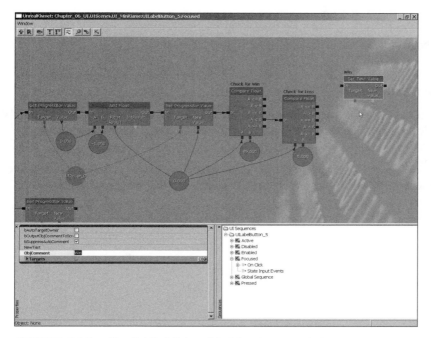

FIGURE 6.63   The Set Text Value object has been created.

b. In the UIScene Editor, select the Label in the center of the layout. In the Kismet Editor, right-click and create a new object variable using UILabel_0. Connect this new variable to the Set Text Value object's Target (see **FIGURE 6.64**).

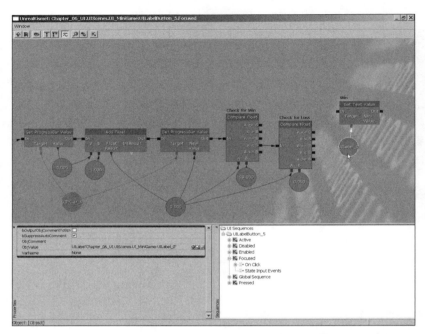

FIGURE 6.64   The new object variable controls which label you're editing.

c. Right-click the New Value input and choose Create New String Variable (see **FIGURE 6.65**). Set the StrValue to You Win!

d. Select the Set Text Value object, as well as the two variables plugged into it, and duplicate them (see **FIGURE 6.66**). Set the ObjComment for the newly duplicated Set Label Text to Loss and then set the StrValue of the duplicated string variable to "You Lose!"

e. Connect the "Win" Set Text Value object's In input to the "Check for Win" A>=B output.

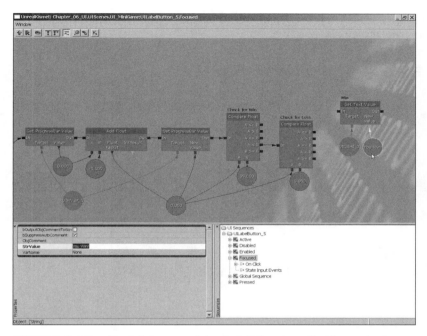

FIGURE 6.65   The label now updates to tell the player that he or she has won.

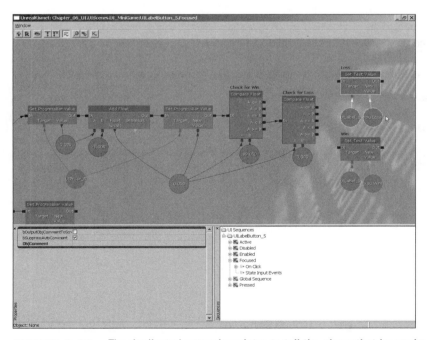

FIGURE 6.66   The duplicated network updates to tell the player that he or she has lost.

f. Connect the "Lose" Set Text Value object's In input to the "Check for Loss" A<=B output (see **FIGURE 6.67**).

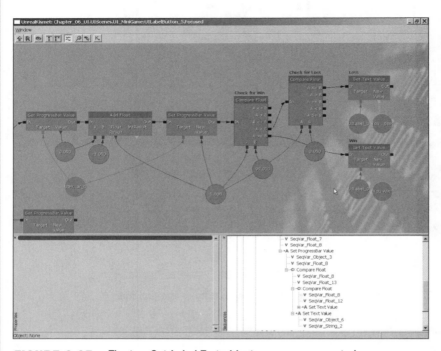

FIGURE 6.67   The two Set Label Text objects are now connected.

6. The last step is to disable the button once the player wins or loses.

a. Create a new Activate UI State object (New Action > UI > Activate UI State) and connect it to the Out outputs of both the Set Text Value objects (see **FIGURE 6.68**).

b. Locate the UILabelButton_0 object variable created in the **TUTORIAL 6.4**. Duplicate it and then connect the duplicate to the Target of the new Activate UI State object (see **FIGURE 6.69**).

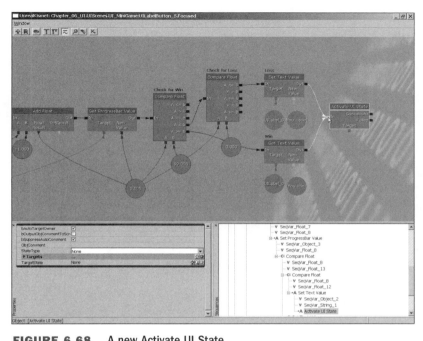

FIGURE 6.68   A new Activate UI State

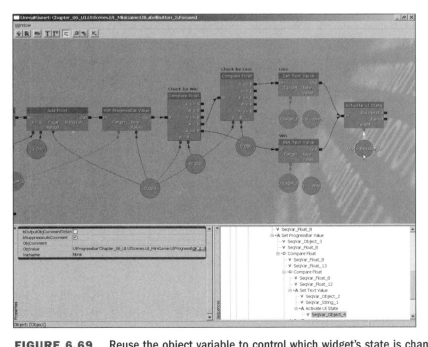

FIGURE 6.69   Reuse the object variable to control which widget's state is changed.

   c. Select the Activate UI State and set its StateType property to UIState_Disabled
   (see **FIGURE 6.70**).

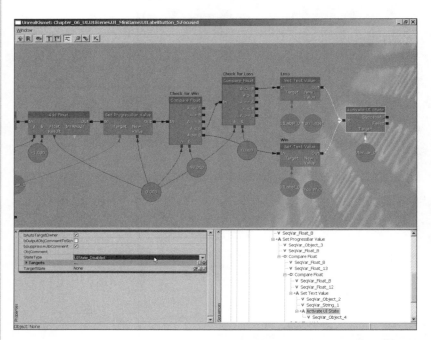

FIGURE 6.70   The StateType property controls which state will be activated.

7. To finish off the game loop, connect the A>B output of the Check for Loss Compare Float
   object to the Start input of the Delay object.

8. Close Kismet and click the background of the viewport of the UIScene editor to view the
   properties of the UIScene itself. In the Properties panel, set bPauseGameWhileActive to
   True.

9. Save your package. Open the DM-CH_06_MiniGame_Start level included on the DVD in the
   files for this chapter. In the Kismet for the level, you will see a Level Beginning event tied
   to an Open Scene action. Select the object variable and use the Generic Browser to set
   the ObjValue to your UI_MiniGame UIScene (see **FIGURE 6.71**).

10. Run the game, and your UI appears. Your game is now playable! Save the level when
   you're finished.

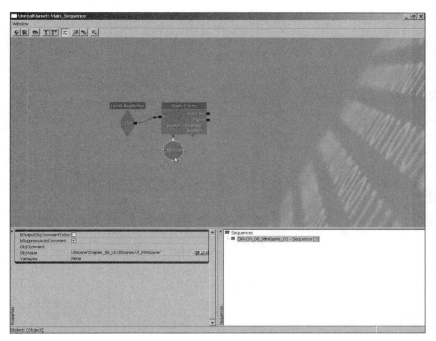

FIGURE 6.71   Use this network to test your UI.

END TUTORIAL 6.5

Widget Navigation and the Focus Chain

When working with UIs, users generally need some way to cycle through the available widgets to send focus from one widget to another. To be more precise, you need a method to put widgets into the Focused state in some sort of order so that the user can navigate your UI. It should be noted, however, that in order to really start talking about navigation, we have to discuss NavFocus events, which are simply input events that result from user input, such as keystrokes. We discuss such events later in the section "Working with User Inputs." For now, it is simply important for you not to confuse them with Kismet events.

Navigation within a UI comes in two distinct flavors: bound and unbound. Bound navigation is pretty simple. Focus progresses linearly from one widget to the next by using NextControl and PreviousControl NavFocus events. To make a long story short, activating these events allows you to cycle linearly through all the widgets in your UI, regardless of the navigation path established by the Focus Chain. This is the idea behind bound navigation (see **FIGURE 6.72**).

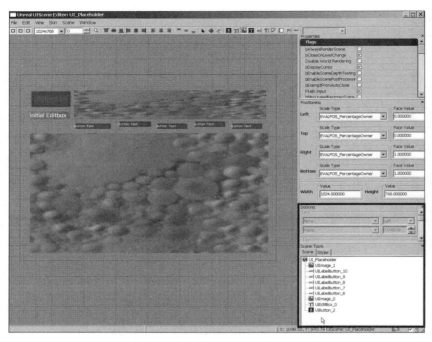

FIGURE 6.72   Bound navigation follows the order that widgets appear in the Scene list.

Unbound navigation requires the Focus Chain. The Focus Chain is a graphical representation of how focus flows from one widget to the next based on NavFocus inputs from the user. There are four primary unbound NavFocus events: NavFocusUp, NavFocusDown, NavFocusLeft, and NavFocusRight. By default, these inputs are slaved to the arrow keys.

The Focus Chain can be seen and edited using the Focus Chain tool ![icon]. Once activated, you will see a series of curved blue lines connecting your selected widget in a network. These lines represent the flow of the Focus Chain (see **FIGURE 6.73**). You will also see four purple diamonds along each of the edges of the widget. These diamonds correspond to one of the unbound NavFocus events. For instance, the topmost diamond is associated with the NavFocusUp event, meaning that the arrow leading from it designates where focus will flow when the user presses the up-arrow key.

Notice that when you select the Focus Chain tool for the first time, the Focus Chain lines are already created. This is because the editor attempts to automatically generate a Focus Chain while you are creating your UI. The Focus Chain tool works best as an editing tool, allowing you to alter the default course of the Focus Chain.

The benefit of using unbound navigation with the Focus Chain is that you have more control over where focus is placed as the user moves from widget to widget. When bound navigation is used, focus simply cycles linearly through the widgets, completely ignoring the Focus Chain. Keep in mind that despite the suggestion of the names, *bound* navigation ignores the Focus Chain, whereas *unbound* navigation utilizes the Focus Chain.

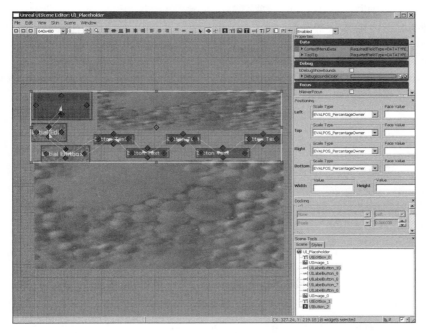

FIGURE 6.73   The Focus Chain appears as a series of blue arrows that link your widgets.

Working with User Inputs

One of the most important aspects to setting up your UI is controlling how it deals with inputs from the user. For our purposes, this pertains primarily to dealing with keyboard keystrokes and mouse inputs, but could also extend to inputs from joysticks, game pads, or even to Xbox 360 and PlayStation 3 controllers, provided you are a licensed developer. No matter your platform, however, all user inputs can be controlled simply through the editing of key bindings.

Working with key bindings requires that you understand input event aliases, which are nothing more than behaviors your widgets will need to perform. By binding these input event aliases to certain keys, you can control how the user works with your UI. For instance, it is generally understood that in most software, clicking a button is the same as highlighting it and pressing Enter. However, what do you do when you need to change such behavior? Or what if your game is designed to use a game pad, so there is no mouse button or Enter key? This is where the editing of key bindings becomes important.

You have two ways to go about editing key bindings: at the global level (meaning that you are affecting all widgets of a particular type) and at the local level (meaning that you are affecting only an individual widget).

Changing key bindings globally requires the Bind UI Event Alias Key Defaults window. This can be accessed by right-clicking within the UIScene Editor viewport or by pressing the F8 key. The Bind UI Event Alias Key Defaults window appears as shown in **FIGURE 6.74**.

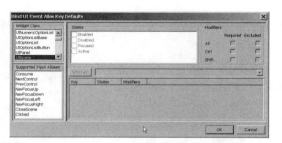

FIGURE 6.74   The Bind UI Event Alias Key Defaults window

In the top-left corner of the window you will find a dropdown that allows you to choose the type of widget you will be editing. As you select a widget, the list of Widget Event Aliases is populated, based on which Event Aliases are available to that type of widget. A Widget Event Alias is simply a type of action that can be performed on the widget. We provide a list of each of the available Widget Event Aliases at the end of this section.

Once you have selected your widget, as well to which Widget Event Alias you want to bind a key, you have only to choose which key you'd like to bind and to click the button with the two arrows pointing to the right. This adds the new key binding to the list.

Using the Bind UI Event Alias Key Defaults window changes the key bindings for all like widgets in a package. For example, if you change the key binding for the Clicked Widget Event Alias for a Button widget, then all buttons in that UI will change as well. More often than not, you will not necessarily want to change every single widget and will instead only be looking to change the input for one individual widget. This process requires the use of Kismet.

If you select a widget, right-click it, and choose Kismet Editor from the context menu, you will see the list of available states for your widget in the sequences browser in the lower-right corner of the screen. Keep in mind that you can alter key bindings not only for each individual widget, but also for each state for that widget. Also, it should be noted that key binding changes made at the local level override any existing at the global level. This means that if you add a new key binding for a key that was already bound by default, you will override that key binding for this widget.

Once you click a given state for a widget, you will see the State Input Event, which holds all the key bindings for that widget in that particular state (see **FIGURE 6.75**). If you double-click this event, you will see a list of all the key bindings that you can apply to the widget's state. Note that if you add a binding to a key that is already bound, you will get an override binding, which supersedes any global bindings (see **FIGURE 6.76**).

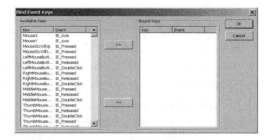

FIGURE 6.75 When you double-click a State Input Event, you can add new key bindings.

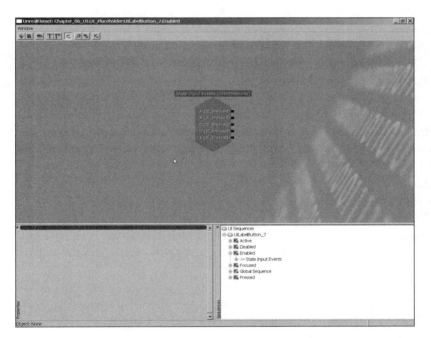

FIGURE 6.76 Newly bound keys appear like so, and can have Kismet actions triggered by them, just like regular events.

Widget input event aliases are used as a means to produce a necessary action using platform-specific keys. For example, a player might take for granted that he or she can press the Backspace key to delete the last letter typed, but what happens when the player is using a gamepad or controller? Widget input event aliases allow you to map certain necessary behavior for each widget to specific keys to solve this problem. The following is a list of the available Widget input event aliases, along with descriptions of their functionality. Note that not all these input event aliases are applicable to every type of widget. You will see which ones are applicable to each widget when you enter the Bind UI Event Alias Key Defaults window. Also be aware that the term *input* pertains to a pressed key that is bound to a particular Widget input event alias.

Consume—This alias kills off any input that is sent into it. It also prevents any inputs from being propagated to other widgets in the scene. For example, you could bind the X button on a game controller to this alias for a given widget, thereby making that button nonfunctional while the widget had focus.

NextControl—This is a navigational alias, allowing you to cycle linearly to the next widget in the UIScene's widget list. The type of navigation produced by this alias is considered to be "bound navigation" because it does not follow the Focus Chain.

Previous Control—This is another navigational alias that cycles linearly to the previous widget in the UIScene's widget list. The type of navigation produced by this alias is considered to be "bound navigation" because it does not follow the Focus Chain.

NavFocusUp—Keys bound to this alias produce "unbound navigation" that does follow the Focus Chain. In this case, focus moves from the Top Focus Chain handle, provided that a link exists to another widget.

NavFocusDown—Keys bound to this alias produce "unbound navigation" that does follow the Focus Chain. Focus moves from the Bottom Focus Chain handle, provided that a link exists to another widget.

NavFocusLeft—Keys bound to this alias produce "unbound navigation" that does follow the Focus Chain. Focus moves from the Left Focus Chain handle, provided that a link exists to another widget.

NavFocusRight—Keys bound to this alias produce "unbound navigation" that does follow the Focus Chain. Focus moves from the Right Focus Chain handle, provided that a link exists to another widget.

Clicked—Any input bound to this alias activates an OnClick Kismet event, from which other actions can be triggered. This alias also places the widget that is receiving the input into the Pressed state, provided that the widget supports that state.

SubmitText—This input event alias is only applicable to widgets that support text entry, such as the Editbox. In most cases, this alias only pertains to widgets that are in the Focused state. Any input bound to this alias activates a SubmitText Kismet event, from which other actions can be triggered. Any text that was stored in the widget is placed within a parameter of the Kismet event for use throughout the sequence. The alias also places the widget receiving the input into the Pressed state.

Char—This input event alias is used with any widgets that support text entry, such as the Editbox. In most cases, this alias only pertains to widgets that are in the Focused state. The alias places whatever bound character was pressed into the text field at the current location of the cursor. This means that you will, in most cases, want to make sure at least all 36 number and letter characters are bound to this alias. However, you should also be aware that in order for the Char alias to work properly, you must have the Character key bound to it as well. As an example, an Editbox has 63 different keys bound to the Char alias by default, including all letters, numbers, punctuation, and the Character key.

BackSpace—This input event alias is used with any widgets that support text entry, such as the Editbox. In most cases, this alias only pertains to widgets that are in the Focused state. When a key is bound to this alias, that key removes the character that sits just before the cursor.

DeleteCharacter—This input event alias is used with any widgets that support text entry, such as the Editbox. In most cases, this alias only pertains to widgets that are in the Focused state. This alias works similarly to the BackSpace alias, except that it removes the character that rests *before* the cursor.

MoveCursorLeft—This input event alias is used with any widgets that support text entry, such as the Editbox. In most cases, this alias only pertains to widgets that are in the Focused state. As the name suggests, this alias moves the cursor to the left, very much like pressing the left-arrow key in most PC applications.

MoveCursorRight—This input event alias is used with any widgets that support text entry, such as the Editbox. In most cases, this alias only pertains to widgets that are in the Focused state. This alias moves the cursor to the right, very much like pressing the right-arrow key in most PC applications.

MoveCursorToLineStart—This input event alias is used with any widgets that support text entry, such as the Editbox. In most cases, this alias only pertains to widgets that are in the Focused state. This alias moves the cursor to the beginning of the text field, very much like pressing the Home key in most PC applications.

MoveCursorToLineEnd—This input event alias is used with any widgets that support text entry, such as the Editbox. In most cases, this alias only pertains to widgets that are in the Focused state. This alias moves the cursor to the end of the text field, very much like pressing the End key in most PC applications.

DragSlider—This alias is only applicable to Slider widgets, and typically only to those that are in the Pressed state, which usually means that you are currently hovering the mouse over the slider and pressing the left mouse button. Once this alias receives input, it starts translating mouse movements into increments or decrements in the slider's value.

IncrementSliderValue—This alias is only applicable to Slider widgets, and generally only applies to the Focused state. This alias causes the value of the slider to increase by the NudgeValue property, located in the SliderValue category.

DecrementSliderValue—This alias is only applicable to Slider widgets, and generally only applies to the Focused state. This alias causes the value of the slider to decrease by the NudgeValue property, located in the SliderValue category.

IncrementNumericValue—This alias is only applicable to Numeric Editbox widgets, and generally only those that are in the Focused state. This alias causes the current value of the numeric field to increase by the NudgeValue property, as specified within the widget's properties.

DecrementNumericValue—This alias is only applicable to Numeric Editbox widgets, and generally only those that are in the Focused state. This alias causes the current value of the numeric field to decrease by the NudgeValue property, as specified within the widget's properties.

Data Stores

Data stores are the primary means of data collection and delivery for UI elements. They are also the way in which you pass data from one widget to the next. For example, say you have a text-entry field for a player's name that updates a label at the top of the screen once the name has been input. You would use a data store to hold that name, and then the label would retrieve the name from the data store and use it to update its text.

Many data stores have been written into Unreal and are available by default. These can be viewed via the Data Store Browser, which is accessed either through the UIScene Editor's Edit menu or by pressing the F7 key. The Data Store Browser is shown in **FIGURE 6.77**.

You can use the Filter field to cycle through the available data stores. However, you will find that most of the default data stores are useful only for very specific purposes. You do have the ability to create your own data stores through UnrealScript; this is, however, beyond the scope of this text.

Attaching your widget to a data store can be done easily through the Data Store Browser. To bind a widget to a data store, simply select it from the browser, right-click your widget, and choose Bind Selected Widgets to <Current Data Store>, where <Current Data Store> is the name of the data store you have selected.

There is a data store that is reserved for use by non-coding designers, and is very useful for passing data between your widgets without having to worry about coding your own data store. This data store is called SceneData. Using

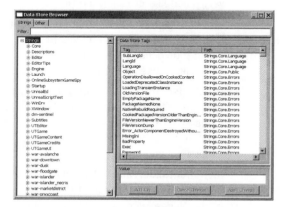

FIGURE 6.77　The Data Store Browser.

this data store requires a particular syntax in the MarkupString property, as well as a specific setup in Kismet. However, the workflow for setting this up is best demonstrated through example. Later in this chapter, we use this technique to create a Video Options UI.

Styles and Skins

You can control the visual look of your UIs through the use of styles and skins. Styles provide the individual control for your widgets, and skins are container that allow you to save a collection of styles into a single object that can be applied to an entire UI. We start by discussing styles and how they can be controlled and created, and then we take a look at skins.

Styles

Styles control the look of your widgets in their various states. Styles are used to modify such things as the way a texture is placed on a widget as well as the font face and alignment of text on a widget's label. For instance, you can have a button appear to be highlighted when the mouse is hovering over it (in the Active state) and then appear to look depressed when clicked (in the Pressed state). Three types of styles are available: Image, Text, and Combo (which includes both Text and Image settings).

All available styles are listed in the Styles panel, which can be seen in the Scene Tools panel on the right side of the UIScene Editor (see **FIGURE 6.78**). Make sure you have activated Scene Tools under the Window menu. The list may seem overwhelming at first, but realize that it includes every style that is applied to every single available widget.

You should be aware that widgets can have more than one style applied to them through the use of a Combo style. For instance, a default Label Button will use a Combo style that is called Default Label Button, and is a combination of the Button Text style and the Button Background style. This means that if you wanted to change the background of the button, you'd need to edit the Button Background style, which would propagate to the Default Label Button style.

Modifying a widget's style can be handled in a few of different ways. You can select a different style from a list of styles available to that widget, or you can edit the style that is currently applied to that widget.

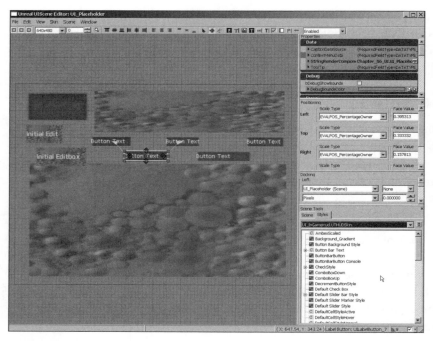

FIGURE 6.78   The Styles panel.

To edit a widget's existing style, simply right-click a particular widget and choose Edit Style, which expands out to show you the styles currently applied to your widget. Choosing one of these styles brings up the Editing Style window. However, doing this means that you will be editing this style for whatever widgets in your scene happen to be using it. For instance, if you edit the Button Background style, the background of all buttons will change. This may be desired, although if you wanted to instead edit only a single widget, you'd need to create a new style and apply this style to that widget.

The Editing Style window has three different appearances, based on the type of style you are editing. **FIGURES 6.79** though **6.81** show the Editing Style window for text styles, image styles, and combo styles, respectively. Notice that when editing a Combo style, you do not have access to a preview window for the image or the text. However, a Combo style does allow you to assign a pre-existing style to both the image and the text, meaning it will likely be simpler to just have a separate Text and Image style and then bring them together within a new Combo style.

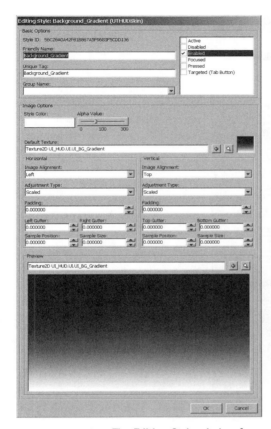

FIGURE 6.79 The Editing Style window for an Image style

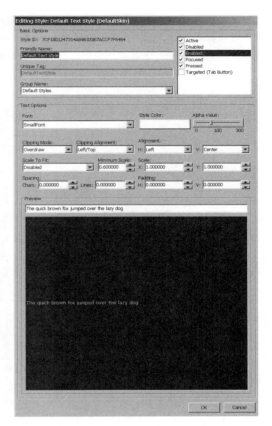

FIGURE 6.80 The Editing Style window for a Text style

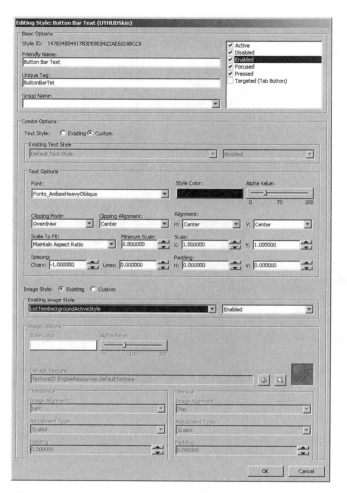

FIGURE 6.81   The Editing Style window for a Combo style. Note that you can reference a Text and an Image style, and that there is no preview area.

Creating a new style is handled in two ways. You can create one from scratch, or you can use an existing style as a template. To create a brand-new style, simply right-click in the Styles list in the Scene Tools and choose Create New Style from the context menu that appears. You are presented with the Create New Style window, which allows you to input some information for the style you're creating (see **FIGURE 6.82**).

Here are the parameters you need to fill in:

FIGURE 6.82   **The Create New Style window.**

> **Style Type**—This allows you to choose between creating a Text, Image, or Combo style.

> **Unique Tag**—This property is the internal name the editor uses to refer to your style. This name cannot have spaces. An example would be vidOptions_buttonBackground.

> **Friendly Name**—This is the name that will be printed in the Style list. This can have spaces. For example, you could use Video Options Button Background.

> **Template**—This allows you to choose the style from which you'd like to derive your new style. If you leave this blank, you create a completely new style. However, if you choose a preexisting style as a template, your new style becomes a child style of the template.

Child styles are the result of creating new styles based on a template. Any changes made to the parent style propagate down to the child, unless those properties were already specifically set within the child. For instance, changing the font size of the parent changes the font size of the child, unless you've already explicitly set the child's font size. Settings made at the child level override those made at the parent level.

Once you have created a new style, you can assign it simply by selecting your widget, right-clicking it, and choosing Select Style from the context menu. This expands to the types of styles you can apply, which are either image or caption styles. This, too, can be expanded, allowing you to see a list of all applicable styles, where you will see the name of the style you just created (see **FIGURE 6.83**).

Skins

A skin is just a collection of styles. By applying a skin, you are essentially activating an entire collection of styles across your widgets, just like choosing different skins on certain media player applications. You must have at least one skin in your game for your UIs to be functional.

FIGURE 6.83   Your new style appears in the context menu.

The UIScene Editor comes with a default skin. Creating a new skin is as simple as clicking the Exclamation Point button ⚠ next to the skin name in the Style tab and then choosing Create New Skin from the context menu that appears. If you plan on making many changes to the various styles of your UI, it is generally a good idea to create a new skin first. All custom skins derive from the original Default skin. When you first create a new skin, you can specify the package name where it will be saved. If the package does not already exist, it will be created for you, although it may not appear until you refresh (close and then reopen) the Generic Browser (see **FIGURE 6.84**).

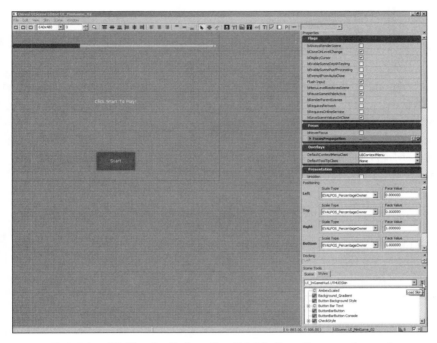

FIGURE 6.84   Clicking the Exclamation Point button allows you to create a new skin.

Once you have created your new skin, you simply need to start overriding the default styles included with it. To do this, locate the package into which you saved your new skin and then double-click the skin. The Skin Editor appears. When you first open this window, you will notice that all the styles listed in the Styles tab are in italics (see **FIGURE 6.85**). This is because the styles are actually referencing the parent style, which is often the default style. By right-clicking these styles and choosing Replace Style in Current Skin, you will make the style unique to the skin, meaning that it will no longer be referencing the parent. At this point, you are free to make changes. Keep in mind, however, that any changes made to the parent still affect those styles that are italicized. This is especially important when a skin other than the Default skin is being used as the parent.

Applying a skin in the editor is fairly simple: You only need to select it from the skin list in the Styles tab. However, this is only a preview. At the time of this writing, you will not see this skin during gameplay by default. To actually use a skin in the game, you must edit the DefaultEngine.ini file.

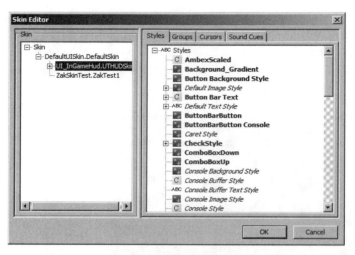

FIGURE 6.85   The styles in italics are being referenced from the template skin. The bold styles are unique to this skin.

Editing the UTUI.ini file is rather simple. First, you need to navigate to it. On most *UT3* installations, it can be found in your Documents folder in the following location:

> Documents\My Games\Unreal Tournament 3\UTGame\Config\

The line shown next must be edited to point to the new PostProcessEffect object, using the notation <PackageName>.<Group>.<Name>.

> DefaultPostProcessName=EngineMaterials.DefaultScenePostProcess

Keep in mind, however, that before changing the UTUI.ini file, you should shut down Unreal Editor and any instances of the game that may be running. Failure to do so could cause the INI file to be overwritten, removing any changes you have made.

Also note that once you're finished, if you would like to set your skin back to the defaults, you simply need shut down all instances of Unreal/Unreal Editor and then delete the UTUI.INI file. Upon the next launch of the game or the editor, the system will notice the missing file and re-create it with its factory default settings

Here is the line of the INI file that will need to be edited is as follows:

> [Engine.UIInteraction]
>
> UISkinName="MyPackageName.MySkinName"

You are only allowed one of these entries in your INI file, because you will only need one skin at a time. Adding multiple entries causes the INI file to overwrite the previous entries with the last entry.

In **TUTORIAL 6.6**, we set up a very simple skin that is derived from the Default skin and change the background image and the text of the button.

Continue from **TUTORIAL 6.5**. If you have not yet completed it, you may use the UI_MiniGame_03 UIScene to complete this tutorial. You will find this object in the Chapter_06_UI package, included on the DVD.

> **NOTE**
>
> MyPackageName will be replaced by the actual name of your package, and MySkinName will of course be the name you gave to your skin. So if your skin is named Fireshelf and is within a package named CustomUISkins, your INI file would read:
>
> UISkinName="CustomUISkins.Fireshelf"

Before we begin, let's get an idea of which styles need to be adjusted in our new skin (see **FIGURE 6.86**). If you're completely new to UI creation, you may not know which styles are associated with certain widgets.

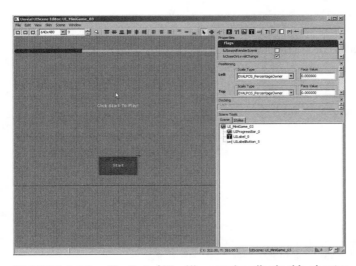

FIGURE 6.86 The Tug-of-War UI created earlier in this chapter.

TUTORIAL 6.6: Creating a Custom Skin

1. In the UIScene Editor, right-click the Label Button and choose Edit Style. This expands to show you which styles are being used for the caption and image on the button. These should be Background Image Style (Button Background Style) and Caption Style (Default Label Button Style), respectively. Make note of these styles for later (see **FIGURE 6.87**).

2. Now we begin to create the new skin, which will contain all our styles. This skin will reference all the Default styles when created, although we have the option of changing all the styles or even adding new ones.

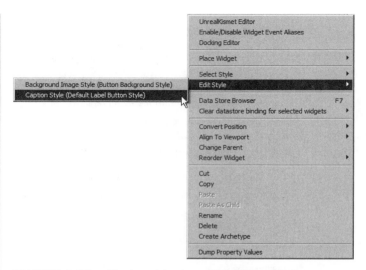

FIGURE 6.87   The two styles in use by the Label Button.

3. In the Scene Tools panel, click the Styles tab and make sure the DefaultSkin is selected from the skin selector dropdown. Click the button with the exclamation point . Choose Create New Skin from the context menu.

4. In the Create New Skin window, set the following properties:

> **Package**: Chapter_06_UI
>
> **Name**: MySkin

Click OK when finished.

5. Your skin will not be immediately visible. You'll need to save your package first, so go ahead and do this now after closing the UIScene Editor. To edit your skin, double-click it in the Generic Browser. The Skin Editor appears (see **FIGURE 6.88**).

When you first enter the Skin Editor, you will notice that all the styles are italicized, meaning that they are being referenced from the DefaultSkin. To change this, we need to replace the styles in this skin. For our example, we are only going to do this for the button background, but you could easily do this with any other style in the skin.

6. Expand the Default Image Style. Then, locate the Button Background Style. Right-click it and choose Replace Style Button Background Style in Current Skin. When you do this, you may get a warning telling you that you need to fully load some packages (see **FIGURE 6.89**).

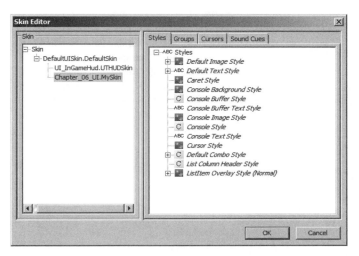

FIGURE 6.88   The Skin Editor window appears when you double-click your new skin.

7. If this is the case, simply right-click the named packages in the Generic Browser's package list, choose Fully Load from the context menu, and then retry the replacement (see **FIGURE 6.90**).

FIGURE 6.89   You may receive a warning such as this when you try to replace the style.

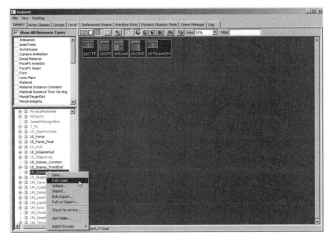

FIGURE 6.90   Fully load the necessary packages and then reattempt the replacement.

8. A new bold version of ButtonBackground should appear. Double-click this new style to open the Editing Style window (see **FIGURE 6.91**).

> **NOTE**
>
> You may receive a second warning telling you that certain elements of your UI are referencing that style. In fact, if you're doing this with *Unreal Tournament 3*, you're probably going to get a list of references that is so long that it won't fit on your screen! Simply click OK (or press Enter if you can't see the OK button) if you receive this warning.

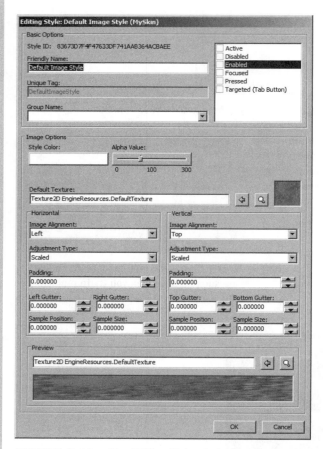

FIGURE 6.91   The Editing Style window for the new style.

9. Use the following steps to alter the style:

   a. We need a new image that we can apply to the style. In the Generic Browser, expand the Textures group within the Chapter_06_UI package. Select the ButtonEnabled texture (see **FIGURE 6.92**).

b. In the Editing Style window, check all the available states for the button, using the small white list of check boxes in the upper corner of the window (see **FIGURE 6.93**).

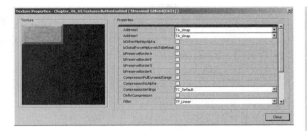

FIGURE 6.92   The ButtonEnabled texture

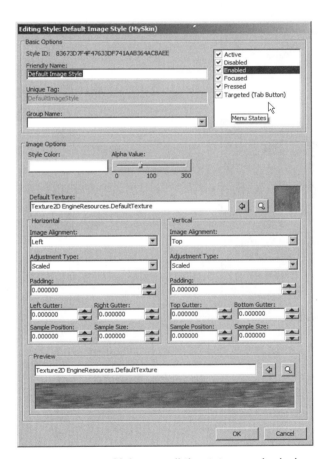

FIGURE 6.93   Make sure all the states are checked.

c. Select the states, one at a time, and for each one click the green arrowed button ⬅ next to the Default Texture field. This places the ButtonEnabled texture into the Default Texture for each state. If it doesn't, make sure the ButtonEnabled texture is still selected in the Generic Browser (see **FIGURE 6.94**).

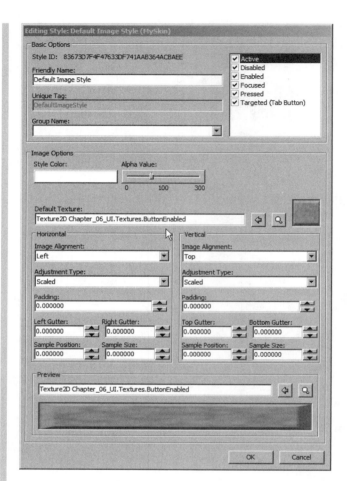

FIGURE 6.94 Place the texture for all states.

d. Select all the states from the state list by clicking while holding down Ctrl and then set the Style Color to white by clicking the Style Color button. Note that this button reads "multiple values" just before you click it (see **FIGURE 6.95**).

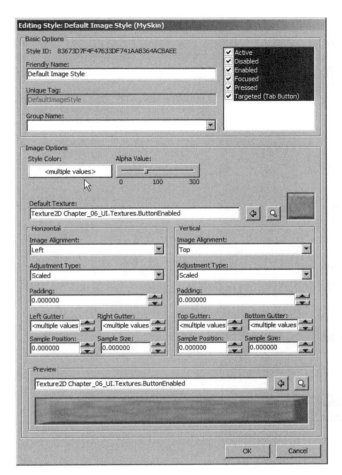

FIGURE 6.95 Notice that the color chooser button reads "multiple values" when you select all the states.

        e. Select only the Pressed state, and set its Style Color to light gray. Then select only the Disabled state, and set its Style Color to dark gray (see **FIGURE 6.96**).

10. Click OK in the Editing Styles window and then click OK in the Skin Editor. Save your package.

11. We now need to assign our skin to the button within our UI. Double-click the UI_MiniGame_03 UIScene included in Chapter_06_UI to open the scene in the UIScene Editor.

12. Select the button at the bottom of the scene. In the Styles tab of the Scene Tools area, choose Chapter_06_UI.MySkin from the dropdown. You will not see an update yet.

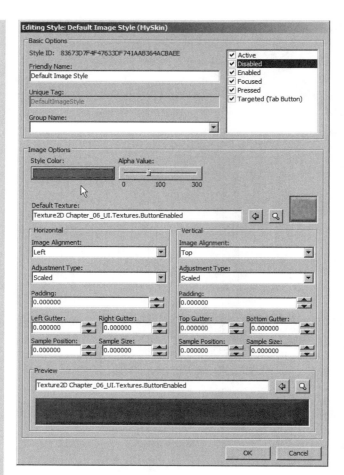

FIGURE 6.96   By setting the color to gray for the Pressed state, you cause the button to appear to darken when clicked.

13. Right-click the button itself. Then, from the context menu, choose Select Style > BackgroundImageStyle > DefaultImageStyle. You should see the button update to show your new graphic.

14. If you were to test your UI right now, you'd notice no changes, even if you had your new skin selected in the Skin dropdown list in the Style tab. This is because you need to update your UTUI.INI file to read your new skin. We will do this in **TUTORIAL 6.7**.

END TUTORIAL 6.6

Continue from **TUTORIAL 6.6**. If you have not yet completed it, you may use the MySkin_01 skin in place of MySkin to complete **TUTORIAL 6.7**. You will find this object in the Chapter_06_UI package, included on the DVD.

> **NOTE**
>
> The steps in **TUTORIAL 6.7** pertain to those using *Unreal Tournament 3* and no other Unreal Engine 3 game.

TUTORIAL 6.7: Editing the ExampleGame.ini File to Read a Custom Skin

1. Close Unreal Editor if it is open.

2. Navigate to the Documents\My Games\Unreal Tournament 3\UTGame\Config\ folder and locate the UTUI.ini file, and open it with any text editor. By default (in Windows) this will open Notepad.

3. Note the very first line under the [Engine.UIInteraction] section. Change it to read as follows:

   ```
   [Engine.UIInteraction]

   UISkinName=Chapter_06_UI.MySkin
   ```

> **NOTE**
>
> Failure to close Unreal Editor will result in your changes being reverted as soon as the game closes, which means you will not be able to edit the INI file. Also, there is no need to back this file up before editing, unless you have made previous edits that you do not want to lose. To set this INI file back to its default settings, simply delete the INI file and restart Unreal Editor. The editor will notice the missing file and re-create it using its internally defined default settings.

4. Save and close the INI file and then restart Unreal Editor. You may get a warning asking if you want to update one of the other INI files. If so, click Yes, and Unreal Editor will begin. If you don't, this is no cause for alarm.

5. Save your package. Open the DM-CH_06_MiniGame_Start level included on the DVD in the files for this chapter. In the Kismet for the level, you will see a Level Beginning event tied to an Open Scene action. Select the object variable and use the Generic Browser to set the ObjValue to your UI_MiniGame UIScene, or use UI_MiniGame_Final.

6. You should now see the button sporting its new skin!

END TUTORIAL 6.7

Style Overrides

Just because a particular style has been applied to a widget does not mean that you are limited to using only the features established within that style. You can override various aspects of the style, such as the particular image used in the case of Image widgets or buttons, or the particular font shown in the case of text labels.

Style overrides can be found in different locations depending on what type of widget you are using and what type of aspect you want to override. For instance, if you want to override the image used on a Button widget, the appropriate StyleOverride property category can be found in the UI Scene Editor's Properties panel within Image > BackgroundImageComponent > StyleOverride. Within this category, you will find the appropriate properties to change the image used on the button, as well as other aspects defined in the style such as alignment, opacity, and more.

If instead you want to change some aspect of the type used on a Label Button widget, such as the font, find the appropriate StyleOverride property category within Data > StringRender Component > StyleOverride. In this category, you will find TextStyleCustomization, within which you will find all the necessary properties to adjust such things as font, alignment, font style (italics, bold, and so on), and many other visual text properties.

There are, however, some special considerations when using style overrides on your widgets. Below is a list of some of the primary things to keep in mind:

- ▶ Style overrides only affect those aspects that you check in the override. All other aspects remain just as they are in the style parameters. For instance, if you override the alignment of text, this will not affect the color.

- ▶ Using style overrides will disable any visual changes to the widget due to a change in state. For example, if you have a button that turns from red to blue when clicked, and you use a style override to change the color to green, then the button will no longer change color – even when clicked – and will always appear green.

- ▶ Due to the fact that using overrides can destroy the interactive nature of certain widgets, style overrides should generally be used for static widgets, such as labels and images.

- ▶ Common usage of overrides includes adjusting text alignment, image color, text wrapping, and UV coordinates for image flipping.

Fonts

Fonts provide you with a way to control the text in your UIScenes. Importing fonts into Unreal is extremely simple, requiring only that you have a few fonts installed on your computer. Unreal Editor will accept any TrueType font as a font source. It then converts that font into a series of textures that can be placed in your UIs. To import a font, simply right-click in the Generic Browser and choose New Font Imported from TrueType. You will then see an import screen where you can choose your font and choose a few settings (see **FIGURE 6.97**).

FIGURE 6.97   The New window has some special options for importing fonts.

One thing to keep in mind when bringing in fonts is that, as of the time of this writing, you will not be able to select different sizes for the font after it is imported. This is because the font is converted to bitmap data upon import, meaning that you really only have a picture of the font, as opposed to access to the vector data of the font itself. Unreal Editor does this by creating a series of textures at a resolution you specify; then it fits as many letters onto a single texture as it can, based on the size of the font. For example, one entire font could be imported onto a 256×256 texture if the font size is only 10, but if the font size is 72, you'd only be able to fit about six letters or so into a 256×256 area. This means you would need multiple textures of that size to import the entire font.

You can, however, export a font back out into an image file and then use any image-editing software you like to make adjustments to the text.

Under the Options area when importing a font, you will find a variety of settings you can adjust to control the final look of your font. Here are some of the more frequently used settings:

> **bCreatePrintableOnly**—This property excludes any characters that are not in the font.

> **bEnableAntiAliasing**—This activates anti-aliasing on the textures that are created for your font.

> **Chars**—Only the characters entered into this property are added to the font. Just type in the alphanumeric characters you want to have in the imported font, and only those characters will be imported.

bEnableItalic—This option imports the italic version of the font.

bEnableLegacyMode—Use this option when you want to import monospace fonts. By default, Unreal adjusts the position and sizes of the texture coordinates for a font texture to maximize overall texture space. With this option activated, coordinate adjustment does not happen, meaning each character receives the same amount of texture space.

bEnableUnderline—This imports the text with underlining enabled.

CharsFilePath—This property is used to set one or more files for localization, allowing you to import fonts in languages other than English. Simply point it at the directory where your localization files are stored.

CharsFileWildcard—This is used in conjunction with the Path property when importing a font with a localization file. You simply type in an asterisk and then the extension of the localization file your using (for example, *.kor).

USize—This sets the width of the texture panels that are generated for your font. The smaller this is, the more textures needed for a larger font.

VSize—This sets the height of the texture panels that generated for your font. The smaller this is, the more textures needed for a larger font.

XPad—This sets the amount of horizontal space between characters on the texture. The size is measured in pixels. This is useful when you notice that letters include portions of their neighbors when typed into the preview window.

YPad—This sets the amount of vertical space between characters on the texture. The size is measured in pixels. This is useful when you notice that letters include portions of their neighbors when typed into the preview window.

TUTORIAL 6.8: Importing a TrueType Font

1. Launch Unreal Editor. In the Generic Browser, right-click and choose New Font Imported from TrueType.

2. In the window that appears, set the following properties:

   Package: Chapter_06_UI

   Group: Fonts

   Name: MyFont

3. Click the Choose Font button and use the window to choose the Verdana font from the list, at size 14. Click OK when finished (see **FIGURE 6.98**).

4. In the Options window, check bCreatePrintableOnly.

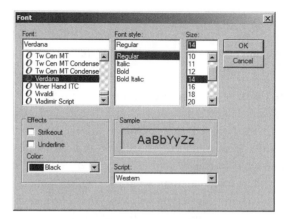

FIGURE 6.98   Make the following settings for your font.

5. Click OK. You may get a warning asking if you'd like to fully load the package, which you do. After a moment, the Font Properties window appears. Click the Preview button, which will open the FontPreview window, where you can type some text to see what your font will look like (see **FIGURE 6.99**).

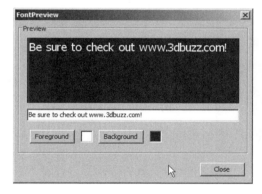

FIGURE 6.99   Test your font in the preview window.

6. Save your package.

END TUTORIAL 6.8

Adding Functionality

As you have already seen in many of the tutorials, all the primary functionality of a UI comes through Kismet. When working with UIs, you will notice that Kismet behaves a bit differently and has a different set of events and actions that all pertain to some type of UI functionality. In fact, each of the widgets in your UIScene has its own Kismet Editor as well as a separate sequence for each of the available states. The particular actions and events you use depend on what it is you're doing with your UI.

When you first right-click a widget and choose Kismet Editor from the context menu, the first thing you see is the contents of the Global Sequence. This state allows you to trigger various Kismet events no matter what state your widget is in. There are three events in this sequence by default: Initialized (which simply outputs once the widget is loaded in the scene, typically when the UIScene is opened), Enter State (which allows you to trigger actions as the widget enters a particular state), and Leave State (which allows you to trigger actions when your widget leaves a particular state). If your widget happens to have any child widgets, you will see a Global Sequence node as well, which you can double-click to see the Global Sequence for the child widget.

When you're working with UI Kismet, it is important to keep in mind which state should be used to house your sequence. For example, if you want to perform some particular action when a button is clicked, you need to create your sequence objects within that button's Pressed state sequence. In many cases, most of the sequences that perform actual functionality take place within the Focused, Global, or Pressed state (see **FIGURE 6.100**).

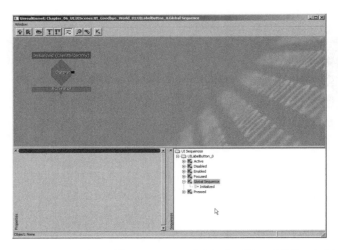

FIGURE 6.100   The sequences list in the Kismet Editor holds the various states that a widget supports.

Inside each of the sequences for the various non-Global states of your widget, you will find a State Input Events placeholder. These exist to hold the various inputs that your widget will respond to while in each state. If you double-click State Input Events, you see a list of all the keys you can bind (see **FIGURE 6.101**). When you add any of these keys, that key will appear inside the State

Input Event as an output, allowing you to use Kismet to attach any actions or events to it that you might need.

An important thing to remember when working with UI Kismet is that, at the time of this writing, all Kismet sequences between different UIScenes are completely independent of one another. This means that sequences that belong to two separate widgets in two separate UIScenes cannot communicate with one another without the use of a custom-written data store. What's more, you cannot easily have actions in one UIScene affect aspects of a separate UIScene. You should also know that interaction between UIScenes and level objects is not handled as it typically would be

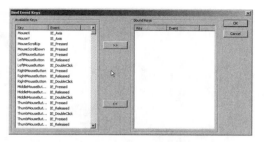

FIGURE 6.101   State Input Events are used for state-specific key bindings.

> **NOTE**
>
> **TUTORIAL 6.9** uses the MySkin UI Skin created earlier in this chapter! You will need to edit your UTUI.INI file as shown in **TUTORIAL 6.7**.

in Kismet, meaning, for example, that you cannot simply bring an object variable for a light source into your UI Kismet sequence in order to toggle the light on and off.

In **TUTORIAL 6.9**, we create a more practical example than the UI game. We're going to set up a Video Options UI such as you might see at the title screen of many video games.

TUTORIAL 6.9: Creating a Video Options UI, Part I: Game Title Screen

1. Launch Unreal Editor. In the Generic Browser, right-click and choose New UIScene. Enter the following values:

   Package: Chapter_06_UI

   Group: UIScenes

   Name: VidOptions_Main

2. Once the UIScene editor is open, create a new Label Button near the center of the viewport. Set the MarkupStrings (located under CaptionDataSource) for this buttons to Start Game.

3. Right-click the button itself, and from the context menu, choose Select Style > BackgroundImageStyle > DefaultImageStyle. You should see the button update to show the gray button graphic.

4. Duplicate this button below the first and then change the markup string for the duplicate to Options (see **FIGURE 6.102**).

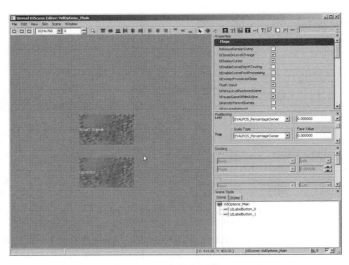

FIGURE 6.102   Create two label buttons as shown.

5. Center the text on *both* buttons by expanding StringRenderComponent >StyleOverride > TextStyleCustomization. Check TextAlignment, and set both UIORIENT_Horizontal and UIORIENT_Vertical to Center (see **FIGURE 6.103**).

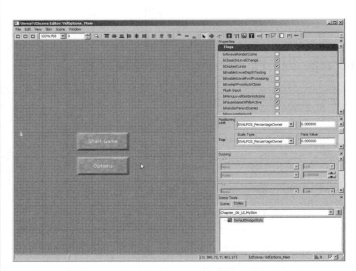

FIGURE 6.103   Center the text on both buttons.

6. Right-click the Start Game button and choose UnrealKismet Editor from the context menu. This time, instead of placing an Enter State event into the Pressed sequence, we're going to change our thought process by using the On Click in the Focused sequence.

7. Select the Focused sequence and notice On Click (see **FIGURE 6.104**).

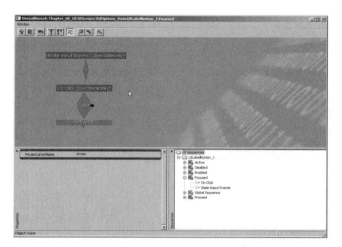

FIGURE 6.104   The Focused sequence already contains an On Click event.

8. Right-click just next to this and choose New Action > UI > Close Scene. Connect this action to the On Click event. In the properties area of this new object, verify that bAutoTargetOwner is checked. This will automatically close our scene, without us having to designate it through an object variable (see **FIGURE 6.105**).

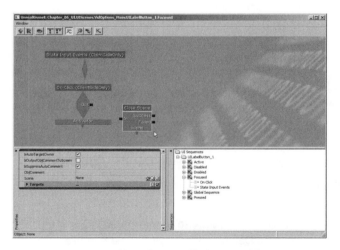

FIGURE 6.105   Close Scene will close our UI.

9. Close the Kismet Editor.

10. Open the DM-CH_06_UITest_Begin.ut3 level included on the DVD in the files for this chapter.

11. In the level's Kismet Editor, select the Open Scene action and set its Scene property to your VidOptions_Main UIScene using the Generic Browser (see **FIGURE 6.106**).

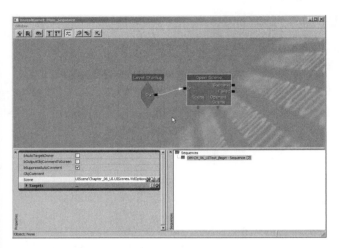

FIGURE 6.106   Use this network to test your UI.

12. Save your package. You can test the UI at this point. Only the Start Game button will be functional, however, because all it does is close the UI.

END TUTORIAL 6.9

Continue from **TUTORIAL 6.9**, or open the VidOptions_Main_01 UIScene included with the files for this chapter. We will now create the UI layout for the Options window.

> **NOTE**
>
> **TUTORIAL 6.10** uses the MySkin UI Skin created earlier in this chapter! You will need to edit your UTUI.INI file as shown in **TUTORIAL 6.7**.

TUTORIAL 6.10: Creating a Video Options UI, Part II: Laying Out the Options UI

1. Create a new UIScene in the Chapter_06_UI package named VidOptions_Opt (see **FIGURE 6.107**).

2. Create a Label Button and set its MarkupString to **640x480**. Center the text using the skills you have gained so far. Also, select the Default Image Style for the button's Background Image Style by right-clicking the button and choosing Select Style > Background Image Style > DefaultImageStyle (see **FIGURE 6.108**).

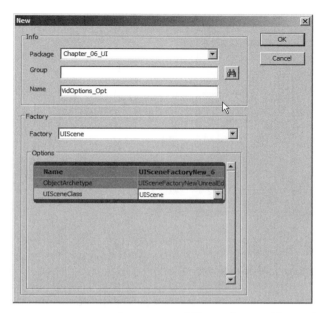

FIGURE 6.107   Create a new UIScene for our video options.

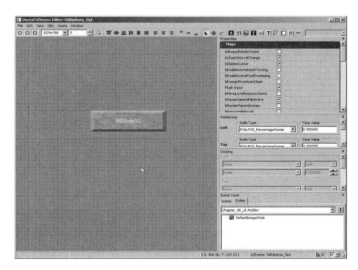

FIGURE 6.108   The new label button for the 640×480 resolution.

3. Duplicate (Ctrl+C, Ctrl+V) to create two more Label Buttons directly below the first, setting their respective MarkupStrings to **800x600** and **1024x768** (see **FIGURE 6.109**).

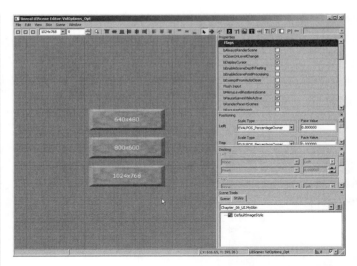

FIGURE 6.109   Two more resolution buttons have been added.

4. Duplicate another Label Button just to the right of the first three, setting its MarkupString to **Apply**.

5. We want the new Apply button to be disabled at first. Using the following steps, we establish this within the button's Kismet:

   a. Right-click the Apply button and choose UnrealKismet Editor. You will see the Global Sequence, which houses the Initialized event.

   b. To the right of the Initialized event, right-click and choose New Action > UI > Activate UI State.

   c. Connect this new Activate UI State to the Output of the Initialized event.

   d. Select the Activate UI State object and set its StateType property to UIState_Disabled. We do not need to specify a target, as long as the bAutoTargetOwner property is set, which it is by default.

   e. Close the Kismet Editor when finished (see **FIGURE 6.110**).

6. Create a Slider widget (right-click and choose Place Widget > UISlider) and then enter **GammaSlider** for the name. Use the scale handles on the left and right sides of the widget to scale it to about half the width of the entire UIScene.

7. Place it just beneath the three resolution buttons. Create a Label just above this Slider and set its MarkupString to **Gamma** (see **FIGURE 6.111**).

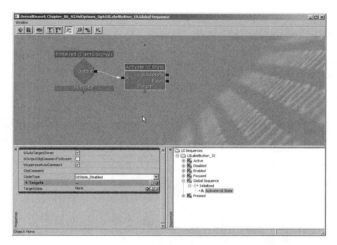

FIGURE 6.110 The new Apply button will begin disabled.

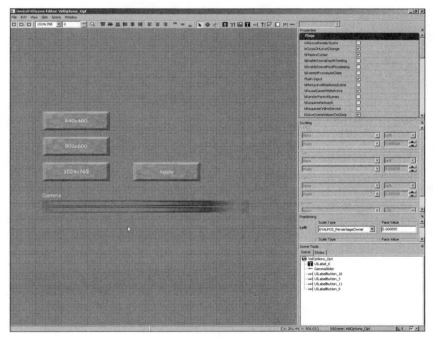

FIGURE 6.111 Create a Slider and a Label that reads "Gamma."

8. Create one more Label Button, set its MarkupString to **Return to Main**, and place it near the bottom of the UI (see **FIGURE 6.112**).

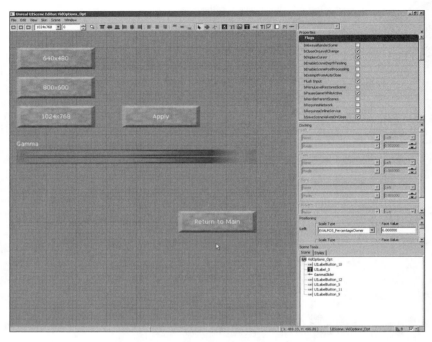

FIGURE 6.112   The Return to Main button closes the UI.

9. We will now dock some of our controls together so that their alignments can be maintained.

   a. Select the 800x600 button. Its docking handles appear as four bright orange circles. Click and drag from the rightmost docking handle to the 640x480 button. As soon as you do this, the docking handles on the upper button appear. Move the mouse over the upper button's rightmost docking handle (it will highlight yellow) and then release the mouse button. A curved blue line appears, meaning you have completed the dock (see **FIGURE 6.113**).

   b. Dock the left handle of the 800x600 button to the left handle of the 640x480 button.

   c. Dock the left and right handles of the 1024x768 button to the left and right handles of the 800x600 button, respectively (see **FIGURE 6.114**).

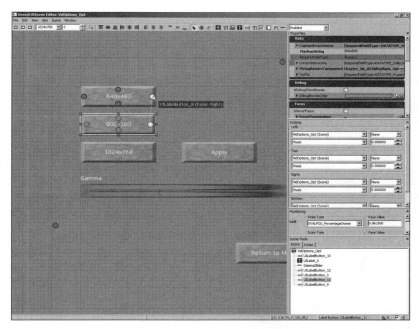

FIGURE 6.113   Dock the right side of the 800x600 button to the right of the 640x480 button.

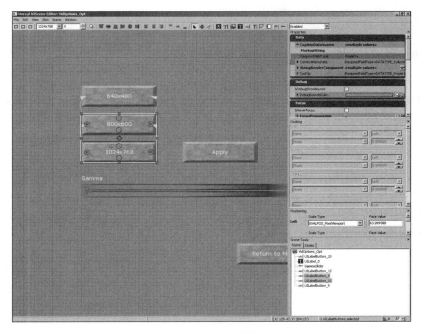

FIGURE 6.114   The left and right sides of the lower two buttons are now docked.

d. Dock the top of the 800x600 button to the bottom of the 640x480 button. This causes the buttons to snap together. Repeat this process to dock the top of the 1024x768 button to the bottom of the 800x600 button (see **FIGURE 6.115**).

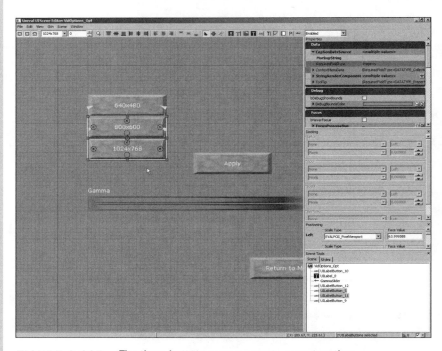

FIGURE 6.115   The three buttons now appear to snap together.

e. Dock the top handle of the Apply button to the top handle of the 1024x768 button. Then dock the left side of the Apply button to the right side of the 1024x768 button, causing them to snap together (see **FIGURE 6.116**).

10. We will now pad our docking to add some spacing back into the layout.

a. Select the 800x600 button, right-click it, and choose Docking Editor. Set the padding for the Top face to 10, using the numerical entry field in the lower-right corner of the Top area (see **FIGURE 6.117**). This creates a 10-pixel gap between the buttons.

b. Open the Docking Editor for the 1024x768 button and set the padding for the Top face to 10.

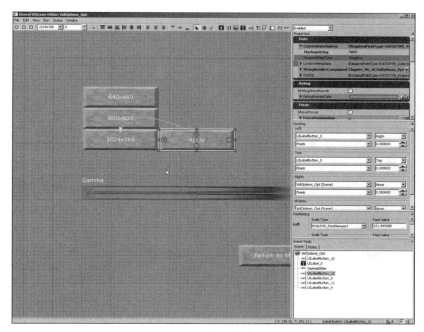

FIGURE 6.116   The Apply button now snaps to the resolution buttons.

    c. Open the Docking Editor for the Apply button and set the padding for the Left
face to 20 (see **FIGURE 6.118**).

FIGURE 6.117   Adjusting the padding creates a 10-pixel gap between the buttons.

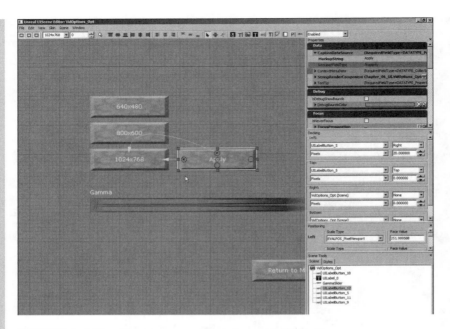

FIGURE 6.118   There are now gaps between all the buttons.

You can now move the 640x480 button, and all the other buttons will move along with it.

11. Save your package.

END TUTORIAL 6.10

Continue from **TUTORIAL 6.10** or open the VidOptions_Opt_01 UIScene included with the files for this chapter. We will set up the initial functionality for our Options UI. This requires the use of the SceneData data store. This data store is present for all UI scenes. We can tap into it to pass data from one widget to another.

> **NOTE**
>
> **TUTORIAL 6.11** uses the MySkin UI Skin created earlier in this chapter! You will need to edit your UTUI.INI file as shown in **TUTORIAL 6.7**.

TUTORIAL 6.11: Creating a Video Options UI, Part III: Adding Functionality

1. Our first step is to create a new entry in the SceneData data store upon the initialization of our UI.

   a. In the Scene Tools window, click the Scene tab. Select the VidOptions_Opt UIScene (at the top of the list). Right-click the UIScene and choose UnrealKismet Editor.

b. By default, you will be looking at the Global sequence for the UIScene. Next to the Initialized event, right-click and choose Add Action > Data Store > Add Data Field. Connect this to the Output of the Initialized event (see **FIGURE 6.119**).

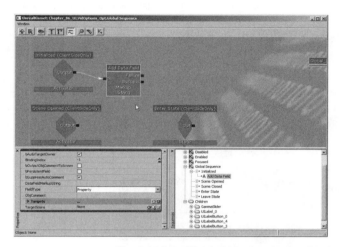

FIGURE 6.119   The Add Data Field object has been added.

c. Right-click the Markup String input of the Add Data Field object and create a new String variable. Set the StrValue property of this new variable to **<SceneData:ResCmd>** (see **FIGURE 6.120**).

d. Close the Kismet Editor for the UIScene.

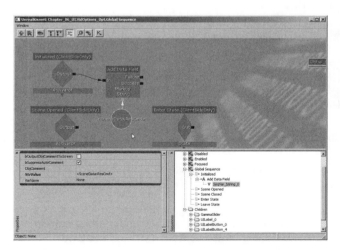

FIGURE 6.120   The markup placed in the string variable directs the Add Data Field to our new SceneData ResCmd data store.

2. Our data store has been set up. We now need to have each of our three resolution buttons record a string using the setres console command and pass it into the data store.

> **NOTE**
>
> The ResCmd portion of the markup is just a variable name. You could use any name you like, as long as you are consistent. You can also create multiple entries in the SceneData data store in this way.

    a. Right-click the 640x480 button and open the Kismet Editor.

    b. In the Global sequence, create the following three objects: an OnClick event (New Event > UI > OnClick), a Set Datastore Value, (New Action > Data Store > Set Datastore Value), and an Activate UI State (New Action > UI > Activate UI State). Wire them all sequentially together as shown in **FIGURE 6.121**.

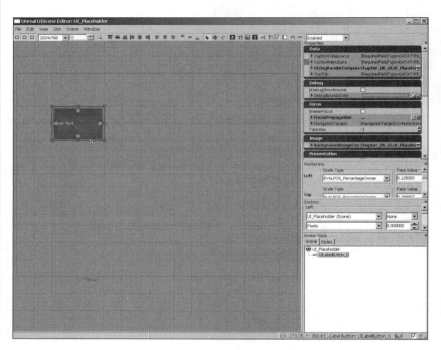

FIGURE 6.121   Create the three objects and connect them like so.

    c. Right-click the Markup String input of the Set Datastore Value and add a new string variable. Set the StrValue of this variable to **<SceneData:ResCmd>** (see **FIGURE 6.122**).

    d. Right-click the String Value input of the Set Datastore Value and add a new string variable. Set the StrValue of this string to **setres 640x480** (see **FIGURE 6.123**).

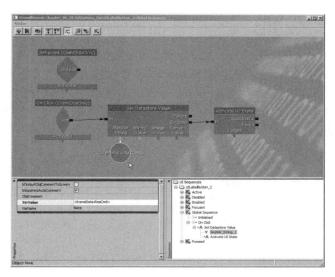

FIGURE 6.122   The new string variable points to the data store.

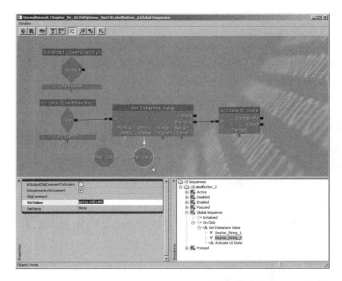

FIGURE 6.123   This new string variable holds the console command.

e. Select the Activate UI State object and set its StateType property to UIState_Enabled.

f. In the UIScene Editor, select the Apply button. Back in Kismet, right-click and choose Create New Object Variable Using…. This creates a new object variable from the Apply button. Attach it to the Target of the Activate UI State.

g. Select OnClick, Set Datastore Value, Activate UI State, the two String variables, and the Object variable and then copy them all with Ctrl+C (see **FIGURE 6.124**).

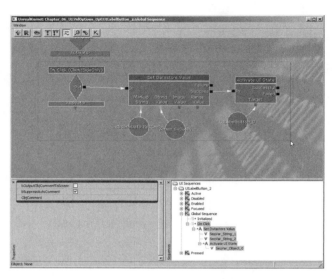

FIGURE 6.124   Copy all the nodes shown in this box.

h. Paste a copy of the sequence objects into the Kismet Editor for the 800x600 button, and set the String Value String Variable's StrValue property to **setres 800x600** (see **FIGURE 6.125**).

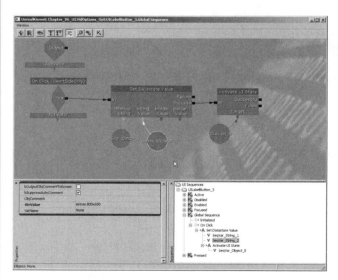

FIGURE 6.125   The nodes have been duplicated. Note that the resolution on the string variable is set to 800x600.

i. Paste another copy into the Kismet Editor for the 1024x768 button, and set the String Value String Variable's StrValue property to **setres 1024x768** (see **FIGURE 6.126**).

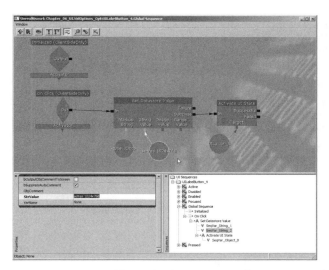

FIGURE 6.126   The nodes have been duplicated a second time. Note that, again, the resolution on the string variable is adjusted accordingly.

3. We will now add functionality for our Apply button.

a. Open the Kismet Editor for the Apply button. In the Global sequence, add a new OnClick event (New Event > UI > OnClick), as shown in **FIGURE 6.127**.

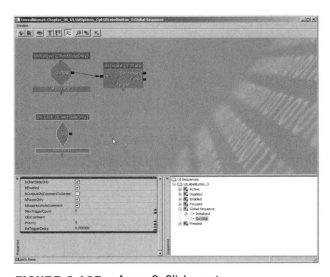

FIGURE 6.127   A new OnClick event.

b. Add a new Get Datastore Value action (New Action > Data Store > Get Datastore Value) and connect it to OnClick (see **FIGURE 6.128**).

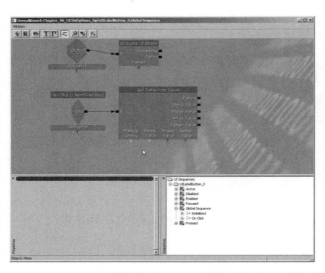

FIGURE 6.128   The Get Datastore Value is triggered by OnClick.

c. Right-click the Markup String variable input on the new Get Datastore Value and create a new String Variable. Set its StrValue property to **<SceneData:ResCmd>** (see **FIGURE 6.129**).

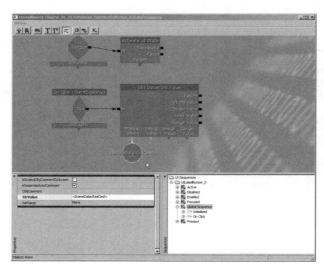

FIGURE 6.129   This new string variable accesses our data store.

d. Right-click the String Value variable connection along the bottom of the Get Datastore Value (not the output along the right side) and create a new String Variable. Set the ObjComment for this variable to **Command Buffer**. We will be referring to this variable as the Command Buffer variable from now on (see **FIGURE 6.130**).

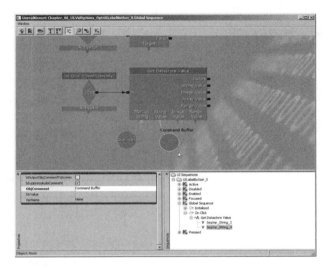

FIGURE 6.130   The string variable with Command Buffer comment

e. Add a Console Command action (New Action > Misc > Console Command) and connect it to the String Value output on the right side of the Get Datastore Value object (see **FIGURE 6.131**).

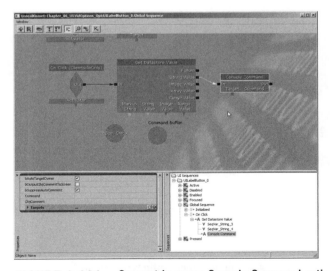

FIGURE 6.131   Connect in a new Console Command action.

f. Connect the Command input of the new Console Command object to the Command Buffer variable (see **FIGURE 6.132**).

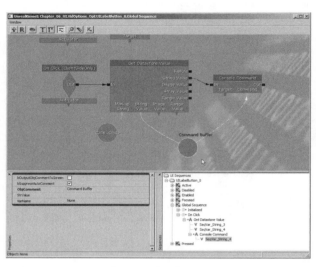

FIGURE 6.132   Connect the Command input like so.

g. Create a new Activate UI State object (New Action > UI > Activate UI State) and connect it to the OnClick event. Set its StateType property to UIState_Disabled. Once again, there is no need to specify a target, as long as the bAutoTargetOwner property is checked, which it is by default (see **FIGURE 6.133**).

h. Close the Kismet Editor when done.

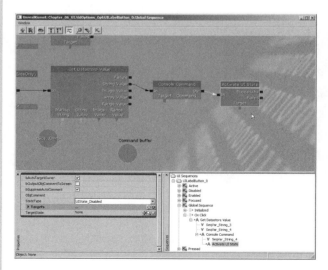

FIGURE 6.133   This new object deactivates the Apply button once settings are applied.

4. In the UIScene Editor, select the Slider widget and set the following properties under the Slider tab's SliderValue category:

> **CurrentValue**: 2.2
>
> **MaxValue**: 5.0
>
> **MinValue**: 1.0

5. We must now add functionality for our Gamma Slider:

> **a.** Open the Kismet Editor for the Slider (see **FIGURE 6.134**). In the Global sequence, add a new Slider Value event (New Event > Value Changed > Slider Value).

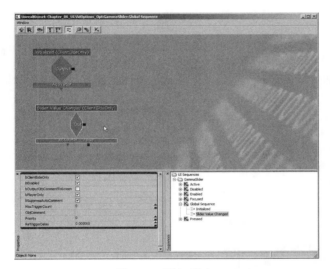

FIGURE 6.134   The new Slider Value event

> **b.** Add a new Set Datastore Value action (New Action > Data Store > Set Datastore Value) and connect it to the Slider Value event (see **FIGURE 6.135**).
>
> **c.** Right-click the Markup String variable input and create a new String variable. Set the StrValue property to **<Display:Gamma>** (see **FIGURE 6.136**). This is a data store that already exists that allows us to adjust the gamma of the game.

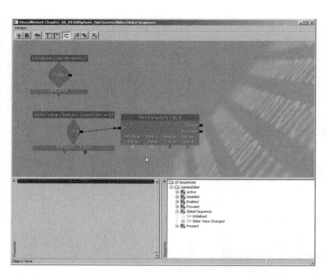

FIGURE 6.135   The Set Datastore Value action connects into the sequence like so.

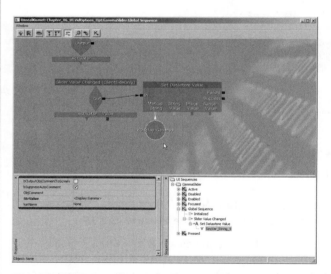

FIGURE 6.136   The new string variable points to the Display:Gamma data store.

d. Create a new Union variable (New Variable > Union) and connect it to the Value of the Slider Value event, as well as to the String Value variable input of the Set Datastore Value object (see **FIGURE 6.137**).

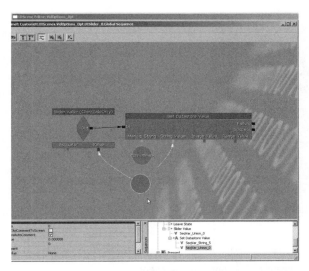

FIGURE 6.137   The Union variable sends the float value of the slider to the String Value of the Set Datastore Value.

6. We now need to set up the functionality for our Return to Main button:

     a. Open the Kismet Editor for the Return to Main label button.

     b. In the Global sequence, create a new OnClick event (New Event > UI > OnClick).

     c. Create a new Close Scene event (New Action > UI > Close Scene) and attach it to the OnClick event. There is no need to set a target because the object automatically targets its owner (see **FIGURE 6.138**).

7. Now we need to make our Options button on the Title Screen send us to the Options screen:

     a. Close the UIScene editor for the VidOptions_Opt scene, and open the UIScene Editor for the VidOptions_Main UIScene.

     b. Select the Options label button and open its Kismet Editor.

     c. In the Global sequence, create a new OnClick event (New Event > UI > OnClick).

     d. Create a new Open Scene event (New Action > UI > Open Scene) and attach it to the OnClick event. Use the Generic Browser to set the Scene property to the VidOptions_Opt UIScene (see **FIGURE 6.139**).

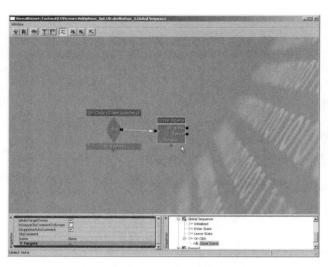

FIGURE 6.138   Connect the Close Scene event to the new OnClick event.

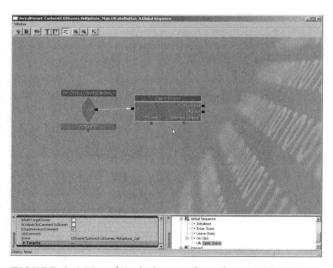

FIGURE 6.139   Attach the new Open Scene to OnClick.

8. Save your package and test your level. Your UI should now be completely functional!

END TUTORIAL 6.11

Continue from **TUTORIAL 6.11** or open the VidOptions_Opt_02 UIScene included with the files for this chapter. In **TUTORIAL 6.12**, we add a background image to our UI that automatically scales based on the current resolution.

TUTORIAL 6.12: Creating a Video Options UI, Part IV: Adding a Background Image

1. We will now associate the first image with our main title screen:

> **a.** Open the UIScene Editor for the VidOptions_Main UIScene.
>
> **b.** Right-click in a blank area of the viewport and choose Place Widget > Image. Use the default name that appears (this will likely be UIImage_0).

> **c.** Select the new Image widget. Make sure the Positioning window is visible (Window menu > Positioning) within it and verify that the Scale Type for all four sides is set to EVALPOS_PercentageOwner (see **FIGURE 6.140**).

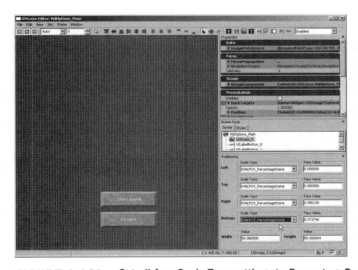

FIGURE 6.140   Set all four Scale Type settings to PercentageOwner.

> **d.** Set the Left and Top Face Values to 0.0, and set the Right and Bottom Face Values to 1.0. This stretches the image across the viewport (see **FIGURE 6.141**).
>
> **e.** In the Properties area, expand the Image tab and the StyleOverride category. Use the Generic Browser to set the ImageRef property to the RandomGameTitleScreen image (see **FIGURE 6.142**).

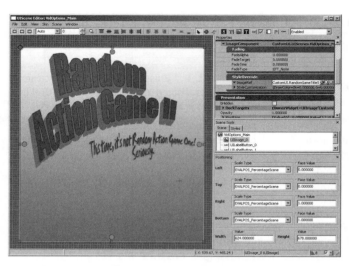

FIGURE 6.141   The image now stretches across the UIScene, but will cover your current UI.

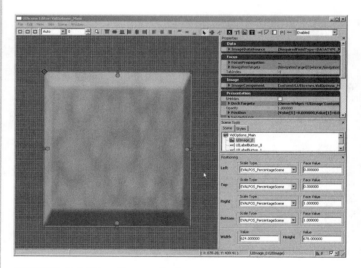

FIGURE 6.142   The new texture appears.

    f. We need to solve the problem of our image covering up our UI. In the Scene Tools, underneath the Scene tab, right-click the Image widget and in the context menu that appears, choose Reorder Widget > Move to Bottom (see **FIGURE 6.143**).

2. Close the VidOptions_Main UIScene Editor and open the VidOptions_Opt UIScene editor. Repeat the process from step 2 of this tutorial to place the RandomGameOptionsScreen image in the background of the UI (see **FIGURE 6.144**).

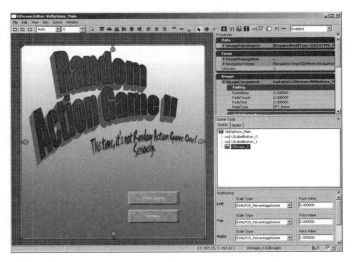

FIGURE 6.143 By moving the Image widget to the bottom of the list, the image appears in the background.

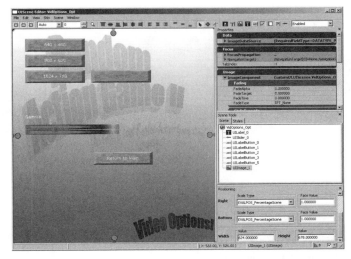

FIGURE 6.144 Set the background for the Options screen as well.

3. Save your package and test your UI. You will now see your image in the background of your UI, and it will scale to fit your new resolutions.

END TUTORIAL 6.12

Sounds

Sound effects can play an important part in your UIs. Fortunately, the UI system in Unreal Editor makes it very easy to associate a sound effect with various aspects of your UI, such as playing an effect when you click the mouse, or through any other event in Kismet.

You have two ways to go about playing sound effects in your UI. The first is through Kismet, using the Play Sound UI sequence object. This sequence behaves very similarly to the Play Sound sequence object as described in Chapter 7, "Sound System," except that the Target (or location of the played sound effect) will always be the Player.

The second and more conventional method for playing sounds in your UI is to set up your SoundCues in your skin. Within the Skin Editor, you will see the SoundCues tab, which allows you to establish which actions trigger a SoundCue, and which SoundCues are associated with each action. Once this is done, you also have the option of playing the sounds you have associated in your skin using the Play UI Sound Cue Kismet sequence. This object can be connected to any action simply by using a string that contains the name of the widget action to which you've assigned a sound effect in your skin. For example, let's say you've associated a particular sound effect to the Clicked action, but want to play it at another event in the UI. You could create your event, attach the Play UI Sound Cue action, and then set the SoundCueName property to Clicked (see **FIGURE 6.145**).

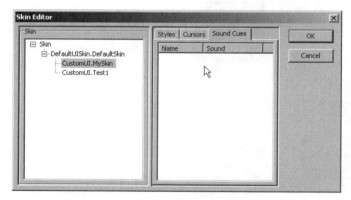

FIGURE 6.145   The Skin Editor holds the Sound Cues tab.

Both methods of playing sounds have their benefits. Going about playing sounds by using Kismet and the Play Sound UI object means that you can create a variety of sounds for individual events on any widget you like. However, setting the sound up in your skin takes care of the sound on a global level, meaning that you do not have to set it up for every single widget.

In **TUTORIAL 6.13**, we implement a simple sound effect into our Video Options UI by doing a global association through our skin. This tutorial uses the Video Options UI created earlier in this chapter. However, you

NOTE

TUTORIAL 6.13 uses the MySkin UI Skin created earlier in this chapter! You need to edit your UTUI.INI file as shown in **TUTORIAL 6.7**.

could technically follow along using any UI that has a custom skin applied to it. In this tutorial, we implement a simple sound effect that plays whenever we click a button on any UI that is using our skin.

TUTORIAL 6.13: Creating a Video Options UI, Part V: Adding Sound Effects

1. In the Generic Browser, open or fully load the Chapter_06_UI package included on the DVD in the files for this chapter.

2. Double-click the MySkin skin object to open the Skin Editor (see **FIGURE 6.146**).

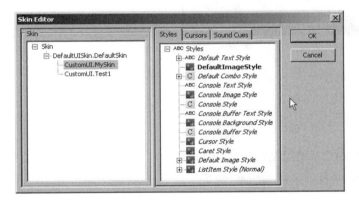

FIGURE 6.146   Open the Skin Editor for the MySkin object.

3. You will see the SoundCues tab. If you click it, you will notice that the list of SoundCues is currently blank. Right-click in the list and choose Add UI SoundCue (see **FIGURE 6.147**).

4. The window that appears has a dropdown that allows you to choose what action you'd like to use to trigger your sound effect. Choose Clicked from the menu.

5. Use the Generic Browser to associate the SoundCue field with the ClickCue sound effect, located in the UISounds package (see **FIGURE 6.148**). Click OK when finished. Click OK in the Skin Editor to close it.

6. Open the UIScene Editor for the VidOptions_Main UIScene. Move the viewport so that you can see a blank area and then click in the blank area to select the UIScene itself. In the Properties window, under the UIScene tab, uncheck the bPauseGameWhileActive property. This is done because sound effects will not play while the game is paused.

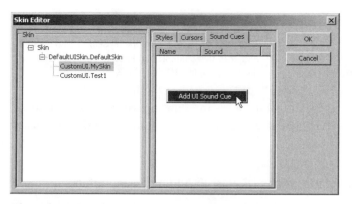

FIGURE 6.147   The option to add a new SoundCue appears upon right-clicking.

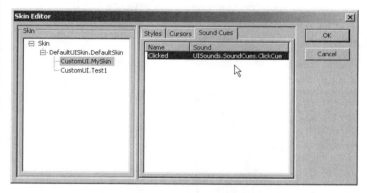

FIGURE 6.148   Your SoundCue window should appear like this.

7. Repeat the previous step for the VidOptions_Opt UIScene.

8. Save your package and test your UI. You will now hear a click whenever you click the mouse on a button!

END TUTORIAL 6.13

Creating HUDs

Head-up displays (HUDs) can be created through the UI system, and they function in very much the same way as a UI, aside from the fact that the user does not interact with them. The purpose of a HUD is to feed important gameplay information to the player during the game. This information could be the player's score, existing health, current ammunition levels, current weapon, distance from a waypoint or target, and so on.

The basics of creating a HUD simply involve laying out the images and other widgets that will be used and then activating a few properties to make the UI noninteractive. The properties for deactivating the interactivity of a UI, essentially making it into a HUD, are outlined here:

- **Splitscreen tab**:

    SceneInputMode: INPUTMODE_None

- **UIScene tab**:

    bDisplayCursor: False (Unchecked)

    bPauseGameWhileActive: False (Unchecked)

When working with *Unreal Tournament 3*, you will find that many of the functions you would typically use for First-Person Shooter–style gameplay (health, ammo, weapons status, and so on) require that you extend the functionality through scripting, which is beyond the scope of this text.

Summary

This chapter has really only touched on the beginning of the possibilities of using the UI System in Unreal Editor. We would like to mention at this point, however, that in order to get really deep into creating advanced user interfaces, it would behoove you to use UnrealScript. This is because at the time of this writing, there is no simple method for pulling information from gameplay and placing it into a data store. At the same time, we hope you find this chapter to have been a useful primer for how the UI System actually functions, and that it has helped you understand UI assembly in Unreal Editor.

Chapter 7

Sound System

No level is complete without ambient sounds, distinct sound effects, and background music. Two options are available for working with sound in Unreal. The first is through the raw sound itself, which is imported from the WAV file format. The second option is known as a *SoundCue*, which is an instruction specifying the way the engine is to play a particular sound. The option you use depends greatly on what it is you're trying to do with sounds in your level.

During the SoundCue creation phase, you have the power to mix sounds, modulate them, cross-fade them, and much more. As you progress through this chapter, you learn how to import sounds into Unreal Editor, as well as how to create SoundCues ranging from simple playback to more complex examples using modulation and attenuation. You also get to use the AmbientSound actors, which provide a way to work with raw WAV files, rather than having to construct SoundCues. Once you have seen that, we look at some ways you can add music to your levels based on your player's location.

Sound Types

Some thought needs to go into what type of sound effects you're creating. In this book, we simplify the kind of sounds you need into three categories: sound effects, ambient sounds, and music. Knowing in advance which type of sound you need helps you determine not only what sounds you will play, but also the manner in which they will be played.

For the purposes of this text, we consider *sound effects* to be sounds that occur when something happens in the level. This includes weapons firing, doors opening, objects colliding, and so on. These are most easily played through a combination of triggers and Kismet sequences, as you'll see in the tutorials later in this chapter.

Ambient sounds are used to give the players some idea of what types of objects are around them. For instance, they may be near some working machinery or a humming computer, or perhaps outside where they can hear birds, running water, or vehicle traffic. These sounds are important to provide the feel of the level and environment.

Music adds a level of feeling and emotion to your game and is an extremely important aspect of the gaming experience. Unreal Editor's extremely robust music system allows you to seamlessly adjust your music based on a nearly infinite number of possible events in your game. You can have a certain type of music for combat, another for when the character's health is low, another when the character enters a particular level, and so on.

USounds Versus SoundCues

In older versions of the Unreal Engine, all sound effects were handled via WAV files, which were played through actors placed within the levels. This is still possible because certain actors allow you to play USounds. A *USound* is an asset derived directly from a WAV file. Although using USounds with actors such as the AmbientSoundSimple does provide a fast-and-easy way to quickly get a sound into a level, Unreal Engine 3 has added the ability to supplement a USound file through the creation of SoundCues.

SoundCues provide you a unique level of flexibility, along with the ability to visualize how your instruction is formed. With a SoundCue, the actual WAV file is really just a component of a greater whole. Visually speaking, SoundCues are made up of the actual sound effect USound file, a base SoundCue node, and a series of instruction nodes in between the two that alter or mix the sound in some way. For example, a single SoundCue could include multiple WAV files for bullet ricochet sound effects. One of these sounds could be pulled at random from the selection of sounds and then mixed in with other effects, modulated to randomize the pitch and have the volume adjusted, and then attenuated on an exact position. This would all be handled by the nodes that make up the SoundCue, as shown in **FIGURE 7.1**.

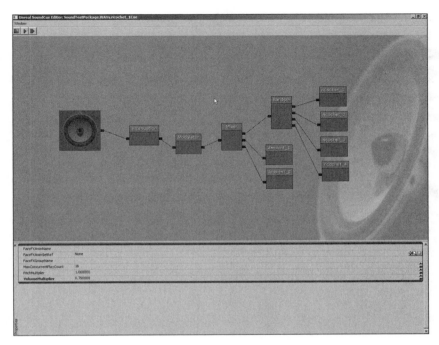

FIGURE 7.1   An example of a SoundCue.

The SoundCue Editor, discussed later in this chapter, provides a visual graph that allows you to see your sound instructions in a network format similar to the Kismet and Material Editors. Because of the level of control afforded by the SoundCue Editor, using SoundCues is the preferred and most common method for working with sounds in Unreal (see **TUTORIAL 7.1**).

TUTORIAL 7.1: Importing WAVs and Creating Your First SoundCues

1. Launch Unreal Editor and open the Generic Browser. From the Generic Browser's File menu, choose Import.

2. In the Import window, locate the sound_1_plink file included on the DVD in the files for this chapter and then click Open. On the SoundFactory window, choose SoundFactory and click OK.

3. The first way to create a SoundCue is to automatically generate one when importing a sound. In the Import window, input the following information for sound_1_plink (see **FIGURE 7.2**):

   ▸ **Package:** MySoundTest

   ▸ **Group:** <none>

   ▸ **Name:** sound_1_plink

Verify that bAutoCreateCue is checked, but uncheck bIncludeAttenuationNode.

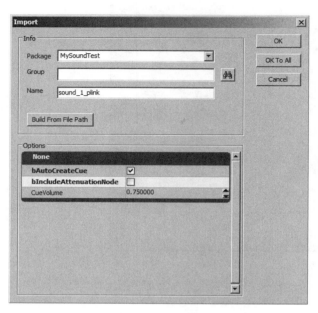

FIGURE 7.2   The Import window should look like this.

When you're finished, click the OK button. The sound file appears in the package, along with a SoundCue object that is automatically connected to the sound file. Be sure to save your package!

4. The second way to create a SoundCue is to import a sound file and then actually create a new SoundCue and attach the sound to it manually. In the Generic Browser, choose File > Import, locate the sound_2_bom file included on the DVD in the files for this chapter, and click Open. The Import window reappears for the sound. Input the following information:

> ▸ **Package:** MySoundTest

> ▸ **Group:** <none>

> ▸ **Name:** sound_2_bom

> **TIP**
>
> You can play either the sound file or the SoundCue by double-clicking its object in the Generic Browser.

Verify that both bAutoCreateCue and bIncludeAttenuationNode are unchecked.

When you're finished, click the OK button. This time a new SoundCue was not created, but we can create one manually (see **FIGURE 7.3**).

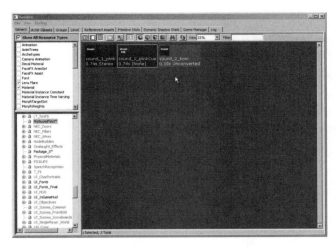

FIGURE 7.3   Notice that because the bAutoCreateCue property was unchecked, we did not get a new SoundCue.

5. Right-click in a blank area of the Generic Browser and choose New SoundCue. Input the following information in the New window:

    ▶ **Package:** MySoundTest

    ▶ **Group:** <none>

    ▶ **Name:** sound_2_bomCue

    ▶ **Factory:** SoundCue

    When you're finished, click the OK button. The new SoundCue Editor appears (see **FIGURE 7.4**). We now connect the sound_2_bom file to this new SoundCue.

6. In the Generic Browser, select the sound_2_bom sound file. Then, in the SoundCue Editor, right-click in a blank area next to the right of the large speaker icon and choose SoundNodeWave:sound_2_bom from the context menu. A new node named after your sound file appears (see **FIGURE 7.5**).

FIGURE 7.4   The SoundCue Editor opens.

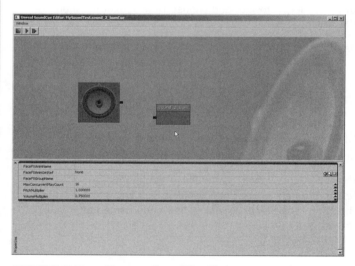

FIGURE 7.5   The new SoundWaveNode appears where you right-clicked.

7. Just as you would in the Kismet Editor, drag a wire from the black box on the left of the new sound node to the small black box on the right of the speaker icon (see **FIGURE 7.6**). This associates the sound file with this SoundCue.

8. Close the SoundCue Editor and save your package. You can now double-click the new SoundCue and hear the sound effect play.

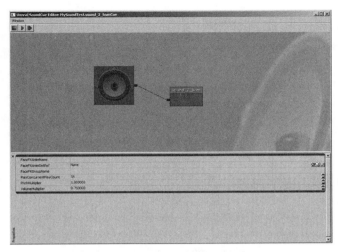

FIGURE 7.6   Notice that the flow of the SoundCue Editor moves from right to left.

END TUTORIAL 7.1

In **TUTORIAL 7.2**, we take a look at the AmbientSoundSimple actor and how it can be used to place sound effects into your level without the need of a SoundCue.

TUTORIAL 7.2: Using the AmbientSoundSimple Actor

1. Launch Unreal Editor and open the SimpleSoundStage level, included on the DVD in the files for this chapter. In the Generic Browser, open the A_Ambient_Loops package, included with your *Unreal Tournament 3* installation.

2. Open the Actor Classes Browser and expand Keypoint. You will see the AmbientSound actor. Expand this, and you will see AmbientSoundSimple; select this actor (see **FIGURE 7.7**). You don't necessarily have to select this actor in the browser, because you automatically get the option to place an AmbientSoundSimple actor whenever you have a sound file selected in the Generic Browser.

3. In the Generic Browser, select the machine_hitek01 USound A_Ambient_Loops package.

4. In the Perspective viewport, right-click and choose Add Actor > AmbientSoundSimple: machine_hitek01 from the context menu (see **FIGURE 7.8**). You cannot place this actor without first selecting a sound file.

5. Open the Properties window (F4), expand the AmbientSoundSimple tab, and expand the Ambient properties. You'll see the option to attenuate and spatialize your sound effect, which we discuss later in this chapter. You'll also see the LPF Min and Max Radius properties, which control low pass filtering. We can ignore these for the time being.

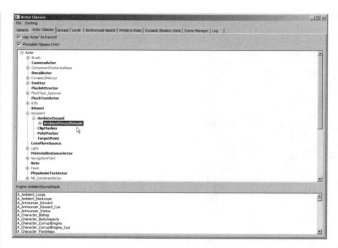

FIGURE 7.7   The AmbientSoundSimple actor is buried underneath the Keypoint actor.

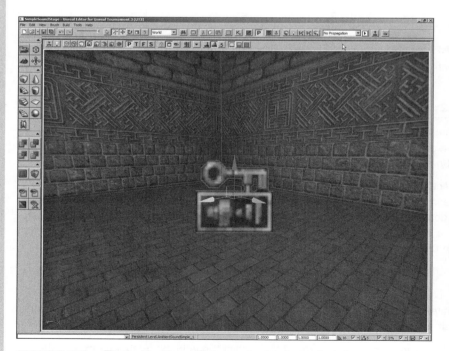

FIGURE 7.8   The AmbientSoundSimple actor has been placed.

6. Take a look at the Min and MaxRadius. These properties allow you to create a sphere of effect within which you can hear the sound. You'll also notice that the Min and MaxRadius properties have their own Min and Max subset of properties. These are to allow a randomization effect, so that you don't always hear the sound pick up in the exact same position.

7. Because we don't want any randomization, click the small blue arrow button 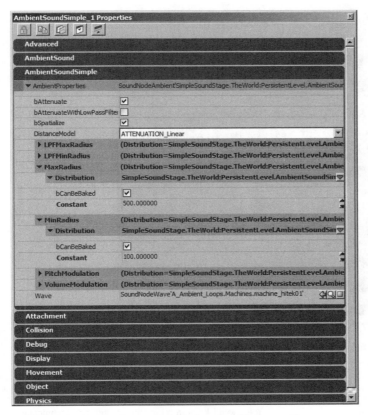 to the right of the MaxRadius property and then choose DistributionFloatConstant from the context menu. Set the new Constant value to 500.

8. Repeat this process for MinRadius, applying a DistributionFloatConstant, but this time set the Constant value to 100 (see **FIGURE 7.9**).

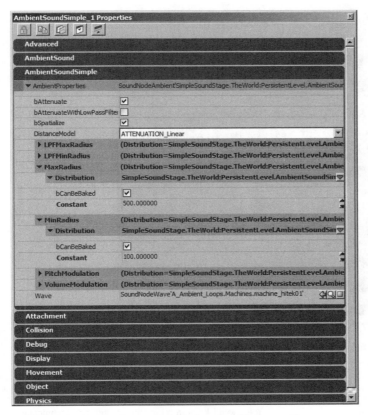

FIGURE 7.9   The Properties window should appear like so.

9. Click the Real Time button in the Perspective viewport and move the camera close to the actor. The sound effect starts to play when you get within the sphere of effect.

> **NOTE**
>
> More information on distributions can be found in Appendix A, "Distributions."

10. Feel free to test the effect by running the level. Because this is only a test, there is no need to save your progress when finished.

END TUTORIAL 7.2

The AmbientSound Actors

Placing a sound in your level can be achieved through a few different methods. An assortment of various actors are specialized to the task. These actors are the primary means for applying ambient sounds into your level (see **FIGURE 7.10**).

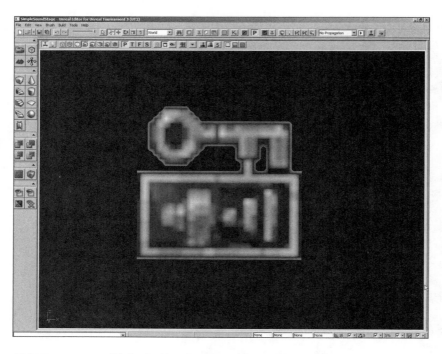

FIGURE 7.10   All the AmbientSound actors use this icon.

AmbientSound

Location in the Actor Classes Browser:

    Keypoint > AmbientSound

The AmbientSound actor allows you to place a sound-emitting actor in your level. It uses a SoundCue rather than a USound file. Its properties are fairly simple because most of your control over the sound comes from the SoundCue assembled with the SoundCue Editor.

> **TIP**
>
> You should keep in mind that sounds can technically be emitted from virtually any actor by using Kismet's Play Sound sequence object by connecting the desired attenuation actor to the Target input.

> **NOTE**
>
> Because all the ambient sound actors use the same icon, we do not show an individual image of each actor.

AmbientSoundSimple

Location in the Actor Classes Browser:

> Keypoint > AmbientSound > AmbientSoundSimple

This actor is rather like the AmbientSound actor, although it accepts a raw sound file rather than having to use a SoundCue. It also comes with internal properties to control low pass filtering, attenuation, spatialization, and modulation (because you do not create such effects with the SoundCue Editor).

AmbientSoundNonLoop

Location in the Actor Classes Browser:

> Keypoint > AmbientSound > AmbientSoundSimple > AmbientSoundNonLoop

The AmbientSoundNonLoop is an extension of the AmbientSoundSimple actor playing a USound file. You need to have this actor selected in the Actor Classes Browser in order to place it in the level. Its benefit is that it does not automatically loop the sound file indefinitely (whereas its parent object, the AmbientSoundSimple actor, does).

AmbientSoundSimpleToggleable

Location in the Actor Classes Browser:

> Keypoint > AmbientSound > AmbientSoundSimple > AmbientSoundSimpleToggleable

This actor is also an extension of the AmbientSoundSimple actor, meaning that it uses a USound rather than a SoundCue. It can be toggled on and off through Kismet sequences. Also, it has its own fade-in and fade-out settings for when it is triggered.

The SoundCue Editor

The SoundCue Editor functions very much like the Kismet and Material Editors, supplying you with a visual interface for working with sounds and the various modifiers that can be applied to them. The interface is divided into three important areas: the preview playback buttons, a visual layout graph, and the property editor (see **FIGURE 7.11**).

The preview buttons include the following buttons:

> **Play SoundCue** ▶—Used to hear the final result of your SoundCue network
>
> **Play Selected Node** ▶—Allows you to hear the result of the network at the selected node
>
> **Stop** ■—Ceases playback

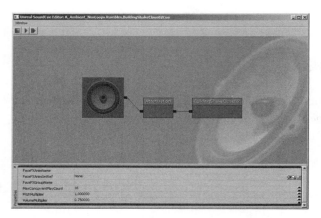

FIGURE 7.11   The SoundCue Editor user interface

When you look at the layout graph, you will see a large speaker icon. This is the icon for the SoundCue itself. If you click it, the properties for the SoundCue appear in the property editor area. These properties exist so that you can change the nature of the entire SoundCue on a global level, rather than on an individual node.

SoundCue Nodes

The true power of the SoundCue Editor lies within the various nodes that you can connect between a WAV file and the SoundCue icon. You can use these nodes to create elaborate networks that transform your sounds into something far more complex and rich. In this section, we discuss the nodes available in the SoundCue Editor at the time of this writing.

SoundNodeWave

This node facilitates the sound files you bring into the SoundCue. Every USound in a SoundCue has its own SoundNodeWave (see **FIGURE 7.12**). Note that the visible name for the node reflects the name of the USound within it.

Attenuation

This commonly used node allows for two of the most important features in game sound creation: attenuation and spatialization (see **FIGURE 7.13**). Attenuation is essentially the ability of a sound to get fainter as the player moves away from it. It works using two radii: MinRadius and MaxRadius. As you move from the sound's origin through the MinRadius, the volume of the sound is at 100%. As you pass between the MinRadius and the MaxRadius, the volume linearly fades between 100% and silence. The rate at which this fade occurs is based on the DistanceModel property, which provides several types of falloff curves to control the volume in between the radii. Once you pass outside the MaxRadius, you're outside the limit of the sound and hear only silence.

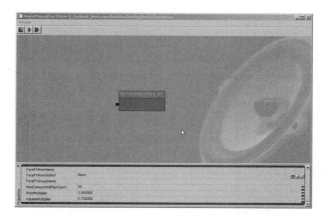

FIGURE 7.12   The SoundWave node

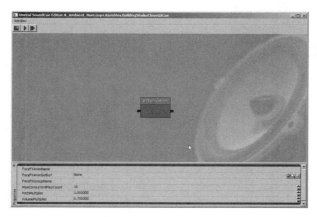

FIGURE 7.13   The Attenuation node

Each of the Min and MaxRadius properties also has its own subset of Min and Max properties. These allow for a randomization of the radii each time the SoundCue is triggered during gameplay. If no randomization is required, set both the Min and Max values to the same number.

Spatialization is the ability of the sound system to localize a sound in 3D space, providing a "surround sound" style of effect. It is based off the bSpatialize property. Without this property active, a sound simply plays equally in both (or all) speakers, with no indication of the direction from which it originated.

If you want your SoundCue to exhibit attenuation and spatialization, you need to have this node connected into your graph with both the bAttenuate and bSpatialize properties set to True (checked).

Concatenator

This node allows you to string two or more sound sources together, playing them in sequence (see **FIGURE 7.14**). You can add more inputs to the node by right-clicking it and choosing Add Input from the context menu. Inputs can be removed by right-clicking an unused input square and choosing Delete Input from the context menu.

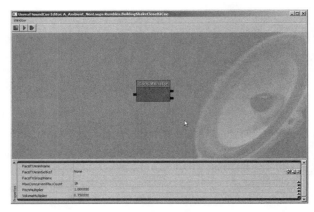

FIGURE 7.14   The Concatenator node

Delay

This node places a delay in seconds, specified by the Min and Max properties within the node (see **FIGURE 7.15**). The range between the Min and Max values designates a randomization each time the SoundCue is triggered. If no randomization is desired, set both values to the same number.

DistanceCrossFade

This node allows you to fade between multiple sounds based on how far away the player is from a sound's origin (see **FIGURE 7.16**). A good example of this would be a change in audible sounds as you approach a large piece of machinery. At a distance, the object might sound like a soft low hum. As you get closer, you may notice that you can hear moving parts within it. Once you're right next to it, you may be able to hear metal clinking and grinding.

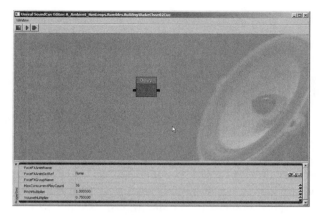

FIGURE 7.15   The Delay node

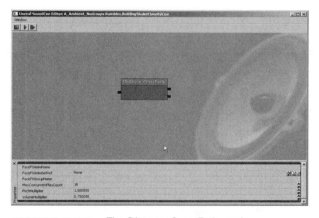

FIGURE 7.16   The DistanceCrossFade node

Each of the inputs has FadeInDistance and FadeOutDistance properties. Both of these properties have a Min and Max value, allowing you to specify the distance over which the fade takes place. For example, suppose your properties look like this:

```
Sound[0]
    FadeInDistance
        Min: 0.00
        Max: 0.00
    FadeOutDistance
        Min: 1000.00
        Max: 1280.00
```

Sound[1]

FadeInDistance

Min: 512.00

Max: 640.00

FadeOutDistance

Min: 1600

Max: 2048

Your behavior would be as follows (if you were moving toward the sound source): At 2048 units from the sound source, Sound[1] would get louder, becoming full volume at 1600. At 1280, Sound[0] would start to fade in, becoming full volume at 1000 units from the source. At this point, both sounds would be playing simultaneously at full volume.

At 640 units from the source, Sound[1] begins to fade away, until it is completely gone once you reach 512 units. From here on in, you only hear Sound[0], which does not fade away until you move beyond 1600 units away from the source. Notice that Sound[0]'s FadeInDistance is set to 0 for both Min and Max, meaning that as long as you are within the FadeOutDistance Min value, you will hear the sound at full volume. A diagram of this behavior is shown in **FIGURE 7.17**.

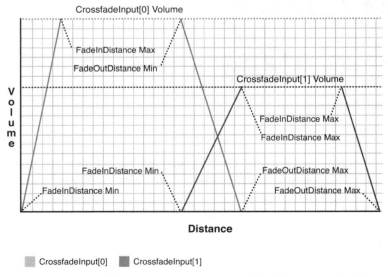

CrossfadeInput[0] Volume

FadeInDistance Max

FadeOutDistance Min

CrossfadeInput[1] Volume

Volume

FadeInDistance Max

FadeInDistance Max

FadeInDistance Min

FadeOutDistance Max

FadeInDistance Min

FadeOutDistance Max

Distance

CrossfadeInput[0]   CrossfadeInput[1]

FIGURE 7.17   **A diagrammatic breakdown of the behavior for the DistanceCrossFade example**

You can add more inputs to the node by right-clicking it and choosing Add Input from the context menu. Inputs can be removed by right-clicking an unused input square and choosing Delete Input from the context menu.

Looping

This node repeats the connected sound the number of times specified in the Min and Max properties (see **FIGURE 7.18**). In this case, Min and Max represent a degree of randomization. If randomization is not desired, then set both of these numbers to the same value. The default setting is 1,000,000, which should be more than enough to consider infinite repetition for most sound effects.

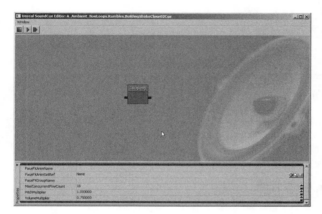

FIGURE 7.18   The Looping node

SoundNodeMature

This node allows you to flag a sound effect as being "mature" so that it could be excluded if your game has its mature content settings deactivated (see **FIGURE 7.19**). For example, if you are stringing together a list of phrases, one of which contains profanity, you could use a SoundNodeMature for the pro-

> **NOTE**
>
> If you're using the Unreal Engine 3 Runtime, mature sounds are controlled by the bAllowMatureLanguage property, which must be set manually within the ExampleEngine.ini file. This is set to False by default.

fane phrase to make sure it does not play if the user has turned off mature content on the game. This only works if the SoundWaveNode has its bMature property set to True (checked).

Mixer

The Mixer node allows you to play back multiple sounds simultaneously (see **FIGURE 7.20**). You can adjust the volume of each inputted sound in the node's properties. You can add more inputs to the Mixer node by right-clicking it and choosing Add Input from the context menu. Inputs can be removed by right-clicking an unused input square and choosing Delete Input from the context menu.

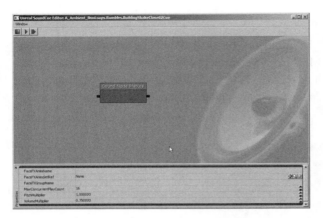

FIGURE 7.19   The SoundNodeMature node

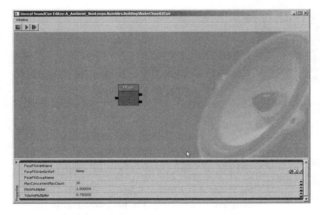

FIGURE 7.20   The Mixer node

Modulator

The Modulator node allows you to adjust the pitch and volume of a sound (see **FIGURE 7.21**). It has two properties, PitchModulation and VolumeModulation, which each have Min and Max values. These values provide a randomization each time the SoundCue is triggered. If no randomization is required, the Min and Max must be set to the same value.

An interesting note about the randomization on this node: If you plug a Looping node into the Modulator's input (moving from right to left), the sound repeats at the same modulated value for the number of times specified

> **NOTE**
>
> The highest amount of modulation possible at the time of this writing is 2, with the lowest amount being 0.2. For best results, keep your modulation values between these limits.

in the loop. However, if you instead plug the Modulator into the Looping node's input, you get a new randomized value each time the loop fires.

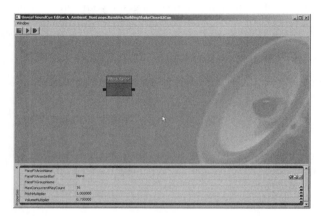

FIGURE 7.21 The Modulator node

ContinuousModulator

This node allows you to modulate the pitch or volume of a sound based on in-game parameters (see **FIGURE 7.22**). For example, you can change the pitch of an engine based on the velocity of the vehicle, or change the volume of a warning beep as a player's health gets too low. However, this node is only extendable through code, and cannot be used effectively within the SoundCue Editor itself.

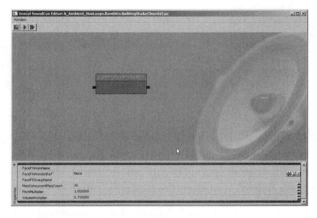

FIGURE 7.22 The ContinuousModulator node

Oscillator

The Oscillator node allows you to modulate the pitch and/or volume of your sound constantly by using a sine wave (see **FIGURE 7.23**). It is perfect for making subtle changes in your sounds over time, or to constantly change looping sounds. Aside from the two properties that control whether you're modulating the pitch or the volume (bModulatePitch and bModulateVolume, respectively), this node has four properties that control the wave itself:

> **Amplitude**—This property controls the height of the wave. It has Max and Min values to provide randomization.
>
> **Center**—This property controls what value the center of the wave has. It also has Max and Min for randomization.
>
> **Frequency**—This property controls how many oscillations take place every second. A value of 1 results in one oscillation per second. Values greater than 1 speed up the oscillation, whereas fractions slow it down.
>
> **Offset**—This property slides the wave to the left or right.

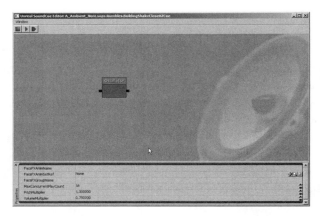

FIGURE 7.23   The Oscillator node

Random

This node takes in any number of inputted sounds and randomly selects one of them each time the SoundCue is triggered (see **FIGURE 7.24**). You can add more inputs to the Random node by right-clicking it and choosing Add Input from the context menu. Inputs can be removed by right-clicking an unused input square and choosing Delete Input from the context menu.

The node includes a Weights list that allows you to adjust the probability that one sound is played over another. If all weight values are equal, all sounds have an even chance of being played.

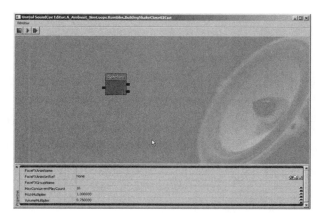

FIGURE 7.24   The Random node

SoundNodeWaveParam

This node allows you to use gameplay code to modify various attributes of the sound itself (see **FIGURE 7.25**). It is extendable only through code, and cannot be effectively used within the SoundCue Editor itself.

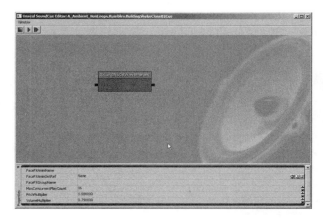

FIGURE 7.25   The SoundNodeWaveParam node

TUTORIAL 7.3: Using Sound Nodes in Your SoundCues

1. Launch Unreal Editor and open the SimpleSoundStage level and the SoundTest package, both included on the DVD in the files for this chapter.

2. Open the Generic Browser and locate the SoundTest package. Right-click the sound_1_plinkCue SoundCue and choose SoundCue Editor from the context menu (see **FIGURE 7.26**).

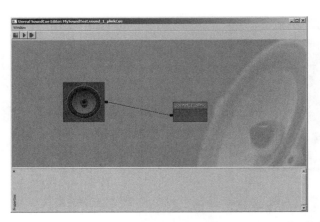

FIGURE 7.26   The SoundCue Editor for the sound_1_plinkCue sound effect

Let's say that we want to spatialize this sound effect to position it properly in 3D space, and we also want to bring its pitch down about 50%. You will find that it helps to know what effect you're looking for before you start slinging nodes around in the SoundCue Editor.

3. Right-click near the speaker icon in the SoundCue and choose Attenuation from the context menu. Connect a wire from the sound_1_plink node to the input (right side) of the Attenuation node, and then another wire from the output (left side) of the Attenuation node into the speaker icon's input (see **FIGURE 7.27**).

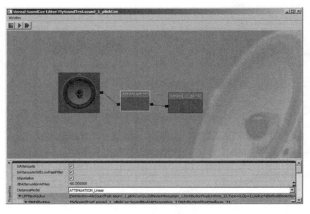

FIGURE 7.27   You must use the Attenuation node any time you want to position your sound in 3D space.

4. Select the new Attenuation node and have a look at its settings in the Properties window. Set the distribution type for MaxRadius to DistributionFloatConstant; then set the Constant value to 1000.

Also apply a DistributionFloatConstant to the MinRadius, setting the Constant value to 500 (see **FIGURE 7.28**).

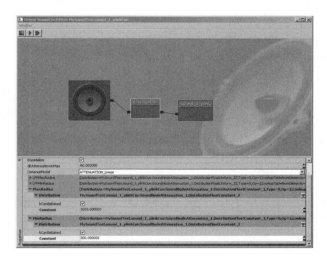

FIGURE 7.28   The properties of the Attenuation node should appear like so.

5. Select the sound_1_plink node and move it to the right a bit (Ctrl-drag) to make room for a new node. Then, right-click and choose Modulator from the context menu. Connect the input (right side) of the new Modulator node to the sound wave node, and connect the output (left side) to the Attenuation node (see **FIGURE 7.29**).

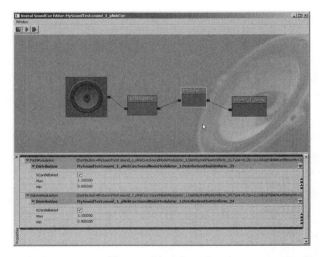

FIGURE 7.29   The new Modulator has been connected.

6. Select the new Modulator and look at its properties. It can modulate both the pitch and the volume, but right now we're only worried about pitch. Under PitchModulation's Distribution, set Max to 2.0 and Min to 0.5, which are the limit values for these properties. This results in a wide range of variation.

7. Click the Play SoundCue 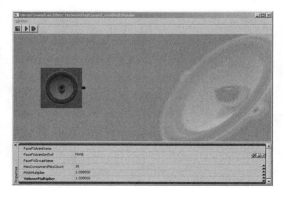 button several times and notice the difference in each playback.

8. Save your package.

END TUTORIAL 7.3

Continue from **TUTORIAL 7.3**, or launch Unreal Editor and open the SimpleSoundStage level included on the DVD in the files for this chapter. Also open the A_Ambient_NonLoops package included in your *Unreal Tournament 3* installation.

In **TUTORIAL 7.4**, we use the SoundCue Editor to create a more sophisticated SoundCue setup. We take a wind sound bite, make a couple versions of it through modulation, and randomly mix it with various sound clips of thunder.

TUTORIAL 7.4: Creating a More Complex Sound Cue

1. Open the Generic Browser and right-click in a blank area. Choose New SoundCue from the context menu. Name this SoundCue using the following information:

   ▸ **Package:** MySoundTest

   ▸ **Group:** <none>

   ▸ **Name:** sound_windAndThunder

   ▸ **Factory:** SoundCue

   Once the new SoundCue appears, right-click it and choose SoundCue Editor from the context menu. Leave the SoundCue Editor open for now, because we jump back and forth between it and the Generic Browser (see **FIGURE 7.30**).

FIGURE 7.30   The new SoundCue, as seen in the SoundCue Editor.

7

2. In the Generic Browser, select the A_Ambient_NonLoops package and then select the WindCaveGust02 USound object. Right-click in the SoundCue Editor and choose SoundNodeWave: WindCaveGust02.

3. Using the same technique as in step 2, open the A_Ambient_NonLoops package and add the following USounds into the SoundCue Editor (see **FIGURE 7.31**):

   ▶ thundersoft01

   ▶ thundersoft02

   ▶ thundersoft03

   ▶ thundersoft04

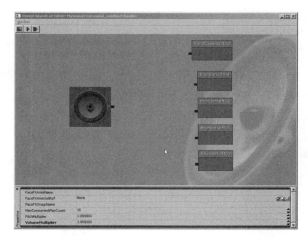

FIGURE 7.31   Place SoundWaveNodes for both the wind and thunder sound effects.

4. Create a new Modulator node and connect the Wind sound node into it. Adjust the PitchModulation Min and Max properties to give a random modulation between 0.8 and 1.5 (see **FIGURE 7.32**). This allows us to randomly raise or lower the pitch of the wind sound effect every time the SoundCue is played, resulting in greater variety with only one actual sound effect.

5. Add a new Mixer node, and connect the Modulator into its topmost input. Because we won't be attenuating this sound effect, you may connect the output of the Mixer directly into the SoundCue's speaker icon (see **FIGURE 7.33**).

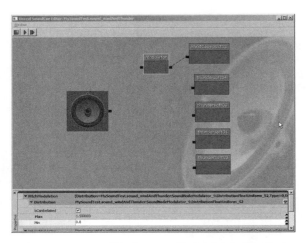

FIGURE 7.32   Attach a new Modulator to the wind.

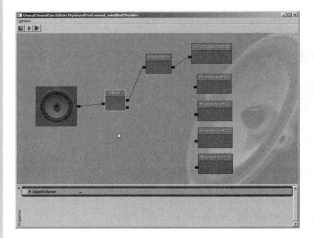

FIGURE 7.33   A Mixer has been added.

6. Create a new Random node, and connect its output to the second input of the Mixer. Then right-click this new Random node and choose Add Input from the context menu. Repeat this process to create a total of eight inputs on the Random node (see **FIGURE 7.34**).

7. Connect the four thundersoft sound wave nodes to the first input of Random. Leave the other inputs unconnected. This results in a 50% chance of no thunder playing, rather than having thunder effects every time the cue is called.

8. In the Random's properties, make sure that bRandomizeWithoutReplacement is unchecked (see **FIGURE 7.35**).

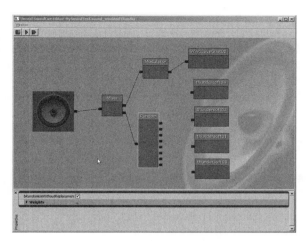

FIGURE 7.34   Create a total of eight inputs for the new **Random**.

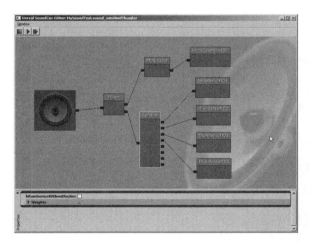

FIGURE 7.35   Your final network should look something like this.

9. Click the Play SoundCue button several times. You will hear a randomly modulated wind sound, with the occasional roll of thunder. Naturally, you could add different variations of thunder to change the effect, and even append other nodes to make the final SoundCue more complex. At this point, however, you should have a good understanding of how to work with the nodes and connections of the SoundCue Editor.

END TUTORIAL 7.4

For **TUTORIAL 7.5**, Launch Unreal Editor and open the SimpleSoundStage level included on the DVD in the files for this chapter.

TUTORIAL 7.5: Using the Distance CrossFade Node

1. Open the Generic Browser and right-click in a blank area. Choose New SoundCue from the context menu. Name this SoundCue using the following information:

   ▶ **Package:** MySoundTest

   ▶ **Group:** <none>

   ▶ **Name:** DCF_Chord_Cue

   ▶ **Factory:** SoundCue

   Once the new SoundCue appears, right-click it and choose SoundCue Editor from the context menu.

2. Add a new SoundWaveNode for each of the following sound effects, all found within the SoundTest package (see **FIGURE 7.36**):

   ▶ sound_C_Tone

   ▶ sound_E_Tone

   ▶ sound_G_Tone

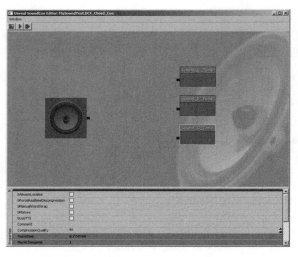

FIGURE 7.36   All three SoundWaveNodes have been added.

3. Right-click in the SoundCue Editor and add a new DistanceCrossFade node. Immediately right-click the new node and choose Add Input from the context menu. Then, connect the sound wave nodes to DistanceCrossFade as follows (see **FIGURE 7.37**):

   ▶ sound_G_Tone → Top input

   ▶ sound_E_Tone → Middle input

- ▸ sound_C_Tone → Bottom input
- ▸ Distance CrossFade Output → SoundCue input

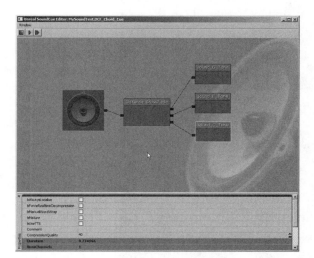

FIGURE 7.37   The tones should be connected to the DistanceCrossFade like so. Note that their order has changed.

4. Select the DistanceCrossFade and look at the Properties window. You can set each of the sounds to fade in and back out at any distance interval you like, but for organizational purposes, we're going to start from the inside and work our way outward. Use the following steps:

> **NOTE**
>
> In this case, we want all the sounds to overlap like a piano chord, so we leave all our FadeInDistance Min and Max values to 0. Although this may seem backward at first, think of it as if you were starting at the location of the sound and hearing the full chord. As you are moving away, one note from the chord drops off every few hundred units.

   a. For element [0] (G_Tone), set the FadeOutDistance Min to 500 and Max to 750.

   b. For element [1] (E_Tone), set the FadeOutDistance Min to 1250 and Max to 1500.

   c. For element [2](C_Tone), set the FadeOutDistance Min to 1750 and Max to 2000.

5. Save your package and then select the DistanceCrossFadeTest SoundCue in the Generic Browser. Near one of the edges of the floor of the level, right-click and choose Add Actor > Add AmbientSound: DistanceCrossFadeTest to place an AmbientSound actor in the level (see **FIGURE 7.38**).

6. Test the level. Even though you cannot see the AmbientSound actor, the sound adds another layer as you get nearer. See if you can use the changing sound to approximate the location of the actor!

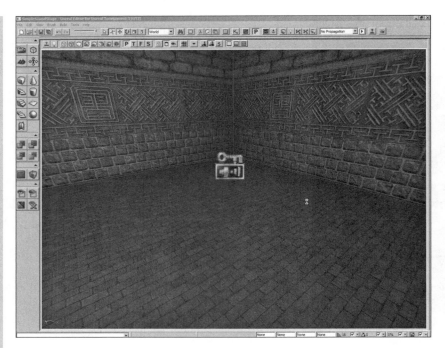

FIGURE 7.38   The AmbientSound actor serves as the source for your sound.

END TUTORIAL 7.5

Kismet Sound Actions

A few Kismet sequence objects are designed to allow sound playback. This section provides an overview of them. Note that this list does not include those Kismet sequences that focus on music playback and control because we discuss those later in this chapter.

Play Sound

The Play Sound sequence object does exactly what its name says it does: It plays a sound effect in your level. Any SoundCue can be applied to it through the object's PlaySound property. The object does not accept USounds (raw audio data). Included in the object's properties you can find the ability to add a delay, fade in and out over X number of seconds, as well as modulate both the pitch and volume (see **FIGURE 7.39**).

By connecting an object variable to the Target input on the bottom of this object, you can spatialize the sound effect, giving it a distinct position in the level. If you would like the sound to play everywhere, you can disregard this connection. You may also connect a Player object variable to the Target, thereby attaching the sound directly to a specific player.

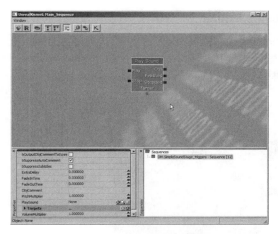

FIGURE 7.39   The Play Sound Kismet action, as seen within the Kismet Editor

Apply Sound Node

At the time of this writing, this node is nonfunctional (see **FIGURE 7.40**).

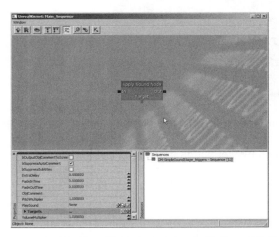

FIGURE 7.40   Here we see the Apply Sound Node action, as shown in the Kismet Editor.

> **NOTE**
>
> Because of the versatile nature of Kismet, there is nearly an infinite number of ways you could go about triggering a sound effect. Therefore, **TUTORIAL 7.6** simply shows you the basics with a few events, leaving the rest up to your experience in working with visual scripting in Unreal.

TUTORIAL 7.6: Triggering a SoundCue Using Kismet

1. Launch Unreal Editor and open the DM-SimpleSoundStageTriggers level and the SoundTest package, both included on the DVD in the files for this chapter. This level shows a visible trigger and a glowing volume (see **FIGURE 7.41**).

FIGURE 7.41   The SimpleSoundStageTrigger level has a Trigger and a Volume within it.

2. Open the Kismet Editor by clicking the Open Kismet button **K**. Right-click and choose New Event > Level Startup. Then, right-click and choose New Action > Sound > Play Sound. Connect the Out output of the Level Startup to the Play input of the Play Sound (see **FIGURE 7.42**).

3. Select the Play Sound and take a look at the Properties window. You will see that you have controls to set an initial delay, fade the sound in and out, and multiply both the pitch and volume.

4. Select the PlaySound property and use the Generic Browser to place the sound_startVoiceCue SoundCue within it (see **FIGURE 7.43**). If you test the level, you will now hear the voice clip play as soon as the level begins.

> **NOTE**
>
> If this sound effect needed to be spatialized, you would need to attach an object variable containing some level actor into the Target input on the bottom of the sequence object. The engine uses the position of this actor (or actors) to position the sound in 3D space.

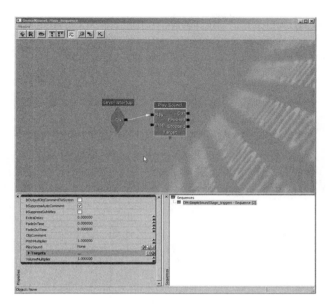

FIGURE 7.42   Your new Kismet network should appear like so.

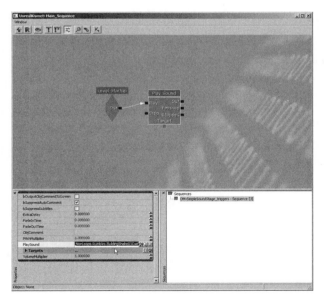

FIGURE 7.43   Your PlaySound's Properties window should look like this.

5. Click the Search for Actors button 🔍 and locate TriggerVolume_0. Double-click it to select it. Then, in the Kismet Editor, right-click and choose Create New Event using TriggerVolume_0 > Touch from the context menu. In the Properties Window, set the MaxTriggerCount property for this event to 0 (see **FIGURE 7.44**).

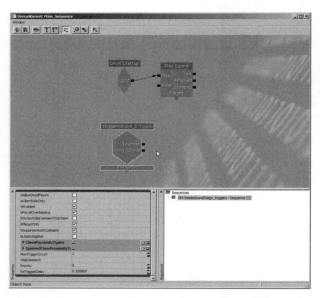

FIGURE 7.44   You have now created a Touch event for TriggerVolume_0.

6. Create a new Play Sound sequence object, and connect it to the Touched output of the new event. Using the skills you gained so far, place the sound_volumeInCue SoundCue in the PlaySound property (see **FIGURE 7.45**).

7. Create a second Play Sound object, placing the sound_volumeOutCue SoundCue into the PlaySound property. Connect this new object to the UnTouched output of the Touch event (see **FIGURE 7.46**).

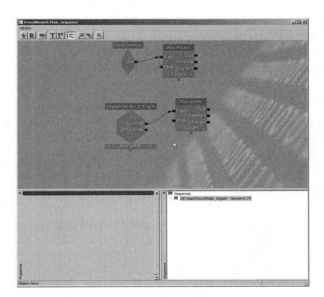

FIGURE 7.45 The new network should look like this.

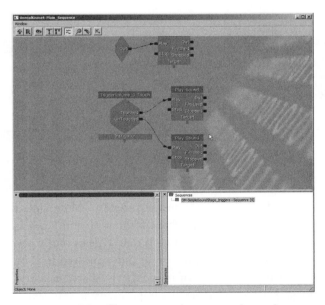

FIGURE 7.46 You can now play a second sound as you exit the volume.

8. Select Trigger_0 in the Perspective viewport. In the Kismet Editor, right-click and choose Create New Event using Trigger_0 > Used from the Context menu. Create a new Play Sound sequence object that plays the sound_triggerCue SoundCue whenever the trigger is used (see **FIGURE 7.47**). Remember to set the Triggers MaxTriggerCount property to 0.

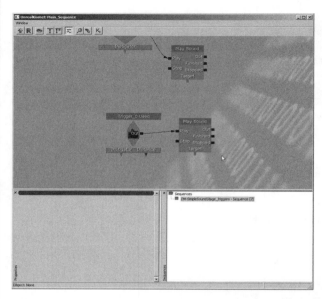

FIGURE 7.47   You will now also hear a sound whenever you use the trigger.

9. Save and test your level, trying out all the new voice clips.

END TUTORIAL 7.6

Working with Music

Adding music to your levels is a little different from simply playing a sound. Unreal provides a robust system that allows for sophisticated control over the playback of multiple music tracks based on a variety of in-game events. For example, you could have a certain type of music play when combat is engaged, or when your player's health gets low. To do this, you need to learn about a few nodes inside of Kismet that allow for the control of music tracks, as well as a little theory on how they work together to make your level's musical compositions as seamless as possible.

But first, you need an overview of how this system is intended to work. The idea of the music system is to provide an easy way for a designer to start a certain piece of music by literally calling it by name. Rather than having many different sequence objects, all set to play different musical selections, you can simply store all your songs into one list, like a jukebox, and call on the one you need when you need it.

MusicTrack

The MusicTrack is simply a Kismet variable that holds a piece of music in the form of a SoundCue (see **FIGURE 7.48**). It has some important parameters, listed under its Music Track property, that allow you to add the appropriate SoundCue to the track, as well as to give it a name, defined by the TrackType property. Also listed are the fade-in and fade-out time parameters and the fade-in and fade-out volumes.

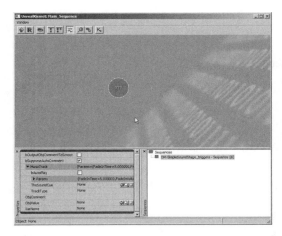

FIGURE 7.48   The MusicTrack variable sequence object

MusicTrackBank

The MusicTrackBank is your list of music (see **FIGURE 7.49**). It allows you to add an index for each music track you want to have available in your level. This can be used as an alternative to multiple Music Tracks, depending on your choice of workflow. Each added index has its own independent controls for fade-in time and volume, as well as independent names for track types. The Music Track Bank can be filled in manually during level design, or dynamically so that the track selections change based on the location of the player.

CrossFadeMusicTracks

The CrossFadeMusicTracks sequence object is the DJ of your musical selection system (see **FIGURE 7.50**). You simply call him up and tell him what kind of music you want to hear, and he'll switch it out for you. Technically speaking, by calling on this sequence object, you can change to any of the tracks stored in your MusicTrackBank simply by passing in a string containing the TrackType you want.

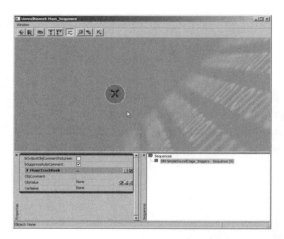

FIGURE 7.49   The MusicTrackBank variable sequence object

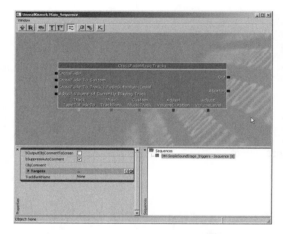

FIGURE 7.50   The CrossFadeMusicTracks sequence object

Set Music Track

If you're not careful, you might start thinking that this sequence object is supposed to play your music. Not so. The Set Music Track object exists so that you can add tracks to your MusicTrack Bank during gameplay, or swap out one type of track for another (see **FIGURE 7.51**).

As an example, let's say you're moving from Level_1 to Level_2. Both levels have their own separate Outdoor music, and both of those music tracks have their TrackType set to Outdoor. By using a Set Music Track object, you can swap out the Outdoor music for Level_1 with the

Outdoor music for Level_2, so that the next time you tell the CrossFadeMusicTracks to play the Outdoor music, you hear the music for Level_2 instead of Level_1.

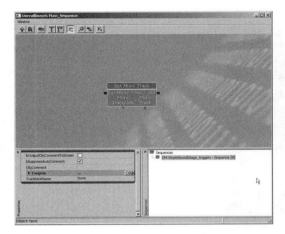

FIGURE 7.51   The Set Music Track sequence object

The UT Map Music Object

Unreal Tournament 3 has a specialized actor—the UT Map Music object—that is designed solely to handle the playback of music in your levels based on a certain set of criteria. For example, you can specify an ambient music track, another track that plays during suspenseful moments, and another that queues during high-action moments. You can also control how each of these tracks blend into each other. The object also allows you to specify a series of "stingers," which are short musical gestures that happen during very specific events, such as a blaring chord when the player gets killed or a triumphant fanfare when an enemy flag is captured.

You can create a UT Map Music object within the Generic Browser by right-clicking and choosing it from the context menu. If you double-click the object, you can see all the different tracks that can be added, along with their labels (see **FIGURE 7.52**).

Once you have specified which tracks will be played for the desired criteria, you need to apply the UT Map Music object to your map. This is done in the World Properties, located under the View menu of the main menu bar. The procedure is fairly simple:

1. Within WorldInfo_0 (World Properties), expand the WorldInfo category.
2. Click the small blue arrow button ▼ next to the MyMapInfo property and add a UTMapInfo.
3. Expand the new UTMapInfo category that appears.

4. Use the Generic Browser to assign your UT Map Music object to the MapMusicInfo property.

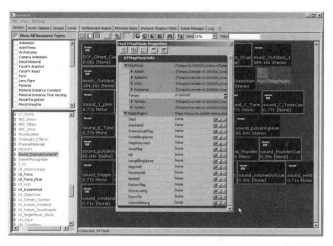

FIGURE 7.52   The properties of the UT Map Music object.

For the purposes of this text, we do not cover the use of the UT Map Music object in terms of a tutorial, because it requires that the user create music in a very specific manner. For best results, each of the musical pieces must work within the same theme and have the same tempo for easy music blending. Rather, we take a look at controlling music through Kismet using MusicTrackBanks.

Working with MusicTrackBanks

You have two primary ways to work with MusicTrackBanks. The first is to fill in your MusicTrackBank manually during the design of your level. This is as simple as selecting your MusicTrackBank in Kismet, expanding its MusicTrackBank property, and adding a new item for each song you'll use in your level. This is a perfectly fine workflow for single levels, although it does become cumbersome should you need to swap a certain song out for another.

A second option is to update your MusicTrackBank dynamically. This method is especially useful for visualizing which songs are in your bank, and it's perfect for streaming levels. Dynamically updating your MusicTrackBank allows each of your streamed levels to have its own selection of musical tracks. As the player moves from one level into the next, your music system can swap out the tracks in the background, meaning the next time you play a certain type of music, you get the version that was designed for the new level. We explore this second method in **TUTORIAL 7.7**.

The benefit of this method is that you only need to send a limited number of commands to the CrossFadeMusicTracks sequence object. You can literally just tell the cross-fader that you want to hear "Outdoor" music, and it plays the outdoor music for one of your levels. The exact same command plays different music if you're in a different level.

> **NOTE**
>
> Before attempting **TUTORIAL 7.7**, make sure City_Persistent, City_Stream_01, and City_Stream_ 02 are copied to your *Unreal Tournament 3* installation's Content/Maps folder. **TUTORIAL 7.7** uses level streaming, and these files all need to be in the Maps folder for it to work properly.

TUTORIAL 7.7: Setting Up a Dynamic Music System, Part I: Establishing the Main Music System

1. Launch Unreal Editor and open the City_Persistent level (see **FIGURE 7.53**). It includes a simplified city that streams through the use of volumes. The persistent world contains a large volume in the center, which we use to cue Transition music.

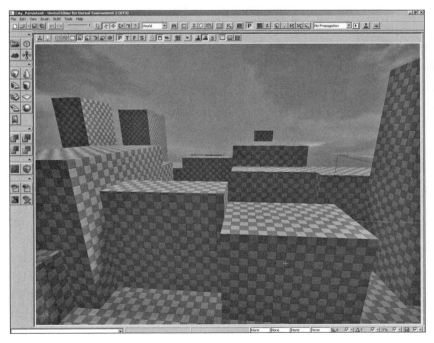

FIGURE 7.53   Our test level is a mockup of a small city.

2. The first thing we need to do is create our constant variables. Complete the following steps:

a. Open the Kismet Editor ![K] and make sure the City_Persistent sequence is high-lighted under the sequences list. This is just to make sure you're adding the following Kismet sequence to the persistent level, and not to the streaming sublevels.

b. Right-click in the Kismet Editor and choose New Variable > Sound > Music Track Bank (see **FIGURE 7.54**).

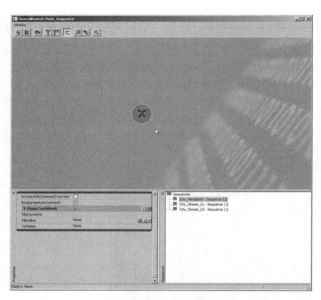

FIGURE 7.54   The MusicTrackBank has been created.

c. Select the new MusicTrackBank and in the Kismet Editor's Properties window, set its VarName property to **MyBank**. Leave all other properties alone for now (see **FIGURE 7.55**).

d. Right-click in the Kismet Editor and choose New Variable > String. Set the VarName property of this new string variable to **TrackName** (see **FIGURE 7.56**).

e. Move these two objects next to one another by Ctrl-dragging them.

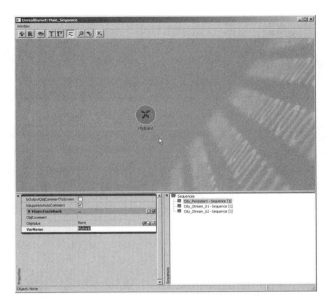

FIGURE 7.55   Notice the name MyBank appears beneath the MusicTrackBank.

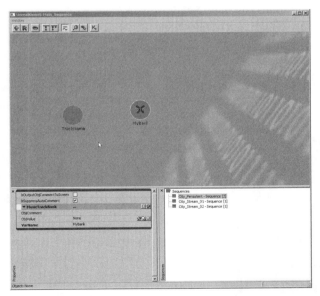

FIGURE 7.56   The variable should display TrackName when finished.

f. While holding down Ctrl+Alt, drag a marquee selection box around both of the variables. Then, right-click and choose New Comment. In the dialog that appears, enter **Variables** and press Enter (see **FIGURE 7.57**).

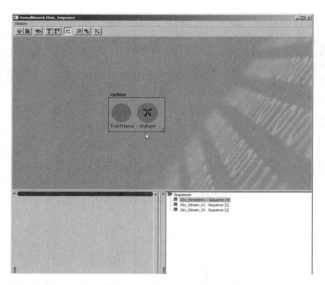

FIGURE 7.57   The variables have been commented.

3. We now need to set up our initial music selections for when the game starts. We could do this dynamically using a Level Startup event and three SetMusicTrack objects, although to simplify our Kismet sequence, we apply them here. Follow these steps:

  a. Select the MyBank MusicTrackBank and open the Generic Browser.

  b. In the Kismet Editor's Properties window, select the MusicTrackBank property and click Add New Item three times (see **FIGURE 7.58**).

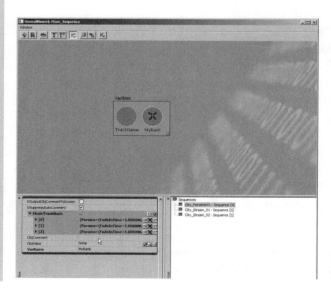

FIGURE 7.58   You need to add three new slots to hold music tracks.

c. Expand element [0], expand its Params property, and set the following values:

- ▶ **FadeInTime**: 1
- ▶ **FadeOutTime**: 2
- ▶ **TrackType**: Outdoor
- ▶ **TheSoundCue**: A_Music_ JesperNecris01_ Action01Cue

> **NOTE**
>
> In substeps c through e, the TheSoundCue property must be set using the Generic Browser; it uses the A_Music_JesperNecris01 package, included with your *Unreal Tournament 3* installation.

d. Expand element [1], expand its Params property, and set the following values:

- ▶ **FadeInTime**: 1
- ▶ **FadeOutTime**: 2
- ▶ **TrackType**: **Indoor**
- ▶ **TheSoundCue**: A_Music_JesperNecris01_Suspense01Cue

e. Expand element [2], expand its Params property, and set the following values:

- ▶ **FadeInTime**: 1
- ▶ **FadeOutTime**: 2
- ▶ **TrackType**: Transition
- ▶ **TheSoundCue**: A_Music_JesperNecris01_Ambient01Cue

4. We now need to set up the "brain" of our music selection system, the CrossFadeMusicTrack object. Complete these steps:

a. Right-click in the Kismet Editor and choose New Action > Sound > CrossFadeMusicTracks. For simplicity, we're going to refer to this as the "CrossFader" from now on (see **FIGURE 7.59**).

b. Select the CrossFader and set its TrackBankName property to **mybank**. Note that if you type the name in all lowercase, the capitalization converts to "MyBank" once the MusicTrackBank is detected.

c. Right-click nearby the green TrackTypeToFadeTo input (not on top of it) and choose New Variable > Named Variable from the context menu. Set the FindVarName property of this new variable to **TrackName**. This means you are "wirelessly" connecting to the TrackName variable created earlier (see **FIGURE 7.60**).

d. Drag a wire from the TrackTypeToFadeTo input to this new named variable.

e. Right-click to the left of the CrossFader and choose New Event > Remote Event from the context menu. Set the MaxTriggerCount of this new event to 0, and set the EventName property to **PlayMusic**.

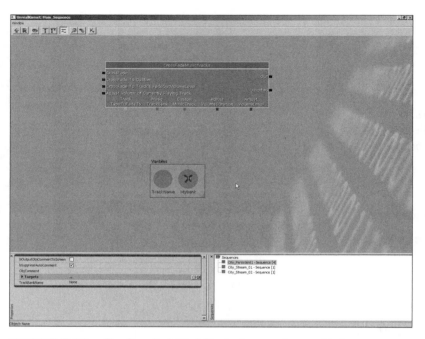

FIGURE 7.59   The CrossFadeMusicTracks has now been added.

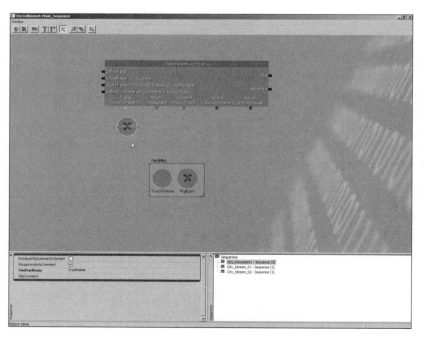

FIGURE 7.60   The new named variable communicates with the TrackName variable created earlier.

f. Connect a wire from the Out output of the Remote Event to the CrossFade property of the CrossFader (see **FIGURE 7.61**).

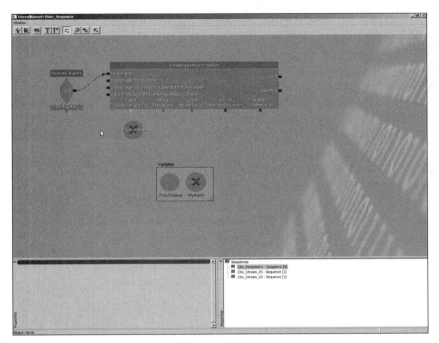

FIGURE 7.61 The new Remote Event handles the switching of songs.

The primary music switching system is now in place.

5. Save your level's progress.

END TUTORIAL 7.7

If you have not yet completed **TUTORIAL 7.7**, do so before proceeding. In **TUTORIAL 7.8**, we establish the initial playback of our level's music.

TUTORIAL 7.8: Setting Up a Dynamic Music System, Part II: Initial Playback and Transitions

1. The first thing we need to do is send a command to our CrossFader, telling it to play the Outdoor music. This is because our PlayerStart actor is located outside. Follow these steps:

a. In the Kismet Editor, right-click and choose New Event > Level Startup from the context menu (see **FIGURE 7.62**).

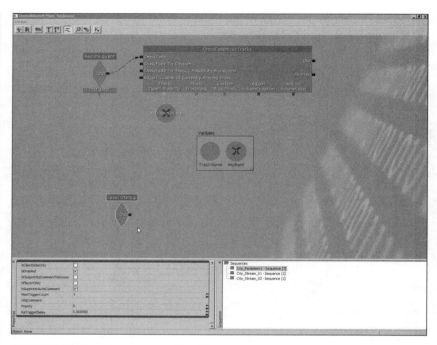

FIGURE 7.62   Create a new Level Startup event.

b. Right-click and choose New Action > Set Variable > String from the context menu. Connect the Out output of the Level Startup event to the In input of this Set String object (see **FIGURE 7.63**).

c. Select the TrackName Named Variable that is currently connected to the CrossFader. Press Ctrl+C, Ctrl+V to duplicate it, and then connect the duplicate to the Target output of the String object (see **FIGURE 7.64**).

7

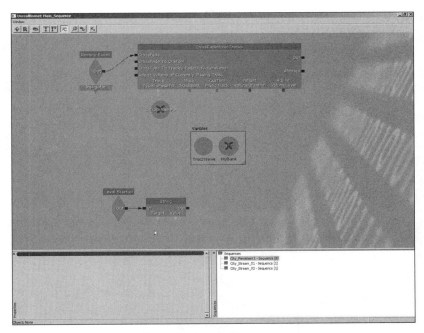

FIGURE 7.63   The wire should connect like so.

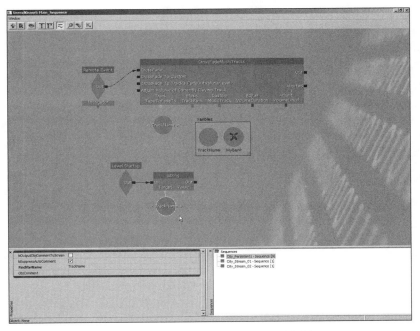

FIGURE 7.64   Duplicate and connect the Named Variable.

d. Right-click the green input box labeled Value on the String object and choose New String Variable from the context menu. This creates a new string variable that is automatically wired to the Value input.

Set the StrValue property of the new String variable to Outdoor (see **FIGURE 7.65**).

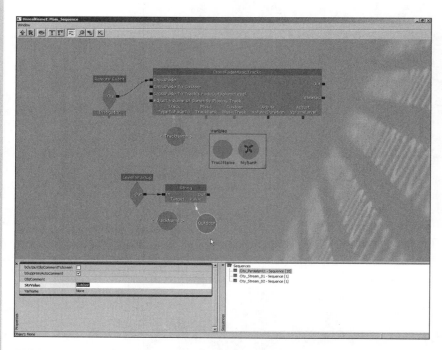

FIGURE 7.65   A new String variable has been added.

e. Right-click to the right of the String object and choose New Action > Event > Activate Remote Event. Connect this action to the Out output of the Set String Variable object, then set the EventName property of this new Activate Remote Event object to PlayMusic. This activates the event currently attached to the CrossFader (see **FIGURE 7.66**).

2. We now want to set up the triggering system that plays the Transition music when we enter the large trigger volume that exists between the two levels. Follow these steps:

a. Click the Search for Actors button ![icon] and locate TriggerVolume_3 (see **FIGURE 7.67**). Double-click it to select this actor.

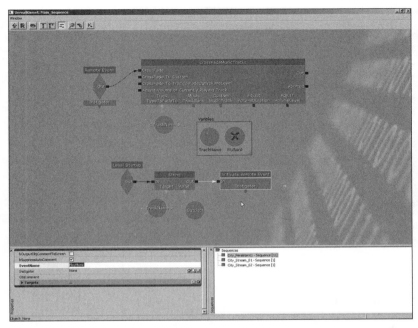

FIGURE 7.66   The Activate Remote event is used to communicate with the CrossFader.

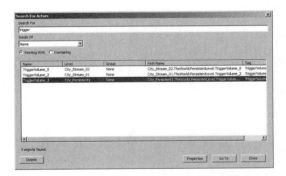

FIGURE 7.67   The Search for Actors window.

b. In the Kismet Editor, right-click and choose Create New Event using TriggerVolume_3 > Touch from the context menu. Set its MaxTriggerCount to 0 (see **FIGURE 7.68**).

c. Holding down Ctrl, select the Set String Variable sequence object created in the previous step, both of the variables plugged into it, as well as the Activate Remote Event object feeding out of it. Duplicate all these sequence objects with Ctrl+C, Ctrl+V (see **FIGURE 7.69**).

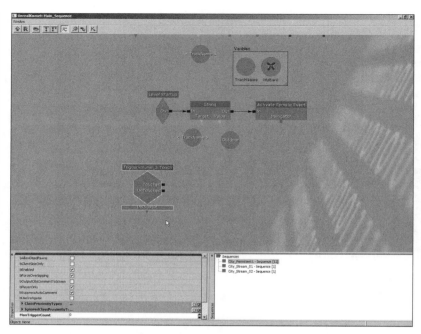

FIGURE 7.68   Create a new Touch event for TriggerVolume_3.

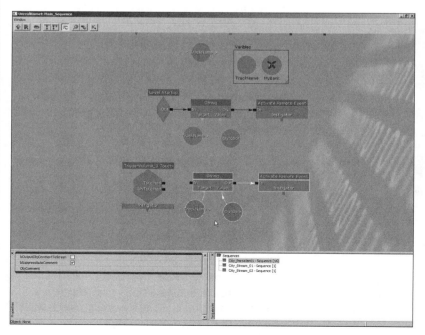

FIGURE 7.69   All the required sequence objects have been duplicated.

d. Wire the Touched output of the Touch event to the In input of the newly duplicated String object (see **FIGURE 7.70**).

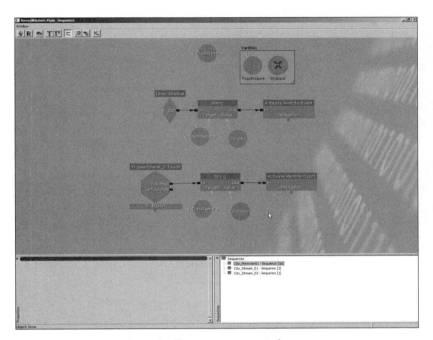

FIGURE 7.70 The new duplicates are connected.

e. Select the string variable attached to the new String object's Value input. Set its StrValue property to Transition (see **FIGURE 7.71**).

3. If you tested the world right now, you'd hear the Outdoor music playing for Level 1, then the Transition music as you pass to the second level. However, the Transition music would continue to play indefinitely because we have not yet called for the Outdoor music to play again once we get to the other level. We fix this problem with the following steps:

a. Select the Set String Variable object currently attached to the Touch event, along with both the variables connected to it. Duplicate them all with Ctrl+C, Ctrl+V.

b. Select the String variable connected to the newly duplicated String object and set its StrValue property to Outdoor.

c. Connect a wire from the UnTouched output of the Touch event to the In input of the new String object (see **FIGURE 7.72**).

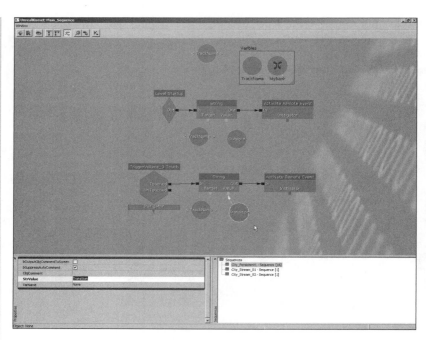

FIGURE 7.71   The volume now queues the Transition music.

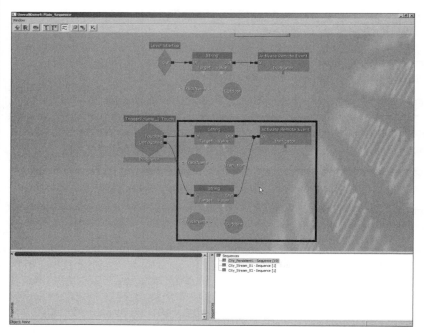

FIGURE 7.72   With the new network in place, the Outdoor music is queued once again.

Now, if you were to test the level, you would find that the Outdoor music for Level 1 begins when the level starts, the Transition music plays as you move through the Transition volume, and the Outdoor music picks back up when you exit the volume. However, we now need to set up the MusicTrackBank so that the tracks for Level 1 are swapped out for the music for Level 2 while you are moving through the Transition volume.

END TUTORIAL 7.8

If you have not yet completed **TUTORIALS 7.7** and **7.8**, do so before proceeding because each of these tutorials builds to the next. In **TUTORIAL 7.9**, we use Kismet to change out the music tracks we are using in our second level. This is because the music for Level 1 has been stored in our MusicTrackBank by default. We now set up Level 2 so we can test our level, and then create the Level 1 sequence in **TUTORIAL 7.9**.

TUTORIAL 7.9: Setting Up a Dynamic Music System, Part III: Setting Music Tracks Dynamically

1. Open the Kismet Editor. In the lower-right corner of the editor, locate the Sequences window and select the sequence for City_Stream_02. You will notice that the sequence already contains a Level Loaded and Visible event. We use this event to change out the tracks in our MusicTrackBank.

2. Right-click to the right of the Level Loaded and Visible object and choose New Action > Sound > Set Music Track from the context menu. Select this new object and set its TrackBankName property to MyBank, and then connect it to the Level Loaded and Visible event (see **FIGURE 7.73**).

3. Right-click the small input box underneath the MusicTrack label and choose New Music Track Variable from the context menu. Select this variable and set its TrackType property to Outdoor, and use the Generic Browser to set its TheSoundCue property to A_Music_JesperNecris01_Victory01Cue (see **FIGURE 7.74**).

> **NOTE**
>
> The A_Music_JesperNecris01_Victory01Cue object, as well as the A_Music_JesperNecris01_Mix01Cue object required in Step 4, are located in the A_Music_JesperNecris01 package, included in your *Unreal Tournament 3* installation.

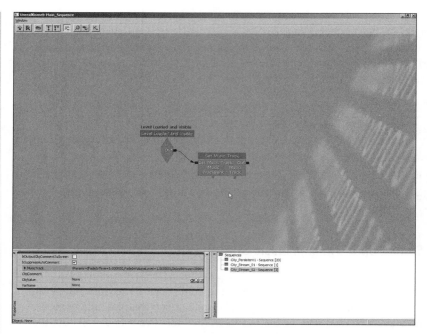

FIGURE 7.73   The new Set Music Track object is used to change our music tracks.

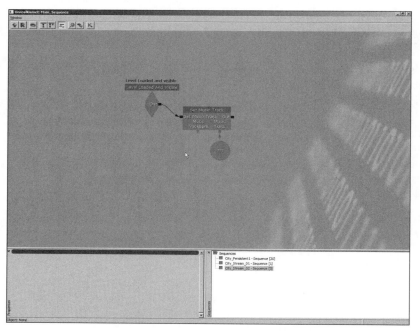

FIGURE 7.74   The MusicTrack variable tells the Set Music Track which song to place into the bank.

4. Select the Set Music Track object, along with the named variable and the String variable. Duplicate them with Ctrl+C, Ctrl+V. Then, select the String variable and set its StrValue property to Indoor, and use the Generic Browser to set its TheSoundCue property to A_Music_JesperNecris01_Mix01Cue. Connect this to the Loaded event as well (see **FIGURE 7.75**).

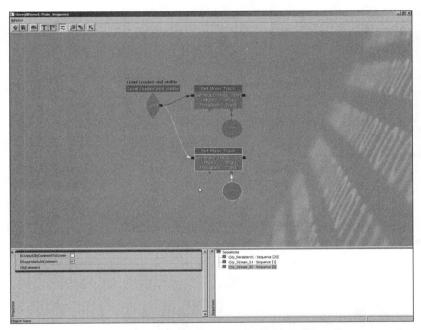

FIGURE 7.75   Now both the Indoor and Outdoor tracks are being adjusted.

5. You now need to set up the trigger that starts the Indoor music when you go into the building. Do this now using the following steps:

   a. Click the Search for Actors button 🔍 and locate TriggerVolume_0. Double-click it to select the volume.

   b. Back in the Kismet Editor, make sure you are still in the City_Stream_02 sequence. Then, right-click and choose New Event using TriggerVolume_0 > Touch (see **FIGURE 7.76**).

   c. In the Sequences window, select the City_Persistent sequence. Then, holding down Ctrl, select both the Set String Variable objects currently connected to the TriggerVolume_3 Touch event, the named variable and String variable connected to each one, as well as the Activate Remote Event object. Once all seven sequence objects are selected, press Ctrl+C to duplicate them (see **FIGURE 7.77**).

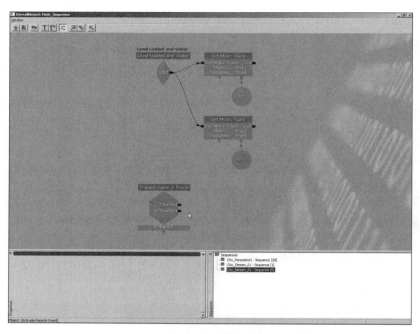

FIGURE 7.76   Create a new Touch event for TriggerVolume_0.

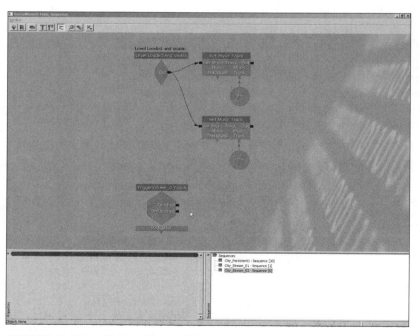

FIGURE 7.77   All the objects within the box should be selected.

d. Go back to the City_Stream_02 sequence and press Ctrl+V to paste the objects into this sequence (see **FIGURE 7.78**). Select the String variable that currently reads Transition and set its StrValue property to Indoor.

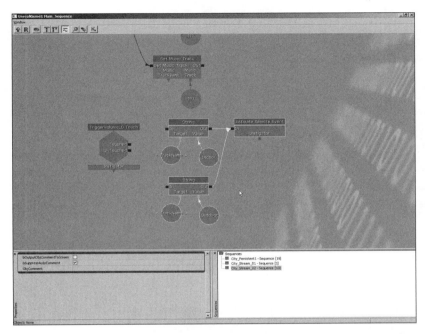

FIGURE 7.78   By duplicating all these nodes, you have saved considerable time.

e. Connect the String object that is attached to the Indoor String variable to the Touched output of the event. Connect the other String object to the UnTouched output (see **FIGURE 7.79**). In the end, you want the Indoor music to play when the character "touches" the volume, and the Outdoor music to play when the character exits the volume.

6. Save and test your level. Make sure you click the Play Level in Editor button ![button]. As the game starts, you'll hear the Level 1 music playing, although the Indoor music is nonfunctional. As you pass over to Level 2, the Transition music kicks in. As you exit the Transition level, the Outdoor music for Level 2 begins. You can now enter the building, and the Indoor music kicks in.

If you were to travel back toward Level 1, the Transition music would start back up, but once you exited the Transition volume, you would find that the Outdoor music for Level 2 would still be playing, even though you've passed to Level 1. We now fix this problem.

7. Click the Search for Actors button and double-click TriggerVolume_2 to select it. Then, back in the Kismet Editor, make sure you're in the City_Stream_01 sequence and create a new Touch event using this trigger (see **FIGURE 7.80**). Be sure to set the event's MaxTriggerCount to 0!

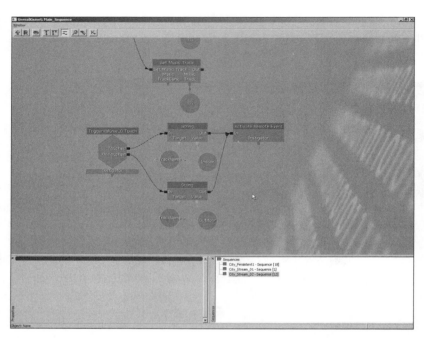

FIGURE 7.79   The Indoor trigger volume is now set up.

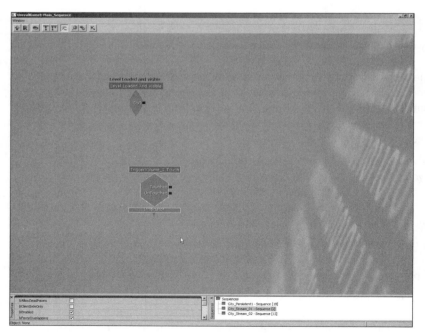

FIGURE 7.80   Create a new Touch event for TriggerVolume_2, placed in the sequence for Level 1.

8. We now create all the necessary actions for this sequence through quick duplication:

   a. Select the City_Stream_02 sequence in the Kismet Editor's sequence window.

   b. Holding down Ctrl, select all non-event sequence objects. This includes all but the Touch event and the Level Loaded and Visible event. Once all these sequence objects are selected, duplicate them with Ctrl+C (see **FIGURE 7.81**).

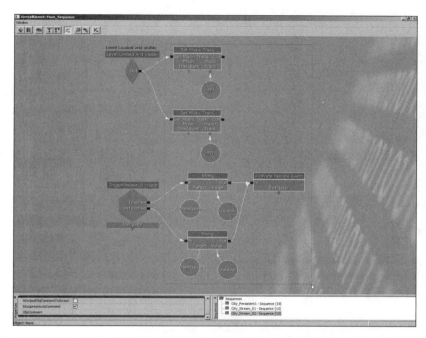

FIGURE 7.81 All the sequence objects within the box should be selected.

   c. Go back to the City_Stream_01 sequence and press Ctrl+V to paste all the sequence objects into the level (see **FIGURE 7.82**).

   d. Connect both of the Set Music Track objects to the Level Loaded and Visible event (see **FIGURE 7.83**).

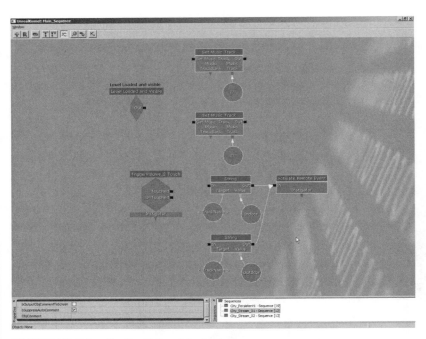

FIGURE 7.82   Paste all the objects at once.

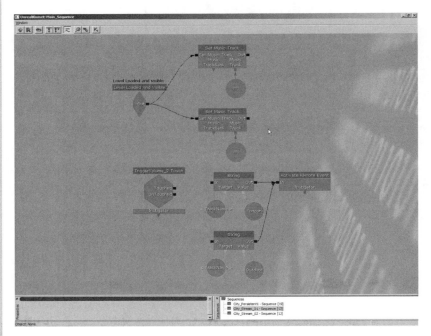

FIGURE 7.83   Connect the Set Music Track objects to the Level Loaded and Visible object.

e. Connect the String object that includes the Indoor variable to the Touched output of the Touch event, and connect the opposite String object to the UnTouched output (see **FIGURE 7.84**).

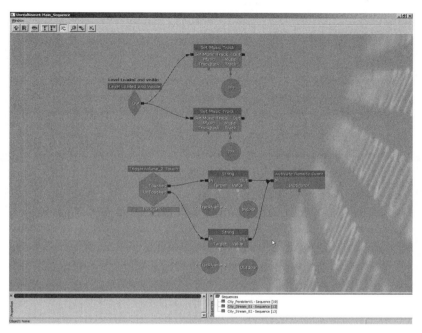

FIGURE 7.84   Wire up the Indoor trigger just as you did for Level 2.

9. Save and test your level.

END TUTORIAL 7.9

At this point, you should now be able to enter the indoor area of Level 1 or Level 2 and hear the appropriate music for that level. You will also notice a seamless transition as you pass from Level 1 to Level 2. There are a great many variations on this setup, depending on what it is you need to accomplish with your music. Once you combine the skills you have gained throughout this book, using the experience you gather as you continue to work with Unreal Editor, you'll find that you have a tremendous amount of flexibility over the sounds and music in your levels.

Summary

Throughout this chapter, we've taken an in-depth look at the features of *Unreal Tournament 3*'s sound system. As you continue to work with it, you will find that you have a tremendous amount of control and flexibility in terms of how your sound and music are presented to the player. Depending on your level of Kismet experience, you should now be ready to set up a variety of different effect and musical layouts. With a bit of practice, you will be able to completely master the use of sounds in Unreal Engine 3!

7

Chapter 8

Post-Process Effects

Post-process effects are responsible for many of the visual effects seen in modern games using Unreal Engine 3. A post-process effect is a form of adjustment or modification that is done to a scene *after* it has been rendered. You can think of it as a special effect that is applied to the camera and affects everything the camera sees. Simple examples include desaturation (going to muted colors or even black and white) and motion blur (see **FIGURE 8.1**). Post-process effects provide a simple way to completely change the overall look and feel of a scene without having to make any changes to existing materials or textures.

Post-process effects can be controlled via a series of properties, but can also be driven by materials. This gives you the power to create a wide variety of effects by implementing the many material expressions available. For example, you could apply a material that inverts the destination color as a post-process effect, which would invert all the colors of your level!

FIGURE 8.1   A post-process effect is being used to create the blur in this scene.

The Four Key Methods of Controlling Post-Processes

Here are the four primary ways of applying post-processes to your levels:

- ▶ **World Settings**—These are DefaultPostProcess settings within a level's WorldInfo.
- ▶ **PostProcessEffects**—These objects are created and then applied before the game.
- ▶ **PostProcessVolumes**—These volumes control post-process effects within a specific area.
- ▶ **Cameras**—Cameras have internal properties for overriding post-process effects, but are only useful when the player is looking through a current camera.

Simpler post-process effects are created by using a few properties in the WorldInfo object of every Unreal level, and are often referred to as the *World Settings*. Post-process effects that can be created in the World Settings include motion blur, depth of field, color adjustment, and light blooms (see **FIGURE 8.2**).

These settings can be supported, amplified, or replaced by the use of PostProcessEffect objects, which can be created in the Generic Browser and then edited using the Post Process Editor, which we will discuss in more depth later in this chapter. Essentially, a PostProcessEffect is comprised of a series of modules that represent bloom, motion blur, material effects, and scene effects.

The World Settings are combined with the current PostProcessEffect object to create the final post-process effect as seen by the player. Other factors can be implemented as well, such as PostProcess Volumes, Kismet sequences, and Matinee sequences. These are discussed later in this chapter. The exact details of this cooperation are covered in the description of the bUseWorldSettings property in the section "Post Process Editor."

It should be noted that many of the post-process effects that take place within Unreal Tournament 3 are accomplished through both the World Settings and the use of PostProcessVolumes. These volumes allow you to designate specific areas of your level where effects are visible. For example, in the Torlan level—as with many of the outdoor levels in *UT3*—you will notice a bright haze that obscures distant objects. If you were to look at the level in the editor, you would notice a large post-process volume that surrounds the entire level and makes this effect happen.

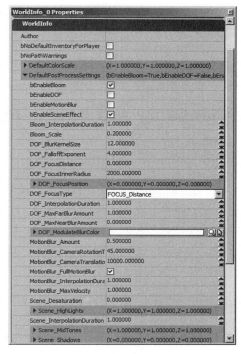

FIGURE 8.2   The WorldInfo properties have settings for global post-process effects.

PostProcessEffect objects, on the other hand, allow you to create effects that are independent of any particular level and have more flexibility because of the use of materials. An example of such an effect in *Unreal Tournament 3* is what happens on the screen when the player takes damage. The red haze that appears on the sides of the screen is the result of the default post-process effect. This means that if you were so inclined, you could edit that effect—or overwrite it with one of your own—to create an entirely new effect.

The key thing to remember is that, generally speaking, any post-process effect that needs to be independent of a level can be achieved with a PostProcessEffect object. Any effect that is to be considered part of the level's environment should be done with a PostProcessVolume instead.

Cameras add further post-process control, but are generally only useful as part of a Matinee cinematic sequence. Every camera comes with a series of properties that may be used to override any current post-processes that are applied to the level. This means that if you cut to an in-game cinematic during gameplay, you can still make use of depth of field, motion blur, bloom, and other effects to alter the "feel" of your scene.

In this chapter, we focus primarily on the actual PostProcessEffect objects that can be created in the Generic Browser, rather than on any other type of post-process effect control. The actual

PostProcessEffect object allows for a great amount of flexibility because it is the only way to apply materials to a post-process. Once you have worked with and mastered this object, you'll find that the other methods for adjusting post-processes come much more easily because they are generally just a series of properties assigned to various actors (volumes, cameras, and so on).

Accessing and Assigning PostProcessEffect Objects

PostProcessEffect objects are created through the Generic Browser, just as most other objects in Unreal. Within the Generic Browser, simply look in the File menu under the New option, or you can right-click in the Generic Browser and choose New PostProcessEffect from the context menu. Upon creation, these objects are available in the Generic Browser just like any other object, such as a texture or material. If you do not see them, make sure you have their options checked in the Resource Type List or that you have checked Show All Resource Types.

At the time of this writing, using a PostProcessEffect in the actual game requires one of three options:

- ▶ Assign the PostProcessEffect by editing the UTEngine.ini file.
- ▶ Overwrite or edit the existing default PostProcessEffect (FX_HitEffects.UTPostProcess).
- ▶ Assign using an UnrealScript (for example, creating a custom Mutator or custom Kismet sequence to handle changing the PostProcessEffect).

The third option is really your best bet in terms of creating a mod that is most easily shared. However, because this book is not intended to teach scripting, and because we do not really want to destroy or alter any permanent game files, we will be focusing on the first option. This is by far the easiest method for learning how post-processes work and can be undone by simply deleting the INI file and letting Unreal create a new one on the next launch.

Editing the UTEngine.ini file is rather simple. First, you need to navigate to it. On most *UT3* installations, it can be found in your Documents folder in the following location:

```
Documents\My Games\Unreal Tournament 3\UTGame\Config\
```

The following line must be edited to point to the new PostProcessEffect object, using the notation *<PackageName>.<Group>.<Name>*.

```
DefaultPostProcessName=EngineMaterials.DefaultScenePostProcess
```

Keep in mind, however, that before changing the ExampleEngine.ini file, you should shut down Unreal Editor and any instances of the game that may be running. Failure to do so could cause the INI file to be overwritten, removing any changes you have made.

Once the change is completed and saved, you may restart your game or the editor, and you should see your PostProcessEffect in use as the default post-process. To complete **TUTORIAL 8.1**, open the PostProcessDemo.ut3 map included on the DVD in the files for this chapter and complete the following steps.

TUTORIAL 8.1: Your First Post-Process Effect

1. In the Generic Browser, right-click the background and choose New Post Process Effect from the context menu. Enter the following information:

   ▶ **Package:** MyPostProcesses

   ▶ **Group:** PostProcesses

   ▶ **Name:** ppe_first_post_process

   Click OK when done, which will open the Post Process Editor (see **FIGURE 8.3**).

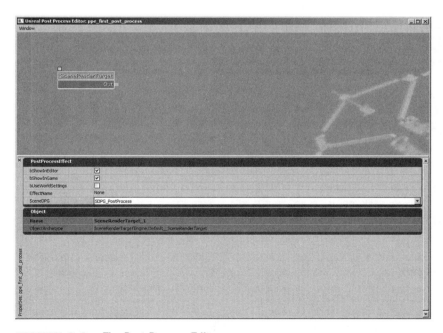

FIGURE 8.3   The Post Process Editor appears.

Although we could start editing this post-process effect now, we will not see the result until we have assigned it as the default post-process effect. This requires that we edit the game's default INI file.

2. Exit the Post Process Editor, save the MyPostProcesses package, and then close Unreal Editor.

3. Navigate to the Documents\My Games\Unreal Tournament 3\UTGame\Config\ folder of your computer, and locate the UTEngine.ini file and open it with any text editor. By default (in Windows) this will open Notepad. Search for (using Ctrl+F) the line that reads as follows:

> **NOTE**
>
> Failure to close Unreal Editor will result in your changes being reverted as soon as the game closes, which means you will not be able to edit the INI file. Also, there is no need to back this file up before editing, unless you have made previous edits that you do not want to lose. To set this INI file back to its default settings, simply delete the INI file and restart Unreal Editor. The editor will notice the missing file and re-create it using its internally defined default settings.

```
DefaultPostProcessName=EngineMaterials.DefaultScenePostProcess
```

This line should be in the [Engine.Engine] section and controls which post-process effect is used in the actual game (when the game is *not* run from within the editor). Change this line to read as follows:

```
DefaultPostProcessName=MyPostProcesses.PostProcesses.ppe_first_post_process
```

4. Now search again for the line that reads as follows (yes, it is the same line as before):

```
DefaultPostProcessName=EngineMaterials.DefaultScenePostProcess
```

This line should be in the [UTEditor.UTUnrealEdEngine[UTEditor.UTUnrealEdEngine] section and controls which post-process effect is used within the editor, as well as when the game is run through the Play In Editor system. Change this line to read as follows:

```
DefaultPostProcessName=MyPostProcesses.PostProcesses.ppe
_first_post_process
```

5. Save the changes to the UTEngine.ini file and close it. Open Unreal Editor again and reopen the PostProcessDemo.ut3 map. Your post-process effect is now in use. However, you will not currently see any significant changes because we have not yet created any particular effects.

6. We will begin by adding a simple depth of field effect, which causes the scene to blur the farther it gets from the camera. Double-click the ppe_first_post_process object in the Generic Browser to open it in the Post Process Editor (see **FIGURE 8.4**).

7. Right-click a blank area of the workspace and choose DOFAndBloomEffect from the context menu. Connect the output (green) of the SceneRenderTarget module to the input (red) of the DOFEffect module. Immediately, you should notice the effects of this in the viewport (see **FIGURE 8.5**).

8

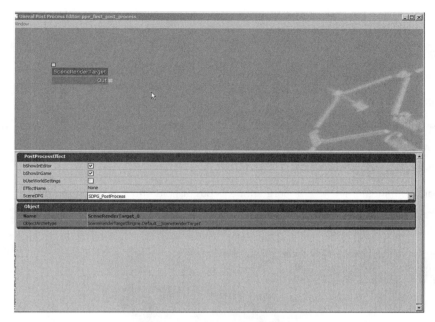

FIGURE 8.4   Currently there is only a SceneRenderTarget in the effect.

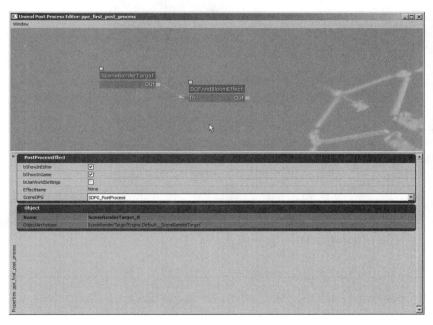

FIGURE 8.5   Connect the SceneRenderTarget to the DOFEffect module.

8. Select the DOFAndBloomEffect module and set the following properties. These properties will be explained later in this chapter.

- ▶ **FalloffExponent**: 1.0

- ▶ **BlurKernelSize**: 4.0

- ▶ **MaxNearBlurAmount**: 0.0

- ▶ **MaxFarBlurAmount**: 0.33

- ▶ **FocusInnerRadius**: 32768

- ▶ **FocusDistance**: 0.0

9. In the viewport, you should now see a more subtle depth of field effect in which the distant hills become blurred (see **FIGURE 8.6**). Make sure to save the package because we will need this post-process effect later on.

FIGURE 8.6   The effect is now very subtle in the level.

END TUTORIAL 8.1

Types of Post-Process Effects

Several types of post-process effects are available to designers. This section goes over each one of them, along with the relevant properties. It should be noted that these properties can be found in different locations, such as in the World Settings, in the properties of PostProcessVolumes, and in the various modules found within the Post Process Editor. Keep in mind, however, that although the names may differ slightly from one location to the other, each property still performs the same function.

Bloom

A bloom effect is a glow that appears on and around very bright objects. Objects that have emissive parts due to the emissive channel of their material can be affected, as well as any objects that have a bright specular highlight. In fact, any object that has a material with a high-intensity color value will be affected by the bloom, at least to some degree (see **FIGURE 8.7**).

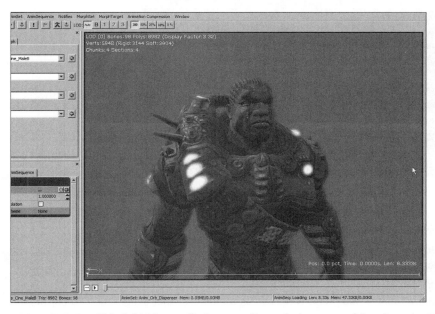

FIGURE 8.7   This light bloom effect causes the emissive areas of the character to glow.

Bloom has one property:

> **BloomScale**—This property serves as a multiplier that scales the amount of bloom to be applied to any bright objects on the screen.

Motion Blur

Motion blur involves the blurring of objects in the scene depending on their velocities relative to that of the camera (see **FIGURE 8.8**). This is seen as a "streaking" that extends from fast-moving objects. Motion blur can be applied in one of two ways:

- ▶ Globally to all objects in the scene, static or dynamic
- ▶ Only to those objects actually moving in the scene

FIGURE 8.8   The blur you see is the result of motion blur applied to a moving camera.

Motion Blur has the following properties:

MaxVelocity—This property serves as an upper limit on the amount of blur applied to any object. For example, any object traveling faster than this value will receive the same amount of blur as an object moving precisely at the value of the property.

MotionBlurAmount—This property serves as a multiplier that scales the amount of blur applied to objects.

FullMotionBlur—This property toggles whether motion blur is applied to every object in the scene or only to those that are moving. If this property is checked, all objects have motion blur; otherwise, only the objects that are in motion have this effect. This property is useful if you want to blur everything while in motion, such as when the camera is flying through the scene at a high rate of speed.

CameraRotationThreshold—The value set in this property serves as the maximum amount of rotation that can happen per frame and still have motion blur applied in the scene. It is measured in degrees per frame. For instance, if the property is set to 5, and the camera rotates more than 5 degrees in a single frame, then motion blur would be disabled during that rotation.

CameraTranslationThreshold—The value set in this property serves as the maximum amount of translation, or linear motion, that can happen per frame and still have motion blur applied in the scene. It is measured in Unreal units per frame. For instance, if the property is set to 15, and the camera moves more than 15 units in a single frame, then motion blur would be disabled during that motion.

Depth of Field

Depth of field is a blurring effect that is applied to objects based on their distance from a designated focus point. You can see this effect in certain photographs and films, where a single object or area seems to be in focus, but other objects that are closer or farther away are blurred out (see **FIGURE 8.9**). It should be noted that this point of focus is at times referred to in Unreal as a *focus plane* and at others as a *focus point*. For the purposes of this text, however, we will use the latter term.

All objects at the focus point receive no blur whatsoever. As objects get farther away from that point, however, the blur becomes more and more pronounced. At the edge and beyond a designated distance (known as the *focus distance*), full blur is applied to all objects.

FIGURE 8.9   Here you can see the results of a depth of field effect.

Depth of field has the following properties:

FalloffExponent—This property controls how quickly blur ramps up to full intensity between the location of the focus point and the focus distance.

A value of 1 results in linear falloff, meaning that the blur is added at a constant rate as you move away from the focus point.

Values less than 1 result in the amount of blur increasing very quickly as you move away from the focus point, but gradually increasing more slowly as you approach the extents of the radius.

Values greater than 1 result in the amount of blur increasing very slowly as you move away from the focus point, but increasing as you approach the radius.

BlurKernelSize—This property controls the maximum distance in pixels that a single pixel can be blurred. Essentially, it controls the maximum amount of blurring possible.

MaxNearBlurAmount—This number represents the amount of blur to apply to objects that are on the near side of the focus point. The value is clamped between 0 and 1.

MaxFarBlurAmount—This number represents the amount of blur to apply to objects that are on the far side of the focus point. The value is clamped between 0 and 1.

ModulateBlurColor—This is a color that will be modulated with the blur itself. Practically speaking, it tints the blur with the selected color.

FocusType—This property allows you to switch between a depth of field effect based on the distance from the camera and one based on a specific point in the world. However, at the time of this writing, the property is nonfunctional.

FocusInnerRadius—This value is the distance from the focus point (both toward and away from the camera) at which objects receive full blur.

FocusDistance—This property controls the distance from the camera that serves as the focus point. Objects at the focus point have no blur applied to them.

FocusPosition—This property allows you to specify a location in the world to be used as the focus point for depth of field calculation. However, it is only functional when the FocusType property is set to FOCUS_Position, which at the time of this writing is nonfunctional.

Material

Material post-process effects are only available through the use of PostProcessEffect objects. These types of post-process effects make use of material expressions to create the final look and are therefore extremely powerful. In essence, this is very much like applying a material to a "virtual lens" placed in front of the camera. Similar to a light gel, the camera "looks through" the material, allowing it to affect the scene (see **FIGURE 8.10**).

FIGURE 8.10 Material post-process effects allow for a wide range of possibilities, such as this inversion effect.

Here's the material post-process effect property:

> **Material**—This property simply holds the material you wish to use for your post-process effect.

Scene Effects

Scene effects are essentially a series of properties you can use to adjust the overall colors and tones of a scene after render time. This allows you control of such things as the overall color of the scene and adjustment of the various tonal parts of the scene (such as shadows and highlights), as shown in **FIGURE 8.11**. You also have the ability to completely desaturate your scene to grayscale or on a percentage basis, washing it out slightly.

These effects can be accessed through the World Settings and from within the UberPostProcess Effect module, inside the Post Process Editor.

FIGURE 8.11   This before and after shot shows the result of adjusting the scene tones to increase contrast.

Here are the scene tones properties:

> **SceneShadows**—This property allows you to control the color that is mapped to black. Any color in the scene with R, G, and B values lower than those specified in this property is transposed to 0 (black). This allows you to push the shadows of the scene toward a particular color.
>
> **SceneHighlights**—This property allows you control of all colors that are mapped to white. Any color with R, G, and B values greater than those specified in this property is transposed to 1 (white). This allows you to drive bright values (such as specular highlights) toward a particular color.
>
> **SceneMidTones**—This property controls the gamma curve, which essentially determines how much contrast exists in the scene once the mapping for SceneShadows and SceneHighlights has taken place. This can also be used on a per-color-component basis, meaning that the gamma curve for only a single color (red, blue, or green) can be affected, provided that is the desired effect.

Here's the scene saturation property:

> **SceneDesaturation**—This property alters the amount of color saturation of the final output. A value of 0 results in no change. A value of 1 results in complete desaturation, driving the scene to monochromatic grayscale. Values less than 0 will oversaturate the scene, driving the colors beyond their original values. Values greater than 1 will start to drive the scene toward the inverse of their origins.

Post-Process Editor

The Post Process Editor is the primary tool for creating and modifying PostProcessEffect objects. This is done through the linking together of various effect modules to create the final desired effect, very much like the SoundCue Editor.

Multiple copies of each type of module can be used to create a particular effect, although the order in which they are connected is very important because each effect builds upon the last. It should also be noted that the flow of the Post Process Editor is from left to right, and that the input of a module is red while the output is green (see **FIGURE 8.12**).

The interface of the Post Process Editor is broken up into two primary panels:

> **Workspace**—This is where the modules of a PostProcessEffect object are placed, arranged, and connected to one another. New modules can be added to this area by right-clicking in a blank area of the workspace and selecting the desired module from the context menu.
>
> **Properties**—This area appears like many of the property windows within Unreal Editor, allowing you to adjust the properties for the currently selected module, or for the last selected module if no module is currently selected.

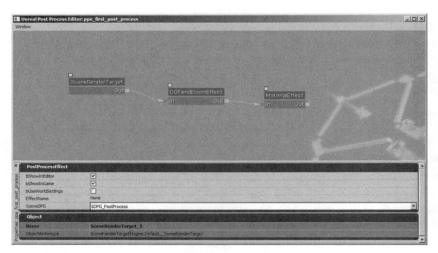

FIGURE 8.12   The Post Process Editor interface.

Post-Process Effects Modules

Here is a list of the available modules within the Post Process Editor. For more information on each of the effects of these modules, as well as the types of unique properties for each one, see "Types of Post-Process Effects," earlier in this chapter.

SceneRenderTarget

This is the base module present in all PostProcessEffects objects. It passes the rendered scene to the other modules, allowing them to perform their various functions on it (see **FIGURE 8.13**).

DOFAndBloomEffect

This module performs both a bloom and a depth of field effect on the scene as it exists when passed into the module. These two effects are applied simultaneously and additively (see **FIGURE 8.14**).

8

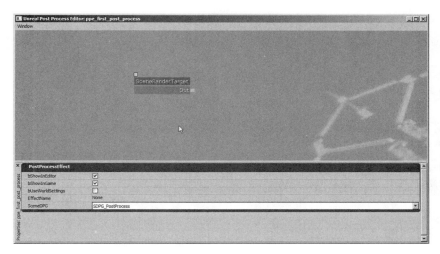

FIGURE 8.13 The SceneRenderTarget

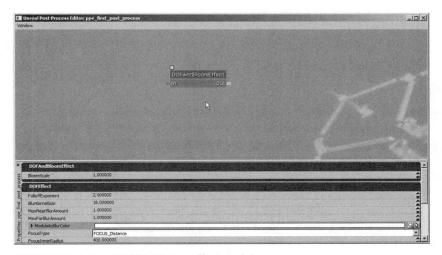

FIGURE 8.14 A DOFAndBloomEffect module

MaterialEffect

This module applies the specified material to the scene as it exists when passed into the module (see **FIGURE 8.15**).

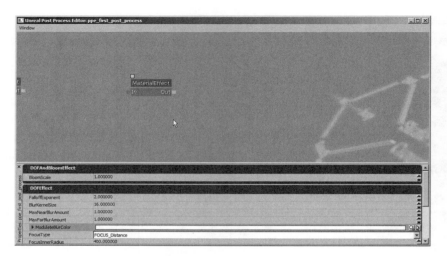

FIGURE 8.15   A MaterialEffect module

MotionBlurEffect

This module applies motion blur to the scene as it is when passed into the module (see **FIGURE 8.16**).

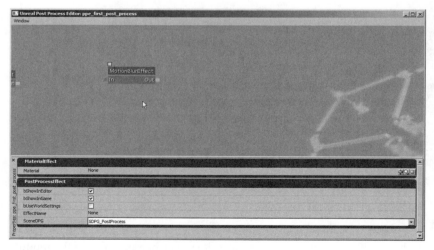

FIGURE 8.16   A MotionBlurEffect module

UberPostProcessEffect

This module performs a scene tone, a bloom, and a depth of field effect to the scene as it exists when passed into the module (see **FIGURE 8.17**). Bloom and depth of field are performed first, and are combined simultaneously in an additive fashion, as with the DOFAndBloomEffect module. The scene tone effect is added last.

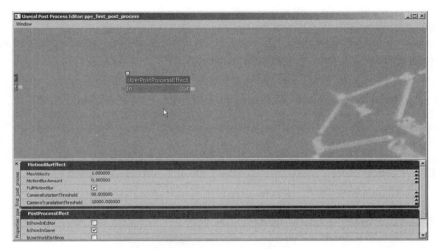

FIGURE 8.17   An UberPostProcessEffect module.

Common Module Properties

The following properties are available in all modules:

> **bShowInEditor**—If this property is checked, and the post-process effect containing this module is the default post-process effect as specified in the INI file, then the effects of this module will be displayed within the editor's Perspective viewport.
>
> **bShowInGame**—If this property is checked, and the post-process effect containing this module is the default post-process effect as specified in the INI file, then the effects of this module will be displayed when the game is played.
>
> **bUseWorldSettings**—If this property is checked, and the post-process effect containing this module is the default post-process effect as specified in the INI file, then the settings in the WorldInfo or those found in any active PostProcessVolumes will override the effects of this module. There is a hierarchy of overriding: WorldInfo settings override module settings, and PostProcessVolumes override WorldInfo settings.
>
> If this property is not checked, the PostProcessEffect module settings are the only settings used for that particular effect, and WorldInfo settings and PostProcessVolumes are ignored.
>
> **EffectName**—This property simply contains the name of the module.
>
> **SceneDPG**—This property contains the Depth Priority Group to which the module belongs. Although the technical details behind Depth Priority Groups are a bit beyond the scope of this book, suffice it to say that all objects within a Depth Priority Group

can access each other's depth information. To keep things simple, you just need to remember that this property is usually set to DPG_PostProcess for most modules. If a material effect is being used that requires actual depth information from the world, then this property should be set to DPG_World.

TUTORIAL 8.2 builds upon **TUTORIAL 8.1**. Open the MyPostProcess package saved at the end of that tutorial, or open the PostProcessChapter package included on the DVD.

TUTORIAL 8.2: Creating a Super-heated Atmosphere Effect, Part I: Adding Effect Modules

1. Double-click the ppe_first_post_process object to open it in the Post Process Editor. If you're using the files included with the book, open ppe_first_post_process_1 instead. Delete the DOFAndBloomEffect module that is already present (see **FIGURE 8.18**). This gives us a clean slate to work with.

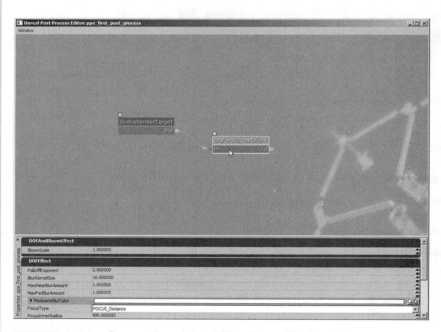

FIGURE 8.18   Remove the existing DOFAndBloomEffect module.

2. Right-click the background of the workspace and choose MaterialEffect from the context menu. A new MaterialEffect module appears in the workspace (see **FIGURE 8.19**).

3. Connect the output of the SceneRenderTarget module to the input of the MaterialEffect module (see **FIGURE 8.20**).

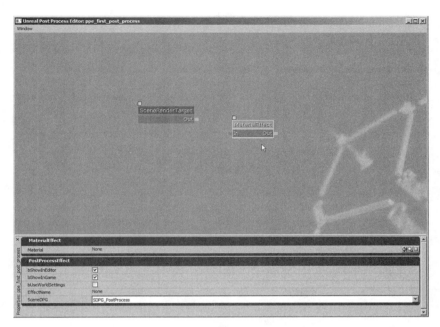

FIGURE 8.19   Create a new MaterialEffect module.

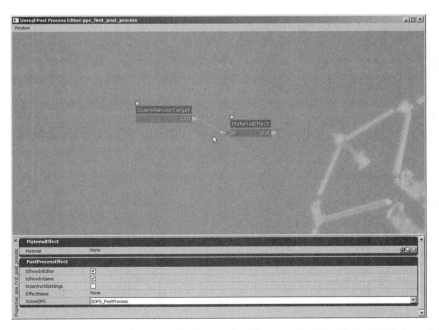

FIGURE 8.20   The SceneRenderTarget should connect to the MaterialEffect module.

4. Right-click the background again and choose MotionBlurEffect to place a new motion blur module (see **FIGURE 8.21**).

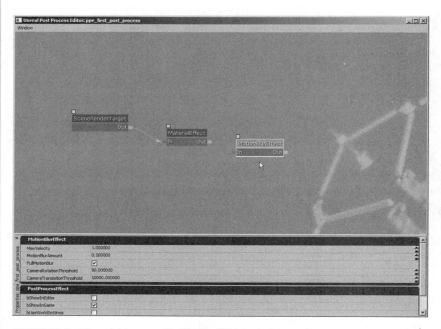

FIGURE 8.21   Add a new MotionBlurEffect module.

5. Connect the output of the MaterialEffect module to the input of the MotionBlurEffect module (see **FIGURE 8.22**).

6. Right-click once more on the background and choose UberPostProcessEffect to place the new module (see **FIGURE 8.23**).

8

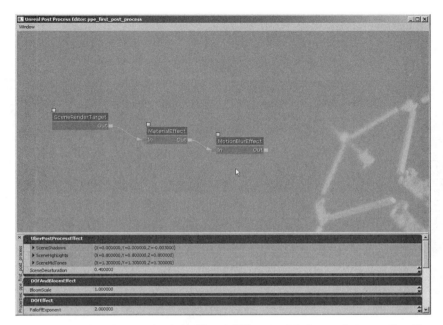

FIGURE 8.22   The result of the MaterialEffect module is now being motion blurred.

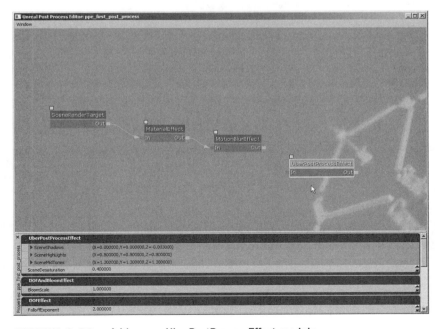

FIGURE 8.23   Add a new UberPostProcessEffect module.

7. Connect the output of the MotionBlurEffect module to the input of the UberPostProcessEffect module (see **FIGURE 8.24**). We now have all the effect nodes necessary to create our effect.

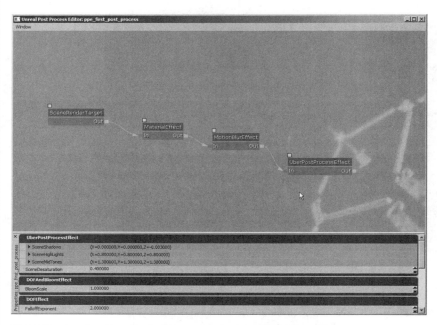

FIGURE 8.24   Your final effect network should look like this.

8. Save your package so you don't lose your changes.

END TUTORIAL 8.2

TUTORIAL 8.3 builds on **TUTORIAL 8.2**. Open the MyPostProcess package saved at the end of that tutorial or open the PostProcessChapter package included on the DVD.

TUTORIAL 8.3: Creating a Super-heated Atmosphere Effect, Part II: UberPostProcessEffect Properties

1. Double-click the ppe_first_post_process object to open it in the Post Process Editor. If you're using the files included with the book, open ppe_first_post_process_2 instead. Select the UberPostProcessEffect module and view its properties. Our goal is to skew the scene toward a reddish-orange tint to give it a heated look.

2. Expand SceneShadows and set the following values:

  ▸ **X**: 0.0

  ▸ **Y**: 0.25

  ▸ **Z**: 0.50

These values cause the green components of any pixel less than 0.25 and the blue components of any pixel below 0.5 to become 0.0, effectively limiting the amount of blue and green in the scene (see **FIGURE 8.25**).

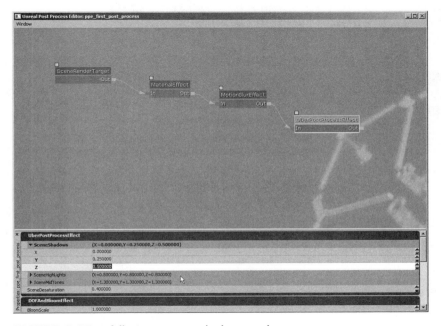

FIGURE 8.25   Adjust your scene shadows as shown.

3. Next, expand SceneHighlights and set these values:

  ▸ **X**: 0.5

  ▸ **Y**: 0.675

  ▸ **Z**: 1.0

These values cause the green components of any pixel greater than 0.675 and the red components of any pixel above 0.5 to become 1.0, effectively augmenting the amount of red and green in the screen (see **FIGURE 8.26**).

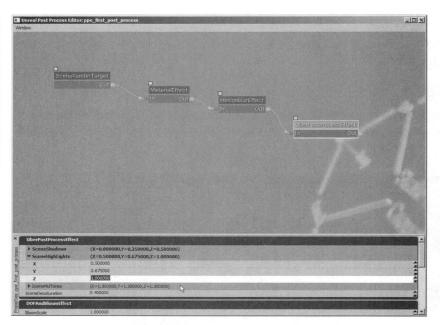

FIGURE 8.26   The SceneHighlights have now been adjusted.

4. Expand SceneMidTones and set the following:

   ▸ **X**: 0.8

   ▸ **Y**: 0.875

   ▸ **Z**: 1.0

5. Verify that SceneDesaturation is set to 0.4. This gives the scene a much more muted and natural look (see **FIGURE 8.27**).

6. Set the BloomScale property down to 0.5 for a little less glow.

7. Now we can start on the depth of field settings located in the DOFEffect section. Set the FalloffExponent to 1.0 to produce a linear falloff. When adjusting the BlurKernelSize, you should make sure to test it in a viewport that is representative of the dimensions at which your game will be played. We are going to use a value of 4.0. This means that each pixel can be blurred a maximum of four pixels in either direction, which can look drastically different on a small viewport in the editor than it might at full-screen settings.

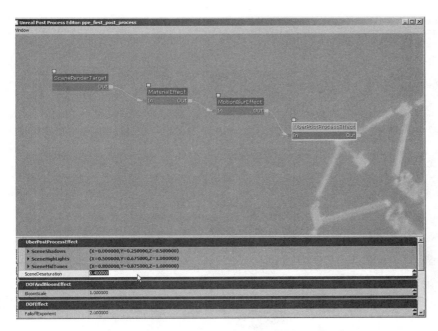

FIGURE 8.27   SceneDesaturation scales down the overall color.

8. Set the FocusDistance to 0.0 so the focus is located at the camera's location. Then set the FocusInnerRadius to 20480.0. That means that objects 20,480 units from the camera or farther are blurred the full amount (as defined by the next two properties).

9. Set the MaxNearBlurAmount to 0.0 (although it really doesn't matter in this case). This represents the amount of blur applied to objects behind the camera, but because of where the focus is located, it will never be seen. Set the MaxFarBlurAmount to 0.75 to give a good amount of blur to objects far away.

10. Make sure bShowInEditor and bShowInGame are both checked and save your package so you don't lose any of your changes. **FIGURE 8.28** shows the final effect.

FIGURE 8.28   You now have a depth of field blur effect visible.

END TUTORIAL 8.3

TUTORIAL 8.4 builds on **TUTORIAL 8.3**. Open the MyPostProcess package saved at the end of that tutorial or open the PostProcessChapter package included on the DVD.

You should note two things: First, **TUTORIAL 8.4** assumes a basic knowledge of the Material Editor. Second, a unique approach is taken in the creation of this material in that we create the material in the order in which the nodes appear when reading from right to left, rather than connecting one effect a piece at a time. This is done strictly for the purposes of speed.

TUTORIAL 8.4: Creating a Super-heated Atmosphere Effect, Part III: Depth-based Heat Wave Material: UV Distortion

1. In the Generic Browser, select the MyPostProcesses package, right-click the background, and choose New Material. Enter the following:

   ▸ **Package**: MyPostProcesses

   ▸ **Group**: Materials

   ▸ **Name**: mat_depth_heat

Click OK to complete the creation process. The Material Editor should open with the newly created material in it (see **FIGURE 8.29**). This material is going to distort the scene, but the amount of this distortion is dependent on the distance from the camera. Objects close to the camera will have less distortion applied than objects far away.

> **NOTE**
>
> Because the ppe_first_post_process is set as the default for the editor, you will notice that the preview window of the Material Editor is tinted as part of the post-process.

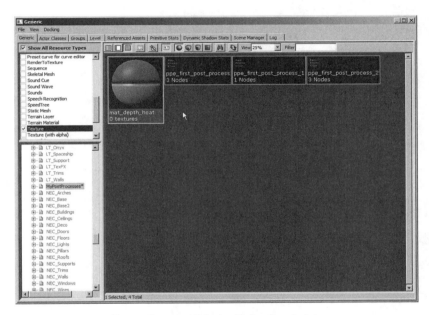

FIGURE 8.29 Create the new mat_depth_heat material.

2. We are going to start building the material from right to left. The first thing we need to do is add a TextureCoordinate expression. Right-click and choose TextureCoordinate (or drag it from the Material Expressions panel). This allows us to control the size of the heat distortion. In the TextureCoordinate expression's properties, set the UTiling and VTiling to 6.0 (see **FIGURE 8.30**). These can always be adjusted later on.

3. Add two Panner expressions to the left of the TextureCoordinate, one above the other. Connect the output of the TextureCoordinate to the Coordinate input of each of the Panner expressions (see **FIGURE 8.31**).

   In the properties of the top panner, set SpeedY to 0.2 and leave SpeedX at 0.0.

   In the properties of the bottom panner, set SpeedX to –0.375 and leave SpeedY at 0.0.

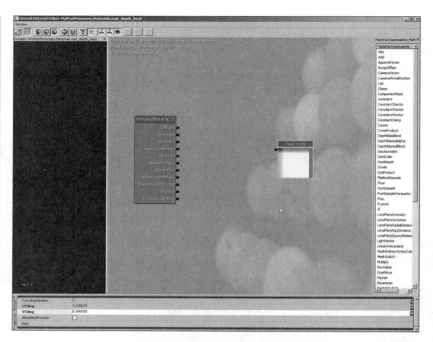

FIGURE 8.30   Begin with a TextureCoordinate, which will help adjust our overall tiling.

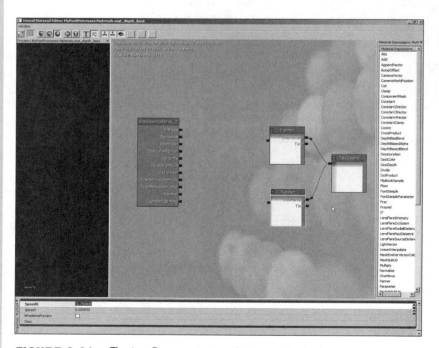

FIGURE 8.31   The two Panners are used to move the texture.

4. In the Generic Browser, open the PostProcessChapter package included on the DVD in the files for this chapter. Select the colored_clouds texture located in the Textures group package. Then, add a new TextureSample to the material. This TextureSample should have the selected texture applied to it automatically. Connect the output of the top Panner to the UVs input of the TextureSample (see **FIGURE 8.32**).

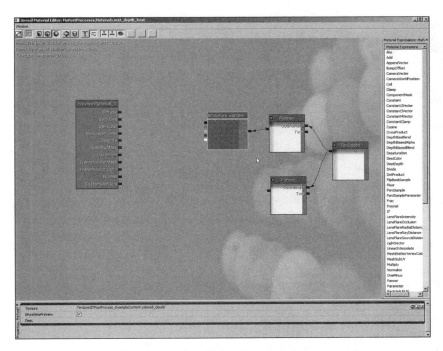

FIGURE 8.32   Bring in the colored_clouds texture and connect it as shown.

5. Add a ComponentMask expression to the left of the TextureSample and connect the RGB output of the TextureSample to the input of the ComponentMask expression. In the ComponentMask expression's properties, check the R and G boxes (see **FIGURE 8.33**).

6. Add an Add expression. Connect the output of the ComponentMask expression to the A input and connect the output of the bottom Panner to the B input (see **FIGURE 8.34**). Basically, we are using the random red and green values of the panning cloud texture to offset the texture coordinates output by the second panner, giving the normal map's output a random wavy appearance.

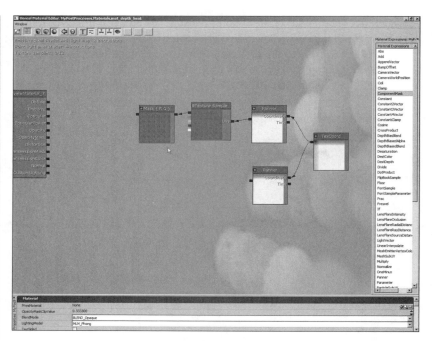

FIGURE 8.33   Bring in a new ComponentMask and connect it accordingly.

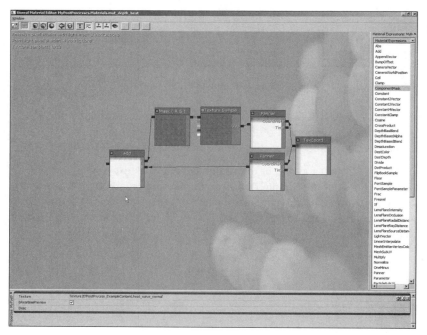

FIGURE 8.34   You are now adding the component mask and the panner.

7. Select the heat_wave_normal texture located in the Textures group of the PostProcessChapter package. Then, add a new TextureSample to the material. This TextureSample should have the selected texture applied to it automatically. Connect the output of the Add expression to the UVs input of the TextureSample (see **FIGURE 8.35**).

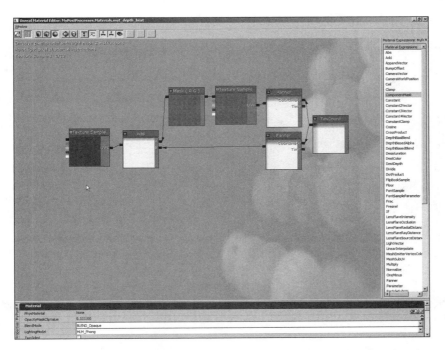

FIGURE 8.35   The network is now being used to perturb the UVs of a normal map.

That is the basis for the distortion. In **TUTORIAL 8.5**, the output will be used to add noise to the actual texture coordinates that are passed to our SceneTexture.

NOTE

At this point, we have made no connections to the actual material node!

8. Save the changes to the material and save your package thus far.

END TUTORIAL 8.4

TUTORIAL 8.5 builds upon **TUTORIAL 8.4**. Open the MyPostProcess package saved at the end of that tutorial or open the PostProcessChapter package included on the DVD.

TUTORIAL 8.5: Creating a Super-heated Atmosphere Effect, Part IV: Depth-based Heat Wave Material: UV Distortion, Cont.

1. Continue by opening the mat_depth_heat material from **TUTORIAL 8.4** in the Material Editor, or open mat_depth_heat_1, included in the MyPostProcess package within the files for this chapter (see **FIGURE 8.36**).

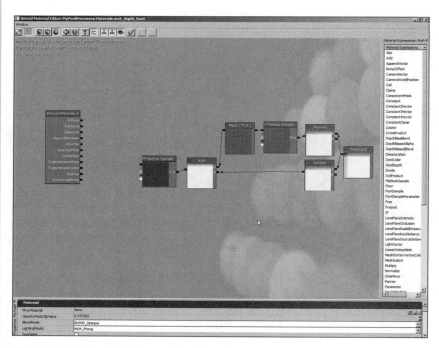

FIGURE 8.36   This figure shows the current progress of our material.

2. Add a Constant expression above the normal map TextureSample. Set the Constant expression's R property to 0.0175 (see **FIGURE 8.37**).

3. Add a Multiply expression and connect the RGB output of the normal map TextureSample and the output of the Constant expression to the Multiply expression's A and B inputs. The order doesn't matter, but keeping links from crossing is usually preferred for clarity (see **FIGURE 8.38**).

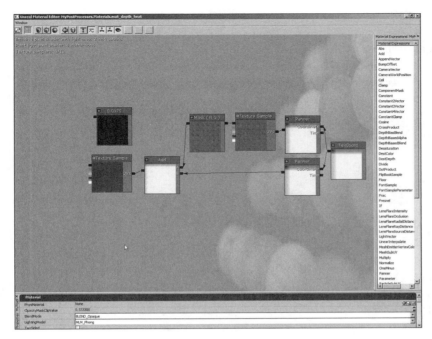

FIGURE 8.37   Create a new Constant expression.

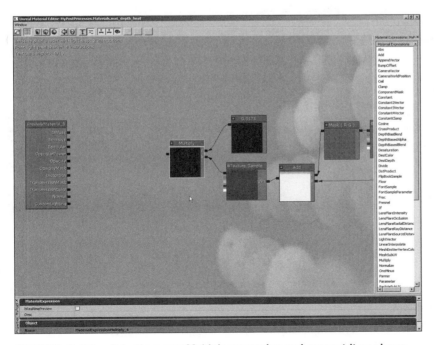

FIGURE 8.38   Bring in a new Multiply expression and connect it as shown.

4. Add a ComponentMask expression to the left of the Multiply expression and connect the output of the Multiply to the input of the ComponentMask (see **FIGURE 8.39**). In the ComponentMask expression's properties, check the R and G boxes.

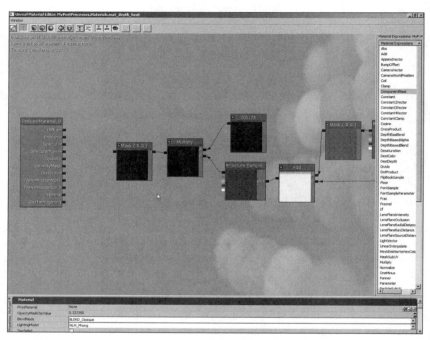

FIGURE 8.39   Connect in a new ComponentMask expression.

5. Add a ScreenPosition expression above the Multiply expression. In its properties, check the ScreenAlign box (see **FIGURE 8.40**).

6. Select the ComponentMask expression you just added and copy it (Ctrl+C and Ctrl+V). Move it to the left of the ScreenPosition expression and connect the ScreenPosition expression's output to the new ComponentMask expression's input (see **FIGURE 8.41**).

8

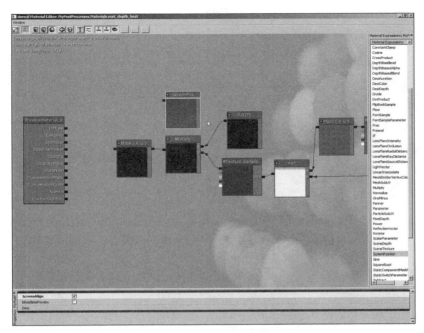

FIGURE 8.40 The new ScreenPosition has been added.

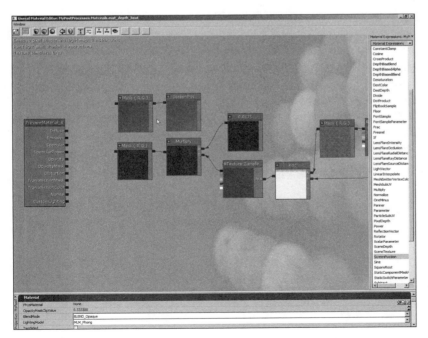

FIGURE 8.41 Duplicate and connect a new ComponentMask.

7. Add an Add expression and connect the outputs of the two ComponentMask expressions to the A and B inputs (see **FIGURE 8.42**). Again, order is not important.

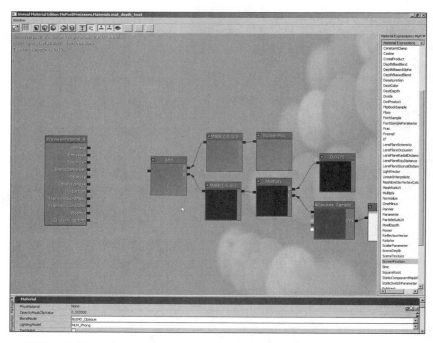

FIGURE 8.42   The component masks are now being combined.

8. Select the Constant-Multiply-ComponentMask-Add chain of expressions and copy them (Ctrl+C and Ctrl+V). Move the duplicates up above the ScreenPosition-ComponentMask chain. Reconnect the normal map's RGB output to the new Multiply's B input, and connect the output of the ComponentMask linked to the ScreenPosition expression to the empty input of the Add expression (see **FIGURE 8.43**). You can reorder the inputs if you wish so the links do not cross.

9. Select the Constant on the top and set its R property to 0.00625.

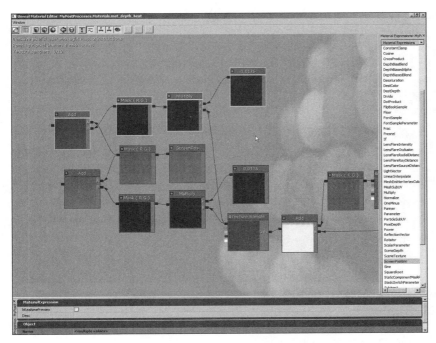

FIGURE 8.43   Duplicate and connect a new ComponentMask.

END TUTORIAL 8.5

That completes the distortion setup. Next, we will create the depth component, which is used to interpolate between the two versions of our scene.

TUTORIAL 8.6 builds on **TUTORIAL 8.5**. Open the MyPostProcess package saved at the end of that tutorial or open the PostProcessChapter package included on the DVD.

TUTORIAL 8.6: Creating a Super-heated Atmosphere Effect, Part V: Depth-based Heat Wave Material: Depth Component

1. Continue by opening the mat_depth_heat material from **TUTORIAL 8.5** in the Material Editor, or open mat_depth_heat_2, included in the MyPostProcess package within the files for this chapter (see **FIGURE 8.44**).

2. To create a depth-based effect, we need to know the depth of the objects in the scene. Add a SceneDepth expression below the existing expressions in the material (see **FIGURE 8.45**). This will give us access to the depth of each pixel in the rendered scene.

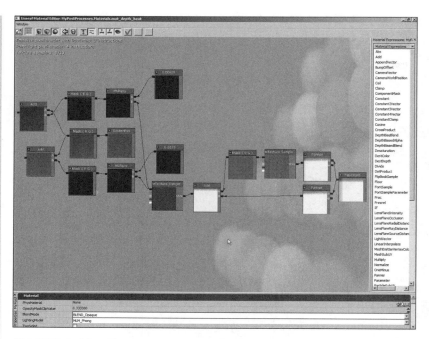

FIGURE 8.44   The current progress of our material.

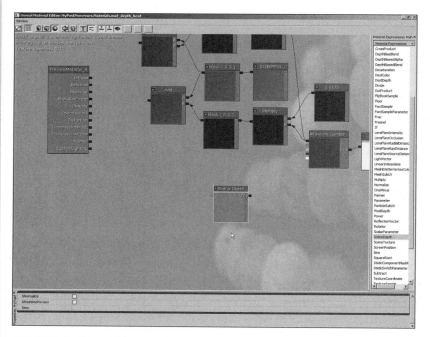

FIGURE 8.45   Add a new SceneDepth expression.

Now, we need to establish a range for the depth. In order for us to use the depth as the alpha input of a LinearInterpolate expression, it needs to be limited to a range of 0 to 1. However, the SceneDepth is going to output depths in Unreal units, which are much larger than 1. We need to map the desired range of depths to the 0-to-1 range to get the proper effect.

3. Add a Constant expression just below the SceneDepth expression and set its R property to 32768 (see **FIGURE 8.46**). This represents the depth mapped to 1, or the distance from the camera where the full amount of distortion is applied.

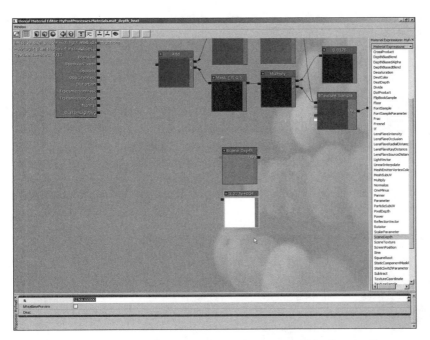

FIGURE 8.46   The new Constant represents our max distortion depth.

4. Add a Divide expression to the left of the SceneDepth expression. Connect the output of the SceneDepth to the A input of the Divide Expression. Then, connect the output of the Constant to the B input of the Divide expression (see **FIGURE 8.47**). Now you should be able to see that when a value of 32768 is output from the SceneDepth and divided by the Constant set to 32768, a value of 1 is output from the Divide expression.

5. That is all well and good, but we don't want values higher than 1 being passed to the LinearInterpolate expression we use in **TUTORIAL 8.7**. Luckily, there is an expression just for this situation. Add a Clamp expression to the left of the Divide expression. Connect the output of the Divide expression to the top input of the Clamp expression (see **FIGURE 8.48**).

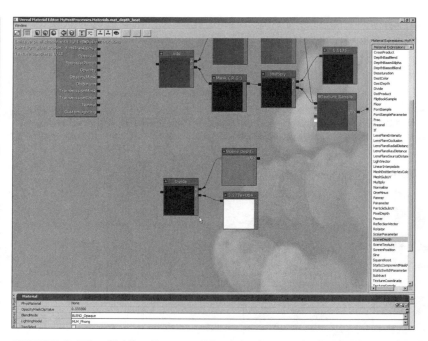

FIGURE 8.47 Dividing the current depth by the max depth provides us with a number we can use for linear interpolation later.

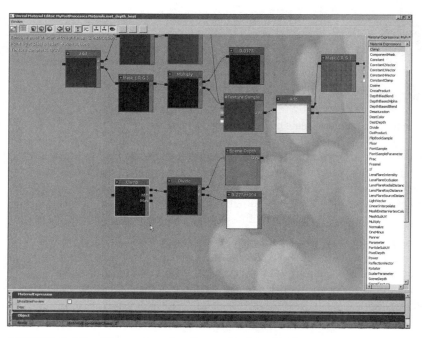

FIGURE 8.48 We are clamping the result of the Divide.

6. Notice the Clamp expression has two more inputs: Min and Max. These allow you to set the values to clamp the top input to. Create a Constant below the Divide expression and connect its output to the Min input of the Clamp expression (see **FIGURE 8.49**). This creates a lower limit of 0. Technically, this is not entirely necessary because the SceneDepth shouldn't pass a negative value, but it is better to be safe.

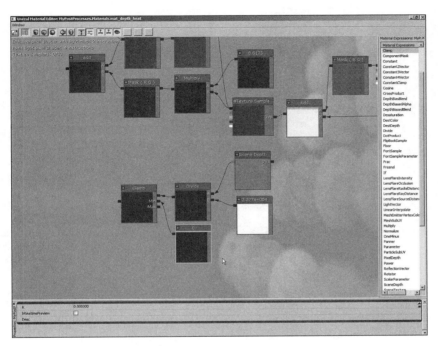

FIGURE 8.49   The Min clamp is now set to 0 by the Constant.

7. Add another Constant expression just below the last Constant expression. Set its R property to 1 and connect its output to the Max input of the Clamp expression (see **FIGURE 8.50**). Now, there should never be a value output from the Clamp expression lower than 0 or higher than 1.

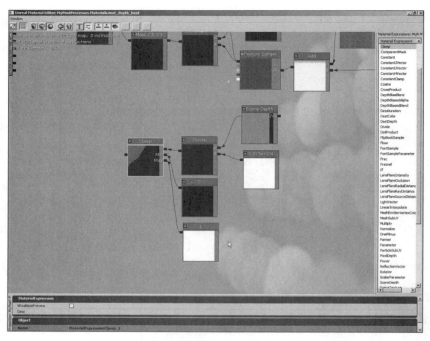

FIGURE 8.50   The max of the clamp is now 1.

END TUTORIAL 8.6

TUTORIAL 8.7 builds on **TUTORIAL 8.6**. Open the MyPostProcess package saved at the end of that tutorial or open the PostProcessChapter package included on the DVD.

TUTORIAL 8.7: Creating a Super-heated Atmosphere Effect, Part VI: Depth-based Heat Wave Material: SceneTexture Interpolation

1. Continue by opening the mat_depth_heat material from **TUTORIAL 8.6** in the Material Editor, or open mat_depth_heat_3, included in the MyPostProcess package within the files for this chapter (see **FIGURE 8.51**).

2. Here is where we put all the parts together to create a coherent effect. The main ingredient to any material post-process effect is the rendered scene. Add a SceneTexture expression to the left of the top Add expression from the distortion tutorials. Connect the output of the Add expression to the UVs input of the SceneTexture (see **FIGURE 8.52**).

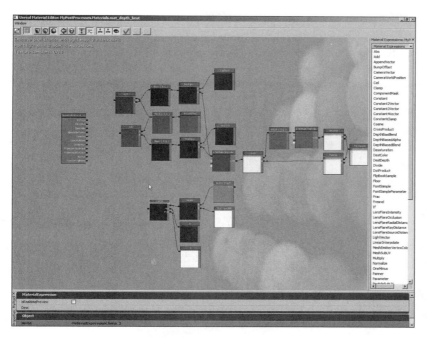

FIGURE 8.51   Our material's progress so far.

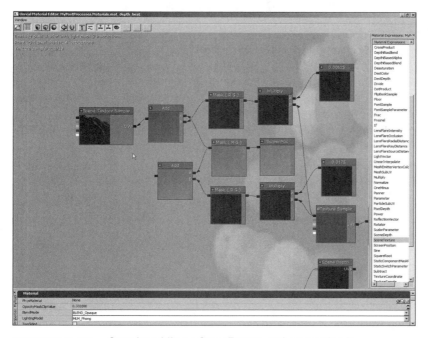

FIGURE 8.52   Start by adding a SceneTexture and connecting it.

3. Make a copy of the SceneTexture expression (Ctrl+C and Ctrl+V) and move it to the left of the bottom Add expression from the distortion tutorials. Connect the output of the Add expression to the UVs input of the SceneTexture expression (see **FIGURE 8.53**).

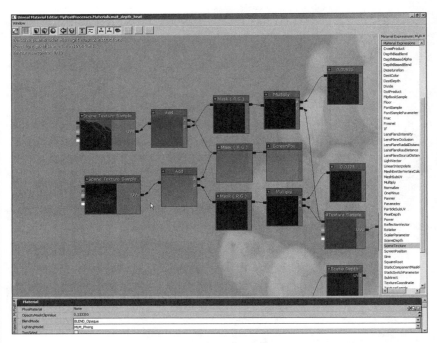

FIGURE 8.53   Duplicate and connect the SceneTexture expression.

4. We need some way to blend, or interpolate, between these two textures. Add a LinearInterpolate expression to the left of the SceneTexture expressions. Connect the RGB output of the top SceneTexture expression to the A input of the LinearInterpolate Expression. Then, connect the RGB output of the bottom SceneTexture expression to the B input of the LinearInterpolate expression (see **FIGURE 8.54**).

5. Connect the output from the Clamp expression to the Alpha input of the LinearInterpolate expression (see **FIGURE 8.55**).

8

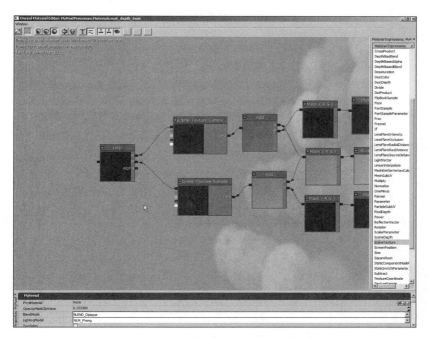

FIGURE 8.54 We are now interpolating between the two SceneTextures.

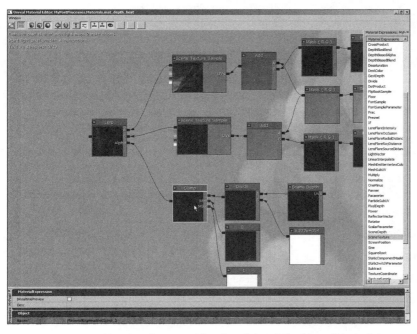

FIGURE 8.55 Use the clamp to drive the alpha of the LinearInterpolate.

6. Connect the output of the LinearInterpolate expression to the Emissive channel of the material node (see **FIGURE 8.56**). Material effects solely use the Emissive channel. If

> **NOTE**
>
> When the final connection is made, the material may turn white when rotated in the preview window.

nothing is connected to the Emissive channel, the scene that's passed out of the MaterialEffect node will be completely black.

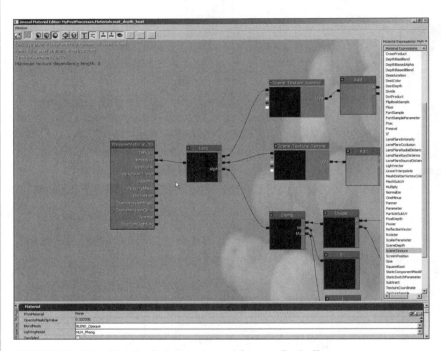

FIGURE 8.56   Use the Emissive channel for your final effect.

7. Select the Material node, and set the LightingModel property to MLM_Unlit. Finally, apply the changes to the material and close the Material Editor.

8. In the Generic Browser, double-click the ppe_first_post_process post-process effect to open it in the Post Process Editor and select the MaterialEffect module to view its properties. Set the following:

- ▶ **bShowInEditor**: True
- ▶ **bShowInGame**: True
- ▶ **SceneDPG**: SDPG_World

> **NOTE**
>
> If you have not completed **TUTORIALS 8.1** through **8.6** and are using the files included with the chapter, you will need to open ppe_first_post_process_3.

9. Select the mat_depth_heat_ material in the Generic Browser and apply it to the Material property of the MaterialEffect module. You should see the heat wave effect in the perspective viewport now, along with the red tint from the UberPostProcessEffect module (see **FIGURE 8.57**).

> **NOTE**
>
> Unless you have altered the UTEngine.ini file as shown in **TUTORIAL 8.1**, you will not see any effect! Also, when you're finished with the effect and want to set Unreal Editor's post-process back to its defaults, be sure to close Unreal Editor, delete the UTEngine.ini file, and then restart Unreal Editor.

FIGURE 8.57   The final effect is now visible.

10. Save your package so your changes are not lost.

END TUTORIAL 8.7

Controlling Post-Process Effects In-Game

Four primary methods are available to alter post-process effects during gameplay. They are via Kismet, Matinee, PostProcessVolume, and script. This particular book does not cover the use of UnrealScript, so we will briefly cover the benefits and limitations of the first three options only.

Kismet

As a powerful visual scripting system, Kismet allows for a great deal of control over various material parameters, which is extremely useful in terms of post-processing effects, especially where material effects are concerned. However, Kismet does not allow the user to control the post-process settings of the player's camera or any cinematic cameras.

This is not to say that you cannot change the post-process effect using Kismet. As mentioned, the ability to adjust settings of material effects provides tremendous control. All you need do is apply a material to a post-process effect and then use Kismet to make changes to that material.

Matinee

Matinee provides the ability to control the post-process settings of cameras through the Float and Vector property tracks. This allows you to tweak various aspects of your post-process effect while a Matinee sequence is going on, which is useful for specialized cinematic sequences.

For more information and an in-depth discussion of using Matinee to control camera settings, see Chapter 10, "Creating Cinematic Sequences."

PostProcessVolumes

One of the most common means of applying post-process effects in areas of a level is to use a PostProcessVolume. A PostProcessVolume allows you to set or alter the post-process settings for a specific area (or areas) of the level. This can be very useful for adding blur underwater and any variety of location-specific effects.

For more information on volumes and a tutorial involving a PostProcessVolume, see Chapter 3, "Working with Volumes."

Summary

8

This chapter has introduced you to a variety of different methods for creating and controlling post-processes in *Unreal Tournament 3*. You will find that post-processes are used widely in many Unreal Engine 3 games to add a variety of feelings to the levels and to increase the visual ambiance of the gaming experience. They can also be used to create the same level of control used by film directors for cinematic sequences—for instance, depth of field can be used to create a camera focus type of effect. From here, you should experiment with what you have learned and find ways to apply different post-process effects to your game levels!

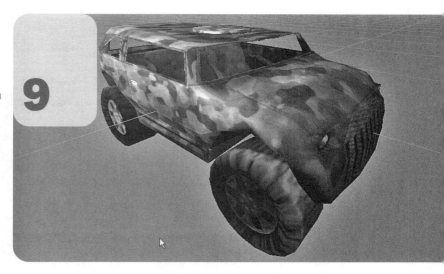

Chapter 9

The Unreal Animation System

When you see a character run across a playing field in a game, you are looking at a polygonal mesh that is changing shape as the character runs. This deformation allows the mesh to move as if it were a human being—or any other kind of character. This is also true of vehicles that have moving parts such as flight control surfaces, turning wheels, suspension, and so on. The animation system within Unreal is responsible for handling this deformation and turning otherwise static models into living and moving elements in your game or project (see **FIGURE 9.1**).

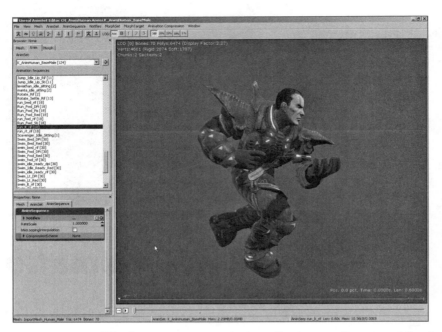

FIGURE 9.1   This character appears to be in motion because bones are deforming the mesh.

The Unreal Animation System

The deformation used by the animation system can come from two primary sources: keyframed animation or blending keyframed animation together to form new animations. Keyframed animation comes in three different types, most of which will be relatively familiar to anyone with experience in 3D animation. These are skeletally based keyframed animation, multimesh morphing, and lip-synching animations created within the FaceFX system. The first two options are typically performed in external applications such as 3ds Max and Maya. We discuss these options early in this chapter. FaceFX is an integrated application within UnrealEd that allows for complex lip-synching animations. FaceFX has its own dedicated section in this chapter, titled "Facial Animation with FaceFX."

All animation applied to a character is done so additively, meaning multiple animations that are affecting different bones can be played simultaneously. For example, you could have one animation where a character is using her arms to reload a weapon, and another where she is using her legs to run forward. You could play both of these animations at the same time, thus allowing the character to run and reload simultaneously.

9

Animation blending is also supported, allowing one animation to flow smoothly into another, or for animations to be combined to form new animations. This blending can take place based on a series of gameplay factors, such as speed and direction. We discuss animation blending later in the "Animation Blending" section.

TUTORIAL 9.1: Setting Up a Basic Animated Skeletal Mesh

1. Open the DM-CH_09_CargoDoor_Begin map. This map is made up of two rooms with an opening between them. Position the camera so that it is facing the opening from the room that is positioned higher (see **FIGURE 9.2**).

FIGURE 9.2   You want the camera to be positioned so that you can see the level like so.

2. Select the CargoBayDoor skeletal mesh from the Chapter_09_Animation package in the Generic Browser. Then, right-click the floor of the room and choose Add Actor > Add SkeletalMesh: SkeletalMesh Chapter_09_Animation.Meshes.CargoBayDoor.

3. Position the new SkeletalMeshActor so that it fits in the opening between the rooms. No rotation should be needed, although a Grid Snap setting of 8 will make it easier (see **FIGURE 9.3**).

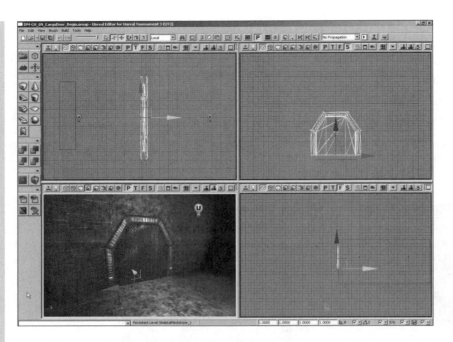

FIGURE 9.3   The CargoBayDoor should close the gap between the rooms.

   4. Press F4 to open the skeletal mesh actor's properties and set the following:

   ▸ **Collision**

       ▸ **CollisionType**: COLLIDE_BlockAll

   ▸ **SkeletalMeshActor**

       ▸ **SkeletalMeshComponent**

       ▸ **bHasPhysicsAssetInstance**: True

       ▸ **PhysicsAsset**: Select the CargoBayDoor_Physics physics asset in the Browser and click Use Current Selection in Browser.

   5. Place a Trigger to one side of the door by right-clicking the floor and choosing Add Actor > Add Trigger. Open the Trigger's properties, expand the Advanced section, and set the following (see **FIGURE 9.4**):

       ▸ **bHidden**: False

   6. With the Trigger selected in the viewport, open Kismet. Right-click and choose New Event Using Trigger_0 > Used. Set the following properties for the Used event:

       ▸ **bAimToInteract**: False

       ▸ **InteractDistance**: 192.0

       ▸ **MaxTriggerCount**: 0

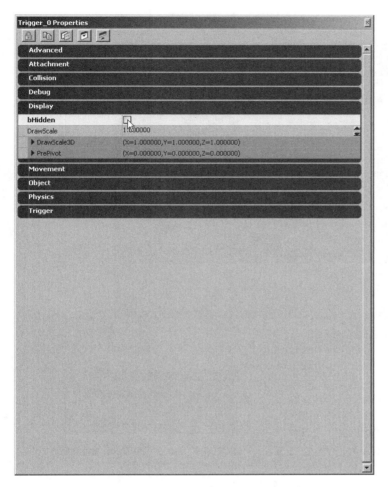

FIGURE 9.4   The Trigger is now visible during gameplay.

7. Select the cargo bay door skeletal mesh actor in the viewport and return to Kismet. Create a new Matinee sequence by right-clicking and choosing New Matinee. Double-click the Matinee object to open the Matinee Editor (see **FIGURE 9.5**).

8. Right-click in the Group List and choose Add New Empty Group. Name the new group **BayDoor**. In the group's properties, add a slot to the GroupAnimSets array by clicking the Add New Item button. Select the AnimSet_cargo_bay_door animation set in the Generic Browser and click Use Current Selection in Browser for slot [0].

9. Right-click the BayDoor group and choose Add New Anim Control Track. With the time slider at Time=0.0, press Enter to place a new key. Choose the Open animation from the dropdown list that appears (see **FIGURE 9.6**).

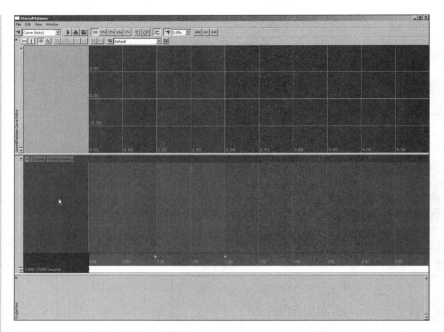

FIGURE 9.5   The Matinee Editor appears.

10. Drag the red Sequence marker at the end of the Matinee sequence to be even with the end of the Open animation so that the sequence ends when the animation ends (see **FIGURE 9.7**).

FIGURE 9.6   The Open animation now plays at time index 0.0.

11. Connect the Out output of the Used event of the trigger to the Play input of the Matinee sequence so that the animation plays when the trigger is used.

12. Test your level. The animation should play when the trigger is used for the first time.

13. If you want to extend this example on your own, you could try to set up a network in Kismet that alternates playing the animation forward and backward each time the trigger is used to simulate the door opening and closing. You could also make it so the direction of the animation cannot be reversed until it is finished playing in its current direction.

14. You may save your work, although we do not use this example in later tutorials.

9

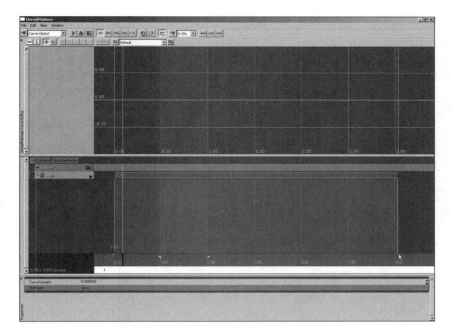

FIGURE 9.7   You want to end the Matinee sequence when the animation is over.

END TUTORIAL 9.1

Skeletal Animation

Skeletal animation is the process of moving the vertices of a model using a hierarchy of digital bones that form a skeletal system within the character. The vertices are then attached to the skeleton through a weighted influence system, allowing particular bones to have a certain percentage of control over each vertex. This weighted influence system allows for smooth bending at the joints rather than harsh changes in direction. The result of this joining of a mesh and a skeleton is referred to as a *skeletal mesh* within Unreal (see **FIGURE 9.8**).

The positions and rotations of the bones are animated inside an external 3D application such as 3ds Max or Maya. The animation is *not* performed within UnrealEd. When animating a skeleton for a character or object, an artist typically uses a system of custom-created controls to drive the bones. The control system that drives the skeleton of a character or object is commonly called a *control rig*. By animating the pieces of the rig, much like controlling a digital puppet, you can animate the skeleton, which in turn drives the vertices of the mesh. You can create animations of a character running, jumping, fighting, and so on, in a manner that is much faster than if the vertices of the mesh had to be moved by hand.

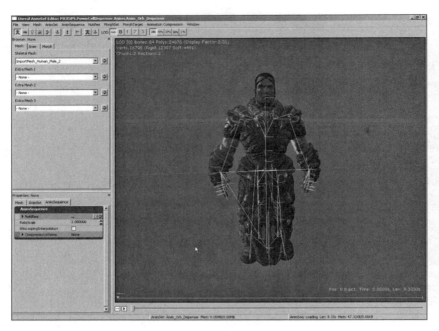

FIGURE 9.8   Here you can see the bones of a character as shown in the AnimSet Editor.

When finished, this skeletal mesh—consisting of the actual mesh itself along with the skeleton that is controlling it—is then imported into Unreal. However, the skeletal mesh is imported separately from its animation. The animation only consists of the positional and rotational changes that take place from one bone to the next. Any rigging or control objects that were driving the skeleton in the 3D package are disregarded. The benefit of separating the skeletal mesh from its animation is that many different objects—such as different characters—can be driven with a single set of animations, rather than having to create a different animation set for each individual object of the same type.

Skeletal Meshes

Examples of skeletal meshes within Unreal include characters, vehicles, and weapons. As mentioned earlier, skeletal meshes are meshes that are attached to a hierarchy of bones. This attachment process is known as *skinning* and is generally handled within an external 3D package. Each vertex of a skeletal mesh receives a percentage of total influence from the different bones around it. For example, a vertex located directly in the center of a character's forearm might receive 100% of its total influence from the forearm bone, because wherever that bone goes, you want the forearm to follow. However, a vertex located at the elbow of the character would receive part of its influence from the forearm bone and part from the bone of the upper arm. This ability to assign different weights to individual vertices allows for smooth transitions of deformation from one bone to the other (see **FIGURE 9.9**).

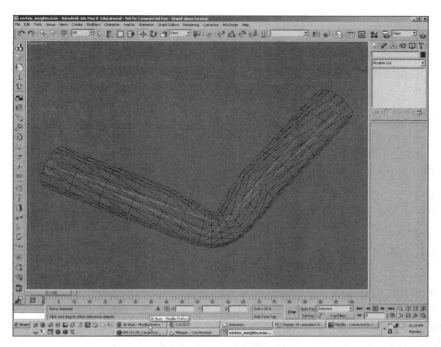

FIGURE 9.9   This object is deforming smoothly because the vertices at the joint are receiving varying percentages of influence from the bones.

Chunks and Sections

For the purposes of skinning inside of Unreal and also for controlling how the mesh is rendered, all skeletal meshes are broken down into individual segments. These segments come in two distinct types, called chunks and sections.

A *section* is made up of all the polygons of the mesh that have the same material applied to them. As you may know, you can apply multiple materials to your meshes in Unreal. A mesh that has three separate materials applied to it is made up of three different sections.

Sections are further divided into smaller segments, based on the number of bones that have some influence over that mesh section. These segments are known as *chunks*. Each chunk can consist of, at most, 75 bones. It should be noted that only bones that have some vertex weighting applied to them are taken into account. Any bone that does not influence the deformation of the mesh is disregarded and is not used in the creation of chunks.

Chunks and sections are important because the more of them your skeletal mesh has, the longer it takes to render to the screen. Therefore, it is important to keep the number of chunks and sections as low as possible. This can be done by using as few materials on the mesh as possible and using as few bones as will give your mesh the appropriate flexibility. For example, a mesh that has several different materials can often have those materials condensed down to only one if proper texturing practices are used. Developing a thorough understanding of the skinning tools in your native 3D application can help you get the deformation you need on your objects without the need for too many bones.

TUTORIAL 9.2: Importing and Viewing Skeletal Meshes and Animations

1. Open the Generic Browser and go to File > Import. In the file browser that appears, navigate to and select the skelMesh_truck_base_LOD.psk file, included on the DVD in the files for this chapter. In the Import window that appears, enter the following information and click OK:

   ▸ **Package**: Chapter_09_Animation

   ▸ **Group**: Meshes

   ▸ **Name**: skelMesh_truck

2. Double-click the skelMesh_truck object in the Generic Browser to open it in the AnimSet Editor (see **FIGURE 9.10**).

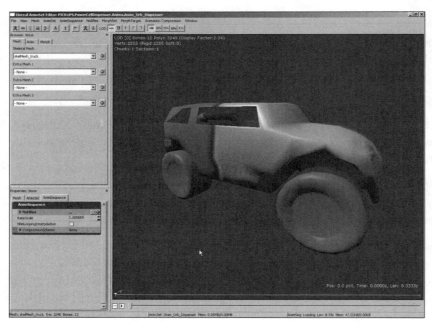

FIGURE 9.10   The new vehicle appears in the AnimSet Editor.

3. The truck has the default material applied to it, which we fix now. In the Generic Browser, select the mat_truck material from the AnimationChapter package. In the AnimSet Editor,

click the Mesh tab in the Properties panel and expand the Materials array. Click the Use Current Selection in Browser ⛯ button for the first, and only, slot in the array. The mesh should now be displayed with the camouflage material applied (see **FIGURE 9.11**).

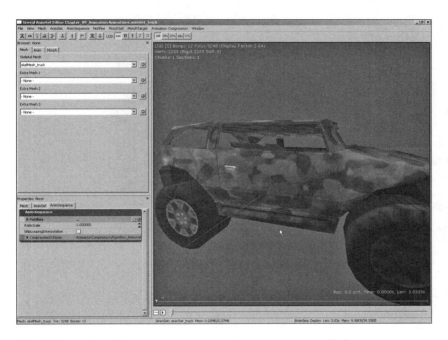

FIGURE 9.11   The appropriate material has now been applied.

4. Next, we import some animations for the mesh. While still in the AnimSet Editor, go to File > New AnimSet. This creates a new container for the animations we import. In the New AnimSet dialog that appears, enter the following information:

- ▶ **Package**: Chapter_09_Animation
- ▶ **Group**: Animations
- ▶ **Name**: animSet_truck

5. Click the Anim tab of the Browser panel and make sure the AnimSet we just created is selected. Then, go back to the File menu and choose Import PSA. In the file browser that appears, navigate to and select the skelMesh_truck.psa file.

The animSet_truck animation set should be populated with four animation sequences: deploy, deployed, retract, and retracted (see **FIGURE 9.12**).

If you try to play the animations now, no animation will be played. This is because these animations are using translation, which is ignored by default. We need to add the bones we wish to use translation on to the UseTranslationBoneNames array in the AnimSet tab of the Properties panel.

FIGURE 9.12   The animations have now been added to the vehicle.

6. Select the AnimSet tab and click the Add New Item button  for the UseTranslationBoneNames array three times to add three slots to the array. Enter the following names in the three slots:

   ▶ **[0]**: Dummy01

   ▶ **[1]**: Dummy02

   ▶ **[2]**: Dummy03

7. Select the deploy animation in the Anim tab and click the Play button in the Preview panel. The animation should begin to play. Make sure you are viewing the rear of the truck because that is where the animation occurs (see **FIGURE 9.13**).

8. Open the Animation Compression dialog from the Animation Compression menu or click the Animation Compression button on the Toolbar. Select the Remove Every Second Key option from the list and set the following options:

   ▶ **bStartAtSecondKey**: true

   ▶ **RotationCompressionFormat**: ACF_Fixed48NoW

   You shouldn't notice any visual difference in the animations after performing the compression. If there were noticeable visual anomalies, you would want to use a less aggressive compression scheme.

9

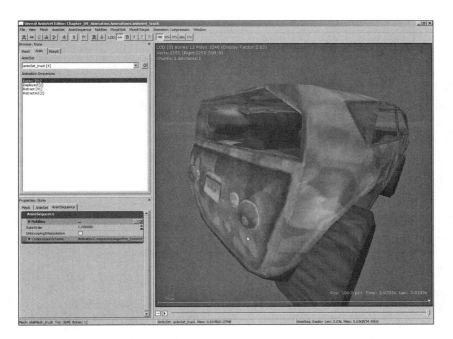

FIGURE 9.13   The rocket launcher should now pop up.

9. Save the Chapter_09_Animation package to preserve your changes.

END TUTORIAL 9.2

Levels of Detail

In terms of skeletal meshes, levels of detail (*LODs* for short) work very much the same way as they do for static meshes. In essence, LODs provide you a way to swap out your skeletal mesh for a simpler mesh based on the object's distance from the camera—or to be more precise, its given screen size. By making a mesh simpler as it gets farther away (or as it gets smaller, depending on how you want to look at it), you can greatly increase the performance of your object. Think about it: If a character is half a mile away in your game, it is only a few pixels in size on the screen. If you're only using a few pixels, then showing a multithousand-polygon character would be inefficient; you couldn't see the detail anyway.

Each level of detail can have its own mesh, as well as its own skeleton. This allows you to create entirely simpler versions of your object that are divided into fewer sections and chunks, which results in shorter rendering times. Each subsequent LOD mesh is simpler (or has fewer vertices) than any meshes for higher levels of detail. Each subsequent LOD skeleton can have fewer bones, but in order to keep animations from breaking, bone names should remain consistent. We discuss in detail the process of importing and editing LOD meshes through the AnimSet Editor later in this chapter.

As we continue setting up our vehicle from **TUTORIAL 9.2**, the mesh is looking nice and animating properly. However, because this is a vehicle and is therefore likely to be able to travel far away from the camera, it would be valuable to cut down the cost of rendering the mesh when it is in the distance. Up close, the amount of polygons in the mesh is necessary to retain visual fidelity, but at a distance there is no need to render that many polygons. In fact, it would be a waste of resources. To combat this issue, we use level of detail meshes that can be switched in and out based on how large the mesh is on the screen in **TUTORIAL 9.3**.

TUTORIAL 9.3: Importing and Setting Up Levels of Detail

1. Continuing from **TUTORIAL 9.2**, double-click the skelMesh_truck to open it in the AnimSet Editor. If you have not completed it, you may use the skelMesh_truck_01 asset located in the Chapter_09_Animation package.

2. Select Import LOD Mesh from the File menu. In the file browser that appears, navigate to and select the skelMesh_truck_lod_1.psk file. Select 1 from the Choose LOD Level dialog that appears next. If successful, you should be greeted with a dialog informing you that "Mesh From LOD 1 Imported Successfully!" Simply click OK to continue (see **FIGURE 9.14**).

FIGURE 9.14   This dialog lets you know that the import process went smoothly.

3. There won't be any immediately apparent change. In order to see the new level of detail, it either needs to be set up in the mesh's properties or forced active through the Toolbar. We set up the LODs in the properties once they are all imported. For now, click the Force LOD 1 button from the Toolbar. The mesh should snap to displaying the mesh just imported (see **FIGURE 9.15**).

> **TIP**
>
> The changes are more apparent when viewing the mesh in the wireframe render mode.

4. Choose Import LOD Mesh from the File menu again. This time, navigate to and select the skelMesh_truck_lod_2.psk file from the file browser. Select 2 from the Choose LOD Level dialog that appears. Again, if the operation is successful, the dialog appears informing you of this fact. Click OK.

5. You can now view the LOD 2 mesh as you did previously with the LOD 1 mesh. Switching back and forth between the available levels gives you a good idea of the changes between them (see **FIGURE 9.16**).

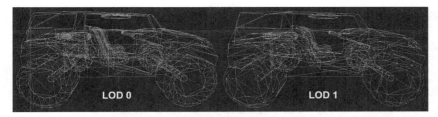

FIGURE 9.15   Notice the difference between the polygonal densities of the two meshes.

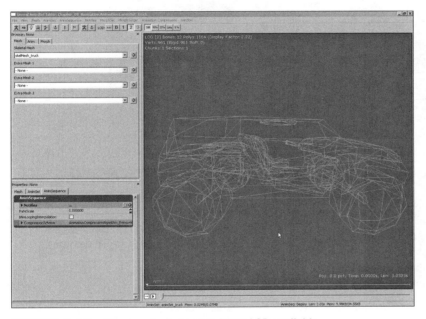

FIGURE 9.16   You now have an even lower LOD available.

6. We can now set up the properties for the levels of detail to tell each mesh when it is to be rendered. Select the Mesh tab of the Properties panel and expand the LODInfo array. You should see three slots in the array corresponding to the three levels of detail of the mesh (see **FIGURE 9.17**).

7. Expand each of the slots so all the properties are visible. The properties for the base LOD (slot [0]) will work fine. Leave them as they are.

8. Set the DisplayFactor for slot [1] to 0.375. This tells the mesh to use this LOD's mesh when the display factor is less than or equal to 0.375. You can test this by zooming in and out in the Preview panel and paying attention to the Display Factor value in the HUD. When it crosses the threshold at 0.375, it should snap to using the new mesh.

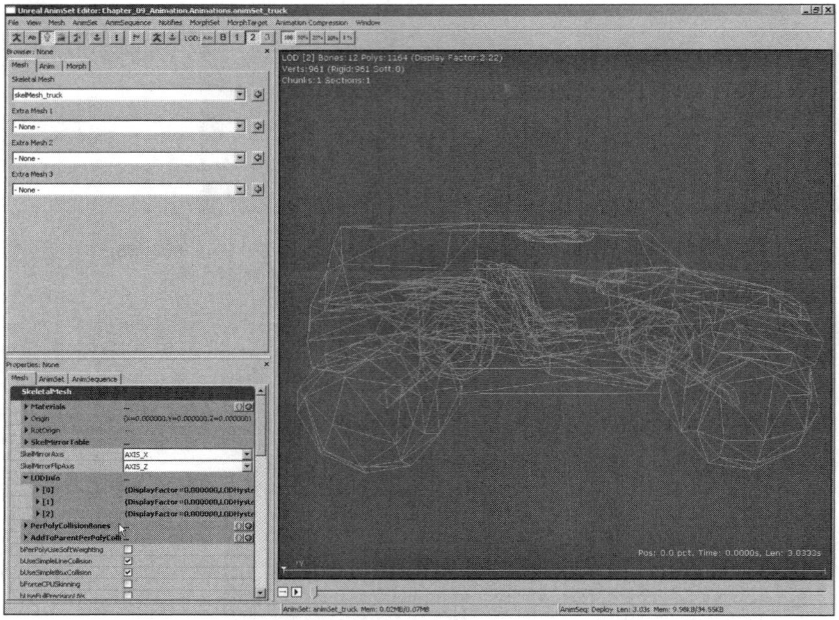

FIGURE 9.17   The three slots appear like so.

9. Set the DisplayFactor for slot [2] to 0.2. Again, this tells the mesh to use this LOD's mesh when the display factor of the mesh is less than or equal to 0.2. Test this out in the Preview panel as before.

> **NOTE**
>
> You must have the Set LOD Auto button toggled on in the Toolbar to observe this in the **Preview** panel.

10. Save the Chapter_09_Animation package to preserve your work.

END TUTORIAL 9.3

Sockets

Sockets are locations associated with bone names that provide a simple method for artists to attach objects to skeletal meshes within the game (see **FIGURE 9.18**). These locations can have a positional and rotational offset from each bone, allowing you, for example, to attach a weapon to the surface of the palm, rather than to the pivot of the bone. Sockets are also given a name that can be used as an alias, which means you can refer to the socket name rather than the bone name when attaching objects through code, such as when attaching a weapon to a hand or a muzzle flash to a weapon.

As an example, you could create a socket with the name WeaponHand that is offset from the hand bone such that it applies any object attached to that socket in a way that it's positioned right at the surface of the palm. You could then simply refer to WeaponHand to attach a weapon to the character's hand, rather than having to remember a particular bone name. Sockets are created and edited in the AnimSet Editor. We cover this process later in the section "AnimSet Editor."

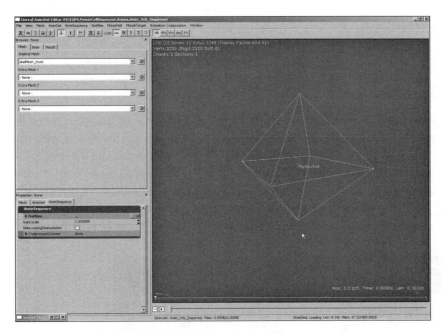

FIGURE 9.18   Sockets appear as named diamonds, as seen here.

AnimSets

An AnimSet is an object that stores a collection of animation sequences that can be associated with a skeletal mesh. For example, you can have an AnimSet that stores all the animations necessary to control a character, such as running, jumping, shooting, and breathing sequences. You can then apply this AnimSet to any character with a skeleton that was created in the same way (having the same names) as the original character for which the animations were created. The new character would now move according to the AnimSet.

AnimSets are created in the Generic Browser and are saved inside of packages. An AnimSet can store two types of items: AnimSequences and AnimNotifies.

AnimSequences are individual keyframed animations of the skeletal hierarchy. These animations can include positional and rotational data for the animated bones. Any animations created for a specific skeletal hierarchy can be used to animate any skeletal mesh using an identical hierarchy. This allows you to share animations between skeletal meshes as long as the skeletons between the meshes are the same.

AnimNotifies, or notifications, are events that are triggered at specific points within the animation sequence. These notifications allow actions to be performed such as shaking the view, playing sounds, and scripting certain functions to be performed by the animation sequences themselves. AnimNotifies can be created and modified within the AnimSet Editor. This process and the various notifications available are discussed in the section "AnimSet Editor."

Morph Animation

The term *morph animation* refers to deformation of the mesh created by the interpolation of its vertices toward the vertex positions of another mesh. Simply put, it's the process of changing the shape of one mesh to look like another through blending. Morphing requires at least two meshes: the original mesh (the one you want to morph) and at least one target mesh. This target mesh must have the exact same topology, meaning that both meshes have the same number of vertices and that those vertices are in the same relation to one another. Basically, this means that the two meshes must be exactly the same, save that one has the vertices shaped differently (see **FIGURE 9.19**).

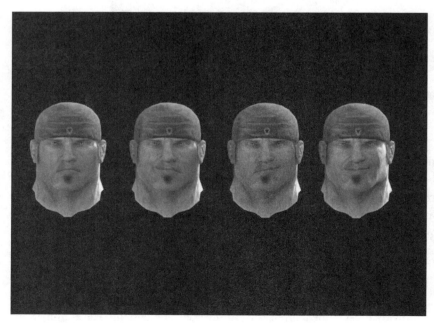

FIGURE 9.19   This figure shows two morph targets used to make the character smile.

A good example of using a morph would be for creating the effect of a character raising her eyebrows. Your original mesh would simply be the character in a normal pose, and the target would be the exact same mesh, but with the eyebrows moved upward or otherwise reshaped to complete the effect. Then, using morph animation, you can blend your original mesh toward the shape of the target. The result would be that the eyebrows of the original mesh appear to rise as you continued the blend. Such changes in shape are perfect for morph animation, although morphing would not be very well suited to motions such as running or jumping.

MorphTargetSets

A *MorphTargetSet* is a collection of morph targets that can be applied to a skeletal mesh. These are simply ways that one can organize *MorphTargets*, which are meshes that are identical to the source skeletal mesh but have different locations for the vertices.

We now have our mesh complete with animations and multiple levels of detail. One thing that adds realism to driving a vehicle around in a game is the vehicle appearing damaged after running into something. Using morph targets provides one method of simulating this damage, which we begin in **TUTORIAL 9.4**.

TUTORIAL 9.4: Simulating Damage Using Morph Targets

1. Continuing from **TUTORIAL 9.3**, double-click the skelMesh_truck to open it in the AnimSet Editor. If you have not completed it, you may use the skelMesh_turck_02 asset instead.

2. In the AnimSet Editor, go to File > New MorphTargetSet. In the New MorphTargetSet dialog that appears, enter the following information and click OK:

   ▶ **Package**: Chapter_09_Animation

   ▶ **Group**: Meshes

   ▶ **Name**: morphSet_truck

3. In the Morph tab of the Browser panel, you should see the morphSet_truck MorphTargetSet listed in the dropdown list (see **FIGURE 9.20**).

4. Now that we have a container for the morph targets created, we need to populate it with some morph targets. Back in the File menu, select Import MorphTarget. In the file browser, navigate to and select the skelMesh_truck_hood_damage.psk file. In the New MorphTarget Name dialog that appears, enter **morph_hood_damage** and click OK.

5. At this point, you should see the effects of the morph target in the Preview panel, but the MorphTargets list in the Browser panel may not have updated due to a bug at the time of this writing. The morph targets can still be selected in the MorphTargets list, but the list appears empty. A simple fix is to close the AnimSet Editor and reopen it by double-clicking the morphSet_truck asset in the Generic Browser. The morph targets should then be visible in the list.

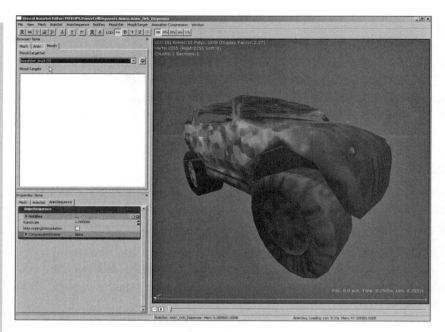

FIGURE 9.20   Make sure the dropdown shows the morphSet_truck morph target set.

6. Repeat this process, importing the following morph target files and giving each the corresponding name (see **FIGURE 9.21**):

   ▶ skelMesh_truck_front_damage.psk → morph_front_damage

   ▶ skelMesh_truck_rear_damage.psk → morph_rear_damage

   ▶ skelMesh_truck_leftdoor_damage.psk → morph_left_damage

   ▶ skelMesh_truck_rightdoor_damage.psk → morph_right_damage

7. Once all the morph targets are imported, cycle through them by selecting each one in the MorphTargets list in the Browser panel to make sure they are all working properly.

8. You may recall that morph targets are additive, yet we are only seeing the effects of each individual morph target at any one time. In **TUTORIAL 9.8**, we hook up these morph targets so that multiple morph targets can be applied at once. For now, save the Chapter_09_Animation package to preserve your work.

FIGURE 9.21 Your new morph targets appear in the list like so.

END TUTORIAL 9.4

AnimSet Editor

The AnimSet Editor is the central area where you can edit skeletal mesh properties as well as preview the mesh's animation sequences and morph targets. The editor has a fairly simple interface, consisting of five key areas: menu bar, toolbar, browser, Properties window, and Preview window (see **FIGURE 9.22**).

Menu bar   Toolbar   Preview

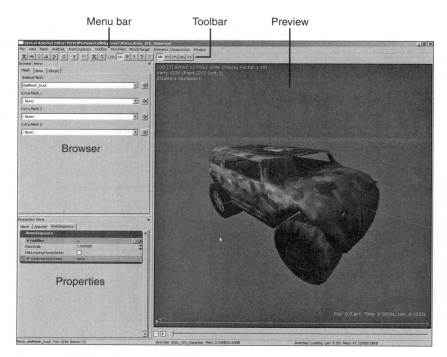

FIGURE 9.22   The AnimSet Editor

Menu Bar

Across the very top of the AnimSet Editor is the menu bar (see **FIGURE 9.23**). The included menus give access to the various functions of the editor.

FIGURE 9.23   The AnimSet Editor's menu bar

File—The File menu contains commands for importing mesh level-of-detail (LOD) models, morph targets, and other AnimSets.

View—The View menu contains a list of Show flags for controlling the visibility of various items in the Preview window. These include such things as showing the floor, skeleton, wireframe view, and several other options.

Mesh—The Mesh menu contains commands that pertain to meshes. This includes switching between LODs, setting up mirror tables, creating sockets, and a variety of other commands.

9

AnimSet—The AnimSet menu contains commands that pertain to AnimSets. This includes resetting the AnimSet (which removes all the sequences from the set) and deleting tracks (which removes the animation information for individual bones from the set).

AnimSequence—The AnimSequence menu provides commands that pertain to animation sequences. These include renaming, deleting, and trimming sequences.

Notifies—The Notifies menu provides commands that pertain to animation notifications. These include creating and sorting notifications.

MorphSet—The MorphSet menu is empty.

MorphTarget—The MorphTarget menu provides commands that are relevant to, and perform functions on, morph targets. These include renaming and deleting morph targets.

Animation Compression—The Animation Compression menu provides access to the Animation Compression dialog.

Window—The Window menu allows the browser and Properties window's visibility to be toggled on or off.

Toolbar

Most of the common functionality of the AnimSet Editor can be found in the toolbar, located at the top of the editor's interface (see **FIGURE 9.24**).

FIGURE 9.24   The AnimSet Editor's toolbar

Show ![icons]—The first five buttons provide quick access to the most commonly used Show flags, which are all available from within the View menu. These are Show Skeleton, Show Bone Names, Show Wireframe, Show Reference Pose, and Show Mirror.

Socket Manager ![icon]—This button opens the Socket Manager, allowing you to edit the sockets of your skeletal mesh.

New Notify ![icon]—This button creates a new animation notification at the current time within the current animation sequence.

Toggle Cloth ![icon]—This button toggles the cloth simulation on or off.

Compression ![icons]—The first button toggles the display of the compressed animation on or off in the Preview. The second button opens the Animation Compression dialog.

LOD ![icons]—These buttons allow for switching between the available levels of detail for the purposes of previewing.

Playback Speed 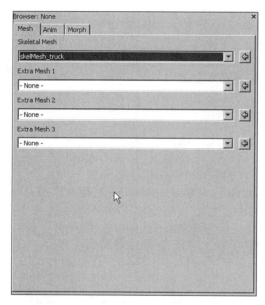 —These buttons provide the ability to adjust the playback speed of the animation sequences in the Preview window.

Browser

The Browser panel displays lists of the available skeletal meshes, animation sets and sequences, and morph target sets and sequences that can be selected for viewing and editing (see **FIGURE 9.25**).

FIGURE 9.25   The AnimSet Editor's Browser panel

Mesh—The Mesh tab has four separate dropdown lists for selecting skeletal meshes. The selection in the first list determines the mesh that is animated and edited within the editor. The remaining lists are for adding extra meshes to the Preview window. These cannot be edited or modified in any way.

Anim—The Anim tab provides a list of all the AnimSets loaded in the Generic Browser from which to select. The selected AnimSet can be edited. Below this is a list of all the animation sequences within the selected AnimSet. The selected animation sequence can be played back and edited.

Morph—The Morph tab provides a list of all the MorphTargetSets loaded in the Generic Browser from which to select. The selected MorphTargetSet can be edited. Below this is a list of all the morph targets within the selected MorphTargetSet. The selected morph target can be morphed to and edited.

9

Preview

The Preview panel displays a perspective view of the animated skeletal mesh along with other information pertaining to the mesh and animations (see **FIGURE 9.26**).

LOD [0] Bones:12 Polys:3248 (Display Factor:1.99)
Verts:2255 (Rigid:2255 Soft:0)
Chunks:1 Sections:1
Pos: 0.0 pct, Time: 0.0000s, Len: 8.3333s

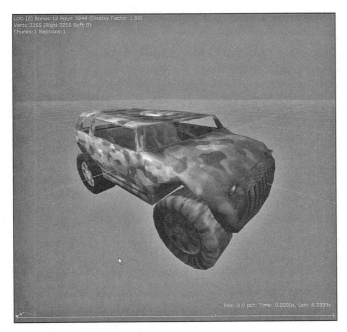

FIGURE 9.26 The AnimSet Editor's Preview window shows your result.

The following controls are used to navigate the viewport:

- Holding down the left mouse button while dragging rotates the viewport.
- Holding down the right mouse button while dragging zooms the viewport.
- Holding down the middle mouse button while dragging pans the viewport.
- Pressing the L key, holding down the left mouse button, and dragging moves the position of the light that lights the scene.

The information HUD in the upper-left corner of the panel displays the current LOD being shown, the DisplayFactor (size on the screen) of the mesh, as well as the number of bones, polygons, vertices, chunks, and sections present in that LOD (see **FIGURE 9.27**).

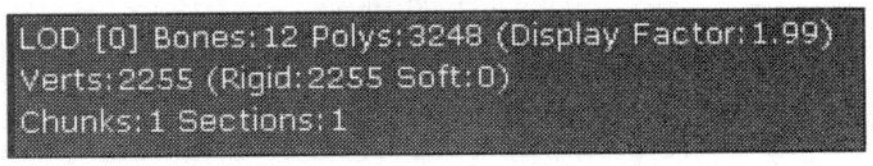
LOD [0] Bones:12 Polys:3248 (Display Factor:1.99)
Verts:2255 (Rigid:2255 Soft:0)
Chunks:1 Sections:1

FIGURE 9.27 A close-up of the Information HUD

The timeline at the bottom of the panel provides playback controls and displays the length of the current animation sequence in seconds as well as the current position within that sequence by percentage and time.

Properties

The Properties area is one of the central locations where you'll edit the behavior of your skeletal mesh. It contains three tabs that allow you to work with the properties of the mesh, the current AnimSet, and the current AnimSequence (see **FIGURE 9.28**).

Mesh Properties

SkeletalMesh

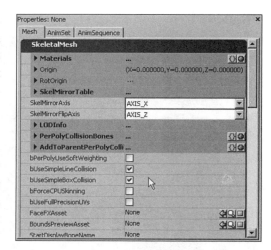

FIGURE 9.28   The Properties area appears like many of the Properties windows inside of UnrealEd.

Materials—This is an array of the materials for this skeletal mesh. The number of items in the array is dependent on the number of materials/shaders/and so on applied to the mesh in the 3D application in which it was created.

Origin—This is a vector specifying a translation offset to apply to the root bone of the skeletal mesh.

RotOrigin—This is a rotation offset to apply to the root bone of the skeletal mesh.

SkelMirrorTable—This is an array of the bone mappings used for mirroring animations. This array is created with the Auto-Build Mirror Table command in the Mesh menu.

SourceIndex—This is the index of the bone from which the current bone should get its animation data. There should always be matching pairs unless the bone is located on the axis over which the mirroring takes place. This means that if the shoulder bones are indices 2 and 4, then the SourceIndex for slot [2] should be 4 and the SourceIndex for slot [4] should be 2.

BoneFlipAxis—This is a bone-level override for the SkelMirrorFlipAxis.

SkelMirrorAxis—This is the axis over which the skeletal mesh should be mirrored when animation mirroring is being used. This is in the mesh's local space before the RotOrigin offset is applied.

SkelMirrorFlipAxis—This is the axis that is flipped after the mirroring takes place to keep the bone from being turned inside-out.

LODInfo—This is an array of all the LOD meshes present. There is always at least one item in this array as the base mesh is LOD 0. LOD meshes are added through the File menu using the Import LOD Mesh command.

DisplayFactor—This value sets the upper bound of the percentage of screen space used by the object for the current level of detail. Once the DisplayFactor of the mesh goes below this value, the mesh associated with this level of detail is used in place of the mesh of the previous level of detail. This has no effect on LOD 0.

LODHysteresis—This is the resistance of the mesh to change to or from this level of detail. This helps to keep the mesh from flickering back and forth between levels of detail when the viewpoint is on the boundaries between levels of detail.

LODMaterialMap—This is an array corresponding to the materials of the mesh that allows the material slots of this level of detail to be remapped to correspond to the correct materials of the base mesh's Materials array.

This is necessary because LOD meshes may sometimes be exported with their materials in a different order than the base mesh's materials. Instead of exporting the mesh again, a simple remapping is done to fix the problem.

PerPolyCollisionBones—This is an array of bone names that should have the polygons used in per-poly collisions.

bUseSimpleLineCollision—If this property is true, the physics asset applied to the skeletal mesh component is used for determining line collisions, or zero-extent collisions.

If this property is false, per-poly collision is used if it has been set up using the PerPolyCollisionBones array.

bUseSimpleBoxCollision—If this property is true, the physics asset applied to the skeletal mesh component is used for determining swept box collisions, or nonzero-extent collisions.

If this property is false, per-poly collision is used if it has been set up using the PerPolyCollisionBones array.

bForceCPUSkinning—If this property is true, CPU skinning is used for this mesh. CPU skinning is slower than GPU skinning, but is necessary for using the cloth simulation.

If this property is false, GPU skinning is used. This is the default.

FaceFXAsset—This is a reference to the FaceFX asset that the current skeletal mesh uses when playing FaceFX animations.

BoundsPreviewAsset—This is the physics asset to use for determining the bounds of the current skeletal mesh.

StartDisplayBoneName—This is the name of the bone to use as the starting point for drawing the bones of a skeletal mesh component that uses the current skeletal mesh. This only affects the displaying of the bone names within the AnimSet Editor.

Cloth

These properties deal with cloth physics simulation. See Chapter 4, "Physics Objects," for an explanation of the properties and their use.

AnimSet Properties

bAnimRotationOnly—If this property is true, only the rotations of the animations are used for the bones of the skeletal mesh, with the exception of the root bone, which always accepts translation from animations.

If this property is false, translations as well as rotations are used from the animations.

UseTranslationBoneNames—This is an array of bone names that should use translations from the animations, effectively overriding the bAnimRotationsOnly property on a per-bone basis.

AnimSequence Properties

Notifies—This is an array of the notifications for the currently selected animation sequence.

Time—This is the number of seconds into the animation sequence that this notification should be fired.

Notify—This is the actual notification object that can be any one of the types of notifications. The various types are described later in this list.

Comment—This is a textual identifier or description that's displayed above the timeline in the Preview viewport at the location of the notification.

Footstep—This is used, in theory, to play a footstep sound by calling the PlayFootStepSound() function within the Pawn class. This function is empty by default, so some setup by a programmer is required for this notification to function.

FootDown—This is used to determine which foot hit the ground: 0 is for the left foot and 1 is for the right foot.

Script—This is used to call a script function within the object that owns the skeletal mesh to which this node is applied.

NotifyName—This is the name of the function to call within the script.

Sound—This is used to play a SoundCue.

SoundCue—This is the SoundCue to play.

bFollowActor—If this property is true, the sound is attached to the mesh and spatialized to the mesh as it moves.

If this property is false, the sound is locked and spatialized to the location of the mesh when the notify was fired.

BoneName—If a valid bone name is entered here, the sound is played at the bone's location.

PlayFaceFXAnim—This plays a FaceFX animation.

FaceFXAnimSetRef—This is the FaceFX AnimSet that contains the animation to be played.

9

GroupName—This is the name of the group within the FaceFX AnimSet that contains the animation to be played.

AnimName—This is the name of the animation to be played.

bOverridePlayingAnim—If this property is true, this animation replaces any FaceFX animations currently playing.

If this property is false, this animation is skipped.

PlayFrequency—This is the probability that the animation is played each time the notification is fired. The valid range of values is 0.0 to 1.0, with 1.0 meaning the animation is played every time the notification is fired. This allows for some randomness.

ViewShake—This causes the camera to shake.

ShakeRadius—This is the distance from the shake's center that players' cameras shake.

Duration—This is the number of seconds the shaking lasts.

RotAmplitude—This is the amount the camera rotates around each axis while shaking.

RotFrequency—This is how quickly the camera rotates around each axis while shaking.

LocAmplitude—This is the distance the camera is offset in each axis while shaking.

LocFrequency—This is the speed at which the camera is offset while shaking.

FOVAmplitude—This is the amount the field of view is altered while the camera is shaking.

FOVFrequency—This is the speed at which the field of view is altered while the camera is shaking.

bUseBoneLocation—If this property is true, the center of the shaking is positioned at the location of the bone specified by the BoneName property.

If this property is false, the center of the shaking is positioned at the location of the object that owns the skeletal mesh the animation sequence is applied to.

BoneName—This is the name of the bone to use as the location for the center of the shaking.

RateScale—This is the rate at which to play the currently selected animation sequence. A value of 1.0 plays back the animation at its normal rate. A value of 2 doubles the rate, 0.5 halves the rate, and so on.

bNoLoopingInterpolation—If this property is true, there is no interpolation of the skeletal mesh between the last and first frames of the current animation sequence when it loops.

If this property is false, the bones of the skeletal mesh interpolate between their positions and rotations in the last frame of the animation sequence and the first frame of the animation sequence when it loops.

CompressionScheme—This displays the current animation compression scheme being used by this sequence. Although it appears the compression can be modified here, all modifications should be done through the Animation Compression dialog. Animation compression is explained in greater detail in the "Animation Compression" section.

Socket Manager

The Socket Manager is a custom dialog in which sockets are created, deleted, and modified (see **FIGURE 9.29**). It is accessed through the Mesh menu or by clicking the Socket Manager button on the toolbar. Here is an overview of its interface.

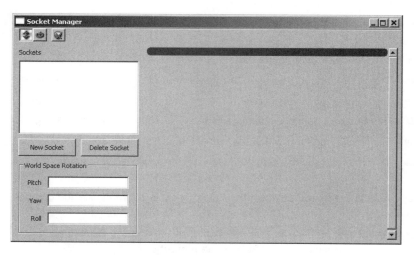

FIGURE 9.29   The Socket Manager interface

Toolbar—The toolbar of the Socket Manager is fairly simplistic. It has only three buttons.

The first two buttons are for switching between the translation widget and the rotation widget that transforms the selected socket in the AnimSet Editor's preview window.

The remaining button removes any meshes, skeletal or static, that have been assigned to the current socket.

Socket List—The socket list contains all the sockets belonging to the skeletal mesh. Sockets in the list can be selected for editing their properties or world space rotation within the Socket Manager or offsets within the preview window (see **FIGURE 9.30**).

FIGURE 9.30   The socket list

Below the list are two buttons for creating and deleting sockets. When you create a new socket, a dialog for choosing the bone that the socket corresponds to appears, followed by a dialog for entering a name for the socket.

World Space Rotation—The Pitch, Yaw, and Roll edit boxes allow the socket to be rotated in world space coordinates instead of relative to the bone on which the socket is based (see **FIGURE 9.31**).

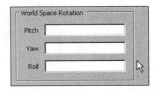

FIGURE 9.31   World Space Rotation section

Properties—This section displays the following properties for the selected socket, assuming a socket is selected (otherwise, it is empty):

SocketName—This displays the name given to the socket upon its creation.

BoneName—This displays the name of the bone to which this socket belongs.

RelativeLocation—This is an offset from the bone's location where the socket should be positioned.

RelativeRotation—This is the rotation of the socket in relation to the bone's rotation.

RelativeScale—This is the scale of the socket in relation to the bone's scale. This scales whatever is attached to that socket.

PreviewSkelMesh—This is the skeletal mesh to attach to the socket for previewing purposes.

PreviewSkelMeshComp—This is the skeletal mesh component of the PreviewSkelMesh. It allows you to set many properties for the attached skeletal mesh so that the preview mirrors the in-game appearance as closely as possible.

PreviewStaticMesh—This is the static mesh to attach to the socket for preview purposes.

In **TUTORIAL 9.5**, we set up a socket for the truck mesh to which we attach a weapon mesh. This could be just for preview purposes to see how the weapon looks attached to the vehicle mesh, it could be to create an attachment point to which the weapon is fastened on the vehicle in the actual game, or both.

TUTORIAL 9.5: Attaching the Plasma Cannon Turret Using Sockets

1. Continuing from **TUTORIAL 9.4**, double-click the skelMesh_truck to open it in the AnimSet Editor. If you have not completed it, you may use the skelMesh_truck_03 asset instead.

2. Open the Socket Manager either from the Mesh menu or by using the Socket Manager button ![button] in the Toolbar. The Socket Manager should appear, looking fairly empty because no sockets have been created for this mesh as of yet (see **FIGURE 9.32**).

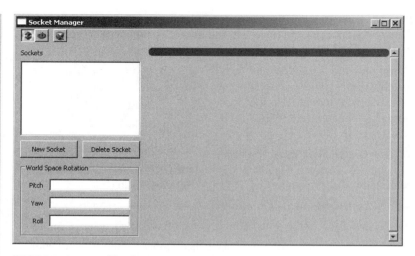

FIGURE 9.32   The Socket Manager

3. Click the New Socket button, choose the Chassis bone from the dropdown list of the New Socket dialog that appears, and then click OK. Enter **Turret** as the Socket Name in the next dialog and click OK. The Sockets list should show the new socket, and the properties for the socket should appear (see **FIGURE 9.33**).

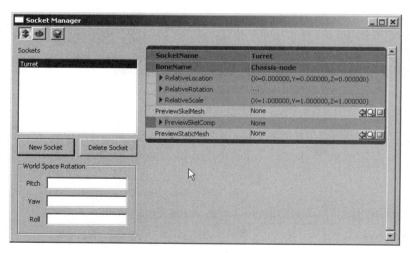

FIGURE 9.33   The socket's properties are now available.

4. The first thing we do is bring in the mesh we attach. This makes it easier to position the socket and make sure the rotation is correct as well. In the Generic Browser, select the skelMesh_truck_gun skeletal mesh from the Chapter_09_Animation package. Then, click the Use Current Selection in Browser button for the PreviewSkeletalMesh property of

the Turret socket. You may not immediately see the mesh because it is inside the vehicle, but you can navigate the viewport to make sure it is there.

5. Move the socket up to the cylindrical platform on top of the vehicle using the translation widget in the Preview panel until it appears to be in the correct position (see **FIGURE 9.34**).

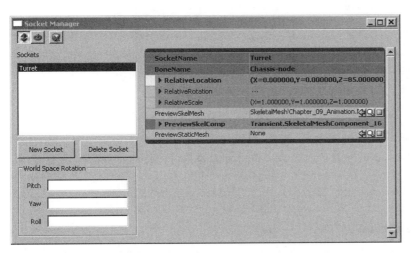

FIGURE 9.34   Relocating the socket moves the cannon as well.

6. Expand the RelativeLocation property in the Socket Manager. You should see the exact coordinates of the socket relative to the Chassis bone there. Set the value for Z to 86.5.

7. In the Socket Manager's toolbar, click the Rotate Socket button. This changes the transform widget in the viewport from translation to rotation (see **FIGURE 9.35**).

8. Using the rotation widget, rotate the socket about the Z-axis (the blue circle). This is referred to as *Yaw*. Turret weapons such as this commonly have limits on their in-game rotations, thus allowing them to shoot only within a certain range. Using the rotation of the socket, we can get an idea for what angles this weapon should be limited to, which can be used later on in the code for the vehicle.

9. Save the Chapter_09_Animation package to preserve your progress.

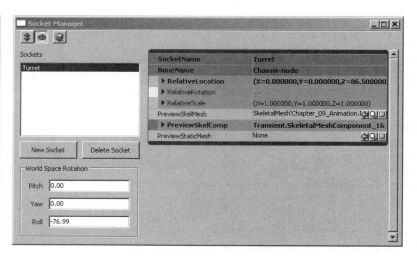

FIGURE 9.35 You now have the ability to rotate the socket in the Preview window.

END TUTORIAL 9.5

Animation Compression

One of the key performance draws for skeletal meshes and their animations is memory. If you have many different characters (or other skeletal meshes) with many different animations, you have the potential to use up vast amounts of computer memory, which in turn drains your frame rate. The amount of memory taken up by animation sequences can be reduced by applying various compression schemes.

Animation compression can be applied individually to a specific animation, or globally to an entire AnimSet. Controlling animation compression requires the use of the Animation Compression dialog, which is found within the AnimSet Editor, in the Animation Compression menu, or by pressing the Animation Compression button located on the toolbar.

The catch is that when compressing animation, you run the risk of lowering overall animation quality to unacceptable levels. Like so many things in game development, this is a battle between the importance of visual accuracy and the necessity for fast gameplay. In the end, you're going to have to work with the settings and figure out which ones give your project the best performance at the least amount of overall quality cost.

The Animation Compression dialog is composed of a list of various compression techniques, properties related to each of these techniques, and buttons for applying the compression to either the AnimSet or the AnimSequence.

Animation Compression Types

Here's a list of the animation compression types available:

Bitwise Compress Only—This compression method only compresses the rotational data of the animation using the RotationCompressionFormat property. The number of keys remains constant, but each key takes up less space in memory. It should be noted that the other compression types also have this ability available to them, because they all have the RotationCompressionFormat property.

RotationCompressionFormat—This property controls the quality of the compression scheme applied to the rotational keys of the animation. The properties themselves are extremely technical in nature—more technical than any level designer or artist would need to worry about—and so this list simply gives you a quality comparison of each one. As a general rule, the visual fidelity of the animation gets lower as you go down the list, but the amount of memory saved gets higher.

ACF_None—This method applies no compression.

ACF_Float96NoW—This compression provides high quality with low memory savings.

ACF_Fixed48NoW—This compression provides medium-high quality with medium-low memory savings.

ACF_IntervalFixed32NoW—This compression provides medium quality with medium memory savings.

ACF_Fixed32NoW—This compression provides medium-low quality with medium-high memory savings.

ACF_Float32NoW—This compression provides low quality with high memory savings.

Remove Every Second Key—This compresses the sequence(s) by removing every other key. This potentially results in a loss of visual fidelity, but should cut the amount of memory needed for each sequence in half. This compression type also provides the option of performing a bitwise compression at the same time to provide even further memory savings (see **FIGURE 9.36**).

MinKeys—This specifies the minimum number of keys a sequence must contain to have key reduction performed. Sequences with fewer keys than this value retain all their keys.

bStartAtSecondKey—If this property is true, every other key is removed starting with the second key (that is, keys 1, 3, 5, 7, and so on).

If false, every other key is removed starting with the first key (that is, keys 0, 2, 4, 6, and so on).

RotationCompressionFormat—Refer to the Bitwise Compress Only entry (earlier in this list) for explanations of the options available here.

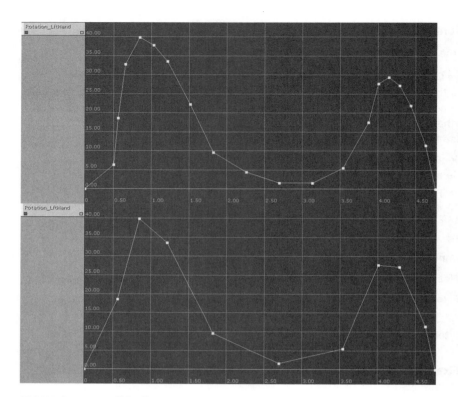

FIGURE 9.36   This diagram shows two curves; the second has had every other key removed.

Remove Trivial Keys—This compresses the sequence(s) by removing any consecutive keys that have identical—or nearly identical—values for translation or rotation. In essence, this removes any redundant keys that have little-to-no influence over the visual appearance of the animation. This compression type also provides the option of performing a bitwise compression at the same time to provide further memory savings (see **FIGURE 9.37**).

MaxPosDiff—This is the maximum deviation that translation values of keys can have and still be considered identical (and thus be removed).

MaxAngleDiff—This is the maximum deviation that rotation values of keys can have and still be considered identical (and thus be removed).

RotationCompressionFormat—Refer to the Bitwise Compress Only section (earlier in this list) for explanations of the options available here.

Revert To Raw—This removes any compression that has been performed, restoring the sequence (or sequences) to its original state.

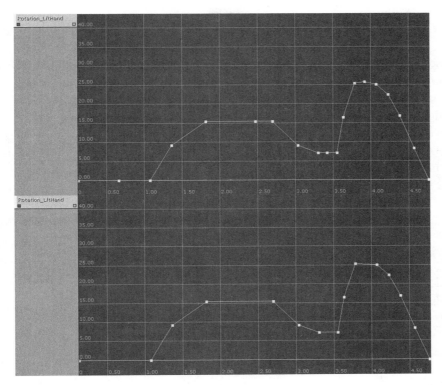

FIGURE 9.37 This is a visual example of trivial key removal. Notice how keys that have very similar (or the same) values have been removed.

Animation Blending

Skeletal animations can be blended together in order to create a more seamless, flowing, and natural look to an object—especially a character—in motion. Also, entirely new animation sequences can be created by combining other animations together. You can blend between animations based on the speed at which a character is moving, the direction in which the character is moving, or whether the character is firing a weapon. Combining animations are useful in instances such as when you have an animation for the character running forward and another for the character running sideways, and you want to combine them so that you can make the character smoothly run in a diagonal direction.

Blending between animations takes place based on weighting. This means you can control how much one animation is used over another, or to put it another way, what percentage of a given animation is represented in the final blended animation. Blending is organized into *AnimTrees*, which represent a hierarchy of how one animation blends into another, and the factors by which that blending takes place.

AnimTrees are used to graphically represent how animations are blended together (see **FIGURE 9.38**). They allow the user to control precisely which animations are played in response to certain events or situations, such as a change in direction or speed. AnimTrees also define the rules by which animations are blended together. The trees themselves are composed of networks of animation, morph, and skeletal controller nodes that, when combined, all form the creation of complex behaviors for your skeletal meshes. AnimTrees are created within the Generic Browser, and double-clicking them opens the AnimTree Editor, where you can create and edit your animation trees. The next section discusses the AnimTree Editor.

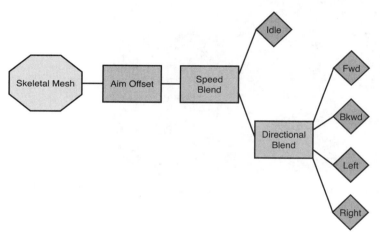

FIGURE 9.38   This illustration shows the concept of an AnimTree.

AnimTree Editor

The AnimTree Editor is accessed by double-clicking an AnimTree object within the Generic Browser. The editor is a node-based visual editor that is very similar in function to the Kismet Editor or the Material Editor (see **FIGURE 9.39**). It allows for the creation of AnimTree networks to make complex animation schemes for your skeletal meshes. These trees are created hierarchically, with the animations themselves being connected to a chain of nodes that controls how they blend together. These node hierarchies flow from left to right, ending in the AnimTree node.

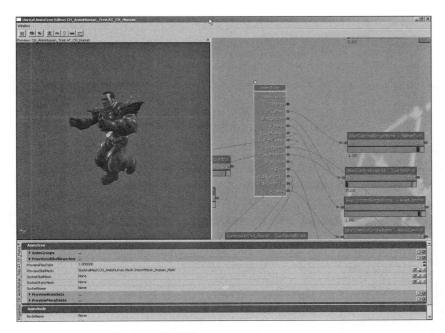

FIGURE 9.39   The AnimTree Editor

The following is a rundown of the AnimTree Editor's user interface.

Menu

There is only one menu: Window. It allows for the showing and hiding of the Preview and Properties panels.

Toolbar

As with most of the specialized editors found within Unreal Editor, the top of the interface contains a toolbar that allows access to the most commonly used functions:

Pause AnimTree ⏸—This toggles the playback in the viewport.

Preview Selected Node 👁—This forces the playback in the viewport to be the result of the selected node. The node being played back is designated by a small yellow square above the top-left corner of the node.

Show Node Weights %—This toggles the display of the weights of each animation node within the viewport.

Show Skeleton 🔨—This toggles the display of the bones within the viewport.

Show Bone Names 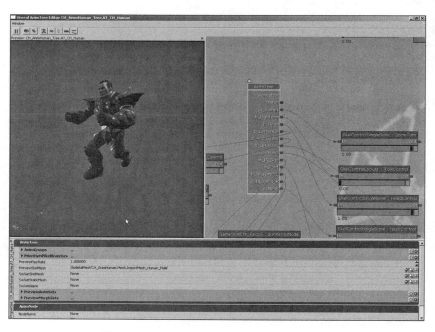—This toggles the display of the bone names in the viewport.

Show Wireframe—This toggles the mesh being rendered in wireframe.

Show Floor—This toggles the display of the floor geometry.

Toggle Curved Connections—At the time of this writing, this item is nonfunctional.

Preview

This window provides a visual playback of the animated skeletal mesh in regard to the final AnimTree. It takes into account all the skeletal and morph animations, as well as the skeletal controllers applied to the mesh (see **FIGURE 9.40**).

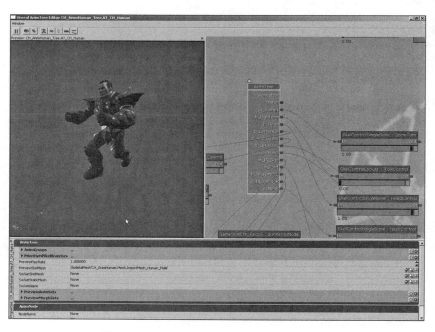

FIGURE 9.40   The AnimTree Editor Preview window shows the result of your tree.

The Preview window can be navigated using the following actions:

▶ Holding down the left mouse button while dragging rotates the viewport.

▶ Holding down the right mouse button while dragging zooms the viewport.

▶ Holding down the middle mouse button while dragging pans the viewport.

▶ Pressing the L key, holding down the left mouse button, and dragging moves the light that is lighting the scene.

Properties

This area displays the properties of the currently selected node for editing purposes. If no node is selected, no properties are displayed.

Workspace

This is where nodes are added and linked together to create the AnimTree networks. The workspace in the AnimTree Editor is essentially identical to the workspaces in the Material Editor or Kismet in terms of selecting and moving nodes (see **FIGURE 9.41**). New nodes can be added by right-clicking and choosing from the list of available nodes.

Copying and pasting nodes is not possible at this time.

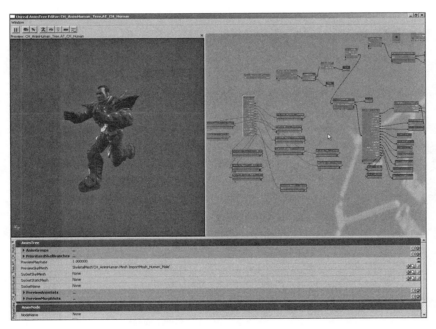

FIGURE 9.41   The workspace is where your AnimTree is assembled.

We now take the truck skeletal mesh we set up in previous tutorials and begin creating an AnimTree for it. In **TUTORIAL 9.6**, we use the SkelControlWheel skeletal controller to set up the wheels for use in-game.

TUTORIAL 9.6: Setting Up a Vehicle, Part I: Wheels

1. Continue from **TUTORIAL 9.5**. If you have not completed it, you may use the skelMesh_truck_4 asset in place of the skelMesh_truck asset when instructed. Right-click in the Generic Browser and choose New AnimTree. Enter the following information in the dialog that appears and then click OK:

   ▶ **Package**: Chapter_09_Animation

   ▶ **Group**: Animations

   ▶ **Name**: animTree_truck

2. The AnimTree Editor appears at this point, but it is empty with the exception of the AnimTree node. Make sure the AnimTree node is selected so its properties are visible (see **FIGURE 9.42**).

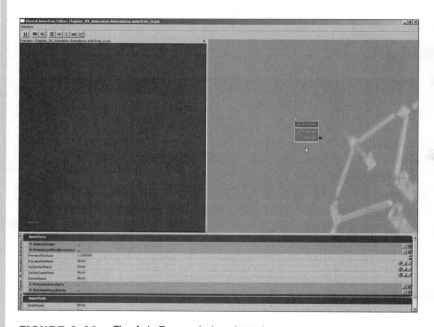

FIGURE 9.42   The AnimTree node is selected.

3. Select the skelMesh_truck skeletal mesh in the Generic Browser and click the Use Current Selection in Browser button ![icon] for the PreviewSkeletalMesh property of the AnimTree node. The truck mesh should appear in the Preview panel of the AnimTree Editor (see **FIGURE 9.43**).

4. Right-click the AnimTree node and choose Add SkelControl Chain. From the New SkelControl Chain dialog that appears, choose the LF_Wheel-node bone and click OK. This creates a new input link on the AnimTree node labeled LF_Wheel-node (see **FIGURE 9.44**).

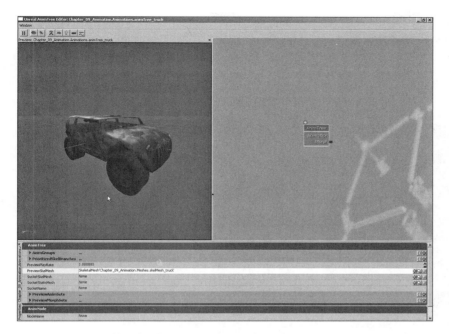

FIGURE 9.43 You should now see the truck mesh.

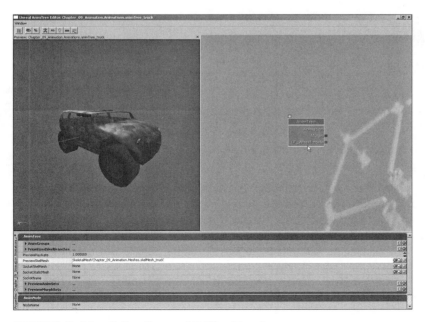

FIGURE 9.44 Notice the new LF_Wheel input.

5. Repeat this process for the RF_Wheel-node, LR_Wheel-node, and RR_Wheel-node bones. After you are finished, the AnimTree node should have an Animation input, a Morph input, an LF_Wheel-node input, an RF_Wheel-node input, an LR_Wheel-node input, and an RR_Wheel-node input (see **FIGURE 9.45**).

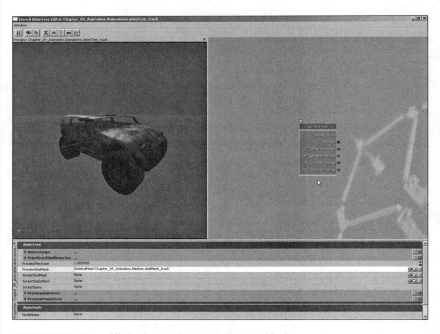

FIGURE 9.45   All the inputs have now been added.

6. Create a new SkelControlWheel node by right-clicking in the AnimTree Editor and choosing SkelControlWheel. Connect the In link of the new node to the LF_Wheel-node input of the AnimTree node (see **FIGURE 9.46**).

7. Repeat this process, connecting each new SkelControlWheel to the subsequent SkelControl Chain link on the AnimTree node (see **FIGURE 9.47**).

8. Select the SkelControlWheel connected to the LF_Wheel-node input. Adjust the WheelSteering and WheelRoll properties to make sure they are using the correct axes. Looking at the left side of the vehicle, the wheel should rotate in the counterclockwise direction when WheelRoll is increased, and vice versa. Increasing WheelSteering should cause the wheel to rotate to the right about the Z-axis as if the vehicle was turning to the right. These should be correct, but if they are not, we would need to make adjustments to WheelRollAxis, WheelSteeringAxis, bInvertWheelRoll, and bInvertWheelSteering so that the wheel behaves as described. Proper setup of the bones in a 3D application should allow the default values to be used.

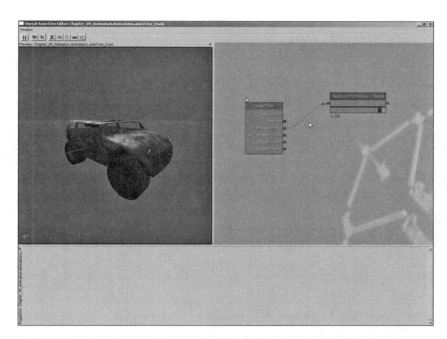

FIGURE 9.46   Connect the new SkelControlWheel to the LF_Wheel input.

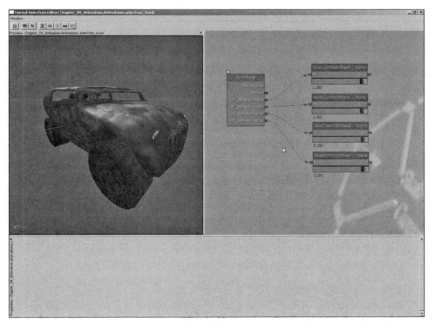

FIGURE 9.47   The wheel controls have now all been connected.

9. Adjust the WheelDisplacement property next. Increase it until the top of the wheel is just below the body of the vehicle, and make a note of the value at that point. It should be around 25.0. This is the value used as the WheelMaxRenderDisplacement. Enter the value in that property now for this SkelControlWheel and the others as well (see **FIGURE 9.48**).

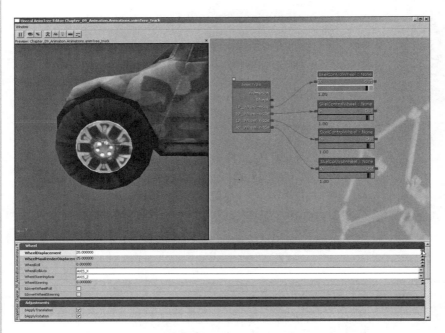

FIGURE 9.48   Use WheelDisplacement to move the wheel upward.

10. Save the Chapter_09_Animation package to preserve your progress.

END TUTORIAL 9.6

TUTORIAL 9.7: Setting Up Vehicle, Part II: Suspension

1. Continue from **TUTORIAL 9.6**. If you have not completed it, you may use the animtree_truck_01 asset in place of the animTree_truck asset when instructed. With the wheels set up, the next step is to set up the suspension system for the vehicle. This is done using the SkelControlLookAt controller. Double-click the animTree_truck asset in the Generic Browser to open it in the AnimTree Editor.

2. Right-click the AnimTree node and choose Add SkelControl Chain. Choose the LF_Strut-node bone from the dropdown list in the dialog that appears. There should be a new input on the AnimTree node labeled LF_Strut-node (see **FIGURE 9.49**).

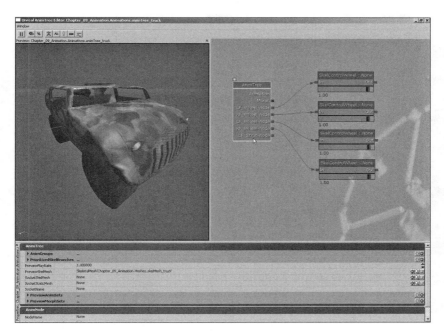

FIGURE 9.49   Notice the new LF_Strut-node input.

3. Right-click in the AnimTree Editor and choose SkelControlLookAt. Connect the In link of the new node to the LF_Strut-node link of the AnimTree node (see **FIGURE 9.50**).

4. We want the LF_Strut-node bone to always point at the LF_Wheel-node bone. To accomplish this, we need to use the TargetLocationSpace property. Setting this to BCS_OtherBoneSpace allows us to specify the name of a bone for the LF_Strut-node bone to look at. Set this property now.

5. We need to specify the bone to use as the target. Set the TargetSpaceBoneName property to LF_Wheel-node.

6. Select the LF_Wheel-node SkelControlWheel node and adjust the WheelDisplacement property to –25.0. The wheel should move down and, if setup has been successful thus far, the suspension should follow along with it (see **FIGURE 9.51**).

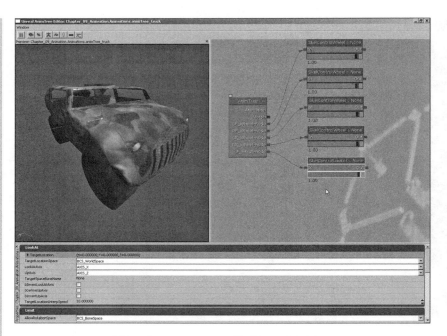

FIGURE 9.50   Add and connect a new SkelControlLookAt.

FIGURE 9.51   Notice that the strut now rotates down to stay with the wheel.

9

7. Reselect the LF_Strut-node SkelControlLookAt node. You may notice that the suspension, while following the wheel, is not looking quite right. You would expect the suspension to appear attached to the center of the wheel on the side nearest to it. The problem here is that the strut bone is looking at the wheel bone, which is located at the very center of the wheel in all axes. We can offset the location of the target from the actual bone's position using the TargetLocation property. If you like, you can use the translation widget in the viewport to drag the target to the desired location. To be precise, simply enter a value of 20.0 for X in the TargetLocation property (see **FIGURE 9.52**).

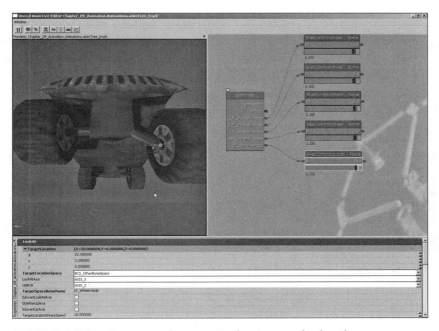

FIGURE 9.52   The suspension now attaches to a precise location.

8. At this point, you can go back and repeat the process of this entire tutorial for each of the other strut bones (RF_Strut-node, LR_Strut-node, and RR_Strut-node), creating a SkelControl Chain link on the AnimTree for each bone and connecting a SkelControlLookAt to each of those links. Then assign the corresponding wheel bone to the TargetSpaceBoneName property and set the TargetLocation.x property to offset the target. The struts on the right use an offset of −20.0 instead of the offset of 20.0 used for the left struts.

9. Save your progress.

END TUTORIAL 9.7

In **TUTORIAL 9.4**, we imported a set of morph targets that can be used to simulate damage to the vehicle. In order to use these, we need to add them to the AnimTree, which we do in **TUTORIAL 9.8**. We only preview the effects in the AnimTree Editor. To see these used in-game, we would, of course, need to set up a working vehicle script as well as have a system set up in that code to take advantage of them.

TUTORIAL 9.8: Setting Up Vehicle, Part III: Morphs

1. Double-click the animTree_truck asset in the Generic Browser to open it in the AnimTree Editor. If you have not completed **TUTORIAL 9.7**, you may open the animTree_truck_02 asset instead (see **FIGURE 9.53**).

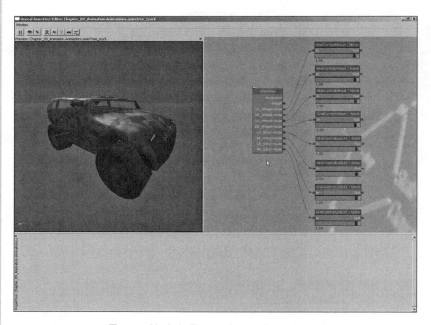

FIGURE 9.53   The truck's AnimTree as it stands at this point

2. In the Generic Browser, select the morphSet_truck asset. Back in the AnimTree Editor, add a new item to the PreviewMorphSets array of the AnimTree node. Then, click the Use Current Selection in Browser button 🔄 for the new item (see **FIGURE 9.54**).

3. Right-click in the AnimTree Editor and choose Morph Pose. Select the new node to view its properties and set MorphName to morph_hood_damage. Also, set the NodeName property to HoodDamage. This gives the node a name by which it can be identified by a programmer in code (see **FIGURE 9.55**).

4. Connect the Out link of the morph node to the Morph link of the AnimTree node. The effects of the morph target should now be visible in the Preview panel.

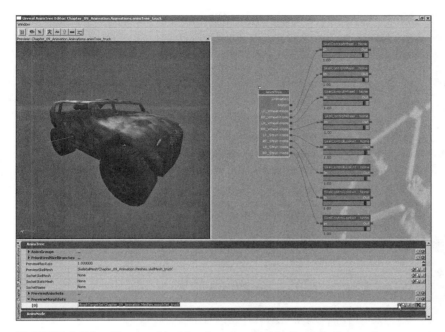

FIGURE 9.54   The morph set has been applied to the AnimTree node.

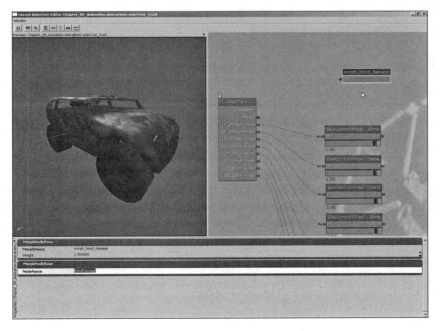

FIGURE 9.55   A new Morph Pose node has been added.

5. With the node selected, hold down Ctrl and press the W key four times to create four more Morph Pose nodes. Assign the following morph targets and node names to them:

- morph_front_damage → FrontDamage

- morph_rear_damage → RearDamage

- morph_left_damage → LeftDamage

- morph_right_damage → RightDamage

6. Connect the Out links of each of these nodes to the Morph link of the AnimTree node. All the morph targets should now be visible on the mesh in the Preview panel simultaneously because of their additive nature (see **FIGURE 9.56**).

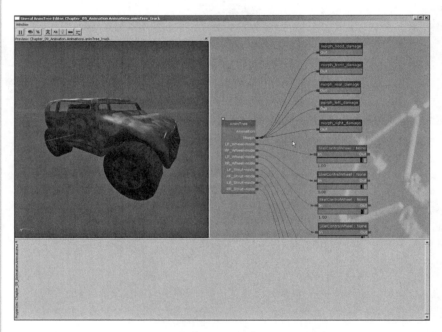

FIGURE 9.56   All the morph poses have now been connected.

In a game situation, some section of code would be created to modify the Weight properties of these nodes based on where the vehicle hit or was hit by some object.

7. Right-click in the AnimTree Editor and choose MorphNodeWeight. Select the new node to view its properties and set the NodeName to DamageControl (see **FIGURE 9.57**).

8. Break the links from the Morph Pose nodes to the Morph link of the AnimTree node and connect the Out link of the DamageControl node in their place.

9. Now make connections between the Out links of each of the Morph Pose nodes to the In link of the DamageControl node (see **FIGURE 9.58**).

9

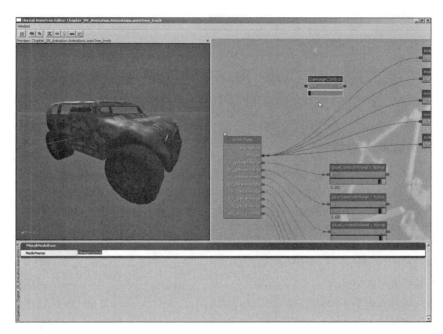

FIGURE 9.57   Add a new MorphNodeWeight.

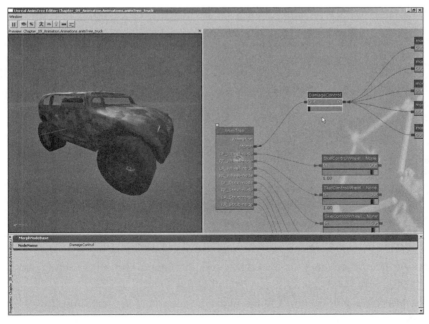

FIGURE 9.58   Connect the new MorphNodeWeight in place of the original Morph Pose nodes.

10. You should be able to drag the slider of the DamageControl node and see the effects of all the morph targets increase or decrease based on the slider's position.

11. Save your progress.

END TUTORIAL 9.8

AnimTree Editor Nodes

Many different nodes are available within the AnimTree Editor, each one designed with a specific purpose in mind. Aside from the main AnimTree node, which serves as the root of the node hierarchy, they are divided by the types of control they provide over certain kinds of objects. Three things can be controlled via AnimTree nodes: animation (which in this case refers to standard keyframed skeletal animation), morph animation, and SkelControls. SkelControls allow you to override the animation being sent to a particular bone if need be.

Each node available within the AnimTree Editor has at least one input and a single output. Many of them can have inputs added if necessary. You do this by right-clicking the node and adding the input through the context menu. Added inputs can be deleted in the same manner. These inputs can hold custom names, making it very easy to see which animations or other nodes should be connected to them.

The following subsections describe the nodes available, dividing them by the type of control they offer.

AnimTreeNode

This default node is present in all AnimTrees (see **FIGURE 9.59**). All other nodes in the AnimTree eventually link to this node. This is analogous to the Material node found within the Material Editor in that it contains channels that take inputs from the network of other nodes in the tree. It uses the information it receives to produce the final animation result.

FIGURE 9.59   The AnimTreeNode

AnimTreeNode Inputs

Animation—The Animation input should be linked to the final output of the network of animation nodes. Only one link may be connected to this input.

Morph—The Morph input is linked to all the morph nodes within the AnimTree. This input can have multiple links connected to it.

SkelControl—SkelControl inputs must be created through the context menu of the AnimTree node and correspond to a single bone within the skeletal mesh. These inputs should have a single skeletal control node linked to them.

AnimTreeNode Properties

AnimGroups—AnimGroups allow for synching a group of animations of varying lengths or play rates so that their notifications are fired correctly when they are blended. AnimGroups can also cause only one animation within the group to fire notifications if that is desired. The play rate of all the animations contained within an AnimGroup can be adjusted as well.

This is often used in the case of the directional movement animations. As an example, it is possible that sound notifications may be used to play footstep sounds, but if the animations are not all the same length the sounds are thrown out of sync when blending between the directions. Placing these animations in the same group keeps them in sync.

GroupName—This is the name of the group. It should be representative of the animations contained within it.

RateScale—This is a multiplier for the play rates of the animations within the group.

PrioritizedSkelBranches—This is an array of bones that need to be updated before the rest of the bones of the skeleton due to some sort of dependence issue.

This is useful when one bone or set of bones using a skeletal controller relies on the position of another bone to be updated properly. If that bone is not updated prior to the dependent bones being updated, the result is the incorrect placement or orientation of the dependent bones.

PreviewPlayRate—This is the rate at which to play back the animations in the preview window of the AnimTree Editor.

PreviewSkelMesh—This is the skeletal mesh to use for previewing the animations within the AnimTree Editor.

SocketSkelMesh—This is the skeletal mesh to attach to the socket specified by the SocketName when previewing socket attachments within the AnimTree Editor.

SocketStaticMesh—This is the static mesh to attach to the Socket when previewing socket attachments within the AnimTree Editor.

SocketName—This is the name of the socket to use when previewing socket attachments within the AnimTree Editor.

PreviewAnimSets—This is an array of AnimSets to use for previewing within the AnimTree Editor.

PreviewMorphSets—This is an array of MorphTargetSets to use for previewing within the AnimTree Editor.

Animation Nodes

Animation nodes control the playing and blending of skeletal animation sequences. Animation nodes are only compatible with other Animation nodes. This means that you cannot connect a Morph node to an Animation node, and vice versa. This also means that Animation nodes always form their own network that is separate from Morph nodes and Skeletal Controller nodes.

Common Properties

Before we jump into the considerable list of Animation nodes available, a couple properties should be mentioned. The following properties can be found on all Animation nodes and are therefore not covered on each individual description:

NodeName—This is the name by which this node is identified and accessed through code.

bSkipTickWhenZeroWeight—If this property is true, this node is not ticked, or updated, when it has no influence on the final deformation of the mesh.

If this property is false, the node is always ticked, or updated, regardless of its influence on the final state of the mesh.

AnimNodeAimOffset

The AnimNodeAimOffset node allows you to specify translation and/or rotation offsets for the bones of a skeletal mesh corresponding to the nine directions LeftUp, CenterUp, RightUp, LeftCenter, CenterCenter, RightCenter, LeftDown, CenterDown, and RightDown and then blend between those offsets based on the value of the Aim property (see **FIGURE 9.60**).

These offsets are then added to the current locations and rotations of the bone animation passed to the Input link of the node and passed on through the Output of the node.

In an actual game situation, a likely use of this would be to use the player's current aim direction so the player model would appear to be pointing its weapon where the player is actually aiming. However, this is not possible without some additional coding because, by default, the node simply uses the value of the Aim property to determine the direction to use.

FIGURE 9.60   An AnimNodeAimOffset node

9

AimOffset Editor

Double-clicking the AnimNodeAimOffset node opens the AimOffset Editor, where the offsets used when aiming can be created. After opening the AimOffset Editor, you should see the following items visible:

Translate/Rotate Socket—These buttons switch between translation and rotation of the selected bone.

Open/Save—These buttons allow for the loading or saving of an aim offset profile.

> **NOTE**
>
> Clicking the Save button without first creating a profile may cause instabilities!

Profile—This section contains a dropdown list of the profiles of this AnimNodeAimOffset node as well as buttons for creating and deleting those profiles.

Aim Direction—This is an array of buttons that switch between the various directions, making a direction active so it can be edited.

Checking the Force Selected Aim box causes the skeletal mesh in the AnimTree Editor's preview window to show the result of the selected direction's offset settings.

Bone Rotation—This section contains edit boxes for manually entering rotation and translation offset values for the selected bone and direction.

Checking the World Space Widget box causes the transform widget to perform the transformations in world space. Unchecking the box causes the transformations to be performed in local space.

Bones—This section contains a list of the bones affected by this node as well as buttons for adding or removing bones from the list.

Aim—This is a 2D vector that determines the direction used by the node to interpolate the mesh between the different poses. The range of values valid here are determined by the HorizontalRange and VerticalRange properties in the current profile.

AngleOffset—This is an offset in each axis that is applied to the Aim value in-game. This is not applied or visible in the editor.

bForceAimDir—If this property is true, the direction specified by ForceAnimDir is used instead of the direction specified by the Aim property.

If this property is false, the direction specified by the Aim property is used.

bBakeFromAnimations—If this property is true, instead of the rotation and translation values for the bones to create the offsets being manually set, the offsets are calculated based on a set of animation sequences specified in the currently selected Profile as indicated by the CurrentProfileIndex.

If this property is false, the offsets must be set manually in the AimOffset Editor.

ForcedAimDir—This allows you to specify a direction from a list of the available directions to use instead of the direction specified by the Aim property, depending on the value of bForceAimDir.

Profiles—This is an array of all the profiles present in the node. Each profile holds a set of offsets and has the following properties:

HorizontalRange—This allows you to set the range used for determining the horizontal direction according to the Aim.X property.

VerticalRange—This allows you to set the range used for determining the vertical direction according to the Aim.Y property.

AnimName_LU/LC/LD/CU/CC/CD/RU/RC/RD—These properties allow you to set animation sequences to be used in calculating the offsets for the node when bBakeFromAnimations is true. AnimName_CC is used as the reference pose, and the other animation sequences are treated as offsets from that reference pose, meaning the locations and rotations of the bones in the AnimName_CC sequence are subtracted from the locations and rotations of the bones in each of the other animation sequences.

CurrentProfileIndex—This is an indicator of the profile that is currently in use by the node. The profile in use is selected in the AimOffset Editor.

AnimNodeBlend

The AnimNodeBlend node simply blends between two inputs based on the position of the slider at the bottom of the node (see **FIGURE 9.61**). The inputs can be the direct output of an AnimSequencePlayer node or the output of a network of nodes.

FIGURE 9.61   An AnimNodeBlend node

AnimNodeBlendByBase

The AnimNodeBlendByBase node blends between two inputs based on whether the skeletal mesh the AnimSet that's applied has a Base matching the specified criteria (see **FIGURE 9.62**).

If the skeletal mesh has no matching Base, the Normal input is passed through. If the skeletal mesh has a matching Base, the Base input is passed through.

FIGURE 9.62   An AnimNodeBlendByBase node

Type—This specifies whether to look for a specific tag or class of the Base of the skeletal mesh.

BBT_ActorTag—This setting tells the node to look for the tag specified in the ActorTag property.

BBT_ActorClass—This setting tells the node to look for the class specified in the ActorClass property.

ActorTag—This specifies the tag of the Base to look for.

ActorClass—This specifies the class of the Base to look for.

bPlayActiveChild—If this property is true, when the active input changes, the animation passed into the new active input will be played if it is not already playing.

If this property is false, the active input will simply be changed accordingly.

AnimNodeBlendByPhysics

The AnimNodeBlendByPhysics node blends between animations depending on the type of physics currently being used by the object that owns the skeletal mesh component to which this node belongs (see **FIGURE 9.63**).

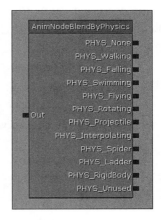

The node has inputs for each physics type that can have an AnimSequencePlayer node or a network of nodes linked to it. The physics of the object is checked and blends to the animation(s) linked to the corresponding input.

> **bPlayActiveChild**—If this property is true, when the active input changes, the animation passed into the new active input will be played if it is not already playing.
>
> If this property is false, the active input will simply be changed accordingly.

FIGURE 9.63 An AnimNodeBlendByPhysics node

AnimNodeBlendByPosture

The AnimNodeBlendByPosture node blends between animations depending on the posture (crouched or standing) of the object that owns the skeletal mesh component to which this node belongs (see **FIGURE 9.64**).

FIGURE 9.64 An AnimNodeBlendByPosture node

The node has inputs for each posture that can have an AnimSequencePlayer node or a network of nodes linked to it. The status of the object is checked and blends to the animation(s) linked to the corresponding input.

> **bPlayActiveChild**—If this property is true, when the active input changes, the animation passed into the new active input will be played if it is not already playing.
>
> If this property is false, the active input will simply be changed accordingly.

AnimNodeBlendBySpeed

The AnimNodeBlendBySpeed node blends between config-urable amounts of inputs based on the speed of the object (which is the magnitude of the vector representing its velocity) that owns the skeletal mesh component to which this node belongs (see **FIGURE 9.65**).

FIGURE 9.65   An AnimNodeBlendBySpeed node

By default, the node has two inputs, but more can be added by right-clicking on the node and choosing Add Input.

> **BlendUpTime**—This is how long in seconds it takes to blend from the current input to the new active input when increasing in speed.
>
> **BlendDownTime**—This is how long in seconds it takes to blend from the current input to the new active input when decreasing in speed.
>
> **BlendDownPerc**—This is the percentage of the distance from one constraint to the next where the change from one input to the next occurs.
>
> **Constraints**—This is an array that determines the range of speeds associated with each input. These should be in order from lowest to highest. The lowest value will be the one at the left end of the slider and the highest value will be the one at the right end of the slider.
>
> **bUseAcceleration**—If this property is true, the node will use the object's acceleration instead of its velocity.
>
> If this property is false, the object's velocity is used.
>
> **bPlayActiveChild**—If this property is true, when the active input changes, the animation passed into the new active input will be played if it is not already playing.
>
> If this property is false, the active input will simply be changed accordingly.

AnimNodeBlendDirectional

The AnimNodeBlendDirectional node blends between inputs based on the direction the object that owns the skeletal mesh component to which this node belongs is moving in relation to the direction it is facing (that is, its rotation). It has four inputs: Forward, Backward, Left, and Right (see **FIGURE 9.66**).

The node's slider can have a value between −180 degrees and 180 degrees. Zero degrees is equivalent to moving in the direction the object is looking. Ninety degrees is equivalent to moving to the right, −90 degrees is equivalent to moving left, and both 180 and −180 degrees are equivalent to moving backward.

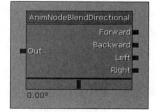

FIGURE 9.66   An AnimNodeBlendDirectional node

DirDegreesPerSecond—This is the number of degrees per second that the directional blend is allowed to change. This keeps animations from being changed several times in succession in a short period of time, which can lead to jerkiness.

AnimNodeBlendList

The AnimNodeBlendList node blends among a list of inputs. You can configure the length of this list by adding inputs through the context menu. In order to switch the active input, a function call must be made in code. When an input is activated, it is linearly blended to over the amount of time specified in the function call to set the new input to active (see **FIGURE 9.67**).

FIGURE 9.67 An AnimNodeBlendList node

> **bPlayActiveChild**—If this property is true, when the active input changes, the animation passed into the new active input will be played if it is not already playing.
>
> If this property is false, the active input will simply be changed accordingly.

AnimNodeBlendMultiBone

At the time of this writing, the AnimNodeBlendMultiBone node is deprecated and non-functional.

AnimNodeBlendPerBone

The AnimNodeBlendPerBone node blends between two inputs on a per-bone basis. The animation input into the Source input is played on all the bones of the skeletal mesh. The animation input into the Target input is played only on the bones specified by the BranchStartBoneName array. The Target animation is blended in based on the value of the node's slider (see **FIGURE 9.68**).

FIGURE 9.68 An AnimNodeBlendPerBone node

> **bForceLocalSpaceBlend**—If this property is true, the blended-in animation will be in local space.
>
> If this property is false, the blended-in animation will be in world space.
>
> **BranchStartBoneName**—This is an array of bone names indicating which bones the Target animation should be applied to. Any bone names entered here and all their children will have the Target animation applied.

AnimNodeCrossfader

The AnimNodeCrossfader node blends between two inputs according to the value of the node's slider (see **FIGURE 9.69**).

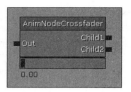

FIGURE 9.69   An AnimNodeCrossfader node

> **DefaultAnimSeqName**—This is the name of the animation sequence that will be played upon initialization of this node if the node linked to the active input has no specified animation sequence.

AnimNodeMirror

The AnimNodeMirror node allows mirroring to be toggled on or off, assuming the skeletal mesh the node is applied to has mirroring set up (see **FIGURE 9.70**).

FIGURE 9.70   An AnimNodeMirror node

> **bEnableMirroring**—If this property is true, the output of the node will be the mirrored skeletal mesh.
>
> If this property is false, the output of the node will be the standard skeletal mesh.

AnimNodePlayCustomAnim

The AnimNodePlayCustomAnim node allows for the overriding of one input, Normal, with another, Custom. A function call in code is necessary to perform the override (see **FIGURE 9.71**).

FIGURE 9.71   An AnimNodePlayCustomAnim node

AnimNodeRandom

The AnimNodeRandom node activates a random input from its list, whose length is configurable, based on parameters set up in the RandomInfo array (see **FIGURE 9.72**).

FIGURE 9.72   An AnimNodeRandom node

> **RandomInfo**—This is an array that holds the parameters used to randomly choose and play back each input of the node.
>
> **Chance**—This is the likelihood this input will be chosen as the random input.
>
> Slots with equal Chance values have an equal likelihood of being chosen. A slot with a higher Chance value has a higher likelihood of being chosen. A slot with a lower Chance value has a lower likelihood of being chosen.

9

These values are normalized in code so that the total of all the values adds up to 1. This means that any values can be used here as long as they are proportionate to each other, thus making it easier for the artist.

LoopCountMin/LoopCountMax—These are the minimum and maximum number of loops the animation of this input will be played. A random value between these two values is used each time this input is randomly chosen.

BlendInTime—This is the number of seconds to spend blending into this animation when it is randomly chosen.

PlayRateRange—This is the rate at which to play this animation. A value of 0.0 plays the animation at its default rate.

X/Y—These are the minimum and maximum rates at which to play the animation. A random value between these two values is used each time this input is chosen.

AnimNodeScalePlayRate

The AnimNodeScalePlayRate node scales the speed at which the input animation is played back (see **FIGURE 9.73**).

FIGURE 9.73 An AnimNodeScalePlayRate node

ScaleByValue—This value is multiplied by the play rate of the animation that is input into this node.

AnimNodeScaleRateBySpeed

The AnimNodeScaleRateBySpeed node scales the speed at which the animation that is input into this node is played back based on the speed of the Object that owns the skeletal mesh component to which this node belongs (see **FIGURE 9.74**).

FIGURE 9.74 An AnimNodeScaleRateBySpeed node

BaseSpeed—This is the speed of the object at which the multiplier for the play rate of the animation will be 1.0. The actual multiplier is calculated by dividing the object's speed by this value. If this value is 0.0, the value of ScaleByValue is used as the multiplier instead.

ScaleByValue—This value is multiplied by the play rate of the animation that is input into this node when BaseSpeed is set to 0.0.

AnimNodeSequenceBlendByAim

The AnimNodeSequenceBlendByAim node, like the AnimNodeAimOffset node, is based on the direction the object that owns the skeletal mesh component to which this node belongs is aiming, but this node simply blends between a set of nine animations instead of using offsets to alter an animation passed to the node (see **FIGURE 9.75**).

Aim—This is a 2D vector that determines the direction used by the node to interpolate the mesh between the different poses. The range of values valid here are determined by the HorizontalRange and VerticalRange properties.

HorizontalRange—This allows you to set the range used for determining the horizontal direction according to the Aim.X property.

FIGURE 9.75   An AnimNodeSequenceBlendByAim node

VerticalRange—This allows you to set the range used for determining the vertical direction according to the Aim.Y property.

AngleOffset—This is an offset in each axis that is applied to the Aim value in game. This is not applied or visible in the editor.

AnimName_LU/LC/LD/CU/CC/CD/RU/RC/RD—These properties allow you to set the animation sequences to be blended between based on the Aim property.

For descriptions of the remaining properties, see the AnimSequencePlayer description.

AnimNodeSlot

The AnimNodeSlot node provides a hook for Matinee or code to override an animation or blend between animations. This is very useful when used in conjunction with one or several AnimNodeBlendPerBone nodes so that individual parts of the skeletal mesh can have one or several animations played on them through Matinee or code (see **FIGURE 9.76**).

FIGURE 9.76   An AnimNodeSlot node

The Source input is the default animation played when Matinee or the code is not overriding the slot. Each Channel input corresponds to one Anim Control Track within Matinee that can be used for overriding the default animation.

The NodeName is very important with this node because it is how the individual slots are identified within Matinee or code.

AnimNodeSynch

The AnimNodeSynch node allows animation sequences to be kept in synch regardless of their lengths or play rates (see **FIGURE 9.77**). This functionality has been replaced by the AnimGroups array contained within the AnimTree node and is still available only to retain compatibility with older AnimTrees created using this node.

FIGURE 9.77   An AnimNodeSynch node

Groups—This is an array of the groups used for synchronization.

GroupName—This is the name of the group. It should be representative of the animations contained within it.

bFireSlaveNotifies—If this property is true, the notifications of all the animation sequences will be fired regardless of their slave status.

If this property is false, only animation sequences not marked as being slaves will have their notifications fired.

RateScale—This is a multiplier for the play rates of the animations within the group.

AnimSequence Player

The AnimSequencePlayer node is extremely important to the AnimTree because it exposes, or plays, an animation sequence within the AnimTree. Think of it as being analogous to the Texture Sample node in the Material Editor (see **FIGURE 9.78**).

FIGURE 9.78 An AnimSequencePlayer node

AnimNodeSequence

AnimSeqName—This is the name of the animation sequence for this node to play. This animation sequence must be contained within one of the AnimSets specified in the PreviewAnimSets array of the AnimTree node.

Rate—This is the speed at which to play the animation. This value is multiplied by the RateScale property of the animation sequence that is set within the AnimSet Editor.

bPlaying—If this property is true, the animation will be playing.

If this property is false, the animation will not be playing.

bLooping—If this property is true, this animation will loop.

If this property is false, this animation will not loop.

bCauseActorAnimEnd—If this property is true, the OnAnimEnd() function is called on the Actor that owns the skeletal mesh to which this node is applied.

bCauseActorAnimPlay—If this property is true, the OnAnimBegin() function is called on the Actor that owns the skeletal mesh to which this node is applied.

bZeroRootRotation—If this property is true, the rotation of the root bone is forced to zero on this animation.

bNoNotifies—If this property is true, this animation sequence will not fire any notifications.

CurrentTime—This is the current position within the animation sequence.

NotifyWeightThreshold—This is the weight that must be given to this node in the final animation in order for its notifications to be fired.

This has no effect when this node is contained within a group for synchronization.

RootBoneOption—This specifies how to treat any root bone movement contained within this animation sequence. The slots [0], [1], and [2] correspond to the X, Y, and Z axes.

RBA_Default—This setting uses the Root's translation as it is in the animation sequence.

RBA_Discard—This setting ignores any root bone translation within the animation sequence.

RBA_Translate—This setting takes the root bone's translation from the animation sequence and applies it as velocity to the Actor owning the skeletal mesh to which this node is applied.

RootRotationOption—This specifies how to treat any root bone rotation contained within this animation sequence. The slots [0], [1], and [2] correspond to Roll, Pitch, and Yaw.

RBA_Default—This setting uses the Root's rotation as it is in the animation sequence.

RBA_Discard—This setting ignores any root bone rotation within the animation sequence.

RBA_Extract—This setting takes the root bone's rotation from the animation sequence and applies it to the Actor owning the skeletal mesh to which this node is applied.

Group

bForceAlwaysSlave—If this property is true, this node is not allowed to be the master of any synchronization group.

bSynchronize—If this property is true, this node will be synchronized when included in a synchronization group.

If this property is false, this node will not be synchronized but will still be included in the group for notification purposes.

SynchGroupName—This is the name of the group to which this node belongs. This should match a name in the AnimGroups array of the AnimTree node or the Groups array of an AnimNodeSynch node.

SynchPosOffset—This is a percentage to offset this node when doing synchronization.

This is useful when trying to synchronize nodes that are not identical on a relative scale. For example, one animation may have its right foot down 25% of the way through the animation, but another may have its right foot down 50% of the way through the animation. In order for synchronization to work properly, you would want to offset one of the animations so they are identical.

Display

bShowTimeLineSlider—If this property is true, a time slider is displayed below this node that shows the current position of the animation as it plays and allows for scrubbing through the animation.

The current position is displayed as a percentage of the total animation length and in seconds.

In **TUTORIAL 9.9**, we begin the process of setting up a fairly basic AnimTree for a character. These can get extremely complex depending on what is required for the game in question and all the circumstances that the character may encounter in said game. We begin by setting up a simple blend between animations based on the direction the player is traveling.

TUTORIAL 9.9: Setting Up Directional Blending

1. Right-click in the Generic Browser and choose New AnimTree. Enter the following information in the dialog that appears and then click OK:

   ▶ **Package**: Chapter_09_Animation

   ▶ **Group**: Animations

   ▶ **Name**: animTree_human

   The AnimTree Editor appears at this point, but it will be empty with the exception of the AnimTree node. Make sure the AnimTree node is selected so its properties are visible (see **FIGURE 9.79**).

2. Select the ImportMesh_Human_Male skeletal mesh in the CH_AnimHuman package in Generic Browser and click the Use Current Selection in Browser button 🔁 for the PreviewSkeletalMesh property of the AnimTree node. The mesh should appear in the Preview panel of the AnimTree Editor (see **FIGURE 9.80**).

3. In the Generic Browser, select the K_AnimHuman_BaseMale asset in the CH_AnimHuman package. Back in the AnimTree Editor, add a new item to the PreviewAnimSets array of the AnimTree node. Then click the Use Current Selection in Browser button 🔁 for the new item.

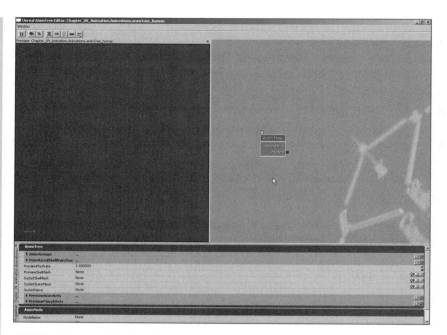

FIGURE 9.79   The AnimTree Editor

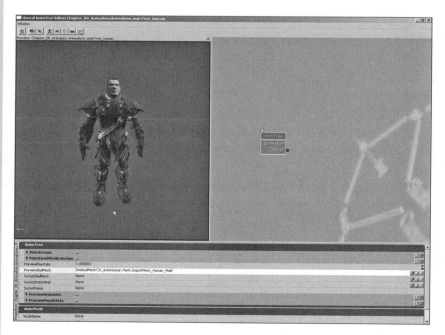

FIGURE 9.80   You should now see the ImportMesh_Human_Male mesh.

4. Right-click in the AnimTree Editor and choose AnimSequence Player. Select the new node to view its properties and then set the following (see **FIGURE 9.81**):

   ▶ **AnimSeqName**: run_fwd_rif

   ▶ **bPlaying**: True

   ▶ **bLooping**: True

   ▶ **NodeName**: FwdAnim

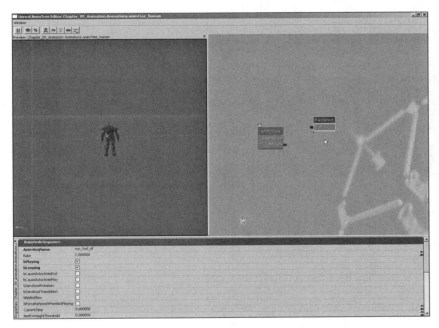

FIGURE 9.81   The new AnimSequence Player has been added.

5. With the node selected, press Ctrl+W three times to create three more AnimSequence Player nodes. Enter the following values into the new nodes (see **FIGURE 9.82**):

   ▶ **Back Animation**

       ▶ **AnimSeqName**: run_bwd_rif

       ▶ **NodeName**: BwdAnim

   ▶ **Left Animation**

       ▶ **AnimSeqName**: run_lt_rif

       ▶ **NodeName**: LeftAnim

> ▶ **Right Animation**
>
>   > ▶ **AnimSeqName**: run_rt_rif
>   >
>   > ▶ **NodeName**: RightAnim

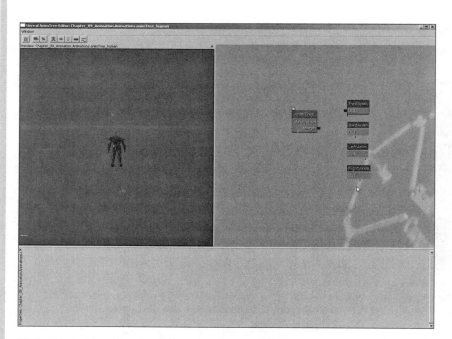

FIGURE 9.82   You should now have four total animation nodes.

6. Right-click in the AnimTree Editor and choose AnimNodeBlendDirectional. Select the new node to view its properties and set the NodeName property to DirNode.

7. Make the following connections (see **FIGURE 9.83**):

> ▶ FwdAnim-Out → DirNode-Forward
>
> ▶ BackAnim-Out → DirNode-Backward
>
> ▶ LeftAnim-Out → DirNode-Left
>
> ▶ RightAnim-Out → DirNode-Right
>
> ▶ DirNode-Out → AnimTree-Animation

8. You can now drag the slider of the DirNode and you should see the animation blend between the various directions.

9. Save your progress.

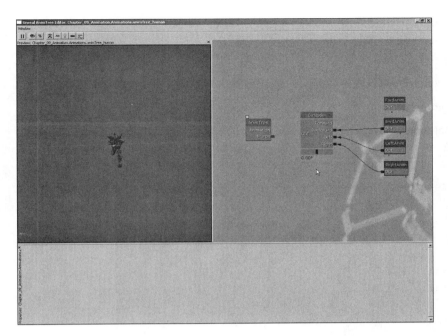

FIGURE 9.83   The nodes should connect like so.

END TUTORIAL 9.9

Following up **TUTORIAL 9.9**, we now implement an additional blending between animations based on the speed of the character. In our case, we blend between the running animations and a single idle animation in **TUTORIAL 9.10**. In an actual game situation, it may also be necessary or desirable to have an additional speed blend for walking animations.

TUTORIAL 9.10: Setting Up Blending by Speed

1. Continuing from the **TUTORIAL 9.9**, double-click the animTree_human asset in the Generic Browser to open it in the AnimTree Editor. If you have not completed it, you may use the animTree_human_01 asset instead.

2. Right-click and choose AnimSequencePlayer. Select the new node to view its properties and then set the following:

   ▶ **AnimSeqName**: idle_ready_rif

   ▶ **bPlaying**: True

   ▶ **bLooping**: True

   ▶ **NodeName**: IdleAnim

3. Right-click and choose AnimNodeBlendBySpeed. Select the new node to view its properties and then set the following (see **FIGURE 9.84**):

- ▶ **BlendUpTime**: 0.15

- ▶ **BlendDownTime**: 0.25

- ▶ **BlendDownPerc**: 0.1

- ▶ **NodeName**: SpeedNode

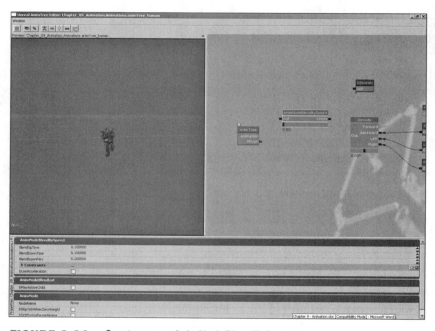

FIGURE 9.84   Create a new AnimNodeBlendBySpeed.

4. Right-click the SpeedNode and choose Add Input. You should see two input links on the node now: Child1 and Child2.

5. Make the following connections (see **FIGURE 9.85**):

- ▶ IdleAnim-Out → SpeedNode-Child1

- ▶ DirNode-Out → SpeedNode-Child2

- ▶ SpeedNode-Out → AnimTree-Animation

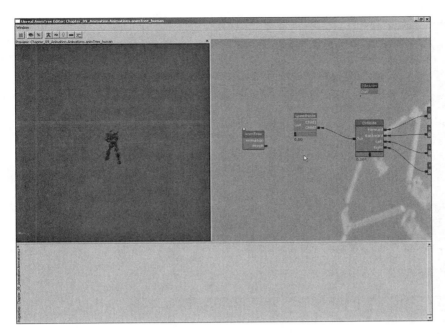

FIGURE 9.85   Make the shown connections.

6. You should be able to drag the slider of the SpeedNode and see the animations blend between the IdleAnim and the currently active input of the DirNode.

7. Save your progress.

END TUTORIAL 9.10

In **TUTORIAL 9.11**, we mask bones from receiving animation, allowing the character to appear to be running and taunting at the same time.

TUTORIAL 9.11: Masking Bones Using AnimNodeBlendPerBone

1. Continuing from **TUTORIAL 9.10**, double-click the animTree_human asset to open it in the AnimTree Editor. If you have not completed it, you may use the animTree_human_02 asset instead.

2. Right-click in the AnimTree Editor and choose AnimNodeBlendPerBone. Select the new node to view its properties and set the following (see **FIGURE 9.86**):

   ▶ **BranchStartBoneName**: Add a new item to this array

      ▶ **[0]**: b_Spine

   ▶ **NodeName**: UpperBody

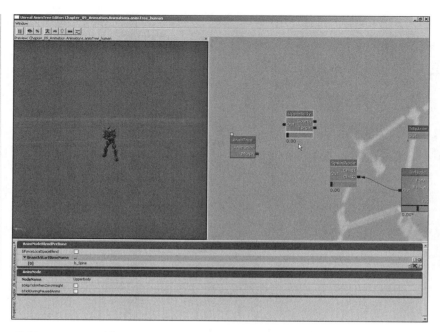

FIGURE 9.86   A new AnimNodeBlendPerBone has been added.

3. Connect the Out link of the SpeedNode to the Source link of the UpperBody node (see **FIGURE 9.87**).

4. Right-click in the AnimTree Editor and choose AnimSequencePlayer. Select the new node to view its properties and then set the following:

> ▸ **AnimSeqName**: Taunt_UB_ComeHere
>
> ▸ **bPlaying**: True
>
> ▸ **bLooping**: True
>
> ▸ **NodeName**: TauntAnim

5. Connect the Out link of the TauntAnim node to the Target link of the UpperBody node (see **FIGURE 9.88**).

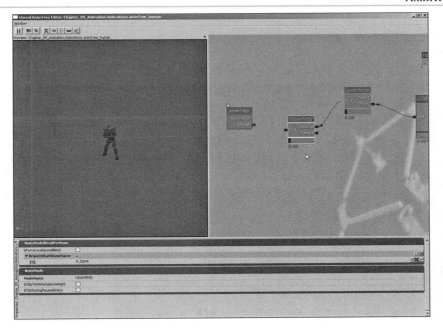

FIGURE 9.87   Connect the new node as shown.

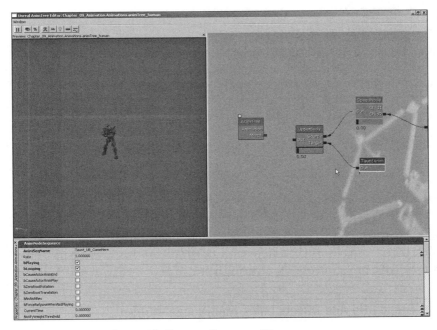

FIGURE 9.88   Connect in the new Sequence Player.

6. Connect the Out link of the UpperBody node to the Animation link of the AnimTree node (see **FIGURE 9.89**).

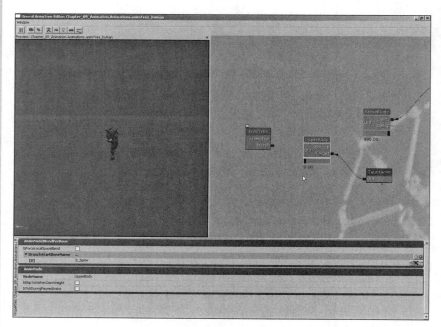

FIGURE 9.89   Connect the UpperBody node to the AnimTree node as shown.

7. Drag the slider of the UpperBody node all the way to the right to give the TauntAnim full weighting. You should now see the taunt animation playing on the upper half of the mesh while the movement animations are still playing on the bottom half of the mesh.

8. Save your progress.

END TUTORIAL 9.11

A nice touch to add to the character's animations is to account for the direction the character's weapon is aiming. Often, you will see the entire mesh rotate as the player turns to aim. More realism and believability can be achieved by using an aim offset node to force certain bones to follow the player's aim while maintaining the current animation. In **TUTORIAL 9.12**, we set up a basic aim offset node by specifying offset rotations for specific bones.

TUTORIAL 9.12: Setting Up Aim Offsets Using AnimNodeAimOffset

1. Continuing from the **TUTORIAL 9.11**, double-click the animTree_human asset in the Generic Browser to open it in the AnimTree Editor. If you have not completed it, you may use the animTree_human_03 asset instead.

2. Right-click in the AnimTree Editor and choose AnimNodeAimOffset. Set the NodeName property to AimNode (see **FIGURE 9.90**).

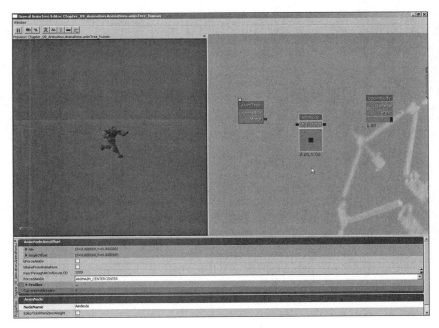

FIGURE 9.90 Create a new AnimNodeAimOffset.

3. Connect the Out link of the UpperBody to the Input link of the AimNode. Then, connect the Out link of the AimNode to the Animation link of the AnimTree node (see **FIGURE 9.91**).

4. Double-click the AimNode to open the AimOffset Editor. Position the AimOffset Editor so that it and the Preview panel are visible.

5. Click the New button in the Profile section of the AimOffset Editor. In the dialog that appears, enter **BaseAim** as the name for the new profile (see **FIGURE 9.92**).

6. In the Bones section, click the Add Bone button and select b_Spine from the list of available bones.

> **NOTE**
>
> If you keep an eye on the AnimTree Editor's preview window while you do this, you'll notice the character update its upper-body aiming.

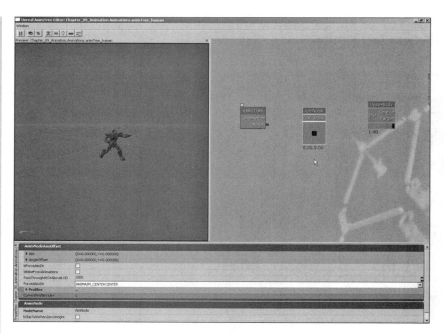

FIGURE 9.91   Connect the nodes as shown.

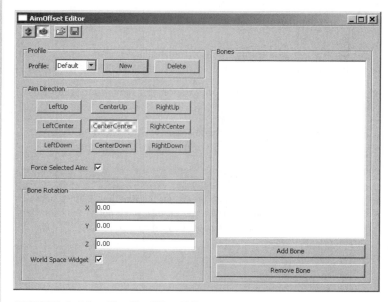

FIGURE 9.92   The AimOffset Editor

7. Click the buttons for each of the directions in the Aim Direction section and enter the following values for each of them using the text boxes of the Bone Rotation section:

- **LeftUp**
    - **X:** −35.0
    - **Y:** 0.0
    - **Z:** −70.0
- **CenterUp**
    - **X:** −35.0
    - **Y:** 0.0
    - **Z:** 0.0
- **RightUp**
    - **X:** −35.0
    - **Y:** 0.0
    - **Z:** 70.0
- **LeftCenter**
    - **X:** 0.0
    - **Y:** 0.0
    - **Z:** −70.0
- **CenterCenter**
    - **X:** 0.0
    - **Y:** 0.0
    - **Z:** 0.0

- **RightCenter**
    - **X:** 0.0
    - **Y:** 0.0
    - **Z:** 70.0
- **LeftDown**
    - **X:** 35.0
    - **Y:** 0.0
    - **Z:** −70.0
- **CenterDown**
    - **X:** 35.0
    - **Y:** 0.0
    - **Z:** 0.0
- **RightDown**
    - **X:** 35.0
    - **Y:** 0.0
    - **Z:** 70.0

8. Just to be safe, click the Save button in the AimOffset Editor and save the profile to a location and with a name of your preference. This way, if the profile gets overridden or altered, you can simply restore it by loading this file.

9. Close the AimOffset Editor.

10. You should be able to drag the mouse around in the AimNode and see the mesh adjust its aim accordingly (see **FIGURE 9.93**).

11. Save your progress.

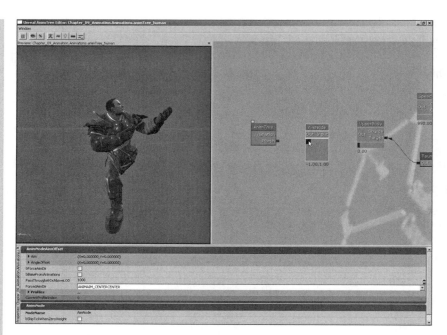

FIGURE 9.93   The character now adjusts his aim.

END TUTORIAL 9.12

Morph Nodes

Morph nodes deal with exposing and modifying the weighting of morph targets. Only morph nodes may be used as inputs into other morph nodes, although multiple morph nodes may be linked to a single input of another morph node.

Morph Node Common Properties

As we did with Animation nodes, let's look at the one property that is common to all morph nodes before we actually jump into the list of nodes available to us:

> **NodeName**—This is the name of this node, used for identification purposes and accessing the node through code.

MorphPose

The MorphPose node exposes one individual morph target within the AnimTree (see **FIGURE 9.94**).

FIGURE 9.94   A MorphPose node

MorphName—This is the name of the morph target this node exposes. The morph target named here must be contained within one of the MorphTargetSets named in the PreviewMorphSets array of the AnimTree node.

Weight—This is the weight (or amount of influence) given to this morph target.

MorphNodeWeight

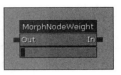

The MorphNodeWeight node adjusts the weighting of each node linked to its In link (see **FIGURE 9.95**). The weight of the morph targets is determined by the slider of the node.

FIGURE 9.95 A MorphNodeWeight node

Skeletal Controller Nodes

Skeletal controller nodes deal with manipulating a single bone or chain of bones directly instead of through the use of animations. This can be useful for making tweaks or adjustments to an animation without having to go back to your original 3D animation package. There are also specific nodes that allow for such things as controlling the wheels of vehicles. Once again, we start by looking at common properties.

Common Properties

ControlName—This is the name by which the node is identified and accessed within code.

ControlStrength—This is the amount of influence the node imparts. This is much like the weighting properties of other node types.

BlendInTime—This is the amount of time in seconds this controller takes to increase its ControlStrength to 1.0 when it is activated.

BlendOutTime—This is the amount of time in seconds this controller takes to decrease its ControlStrength to 0.0 when it is deactivated.

bSetStrengthFromAnimNode—If this property is true, this controller's ControlStrength is linked to the weighting of the animation nodes listed in the StrengthAnimNodeNameList. The value used is the sum of the weights of all the nodes in the list.

bPropagateSetActive—If this property is true, when activated, this controller causes the controller into which it is input to be activated as well.

StrengthAnimNodeNameList—This is an array of the names of the animation nodes from which to draw the value to use for the ControlStrength when bSetStrengthFromAnimNode is true.

BoneScale—This is a multiplier to apply to the scale of the bone to which this controller is applied.

Bone Control Space

Several properties within the various skeletal controller nodes require a control space from the bone to determine the reference frame in which the controller is applied. The options for those properties are defined here:

>**BCS_WorldSpace**—The location represents absolute coordinates in world space.
>
>**BCS_ActorSpace**—The location specified is relative to the Actor owning the skeletal mesh to which this node is applied (that is, local space).
>
>**BCS_ComponentSpace**—The location specified is relative to the origin of the skeletal mesh to which this node is applied (that is, relative to the Root).
>
>**BCS_ParentBoneSpace**—The location specified is relative to the location of the parent bone of the bone this node controls.
>
>**BCS_BoneSpace**—The location specified is relative to the location of the bone this node controls.
>
>**BCS_OtherBoneSpace**—The location specified is relative to the bone specified by a name entered into a supporting property within the node. This property's name usually ends in *BoneName*.

SkelControlLimb

This controller creates an IK solver over a two-bone chain. It is specifically designed for limbs or extremities that have a single joint between two bones. The bone this controller is applied to should be the last bone in the chain (see **FIGURE 9.96**).

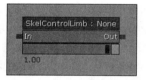

FIGURE 9.96   A SkelControlLimb node

Because the SkelControlLimb node can only create an IK solver across two bones, artists will run into an interesting problem if they are using limb rig setups that employ "roll" bones, such as bones at the location of the bicep and center of the forearm that allow for smoother twisting. If these roll bones are part of a standard bone chain hierarchy as is common in most 3D packages, the node does not work properly as there will be more than two bones in the chain. To make roll bones work, a special joint hierarchy is needed in which the roll bones are not part of a straight hierarchy, but are instead parented in such a way that there are only two bones between the shoulder and the wrist, as shown in **FIGURE 9.97**.

The target location for the affected bone is designated in the viewport by a purple diamond and a translation widget for visually manipulating its location.

A target for the joint between the bones to bend toward is also provided and is designated in the viewport by a pink diamond and a translation widget for visually manipulating its location.

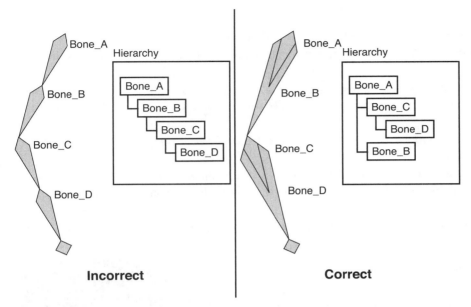

FIGURE 9.97   To the left is the incorrect setup typical of most 3D applications. To the right is the necessary roll bone setup for Unreal.

Effector

EffectorLocation—This is the location at which the controller attempts to place the bone. The bone will actually be placed as close to this location as possible within the constraints of the skeleton.

EffectLocationSpace—This determines what coordinate system to use when interpreting the location specified by the EffectorLocation. See the "Bone Control Space" section of the "Skeletal Controller Nodes" section for complete descriptions of the options for this setting.

EffectSpaceBoneName—This is the name of the bone to use when the EffectorLocationSpace is set to BCS_OtherBoneSpace.

Joint

JointTargetLocationSpace—This determines what coordinate system to use when interpreting the location specified by the JointTargetLocation. See the "Bone Control Space" section of the "Skeletal Controller Nodes" section for complete descriptions of the options for this setting.

JointTargetLocation—This is the location that the joint bends toward as the controller attempts to place the affected bone at the target location.

JointTargetSpaceBoneName—This is the name of the bone to use when the JointTargetLocationSpace is set to BCS_OtherBoneSpace.

Limb

BoneAxis—This is the axis that points along the length of the bones within the chain.

JointAxis—This is the axis that the joint in between the two bones in the chain bends around.

bInvertBoneAxis—If this property is true, the opposite of the axis specified in BoneAxis will be used. For example, if BoneAxis is set to Z, setting this value to True causes you to use –Z.

bInvertJointAxis—If this property is true, the opposite of the axis specified in JointAxis is used.

bMaintainEffectorRelRot—If this property is true, the rotation of the controlled bone is altered as the bone is moved. This helps to keep the limb from becoming all twisted up in certain situations.

If this property is false, the rotation of the controlled bone will not be changed.

SkelControlFootPlacement

The SkelControlFootPlacement node performs line checks to determine the distance to the surface beneath the skeletal mesh and attempts to place the bone to which this controller is applied on that surface (see **FIGURE 9.98**).

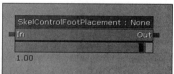

FIGURE 9.98   A SkelControlFootPlacement node

The target location to place the bone is designated by a purple diamond in the viewport and a translation widget, but the location is locked in the viewport because the actual location is determined by code during play.

The target direction for the joint to bend toward is designated in the viewport by a pink diamond and a translation widget for manipulating its location.

Many of the properties of the SkelControlFootPlacement controller are inherited from the SkelControlLimb controller. See its description for explanations of those properties.

FootOffset—This is the amount to offset the affected bone along the direction from the hip bone to the foot bone.

FootUpAxis—This is the axis of the bone that will be aligned to the surface when bOrientFootToGround is true.

FootRotOffset—This is a set of rotational offsets in each axis that will be applied prior to aligning the bone to the surface.

bInvertFootUpAxis—If this property is true, the opposite of the FootUpAxis is used.

If this property is false, the FootUpAxis is used as is.

bOrientFootToGround—If this property is true, the bone will be aligned to the surface in the axis defined by FootUpAxis.

If this property is false, the bone will simply be placed translated to the intersection point with the surface.

bOnlyEnableForUpAdjustment—If this property is true, this node will only affect the bone when it is below the surface and needs to be adjusted upward.

If this property is false, this node will adjust the bone when it is above or below the surface. This could be problematic if the character can jump or is falling.

MaxUpAdjustment—This is the maximum distance below the surface that the node will have any effect.

MaxDownAdjustment—This is the maximum distance above the surface that this node will have any effect.

MaxFootOrientAdjust—This is the maximum amount of degrees the bone will be rotated in an attempt to orient the bone to the surface.

SkelControlLookAt

The SkelControlLookAt node causes the controlled bone to be oriented toward a target location (see **FIGURE 9.99**).

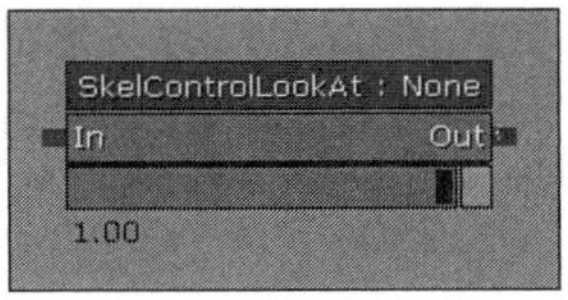

FIGURE 9.99 A SkelControlLookAt node

LookAt

TargetLocation—This is the location toward which the bone will be oriented.

TargetLocationSpace—This determines how the location specified in the TargetLocation is interpreted.

LookAtAxis—This is the axis of the controlled bone that should point toward the TargetLocation.

UpAxis—This is the axis of the controlled bone that should point in the world's positive Z-axis.

This cannot be the same axis as the LookAtAxis.

TargetSpaceBoneName—This is the name of the bone to use when TargetLocationSpace is set to BCS_OtherBoneSpace.

bInvertLookAtAxis—If this property is true, the controller will use the opposite of the LookAtAxis. This could also be seen as the controller forcing the LookAtAxis to face away from the TargetLocation.

If this property is false, the controller will use the LookAtAxis as specified.

bDefineUpAxis—If this property is true, the controller will attempt to force the UpAxis to point up.

If this property is false, the controller will ignore the UpAxis.

bInvertUpAxis—If this property is true, the controller will use the opposite of the UpAxis. This could also be seen as the controller forcing the UpAxis to point in the world's negative Z-axis.

If this property is false, the controller will use the UpAxis as specified.

TargetLocationInterpSpeed—This is the rate at which the current location of the target interpolates to the new location of the target.

Limit

AllowRotationSpace—This is the reference frame that is used for determining the limits of the bone's rotation.

bEnableLimit—If this property is true, the angle the controlled bone is allowed to rotate is limited.

If this property is false, the controlled bone is allowed to rotate freely.

bLimitBasedOnRefPose—If this property is true, the limited rotation is based on the rotation of the bone in the skeletal mesh's reference pose.

If this property is false, the limited rotation is based on the current orientation of the bone.

bDisableBeyondLimit—If this property is true, when the bone's rotation exceeds the limit, it will be interpolated back to its original orientation.

If this property is false, when the bone's rotation exceeds the limit, it will simply not rotate any farther.

bNotifyBeyondLimit—If this property is true, when the bone's rotation exceeds the limit, an event is fired off notifying the actor that owns the skeletal mesh to which this control is applied.

If this property is false, no event is fired when the limit is exceeded.

bShowLimit—If this property is true, a visual representation of the limit is drawn in the viewport. This appears as a green cone.

bAllowRotationX—If this property is true, the bone is allowed to rotate around the X-axis in an attempt to face the target.

If this property is false, the bone is not allowed to rotate around the X-axis as a result of this controller.

bAllowRotationY—If this property is true, the bone is allowed to rotate around the Y-axis in an attempt to face the target.

If this property is false, the bone is not allowed to rotate around the Y-axis as a result of this controller.

bAllowRotationZ—If this property is true, the bone is allowed to rotate around the Z-axis in an attempt to face the target.

If this property is false, the bone is not allowed to rotate around the Z-axis as a result of this controller.

MaxAngle—This is the maximum angle the bone is allowed to rotate in all axes.

DeadZoneAngle—This is the maximum angle between the current orientation of the bone and the orientation that would result in the bone looking directly at the target where the bone is considered to be facing the target.

AllowRotationOtherBoneName—This is the name of the bone to use when AllowRotationSpace is set to BCS_OtherBoneSpace.

SkelControlSingleBone

The SkelControlSingleBone node controls, either by over-riding or adding to, the translation and/or rotation of a single bone (see **FIGURE 9.100**).

FIGURE 9.100   A SkelControlSingleBone node

Adjustments

bApplyTranslation—If this property is true, this controller will affect the translation of the controlled bone.

If this property is false, this controller will not affect the translation of the controlled bone.

bApplyRotation—If this property is true, this controller will affect the rotation of the controlled bone.

If this property is false, this controller will not affect the rotation of the controlled bone.

Translation

bAddTranslation—If this property is true, the specified offset is added to the bone's current location.

If this property is false, the specified offset overrides the bone's current location.

BoneTranslation—This is the offset to apply to the bone's location.

BoneTranslationSpace—This determines how the specified offset will be interpreted.

TranslationSpaceBoneName—This is the name of the bone to use when the BoneTranslationSpace is set to BCS_OtherBoneSpace.

Rotation

bAddRotation—If this property is true, the specified rotation is added to the bone's current rotation.

If this property is false, the specified rotation overrides the bone's current rotation.

BoneRotationSpace—This is the name of the bone to use when the BoneRotationSpace is set to BCS_OtherBoneSpace.

BoneRotation—This is the offset to apply to the bone's rotation.

RotationSpaceBoneName—This is the name of the bone to use when the BoneRotationSpace is set to BCS_OtherBoneSpace.

SkelControlSpline

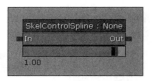

The SkelControlSpline node causes the controlled bone and a specified number of parent bones to be oriented along a spline (see **FIGURE 9.101**).

FIGURE 9.101   A SkelControlSpline node

SplineLength—This is the number of parent bones to align to the spline.

SplineBoneAxis—This is the axis that determines the direction the spline travels as it leaves the controlled bone.

BoneRotMode—This determines the rotational behavior of the bones that are aligned to the spline.

SCR_NoChange—This setting will not change the rotation of the bones at all.

SCR_AlongSpline—This setting causes the axis specified by SplineBoneAxis to be aligned with the curve.

SCR_Interpolate—This setting causes the rotation of the bones to be interpolated between the rotations of the bones at each end of the spline.

bInvertSplineBoneAxis—If this property is true, the direction the spline travels when leaving the bone is the opposite of the SplineBoneAxis.

If this property is false, the SplineBoneAxis is used as is.

EndSplineTension—This is the strength of the tangent of the spline as it leaves from the controlled bone.

StartSplineTension—This is the strength of the tangent of the spline as it approaches the bone at the opposite end from the controlled bone.

SkelControlTrail

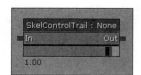

The SkelControlTrail node causes a chain of bones to trail behind a parent bone (see **FIGURE 9.102**).

FIGURE 9.102 A SkelControlTrail node

ChainLength—This is the number of bones to include in the chain, including the controlled bone.

ChainBoneAxis—This is the axis of the bones that should point in the direction of the chain.

bInvertChainBoneAxis—If this property is true, the direction of the chain is the opposite of the ChainBoneAxis.

If this property is false, the ChainBoneAxis is used as is.

bLimitStretch—If this property is true, the bones included in the chain will have the amount they can stretch limited.

If this property is false, the stretching of the bones is not limited at all.

TrailRelaxation—This is how tightly the chain follows the parent bone. Higher values make the trail effect less noticeable.

StretchLimit—This is the maximum amount the bones are allowed to stretch beyond their length in the reference pose of the skeletal mesh when bLimitStretch is true.

SkelControlWheel

The SkelControlWheel node is used to set up and control vehicle wheels (see **FIGURE 9.103**).

FIGURE 9.103   A SkelControlWheel node

> **WheelDisplacement**—This offsets the controlled bone in the Z-axis for preview purposes. This property can be used to determine the proper value for the WheelMaxRenderDisplacment property.

WheelMaxRenderDisplacement—This is the maximum distance the controlled bone is allowed to be offset in either direction of the Z-axis.

WheelRoll—This rotates the controlled bone around the WheelRollAxis for preview purposes.

WheelRollAxis—This determines the axis that the wheel rotates around when the vehicle is moving forward or backward.

WheelSteeringAxis—This determines the axis that the wheel rotates around when the vehicle is turning left or right.

WheelSteering—This rotates the controlled bone around the WheelSteeringAxis for preview purposes.

bInvertWheelRoll—If this property is true, the wheel rotates in the opposite direction when rolling.

bInvertWheelSteering—If this property is true, the wheel rotates in the opposite direction when steering.

You may have noticed that the animations have the character steadying his weapon (or imaginary weapon as it is) with his off hand. In **TUTORIALS 9.13** through **9.17**, we alter the animations so that the weapon would just be resting on the forearm of the off arm as if the player had injured his hand or was otherwise unable to physically grip the weapon with his hand.

TUTORIAL 9.13: Altering Animations Using SkelControlLimb and SkelControlSingleBone, Part I: Forward Animation

1. Continuing from **TUTORIAL 9.12**, double-click the animTree_human asset in the Generic Browser to open it in the AnimTree Editor. If you have not completed it, you may use the animTree-Human_04 asset instead (see **FIGURE 9.104**).

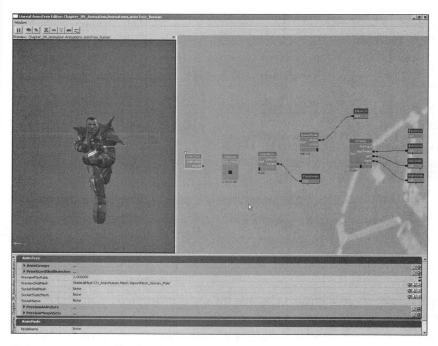

FIGURE 9.104   The AnimTree as it currently appears

2. Right-click the AnimTree node and choose Add SkelControl Chain. Select the b_LeftHand bone from the list in the dialog that appears and click OK. There should be a new link created on the AnimTree node labeled b_LeftHand (see **FIGURE 9.105**).

   We link a chain of SkelControlLimb nodes to the b_LeftHand link and a chain of SkelControlSingleBone nodes to the LftShoulder link. The reason for using a chain of nodes is that we need different settings depending on which animation is being played. Because of this, we use one node for each animation and link the weight of that skeletal controller to the weight of the AnimSequence Player node for the corresponding animation. That way, the effects of each skeletal controller will only be seen when the associated animation is playing.

3. Right-click in the AnimTree Editor and choose SkelControlLimb. Connect the In link of the new node to the b_LeftHand link of the AnimTree node (see **FIGURE 9.106**).

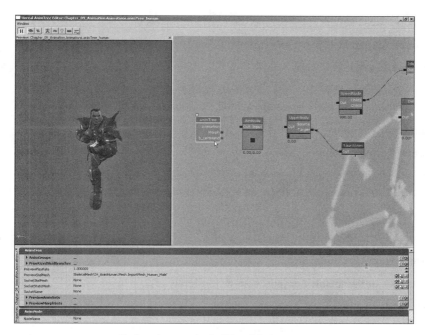

FIGURE 9.105 Notice the new b_LeftHand link.

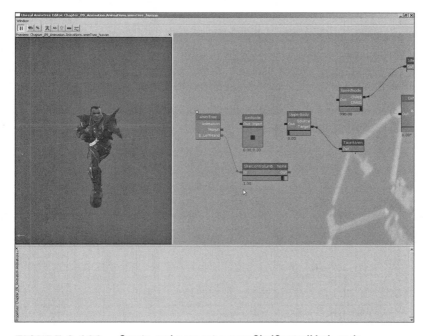

FIGURE 9.106 Create and connect a new SkelControlLimb node.

4. Select the new node to view its properties and then set the following:

▶ **EffectorLocationSpace**: BCS_OtherBoneSpace

▶ **EffectorSpaceBoneName**: b_Spine

This sets the location in relation to the b_Spine bone, which will account for any modifications caused by the aim offset node we implemented previously.

▶ **JointTargetLocationSpace**: BCS_OtherBoneSpace

▶ **JointTargetSpaceBoneName**: b_Spine

As before, this sets the location in relation to the b_Spine bone, which will account for any modifications caused by the aim offset node we implemented previously.

▶ **bMaintainEffectorRelRot**: True

▶ **ControlName**: FwdLimb

▶ **bSetStrengthFromAnimNode**: True

▶ **StrengthAnimNodeNameList**: Add one item to the array

▶ **[0]**: FwdAnim

5. Because we haven't set the actual locations of the effector or joint target yet, the preview looks quite distorted at this point, assuming the forward animation is currently playing (see **FIGURE 9.107**). If it is not, adjust the DirNode so that the FwdAnim node has full weighting. Currently, both the effector and joint target are simply placed at the location of the b_Spine bone. To make adjusting the locations easier, click the Pause AnimTree button in the Toolbar.

6. Using the translation widget, move the pink-colored diamond in front and slightly to the left of the mesh relative to the direction it is facing (see **FIGURE 9.108**).

7. Using the translation widget, move the blue diamond in front and to the right of the character in relation to the direction it is facing.

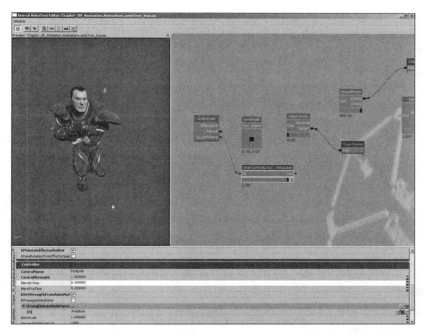

FIGURE 9.107   The character's arm looks heavily distorted at this point.

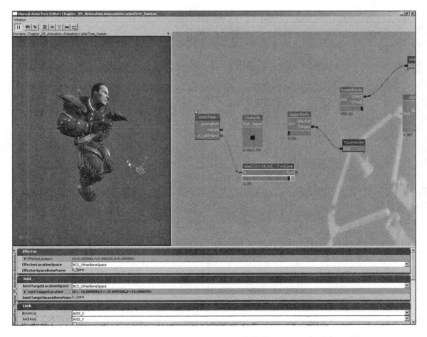

FIGURE 9.108   Position the pink diamond (joint target) object like so.

8. Tweak the positions of the effector and joint target until the character appears to be holding his arm crossed in front of him in a position that the weapon he is holding seems to rest on it. Here are some values to help you (see **FIGURE 9.109**):

- ▶ **EffectorLocation**:
    - ▶ **X:** 15.0
    - ▶ **Y:** –24.0
    - ▶ **Z:** 4.0
- ▶ **JointTargetLocation**:
    - ▶ **X:** –10.0
    - ▶ **Y:** –32.0
    - ▶ **Z:** 25.0

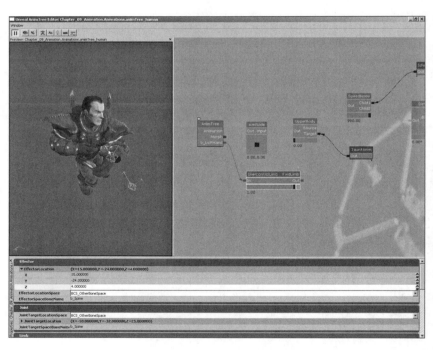

FIGURE 9.109   Use the effector and the joint target to position the arm like so.

9. Right-click in the AnimTree Editor and choose SkelControlSingleBone. Connect the In link of the FwdLimb node to the Out link of the new node and connect the In link of the new node to the b_LeftHand link of the AnimTree node (see **FIGURE 9.110**). This node will apply a slight adjustment to get the hand position just right.

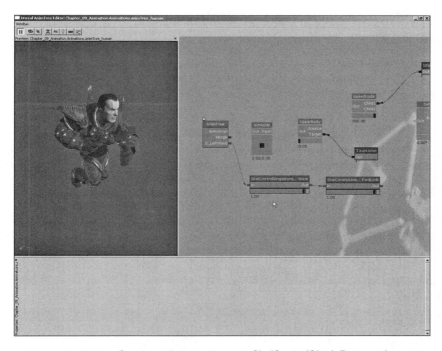

FIGURE 9.110   Create and connect a new SkelControlSingleBone node.

10. Select the new node to view its properties and then set the following:

- ▸ **bApplyRotation**: True

- ▸ **BoneRotationSpace**: BCS_OtherBoneSpace

- ▸ **BoneRotation**:

> **NOTE**
>
> It may help if you occasionally unpause the animation to see the update.

  - ▸ **Pitch**: –58.0

  - ▸ **Yaw**: –50.0

  - ▸ **Roll**: 273.0

- ▸ **RotationSpaceBoneName**: b_Spine

- ▸ **ControlName**: FwdBone

- ▸ **bSetStrengthFromAnimNode**: True

- ▸ **StrengthAnimNodeNameList**: Add an item to this array

  - ▸ **[0]**: FwdAnim

11. Save your progress.

END TUTORIAL 9.13

TUTORIAL 9.14: Altering Animations Using SkelControlLimb and SkelControlSingleBone, Part II: Backward Animation

1. Continuing from **TUTORIAL 9.13**, double-click the animTree_human asset in the Generic Browser to open it in the AnimTree Editor. If you have not completed it, you may use the animTree_human_05 asset instead.

2. Right-click in the AnimTree Editor and choose SkelControlLimb. Connect the In link of the new node to the Out link of the FwdLimb node (see **FIGURE 9.111**).

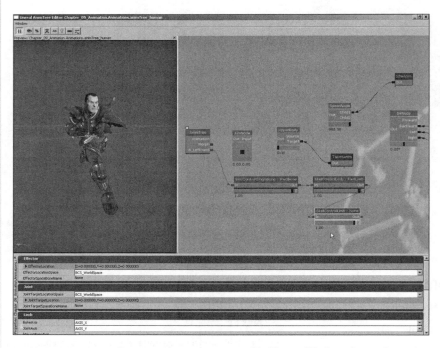

FIGURE 9.111   Create and connect a new SkelControlLimb node as shown here.

3. Select the new node to view its properties and then set the following:

   ▸ **EffectorLocationSpace**: BCS_OtherBoneSpace

   ▸ **EffectorSpaceBoneName**: b_Spine

   This sets the location in relation to the Spine bone, which will account for any modifications caused by the aim offset node we implemented previously.

   ▸ **JointTargetLocationSpace**: BCS_OtherBoneSpace

   ▸ **JointTargetSpaceBoneName**: b_Spine

As before, this sets the location in relation to the Spine bone, which will account for any modifications caused by the aim offset node we implemented previously.

- ▶ **bMaintainEffectorRelRot**: True
- ▶ **ControlName**: BwdLimb
- ▶ **bSetStrengthFromAnimNode**: True
- ▶ **StrengthAnimNodeNameList**: Add one item to the array
  - ▶[0]: BwdAnim

4. If it is not already, adjust the DirNode so that the BwdAnim node has full weighting. Currently, both the effector and joint target are simply placed at the location of the b_Spine bone. To make adjusting the locations easier, click the Pause AnimTree button in the Toolbar (see **FIGURE 9.112**).

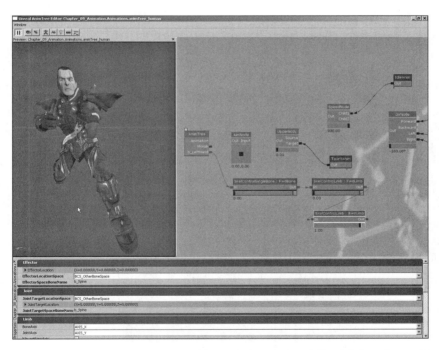

FIGURE 9.112   If your new SkelControlLimb node has full weighting, the mesh's arm appears heavily distorted.

5. Using the translation widget, move the pink-colored diamond in front and slightly to the left of the mesh relative to the direction it is facing.

6. Using the translation widget, move the blue diamond in front and to the right of the character in relation to the direction it is facing.

7. Tweak the positions of the effector and joint target until the character appears to be hold-ing his arm crossed in front of him in a position that the weapon he is holding seems to rest on it. Here are some values to help you (see **FIGURE 9.113**):

- ▶ **EffectorLocation**:
    - ▶ **X**: 9.0
    - ▶ **Y**: −24.0
    - ▶ **Z**: 4.0
- ▶ **JointTargetLocation**:
    - ▶ **X**: −20.0
    - ▶ **Y**: 0.0
    - ▶ **Z**: 39.0

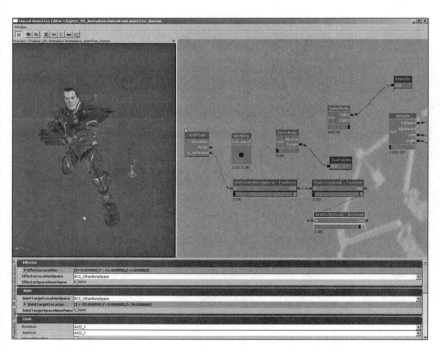

FIGURE 9.113   Your character should look something like this when finished.

8. Right-click in the AnimTree Editor and choose SkelControlSingleBone. Connect the In link of the BwdLimb to the Out link of the new node and then connect the In link of the new node to the Out link of the FwdLimb. Again, this node will apply a slight adjustment to get the hand position just right.

9. Select the new node to view its properties and then set the following (see **FIGURE 9.114**):

- ▶ **bApplyRotation**: True
- ▶ **BoneRotationSpace**: BCS_OtherBoneSpace
- ▶ **BoneRotation**:
    - ▶ **Pitch**: −49.0
    - ▶ **Yaw**: −94.0
    - ▶ **Roll**: −75.0
- ▶ **RotationSpaceBoneName**: b_Spine
- ▶ **ControlName**: BwdBone
- ▶ **bSetStrengthFromAnimNode**: True
- ▶ **StrengthAnimNodeNameList**: Add an item to this array
    - ▶ **[0]**: BwdAnim

> **NOTE**
>
> It may help if you occasionally unpause the animation to see the update.

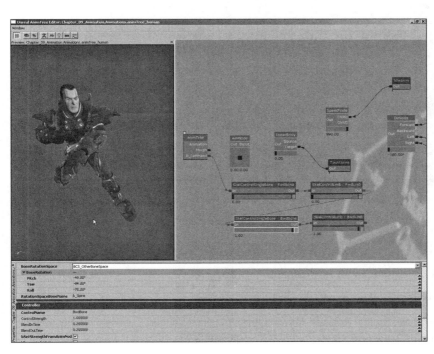

FIGURE 9.114   The arm has now been adjusted for the backward running animation.

10. Save your progress.

END TUTORIAL 9.14

TUTORIAL 9.15: Altering Animations Using SkelControlLimb and SkelControlSingleBone, Part III: Left Animation

1. Continuing from the **TUTORIAL 9.14**, double-click the animTree_human asset in the Generic Browser to open it in the AnimTree Editor. If you have not completed it yet, you may use the animTree_human_06 asset instead.

2. Right-click in the AnimTree Editor and choose SkelControlLimb. Connect the In link of the new node to the Out link of the BwdLimb node (see **FIGURE 9.115**).

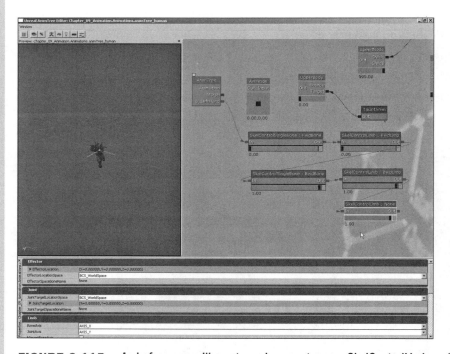

FIGURE 9.115   As before, you will create and connect a new SkelControlLimb node.

3. Select the new node to view its properties and then set the following:

   ▶ **EffectorLocationSpace**: BCS_OtherBoneSpace

   ▶ **EffectorSpaceBoneName**: b_Spine

   This sets the location in relation to the Spine bone, which accounts for any modifications caused by the aim offset node we implemented previously.

   ▶ **JointTargetLocationSpace**: BCS_OtherBoneSpace

   ▶ **JointTargetSpaceBoneName**: b_Spine

   As before, this sets the location in relation to the Spine bone, which accounts for any modifications caused by the aim offset node we implemented previously.

- ▶ **bMaintainEffectorRelRot**: True

- ▶ **ControlName**: LeftLimb

- ▶ **bSetStrengthFromAnimNode**: True

- ▶ **StrengthAnimNodeNameList**: Add one item to the array

  - ▶ **[0]**: LeftAnim

4. If it is not already, adjust the DirNode so that the LeftAnim node has full weighting. Currently, both the effector and joint target are simply placed at the location of the b_Spine bone. To make adjusting the locations easier, click the Pause AnimTree button in the Toolbar.

5. As before, you can tweak the positions of the effector and joint target until the character appears to be holding his arm crossed in front of him in a position that the weapon he is holding seems to rest on it. Here are some values to help you:

- ▶ **EffectorLocation**:

  - ▶ **X**: 8.0

  - ▶ **Y**: −24.0

  - ▶ **Z**: −6.0

- ▶ **JointTargetLocation**:

  - ▶ **X**: 3.0

  - ▶ **Y**: −17.0

  - ▶ **Z**: 37.0

6. Right-click in the AnimTree Editor and choose SkelControlSingleBone. Connect the In link of the LeftLimb to the Out link of the new node and then connect the In link of the new node to the Out link of the BwdLimb. Again, this node will apply a slight adjustment to get the hand position just right (see **FIGURE 9.116**).

7. Select the new node to view its properties and then set the following:

- ▶ **bApplyRotation**: True

- ▶ **bAddRotation**: True

- ▶ **BoneRotationSpace**: BCS_OtherBoneSpace

- ▶ **BoneRotation**:

  - ▶ **X**: −13.0

  - ▶ **Y**: 69.0

  - ▶ **Z**: −22.0

NOTE

It may help if you occasionally unpause the animation to see the update.

▶ **RotationSpaceBoneName**: b_Spine

▶ **ControlName**: LeftBone

▶ **bSetStrengthFromAnimNode**: True

▶ **StrengthAnimNodeNameList**: Add an item to this array

    ▶ **[0]**: LeftAnim

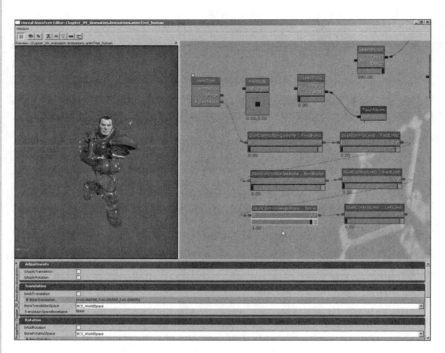

FIGURE 9.116   Create and connect the new SkelControlSingleBone node.

8. Save your progress.

END TUTORIAL 9.15

TUTORIAL 9.16: Altering Animations Using SkelControlLimb and SkelControlSingleBone, Part IV: Right Animation

1. Continuing from **TUTORIAL 9.15**, double-click the animTree_human asset in the Generic Browser to open it in the AnimTree Editor. If you have not completed it yet, you may use the animTree_human_07 asset instead.

2. Right-click in the AnimTree Editor and choose SkelControlLimb. Connect the In link of the new node to the Out link of the LeftLimb node (see **FIGURE 9.117**).

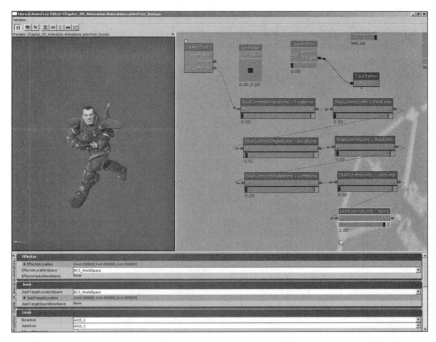

FIGURE 9.117   Create and connect a SkelControlLimb node for the Right animation.

3. Select the new node to view its properties and set the following:

▶ **EffectorLocationSpace**: BCS_OtherBoneSpace

▶ **EffectorSpaceBoneName**: b_Spine

This sets the location in relation to the Spine bone, which will account for any modifications caused by the aim offset node we implemented previously.

▶ **JointTargetLocationSpace**: BCS_OtherBoneSpace

▶ **JointTargetSpaceBoneName**: b_Spine

As before, this sets the location in relation to the Spine bone, which will account for any modifications caused by the aim offset node we implemented previously.

▶ **bMaintainEffectorRelRot**: True

▶ **ControlName**: RightLimb

▶ **bSetStrengthFromAnimNode**: True

▶ **StrengthAnimNodeNameList**: Add one item to the array

  ▶ **[0]**: RightAnim

4. If it is not already, adjust the DirNode so that the RightAnim node has full weighting. Currently, both the effector and joint target are simply placed at the location of the b_Spine bone. To make adjusting the locations easier, click the Pause AnimTree button in the Toolbar (see **FIGURE 9.118**).

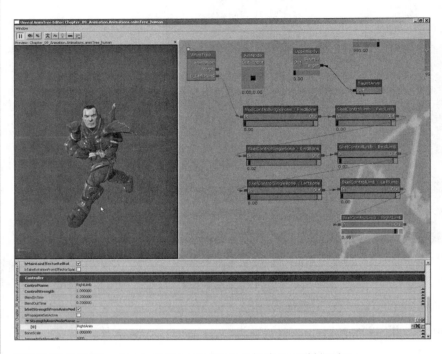

FIGURE 9.118   As usual, the arm appears broken at this point.

5. Tweak the positions of the effector and joint target until the character appears to be holding his arm crossed in front of him in a position that the weapon he is holding seems to rest on it. Here are some values to help you (see **FIGURE 9.119**):

   ▸ **EffectorLocation**:

      ▸ **X**: 12.0

      ▸ **Y**: –22.0

      ▸ **Z**: 15.0

   ▸ **JointTargetLocation**:

      ▸ **X**: 0.0

      ▸ **Y**: –1.0

      ▸ **Z**: 21.0

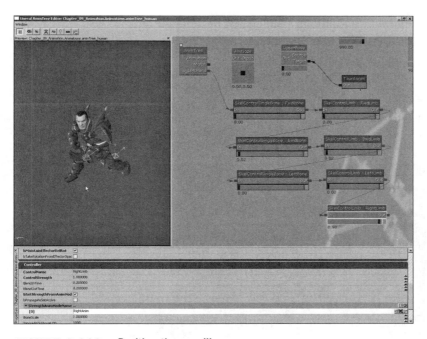

FIGURE 9.119 Position the arm like so.

6. Right-click in the AnimTree Editor and choose SkelControlSingleBone. Connect the In link of the RightLimb to the Out link of the new node and then connect the In link of the new node to the Out link of the LeftLimb. Again, this node will apply a slight correction to get the arm position just right due to the way the COG_Grunt_AMesh skeleton is set up.

7. Select the new node to view its properties and then set the following:

▸ **bApplyRotation**: True

▸ **bAddRotation**: True

▸ **BoneRotationSpace**: BCS_OtherBoneSpace

▸ **BoneRotation**:

    ▸ **Pitch**: –94.0

    ▸ **Yaw**: –18.0

    ▸ **Roll**: 23.0

▸ **RotationSpaceBoneName**: b_Spine

▸ **ControlName**: RightBone

▸ **bSetStrengthFromAnimNode**: True

▸ **StrengthAnimNodeNameList**: Add an item to this array

    ▸ **[0]**: RightAnim

8. Save your progress.

> **NOTE**
>
> It may help if you occasionally unpause the animation to see the update.

END TUTORIAL 9.16

TUTORIAL 9.17: Altering Animations Using SkelControlLimb and SkelControlSingleBone, Part IV: Idle Animation

1. Continuing from **TUTORIAL 9.16**, double-click the animTree_human asset in the Generic Browser to open it in the AnimTree Editor. If you have not completed it yet, you may use the animTree_human_08 asset instead.

2. Right-click in the AnimTree Editor and choose SkelControlLimb. Connect the In link of the new node to the Out link of the RightLimb node (see **FIGURE 9.120**).

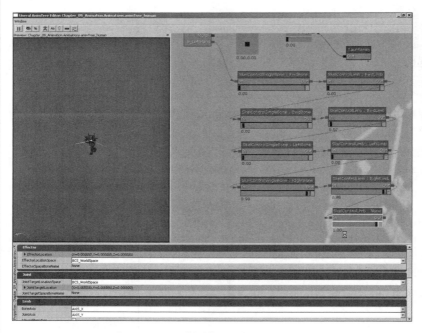

FIGURE 9.120   Create a new SkelControlLimb node.

3. Select the new node to view its properties and then set the following:

   ▶ **EffectorLocationSpace**: BCS_OtherBoneSpace

   ▶ **EffectorSpaceBoneName**: Spine

   ▶ **JointTargetLocationSpace**: BCS_OtherBoneSpace

   ▶ **JointTargetSpaceBoneName**: Spine

   ▶ **bMaintainEffectorRelRot**: True

   ▶ **ControlName**: IdleLimb

   ▶ **bSetStrengthFromAnimNode**: True

   ▶ **StrengthAnimNodeNameList**: Add one item to the array

      ▶ **[0]**: IdleAnim

4. If it is not already, adjust the SpeedNode so that the IdleAnim node has full weighting. Currently, both the effector and joint target are simply placed at the location of the b_Spine bone. To make adjusting the locations easier, click the Pause AnimTree button in the Toolbar.

5. Tweak the positions of the effector and joint target until the character appears to be holding his arm crossed in front of him in a position that the weapon he is holding seems to rest on it. Here are some values to help you:

- ▶ **EffectorLocation**:
    - ▶ **X**: 16.0
    - ▶ **Y**: −25.0
    - ▶ **Z**: 5.0
- ▶ **JointTargetLocation**:
    - ▶ **X**: 0.0
    - ▶ **Y**: −9.0
    - ▶ **Z**: 17.0

6. Right-click in the AnimTree Editor and choose SkelControlSingleBone. Connect the In link of the IdleLimb to the Out link of the new node and then connect the In link of the new node to the Out link of the RightLimb. Again, this node will apply a slight adjustment to get the hand position just right.

7. Select the new node to view its properties and set the following (see **FIGURE 9.121**):

- ▶ **bApplyRotation**: True
- ▶ **BoneRotationSpace**: BCS_OtherBoneSpace
- ▶ **BoneRotation**:
    - ▶ **X**: −44.0
    - ▶ **Y**: 80.0
    - ▶ **Z**: −28.0

> **NOTE**
>
> It may help if you occasionally unpause the animation to see the update.

- ▶ **RotationSpaceBoneName**: b_Spine
- ▶ **ControlName**: IdleBone
- ▶ **bSetStrengthFromAnimNode**: True
- ▶ **StrengthAnimNodeNameList**: Add an item to this array
    - ▶ **[0]**: IdleAnim

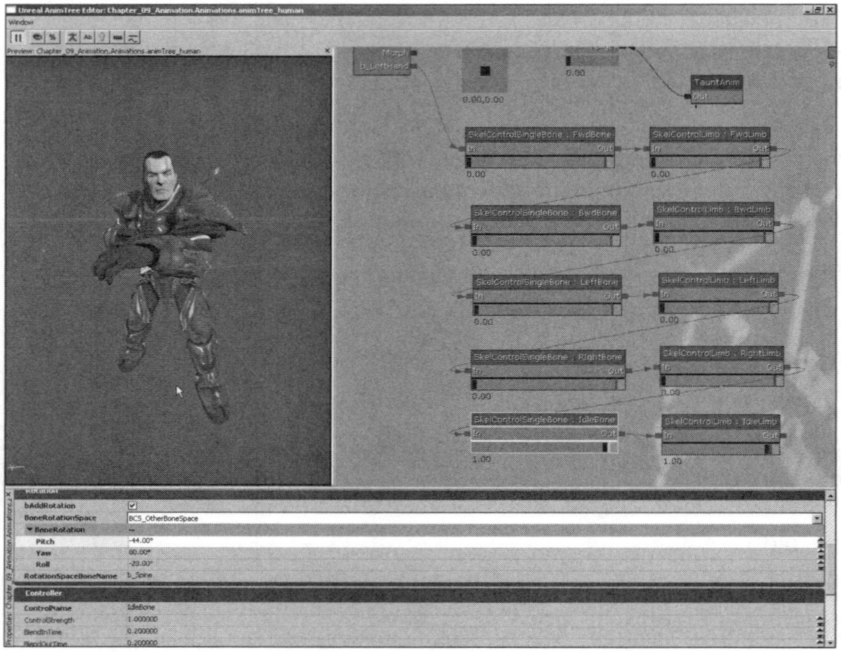

FIGURE 9.121   Your character's arm should be fully adjusted.

8. Save your progress.

END TUTORIAL 9.17

In **TUTORIAL 9.18**, we duplicate the "blend by speed and direction" network and use an AnimNodeBlend node to blend between the original network and the duplicated network. The duplicated network has the names of the animation nodes cleared out so they do not influence the skeletal controllers making this network play the standard animations. This gives us the ability to switch between the standard animations and the altered animations at will.

In common circumstances, this blend would be driven through code, such as when the character picks up different weapons.

9

TUTORIAL 9.18: Altering Animations Using SkelControlLimb and SkelControlSingleBone, Part IV: Finishing Touches

1. Continuing from the **TUTORIAL 9.17**, double-click the animTree_human asset in the Generic Browser to open it in the AnimTree Editor. If you have not completed it yet, you may use the animTree_human_09 asset instead.

2. Marquee select the SpeedNode, DirNode, IdleAnim, FwdAnim, BackAnim, LeftAnim, and RightAnim nodes by holding down Ctrl and Alt and dragging the mouse (see **FIGURE 9.122**).

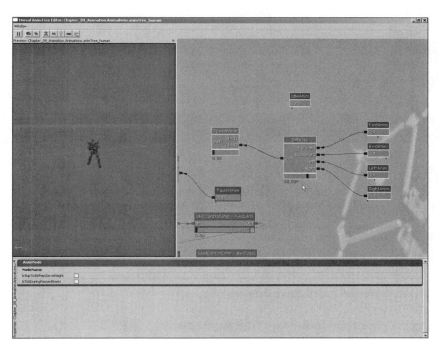

FIGURE 9.122   Select the nodes shown above.

3. Press Ctrl+W to duplicate the nodes and move the new nodes above the originals (see **FIGURE 9.123**).

4. Select all the AnimSequence Player nodes in the duplicated network and set their NodeName properties to None. Don't bother trying to do this one at a time; if they're all selected at once, you can change them simultaneously.

5. Right-click in the AnimTree Editor and choose AnimNodeBlend. Position the new node between the speed/direction networks and the aim offset node (see **FIGURE 9.124**).

6. Connect the Out links of each of the "blend by speed" nodes to the Child1 and Child2 links of the new node.

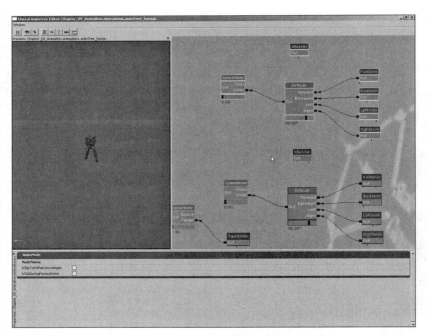

FIGURE 9.123   Position the new nodes above their originals.

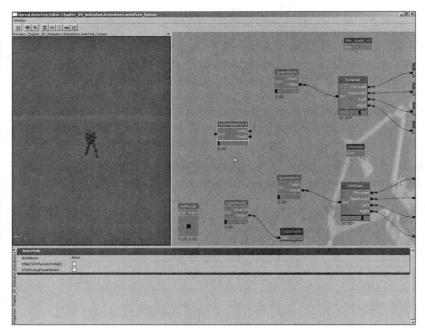

FIGURE 9.124   A new AnimNodeBlend has been added.

7. Connect the Out link of the new node to the Source link of the UpperBody node (see **FIGURE 9.125**).

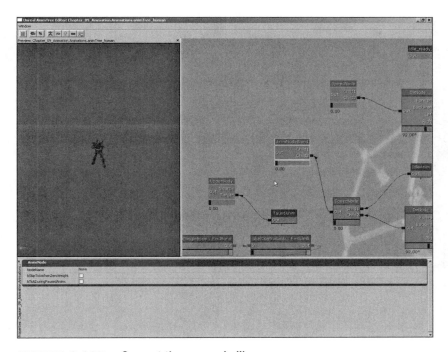

FIGURE 9.125   Connect the new node like so.

8. Dragging the slider of the new blend node should cause the animation being played to gradually blend from the standard animation to the altered animation.

9. Save your progress.

END TUTORIAL 9.18

In **TUTORIALS 9.19** through **9.21**, we set up a skeletal mesh to play multiple animations with blending and masking all controlled through Matinee. We use the SkeletalMeshActorMAT actor for this and it requires setting up a network of nodes in the AnimTree in order to work properly. Then, we set up a few tracks in Matinee to play the various animations. To begin with, we create the necessary nodes in the AnimTree in **TUTORIAL 9.19**.

TUTORIAL 9.19: Animation Blending Using Matinee, Part I: Creating Slots in AnimTree

1. Continuing from the **TUTORIAL 9.18**, double-click the animTree_human asset in the Generic Browser to open it in the AnimTree Editor. If you have not completed it yet, you may use the animTree_human_10 asset instead.

2. Right-click in the AnimTree Editor and choose AnimNodeSlot. Position the new node between the aim offset node and the AnimTree node (see **FIGURE 9.126**).

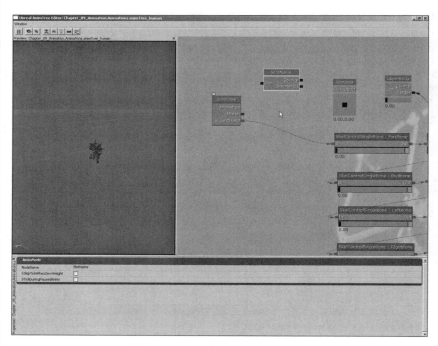

FIGURE 9.126   Create and position a new AnimNodeSlot node.

3. With the new node selected, press Ctrl+W to duplicate it and move the new node below the original node.

4. Select the top AnimNodeSlot node and set its NodeName to SlotFull.

5. Select the bottom AnimNodeSlot node and set its NodeName to SlotUpper (see **FIGURE 9.127**).

6. Right-click the SlotUpper node and choose Add Input. This should add a new link to the node.

7. Right-click in the AnimTree Editor and choose AnimSequence Player. Position this node to the right of the Channel 01 link of the SlotFull node and set its NodeName to FullAnim (see **FIGURE 9.128**).

8. With the AnimSequence Player node selected, press Ctrl+W to duplicate the node and move the new node adjacent to the Channel 0 link of the SlotUpper node. Set this node's NodeName to UpperAnim1.

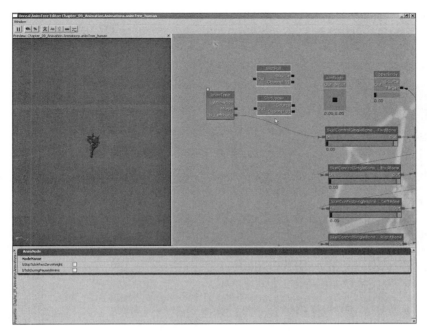

FIGURE 9.127 Both nodes have now been renamed.

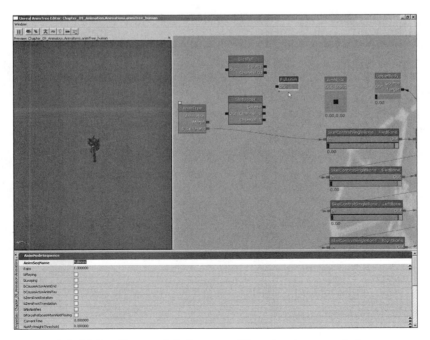

FIGURE 9.128 The new AnimSequence Player has been created.

9. Duplicate the AnimSequence Player node and move it down adjacent to the Channel 1 link of the SlotUpper node. Set this node's NodeName to UpperAnim2 (see **FIGURE 9.129**).

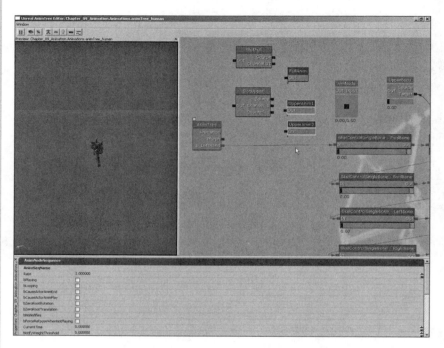

FIGURE 9.129   There are now two duplicates of the AnimSequence Player node.

10. Right-click in the AnimTree Editor and choose AnimNodeBlendPerBone. Position the new node to the left of the SlotFull and SlotUpper nodes.

11. Select the new node to view its properties. Add an item to the BranchStartBoneName array and enter b_Spine in slot [0]. Then, set the NodeName property to UpperBlend.

12. Make sure that the slider for this node is set all the way to the right (1.00).

13. To finish up, make the following connections (see **FIGURE 9.130**):

- ▶ Aim Node-Out → SlotFull-Source
- ▶ Aim Node-Out → SlotUpper-Source
- ▶ FullAnim-Out → SlotFull-Channel 01
- ▶ UpperAnim1-Out → SlotUpper-Channel 0
- ▶ UpperAnim2-Out → SlotUpper-Channel 1
- ▶ SlotFull-Out → UpperBlend-Source

9

- ▸ SlotUpper-Out → UpperBlend-Target

- ▸ UpperBlend-Out → AnimTree-Animation

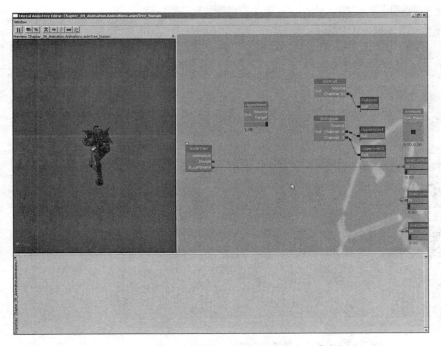

FIGURE 9.130   Your network should look like this when finished.

14. Save your progress.

TUTORIAL 9.20: Animation Blending Using Matinee, Part II: Placing Nodes in AnimTree

1. Continuing from **TUTORIAL 9.19**, open the DM-CH_09_AnimDemo_Begin map. This is just a basic map to give us somewhere to display the character and animation. If you have not completed it, you may use the animTree_human_11 asset in place of the animTree_human asset when instructed.

2. Select the ImportMesh_Human_Male asset from the CH_AnimHuman package in the Generic Browser. Right-click in the viewport and choose Add Actor > SkeletalMeshActorMAT: SkeletalMesh CH_AnimHuman.Mesh.ImportMesh_Human_Male to place the actor in the map.

3. Select the actor. Using the Front or Side viewport, move the actor up until the feet are resting on the surface (see **FIGURE 9.131**).

FIGURE 9.131   Make sure the character's feet appear planted.

4. Press F4 to open the actor's properties and then expand the SkeletalMeshActor section and the SkeletalMeshComponent section. Then, scroll down to the SkeletalMeshComponent subsection. Select the animTree_human asset in the Generic Browser and click the Use Current Selection In Browser button ◄ for the AnimTreeTemplate property (see **FIGURE 9.132**).

5. With the SkeletalMeshActorMAT actor still selected, open Kismet. Create a new Matinee sequence by right-clicking and choosing New Matinee. Set the Matinee sequence's bLooping property to True. Double-click the Matinee object to open the Matinee Editor.

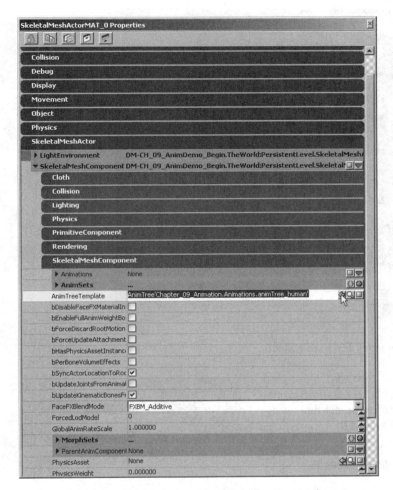

FIGURE 9.132   This assigns our new AnimTree to our character.

6. Right-click in the Group List and choose Add New Empty Group. Name the new group **BlendAnim**. In the group's properties, add a slot to the GroupAnimSets array by clicking the Add New Item button. Select the K_AnimHuman_BaseMale animation set from the CH_AnimHuman package in the Generic Browser and click the Use Current Selection in Browser button ◀ for slot [0] (see **FIGURE 9.133**).

7. Right-click the BlendAnim group and choose Add New Anim Control Track. Select the SlotFull slot from the dialog that appears (see **FIGURE 9.134**).

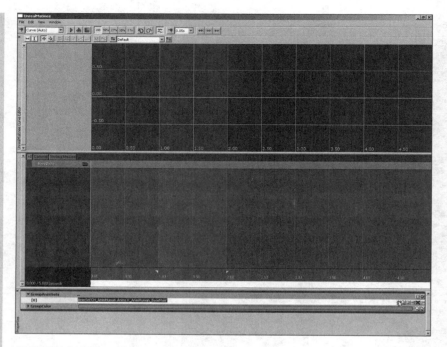

FIGURE 9.133   The new group has been added.

8. With the time slider at Time=0.0, press Enter to place a new key. Choose the run_fwd_rif animation from the dropdown list that appears (see **FIGURE 9.135**).

9. Right-click the run_fwd_rif animation sequence in the timeline and choose Set Looping.

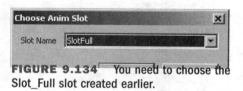

FIGURE 9.134   You need to choose the Slot_Full slot created earlier.

10. Send the track's info to the Curve Editor and then open the Curve Editor. Holding down Ctrl, click the left mouse button on the curve in the curve editor near Time=0.0 and drag the new point up to a value of 1.0. This moves the entire curve up to a value of 1.0.

11. Save your progress so far.

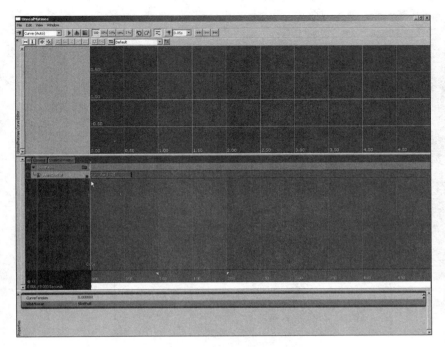

FIGURE 9.135   Add the run_fwd_rif animation at Time=0.0.

END TUTORIAL 9.20

In **TUTORIAL 9.21**, we now create two more animation tracks that oscillate the character's animation for the upper body between a weapon-firing sequence and idle animation. This requires that we create custom animation curves that dictate when each one of these animations is being applied. Matinee then blends in between the curves, and thereby blends between the two animation cycles on the character.

TUTORIAL 9.21: Animation Blending Using Matinee, Part III: Finishing the Matinee Sequence

1. Continue from **TUTORIAL 9.20**. If you have not completed it, you may open the DM-CH_09_AnimDemo_01 map. In the Matinee Editor, right-click the BlendAnim group and choose Add New Anim Control Track. Select the SlotUpper slot from the dialog that appears (see **FIGURE 9.136**).

2. With the new track selected and the time slider at Time=0.0, press Enter to place a new key. Choose the Taunt_UB_ComeHere animation from the dropdown list that appears.

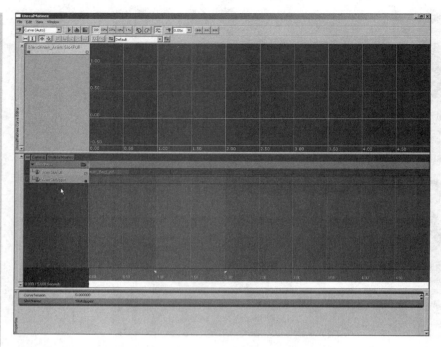

FIGURE 9.136   The new track has been placed.

3. Right-click the Taunt_UB_ComeHere animation sequence in the timeline and choose Set Looping.

4. Send the track's info to the Curve Editor and then open the Curve Editor. Holding down Ctrl, click the left mouse button on the curve in the Curve Editor near Time=0.0 and drag the new point up to a value of 1.0. This moves the entire curve up to a value of 1.0 (see **FIGURE 9.137**).

5. Right-click the BlendAnim group and choose Add New Anim Control Track. Select the Slot_Upper slot from the dialog that appears.

6. With the time slider at Time=0.0, press Enter to place a new key. Choose the Taunt_FB_Victory animation from the dropdown list that appears.

7. Right-click the Taunt_FB_Victory animation sequence in the timeline and choose Set Looping.

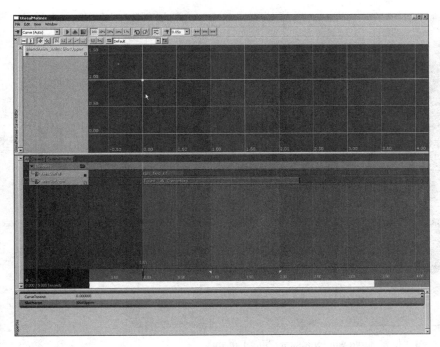

FIGURE 9.137   Your final curve will look like a straight line.

8. Send the track's info to the Curve Editor and then open the Curve Editor. Set points on the curve at the following times with the corresponding values (see **FIGURE 9.138**):

   ▸ 2.0 → 0.0

   ▸ 2.25 → 1.0—Set InterpMode to Linear

   ▸ 4.5 → 1.0

   ▸ 4.75 → 0.0—Set InterpMode to Linear

   ▸ 6.6 → 0.0

   ▸ 6.85 → 1.0—Set InterpMode to Linear

   ▸ 9.1 → 1.0

   ▸ 9.35 → 0.0

9. Drag the red sequence marker to Time=9.35 so the sequence lasts 9.35 seconds.

10. Close Matinee. In Kismet, create a new Level Startup event and connect its Out link to the Play input of the Matinee sequence (see **FIGURE 9.139**).

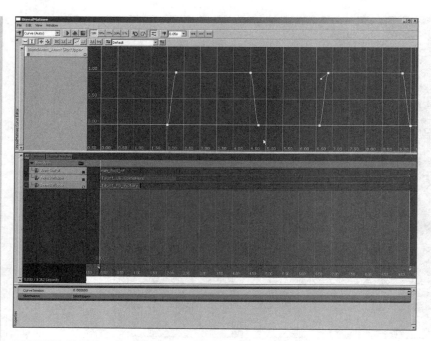

FIGURE 9.138   Your final curve will look something like this.

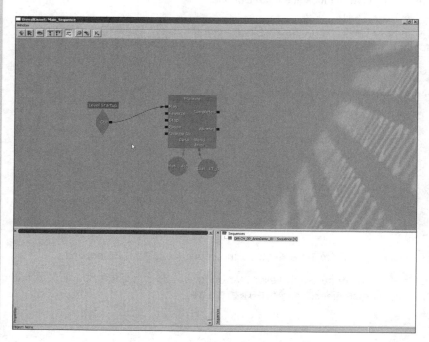

FIGURE 9.139   Connect your Kismet sequence as shown.

11. Playtest the map. You should see the mesh playing the run animation on the lower body (though he will be running in place) and alternating between the idle and firing animations on the upper body.

12. Save your progress.

END TUTORIAL 9.21

Facial Animation with FaceFX

Facial animation is a key factor in animating your characters so that they are believable as in-game personas. The face is where you can truly add personality to your characters; a mere change of expression can turn a character from the hopeful hero to the diabolical villain. In UnrealEd, facial animation can be created by combining skeletal and morph animations specifically in the region of the face (see **FIGURE 9.140**).

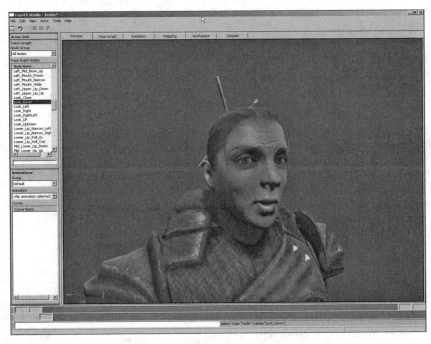

FIGURE 9.140   Good facial animation makes characters more believable.

This is done with FaceFX, a program that is integrated into Unreal Engine 3 and deals strictly with facial animation. It allows you to create custom facial animation sequences by hand, as well as to create animations directly from SoundCues that you can then tweak to perfection. This process is much faster and much more efficient than setting up the entire animation by hand in a 3D package. FaceFX can also control material parameters, allowing you the ability to apply such effects as a character's face turning red when he or she is angry, along with the ability to use morph targets to create expressions to go along with the mouth movements of the lip-sync animation.

FaceFX requires that an artist first create several poses for the character's face in his or her native 3D package. Those poses are referred to as *bone poses* (though they can easily be morphs as opposed to bone-driven poses, or any combination of morphs and bone poses). These poses are imported into FaceFX Studio using an FXA file. The artist then creates relationships between the different poses using FaceFX Studio's Face Graph. Then, audio is used to drive an initial animation based on this initial data. This animation is tweaked using the curves created by FaceFX, perfecting its motion.

FaceFXAssets are the basic building blocks of facial animations in the FaceFX system. They contain all the necessary data to play the facial animations you need based on a sound file and your custom settings. Animations are applied to FaceFXAssets by way of FaceFX AnimSets, discussed later.

FaceFXAssets are created within the Generic Browser and are populated with data by importing FXA files, which are created within Max or Maya using the FaceFX export plug-ins. In essence, you simply need to create a face that has a series of bones to control facial poses. These poses are then imported into FaceFX.

FaceFX Studio

FaceFX Studio is a fully functional application integrated into UnrealEd that provides the ability to create and edit facial animations. It is the heart of the FaceFX system and the key way to animate faces for Unreal Engine 3. FaceFX Studio is accessed by double-clicking any FaceFXAsset or FaceFX AnimSet in the Generic Browser (see **FIGURE 9.141**).

Phonemes

A *phoneme* is a conceptual representation of a spoken sound. In all languages, many words, though spelled differently, contain similar sounds. Take, for example, the words *be*, *bee*, and *beat*. Each of the words has a different spelling, though they all create the same type of sound in the case of a hard *E*. A single phoneme is used to represent this hard *E*, regardless of the spelling of the actual word. This concept is used by most dictionaries to provide the pronunciation of a word by showing the word phonetically spelled out. The individual parts of the pronunciation are phonemes (see **FIGURE 9.142**).

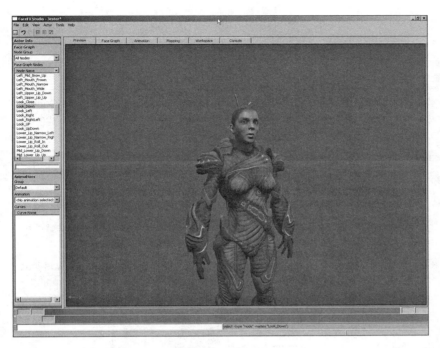

FIGURE 9.141   The FaceFX Studio interface

FIGURE 9.142   Some examples of phonemes.

When dealing with syncing animations to words, all that matters is how the words are said. More specifically, all that matters is the sounds that are produced when the words are spoken. This is why phonemes are so useful. Dialog is broken down into phonemes, which are used to drive animation curves that in turn blend between a set of mesh poses that each represent the various sounds. The final result of all this is that spoken dialogue is used to drive the facial animation of a character such that it appears the character is speaking the dialogue.

The following series of tutorials guides you through the creation of a facial animation using FaceFX—from the creation of the FaceFXAsset inside of UnrealEd through the final lip-synch animation. The process of creating, rigging, and posing the mesh in 3ds Max or Maya and export-ing using the FaceFX plug-ins for those applications are not covered.

TUTORIAL 9.22: Creating a Facial Animation, Part I: Initial Setup

1. Select the skelMesh_facefx asset from the Chapter_09_Animation package in the Generic Browser. Right-click it and choose Create New FaceFX Asset. Enter the following in the dia-log that appears:

   ▶ **Package**: Chapter_09_Animation

   ▶ **Group**: FaceFX

   ▶ **Name**: fxa_facefx

2. Right-click the fxa_facefx asset and choose Import From .FXA. Navigate to and select the FaceFX_Demo.fxa file.

3. Double-click the fxa_facefx asset to open it in FaceFX Studio. Because the asset was just created, there are no phoneme mappings, but FaceFX Studio assigns a default mapping for you (see **FIGURE 9.143**).

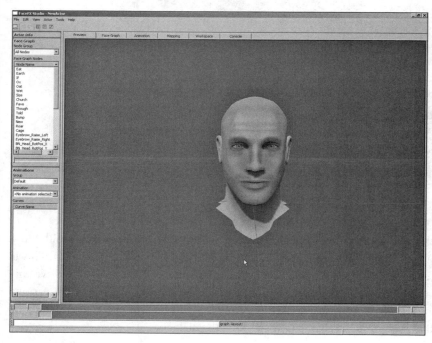

FIGURE 9.143   FaceFX Studio now appears.

4. Back in the Generic Browser, select the facefx_target_acquiredCue from the Chapter_09_Animation package. Then, open the Animation Manager in FaceFX Studio from the Actor menu or by using the button on the toolbar (see **FIGURE 9.144**).

FIGURE 9.144   Once the SoundCue is selected in the Generic Browser, click the Animation Manager button.

5. Click the New Group... button and name the new group **MasteringUnreal**. Click OK.

6. Click the Create Animation... button. The Create Animation Wizard appears (see **FIGURE 9.145**).

Select Automatically generate gesture speech curves and then click Next.

7. The selected sound cue should be placed in the text box of the next page, which is exactly what we want. Click Next again.

8. There is only one SoundNodeWave in the sound cue, so simply click Next again.

9. We want to specify a text file to use in analyzing the audio. This is not mandatory, but it results in a better analysis and thus less tweaking afterward. Click the Browse button. Navigate to and select the target_acquired.txt file. The text of the file should be visible in the Analysis Text: box on the page (see **FIGURE 9.146**). Click Next.

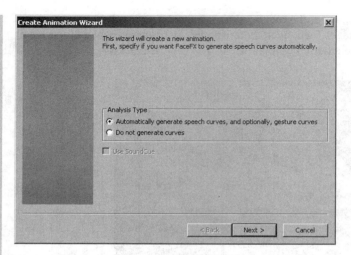

FIGURE 9.145   The Create Animation Wizard

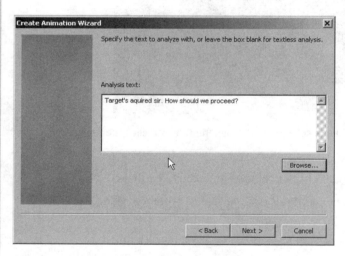

FIGURE 9.146   You should see text appear in the window.

10. The default settings of the next page will work fine for our purposes. If you wanted to use different configurations or were using a language other than English, you would select those here. Click Next.

11. The default name for the animation is the name of the sound, which will work fine. Click Finish.

12. A quick progress bar appears and then the new animation is listed in the Animation Manager. Click OK to close the Animation Manager.

13. Click the Save Actor button in the toolbar to save your progress. Then close FaceFX Studio and save the Chapter_09_Animation package.

END TUTORIAL 9.22

In **TUTORIAL 9.22**, we created an animation from a sound cue. In **TUTORIAL 9.23**, we take a look at that animation and make any adjustments to the phonemes that may be necessary to make the facial animation match the audio as closely and realistically as possible.

TUTORIAL 9.23: Creating a Facial Animation, Part II: Tweaking Phonemes

1. Double-click the fxa_facefx asset from the AnimationChapter package in the Generic Browser to open it in FaceFX Studio. If you have not completed **TUTORIAL 9.22** yet, you may use the fxa_facefx_01 asset instead. Note the fxa_facefx_01 asset has no skeletal mesh associated with it at this point. You must open the skelMesh_facefx mesh and assign the asset to the FaceFXAsset property in the Mesh tab before you can open the asset in FaceFX (see **FIGURE 9.147**).

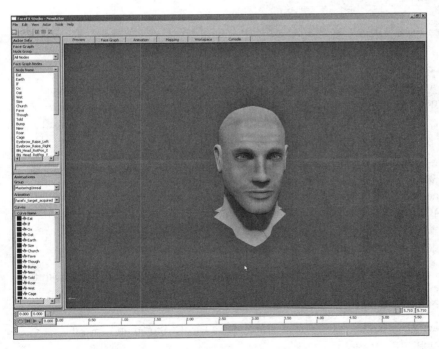

FIGURE 9.147   Open your FaceFX asset in FaceFX Studio.

We need to view both the Animation tab and the Preview tab in order to effectively tweak the phonemes. Double-click the Preview tab to undock it from the main FaceFX Studio window and move it off to the side. You may need to adjust the sizes of the FaceFX Studio window and the Preview window to make them fit on your screen, depending on how much screen space you have (see **FIGURE 9.148**). Of course, this will work a little better if you happen to have a second monitor.

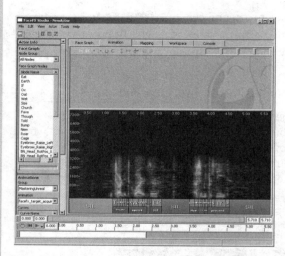

FIGURE 9.148   You need to reconfigure your windows.

2. Select the Animation tab so it is visible in the main window. At the bottom you should see all the phonemes as well as the words they are assigned to.

3. Play the animation a few times to get an idea of what might need to be adjusted. You can click the Toggle Looped Playback button [icon] to make this easier.

4. Zoom in on the word *Targets* and scrub the timeline through that word. Drag the ends of the phonemes to position them until you are happy with them. You can always add or delete phonemes. This is done by right-clicking the phoneme and choosing Delete Phoneme. You can also change one phoneme to another by right-clicking and choosing Change Phoneme and then selecting the phoneme from the popup that appears.

   The important thing is that the animation appears to say the words.

5. Repeat this process for the remaining words in the animation until you are happy with the entire animation. Remember, you can always come back later and tweak the phonemes more (see **FIGURE 9.149**).

6. Click the Save Actor button in the toolbar. Then, close FaceFX Studio and save the AnimationChapter package.

9

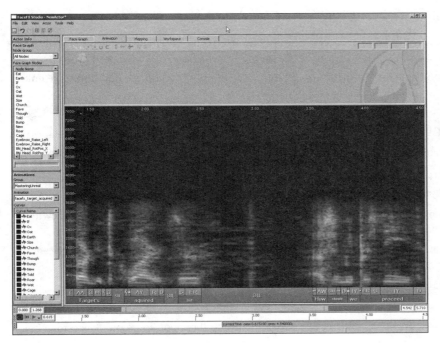

FIGURE 9.149   An example of what the phonemes might look like when you are finished

END TUTORIAL 9.23

Nodes

Nodes should be a relatively familiar concept by now. They are used extensively throughout Unreal Engine 3 and its various editors. Just as in the other editors, nodes in FaceFX studio are self-contained objects that perform a specific function on data passed to them and output the result of that function.

Nodes in FaceFX Studio have a slightly different appearance than the nodes used throughout the rest of UnrealEd. The reason for this is that FaceFX Studio is actually a standalone application that has been integrated into UnrealEd. Despite this slightly different appearance, they are structurally the same as UnrealEd's nodes, meaning they are rectangular in shape with input and output links on the sides.

The value of a node at any time determines the amount of influence the node has over the final appearance of the animation. This value is the sum of its combined input values and the value for the current point in the animation of the curve associated with the node.

Types of Nodes

Six types of nodes are available in FaceFX Studio. The artist can only manually create five of these. The FxBonePoseNode is created automatically for each of the bone poses brought in for the face. Each node is responsible for performing a different type of operation on the nodes that are linked to its inputs.

Common Properties

The following properties are common to all nodes in FaceFX Studio.

> **NOTE**
>
> The names visible on the images of these nodes were applied at the time of creation. The nodes have no default name.

Node Name—This is the name by which the node is identified.

Minimum Value—This is the minimum value this node can have. Any values below this will be clamped to this value.

Maximum Value—This is the maximum value this node can have. Any values above this will be clamped to this value.

Input Operation—This determines the method used to combine the input values.

Sum Inputs—This causes the values input into this node to be added together.

Multiply Inputs—This causes the values input into this node to be multiplied together.

FxBonePoseNode

This is the one node that the user does not manually create. It is automatically created when the user Bone pose nodes hold bone position, rotation, and scale information (see **FIGURE 9.150**).

FIGURE 9.150   An FxBonePoseNode

FxBonePoseNodes combine the values that are passed into their inputs, use that value to determine how far to interpolate toward the bone pose, and also output the combined result.

These nodes can have any number of inputs or outputs.

FxCombinerNode

Combiner nodes do exactly what their name suggests. They combine the values that are passed into their inputs and then output the result (see **FIGURE 9.151**).

These nodes can have any number of inputs or outputs.

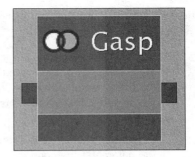

FIGURE 9.151   An FxCombinerNode

FxCurrentTimeNode

Current time nodes are very self-explanatory because they simply output the current time (see **FIGURE 9.152**). These nodes do not function properly inside of FaceFX Studio. Their effects are only visible inside the game.

These nodes can have any number of outputs, but no inputs at all. Therefore, they do not use the Input Operation property.

FIGURE 9.152   An FxCurrentTimeNode

FxDeltaNode

Delta nodes calculate the difference between the value of the node at the current frame and the value of the node at the previous frame (see **FIGURE 9.153**). The value of the node is the value of its input.

These nodes can have any number of outputs, but only one input. These nodes do not make use of the Minimum Value and Maximum Value properties.

FUnrealFaceFXMaterialParameterNode

Material parameter nodes are used to drive parameters inside of the material(s) applied to the mesh to which the FaceFX animation is applied (see **FIGURE 9.154**). They combine the values that are passed into their inputs, pass that value to the material parameter, and also output the combined result.

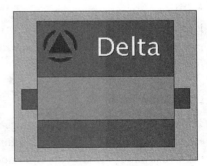

FIGURE 9.153   An FxDeltaNode

These nodes can have any number of inputs or outputs.

> **Material_Slot_Id**—This is the slot in the Materials array of the mesh corresponding to the material that contains the parameter the node controls. This is a zero-based index.
>
> **Parameter_Name**—This is the name of the parameter the node controls.

FIGURE 9.154   An FUnrealFaceFXMaterialParameterNode

FUnrealFaceFXMorphNode

Morph nodes hold a reference to a morph target. They combine the values that are passed into their inputs, use that value to determine how far to interpolate toward the morph target, and also output the combined result (see **FIGURE 9.155**).

These nodes can have any number of inputs or outputs.

> **Target_Name**—This is the name of the morph target this node uses.

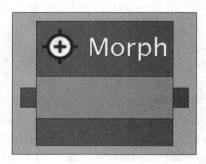

FIGURE 9.155   An FUnrealFaceFXMorphNode

Links

Links are connections between nodes that allow for the passing of data. This makes creating complex animations possible. Links control this passage of data from one node to the next using *link functions*.

Link Functions

The value of the parent node is plugged into the link function used by the link between the parent node and the child node. That function is then evaluated using that value, and the result is the actual value passed to the child node.

These functions can be set and modified by using the Link Function Editing dialog, which is accessed by right-clicking a node's link and choosing Edit Link Properties or by double-clicking the Link Function of a link in the Input Links or Output Links area of the Face Graph.

9

Linear

This function uses a linear equation of the form $y = m * x + b$ to determine the value passed to the child node. In the equation, y is the value passed to the child node, x is the value of the parent node, m is the slope of the line, and b is a vertical offset of the line.

The values of m and b can be modified by the designer.

Quadratic

This function uses a quadratic equation of the form $y = a * x^2$ to determine the value passed to the child node. In the equation, y is the value passed to the child node, x is the value of the parent node, and a is how quickly the slope of the curve increases.

The value of a can be modified by the designer.

Cubic

This function uses a cubic equation of the form $y = a * x^3$ to determine the value passed to the child node. In the equation, y is the value passed to the child node, x is the value of the parent node, and a is how quickly the slope of the curve increases.

The value of a can be modified by the designer.

Square Root

This function uses an equation of the form $y = a * \text{sqrt}(x)$ to determine the value passed to the child node. In the equation, y is the value passed to the child node, x is the value of the parent node, and a is how quickly the slope of the curve decreases.

The value of a can be modified by the designer.

Negate

This function uses an equation of the form $y = -x$ to determine the value passed to the child node. In the equation, y is the value passed to the child node and x is the value of the parent node.

Inverse

This function uses an equation of the form $y = 1 / x$ to determine the value passed to the child node. In the equation, y is the value passed to the child node and x is the value of the parent node.

One Clamp

For values of x less than or equal to 1.0, this function uses an equation of the form $y = 1$ to determine the value passed to the child node. In the equation, y is the value passed to the child node and x is the value of the parent node.

For values of x greater than 1.0, this function uses an equation of the form $y = 1 / x$ to determine the value passed to the child node. In the equation, y is the value passed to the child node and x is the value of the parent node.

Constant

This function causes the value passed to the child node to always be a constant value c.

Corrective

This function causes the value of the child node to be modified according to the Correction_Factor only when the parent node's value is not 0.0.

The correction is applied in the opposite direction as the value of the parent node. So, a positive Correction_Factor coupled with a positive value of the parent node would decrease the value of the child node, whereas a negative value of the parent node with the same Correction_Factor would increase the value of the child node.

From some testing, it appears that a Correction_Factor value of 33.33 causes amount of correction to be 1 to 1 with the value of the parent node.

Clamped Linear

This function uses a linear equation of the form $y = m * x$ to determine the value passed to the child node, but allows for clamping the value as well.

In the linear equation, y is the value passed to the child node, x is the value of the parent node, and m is the slope of the line. The value of m can be modified by the designer.

> **clampx**—This specifies the value of the parent node where the clamping will begin. This property also has the effect of offsetting the line horizontally.
>
> **clampy**—This specifies the value being passed to the child node where the clamping will begin. This property also has the effect of offsetting the line vertically.
>
> **clampdir**—This determines whether the clamping occurs to the left or right of the points specified by (clampx,clampy).
>
> If the value is positive, the linear function is used to the right of the point and the clamping occurs to the left of the point. If the value is less than or equal to 0.0, the linear function is used to the left of the point and the clamping occurs to the right of the point.

Edit Link Function Dialog

This dialog provides functionality for changing the type of link function used by a link and editing that link function. At the top of the dialog is a textual description of the current link function and its values.

A dropdown list contains all the types of link functions and allows for selecting the type to be used by the current link.

A graph shows a visual representation of the link function with the Input Node's value along the horizontal axis and the Output Node's value along the vertical axis. In this graph, red designates negative values and green designates positive values.

At the bottom of the dialog, the properties of the link function are displayed and can be modified.

Once the phonemes have been adjusted and the mouth appears to be saying the words correctly, you may notice that the animation is still rather lifeless. There are no gestures or expressions or movement of any kind, even though, as you may recall, we told FaceFX to create the gesture curves automatically. The problem is that, although it did create the curves, FaceFX did not create combiners that correspond to those curves that drive the bone pose nodes. Over **TUTORIALS 9.24** through **9.29**, we create them.

TUTORIAL 9.24: Creating a Facial Animation, Part III: Combiners for Blink and Eyebrow Raise

1. Double-click the fxa_facefx asset from the Chapter_09_Animation package in the Generic Browser to open it in FaceFX Studio. If you have not completed **TUTORIAL 9.23** yet, you may use the fxa_facefx_02 asset instead. Note the fxa_facefx_02 asset has no skeletal mesh associated with it at this point. You must open the skelMesh_facefx mesh and assign the asset to the FaceFXAsset property in the Mesh tab before you can open the asset in FaceFX.

2. Select the Face Graph tab. Then, right-click and choose Create Speech Gestures Setup. This creates all the nodes we need for the speech gestures and creates some connections between them. We still need to hook them up to the correct pose nodes, though.

3. Click the Layout Graph button in the toolbar to rearrange all the nodes. Then, locate the Blink node and position it so that it is to the left of the Blink_Left_Pose and Blink_Right_Pose nodes (see **FIGURE 9.156**).

4. Drag a link from the Blink node to the Blink_Left_Pose node. Then, drag a link from the Blink node to the Blink_Right_Pose node (see **FIGURE 9.157**).

   The Blink node now causes the character to blink its eyes. You can test it out to be sure it is connected properly by selecting the Blink node in the Face Graph section of the Actor Panel. Once this is selected, you can drag the slider at the bottom of the Face Graph section and the character's eyes should close.

5. Locate the Eyebrow_Raise node and position it to the left of the Eyebrow_Raise_Left and Eyebrow_Raise_Right nodes.

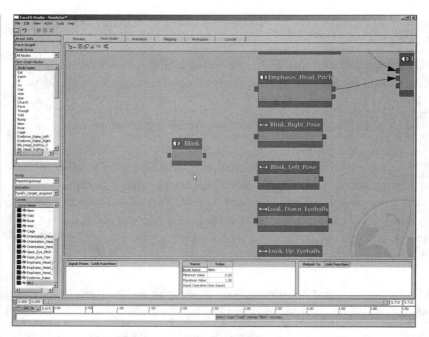

FIGURE 9.156   Position the Blink node as shown.

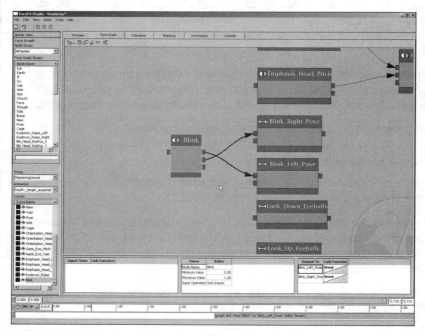

FIGURE 9.157   Create the shown links.

6. Drag a link from the Eyebrow_Raise node to the Eyebrow_Raise_Left node. Then, drag a link from the Blink node to the Eyebrow_Raise_Right node (see **FIGURE 9.158**).

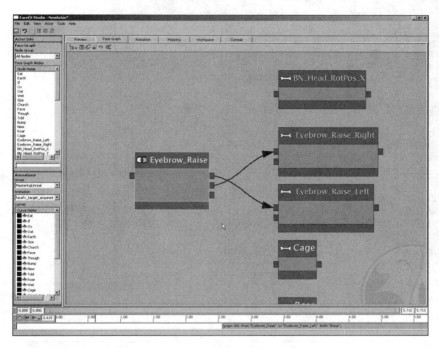

FIGURE 9.158   Position and connect the Eyebrow_Raise node as shown.

7. The Eyebrow_Raise node now causes the character to raise its eyebrows. You can test it out to be sure it is connected properly by selecting the Eyebrow_Raise node in the Face Graph section of the Actor panel. Once this is selected, you can drag the slider at the bottom of the Face Graph section and the character's eyebrows should raise (see **FIGURE 9.159**).

8. Click the Save Actor button in the toolbar. Then, close FaceFX Studio and save the Chapter_09_Animation package.

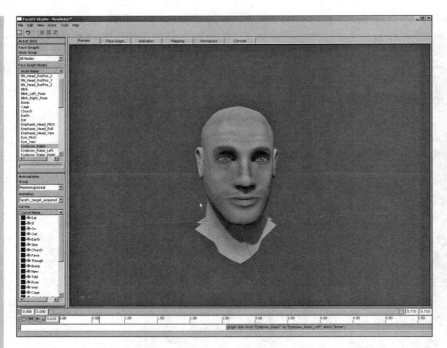

FIGURE 9.159   You can now raise the eyebrows and blink the eyelids.

END TUTORIAL 9.24

TUTORIAL 9.25: Creating a Facial Animation, Part IV: Creating Combiners
for Eye Pitch

---

1. Double-click the fxa_facefx asset from the Chapter_09_Animation package in the Generic
   Browser to open it in FaceFX Studio. If you have not completed **TUTORIAL 9.24** yet, you
   may use the fxa_facefx_03 asset instead. Note the fxa_facefx_03 asset has no skeletal
   mesh associated with it at this point. You must open the skelMesh_facefx mesh and
   assign the asset to the FaceFXAsset property in the Mesh tab before you can open the
   asset in FaceFX.

2. Select the Face Graph tab and locate the Eye_Pitch node and position it to the left of the
   Look_Up_Eyeballs and Look_Down_Eyeballs nodes.

3. Drag a link from the Eye_Pitch node to the Look_Down_Eyeballs node. Then, drag a link
   from the Eye_Pitch node to the Look_Up_Eyeballs node (see **FIGURE 9.160**).

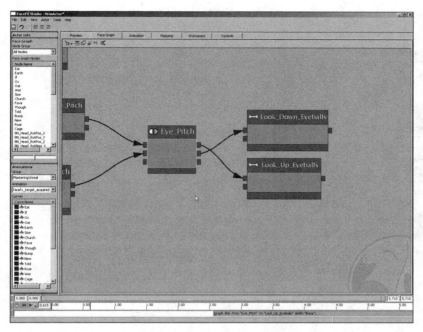

FIGURE 9.160   Connect Eye_Pitch to the Look_Down_Eyeballs node.

4. With the Eye_Pitch node selected, double-click the Look_Down_Eyeballs link function in the Output Links' Properties section to open the Link Function Editor.

5. Set the m property of the link function to –1.0 and click OK (see **FIGURE 9.161**).

6. Locate the Look_Up_Lids and Look_Down_Lids nodes and position them to the right of the Look_Up_Eyeballs and Look_Down_Eyeballs nodes.

7. Drag a link from the Look_Up_Eyeballs node to the Look_Up_Lids node. Then, drag a link from the Look_Down_Eyeballs node to the Look_Down_Lids node (see **FIGURE 9.162**).

8. The Eye_Pitch node now causes the character's eyes to look up and down. You can test it out in the Face Graph section of the Actor panel (see **FIGURE 9.163**).

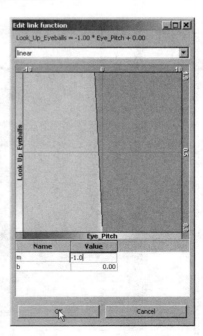

FIGURE 9.161   The Edit Link Function dialog

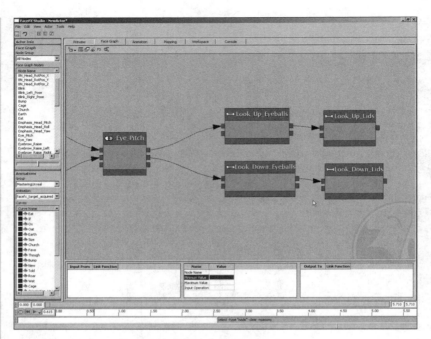

FIGURE 9.162   Create the links as shown.

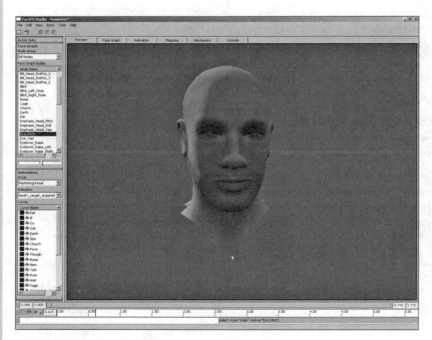

FIGURE 9.163   The character can now look up and down.

9. Click the Save Actor button in the toolbar. Then, close FaceFX Studio and save the Chapter_09_Animation package.

END TUTORIAL 9.25

TUTORIAL 9.26: Creating a Facial Animation, Part V: Creating Combiners for Eye Yaw

1. Double-click the fxa_facefx asset from the Chapter_09_Animation package in the Generic Browser to open it in FaceFX Studio. If you haven't completed **TUTORIAL 9.25** yet, you may use the fxa_facefx_04 asset instead. Note the fxa_facefx_04 asset has no skeletal mesh associated with it at this point. You must open the skelMesh_facefx mesh and assign the asset to the FaceFXAsset property in the Mesh tab before you can open the asset in FaceFX.

2. Select the Face Graph tab and locate the Eye_Yaw node and position it to the left of the Look_Right_Eyeballs and Look_Left_Eyeballs nodes (see **FIGURE 9.164**).

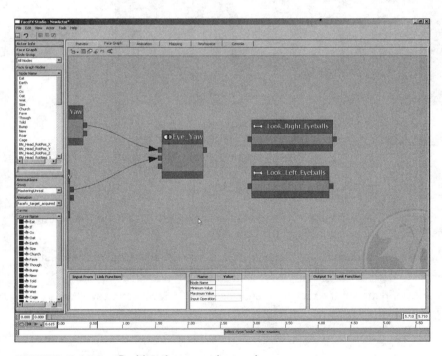

FIGURE 9.164   Position the eye nodes as shown.

3. Drag a link from the Eye_Yaw node to the Look_Left_Eyeballs node. Then, drag a link from the Eye_Yaw node to the Look_Right_Eyeballs node.

4. With the Eye_Yaw node selected, double-click the Look_Left_Eyeballs link function in the Output Links' Properties section to open the Link Function Editor.

5. Set the m property of the link function to –1.0 and click OK.

6. Locate the Look_Right_Lids and Look_Left_Lids nodes and position them to the right of the Look_Right_Eyeballs and Look_Left_Eyeballs nodes (see **FIGURE 9.165**).

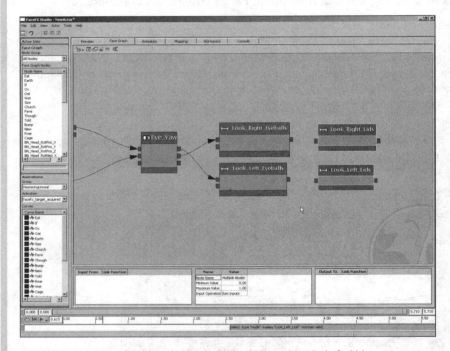

FIGURE 9.165   Position the Look_Right_Lids and Look_Left_Lids.

7. Drag a link from the Look_Right_Eyeballs node to the Look_Right_Lids node. Then, drag a link from the Look_Left_Eyeballs node to the Look_Left_Lids node.

   The Eye_Yaw node now causes the character's eyes to look left and right. You can test it out in the Face Graph section of the Actor panel (see **FIGURE 9.166**).

8. Click the Save Actor button in the toolbar. Then, close FaceFX Studio and save the Chapter_09_Animation package.

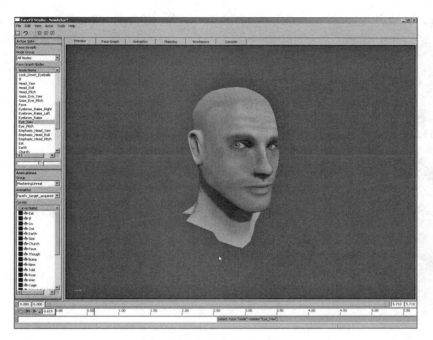

FIGURE 9.166   The character can now look left and right.

END TUTORIAL 9.26

TUTORIAL 9.27: Creating a Facial Animation, Part VI: Creating Combiners for Head Pitch

1. Double-click the fxa_facefx asset from the Chapter_09_Animation package in the Generic Browser to open it in FaceFX Studio. If you have not completed **TUTORIAL 9.26** yet, you may use the fxa_facefx_05 asset instead. Note the fxa_facefx_05 asset has no skeletal mesh associated with it at this point. You must open the skelMesh_facefx mesh and assign the asset to the FaceFXAsset property in the Mesh tab before you can open the asset in FaceFX.

2. Select the Face Graph tab, locate the Head_Pitch node, and position it to the left of the BN_Head_RotPos_X and BN_Head_RotNeg_X nodes.

3. Drag a link from the Head_Pitch node to the BN_Head_RotNeg_X node. Then, drag a link from the Head_Pitch node to the BN_Head_RotPos_X node (see **FIGURE 9.167**).

4. With the Head_Pitch node selected, double-click the BN_Head_RotPos_X link function in the Output Links' Properties section to open the Link Function Editor.

5. Set the m property of the link function to –1.0 and click OK.

    The Head_Pitch node now causes the character's head to look up and down. You can test it out in the Face Graph section of the Actor panel (see **FIGURE 9.168**).

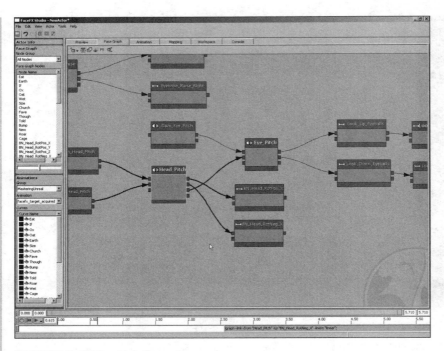

FIGURE 9.167   Link the nodes as shown.

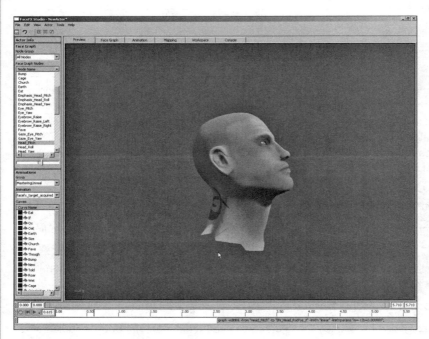

FIGURE 9.168   The character can now nod its head up and down.

6. Click the Save Actor button in the toolbar. Then, close FaceFX Studio and save the Chapter_09_Animation package.

END TUTORIAL 9.27

TUTORIAL 9.28: Creating a Facial Animation, Part VII: Creating Combiners for Head Yaw

1. Double-click the fxa_facefx asset from the Chapter_09_Animation package in the Generic Browser to open it in FaceFX Studio. If you have not completed **TUTORIAL 9.27** yet, you may use the fxa_facefx_06 asset instead. Note the fxa_facefx_06 asset has no skeletal mesh associated with it at this point. You must open the skelMesh_facefx mesh and assign the asset to the FaceFXAsset property in the Mesh tab before you can open the asset in FaceFX.

2. Select the Face Graph tab, locate the Head_Yaw node, and position it to the left of the BN_Head_RotPos_Y and BN_Head_RotNeg_Y nodes.

3. Drag a link from the Head_Yaw node to the BN_Head_RotNeg_Y node. Then, drag a link from the Head_Yaw node to the BN_Head_RotPos_Y node (see **FIGURE 9.169**).

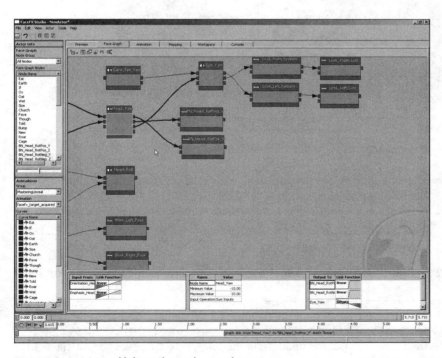

FIGURE 9.169   Link up the nodes as shown.

4. With the Head_Yaw node selected, double-click the BN_Head_RotNeg_Y link function in the Output Links' Properties section to open the Link Function Editor.

5. Set the m property of the link function to –1.0 and click OK.

6. The Head_Yaw node now causes the character's head to look left and right. You can test it out in the Face Graph section of the Actor panel (see **FIGURE 9.170**).

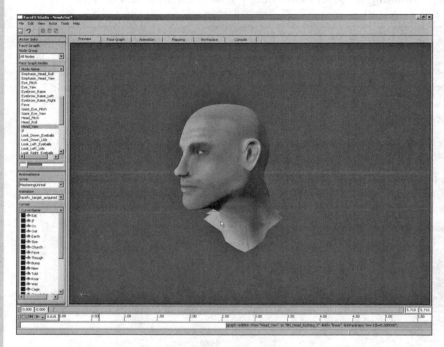

FIGURE 9.170   The character can now turn its head left and right.

7. Click the Save Actor button in the toolbar. Then, close FaceFX Studio and save the Chapter_09_Animation package.

END TUTORIAL 9.28

TUTORIAL 9.29: Creating a Facial Animation, Part VIII: Creating Combiners for Head Roll

1. Double-click the fxa_facefx asset from the Chapter_09_Animation package in the Generic Browser to open it in FaceFX Studio. If you haven't completed **TUTORIAL 9.28** yet, you may use the fxa_facefx_07 asset instead. Note the fxa_facefx_07 asset has no skeletal mesh associated with it at this point. You must open the skelMesh_facefx mesh and assign the asset to the FaceFXAsset property in the Mesh tab before you can open the asset in FaceFX.

2. Select the Face Graph tab, locate the Head_Roll node, and position it to the left of the BN_Head_RotPos_Z and BN_Head_RotNeg_Z nodes.

3. Drag a link from the Head_Roll node to the BN_Head_RotNeg_Z node. Then, drag a link from the Head_Roll node to the BN_Head_RotPos_Z node (see **FIGURE 9.171**).

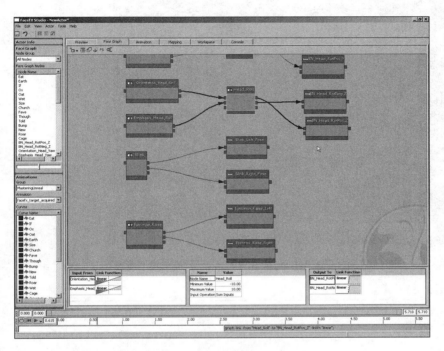

FIGURE 9.171 Connect the nodes together as shown.

4. With the Head_Roll node selected, double-click the BN_Head_RotNeg_Z link function in the Output Links' Properties section to open the Link Function Editor.

5. Set the m property of the link function to –1.0 and click OK.

6. The Head_Roll node now causes the character to tilt its head. You can test it out in the Face Graph section of the Actor panel (see **FIGURE 9.172**).

7. Click the Save Actor button in the toolbar. Then, close FaceFX Studio and save the Chapter_09_Animation package.

FIGURE 9.172   The character can now roll its head to the left and to the right.

END TUTORIAL 9.29

Curves

In order to provide control of a node's value over the course of the animation, a curve can be added to the animation associated with a particular node. That curve can then be edited to modify the value of the node during the animation.

There are two basic types of curves within FaceFX Studio. FaceFX uses *ownership* or, more accurately, what the curve is "owned by" to differentiate between these two types of curves.

First, a curve that is *owned by analysis* is automatically generated during the animation-creation process. Such curves are also re-created anytime the audio is analyzed, phonemes are adjusted, or any changes are made to the Phoneme bar. These curves cannot be modified by the user. Speech gesture curves are an example of curves that are owned by analysis.

Second, a curve that is *owned by the user* is manually added to the animation by the user through the Curve Manager. Such curves are not affected by changes to the Phoneme bar. These curves are completely editable by the user and provide a great deal of power to make animations really shine.

Curves can be switched from one type to another through the Curve Properties dialog. Curves that are set to Owned by Analysis should be left that way until the phoneme positions and durations are finalized, at which time they can be switched to Owned by the User to make tweaks and adjustments.

Once a curve is switched to Owned by the User, it should never be switched back to Owned by Analysis because that creates the potential for any customization to be lost if it is decided that any adjustments to the phonemes need to be made.

The Curve Properties dialog is accessed through the context menu of the Animations panel of the Actor panel. It is fairly simple and provides only two functions:

> **Curve Color**—This allows the color of the curve to be modified, making it easier to differentiate between curves in the Curve Editor.
>
> **Owned by Analysis**—This check box allows the curve to be toggled between the two settings: Owned by Analysis and Owned by the User.
>
> If this box is checked, the curve is owned by analysis. Otherwise, the curve is owned by the user.

Now that the gesture combiners have been created, the automatically created gesture curves should be having an effect on the animation. If you play through the animation, though, you will notice that the gestures are not exactly subtle. We can fix that by adjusting the curves for the gestures. To do this, we have to switch the curves from being owned by analysis to being owned by the user in **TUTORIAL 9.30**.

TUTORIAL 9.30: Creating a Facial Animation, Part IX: Tweaking Gesture Curves

1. Double-click the fxa_facefx asset from the Chapter_09_Animation package in the Generic Browser to open it in FaceFX Studio. If you haven't completed **TUTORIAL 9.29** yet, you may use the fxa_facefx_08 asset instead. Note the fxa_facefx_08 asset has no skeletal mesh associated with it at this point. You must open the skelMesh_facefx mesh and assign the asset to the FaceFXAsset property in the Mesh tab before you can open the asset in FaceFX.

2. Select the Animation tab and then select the Empahsis_Head_Pitch curve in the Animations section of the Actor panel. You should see the curve for the Empahsis_Head_Pitch in the Curve View, but there are no points visible. This is because it is owned by analysis currently. We need to switch it to be owned by the user so it can be edited (see **FIGURE 9.173**).

3. Right-click the Empahsis_Head_Pitch curve in the Animations section of the Actor panel and choose Curve Properties. In the Curve Properties dialog, uncheck the Owned by Analysis box and click OK. The points on the curve should now be visible and editable (see **FIGURE 9.174**).

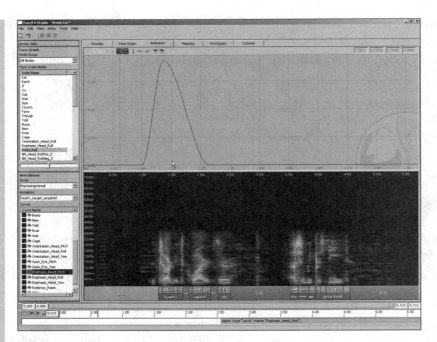

FIGURE 9.173   Notice that the curve has no points.

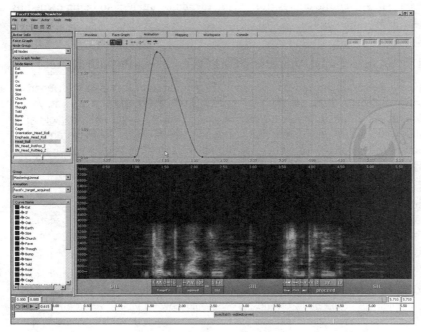

FIGURE 9.174   The curve now has editable points.

You are looking for a mostly random curve during the animation so the head does not appear rigid. You can adjust the points along the curve by clicking them and dragging. New points can be added by pressing the Insert key and then clicking in the Curve View. Values in the range between −0.15 and 0.15 should give good results (see **FIGURE 9.175**).

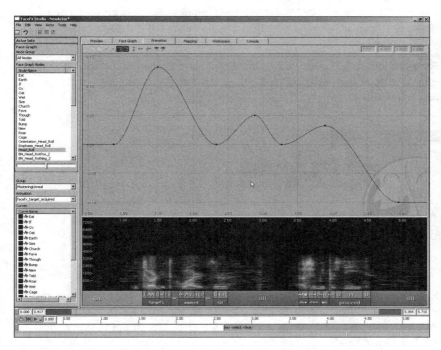

FIGURE 9.175   Make your curve look something like this.

Once you have the Emphasis_Head_Pitch curve adjusted, tweaking the other curves should be easier. Follow the same procedure for converting the other curves you wish to change to be owned by the user.

The curves you may want to adjust are Emphasis_Head_Yaw, Gaze_Eye_Yaw, Eyebrow_Raise, and Blink. Feel free to experiment, and then play back your results to see what you've done.

4. When you are satisfied with the results of the adjusted curves, click the Save Actor button in the toolbar. Then, close FaceFX Studio and save the Chapter_09_Animation package.

END TUTORIAL 9.30

One of the nice features of FaceFX is that it has the ability to drive material parameters. In **TUTO-RIAL 9.31**, we set up a node that drives a parameter in the material applied to the eyes of the mesh.

TUTORIAL 9.31: Creating a Facial Animation, Part X: Driving Material Parameters

1. Double-click the fxa_facefx asset from the Chapter_09_Animation package in the Generic Browser to open it in FaceFX Studio. If you have not completed **TUTORIAL 9.30** yet, you may use the fxa_facefx_09 asset instead. Note the fxa_facefx_09 asset has no skeletal mesh associated with it at this point. You must open the skelMesh_facefx mesh and assign the asset to the FaceFXAsset property in the Mesh tab before you can open the asset in FaceFX.

2. Select the Face Graph tab, right-click in the Face Graph, and choose Add Node > FxMaterialParameterNode (see **FIGURE 9.176**). In the dialog that appears, enter the name **EyeMat** and click OK.

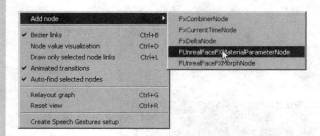

FIGURE 9.176   The FxMaterialParameterNode can be found in the context menu.

3. Select the EyeMat node and set its Parameter_Name property to Bloodshot. This is the name of the parameter in the material this node controls. The material is applied to slot [0] of the skeletal mesh's Materials array, so having Material_Slot_Id set to 0 is perfect (see **FIGURE 9.177**).

4. Open the Curve Manager either from the Actor menu or by using the button in the toolbar. Select the EyeMat curve in the list on the right and then click the Current Anim button to add the curve to the animation.

5. Select the EyeMat curve in the Animations section of the Actor panel. Then select the Animation tab to view the curve. This curve defaults to being owned by the user because it was created by us, so it is ready to be edited.

6. Press the Insert key and then click in the Curve View to place a key at Time=2.5, with a value of 0.0. The edit boxes in the top-right corner can be used to enter exact values (see **FIGURE 9.178**).

9

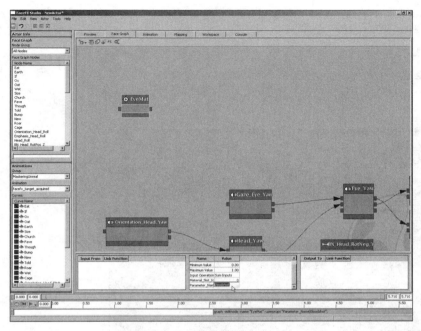

FIGURE 9.177   Set the properties as shown.

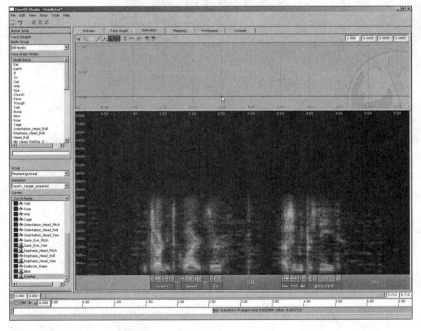

FIGURE 9.178   Place a key at 2.5.

7. Add keys at the following times with the corresponding values to finish off the curve (see **FIGURE 9.179**):

   ▸ 3.5 → 1.0

   ▸ 4.5 → 1.0

   ▸ 5.5 → 0.0

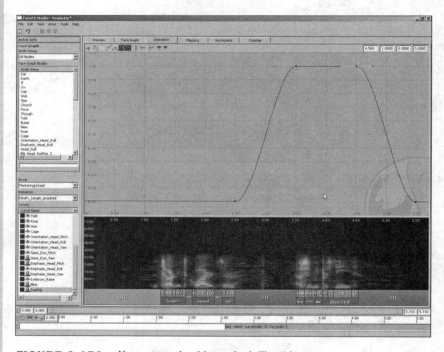

FIGURE 9.179   Your curve should now look like this.

Now you can play the animation to see the effect of the material parameter and make sure everything is working properly.

8. Click the Save Actor button in the toolbar. Then, close FaceFX Studio and save the Chapter_09_Animation package.

END TUTORIAL 9.31

FaceFX Studio User Interface

The following is an overview of the FaceFX Studio user interface. Note that this interface is quite extensive because FaceFX Studio is a fully integrated yet separately designed application (see **FIGURE 9.180**).

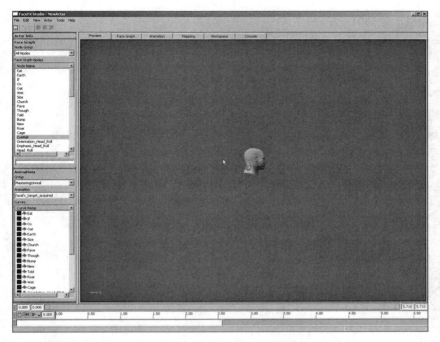

FIGURE 9.180   The FaceFX Studio interface appears like this when first opened.

Menu Bar

FaceFX Studio has a conventional menu bar that provides access to its key functionality features (see **FIGURE 9.181**).

> **File**—The File menu provides functionality for saving the FaceFXAsset being edited as well as closing FaceFX Studio.
>
> **Edit**—The Edit menu provides functionality for the searching and replacing of names as well as undo and redo.
>
> **View**—The View menu provides functionality for toggling the window to full screen and resetting the view in the Face Graph.
>
> **Actor**—The Actor menu provides functionality for the following operations:
>
> > ▸ Renaming the FaceFXAsset
> >
> > ▸ Opening the Node Group, Animation, and Curve Managers
> >
> > ▸ Exporting and syncing to templates
> >
> > ▸ Editing bone weights
>
> **Tools**—The Tools menu provides access to the application, Phoneme bar, Audio View, and Face Graph Options dialog.

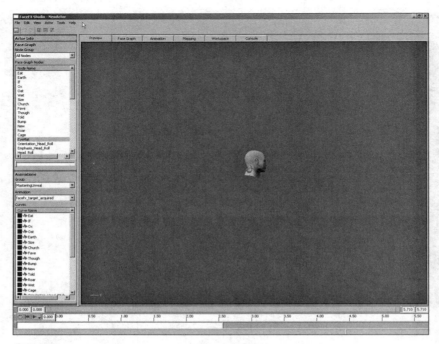

FIGURE 9.181   The FaceFX Studio menu bar

Toolbar

As with most interface elements in Unreal Editor, FaceFX studio provides access to common functions through its toolbar (see **FIGURE 9.182**).

> **Save Actor** 🖫—This button saves the FaceFXAsset being edited.
>
> **Undo/Redo** ↺↻—This will undo or redo the last command.
>
> **Node Group/Animation/Curve Managers** 🗎 🗎 🗎—These buttons open the corresponding manager dialog.

Actor Panel

The actor panel contains several areas dedicated to viewing and controlling your animated asset (see **FIGURE 9.183**).

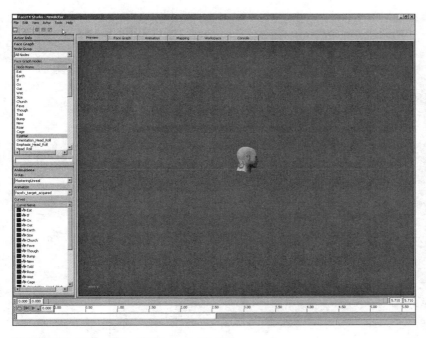

FIGURE 9.182   FaceFX Studio toolbar

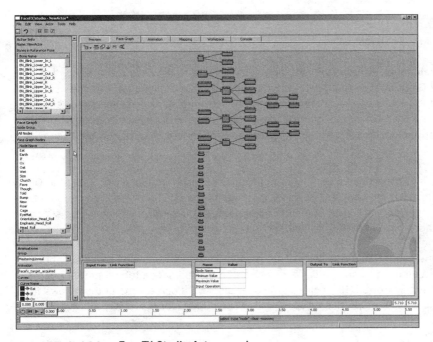

FIGURE 9.183   FaceFX Studio Actor panel

Actor Info panel—This panel simply lists the name of the FaceFXAsset as well as all the bones present in the reference pose of the asset (see **FIGURE 9.184**).

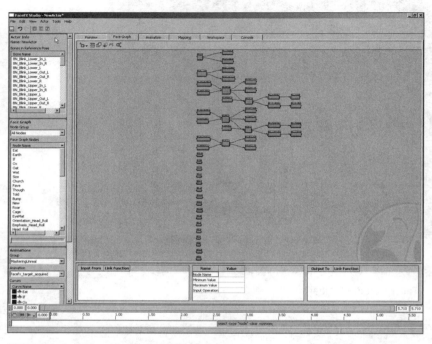

FIGURE 9.184   The Actor Info panel

Face Graph panel—This panel lists the nodes present in the Face Graph according to the Node Group that is selected in the dropdown list. Selecting a node in the list focuses the Face Graph on that particular node. Depending on the Face Graph's options settings, the Face Graph can actually interpolate to the new node in order to give you an idea of the location of the selected node to your current viewpoint in the Face Graph.

The effects of the selected node can be previewed quickly and easily by using the Quick Preview Slider below the list. The slider remembers the position set for each node, thus allowing you to create a new Combiner node using the current positions of the sliders for each node (see **FIGURE 9.185**).

Animations panel—This lists the curves present in the currently selected animation of the current group. Selecting a curve displays it in the Animation tab so that it may be edited or simply viewed. Right-clicking a curve displays a context menu that allows for setting the curve's properties or opening the Curve Manager (see **FIGURE 9.186**).

9

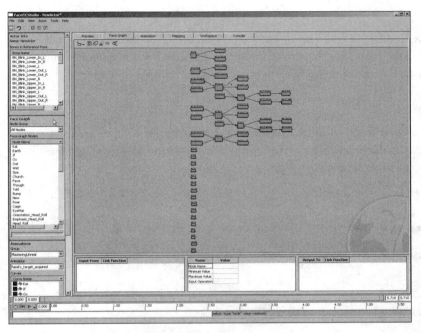

FIGURE 9.185 The Face Graph panel

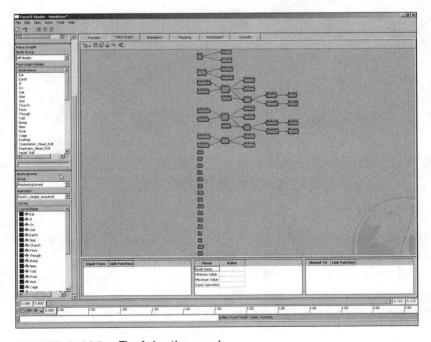

FIGURE 9.186 The Animation panel

Tab Bar

The majority of the interface is taken up by the tabs. These can be reordered in the tab bar by clicking and dragging the tabs. They can also be undocked and made into standalone windows by double-clicking the tabs. To dock the standalone windows again, simply close them.

Face Graph Tab

The Face Graph is a node-based editor that determines how animation curves are used in conjunction to create the final animation data that is output and used for transforming bones, morphing, or driving material parameters.

The Face Graph itself is broken up into a toolbar and four panels (see **FIGURE 9.187**).

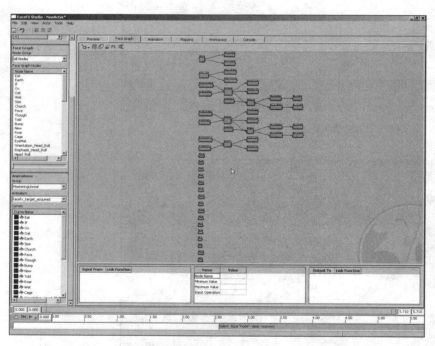

FIGURE 9.187   The Face Graph tab.

Toolbar—The toolbar provides quick access to commonly used functions. Most of these functions are available through the context menu as well.

Add Node —This adds a node of the selected type to the Face Graph.

Toggle Node Visualization —This toggles whether the current values of the nodes are displayed or not.

Layout Graph 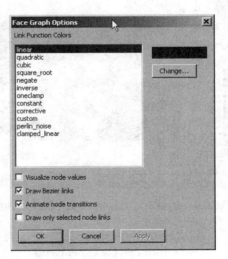—This positions all the nodes in the Face Graph in a logical manner (that is, connected nodes are near each other, with parent nodes to the left of child nodes).

Reset View —This zooms out so that all the nodes are visible and centered in the Face Graph work area.

Find Selected Node(s) F5 —This focuses the Face Graph work area on the selected node.

Create Speech Gestures Setup —This creates the nodes that correspond to the default speech gestures' curves, which can then be linked to the appropriate nodes to allow them to control the animation.

Work area—The work area is where nodes are manipulated and links are created. The context menu of the work area provides similar functionality to the toolbar functions.

Input links—This area in the lower-left corner of the Face Graph shows any input links belonging to the selected node, along with the functions used by those input links.

Node properties—This area to the right of the input links area allows editing of the properties of the currently selected node.

Output links—This area in the lower-right corner of the Face Graph shows any output links belonging to the selected node as well as the functions used by those output links.

The Face Graph Options dialog contains settings that determine the appearance and behavior of the Face Graph (see **FIGURE 9.188**). The following options are available:

Link Function Colors—This provides a list of the various types of link functions and allows different colors to be set for the various types so they can easily be distinguished in the Face Graph.

Visualize node values—If this box is checked, the values of the nodes are displayed in the Face Graph.

Draw Bezier links—If this box is checked, the links between the nodes in the Face Graph will be curves. Otherwise, the links will be straight lines.

FIGURE 9.188   The Face Graph Options dialog

Animate node transitions—If this box is checked, the transition to displaying the selected node will be animated. Otherwise, the view will instantaneously snap to the selected node.

Draw only selected node links—If this box is checked, only the links into or out of the selected node will be displayed. Otherwise, all links will be displayed at all times.

Animation Tab

The Animation tab is split into three sections: the Curve Editor, the Phoneme bar, and the Audio View. This is where the phonemes and animation curves are edited.

Curve Editor

This is where curves, when selected in the Animations panel, can be edited by adjusting the locations of keys (see **FIGURE 9.189**). The Curve Editor toolbar provides the following buttons:

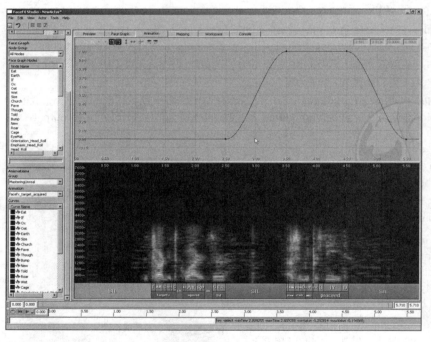

FIGURE 9.189   The Animation Curve Editor

Cut/Copy/Paste —These buttons cut, copy, and paste the selected keys.

Lock/Unlock Tangents — These buttons break or unify the tangents of the selected keys.

> **NOTE**
>
> Only curves that are owned by the user are actually editable in the Curve Editor. See the "Curves" section of this chapter for an in-depth explanation of the difference between curves owned by the user versus owned by analysis.

Snap to Value/Time Grid Lines 🔲🔲—These buttons toggle whether keys should snap to the grid lines of the Curve View.

Fit Curve in Value/Time Axis 🔲🔲—These buttons zoom to fit the keys of the visible curves in the Curve View.

View All Active Curves 🔲—This button makes all the curves belonging to the animation visible in the Curve View.

Previous/Next Key 🔲🔲—These keys will cycle through the keys of the visible curves forwards or backwards.

Time/Value/Derivative Edit Boxes `2.500` `0.0000` `0.0000` `0.0000` —These edit boxes allow the Time, Value, and Tangents of a key to be set precisely.

Curve View

The Curve View is where the actual curves are displayed and visually edited by the user. Curves are displayed using the color set for the curve in the Curve Properties dialog. The curves can be displayed as solid and/or dotted lines. If you remember our discussion of nodes, we talked about how the actual value of a node is based on its curve's value and the combined value of all its inputs.

In the Curve View, the solid curve represents the value of the node's curve. The dotted curve represents the actual value of the node after taking its inputs into account. The dotted curve is only visible if the node has inputs that are passing a value other than 0.0 to the node.

The Curve View can be navigated as follows:

▶ Keys are drawn as points along the curves and can be selected by clicking them. Once selected, the key's tangent handles become visible.

▶ Clicking the left mouse button on the key and dragging moves the key.

▶ Holding down Shift, clicking the left mouse button anywhere, and dragging the mouse moves the selected keys.

▶ Clicking the left mouse button on a tangent handle and dragging the mouse modifies the tangent.

▶ Clicking the left mouse button and dragging on empty space creates a marquee selection that overrides any previous selections.

▶ Holding down Ctrl, clicking the left mouse button, and dragging on empty space creates a marquee selection that toggles the selection of any keys within it.

▶ Pressing the Insert key turns on key creation mode. Clicking with the left mouse button then inserts a new key for all the selected curves.

▶ Clicking the middle mouse button and dragging pans the Curve View.

Phoneme Bar

This is where curves that deal with the actual lip syncing are edited by adjusting the phonemes' locations and durations (see **FIGURE 9.190**). These curves are then automatically generated according to the phonemes.

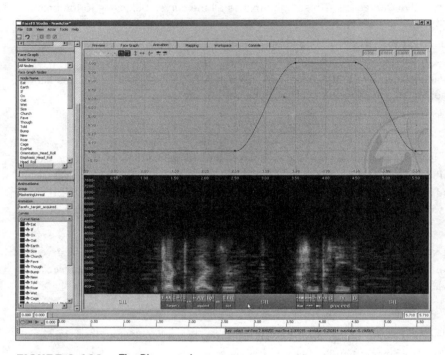

FIGURE 9.190   The Phoneme bar

The Phoneme bar can be navigated as follows:

▶ Clicking the left mouse button on a phoneme or word selects the item.

▶ Holding down Shift and clicking the left button on a phoneme or word adds all the phonemes or words from the current selection and the phoneme that was clicked. If nothing is currently selected, only the phoneme that was clicked is selected.

▶ Clicking the left mouse button on the boundary of a phoneme or word and dragging the mouse adjusts the duration of the adjacent phonemes or words.

▶ Holding down Ctrl while clicking the left mouse button on the boundary of a phoneme or word and dragging the mouse shifts all the phonemes or words to the right of that boundary while maintaining their current durations, effectively lengthening or shortening the overall animation.

▶ Double-clicking the left mouse button on a phoneme or word plays the audio corresponding to that item.

Phoneme bar's context menu, shown in **FIGURE 9.191**, provides the following options:

> **Delete Selection**—This deletes the phoneme or word that is selected.
>
> **Insert Phoneme**—This inserts a new phoneme prior to the selected phoneme.
>
> **Change Phoneme**—This is a set of menus containing all the available phonemes from which a new phoneme can be chosen to replace the selected phoneme.

FIGURE 9.191   The Phoneme Bar context menu

> **Quick Change Phoneme**—This opens a dialog that lists all the available phonemes from which a new phoneme can be chosen to replace the selected phoneme.
>
> **Group To Word**—This groups the selected phonemes to a word. When the boundary of a word is moved, each phoneme grouped to that word is resized proportionately.
>
> **Rename Word**—This allows you to rename the selected word.
>
> **Ungroup Word**—The deletes the selected word, effectively breaking the group.
>
> **Play Phoneme/Word**—This plays the audio that corresponds to the selected phonemes and/or words.
>
> **Reset View**—This zooms the entire contents of the Animation tab to show the animation in its entirety.
>
> **Zoom Selection**—This zooms the entire contents of the Animation tab to show only the selected phonemes and/or words.
>
> **Reanalyze Selection**—This causes the audio corresponding to the selected phonemes and/or words to be reanalyzed. This causes any curves that are owned by analysis to be re-created.

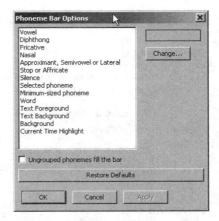

The Phoneme Bar Options dialog provides the following settings for determining the appearance and behavior of the Phoneme bar (see **FIGURE 9.192**):

> **Phoneme colors**—This lists the colors of the different phoneme types and other components of the Phoneme bar so they can be more easily distinguished. These colors can be changed.

FIGURE 9.192   The Phoneme Bar Options dialog

Ungrouped phonemes fill the bar—If this box is checked, phonemes that are not grouped to a word fill the Phoneme bar vertically.

If this box is unchecked, phonemes that are not grouped to a word only fill the top half of the Phoneme bar.

Audio View

The Audio View displays either a spectral graph or waveform plot of the audio file used in the current animation. The spectral graph is the default view type and is preferred in most cases because it allows the boundaries of the words in the audio to be seen more clearly.

To switch between the two types of views, select the Audio View and press Ctrl+T. The Audio View Options dialog provides the following settings for determining the appearance and behavior of the Audio View (see **FIGURE 9.193**).

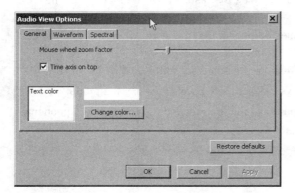

FIGURE 9.193   The Audio View Options dialog

General tab:

Mouse wheel zoom factor—This allows the amount the mouse wheel zooms in or out on the Audio View to be adjusted.

Time axis on top—If this box is checked, the labels of the Time axis are at the top of the Audio View.

If this box is unchecked, the Time axis labels will be at the bottom of the Audio View.

Text Color—This allows the color used for the axis labels to be set.

Waveform tab:

Colors—This allows the colors used for the various aspects of the waveform plot to be set.

9

Spectral tab:

Window Length—This is the window length used for the selected window function.

Window Function—This is the window function used to create the spectral graph.

Colors—This allows the colors of the various aspects of the spectral graph to be set.

Reverse spectral colors—If this box is checked, the colors of the spectral graph will be reversed.

If this box is unchecked, the spectral graph's colors are used as specified.

Color gamma—This sets the gamma of the spectral graph.

Mapping Tab

The Mapping tab shows the weighting of each of the targets, or bone poses, to the different phonemes (see **FIGURE 9.194**). Any time a phoneme is encountered in the Phoneme bar, keys are added to the curves of the targets that have weighting to that phoneme. The peak of the curve formed by those keys is the value specified in the mapping.

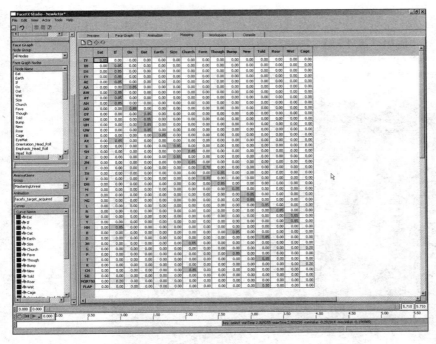

FIGURE 9.194   The Mapping tab

FaceFX Studio provides a default mapping of targets to phonemes, which is a good starting point from which to make tweaks. The mappings can be reset to the default at any time. Additional targets can be added to the mapping through the context menu that is accessed by right-clicking any of the targets or phonemes along the top or left of the grid and choosing Add New Target to Mapping….

Once tweaks have been made, the current mapping values can be set as the default mapping through the context menu by choosing Make Default Mapping.

The Mapping tab's toolbar provides the following options:

> **New Mapping** 📄—This deletes all mappings present.
>
> **New Default Mapping** 📄—This replaces the current mappings with the default mappings.
>
> **Add Target to Mapping** ⊕—This opens a dialog with a list of all the nodes present in the Face Graph from which to choose a new target to be added to the mapping.
>
> **Sync Current Animation to Mapping** 🔄—This adds any speech target curves to the current animation that are not currently present and deletes any curves from the current animation which are not speech target curves and are owned by the analysis.

Preview Tab

The Preview tab is nothing more than a perspective view of the skeletal mesh the FaceFXAsset is associated with (see **FIGURE 9.195**).

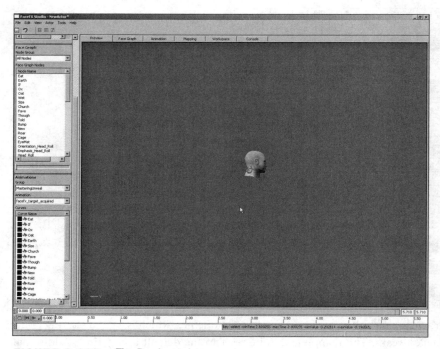

FIGURE 9.195   The Preview tab

The mesh deforms according to the curves and node networks for the current animation, allowing values and timings to be tweaked with real-time visual feedback.

The Preview tab can be navigated as follows:

- ▶ Clicking the left mouse button and dragging the mouse rotates the viewport.
- ▶ Clicking the right mouse button and dragging the mouse zooms in and out in the viewport.
- ▶ Clicking the middle mouse button and dragging the mouse pans the viewport.

> **NOTE**
>
> Clicking the right mouse button brings up the standard UnrealEd viewport context menu. There is no use for this in FaceFX.

Workspace Tab

The Workspace tab allows sets of sliders to be set up in groups called *workspaces*, which can then be used to animate the values of nodes over the length of an animation.

One of the main benefits of this workflow is that these sliders can be two-dimensional. This means that movement in the horizontal axis can control one node and movement in the vertical axis can control a different node. This is extremely useful for controlling and animating the look direction of the eyes of a character, for example.

In the standalone version of FaceFX Studio, using the Workspace tab is most likely the preferred animation workflow. This is because the background of each workspace can be a viewport with its own camera position. This allows the sliders to be placed strategically on top of that viewport and even rotated to fit their intended use, thus making animating very intuitive. This allows real-time visual feedback directly within the Workspace tab. Unfortunately, the integrated version does not currently offer the ability to use a viewport, which limits the usefulness of the Workspace tab. To get similar results, the Workspace tab or Preview tab needs to be separated from the main window (done by double-clicking each tab itself) so they are both visible simultaneously. This requires a great deal more screen real estate, which may not be available to the user.

The Workspace tab has two main modes: Edit Mode and Normal Mode. In Edit mode, the workspace is set up for use and in Normal Mode, the actual work is done.

Normal Mode

This is the default mode in which the Workspace tab starts. It is used mainly for animating the values of nodes over the length of the animation, but can also be used to create new Combiner nodes to control multiple other nodes, as well as to set up mapping relationships (see **FIGURE 9.196**).

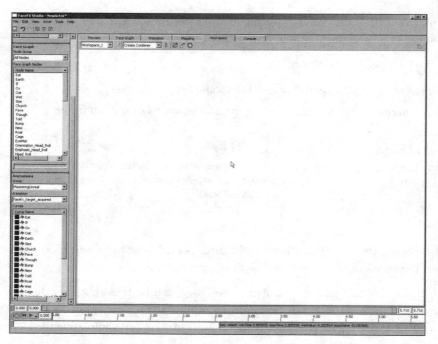

FIGURE 9.196   The Workspace tab in Normal mode

The Normal mode toolbar contains buttons that perform functions essential to using the Workspace. Parts of the toolbar in Normal mode change depending on the current mode it is in. The constant components are listed here:

Workspace List [Workspace_1 ▼]—This is a list of all the workspaces present from which an active workspace can be chosen.

Enter Workspace Edit Mode [✎]—This button switches the Workspace tab into Edit mode.

Workspace Mode List [Create Combiner ▼]—This is a list of the various modes available within the Normal mode. They include Create Combiner, Animate, and Visual Mapping. Each of these is explained in greater detail later in this chapter.

Always Display Slider Names [⚏]—This toggles whether the names of the sliders, or rather the names of the nodes to which the sliders correspond, are always displayed or just displayed when the mouse is hovering over a slider.

Workspace—The workspace takes up the majority of the Workspace tab and is where all the work in Normal mode is done.

All the sliders that are present in the currently selected workspace will be displayed and can be manipulated here.

Normal mode contains three submodes: Create Combiner, Animate, and Visual Mapping. We discuss these submodes next.

Create Combiner mode is a submode of Normal mode that allows slider values to be set manually or according to their values in the current frame. From these slider values, a new Combiner node can be created that allows for blending between the default value and whatever value the slider held at the time the new combiner was created.

Clicking the left mouse button inside a slider snaps the value of the slider to the location of the click. Clicking the right mouse button on a slider resets the slider to its default value.

This is useful for making master controls that can drive many nodes to specific values to create complex poses or effects, such as making a character wink. This node could cause one eye to close completely, the eyebrow above that eye to move downward slightly, the cheek below that eye to move upward slightly, as well as certain normal maps to be blended to a certain degree into the material through parameters. Having one combiner that, when driven to its maximum value, causes all the aforementioned nodes to be driven to specific values within their set range of possible values makes animating a wink much more efficient, especially if it is to be used multiple times.

Finally, the Create Combiner mode toolbar provides the following options:

Reset All Sliders 🚫—This resets all the sliders, including those in the Face Graph panel of the Actor panel, to their default values.

Load The Current Frame 🔧—This sets the sliders in the workspace and in the Face Graph panel to their values at the current frame the timeline is at.

Create Combiner Node 🔘—This creates a new Combiner node controlling all the sliders, either in the workspace or in the Face Graph panel, that are not at their default values.

A dialog will open allowing you to enter a name for the new node. Then another dialog opens, displaying the properties of the new node and the links the new node will have. Links can be removed from the node in this dialog if desired. Once you click Create, the node will finally be created.

The Animate submode allows you to animate the values of the sliders present in the workspace using keyframes by navigating the timeline to a specific frame and setting the value of the slider(s).

Clicking the left mouse button on the slider snaps the value of the slider to the location of the click. Right-clicking the slider resets the slider to its default value. Clicking the middle mouse button on the slider creates a new key for that slider on the current frame with the slider's current value.

The bar representing the value of the slider is displayed in one of three colors. If the slider's bar is green, the value is in sync with the curve, meaning that setting a key at that value for the current frame would not alter the ani-mation curve at all. If the slider's bar is yel-

> **NOTE**
>
> When a key is already present at the current frame, a new key must be set in order to change the value of that key. Simply changing the value of the slider has no permanent effect on the animation curve.

low, the value of the slider is not in sync with the curve and setting a key would alter the animation curve. If the slider's bar is red, there is a key set for that slider on the current frame and setting a key will override the current key.

The Animate submode's toolbar provides the following options:

Auto-key 🔲—This toggles automatic key creation on or off. When it's on, a new key is automatically created when the value of the slider is manually changed by the user.

Key All Sliders 🔲—This sets a key for all the sliders in the workspace at the current frame with their current values.

Previous Key 🔲—This causes the timeline to jump to the location of the previous key for any of the sliders in the workspace.

Next Key 🔲—This causes the timeline to jump to the location of the next key for any of the sliders in the workspace.

The Visual Mapping submode of Normal Mode allows mapping relationships that are normally set up in the Mapping tab to be created and adjusted within the Workspace tab. This allows the designer to preview the results in real time, thus making setting up mappings a much more visual process.

Clicking the left mouse button on a slider in this submode snaps the value of the slider to the location of the click. Clicking the right mouse button resets the slider to its default value.

The Visual Mapping submode's toolbar provides the following options:

Reset All Sliders 🔲—This resets all the sliders, including those in the Face Graph panel of the Actor panel, to their default values.

Load the Current Frame 🔲—This sets the sliders in the workspace and in the Face Graph panel to their values at the current frame the timeline is at.

Apply to Mapping 🔲—This creates a new entry in the mapping for any nodes present in the workspace and sets their mapping values.

If an entry already exists for any of the nodes, the values will simply be updated.

Mapping List 🔲—This is a list of all the phonemes. The mapping values of the sliders in the workspace are applied to the currently selected phoneme.

Edit Mode

Edit mode allows you to create your own slider-style controls to manipulate various aspects of the character's face (see **FIGURE 9.197**). When in Edit mode, the Workspace interface changes, providing you with a list of all the nodes available within the Face Graph. These nodes can then be dragged-and-dropped into the workspace in order to create simple 2D sliders.

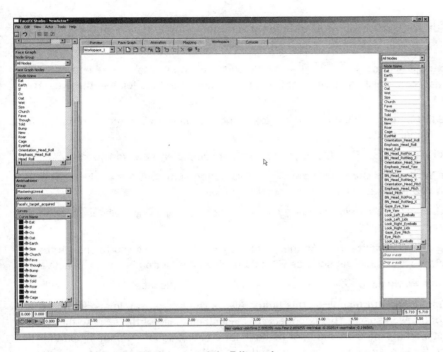

FIGURE 9.197   The Workspace tab in Edit mode

By manipulating these sliders, you can animate the face manually. However, these sliders can only be used in Normal mode. While in Edit mode, the workspace is still considered to be "under construction" so to speak, allowing you to change the size and orientation of each slider.

If so desired, you can create two-dimensional sliders as well, which is great for instances in which you would want to animate a specific component on more than one axis, such as the rotation of the eyes. The process for creating a 2D slider is quite simple. At the bottom of the Node List while in Edit mode, you will see a small window located just beneath two small fields. Simply drag whichever node you want to be controlled by the slider's X-axis into the first field, and the node you want to be controlled by the Y-axis into the other. When you're finished, a new control will appear in the window beneath the fields. Drag this node into your workspace, and you have a new 2D slider.

The Workspace Creation Wizard provides a way for you to create a workspace for your FaceFX project without having to spend any time creating or positioning sliders. When you click the Run the Workspace Creation Wizard button ![], a dialog appears from which you choose which nodes you'd like to control. These nodes are added to a new list. Once you're happy with that list, you can choose the layout for the nodes, click OK, and the workspace will be created for you automatically.

The interface of the Workspace tab while in Edit mode is quite simple. Here is an overview of the toolbar, as well as a look at slider placement and control:

Workspace dropdown [Workspace_1 ▾]—This dropdown allows you to choose between multiple workspaces, which is convenient if you have different setups for, say, the eyes and the mouth.

Leave Edit Mode ![X]—As its name suggests, this button exits Edit mode, placing you back in Normal mode.

New Workspace ![]—This allows you to create a completely new workspace.

Run the Workspace Creation Wizard ![]—This button summons the Workspace Creation Wizard for automatic workspace generation.

Apply Changes to This Workspace ![]—This button commits any changes made to the workspace.

Rename this Workspace ![]—As the name suggests, this allows you to change the name of the workspace. As soon as you add a slider, this button becomes deactivated.

Delete this Workspace ![]—This removes the current workspace.

Add a Background Bitmap ![]—This button allows you to place an image in the background of the workspace. This is perfect for placing an image of the face so that you can position the sliders around it, or perhaps for creating an image showing all the phoneme facial poses for the pertinent nodes, allowing you to place a slider directly underneath each image. You may add as many images as you like. They are positioned the same way as any other workspace element, although they cannot be rotated.

Add a Viewport ![]—This allows you to add a viewport and position a camera so that you can associate a particular view with the current workspace. At the time of this writing, this button is nonfunctional.

Delete Workspace Element ![X]—This removes the selected slider or image from the workspace.

Change the Workspace's Text Color ![]—This allows you to change the color of the textual captions for each workspace element.

Placing sliders and images (referred to as *elements*) in your workspace is quite simple. For one-dimensional sliders, simply drag the name of the node from the node list onto the workspace. For 2D sliders, place the X- and Y-axis nodes into their assigned fields beneath the node list, and then drag the new element from below them onto the workspace. Finally, for images, simply click the Add a Background Bitmap button on the toolbar and choose your image from the dialog.

Once an element is placed on the workspace, you have several options for its positioning. By dragging the small green dot in the center of the element, you can reposition it. Dragging the dots located at the corners and at the center of each edge will scale the element, and dragging the green dot just above the element will rotate it.

Bitmaps that are added to your workspace are adjusted in the same manner, although it should be noted that they cannot be rotated.

Although Edit mode does allow for considerable power over the workspace you use while animating your face, in may computer setups it will not always be so easy to use. As you may have already noticed, the Workspace tab sits directly over the Preview tab, meaning that you cannot see them both at the same time.

Fortunately, you can undock any of the tabs by double-clicking them, and then you can re-dock them by closing the undocked version. This means that if you want to see the Workspace and Preview tabs at the same time, you need only undock one of them and move it out of the way. The only problem with doing this is that if you are using only a single monitor, your screen space will be quite limited. A second monitor will make the use of the Workspace area much more appropriate, although with a little bit of adjustment (and a little patience) there's no reason you can't use FaceFX very well with only one screen.

Console Tab

The Console tab displays the FaceFX log file. The contents of this file provide useful information such as errors, warnings, and echoes of the commands performed within the program in the form of console commands.

- ▶ Errors are displayed highlighted in red.
- ▶ Warnings are displayed highlighted in yellow.
- ▶ Comments are displayed as green text.

Anything not formatted in one of these methods is a FaceFX command. These commands can be copied and pasted into the command line or into FaceFX batch files.

The Console tab shows the last 250 lines of the log file.

Scrub Bar

The scrub bar is used to display and manipulate the length of the current animation and the portion of that animation that is visible within the timeline and Animation tab (see **FIGURE 9.198**). The scrub bar area consists of four edit boxes, two to each side, and the actual "scrub bar" in the center. The two outer (farthest left and right) edit boxes control the length of the animation. The two inner edit boxes control the length of the scrub bar itself.

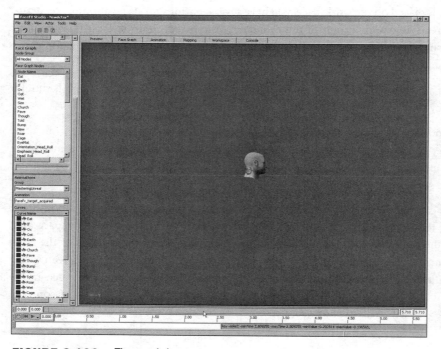

FIGURE 9.198   The scrub bar

Clicking the left mouse button on the small squares at either end of the scrub bar and dragging the mouse alters the length of the scrub bar. Clicking the left mouse button on the rest of the scrub bar and dragging will scrub the bar back and forth, thus altering the portion of the animation that is active.

Timeline

The timeline displays the length of the active portion of the animation and the current position within that portion (see **FIGURE 9.199**). It also contains controls for playing back the animation. The current position is displayed within an edit box just to the right of the actual timeline and by a small black bar drawn on the actual timeline itself.

Clicking the left mouse button within the timeline snaps the current position to that location or frame. Clicking the left mouse button on the timeline and dragging the mouse scrubs through the animation.

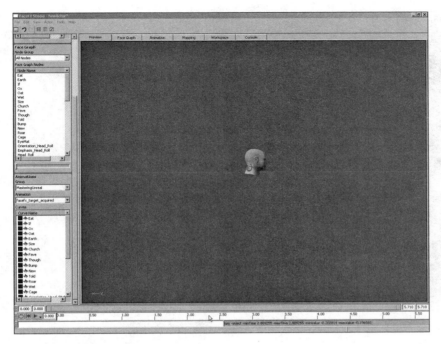

FIGURE 9.199   The timeline

The timeline offers the following buttons:

> **Toggle Looped Playback**—This toggles whether or not the animation should loop back to the beginning when it reaches the end.
>
> **Reset Cursor To Beginning of Time Range**—This sets the current position back to the beginning of the timeline.
>
> **Play Current Time Range**—This begins playback of the animation from the current position. Clicking the button while the animation is playing stops playback and sets the current position to the beginning of the timeline.
>
> Clicking the right side of the button with the small down arrow displays a flyout list of playback speeds from which to choose.

Command Line

The command line allows you to input and execute FaceFX commands directly (see **FIGURE 9.200**).

The left side is where commands are typed in. The right side displays the result of the last command.

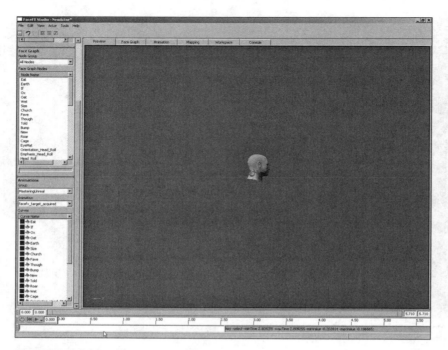

FIGURE 9.200   The command line

Node Group Manager

The Node Group Manager allows nodes to be organized into groups for use in the Face Graph panel (see **FIGURE 9.201**). The Node Group Manager is divided into two sections: Face Graph and Node Groups. The following lists detail the options available in each section.

Face Graph section:

Node Type Filter—This is a list of the types of nodes present in the Face Graph. If no instance of a particular type of node exists, that type will not be an option in this list.

Selecting a type from this list will filter out all the nodes that are not of that type, leaving only the nodes of that type in the Face Graph Nodes list.

Face Graph Nodes—This is a list of all the nodes of the type selected in the Node Type Filter list.

Add to Current Group—This button becomes active when at least one node is selected in the Face Graph Nodes list. Clicking this button adds the selected nodes to the current group selected in the Group list.

9

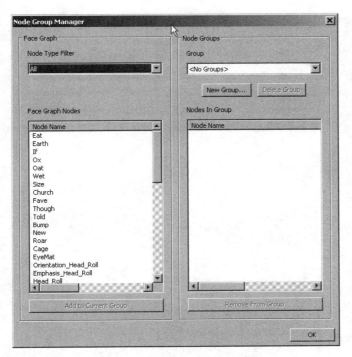

FIGURE 9.201   The Node Group Manager

Node Groups section:

> **Group**—This is a list of all the groups present in this FaceFXAsset. Selecting a group from this list will filter out all the nodes that do not belong to the group, leaving only the nodes that do belong to the group in the Nodes In Group list.
>
> **New/Delete Group**—These buttons are used to create a new group and delete the currently selected group, respectively.
>
> **Nodes In Group**—This is a list of all the nodes belonging to the currently selected group in the Groups list.
>
> **Remove From Group**—This button becomes active when at least one node is selected in the Nodes In Group list. Clicking this button removes the selected nodes from the current group.

Animation Manager

The Animation Manager allows animations to be created as well as placed into, copied into, and moved between groups for organizational purposes (see **FIGURE 9.201**). The Animation Manager is divided into two sections: Primary and Secondary. The following lists detail the options available in each section.

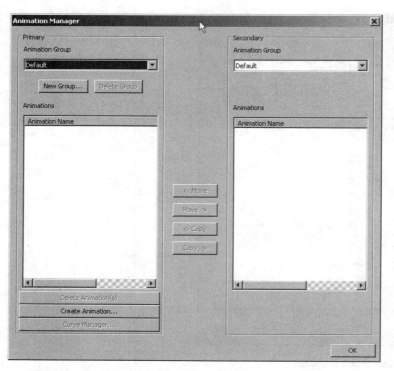

FIGURE 9.201   The Animation Manager

Primary section:

Animation Group—This is a list of all the groups present in the FaceFXAsset. Selecting a group displays the animations the group contains.

New/Delete Group—These buttons create a new group and delete the currently selected group, respectively.

Animations—This displays a list of all the animations contained within the group selected in the Animation Group list.

Delete Animation(s)—This button deletes the selected animation(s) from the currently selected group.

Create Animation—This opens the Create Animation Wizard, which walks you through creating an animation from the Curve Manager.

<- Move / Move ->—These buttons remove the selected animation from one group and place it into another.

<- Copy / Copy ->—These buttons make a copy of the selected animation and place it into the other group.

Secondary section:

> **Animation Group**—This is a list of all the groups present in the FaceFXAsset. Selecting a group displays the animations the group contains.
>
> **Animations**—This displays a list of all the animations contained within the group selected in the Animation Group list.

Curve Manager

The Curve Manager allows curves to be added to an animation, to all animations within a group, or to all animations belonging to the FaceFXAsset (see **FIGURE 9.203**). The Curve Manager is divided into two sections: Curve Target and Curve Source. The following lists detail the options available in each section.

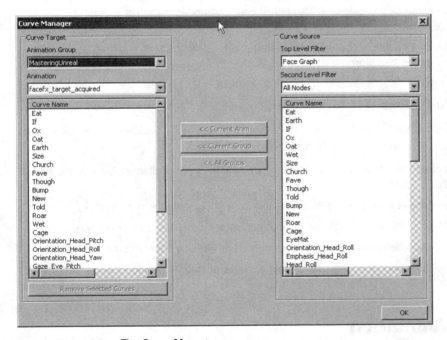

FIGURE 9.203   The Curve Manager

Curve Target section:

> **Animation Group**—This is a list of all the groups present in the FaceFXAsset.
>
> Selecting a group displays the animations the group contains.
>
> **Animation**—This displays a list of all the animations contained within the group selected in the Animation Group list.

Curve List—This is a list of all the curves currently in the selected animation.

<< Current Anim—This button adds the selected curve(s) to the currently selected animation only.

<< Current Group—This button adds the selected curve(s) to all the animations within the currently selected group.

<< All Groups—This button adds the selected curve(s) to all the animations within all the groups.

Curve Source section:

Top Level Filter—This filter lists the Face Graph and any animation groups in the FaceFXAsset.

Second Level Filter—This is populated with either a list of animations belonging to the group selected or a choice of All Nodes or only root nodes if the Face Graph is selected.

Curve List—This list is populated with all the curves/nodes that fit within the restrictions set by the two filters.

FaceFX Studio Options

The Time Grid format group contains various options for controlling the display and use of time in the curve editor. Within it, you will find the following settings.

Curve Editor Time Format—This determines how the time is displayed along the X-axis of the Curve Editor.

Timeline Format—This determines how the time is displayed in the timeline.

Frame Rate (FPS)—This sets the normal playback rate in frames per second.

Phonetic Alphabet—This allows the phoneme set used by FaceFX to be set.

Colors—This allows the colors of certain aspects of FaceFX Studio to be set.

Physical Animation

The animation system is not limited to using only skeletal and morph animation. Physical animation can be employed as well. This means that you can have the bones of your character be affected by physical forces such as gravity and collision. This simulated animation can then be blended with the skeletal animation on a per-bone basis, making realistic weapon hit and death sequences possible. The animation is calculated thus: First, the original skeletal animation is calculated. Then, any skeletal controllers that are affecting the bones of the character or object are applied. Finally, the physical simulation is added to the mix to create the final output.

9

The one major drawback to the use of physical animation is that outside of working with an already completed game that employs it, it must be created via close cooperation between the artist and the programmer, and it does require some coding. This is so that the engine knows precisely under what conditions physical animation is to be applied to the character. Because achieving this process requires programming, its use is beyond the scope of this book. However, it is covered here as a way to introduce the concept, and to make existing programmers aware of the capability.

In **TUTORIAL 9.32**, we set up a skeletal mesh playing a running animation and then combine that with a physics simulation on part of the body (specifically the left arm) to give the appearance of physical injury.

TUTORIAL 9.32: Simulating Injury Using Physical Animation

1. Open the DM-CH_09_PhysAnim_Begin map. This is just a basic map to give us somewhere to display the character and animation.

2. Select the ImportMesh_Human_Male asset from the CH_AnimHuman package in the Generic Browser. Right-click in the viewport and choose Add Actor > SkeletalMeshActor: SkeletalMesh CH_AnimHuman.Mesh.ImportMesh_Human_Male to place the actor in the map (see **FIGURE 9.204**).

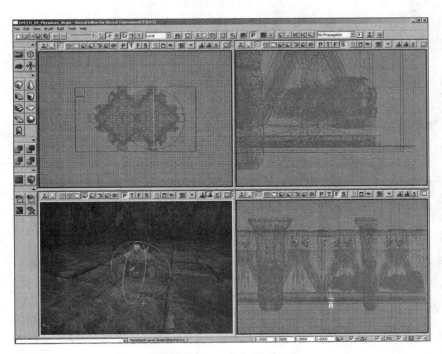

FIGURE 9.204   Place the skeletal mesh in the level.

3. Select the actor. Using the Front or Side viewport, move the actor up until the feet are resting on the surface.

4. Press F4 to open the actor's properties and then expand the SkeletalMeshActor section and the SkeletalMeshComponent section. Scroll down to the SkeletalMeshComponent subsection and set the following properties:

   ▶ **bEnableFullAnimWeightBodies**: True

   ▶ **bHasPhysicsAssetInstance**: True

   ▶ **bUpdateJointsFromAnimation**: True

   ▶ **PhysicsWeight**: 1.0

5. Select the SK_CH_BaseMale_Physics asset from the Chapter_09_Animation package in the Generic Browser and click the Use Current Selection In Browser button 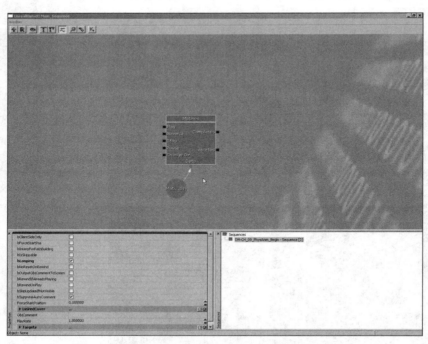 for the PhysicsAsset property of the actor.

6. Select the skeletal mesh actor in the viewport and open Kismet. Create a new Matinee sequence by right-clicking and choosing New Matinee. Set the Matinee sequence's bLooping property to True. Double-click the Matinee object to open the Matinee Editor (see **FIGURE 9.205**).

FIGURE 9.205   Create a new Matinee sequence in Kismet.

7. Right-click in the Group List and choose Add EmptyNew Group. Name the new group **DeadArm**. In the group's properties, add a slot to the GroupAnimSets array by clicking the Add New Item button. Select the K_AnimHuman_BaseMale animation set from the CH_AnimHuman package in the Generic Browser and click Use Current Selection in Browser button ![icon] for slot [0].

8. Right-click the DeadArm group and choose Add New Anim Control Track. With the time slider at Time=0.0, press Enter to place a new key. Choose the run_fwd_rif animation from the dropdown list that appears (see **FIGURE 9.206**).

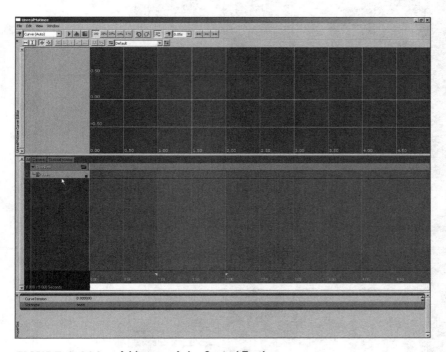

FIGURE 9.206   Add a new Anim Control Track.

9. Drag the red Sequence marker at the end of the Matinee sequence to be even with the end of the run_fwd_rif animation so that the sequence ends when the animation ends. You may need to disable snapping in Matinee for this.

10. Now we need to set up the physics asset. Double-click the SK_CH_BaseMale_Physics asset from the Chapter_09_Animation package in the Generic Browser to open it in PhAT (see **FIGURE 9.207**).

11. Select the b_LeftArm body in the Tree list and set its bAlwaysFullAnimWeight property to True. Now, set this property for the b_LeftForeArm and b_LeftHand bodies in the Tree list (see **FIGURE 9.208**).

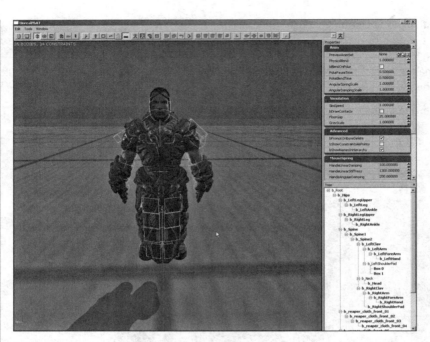

FIGURE 9.207   Open the physics asset in PhAT.

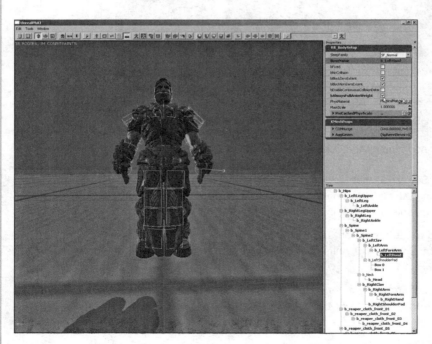

FIGURE 9.208   Make sure that the bAlwaysFullAnimWeight property is set for all bones.

12. Click the Editing Mode button (or press the B key) in the toolbar to switch to Constraint Mode and select the b_LeftHand constraint in the Tree list.

13. Click the Instance Properties button (or press the I key) in the toolbar to view the instance properties of the constraint. Set the following:

   ▸ **bSwingPositionDrive**: True

   ▸ **bTwistPositionDrive**: True

14. Close PhAT. In the Matinee Editor, connect a new Level Startup event to the Play input of the Matinee Sequence (see **FIGURE 9.209**).

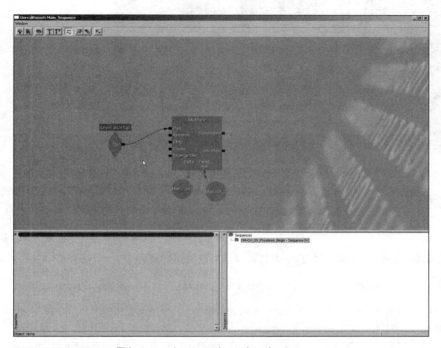

FIGURE 9.209   This network starts the animation.

15. Playtest the map. You should see the character running with his arm dangling (see **FIGURE 9.210**).

16. Save the map if you wish to preserve your progress.

FIGURE 9.210   The character's arm is now dangling as if broken.

END TUTORIAL 9.32

Setup Procedure for Physical Animation

This section outlines the noncoding requirements for a skeletal mesh to use physical simulations.

First, before the skeletal mesh can make use of physical animation, the mesh needs a physics asset created for it from within PhAT. Any of the physics asset's bodies that are to be influenced by the physics simulation should have their bAlwaysFullAnimWeight set to True. The process of creating a physics asset is covered in detail in Chapter 4, "Physics Objects."

The bHasPhysicsAssetInstance property on the skeletal mesh component must be set to True. This sets up the physics engine data necessary for creating the physical simulation.

The PhysicsWeight property on the skeletal mesh component should be set to a value higher than 0.0. A value of 0.0 means that the physical simulation has no influence, whereas a value of 1.0 results in full influence from the physical animation.

Finally, the bEnableFullAnimWeightBodies should be set to True in the skeletal mesh component.

9

Skeletal Mesh Actors

Skeletal meshes are used for a variety of different in-game objects, such as pawns, vehicles, weapons, and even some noninteractive objects. Most of these actors are set up using coding and are not commonly used by level designers apart from placement within a level.

This placement is done using one of two actors; either the SkeletalMeshActor or the SkeletalMeshActorMAT. The one you use will depend on what your skeletal mesh will be doing inside your level. If the mesh is simply playing through a single animation, you will only need the SkeletalMeshActor. However, if the mesh needs to blend between different animations, it will need the SkeletalMeshActorMAT actor. This actor uses Matinee to allow for blending between different animations. The process for doing this is covered in Chapter 10, "Creating Cinematic Sequences."

Skeletal Mesh Component

All actors that make use of skeletal meshes do so through the skeletal mesh component. This contains a reference to which skeletal mesh will be used for the actor, as well as all the properties that pertain to that particular skeletal mesh's behavior. These properties are listed and described next:

>**Animations**—This is this skeletal mesh component's instance of the AnimTree.
>
>**AnimSets**—This is an array of the AnimSets from which this skeletal mesh can use animation sequences.
>
>**AnimTreeTemplate**—This is a reference to the AnimTree for this skeletal mesh.
>
>**bDisableFacefXMaterialInstanceCreation**—If this property is true, FaceFX will not create material instances for this skeletal mesh.
>
>**bEnableFullAnimWeightBodies**—If this property is true, bodies that have bAlwaysFullAnimWeight set to true will be enabled, allowing them to use the physics simulation to drive their position and rotation.
>
>If this property is false, all bodies will respect the animation, only dismissing any physics influence.
>
>**bForceDiscardRootMotion**—If this property is true, any root motion within the animations applied to this skeletal mesh will be ignored regardless of the settings within the AnimSequencePlayer node for that animation sequence of this skeletal mesh's AnimTree.
>
>If this property is false, the root motion of animation sequences will be used according to the settings within the AnimSequencePlayer node for that animation sequence of this skeletal mesh's AnimTree.
>
>**bHasPhysicsAssetInstance**—If this property is true, this skeletal mesh will have an instance set up within the physics engine.

bPerBoneVolumeEffects—If this property is true, each body of this skeletal mesh will be tested individually against physics volumes to determine whether they overlap and the effects of the volume will be applied accordingly.

bSyncActorLocationToRootRigidBody—If this property is true, the location of the Actor that owns this skeletal mesh component will be set to the root bone's location when using PHYS_RigidBody physics.

bUpdateJointsFromAnimation—If this property is true, the position of the joints will be updated each frame to match the animation playing on the skeletal mesh.

bUpdateKinematicBonesFromAnimation—If this property is true, the position of bones with bFixed set to true will be updated each frame to match the animation playing on the skeletal mesh.

FaceFXBlendMode—This determines how transformations due to FaceFX are handled.

FXBM_Overwrite—This mode causes the transformations to replace the transforms of the relevant bones.

FXBM_Additive—This mode causes the transformations to be added to the transformations of the relevant bones.

MorphSets—This is an array of the MorphTargetSets this skeletal mesh can use.

ParentAnimComponent—This is a reference to the parent component used for compositing skeletal meshes.

PhysicsAsset—This is a reference to the physics asset for this skeletal mesh.

PhysicsWeight—This is the amount of influence the physical animation simulation will have on the final rendered mesh. A value of 0.0 means only the skeletal animation is used. A value of 1.0 means only the physical animation is used.

RootMotionMode—This determines how root motion is handled with respect to the Actor that owns this skeletal mesh component.

RMM_Translate—This mode moves the Actor owning the skeletal mesh according to the root's motion.

RMM_Velocity—This mode uses the root motion's speed to limit the owning Actor's velocity with that value.

RMM_Ignore—This mode causes the root motion to be ignored by the owning Actor.

RMM_Accel—This mode uses the velocity from the root motion to determine the acceleration of the owning Actor.

RootMotionRotationMode—This determines how the rotation of the root bone is handled by the owning Actor.

RMRM_Ignore—This mode causes the root rotation to be ignored by the owning Actor.

RMRM_RotateActor—This mode applies the rotation of the root bone to the Actor that owns this skeletal mesh component.

SkeletalMesh—This is a reference to the skeletal mesh this component uses.

Summary

There are many aspects to the Animation System in Unreal Editor. In fact, despite this being one of the largest chapters in this book, we've really only scratched the surface of what is possible. We hope that from here, you are able to walk away with enough knowledge to start striking out on your own in creating animations, either from scratch, by way of 3D animation software, or by manipulating and working with the existing animations included with *Unreal Tournament 3*!

Chapter 10

Creating Cinematic Sequences

Cinematic sequences (often called *cut scenes* or *machinima*) are essentially short virtual films shown as intermissions between levels or missions, as prologues to the next level, or as epilogues to the level just completed. Most often, these are completely noninteractive because the player has limited to no control over the action that happens or the manner in which he or she experiences the cinematic. Cinematic sequences provide designers and art directors with the power to present their story precisely in the manner they wish the player to receive it.

Cinematic Sequences

Although cinematic sequences provide the primary way for game designers to push character development and explain the storyline with complete control, they do present some considerable challenges—especially those that are completely noninteractive. Keeping the viewer interested and entertained is extremely important, but will often prove difficult at the same time. If at all possible, you want to avoid having the scene devolve into a series of talking heads. This becomes more difficult when a lot of info needs to be conveyed to the player, such as mission objectives or integral story lines. Keeping the scene moving is a great way to keep the action flowing and keep the player's attention when he or she is not in control. This can be done using a combination of moving the actors, moving the camera, and moving through edits (such as camera cuts).

Moving the Actors

Moving the actors is fairly self-explanatory. In essence, as the director, you are moving the characters in the scene around to keep the scene from being monotonous and stale (see **FIGURE 10.1**). This not only creates the feeling of action taking place even when the camera is relatively static, but it also creates opportunities for the other methods (camera movement and camera edits).

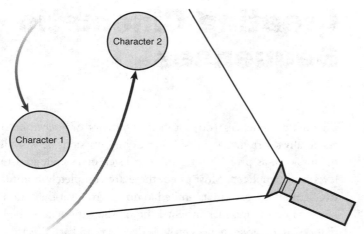

FIGURE 10.1   This diagram illustrates the actors of a scene moving about while the camera remains stationary.

Moving the Camera

Moving the camera refers to physically trucking the camera around in space during the sequence. This is a great way to make use of single-camera shots while keeping the scene lively. It also presents the opportunity to display the environments in which the characters in the scene find themselves (see **FIGURE 10.2**).

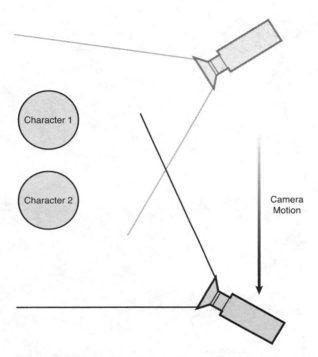

FIGURE 10.2 This diagram illustrates the camera moving about or through the scene.

Moving Through Edits

Moving through edits refers mainly to the use of camera cuts, but also to fading and zooming or even the use of slow-motion. Any or all of these editing techniques can be used to keep the scene moving along and interesting to the player. In larger scenes where the characters are more spaced out, it may be difficult or even impossible to shift focus from one character to another simply through moving the camera or moving the actors themselves. Having multiple cameras and cutting between them can be invaluable in situations like these (see **FIGURE 10.3**).

Rendered In-Game Versus Prerendered

One of the aspects of cut scenes—especially in the past—that has put off some gamers and enticed others is the distinction between in-game cinematic sequences and prerendered sequences. In-game cinematics are produced in real time and are rendered using the game's own art assets and rendering engine. Prerendered cinematics are different in that they are created using separate high-resolution art assets and are generally created with and rendered out from 3D applications. The resulting movie is simply played back as a movie in the game.

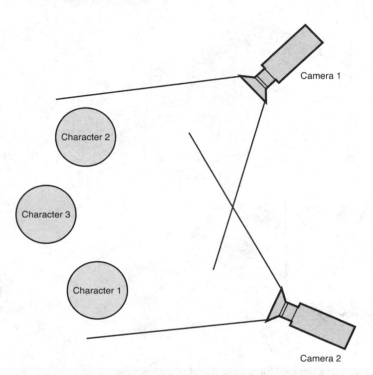

FIGURE 10.3   This diagram shows multiple cameras focusing on the subjects. These cameras could then be cut in between using edits.

With the advent of Unreal Engine 3 and the quality of its rendering system, the line between these techniques has been blurred. The art assets used in-game—and therefore in the in-game cinematics—have the same high visual fidelity as the high-resolution art assets used in many modern films. The Matinee system has also been completely overhauled into a fully featured non-linear editor. Cinematic sequences that rival the quality previously only found in prerendering in the past can now be created directly inside of UnrealEd and rendered in real time as the game plays, and they can be created much more easily.

What this means for developers is that art assets can now be shared between the game and the cinematic sequences used in the game as well as used for marketing purposes. This means less time spent working on the cinematic sequences in-house and less money spent outsourcing the creation of the cinematics to other studios. It also means that there is no gap between the look of the cinematic sequences and the actual gameplay. This has been a sticking point for gamers for the longest time. The commercial for a game would look amazingly lifelike; however, once the gamer got it home and began playing it, he or she would find out the game looks nothing like the commercial. With the power provided in Unreal Engine 3, this gap is a thing of the past.

Camera Actor

The camera actor is used in Unreal Engine 3 as a virtual representation of a real-world camera (see **FIGURE 10.4**). The currently active camera serves as the viewpoint through which the scene is rendered. Through the use of the Director track in Matinee, cameras can be cut between and faded in and out to create transitions much like those found in traditional films. Cameras can also zoom in and out to focus on specific areas or reveal more of the scene to the player. Each camera has its own set of post-processing settings as well, which can be used to override the current post-processing settings of the level, thus creating the possibility for unique effects applicable only to each individual camera.

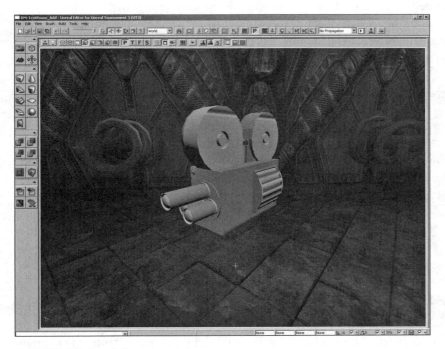

FIGURE 10.4   A Camera actor

A camera actor has the following properties that can be used to modify the look of the scene as rendered from that camera:

> ▶ **AspectRatio**—This sets the ratio of width to height of the rendered scene. Standard aspect ratios are 1.33 (the aspect ratio of a standard television or computer monitor) and 1.78 (the aspect ratio of a widescreen television or computer monitor).

> ▶ **bConstrainAspectRatio**—This determines if the rendered scene is restricted to the aspect ratio specified in the AspectRatio property, if the extra space in the window is letterboxed if not the same aspect ratio as the camera, or if the rendered scene simply fills the entire window regardless of the aspect ratio of the window or camera.

> ▶ **FOVAngle**—This sets the field of view (or the amount of degrees displayed) for the camera. Adjusting this property effectively causes the camera to zoom in or out.

> ▶ **bCamOverridePostProcess**—If this property is true, the CamOverridePostProcess settings of this camera override the current post-process settings when this camera is active.

> If this property is false, the CamOverridePostProcess settings of this actor are ignored.

> ▶ **CamOverridePostProcess**—This is a group of post-process settings that are used depending on the bCamOverridePostProcess property of this camera. Complete descriptions of these properties can be found in Chapter 8, "Post-Process Effects."

Camera Effects

As mentioned previously, when you create a cinematic sequence, you are essentially creating a virtual film that is shown to the player during the game. One way to make these virtual films more interesting and believable is to add effects, such as depth of field or motion blur. These effects would generally be created by traditional film cameras and lenses simply because of how they work and interact with the scene. Unreal Engine 3, through the use of post-process effects and other features, takes the methods traditional filmmakers use and breaks them down into their individual parts in an attempt to mimic the film-creation process. This makes knowledge of how effects are created using cameras and film extremely valuable when creating cinematic sequences within Unreal Engine 3.

Depth of Field

Depth of field is used to give focus to objects at a certain depth while causing other objects to appear out of focus or blurry. This can be a great way to direct the player's attention to a certain area in the scene. It can also be used to create the effect of a scene being viewed through a camera that loses focus or even through the eyes of a player as he wakes up from sleeping or being knocked unconscious.

With cameras in the real world, depth of field is based on what is known as the *f-number* (often referred to as *f-stops*) or *relative aperture*. This is the ratio of the focal length of the lens to the diameter of the entrance pupil, or the entrance for light into the camera. Increasing the f-number increases the depth of field effect, but also decreases the amount of light received.

In Unreal Engine 3, depth of field is created by rendering objects at a certain distance (the FocusDistance) from the camera clearly, while applying a graduated blur effect to other objects in the scene out to the FocusInnerRadius. Unlike in the real world, depth of field is not limited by light inside of Unreal Engine 3, but its main principles and its final result remain the same (see **FIGURE 10.5**).

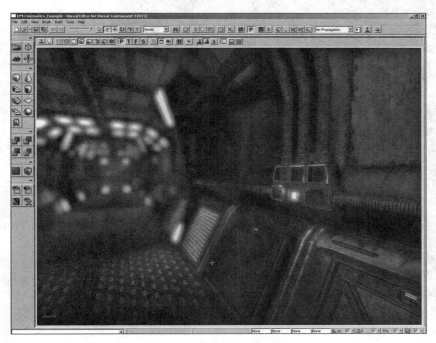

FIGURE 10.5   Here you can see the result of depth of field.

Motion Blur

Motion blur makes objects in the scene that are moving in relation to the camera appear blurred along their direction of movement. This can be used to exaggerate the amount of motion for objects in the scene or make that motion more apparent to the player. It can also be used to make abrupt camera movements more realistic.

In the real world, motion blur is based on the amount of incoming light and the length of time the film is exposed to that light. In essence, the film is capturing the scene and thus the position of objects moving within the scene in relation to the camera, over a period of time as determined by the shutter speed. This gives those moving objects their blurred appearance.

In Unreal Engine 3, rendering the scene multiple times and compositing those renders into a single image for each frame is not feasible in order to keep the game running at an acceptable frame rate. Instead, a graduated blur based on the rate of motion is applied to the area covered by moving objects, which when used wisely can give the appearance of motion that standard motion blur provides. This can be applied either to individual objects that are moving in the scene or to the entire scene, such as in a case where the camera is moving very quickly (see **FIGURE 10.6**).

FIGURE 10.6   Motion blur causes this object to be blurred as it passes by the camera.

Field of View

Field of view is the angular extent, or number of degrees, that can be seen by the camera at any one time. Adjusting the field of view is a way to zoom in on certain areas in the scene to show fine details or just to focus the player's attention on what he or she needs to see.

When you're dealing with real-world cameras, field of view is determined by the size of the film, the focal length of the lens being used, and the amount of distortion caused by that lens. Lenses are often classified in terms of their field of view, such as wide-angle or telephoto. Lenses of these types need to be swapped out to get different fields of view. Also, zoom lenses are available that allow their focal lengths to be adjusted, thus producing a zooming effect.

In Unreal Engine 3, each camera has its own field of view setting called *FOV* (see **FIGURE 10.7**). The value of this property is the number of degrees the camera can see, just as with real cameras. The FOV of a camera can be adjusted during the cinematic to zoom in on characters or the environment when the player's attention is required. Increasing the FOV gives the result of zooming out, and decreasing zooms in.

10

FIGURE 10.7   These two shots show the camera zooming in through the use of FOV.

Scene Effects

Scene effects are used to modify the color range, saturation, or contrast of the scene. This can be a great way to create a specific mood or atmosphere in your cinematic sequence. Scene effects can be used to create a sepia-tone image or even a simple black-and-white image. This technique can be used during a flashback sequence to give a sense of time shifting or to evoke emotions or sense of nostalgia. The possibilities are virtually limitless.

With traditional cameras and film, effects such as these are created by either directly manipulating the film during the developing process or through the use of lens filters. Several kinds of filters are available that can cancel out certain colors, boost specific colors, increase contrast, and perform a myriad of other functions.

Camera actors in Unreal Engine 3 give the designer control over the red, green, and blue channels of the lowlights (SceneShadows) and highlights (SceneHighlights), allowing individual color components to be boosted or limited. Control of the gamma curve, which allows contrast to be modified, is also provided through the SceneMidtones property. The entire scene can also be desaturated by adjusting the SceneDesaturation property (see **FIGURE 10.8**).

FIGURE 10.8   On the left is the original shot; on the right, the same shot with scene effects applied.

Image Separation Through Lighting

With the improved graphical capabilities of Unreal Engine 3 and the consistent lighting across surfaces, it is much easier for the characters and environment to appear integrated into one coherent scene. At times, this almost works too well and the characters blend into the scene so perfectly that they are difficult to distinguish. Separating the characters from the environment becomes important in situations like this and can be achieved using subtle lighting cues, such as rim lighting.

Rim lighting is basically creating highlights along the silhouette of the character using accent lights or shader setups. This not only creates a nice visual look, but draws the characters out of the scene just enough to keep them set as the focus of the scene. It is important to keep the effect subtle, though, because too much rim lighting can destroy the scene's sense of realism.

DumpMovie Command

Unreal Engine 3 also provides the ability to render out each frame of the cinematic sequence to individual image files that can be composited into a single movie file in an external application. These standalone movie files can potentially be used for the purpose of promoting a game or mod (taking legal issues into account of course) by making it available on the Internet or by including it in commercials. The process is extremely simple once the cinematic is created. All you need to do is launch the game's executable file from the command line, specifying the name of the map file the cinematic resides in followed by the -dumpmovie switch. This causes a BMP image file for each frame to be created inside the Screenshots folder for the game. Additionally, the -benchmark switch may be used to limit the game to running at 30 frames per second. If you wish to, you may also specify the resolution for running the game using the -ResX= and -ResY= switches. The full command would look something like this:

```
ExampleGame CinematicsDemo -dumpmovie -benchmark -resx=1280 -resy=720
```

This command launches the ExampleGame running the CinematicsDemo map at a resolution of 1280×720 and at 30 frames per second while creating an image of each frame.

Putting It All Together

Through the use of the tools, techniques, and effects mentioned throughout this chapter, along with a good filmmaking sense and a flare for the dramatic, designers can use Unreal Engine 3 to create engaging stories with fully developed characters, exciting gameplay, and film-quality visual progression. Cinematic sequences can take over a scene, be integrated into the scene, or be rendered out as frames by the game and composited into a standalone movie. The only real limitations are your own imagination and creativity.

10

Over the course of this set of tutorials, we create a cinematic sequence, or cut scene, in which the character runs down a hallway. Four explosions occur, knocking the player around on his way. The sequence contains two camera cuts and the use of fades and slow-motion (slomo). We will also modify certain properties of the camera actors themselves, such as the depth of field post-processing settings as well as the field of view (FOV). The entire sequence is backed by a musical score for a more cinematic atmosphere.

TUTORIAL 10.1: Character Setup

1. Open the DM-CH_10_Cine_Begin map. This map is the scene for the cinematic sequence we are going to create (see **FIGURE 10.9**). It consists of the long hallway the character will be running down while being thrown about by explosions.

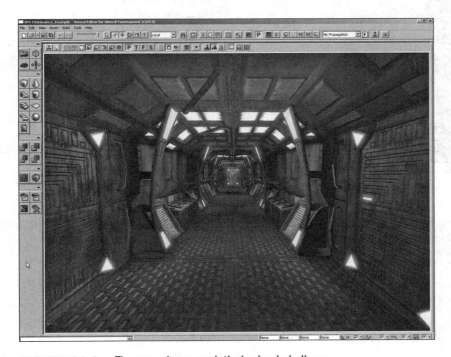

FIGURE 10.9 The map shows a relatively simple hallway.

2. The first thing that needs to be done is to place the character in the level. We will be using a special actor called SkeletalMeshActorMAT that allows for the blending of animations within Matinee. In the Generic Browser, select the COG_Grunt_AMesh asset from the COG_Grunt package provided in the files on the DVD for this chapter. Then, right-click the floor

> **NOTE**
>
> The topic of blending animations is discussed in depth in Chapter 9, "The Unreal Animation System."

of the hallway in the perspective viewport and choose Add Actor > SkeletalMeshActorMAT: SkeletalMesh COG_Grunt.COG_Grunt_AMesh to place the actor (see **FIGURE 10.10**).

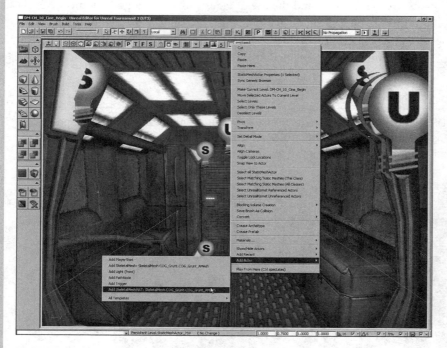

FIGURE 10.10   Place the actor in the level.

3. Move the character's pivot so that it rests in the center of the hallway. Note that this will cause the character to appear to be off to the side of the hallway.

4. Select the actor and press F4 to open its properties.

5. Under the Movement section, set the Physics property to PHYS_Interpolating. This will be necessary because we are going to use Matinee to control the movement of the player.

6. Expand the SkeletalMeshActor section. Then expand the LightEnvironment section and select the bEnabled property under LightEnvironmentComponent.

7. Under the SkeletalMeshActor section, expand the SkeletalMeshComponent section and then scroll down to the SkeletalMeshComponent subsection.

8. In the Generic Browser, select the animTree_Grunt_cinematic asset from the Chapter_10_Cinematics package provided on the DVD with the files for this chapter. Then click the Use Current Selection in Browser button for the AnimTreeTemplate property. This AnimTree is set up to allow for the blending of animations.

10

9. Position the actor at the top end of the hallway looking at it in the Top viewport. It should be centered on the hallway in the Y-axis and about 144 units from the end of the hallway in the X-axis. Also, move the actor up so the mesh's feet are even with the floor of the hallway. Then, rotate it so the character is facing the opposite end.

10. Make sure the pivot is in the center of the hallway, not the mesh. If it's positioned properly, you should just barely see the character's hand coming through the wall (see **FIGURE 10.11**).

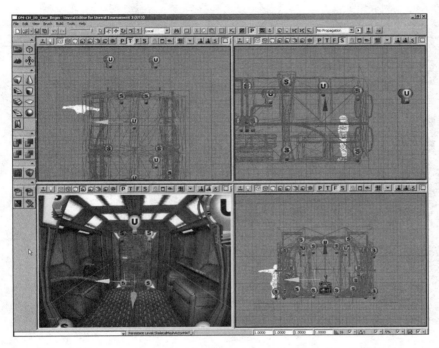

FIGURE 10.11 Notice that the pivot rests in the middle of the hallway; you can just barely notice the character's hand sticking through the wall.

11. Save the map to preserve your work.

END TUTORIAL 10.1

Complete **TUTORIAL 10.1** before proceeding. If you have not, you may open the DM-CH_10_Cine_01 map to begin **TUTORIAL 10.2**.

TUTORIAL 10.2: Initial Kismet Setup

1. We need to set up a network in Kismet that toggles Cinematic Mode on and off, play the Matinee sequence, and hide the skeletal mesh actor once the animation is complete. Open Kismet and right-click in the workspace. Choose New Event > Level Startup (see **FIGURE 10.12**).

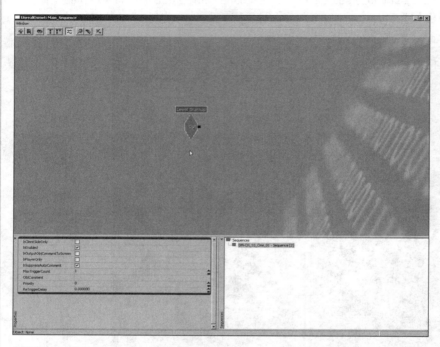

FIGURE 10.12   Add a Level Startup.

2. To the right of the Level Startup event, add a Toggle Cinematic Mode action by right-clicking and choosing New Action > Toggle > Toggle Cinematic Mode (see **FIGURE 10.13**). The default settings for the properties of this action will work fine for our purposes. This action disables all input and movement of the player and hides the player's mesh and the HUD.

3. Create a new Player variable by right-clicking and choosing New Variable > Object > Player. Connect the Player variable to the Target link of the Toggle Cinematic Mode action (see **FIGURE 10.14**).

10

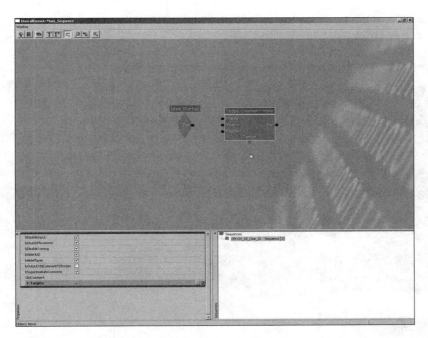

FIGURE 10.13   This node initiates Cinematic Mode.

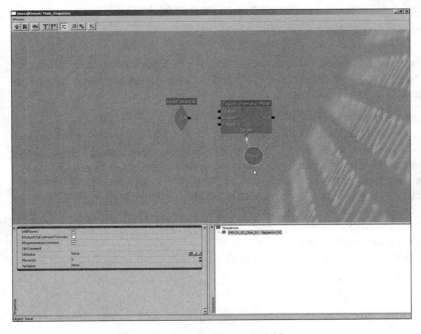

FIGURE 10.14   Connect in the new Player variable.

4. Connect the Out link of the Level Startup event to the Enable link of the Toggle Cinematic Mode action (see **FIGURE 10.15**).

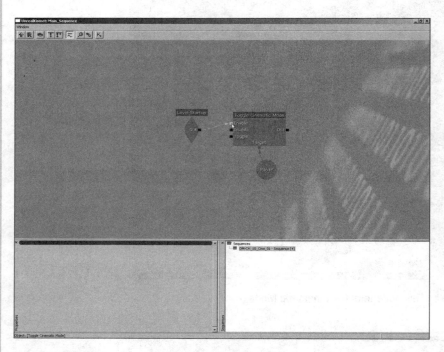

FIGURE 10.15   Connect the nodes like so.

5. To the right of the Toggle Cinematic Mode action, create a new Matinee by right-clicking and choosing New Matinee. Connect the Out link of the Toggle Cinematic Mode to the Play link of the Matinee (see **FIGURE 10.16**).

6. Select the Toggle Cinematic Mode and Player variables created earlier and duplicate them by pressing Ctrl+C and Ctrl+V. Disconnect any wires that run to the Matinee sequence, and move the new objects to the right of the Matinee. This action unhides the player's mesh and the HUD as well as enables input and movement, essentially returning to normal play (see **FIGURE 10.17**).

> **NOTE**
>
> The Matinee sequence object is going to grow considerably as we add new groups and tracks. It may be wise to move this and all subsequent sequence objects way off to the right (or up or down) to avoid overlapping.

7. Connect the Completed link of the Matinee to the Disable link of the new Toggle Cinematic Mode action.

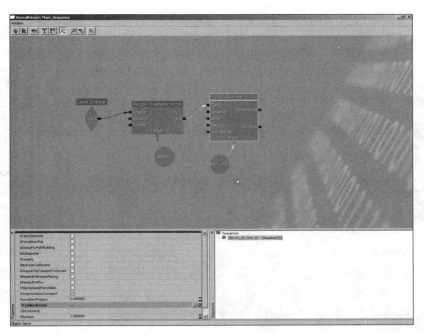

FIGURE 10.16   Create and connect a new Matinee.

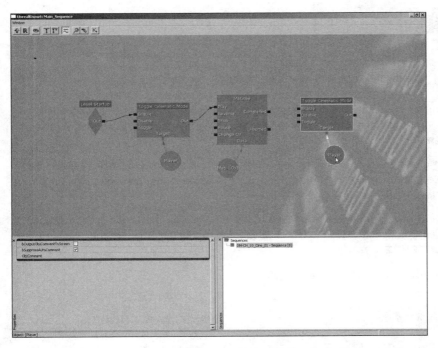

FIGURE 10.17   Duplicate and position the Toggle Cinematic Mode and Player nodes.

8. To the right of the new Toggle Cinematic Mode action, right-click and choose New Action > Actor > Teleport. Connect it to the Out of the new Toggle Cinematic Mode, and connect the Player variable to the Target link of the Teleport. The teleport places the player's mesh at the position of the mesh when the cinematic sequence ended (see **FIGURE 10.18**).

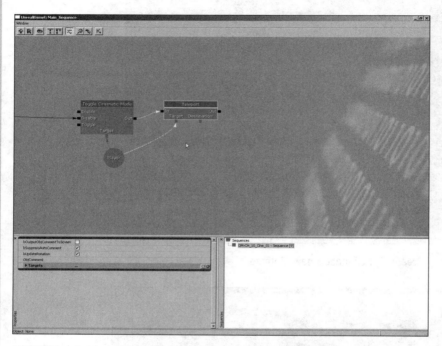

FIGURE 10.18   Create and connect a new Teleport node.

9. In the viewport, select the SkeletalMeshActorMAT. Then, right-click the Destination link of the Teleport action and choose New Object Var Using SkeletalMeshActorMat_0 (see **FIGURE 10.19**).

10. To the right of the Teleport action, create a Toggle Hidden action by right-clicking and choosing New Action > Toggle > Toggle Hidden. This action hides the skeletal mesh actor so it is no longer seen.

11. Connect the Out link of the Teleport action to the Hide link on the Toggle Hidden action. Then, connect the SkeletalMeshActorMAT_0 variable to the Target link of the Toggle Hidden action (see **FIGURE 10.20**).

12. Save the map to preserve your work.

10

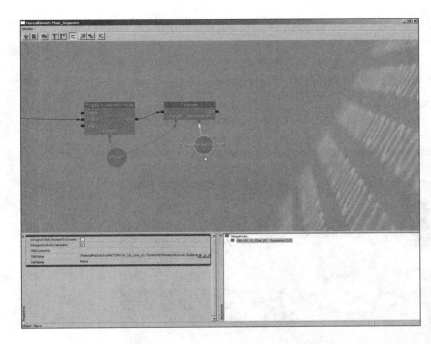

FIGURE 10.19
Your teleport should now connect to the skeletal mesh.

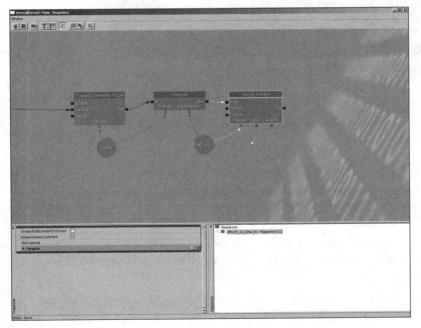

FIGURE 10.20
This hides the skeletal mesh after the teleport.

END TUTORIAL 10.2

Complete **TUTORIAL 10.2** before proceeding. If you have not, you may open the DM-CH_10_ Cine_02 map to begin **TUTORIAL 10.3**.

TUTORIAL 10.3: Blocking Out Character Movement

1. Select the SkeletalMeshActorMAT in the viewport and open Kismet. Then, double-click the Matinee sequence to open the Matinee Editor (see **FIGURE 10.21**).

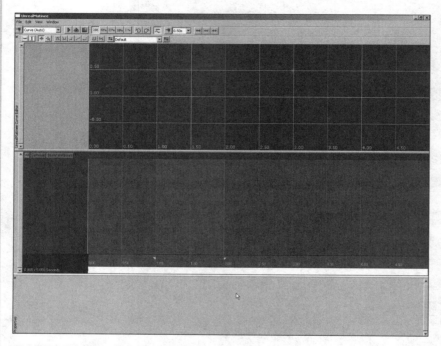

FIGURE 10.21   The Matinee Editor

2. Create a new group by right-clicking in the Group/Track List and choosing Add New Empty Group. In the dialog that appears, name the new group **Grunt** and click OK. This creates a new group as well the selected actor connected to it, causing any tracks in this group to affect the SkeletalMeshActorMAT we placed earlier (see **FIGURE 10.22**).

3. Right-click the Grunt group that was just created and choose Add New Movement Track. A new track should be added to the Grunt group with an initial key set at Time=0.0 (see **FIGURE 10.23**).

4. Move the sequence end indicator (small red triangle) to Time=13.0, which causes the duration of the sequence to be 13 seconds.

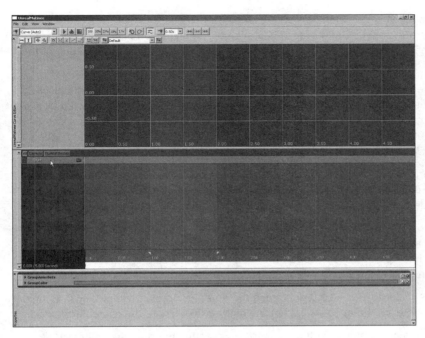

FIGURE 10.22   Create a new Grunt group.

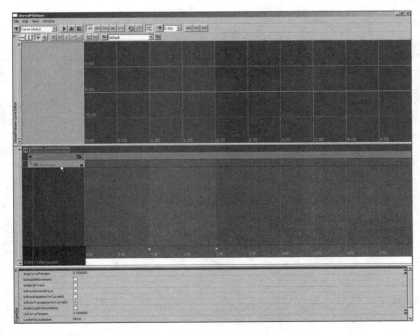

FIGURE 10.23   Add a new movement track.

5. Right-click the initial key at Time=0.0 and choose Interp Mode > Linear. This causes the actor to move at a constant rate over the duration of the animation instead of easing in and out, or moving slowly at the beginning, speeding up through the center portion of the animation, and then slowing down near the end.

6. Move the time slider to Time=4.3 and press the Enter key to place a new key. Right-click the new key and choose Interp Mode > Linear. Make sure the new key is selected by clicking it. This puts the editor into the key-editing mode, which can be verified by looking for the text "ADJUST KEY 1" in the lower-left corner of the viewports as well as the appearance of " · KEY 1" in the lower-left corner of the Matinee Editor.

7. In the viewports, the SkeletalMeshActorMAT should be selected automatically. Using the Top viewport, drag the actor halfway down the hall. It should be even with the control panels on the side of the hallway.

8. Move the time slider to Time=5.8 and press the Enter key again to place a new key. Right-click the new key and choose Interp Mode > Linear. With the key selected, move the character so that it is approximately even with the doors on each side of the hallway near the opposite end of the hallway from where the character started.

9. Move the time slider to Time=10.0 and press the Enter key to place a new key. This time move the character to the opposite end of the hallway from where the character started.

   You should see a curve appear in the viewport representing the path the actor will follow during the Matinee sequence from one end to the opposite end of the hallway (see **FIGURE 10.24**).

10. With the time slider at the beginning of the sequence, click the Play button ▶ in the Matinee Editor to preview the movement of the SkeletalMeshActorMAT. It should go from one end of the hallway to the other at a constant rate.

> **NOTE**
>
> You may need to move the looping indicators (small green triangles) in Matinee to allow the entire sequence to play.

11. Save the map to preserve your progress.

10

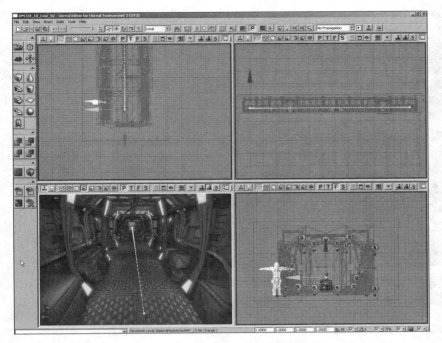

FIGURE 10.24   A line should appear showing the mesh's trajectory.

END TUTORIAL 10.3

Complete **TUTORIAL 10.3** before proceeding. If you have not, you may open the DM-CH_10_Cine_03 map to begin **TUTORIAL 10.4**.

TUTORIAL 10.4: Base Animation Track

1. Open Kismet and double-click the Matinee sequence to open the Matinee Editor.

   We are going to play one base animation throughout the entire sequence and blend in other animations later. In this tutorial, we set up this base animation.

2. Select the COG_Grunt_BasicAnims asset from the COG_Grunt package in the Generic Browser. Then, select the Grunt group in Matinee and add two new items to the GroupAnimSets array in its properties (see **FIGURE 10.25**). Click the Use Current Selection In Browser button ![icon] for slot [0].

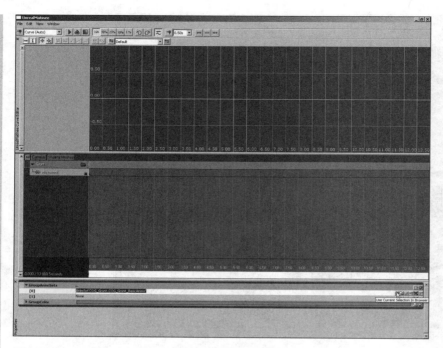

FIGURE 10.25   Add the basic animations to the GroupAnimSets property's slot [0].

3. Select the COG_Grunt_EvadeAnims asset from the COG_Grunt package in the Generic Browser and click the Use Current Selection In Browser button for slot [1].

4. Right-click the Grunt group and choose Add New Anim Control Track. Select the FullBody slot from the list in the dialog that appears and click OK (see **FIGURE 10.26**).

5. With the time slider at Time=0.0, press the Enter key to place a key. Select the Run_Fwd_Rdy_01 animation from the list in the dialog that appears and click OK. The animation should appear as a blue bar running the length of the animation.

6. Right-click the key and choose Set Looping. The animation should now run the length of the sequence.

7. Send the track's curve information to the Curve Editor by clicking the small box in the lower-right corner of the track, and open the Curve Editor if it is not already open by clicking the Toggle Curve Editor button in the Toolbar.

8. The curve information represents the weighting of the animation being played. Hold down the Ctrl key and left-click the curve at Time=0.0. Right-click the new point and choose Set Value. Set the value to 1.0. This causes this animation to have full weighting (see **FIGURE 10.27**).

10

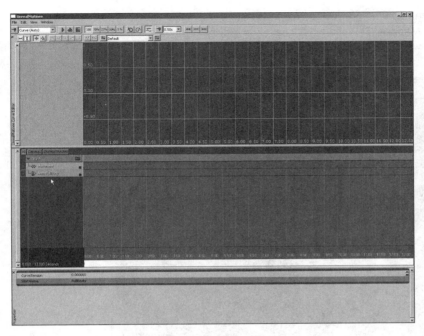

FIGURE 10.26   Create a new animation control track.

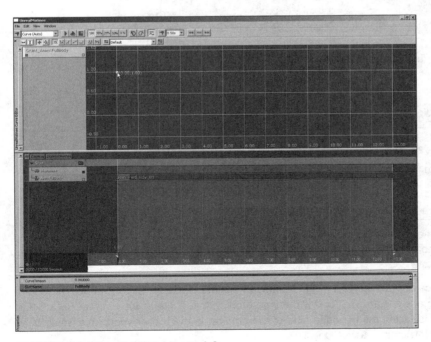

FIGURE 10.27   Set the value to 1.0.

9. Make sure the real-time preview is enabled in the perspective viewport and click the Play button ![play] in Matinee. The character should be playing a running animation as he moves down the hallway (see **FIGURE 10.28**).

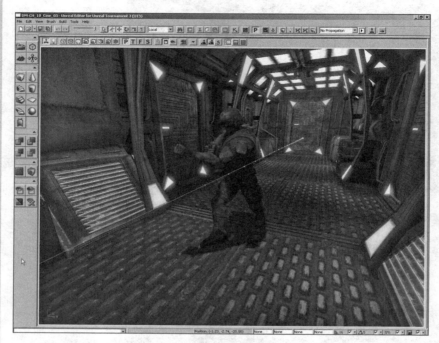

FIGURE 10.28   The character is now running.

10. Save the map to preserve your progress.

END TUTORIAL 10.4

Complete **TUTORIAL 10.4** before proceeding. If you have not, you may open the DM-CH_10_Cine_04 map to begin **TUTORIAL 10.5**.

TUTORIAL 10.5: Camera 1 Setup and Blocking

1. Open the Generic Browser and select the Actor Classes tab. Select the CameraActor class from the tree list, right-click in the viewport, and choose Add CameraActor Here (see **FIGURE 10.29**).

2. Position the camera at the end of the hallway where the character begins, above the door to the character's left and just below the pipe running the length of the hallway. Rotate the camera so it is facing the opposite side of the hallway. In the top viewport, this would be facing to the left (see **FIGURE 10.30**).

10

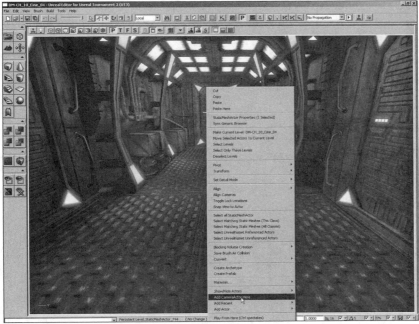

FIGURE 10.29   Place a new Camera actor.

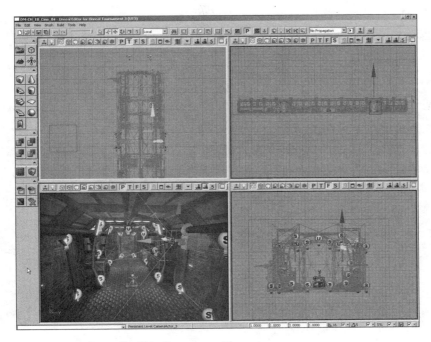

FIGURE 10.30   Position the camera like so.

3. With the camera selected, press F4 to open the camera's properties. Under the CameraActor section, check the bCamOverridePostProcess property and uncheck the bConstrainAspectRatio property.

4. Expand CamOverridePostProcess and set the following:

   - **bEnableDOF**: True
   - **bEnableMotionBlur**: True
   - **BloomScale**: 0.5
   - **DOF_BlurKernelSize**: 4.0
   - **DOF_FocusInnerRadius**: 750.0
   - **Scene_Desaturation**: 0.425
   - **Scene_Highlights**:
     - **X**: 0.7
     - **Y**: 0.8
     - **Z**: 0.9
   - **Scene_MidTones**:
     - **X**: 1.2
     - **Y**: 1.1
     - **Z**: 1.0
   - **Scene_Shadows**:
     - **X**: 0.0
     - **Y**: 0.005
     - **Z**: 0.01

5. With the camera selected, open Kismet and double-click the Matinee sequence to open the Matinee Editor.

6. Right-click in the empty space of the Group/Track List and choose Add New Empty Group. Name the new group **Camera1** and click OK (see **FIGURE 10.31**).

7. Right-click the Camera1 group and choose Add New Movement Track (see **FIGURE 10.32**).

10

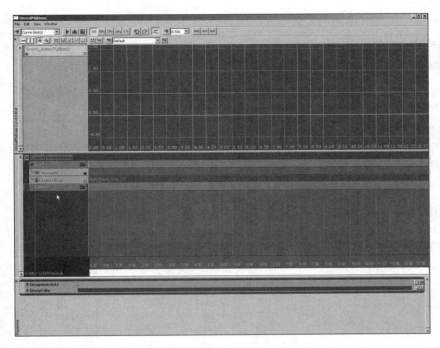

FIGURE 10.31   Add a new Camera1 group.

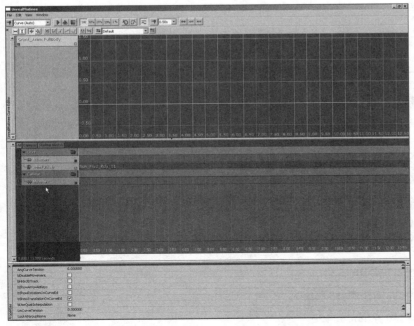

FIGURE 10.32   Create a new movement track for the camera.

8. In the movement track's properties, set the following:

   ▶ **LookAtGroupName**: Grunt

   ▶ **RotMode**: IMR_LookAtGroup

   This causes the camera to always face directly at the actor connected to the Grunt group, which will be the SkeletalMeshActorMAT.

9. There is already an initial key at Time=0.0. Place the time slider at Time=13.0 (or the end of the sequence) and press the Enter key to place another key. There is no need to do any adjusting to the position of the camera at either key because this camera is simply going to rotate to follow the character, and that is all handled by the LookAtGroup settings of the track.

10. Make sure Realtime Preview is turned on in the perspective viewport. Click the small camera icon to the right of the Camera1 group name to force the perspective viewport to render the scene from the viewpoint of the group (in this case, the camera 0).

11. Click the Play button ▶ in Matinee. The viewport should follow the character as it moves down the hallway.

12. Save the map to preserve your progress.

END TUTORIAL 10.5

Complete **TUTORIAL 10.5** before proceeding. If you have not, you may open the DM-CH_10_Cine_05 map to begin **TUTORIAL 10.6**.

TUTORIAL 10.6: Camera 2 Setup and Blocking

1. Using the skills you've gained so far, create a second CameraActor positioned at the opposite end of the hallway, above the door on the opposite side of the hallway (see **FIGURE 10.33**).

2. With the camera selected, press F4 to open the camera's properties. Under the Camera section, check the bCamOverridePostProcess property and uncheck the bConstrainAspectRatio property.

3. Expand CamOverridePostProcess and set the following:

   ▶ **bEnableDOF**: True

   ▶ **bEnableMotionBlur**: True

   ▶ **BloomScale**: 0.5

   ▶ **DOF_BlurKernelSize**: 4.0

   ▶ **DOF_FocusInnerRadius**: 750.0

   ▶ **Scene_Desaturation**: 0.425

- **Scene_Highlights**:
  - **X**: 0.7
  - **Y**: 0.8
  - **Z**: 0.9
- **Scene_MidTones**:
  - **X**: 1.2
  - **Y**: 1.1
  - **Z**: 1.0
- **Scene_Shadows**:
  - **X**: 0.0
  - **Y**: 0.005
  - **Z**: 0.01

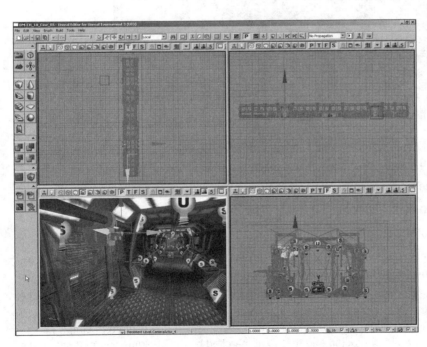

FIGURE 10.33   The new camera should look back down the hallway.

4. With the camera selected, open Kismet and double-click the Matinee sequence to open the Matinee Editor.

5. Right-click in the empty space of the Group/Track List and choose Add New Empty Group. Name the new group **Camera2** and click OK (see **FIGURE 10.34**).

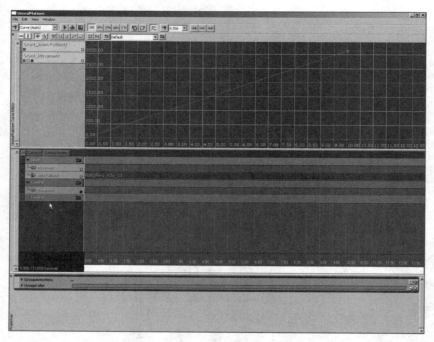

FIGURE 10.34   Add a new Camera2 group.

6. Right-click the Camera2 group and choose Add New Movement Track (see **FIGURE 10.35**).

7. In the movement track's properties, set the following:

   ▶ **LookAtGroupName**: Grunt

   ▶ **GruntRotMode**: IMR_LookAtGroup

   This causes this camera, as was the case with the first camera, to always face directly at the actor connected to the Grunt group, which will be the SkeletalMeshActorMAT.

8. There is already an initial key at Time=0.0. Place the time slider at Time=13.0, or the end of the sequence, and press the Enter key to place another key. There is no need to do any adjusting to the position of the camera at either key because this camera is simply going to rotate to follow the character, and that is all handled by the LookAtGroup settings of the track.

9. Make sure Realtime Preview is turned on in the perspective viewport. Click the small camera icon to the right of the Camera2 group name to force the perspective viewport to render the scene from the viewpoint of the group (in this case, the camera).

10

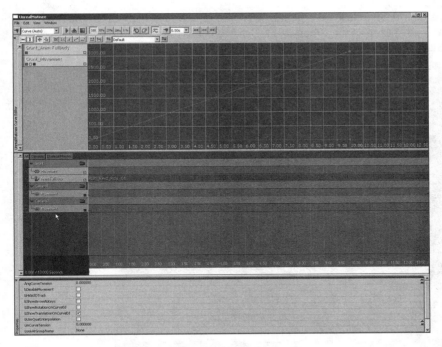

FIGURE 10.35   Add a new movement track to the group.

10. Click the Play button ▶ in Matinee. The viewport should follow the character as it moves down the hallway.

11. Save the map to preserve your progress.

END TUTORIAL 10.6

Complete **TUTORIAL 10.6** before proceeding. If you have not, you may open the DM-CH_10_Cine_06 map to begin **TUTORIAL 10.7**.

We have some very basic blocking in place now as the character moves from one end of the hallway to the other and the two cameras follow the character. Now, we are going to lay down the music that provides the score for the cinematic. This gives us something to use as a basis for timing events.

TUTORIAL 10.7: Music Track

1. In the Generic Browser, select the cinematic_scoreCue asset from the Chapter_10_Cinematics package.

2. Open Kismet and double-click the Matinee sequence to open the Matinee Editor. Right-click in the empty space of the Group/Track List and choose Add New Empty Group. Name the new group **Score** and click OK (see **FIGURE 10.36**).

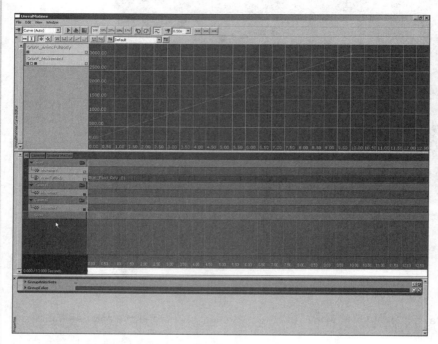

FIGURE 10.36   Create a new Score group.

3. Right-click the Score group and choose Add New Sound Track.

4. With the time slider at Time=0.0, press the Enter key to place a new key. This shows up as a green bar the length of the sound cue and displays the name of the SoundCue (see **FIGURE 10.37**).

5. Select the key and right-click it. Choose Set Sound Volume and set the volume to 2.0.

6. Click the Play button ▶ in Matinee to play the sequence. The musical score should now be playing along with the sequence. You'll notice it has a few distinct parts to it. These are our cues for placing camera cuts in **TUTORIAL 10.8**.

7. Save the map to preserve your progress.

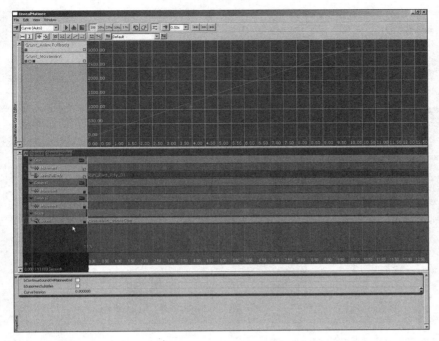

FIGURE 10.37   You can now visualize the duration of the sound.

END TUTORIAL 10.7

Complete **TUTORIAL 10.7** before proceeding. If you have not, you may open the DM-CH_10_Cine_07 map to begin **TUTORIAL 10.8**.

TUTORIAL 10.8: Camera Edits, Part I: Slomo

1. Open Kismet and double-click the Matinee sequence to open the Matinee Editor.

2. Right-click in the empty space of the Group/Track List and choose Add New Director Group. There should be a new group added named DirGroup with a Director track (see **FIGURE 10.38**). This track is used to create the camera cuts for the cinematic in **TUTORIAL 10.9**.

3. Right-click the DirGroup group and choose Add New Slomo Track. This track is used to put the action in the cinematic into slow-motion during the time that the Camera2 camera is active (see **FIGURE 10.39**).

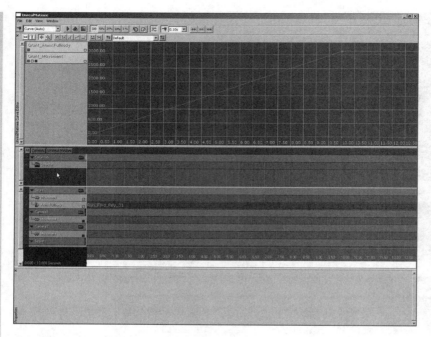

FIGURE 10.38   Create a new Director track.

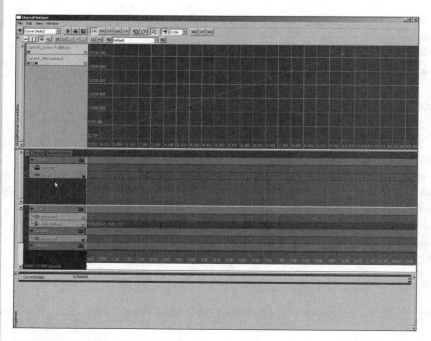

FIGURE 10.39   Add a new Slomo track.

10

4. Select the initial key at Time=0.0, right-click it, and choose Set Value. The value of the key should be set to 1.0 by default, but if it is not, set the value of the key to 1.0 (see **FIGURE 10.40**).

FIGURE 10.40   Verify the first key has a value of 1.

5. Right-click the key again and choose Interp Mode > Constant. This causes the value of the curve for the track to remain at that value and then snap to the value of the next key when it is reached.

6. Move the time slider to Time=3.7 (or as close as you can get) and press the Enter key again to place another key.

7. Select the new key and right-click it. Choose Set Time and set the time for the key to 3.7.

8. Right-click the key again and choose Set Value. Set the value of this key to 0.2. This causes the action in the scene to play back at 20% of its normal speed (see **FIGURE 10.41**).

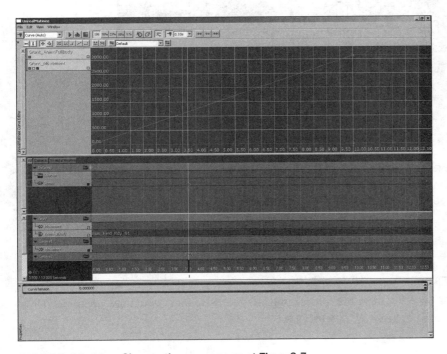

FIGURE 10.41   Slow-motion now occurs at Time=3.7.

9. Right-click the key yet again and choose Interp Mode > Constant.

10. Move the time slider to Time=5.8 (or again, as close as you can get it) and press the Enter key to create a new key.

11. Select the new key and right-click it. Choose Set Time and set the time for the key to 5.8.

12. Right-click the key again and choose Set Value. Set the value of this key to 1.0 (see **FIGURE 10.42**).

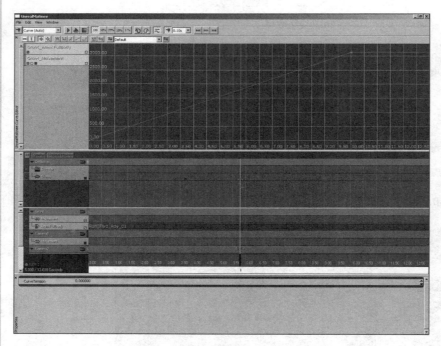

FIGURE 10.42   Speed now returns to normal at Time=5.8.

13. Make sure Realtime Preview is turned on in the perspective viewport and click the Play button ▶ in Matinee. You should notice that the slomo coincides with the changes in the music set in **TUTORIAL 8.7**. We use this as the basis for the camera cuts in **TUTORIAL 10.9**.

14. Save the map to preserve your work.

END TUTORIAL 10.8

Complete **TUTORIAL 10.8** before proceeding. If you have not, you may open the DM-CH_10_Cine_08 map to begin **TUTORIAL 10.9**.

TUTORIAL 10.9: Camera Edits, Part II: Cuts

1. Open Kismet and double-click the Matinee sequence to open the Matinee Editor.

2. Play through the sequence a couple times and make notes as to where the music changes. The changes should occur at about Time=3.7 and Time=5.8. These are the times we will use when placing the keys for the camera cuts.

3. With the time slider at Time=0.0, select the Director track and press the Enter key to add a new key. Choose the Camera1 group from the dropdown list in the dialog that appears and then click OK. This causes the camera attached to the Camera1 group to be active when the sequence begins.

4. Move the time slider to Time=3.7 (or as close as you can get—the exact placement of the key can be set after creation) and press the Enter key again to place another key. This time, choose the Camera2 group from the dropdown list and click OK (see **FIGURE 10.43**).

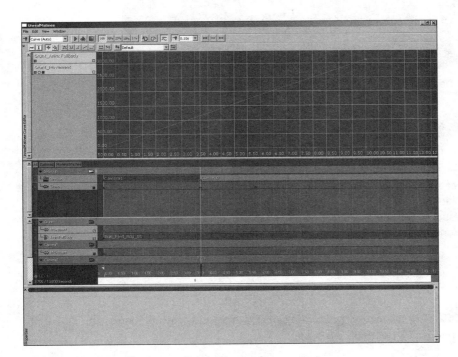

FIGURE 10.43   You now switch to Camera2.

5. Select the new key and right-click it. Choose Set Time and set the time for the key to 3.7.

6. Move the time slider to Time=5.8 (or again, as close as you can get it) and press the Enter key to create a new key. Choose the Camera1 group for this key and click OK.

7. Select the new key and right-click it. Choose Set Time and set the time for the key to 5.8 (see **FIGURE 10.44**).

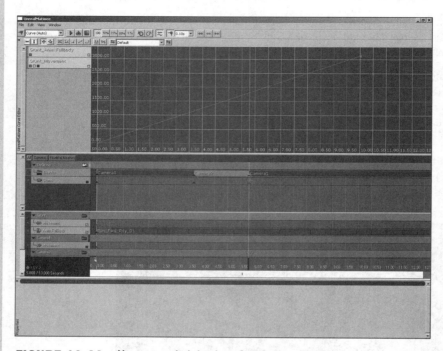

FIGURE 10.44   You now switch back to Camera1 at Time=5.8.

8. Click the camera icon for the DirGroup to highlight it if it is not already and click the Play button ▶ in Matinee. Make sure Realtime Preview is turned on in the perspective viewport. You should see the sequence playing from the perspective of the first camera, a cut to the second camera, and finally a cut back to the first camera.

9. Save the map to preserve your work.

END TUTORIAL 10.9

Complete **TUTORIAL 10.9** before proceeding. If you have not, you may open the DM-CH_10_Cine_09 map to begin **TUTORIAL 10.10**.

TUTORIAL 10.10: Camera Edits, Part III: Fades

1. Open Kismet and double-click the Matinee sequence to open the Matinee Editor.

2. Right-click the DirGroup group and choose Add New Fade Track (see **FIGURE 10.45**). This track is used to fade the scene in at the beginning of the sequence and out at the end.

10

FIGURE 10.45 Add a new Fade track.

3. With the time slider at Time=0.0, press the Enter key to add a new key. This is used to set the initial value of the Fade track.

4. The value of the key should be set to 0.0, which means the scene is completely visible, by default. We want the scene to begin completely faded out. Select the key, right-click it, and choose Set Value. Set the value of the key to 1.0 (see **FIGURE 10.46**).

FIGURE 10.46 This causes the scene to be blacked out when it is launched.

5. Move the time slide to Time=1.0 and press the Enter key to place a new key. Select the key and right-click it. Choose Set Value and set the value of this key to 0.0 (see **FIGURE 10.47**).

6. Move the time slider to Time=9.5 and press the Enter key to place a new key. This is the beginning of the fade out.

> **NOTE**
>
> The times for the placement of keys in **TUTORIAL 10.10** do not need to be as exact as in **TUTORIAL 10.9**, but you can use the Set Time function from the right-click menu to set them precisely if you wish.

The value of this key should be set to 0.0, which is what we want. You can right-click it and choose Set Value to be absolutely sure and set it if necessary.

FIGURE 10.47   This fades the scene in at Time=1.0.

7. Move the time slider to Time=11.0 and press the Enter key one last time to place the final key for the track. Select the key and right-click it. Choose Set Value and set the value of this key to 1.0.

8. Make sure that Realtime Preview is enabled in the perspective viewport and click the Play button ▶ in Matinee. The scene should fade in at the beginning and fade out near the end.

9. Save the map to preserve your progress.

END TUTORIAL 10.10

Complete **TUTORIAL 10.10** before proceeding. If you have not, you may open the DM-CH_ 10_Cine_10 map to begin **TUTORIAL 10.11**.

TUTORIAL 10.11: Camera 1 Basic Depth of Field Effect, Part I: Recording Values

1. Open Kismet and double-click the Matinee sequence to open the Matinee Editor.

   In this tutorial, we create a track to control the DOF_FocusDistance property of Camera1. This serves to keep the character in focus as it moves along the hallway. In order to do this, we need to know the distance between the character and the camera. A simple Kismet network will be created to display the distance as the character makes its way down the hallway. We then use these values as guidelines to set keys for the track within Matinee in **TUTORIAL 10.12**.

2. Right-click the Camera1 group and choose Add New Float Property Track (see **FIGURE 10.48**). Select the DOF_FocusDistance from the list of available properties in the dialog that appears and click OK. This creates a new track named DOF_FocusDistance.

Before we can begin placing keys, we really need some values to assign to those keys. As mentioned previously, using a network in Kismet gives us the values we need without resorting to guesswork.

> **NOTE**
>
> You may need to resize the dialog displaying the available properties because it can be quite small, obscuring the names of the properties.

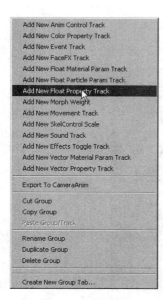

Add New Anim Control Track
Add New Color Property Track
Add New Event Track
Add New FaceFX Track
Add New Float Material Param Track
Add New Float Particle Param Track
Add New Float Property Track
Add New Morph Weight
Add New Movement Track
Add New SkelControl Scale
Add New Sound Track
Add New Effects Toggle Track
Add New Vector Material Param Track
Add New Vector Property Track

Export To CameraAnim

Cut Group
Copy Group
Paste Group/Track

Rename Group
Duplicate Group
Delete Group

Create New Group Tab...

FIGURE 10.48   Create a new float property track.

3. In Kismet, create a Get Distance action below and to the right of the Level Startup event by right-clicking and choosing New Action > Actor > Get Distance (see **FIGURE 10.49**).

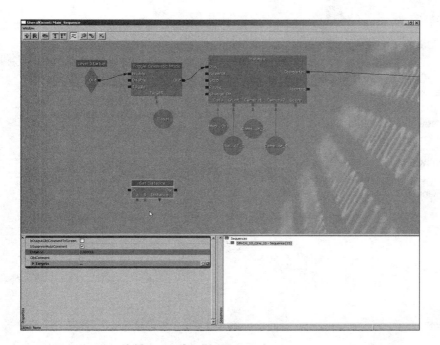

FIGURE 10.49   Add a new Get Distance action.

4. Connect the Out link of the Level Startup event to the In link of the Get Distance action (see **FIGURE 10.50**).

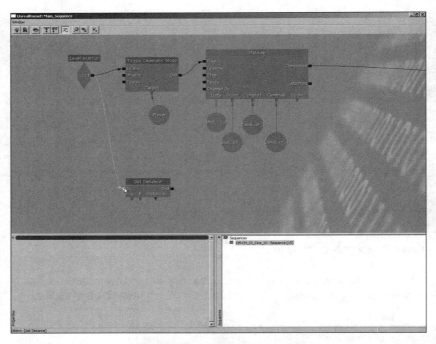

FIGURE 10.50   Connect the Level Startup to the Get Distance action.

5. Select CameraActor_0 (the first camera) in the viewport. Then, right-click the A link of the Get Distance action and choose New Object Var Using CameraActor_0 (see **FIGURE 10.51**).

> **NOTE**
>
> The name of the actual camera actor may not be the same. Just make sure you have selected the first camera that was created.

6. Back in the viewport, select the SkeletalMeshActorMAT (the character), right-click the B link of the Get Distance action, and choose New Object Var Using SkeletalMeshActorMAT_0 (see **FIGURE 10.52**).

10

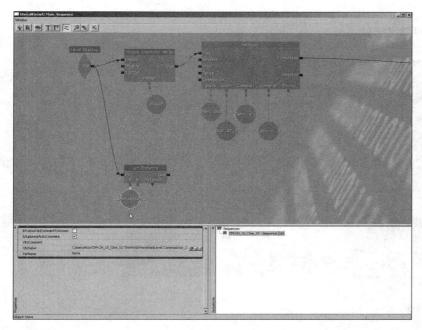

FIGURE 10.51 Add a new variable for the first camera.

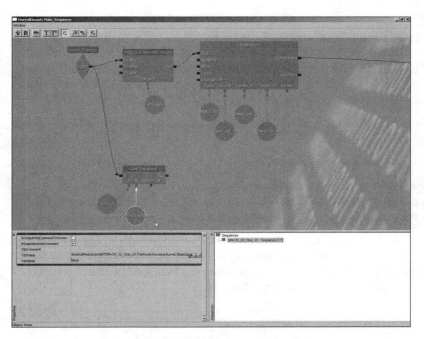

FIGURE 10.52 You now get the distance between the skeletal mesh and Camera1.

7. Right-click the Distance link of the Get Distance action and choose Create New Float Variable (see **FIGURE 10.53**).

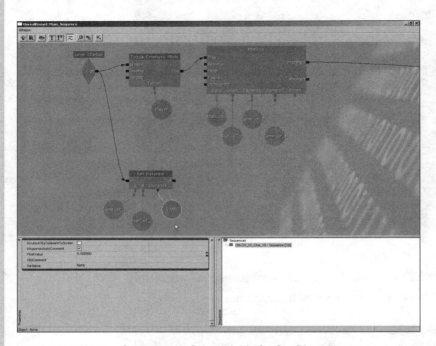

FIGURE 10.53   Create a new float variable for Get Distance.

8. To the right of the Get Distance action, create a new Log action by pressing the L key and left-clicking. Right-click the Log action and choose Expose Variable > Float. The Float link should become visible on the Log action.

9. Connect the Float link of the Log action to the float variable connected to the Distance link of the Get Distance action.

10. Connect the Out link of the Get Distance action to the In link of the Log action.

11. Connect the Out link of the Log action back around to the In link of the Get Distance action to form a loop. Right-click the Out link of the Log action and choose Set Activate Delay. Set the delay for the link to 0.2 (see **FIGURE 10.54**).

12. You will also need to bypass the Toggle Cinematic Mode action in order to see the Log output on the screen. Delete the connection from the Level Startup to the Toggle Cinematic Mode and from the Toggle Cinematic mode to the Matinee. Then, drag a new connection from the Level Startup to the Play input of the Matinee.

10

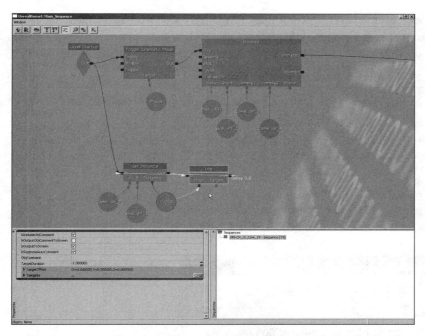

FIGURE 10.54   You now log the value of the distance to the screen.

13. Play the map in the editor and take notes of the distance values at certain landmarks, such as the beginning of the sequence, when the character is directly in front of the camera, at the time of the first camera cut, at the time of the second camera cut, and at the end of the sequence. Here are some values to compare to your own (they should be relatively similar):

- ▶ 600.0
- ▶ 200.0
- ▶ 700.0
- ▶ 1800.0
- ▶ 2200.0

> **NOTE**
>
> The Matinee Editor will have to be closed in order to play the map. UnrealEd will prompt you with the option to do so if you forget.

14. Once you have the values recorded, re-create the connections between the Level Startup, Toggle Cinematic Mode, and the Matinee, and then delete the connection from the Level Startup to the Matinee.

15. Save the map to preserve your progress.

END TUTORIAL 10.11

Complete **TUTORIAL 10.11** before proceeding. If you have not, you may open the DM-CH_10_Cine_11 map to begin **TUTORIAL 10.12**.

TUTORIAL 10.12: Camera 1 Basic Depth of Field Effect, Part II: Setting Keys

1. Open Kismet and double-click the Matinee sequence to open the Matinee Editor.

   In this tutorial, we use the values gathered in **TUTORIAL 10.11** to create the keys for the track controlling the DOF_FocusDistance property of the first camera. The tutorial uses the values specified in **TUTORIAL 10.11**. Feel free to substitute the values you recorded on your own.

2. Select the Camera_DOF_FocusDistance track of the Camera1 group. With the time slider at Time=0.0, press the Enter key to place an initial key. Right-click the new key and choose Set Value. Set the value to 600.0 (see **FIGURE 10.55**).

FIGURE 10.55   Set the first key to a value of 600.0.

3. Move the time slider to Time=1.5 and press the Enter key to place a new key. Right-click the key and choose Set Value. Set the value to 200.0.

4. Move the time slider to Time=3.7 (or the time of the first camera cut) and press the Enter key to create a new key. Right-click the new key and choose Set Value. Set the value of this key to 700.0.

5. Move the time slider to Time=5.8 (or the time of the second camera cut) and press the Enter key to place a new key. Right-click the key and choose Set Value. Set the value of the key to 1800.0.

6. Move the time slider to the end of the sequence and press the Enter key one last time to place the final key. Right-click the key and choose Set Value. Set the value of this key to 2200.0.

7. Make sure that Realtime Preview is enabled in the perspective viewport and click the Play button ▶ in Matinee. Check to make sure the character, when viewed from the first camera, appears in focus throughout the sequence (see **FIGURE 10.56**).

8. Save the map to preserve your work.

10

FIGURE 10.56   You should notice the background behind the character blur at some points.

END TUTORIAL 10.12

Complete **TUTORIAL 10.12** before proceeding. If you have not, you may open the DM-CH_10_Cine_12 map to begin **TUTORIAL 10.13**.

TUTORIAL 10.13: Camera 1 Zoom

1. Open Kismet and double-click the Matinee sequence to open the Matinee Editor.

   We are going to cause Camera1 to zoom in on the character as it gets farther away from the camera as well as add a quick auto-focus effect as the camera cuts back to Camera1.

2. Right-click the Camera1 group and choose New Float Property Track. In the dialog that appears, choose FOVAngle and click OK. This creates a new track that controls the FOVAngle property of the camera actor (see **FIGURE 10.57**).

3. Move the time slider until the character is directly in front of the camera (or about Time=1.5) and press the Enter key to place a

FIGURE 10.57   Add a new float property track that affects the FOV angle.

new key. The value of this key will be the value of the FOVAngle property of the camera as set in its properties, which is the default value of 90.0 degrees. That is fine because this is just a key to provide a baseline for the curve.

4. Move the time slider to Time=3.0 and press Enter to place a new key. Right-click the key and choose Set Value. Set the value of this key to 50.0.

5. Move the time slider to Time=5.8 (the time where the second camera cut takes place) and press the Enter key to place a new key. Right-click the key and choose Set Value. Set the value of this key to 25.0.

6. Move the time slider to Time=5.9 and press the Enter key to place a new key. Right-click the key and choose Set Value. Set the value of the key to 12.0.

7. Move the time slider to Time=6.1 and press the Enter key to place a new key. Right-click the key and choose Set Value. Set the value of this key to 17.5.

8. Move the time slider to Time=6.4 and press the Enter key to place a new key. Right-click the key and choose Set Value. Set the value of this key to 13.5.

9. Move the time slider to Time=7.0 and press Enter to place the last key. Right-click the key and choose Set Value. Set the value of the key to 15.0.

10. Make sure that Realtime Preview is enabled in the perspective viewport and click the Play button ▶ in Matinee. You should see the camera perform a smooth zoom as the character runs away from the first camera and a quick zoom in on the character with a little recoil just after the second camera cut. In **TUTORIAL 10.14**, a blur effect will be added to the zoom in and recoil to give it the appearance of the camera trying to gain focus on the character.

11. Save the map to preserve your work.

END TUTORIAL 10.13

Complete **TUTORIAL 10.13** before proceeding. If you have not, you may open the DM-CH_10_Cine_13 map to begin **TUTORIAL 10.14**.

TUTORIAL 10.14: Camera 1 Advanced Depth of Field Effect, Part I: DOF_FocusInnerRadius

1. Open Kismet and double-click the Matinee sequence to open the Matinee Editor.

    In this tutorial, we continue the process of creating the auto-focus effect by modifying the radius of the camera's depth of field effect. We basically collapse the radius of the effect to 0.0 in order to blur the entire scene. Then, in **TUTORIAL 10.15**, we animate the amount of blur being used.

10

2. Right-click the Camera1 group and choose Add New Float Property Track. Select the DOF_FocusInnerRadius property from the list in the dialog that appears and click OK (see **FIGURE 10.58**).

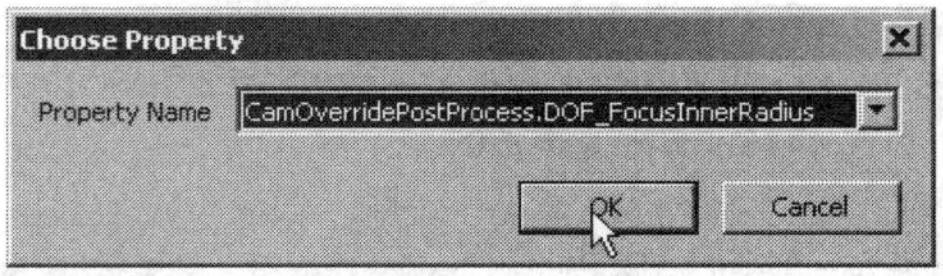

FIGURE 10.58   Create a new float property track to control the DOF inner radius.

3. Move the time slider to Time=5.8 (the time of the second camera cut) and press the Enter key to place a new key. Right-click the key and choose Set Value. Make sure the value is set to 750.0.

4. Move the time slider to Time=5.9 and press the Enter key again to place a key. Right-click the key and choose Set Value. Set the key's value to 0.0.

5. Right-click the key again and choose Interp Mode > Linear. This keeps the curve from going below zero between this point and the next, which is necessary because the depth of field effect requires a radius of zero or greater (see **FIGURE 10.59**).

FIGURE 10.59   Set the Interp Mode to Linear.

6. Move the time slider to Time=6.4 and press the Enter key to create a new key. Right-click this key and choose Set Value. Set the value of the key to 0.0.

7. Move the time slider to Time=7.0 and press the Enter key one last time to place the final key. Right-click the key and choose Set Value. Set the value of the last key to 750.0.

8. Scrub through the sequence and make sure the scene completely blurs out during this period.

9. Save the map to preserve your progress.

END TUTORIAL 10.14

Complete **TUTORIAL 10.14** before proceeding. If you have not, you may open the DM-CH_10_Cine_14 map to begin **TUTORIAL 10.15**.

TUTORIAL 10.15: Camera 1 Advanced Depth of Field Effect, Part II: DOF_BlurKernelSize

1. Open Kismet and double-click the Matinee sequence to open the Matinee Editor.

As mentioned in **TUTORIAL 10.14**, we will alter the amount of blur used in the depth of field effect in this tutorial to give the appearance that the camera is trying to focus. The shape of the curve we are creating is basically a decaying oscillation.

2. Right-click the Camera1 group and choose Add New Float Property Track. Select the DOF_BlurKernelSize property from the list in the dialog that appears and click OK (see **FIGURE 10.60**).

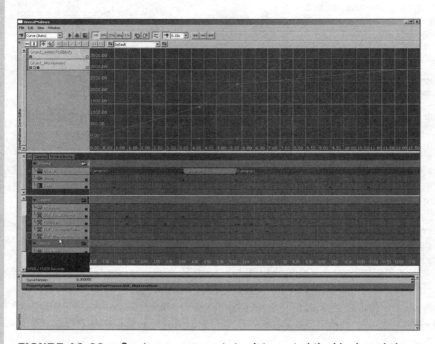

FIGURE 10.60   Create a new property track to control the blur kernel size.

3. Move the time slider to Time=5.8 (again, the time of the second camera cut) and press the Enter key to place an initial key. Right-click the key and choose Set Value. Set the value of the key to 4.0 if it is not already.

4. Move the time slider to Time=5.9 and press the Enter key again to place a new key. Right-click the key and choose Set Value. Set the value of the key to 90.0. This causes the scene to become extremely blurry.

5. Move the time slider to Time=6.0 and press the Enter key to place a new key. Right-click the key and choose Set Value. Set the value of the key to 16.0.

6. Move the time slider to Time=6.1 and press the Enter key to create a new key. Right-click the key and choose Set Value. Set the value of the key to 65.0.

7. Move the time slider to Time=6.25 and press the Enter key to place a new key. Right-click the key and choose Set Value. Set the value of the key to 8.0.

8. Move the time slider to Time=6.4 and press the Enter key to create a new key. Right-click the key and choose Set Value. Set the value of this key to 25.0.

9. Move the time slider to Time=7.0 and press the Enter key one last time to place the final key. Right-click the key and choose Set Value. Set the last key's value back to 4.0.

10. Make sure Realtime Preview is enabled in the perspective viewport and click the Play button ▶ in Matinee (see **FIGURE 10.61**). If you would like to make any tweaks or changes to the effect, feel free to do so.

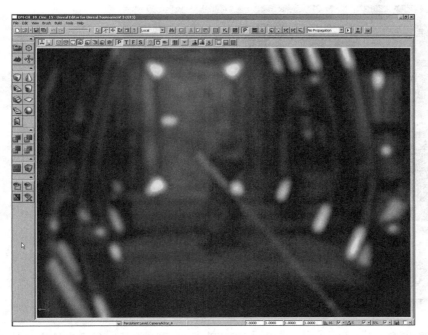

FIGURE 10.61   Your scene should now have a motion blur effect that changes over time.

11. Save the map to preserve your work.

END TUTORIAL 10.15

Complete **TUTORIAL 10.15** before proceeding. If you have not, you may open the DM-CH_10_Cine_15 map to begin **TUTORIAL 10.16**.

TUTORIAL 10.16: Camera 2 Zoom

1. Open Kismet and double-click the Matinee sequence to open the Matinee Editor.

   In this tutorial, the second camera begins zoomed in tight on the character and zooms out as the character approaches the camera.

2. Right-click the Camera2 group and choose Add New Float Property Track. Choose the FOVAngle property from the list in the dialog that appears and click OK (see **FIGURE 10.62**).

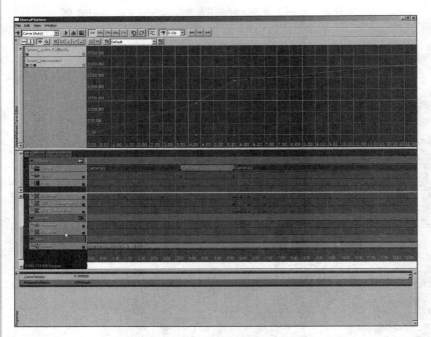

FIGURE 10.62   This new track controls Camera2's FOV angle.

3. Move the time slider to Time=3.7 (the time of the first camera cut and when the second camera becomes active) and press the Enter key to place a new key.

4. Right-click the key and choose Set Value. Set the value of the key to 10.0. This causes the character to fill most of the view.

5. Move the time slider to Time=5.8 (the time of the second cut and when the second camera is no longer active) and press the Enter key again to place a key.

6. Right-click the new key and choose Set Value. Set the value of this key to 90.0. This is the default field of view for the camera and will cause the camera to zoom out as the character approaches (see **FIGURE 10.63**).

10

FIGURE 10.63   The camera is now zoomed out to normal at Time=5.8.

7. Send the track's curve to the Curve Editor by clicking the little box in the lower-right corner and then open the Curve Editor (if it is not already) by clicking the Toggle Curve Editor button ⌇ in the toolbar.

8. Select the second point on the curve in the Curve Editor to make its tangent handles visible. Left-click the left tangent handle and drag the mouse down until the curve takes on the shape of the right half of a *U* instead of an *S* shape. This causes the zoom to be slow at first but to quicken as the character approaches (see **FIGURE 10.64**).

9. Make sure that Realtime Preview is enabled in the perspective viewport and click the Play button ▶ in Matinee to preview the zoom. If you need to make any adjustments, feel free to do so.

10. Save the map to preserve your progress.

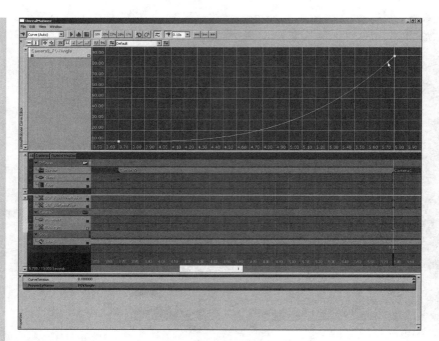

FIGURE 10.64   Shape your curve like so.

END TUTORIAL 10.16

Complete **TUTORIAL 10.16** before proceeding. If you have not, you may open the DM-CH_10_Cine_16 map to begin here. **TUTORIAL 10.17** continues with the second camera by setting the focus distance of the depth of field effect, much in the same manner it was set up for the first camera. We use the same Kismet network to record the distance, but this time it will be between the character and second camera (see **FIGURE 10.65**).

TUTORIAL 10.17: Camera 2 Depth of Field Effect

1. Select the second camera in the viewport and open Kismet.

2. Right-click the variable connected to the A link of the Get Distance action and choose Assign CameraActor_1 to Object Variable(s).

> **NOTE**
>
> The actual name of the camera actor in your level may differ. Be sure you are connecting the second camera.

3. As before, you must break the links between the Level Startup, Toggle Cinematic Mode, and the Matinee and then connect the Level Startup directly to the Play of the Matinee for the Log outputs to be displayed on the screen.

10

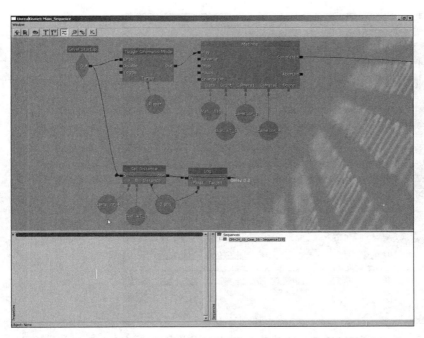

FIGURE 10.65   You can now get the distance from the skeletal mesh to Camera2.

4. You can now play the map in the editor as before and take notes on the distance value output to the screen. You are looking for the values at the time of each camera cut. Here are some values to compare to yours:

   ▸ 800.0

   ▸ 200.0

5. Once you have the values, re-create the connections between the Level Startup, Toggle Cinematic Mode, and the Matinee and then delete the link from the Level Startup to the Matinee.

6. Double-click the Matinee sequence to open the Matinee Editor.

7. Right-click the Camera2 group and choose Add New Float Property Track. From the dialog that appears, select the DOF_FocusDistance property and click OK (see **FIGURE 10.66**).

8. Move the time slider to Time=3.7 (the time of the first camera cut) and press the Enter key to place an initial key.

9. Right-click the key and choose Set Value. Set the value of this key to 800.0.

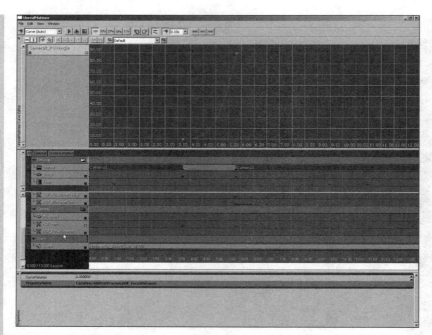

FIGURE 10.66   Add a new float property track to control the DOF focus distance.

10. Move the time slider to Time=5.8 (the time of the second camera cut) and press the Enter key to create a new key.

11. Right-click the key and choose Set Value. Set the value of the key to 200.0.

12. Make sure that Realtime Preview is enabled in the perspective viewport and click the Play button ▶ in Matinee. Make any adjustments to the values of these keys you feel are necessary (see **FIGURE 10.67**).

13. Save the map to preserve your progress.

10

FIGURE 10.67   Camera2 now exhibits a depth of field effect.

END TUTORIAL 10.17

Complete **TUTORIAL 10.17** before proceeding. If you have not, you may open the DM-CH_10_Cine_17 map to begin **TUTORIAL 10.18**.

In the "Image Separation Through Lighting" section, using rim lighting was discussed as a way to subtly draw characters out from their environment. You may have noticed over the course of the previous tutorials that the character seems to almost disappear at times because of the darkness of the scene and the limited range of the color palette. In **TUTORIAL 10.18**, we add in some accent lights (three to be exact) to give the character some highlights in order to distinguish it from the background.

TUTORIAL 10.18: Accent Lighting, Part I: Placing Lights

1. Open the Generic Browser and select the Actor Classes tab. Select the PointLightMovable class under Actor > Light > PointLight. Then, right-click in the viewport and choose Add New PointLightMovable Here (see **FIGURE 10.68**).

> **NOTE**
>
> These instructions are relative to the direction the character's mesh is facing.

2. Position this light at the end of the hallway, slightly behind, above, and to the right of the character.

3. With the light selected, press F4 to open its properties.

4. Expand LightingChannels and make sure that only the Cinematic1 channel is selected. This is because we only want these lights to affect the character. In the next step, we set the SkeletalMeshActorMAT to use this channel as well.

5. Select the character and press F4 to open its properties. Expand the LightingChannels and select the Cinematic1 channel. Leave the other channels as they are.

6. Holding down the Alt key to create a duplicate, move the light 224 units in the positive Y direction. This should create a new light to the character's left.

7. Holding down the Alt key again to create a duplicate, move the new light 544 units in the negative X direction. This should create a new light in front of the character and to its left side (see **FIGURE 10.69**).

8. We now need to attach these three lights to the character so they follow the character as it moves. Select all three lights and open the Properties window. Click the Lock to Selected Actors button 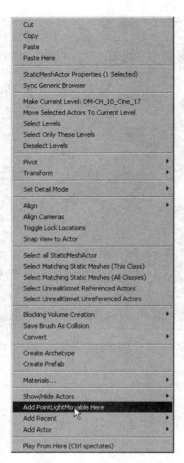 and then select the charac- ter. Back in the Properties window, expand Attachment and click the Use Current Selection button ◄┤ for the Base property.

9. Save the map to preserve your progress.

FIGURE 10.68   Create a new PointLightMovable.

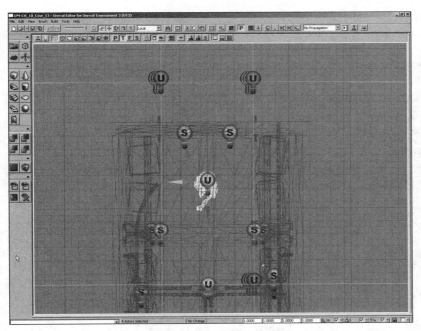

FIGURE 10.69 The character now has three lights around it.

END TUTORIAL 10.18

Complete **TUTORIAL 10.18** before proceeding. If you have not, you may open the DM-CH_10_Cine_18 map to begin **TUTORIAL 10.19**.

TUTORIAL 10.19: Accent Lighting, Part II: Left Rear Brightness Track

1. Open Kismet and double-click the Matinee sequence to open the Matinee Editor.

   In this tutorial, we begin creating tracks to control the brightness of the accent lights because we only need one of them to be lighting the mesh at any one time.

2. Select the light behind and to the left of the character. Then, right-click in the empty space of the Group/Track List and choose Add New Empty Group. Name the new group **RimLightRearLeft** and click OK (see **FIGURE 10.70**).

FIGURE 10.70   Create a new group named RimLightRearLeft.

3. Right-click the RimLightRearLeft group and choose Add New Float Property Track. Select the Brightness property in the dialog that appears and click OK (see **FIGURE 10.71**).

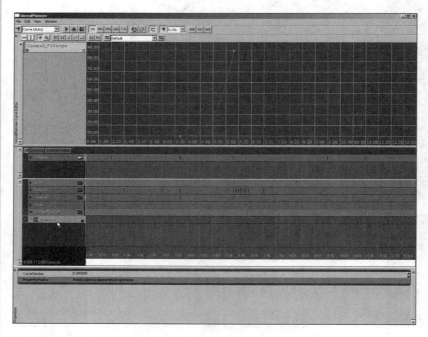

FIGURE 10.71   This new track controls the brightness.

4. With the time slider at Time=0.0, press the Enter key to place an initial key. Right-click the key and choose Set Value. Set the value of the key to 0.5.

5. Move the time slider to Time=1.5 and press the Enter key to place a key. Right-click the key and choose Set Value. Set the value of this key to 0.0. This fades the light out as the character approaches the camera.

6. Save the map to preserve your progress.

END TUTORIAL 10.19

Complete **TUTORIAL 10.19** before proceeding. If you have not, you may open the DM-CH_10_Cine_19 map to begin **TUTORIAL 10.20**.

10

TUTORIAL 10.20: Accent Lighting, Part III: Right Rear Brightness Track

1. Open Kismet and double-click the Matinee sequence to open the Matinee Editor.

   In this tutorial, we continue creating tracks to control the brightness of the accent lights.

2. Select the light behind and to the right of the character. Then, right-click in the empty space of the Group/Track List and choose Add New Empty Group. Name the new group **RimLightRearRight** and click OK (see **FIGURE 10.72**).

FIGURE 10.72   Create a new group for the rear rim light.

3. Right-click the RimLightRearRight group and choose Add New Float Property Track. Select the Brightness property in the dialog that appears and click OK (see **FIGURE 10.73**).

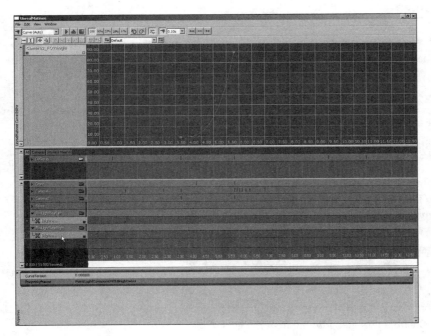

FIGURE 10.73   This new track controls the brightness of the light.

4. With the time slider at Time=1.5, press the Enter key to place an initial key. Right-click the key and choose Set Value. Set the value of the key to 0.0.

5. Move the time slider to Time=3.0 and press the Enter key to place a new key. Right-click the key and choose Set Value. Set the value of the key to 0.5.

6. Right-click the key again and this time choose Interp Mode > Constant to create a stepped curve between this key and the next (see **FIGURE 10.74**).

FIGURE 10.74   The value is now held from one key to the next.

7. Move the time slider to Time=3.7 and press the Enter key to create a new key. Right-click the key and choose Set Value. Set this key's value to 0.0.

8. Right-click this key again and choose Interp Mode > Constant again to create a stepped curve.

9. Move the time slider to Time=5.8 and press the Enter key to create a key. Right-click the key and choose Set Value. Set the value of this key to 0.5.

10. Save the map to preserve your work.

END TUTORIAL 10.20

Complete **TUTORIAL 10.20** before proceeding. If you have not, you may open the DM-CH_10_Cine_20 map to begin **TUTORIAL 10.21**.

TUTORIAL 10.21: Accent Lighting, Part IV: Front Brightness Track

1. Open Kismet and double-click the Matinee sequence to open the Matinee Editor.

   In this tutorial, we continue creating the tracks to control the brightness of the accent lights.

2. Select the light behind and to the left of the character. Then, right-click in the empty space of the Group/Track List and choose Add New Empty Group. Name the new group **RimLightFront** and click OK (see **FIGURE 10.75**).

FIGURE 10.75   Create a new group for the front rim light.

3. Right-click the RimLightFront group and choose Add New Float Property Track. Select the Brightness property in the dialog that appears and click OK.

4. With the time slider at Time=0.0, press the Enter key to place an initial key. Right-click the key and choose Set Value. Set the value of the key to 0.0.

5. Right-click this key again and choose Interp Mode > Constant.

6. Move the time slider to Time=3.7 and press the Enter key to place a new key. Right-click the key and choose Set Value. Set the value of the key to 0.5.

7. Right-click the key again and choose Interp Mode > Linear.

8. Move the time slider to Time=5.4 and press the Enter key to place a key. Right-click the key and choose Set Value. Make sure the key's value is set to 0.5.

9. Move the time slider to Time=5.8 and press the Enter key to create a new key. Right-click the key and choose Set Value. Set the value of the key to 0.0.

10. Make sure that Realtime Preview is enabled in the perspective viewport and click the Play button ▶ in Matinee. You should notice the lit silhouette of the character as the cinematic plays (see **FIGURE 10.76**).

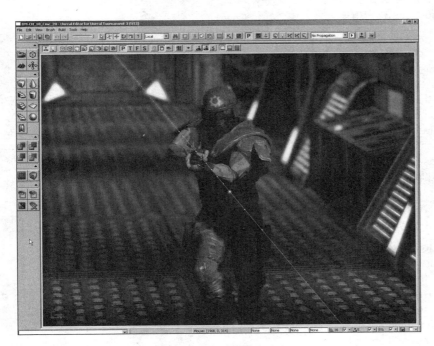

FIGURE 10.76   The character is now illuminated.

11. Save the map to preserve your progress.

END TUTORIAL 10.21

Complete **TUTORIAL 10.21** before proceeding. If you have not, you may open the DM-CH_10_Cine_21 map to begin **TUTORIAL 10.22**.

At this point, we have successfully set up the skeleton of the cinematic sequence, but it is still pretty boring. There just isn't really anything happening. We need to add some meat (by way of action) to those bones. In the explanation of the series of tutorials, some explosions were mentioned. It is now time to begin adding those explosions in to make the sequence more dynamic and exciting.

TUTORIAL 10.22: Explosion Particle Effects, Part I: Placing Emitters

1. In the Generic Browser, select the part_explosion asset from the Chapter_10_Cinematics package. Then, right-click in the viewport and choose Add Actor > Emitter: part_explosion (see **FIGURE 10.77**).

   The question of where to place the emitter comes up next. The positioning really depends on the timing of when the explosion is supposed to occur. This can be very subjective and based on personal preference of what feels right. For these tutorials, the timing of the explosions was worked out ahead of time and that timing will be used. As always, feel free to experiment on your own.

   The first explosion takes place just after the character passes the control boxes at the halfway point of the hallway. These control boxes are found at several points along the hallway, and they are designated by the red and green lights on the front of them. This is where the first emitter will be placed.

2. Position the emitter centered on the control box on the left side of the hallway looking in the Top viewport (this would be to the

FIGURE 10.77   Add a new emitter actor.

character's right as it passes the control box). It may help to open Matinee and move the time slider to Time=4.3. Then, you can find the character's position in the viewport, and the control box should be right there to its right. If for some reason the character has not yet reached the control box (or is already beyond it), simply close Matinee and then reposition the skeletal mesh in the X axis to change its starting location. However, you will likely want to tweak the camera's position as well if you do this (see **FIGURE 10.78**).

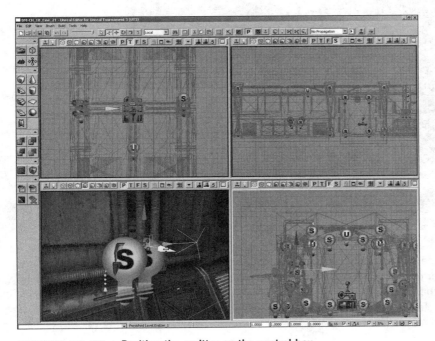

FIGURE 10.78   Position the emitter on the control box.

3. With the emitter selected, press F4 to open its properties. Deselect bAutoActivate so the emitter will not initially be emitting particles. The emitters for the explosions will be triggered via Matinee in subsequent tutorials.

4. With the emitter still selected, set the DrawScale3D setting at the bottom of the UnrealEd interface to 4.0. This makes the explosion four times larger than its original size.

5. Hold down the Alt key and drag the emitter across the hallway to create a duplicate. Now, move the time slider in Matinee to Time=4.7 and find the character's position at that time. There is a support beam to its left and some metal tubing that runs behind the support. Position the new emitter where the tubing and the support meet (see **FIGURE 10.79**).

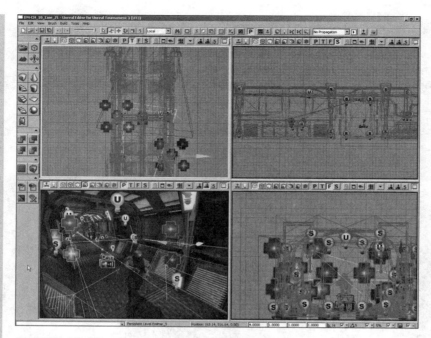

FIGURE 10.79   Position the next emitter as shown.

6. Hold down the Alt key again and drag the emitter back to the other side of the hallway, creating another duplicate. Move the time slider in Matinee to Time=5.075 and find the position of the character at that time in the viewports. There should be a row of four terminals to the character's right. Position the emitter at the second terminal in the row (see **FIGURE 10.80**).

7. Hold down Alt yet again and drag the emitter to the opposite side of the hallway, creating a fourth emitter. Move the time slider in Matinee to Time=5.45 and find the character in the viewports. To the character's left is another support beam with a pipe running behind it along the ceiling. Position the last emitter 64 units below where the pipe meets the support beam. The emitter is moved down 64 units because it would barely be seen based on the angle of the camera at that point during the cinematic. This ensures it is seen by the player (see **FIGURE 10.81**).

8. Save the map to preserve your progress.

10

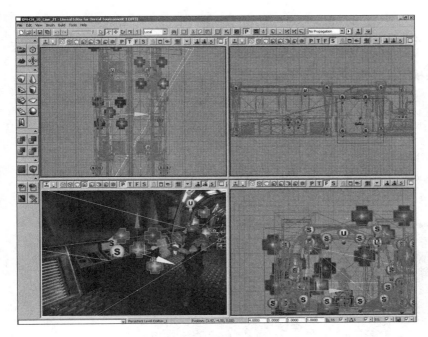

FIGURE 10.80
The third emitter
should go at the
second terminal.

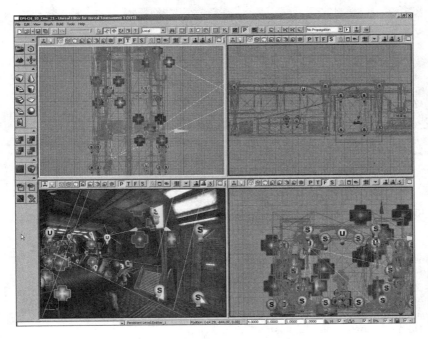

FIGURE 10.81
Place the fourth
emitter below
where the pipe
meets the beam.

END TUTORIAL 10.22

Complete **TUTORIAL 10.22** before proceeding. If you have not, you may open the DM-CH_10_Cine_22 map to begin **TUTORIAL 10.23**.

TUTORIAL 10.23: Explosion Particle Effects, Part II: Particle Toggle Tracks

1. Open Kismet and double-click the Matinee sequence to open the Matinee Editor.

2. Select the first emitter located at the control box. Right-click in the empty space of the Groups/Tracks List and choose Add New Empty Group. Name the new group **ExplosionEmitter1** and click OK.

3. Right-click the ExplosionEmitter1 group and choose Add New Effects Toggle Track (see **FIGURE 10.82**).

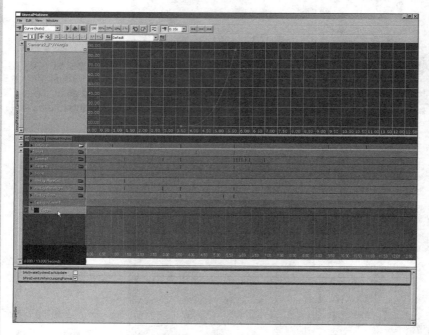

FIGURE 10.82   The new toggle track turns the particles on and off.

4. Move the time slider to Time=4.3 and press the Enter key to place a new key. Select On from the list in the dialog that appears and click OK. This causes the emitter to begin emitting its particles.

5. Select the second emitter located at the intersection of the metal tubing and the support beam. Right-click in the empty space of the Groups/Tracks List and choose Add New Empty Group. Name the new group **ExplosionEmitter2** and click OK.

6. Right-click the ExplosionEmitter2 group and choose Add New Effects Toggle Track (see **FIGURE 10.83**).

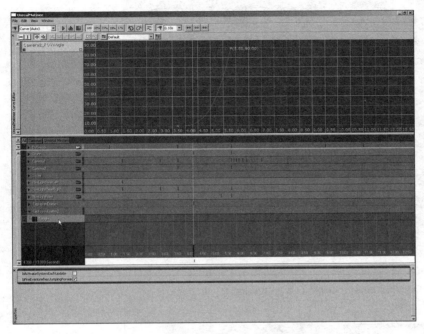

FIGURE 10.83   A new group and toggle track have been added for the second emitter.

7. Move the time slider to Time=4.7 and press the Enter key to place a new key. Select On from the list in the dialog that appears and click OK. This cause the emitter to begin emitting its particles.

8. Select the next emitter located at the terminal. Right-click in the empty space of the Groups/Tracks List and choose Add New Empty Group. Name the new group **ExplosionEmitter3** and click OK.

9. Right-click the ExplosionEmitter3 group and choose Add New Effects Toggle Track (see **FIGURE 10.84**).

10. Move the time slider to Time=5.075 and press the Enter key to place a new key. Select On from the list in the dialog that appears and click OK. This causes the emitter to begin emitting its particles.

11. Select the first emitter located at the control box. Right-click in the empty space of the Groups/Tracks List and choose Add New Empty Group. Name the new group **ExplosionEmitter4** and click OK.

12. Right-click the ExplosionEmitter4 group and choose Add New Effects Toggle Track (see **FIGURE 10.85**).

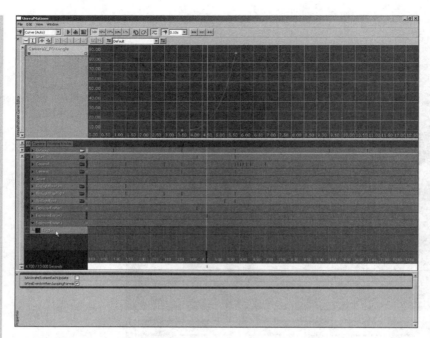

FIGURE 10.84   The third emitter now has a group and toggle track.

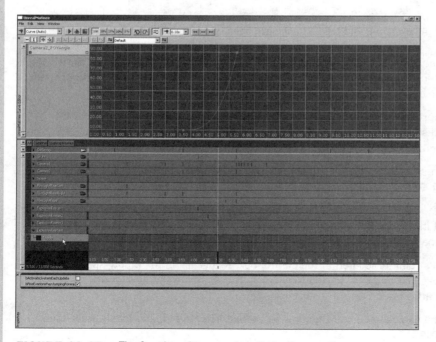

FIGURE 10.85   The fourth emitter now has its track as well.

10

13. Move the time slider to Time=5.45 and press the Enter key to place a new key. Select On from the list in the dialog that appears and click OK. This causes the emitter to begin emitting its particles.

14. Make sure that Realtime Preview is enabled in the perspective viewport and click the Play button ▶ in Matinee. The explosion effects should trigger as the character runs by them (see **FIGURE 10.86**).

FIGURE 10.86   You can now see the explosions going off.

There is one small problem. If you loop the playback, you'll notice that during subsequent viewings, the emitters don't seem to work. The fact is that they're just smoking, and have not been queued to explode again.

15. You can easily fix this by keying each emitter to be off when the sequence starts. Using the skills you have gained so far, add a key at Time=0 for each emitter, switching it off at the beginning of the sequence.

16. Save the map to preserve your work.

END TUTORIAL 10.23

Complete **TUTORIAL 10.23** before proceeding. If you have not, you may open the DM-CH_10_Cine_23 map to begin **TUTORIAL 10.24**.

The explosions are now in place and firing as the character runs by, but there are a few things missing, such as the light an explosion would give off and the sound it makes. In **TUTORIAL 10.24**, we place lights at each emitter's location that have their Brightness properties driven by tracks created in **TUTORIAL 10.23**. Explosion sound effects are added in **TUTORIAL 2.26**.

TUTORIAL 10.24: Explosion Lights, Part I: Placing Lights

1. Open the Generic Browser and select the Actor Class tab. Select the PointLightToggleable located under Actor > Light > PointLight.

2. Right-click in the viewport on the control box where the first emitter is located and choose Add PointLightToggleable Here (see **FIGURE 10.87**).

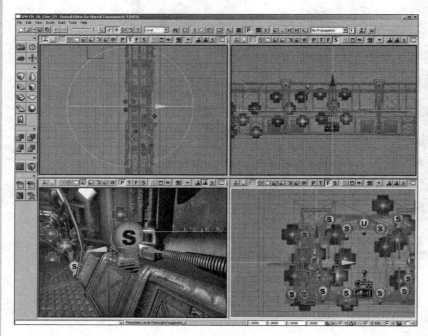

FIGURE 10.87   Create a point light toggleable where the first emitter is located.

3. With the light selected, press F4 to open its properties. Set the LightColor property to the following:

> **A**: 0
>
> **B**: 0
>
> **G**: 128
>
> **R**: 255

4. Set the Radius to 512.0 and the Brightness to 0.0.

5. Hold down the Alt key and move the light to the location of the second emitter, creating a duplicate.

6. Hold down the Alt key again and move the light to the location of the third emitter, creating yet another duplicate light.

7. Hold down the Alt key and move the light to the location of the final emitter, creating one last duplicate light.

8. Save the map to preserve your progress.

END TUTORIAL 10.24

Complete **TUTORIAL 10.24** before proceeding. If you have not, you may open the DM-CH_10_Cine_24 map to begin **TUTORIAL 10.25**.

TUTORIAL 10.25: Explosion Lights, Part II: Brightness Tracks

1. Open Kismet and double-click the Matinee sequence to open the Matinee Editor.

2. Select the light located at the first explosion emitter. Then, right-click in the empty space of the Groups/Tracks List in Matinee and choose Add New Empty Group. Name the new group **ExplosionLight1** and click OK (see **FIGURE 10.88**).

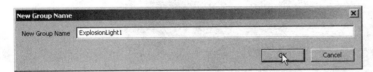

FIGURE 10.88   Create a new group for the first explosion light.

3. Add a new Float Property Track to the group and then set the property to Brightness.

4. Move the time slider to Time=4.3 and press the Enter key to set a key. Right-click the key and choose Set Value. Set the value of the key to 0.0.

5. Move the time slider to Time=4.35 and press the Enter key again to place another key. Right-click the key and choose Set Value. Set the value of this key to 2.0.

6. Move the time slider to Time=4.7 and press the Enter key to create a new key. Right-click the key and choose Set Value. Set the value of this key to 0.0.

7. Select the ExplosionLight1 group and right-click it. Choose Duplicate Group and name the new group **ExplosionLight2** (see **FIGURE 10.89**).

FIGURE 10.89   Copy the group to get a second version.

8. Select the light located at the second explosion emitter in the viewport. In Kismet, right-click the ExplosionLight2 link and choose New Object Var Using PointLightToggleable_2.

> **NOTE**
>
> The actual name of the light may not be the same as that stated earlier.

9. Move the keys of the ExplosionLight2 group to the following times, corresponding to the keys from left to right (see **FIGURE 10.90**):

> **First key**: Time = 4.7
>
> **Second key**: Time = 4.75
>
> **Third key**: Time = 5.075

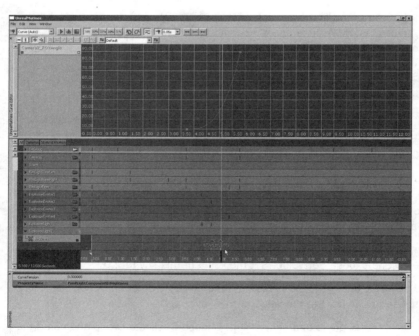

FIGURE 10.90   This offsets the light for the second explosion.

10

10. Select the ExplosionLight2 group and right-click it. Choose Duplicate Group and name the new group **ExplosionLight3**.

11. Select the light located at the second
    explosion emitter in the viewport. In
    Kismet, right-click the ExplosionLight3
    link and choose New Object Var Using
    PointLightToggleable_3.

> **NOTE**
>
> The actual name of the light may not be the same as that stated earlier.

12. Move the keys of the ExplosionLight3 group to the following times, corresponding to the
    keys from left to right:

> **First key**: Time = 5.075
>
> **Second key**: Time = 5.125
>
> **Third key**: Time = 5.45

13. Select the ExplosionLight3 group and right-click it. Choose Duplicate Group and name the
    new group **ExplosionLight4** (see **FIGURE 10.91**).

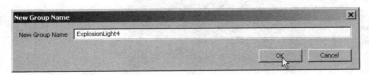

FIGURE 10.91 Copy the third group to create a fourth.

14. Select the light located at the second
    explosion emitter in the viewport. In
    Kismet, right-click the ExplosionLight4
    link and choose New Object Var Using
    PointLightToggleable_0.

> **NOTE**
>
> The actual name of the light may not be the same as that stated earlier.

15. Move the keys of the ExplosionLight4 group to the following times, corresponding to the
    keys from left to right:

> **First key**: Time = 5.45
>
> **Second key**: Time = 5.5
>
> **Third key**: Time = 5.85

16. Make sure the Realtime Preview is enabled in the perspective viewport and click the Play
    button ▶ in Matinee. The lights should turn on in time with the explosion effects (see
    FIGURE 10.92).

17. Save the map to preserve your progress.

FIGURE 10.92   The explosions now illuminate the scene.

END TUTORIAL 10.25

Complete **TUTORIAL 10.25** before proceeding. If you have not, you may open the DM-CH_10_Cine_25 map to begin **TUTORIAL 10.26**.

TUTORIAL 10.26: Explosion Sounds

1. Open Kismet and double-click the Matinee sequence to open the Matinee Editor.

2. In the Generic Browser, select the soundCue_explosion asset from the Chapter_10_Cinematics package.

3. Back in Matinee, right-click in the empty area of the Groups/Tracks List and choose Add New Empty Group. Name the new group **ExplosionSounds** and click OK (see **FIGURE 10.93**).

FIGURE 10.93   Create a new group named ExplosionSounds.

4. Right-click the ExplosionSounds group and choose Add New Sound Track.

5. Move the time slider to Time=4.3 and press the Enter key to place a new key. Right-click the key and choose Set Sound Pitch. Set the pitch to 0.5.

6. Right-click the ExplosionSounds group and choose Add New Sound Track.

7. Move the time slider to Time=4.7 and press the Enter key to place a new key. Right-click the key and choose Set Sound Pitch. Set the pitch to 0.5.

8. Right-click the ExplosionSounds group and choose Add New Sound Track.

9. Move the time slider to Time=5.075 and press the Enter key to place a new key. Right-click the key and choose Set Sound Pitch. Set the pitch to 0.5.

10. Right-click the ExplosionSounds group and choose Add New Sound Track.

11. Move the time slider to Time=5.45 and press the Enter key to place a new key. Right-click the key and choose Set Sound Pitch. Set the pitch to 0.5 (see **FIGURE 10.94**).

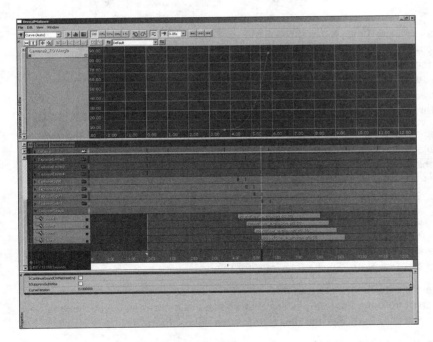

FIGURE 10.94   Four separate explosion sounds now play.

12. Make sure the Realtime Preview is enabled in the perspective viewport and click the Play button ▶ in Matinee. The explosion sounds should now play in time with the explosion effects.

13. Save the map to preserve your progress.

END TUTORIAL 10.26

Complete **TUTORIAL 10.26** before proceeding. If you have not, you may open the DM-CH_10_Cine_26 map to begin **TUTORIAL 10.27**.

TUTORIAL 10.27: Evasion Animation Track, Part I: Key Creation

1. Open Kismet and double-click the Matinee sequence to open the Matinee Editor.

   Now that we have our base animation playing, we need to add (or blend in) the evasion animations at the points in the sequence where the explosions occur.

2. Right-click the Grunt group and choose Add New Anim Control Track (see **FIGURE 10.95**). Select the FullBody slot from the list in the dialog that appears and click OK.

3. Move the time slider to Time=4.3 and press the Enter key to place a key. Select the DvLt01 animation from the list in the dialog that appears and click OK. Right-click the new key and select Set Play Rate. Set the play rate for this animation to 3.0. This speeds up the animation.

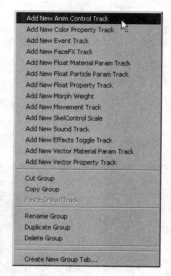

4. Move the time slider to Time=4.7 and press the Enter key to place a key. Select the DvRt01 animation from the list in the dialog that appears and click OK. Right-click the new key and select Set Play Rate. Set the play rate for this animation to 3.38.

FIGURE 10.95   Add a new animation control track to the Grunt group.

5. Move the time slider to Time=5.075 and press the Enter key to place a key. Select the DvLt01 animation from the list in the dialog that appears and click OK. Right-click the new key and select Set Play Rate. Set the play rate for this animation to 3.25.

6. Move the time slider to Time=5.45 and press the Enter key to place a key. Select the DvFd01 animation from the list in the dialog that appears and click OK. Right-click the new key and select Set Play Rate. Set the play rate for this animation to 3.0.

7. Move the time slider to Time=5.83 and press the Enter key to place a key. Select the Run_Fwd_Rdy_01 animation from the list in the dialog that appears and click OK. Right-click the new key and select Set Play Rate. Set the play rate for this animation to 0.25 (see **FIGURE 10.96**).

8. Right-click the last key and choose Set Looping.

9. Save the map to preserve your work.

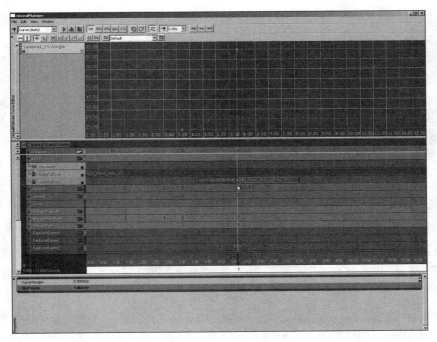

FIGURE 10.96 The final animation has been added.

END TUTORIAL 10.27

Complete **TUTORIAL 10.27** before proceeding. If you have not, you may open the DM-CH_10_Cine_27 map to begin **TUTORIAL 10.28**.

TUTORIAL 10.28: Evasion Animation Track, Part II: Curve Adjustment

1. Open Kismet and double-click the Matinee sequence to open the Matinee Editor.

   Now that the keys for playing the individual animations are in place, we need to adjust the curve for this track so that its animations will override those of the base animation track.

2. Send the second Anim Control track's curve information to the Curve Editor by clicking the little box in the lower-right corner of the track and then open the Curve Editor (if it is not already open) by clicking the Toggle Curve Editor button ⇄ in the Toolbar. Currently, the curve appears as a straight line.

3. Create a point on the curve at Time=0.0 with a value of 0.0 by holding down the Ctrl key and left-clicking the curve. With this point selected, click the Constant Tangent button ⬔ in the Curve Editor's toolbar (see **FIGURE 10.97**).

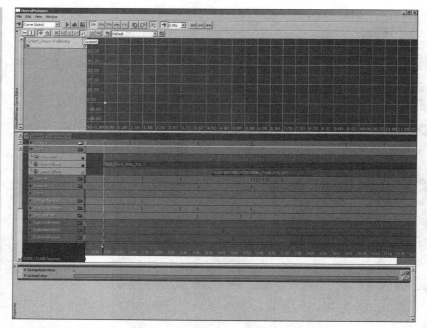

FIGURE 10.97   Create a constant key at Time=0.0.

4. Create a new point on the curve at Time=4.3 by holding down the Ctrl key and left-clicking the curve. Right-click the point and choose Set Value. Set the value of the point to 1.0. With this point selected, click the Linear Tangent button in the Curve Editor's toolbar.

   This causes the animations of this track to override the base animations starting at Time=4.3, which is the time of the first explosion (see **FIGURE 10.98**).

5. Create a new point on the curve at Time=5.75 and a value of 1.0 by holding down the Ctrl key and left-clicking the curve.

6. Create a new point on the curve at Time=5.85 by holding down the Ctrl key and left-clicking the curve. Right-click the point and choose Set Value. Set the value of this point to 0.0.

   This causes the animations of this track to blend back to the base animation after the last explosion.

7. Create a new point on the curve at Time=10.0 by holding down the Ctrl key and left-clicking the curve. Right-click the point and choose Set Value. Set the value of this point to 1.0.

   This causes the running animation of this track to slowly blend in with the base running animation over a period of time, creating a slow-motion-type effect that only affects the character (see **FIGURE 10.99**).

10

FIGURE 10.98   The animation on this track now overrides the base run track created earlier.

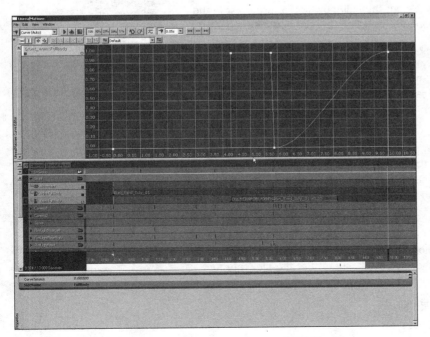

FIGURE 10.99   The final curve should look something like this.

8. Make sure the Realtime Preview is enabled in the perspective viewport and click the Play button ▶ in Matinee. The character should be playing a running animation as it runs down the hallway, but when the explosions occur, the character should perform a roll to the left, then a roll to the right, then a roll to the left, and finally a somersault forward. The character's animation should also blend from a full-speed run to a slow run after the explosions.

9. Save the map to preserve your progress.

END TUTORIAL 10.28

Complete **TUTORIAL 10.28** before proceeding. If you have not, you may open the DM-CH_10_Cine_28 map to begin **TUTORIAL 10.29**.

TUTORIAL 10.29: Additional Animation Track, Part I: Key Placement

1. Open Kismet and double-click the Matinee sequence to open the Matinee Editor.

    Now that we have our base animation playing along with blending in the evasion animations, we will also blend in the front somersault animation with the three side-roll animations. This is just to give those roll animations a touch of forward motion because the character's momentum would carry it in that direction.

2. Right-click the Grunt group and choose Add New Anim Control Track. Select the FullBody slot from the list in the dialog that appears and click OK (see **FIGURE 10.100**).

3. Move the time slider to Time=4.3 and press the Enter key to place a key. Select the DvFd01 animation from the list in the dialog that appears and click OK. Right-click the new key and select Set Play Rate. Set the play rate for this animation to 3.0.

4. Move the time slider to Time=4.7 and press the Enter key to place a key. Select the DvFd01 animation from the list in the dialog that appears and click OK. Right-click the new key and select Set Play Rate. Set the play rate for this animation to 3.38.

5. Move the time slider to Time=5.075 and press the Enter key to place a key. Select the DvFd01 animation from the list in the dialog that appears and click OK. Right-click the new key and select Set Play Rate. Set the play rate for this animation to 3.25.

FIGURE 10.100   Add yet another animation control track to the Grunt group.

6. Save your progress.

END TUTORIAL 10.29

Complete **TUTORIAL 10.29** before proceeding. If you have not, you may open the DM-CH_10_Cine_29 map to begin **TUTORIAL 10.30**.

TUTORIAL 10.30: Additional Animation Track, Part II: Curve Adjustment

1. Open Kismet and double-click the Matinee sequence to open the Matinee Editor.

   Now that the keys for playing the additional animations are in place, we need to adjust the curve for this track so that its animations will blend with those of the evasion animation track.

2. Send the third Anim Control track's curve information to the Curve Editor by clicking the little box in the lower-right corner of the track and then open the Curve Editor (if it is not already open) by clicking the Toggle Curve Editor button ⤳ in the Toolbar. The curve will be a flat line when you begin (see **FIGURE 10.101**).

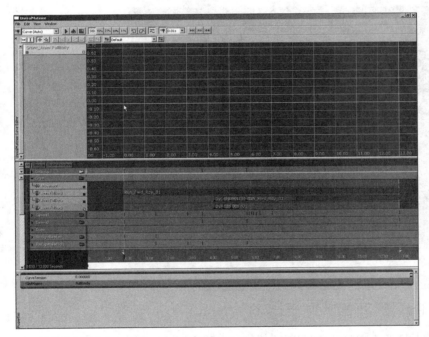

FIGURE 10.101   Your curve will start out looking like this.

3. Create a point on the curve at Time=4.3 with a value of 0.0 by holding down the Ctrl key and left-clicking the curve.

4. Create a new point on the curve at Time=4.4 by holding down the Ctrl key and left-clicking the curve. Right-click the point and choose Set Value. Set the value of the point to 0.5.

5. Create a new point on the curve at Time=4.7 by holding down the Ctrl key and left-clicking the curve. Right-click the point and choose Set Value. Set the value of the point to 0.0.

6. Create a new point on the curve at Time=4.8 by holding down the Ctrl key and left-clicking the curve. Right-click the point and choose Set Value. Set the value of this point to 0.375.

7. Create a new point on the curve at Time=5.075 by holding down the Ctrl key and left-clicking the curve. Right-click the point and choose Set Value. Set the value of this point to 0.0.

8. Create a new point on the curve at Time=5.175 by holding down the Ctrl key and left-clicking the curve. Right-click the point and choose Set Value. Set the value of the point to 0.25.

9. Create a new point on the curve at Time=5.4 by holding down the Ctrl key and left-clicking the curve. Right-click the point and choose Set Value. Set the value of this point to 0.0 (see **FIGURE 10.102**).

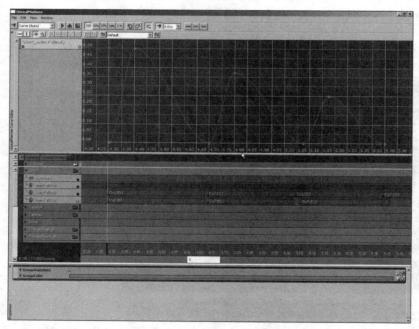

FIGURE 10.102   Your final curve will appear like so.

10. Make sure the Realtime Preview is enabled in the perspective viewport and click the Play button ▶ in Matinee. The difference is very subtle, but it adds to the believability of the animations. The character's animation should also blend from a full-speed run to a slow run after the explosions.

11. Save the map to preserve your progress.

END TUTORIAL 10.30

10

Complete **TUTORIAL 10.30** before proceeding. If you have not, you may open the DM-CH_10_Cine_30 map to begin **TUTORIAL 10.31**.

TUTORIAL 10.31: Finalize Character Movement

1. Open Kismet and double-click the Matinee sequence to open the Matinee Editor.

   Now that the animations of the character evading the explosions are finalized, we are going to adjust the movement track of the character to match those animations. Make sure you have the Movement track selected.

2. Select the key at Time=4.3. With this key selected, move the character in the viewport so that it's about 48 units to the character's right of the center of the hallway. This moves the character closer to where the explosion will go off (see **FIGURE 10.103**).

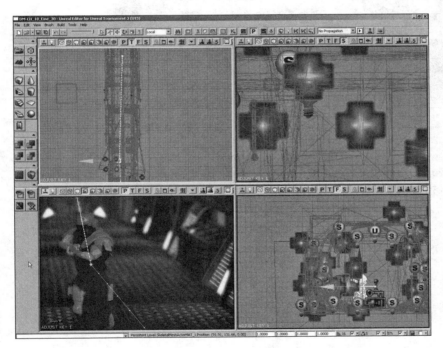

FIGURE 10.103   The first key moves the character to the right.

3. Move the time slider to Time=4.7 and press the Enter key to place a new key. With this key selected, move the character in the viewport so that it's about 48 units to the character's left of the center of the hallway (see **FIGURE 10.104**).

4. Move the time slider to Time=5.075 and press the Enter key to place a new key. With this key selected, move the character in the viewport so that it's about 48 units to the character's right of the center of the hallway.

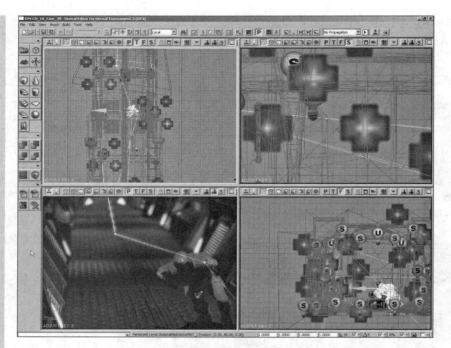

FIGURE 10.104   This causes the character to appear to leap back to the left.

5. Move the time slider to Time=5.45 and press the Enter key to place a new key. With this key selected, move the character in the viewport so that it's about 48 units to the character's left of the center of the hallway.

6. Select the key at Time=5.80 and make sure the character is in the center of the hallway (see **FIGURE 10.105**).

7. Make sure the Realtime Preview is enabled in the perspective viewport and click the Play button ▶ in Matinee. The character should now appear to be actually evading, or being banged around by, the explosions while running down the hallway.

8. Save the map to preserve your progress.

10

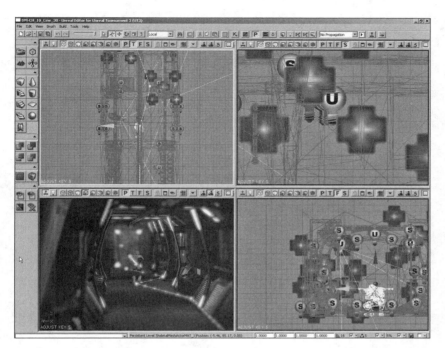

FIGURE 10.105   Verify the character moves back to the center of the hallway.

END TUTORIAL 10.31

Summary

In the end, creating a cinematic sequence is not an exact science. Even as you progress through these tutorials, you will likely find areas where it might make more sense to go your own way and make small tweaks or even major changes. It depends on where you place certain objects, the timing of your animation, and, above all, your own sense of style. Feel free to experiment and make adjustments as you like, and, of course, make sure you practice. Plus, if you want to become an effective storyteller, remember that even though you're in Unreal, you're essentially a cinematographer. Therefore, it helps to study cinematography and storytelling through video.

Appendix A

Distributions

Distributions provide tremendous flexibility to level designers by allowing them to choose how they would like the value of a property to be defined. The sheer number of different types of distributions, along with their similarities to one another, can make distributions seem a little daunting at first. However, upon closer examination, you'll find that although they can appear to be a bit complex, there's really nothing to fear about them, and they can give you a lot of power over the look of your particle systems, the sound of your audio files, and much more.

Overview

In a nutshell, distributions are just ways to control what kind of numeric value is assigned to your property. Sometimes you don't just want a single number to apply to your objects. Instead, you need a random number between a certain range for variety, or you need a value along a graphical curve. Other times, you may need to reach the value of a given property via a parameter through scripting or Kismet.

A

However, even though the general concept of a distribution is fairly simple, the number of available distributions can become confusing to the beginner. Therefore, we're going to break everything down gradually, and build up the concept, keeping the complete beginner in mind. If you're already experienced with assigning different distributions, you might do well to skip ahead and just check out the definitions of each one.

At the simplest level, four basic types of distributions are available:

> **Constant**—A single, unchanging value, such as the number 42.
>
> **Uniform**—A random value that will fall between a user-defined range, such as any random number between 86.7 and 530.9.
>
> **Curve**—A value that changes over time and can be plotted on a graphical curve. This is extremely useful for situations such as when you want a particle to get bigger over its lifespan.
>
> **Parameter**—A value that can be accessed and changed during gameplay via Kismet, Matinee, or UnrealScript.

Each of these four types can come in one of two different forms—float or vector—depending on what type of property you are trying to define. For example, if you are defining a property such as a particle's Lifetime, you would only need a single number, and so a float would be called for. However, if you're defining the color of a particle (RGB), you need a vector, which holds three values. This means we now have a total of eight different types of distributions, based on the type we choose and the kind of property we are editing. Fortunately, Unreal automatically handles which of the two forms you need based on the type of property you're defining. For example, you won't be able to assign a Float Constant distribution to a Vector property.

Curves are special cases because they are used to change the value of a property over time. However, curves themselves can come in two separate types:

> **Constant Curve**—A single curve that spans a property over time. At any point along the timeline, a single value can be defined.
>
> **Uniform Curve**—Two separate curves, both defining a property over time. One curve defines a minimum, the other defines a maximum. At any point along the timeline, a random value is calculated that falls between the two curves.

If you're a more visual person, we've put together some graphs that show how each of these concepts work. For more information, see the "Curve Distributions" subsection.

Now that we have defined all these special cases, we are left with 10 separate types of distributions to be found within the editor:

Float Constant	Vector Constant
Float Uniform	Vector Uniform
Float Constant Curve	Vector Constant Curve
Float Uniform Curve	Vector Uniform Curve
Float Parameter	Vector Parameter

Distribution Types In-Depth

In this section we discuss the available distributions. We begin by taking a look at Constant and Uniform distributions for both Float and Vector. From there we move on to working with Curve distributions, and finally wrap up with a discussion of Parameter distributions.

Constant Distributions

As mentioned earlier, Constant is the simplest type of distribution because it provides the user with a single value (either a float value or a vector) that remains unchanged at all times. This type of distribution has only one key property.

Float Constant Property

Constant—This property holds the single float that provides the value for this distribution type.

Vector Constant Properties

Constant—As with the Float Constant, this property holds a single value for the distribution type. However, because this is a vector-type property, it has X, Y, and Z values. These values can represent axes, RGB colors, or any other set of values the property requires.

LockedAxes—This property allows the specified axes to be locked, or forced to have the same values as another axis. When axes are locked, the values in the property window will not update accordingly. This property contains the following settings:

EDVLF_None—This setting causes each value to be independent.

EDVLF_XY—This setting causes Y to use the value of X.

EDVLF_XZ—This setting causes Z to use the value of X.

EDVLF_YZ—This setting causes Z to use the value of Y.

EDVLF_XYZ—This setting causes Y and Z to use the value of X.

A

Uniform Distributions

This is the ranged distribution. It allows you to establish a minimum and maximum value (designated Min and Max) and will randomly choose a value between them.

How often this calculation occurs depends on the application. In terms of particles, when or how often this random selection is calculated for each particle depends on the type of module being used. "Over Life" and similar modules calculate and apply the random value each time the system is updated. Most other modules only evaluate and apply the value once at the spawn of the particle.

When you're working with sounds, a Uniform distribution generally calculates a random value whenever a particular SoundCue node is called. For instance, you can modulate the pitch of a sound using a Uniform distribution containing a widespread Min and Max. Each time you play back the SoundCue, a new random value is calculated, resulting in variation (see **FIGURE A.1**).

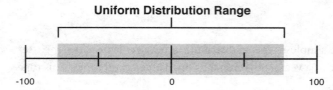

FIGURE A.1   Uniform distributions can be thought of as a range along a number line.

Float Uniform Properties

Min—This is the lower bound used to choose the random value.

Max—This is the upper bound used to choose the random value.

Vector Uniform Properties

Min—This is the lower bound used to choose the random value. It contains separate subproperties for X, Y, and Z.

Max—This is the upper bound used to choose the random value. It contains separate subproperties for X, Y, and Z.

bUseExtremes—When this property is true, the value for each axis chosen will either be the Min or the Max.

LockedAxes—See the section "Vector Constant Properties" for an explanation of this property.

MirrorFlags—Allows for mirroring the Min/Max values for each component of the value. This property has the following settings:

EDVMF_Same—This setting uses the Max value in place of Min, effectively making it behave like a constant.

EDVMF_Different—This setting uses the values as entered. This is the default.

EDVMF_Mirror—This setting uses the opposite of the Max value in place of the Min value. For example, if Max is set to 30, Min is automatically set to –30.

Curve Distributions

Curve distributions can be a little intimidating because they are easily the most inherently complex of the available distribution types. As mentioned earlier, they allow the value of a property to be determined through the evaluation of a curve. This curve graphs the value of the property over a specified period of time, usually the Lifetime of an individual particle. If you are coming into this topic from a background in computer animation, you can think of this as being very similar to working with keyframes and function curves (see **FIGURE A.2**).

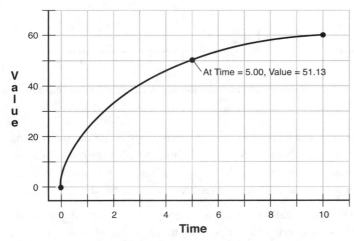

FIGURE A.2   Curve distributions are evaluations of a curve that measure the value of a property over time.

If you've ever sat through an algebra class, you know that a curve is merely a line that moves through a series of points. This is no different in Unreal. In order to define your curve, and thus the behavior of your property over time, you need to create points that specify what the value for that property will be at a given time. For example, you could say that the DrawScale3D of a particle will be 0 at its birth (which would translate to 0 along its Lifetime), and will expand to a value

A

of 5 after the particle has been alive for 3 seconds. To do this, you would create two points that specify each of these relationships (value over time). The engine then interpolates a curve between those two points to establish the curve that will define the property.

You can also change the behavioral characteristics used by the curve to control how it enters and exits each point by editing the tangents of each point created. This is important because it allows the user to create more complex behaviors, such as variations in rate of change (acceleration and deceleration). For example, if you had two points with a straight line connecting them, the value would change at a constant rate as time progresses. However, if the curve gradually sweeps upward and then back down forming an S-like shape, your property would accelerate while changing, and then slow back down before reaching its final value. Consider the graphs shown in **FIGURE A.3**.

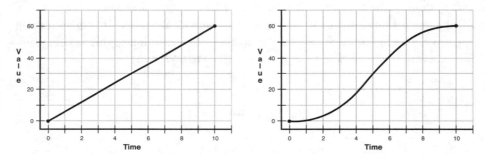

FIGURE A.3   The graph on the left is a linear graph, whereas the one on the right is an "ease in, ease out" type of graph.

The properties that control your curves can be edited in two different ways: either manually using the properties of the distribution itself or through the Curve Editor. In this section, we focus on the property values and their functions in controlling the curves. For more information on using the Curve Editor available within the Unreal Editor, see its section in this appendix.

Although a total of four separate Curve distributions are available, you may have noted earlier that there are really only two types of distributions that use curves. These are Constant and Uniform Curves. Although many of the properties of both of these distributions are essentially the same, there are minor changes to account for, depending on whether the curve is using a Constant or Uniform distribution and whether the property in question is a float or a vector. Next, we outline the properties for Constant and Uniform Curves. Any time a property is different in regard to using a float- or vector-type of property, the difference is noted in the definition.

It is important to keep in mind that the key difference between using a float-based curve and a vector-based curve is that a float-based curve is defined by only a single curve. A vector-based curve, on the other hand, is actually three independent curves—one for each axis (X, Y, and Z)—each of which is capable of defining separate behavior.

Constant Curves

A constant curve is a single interpolation curve that travels through points that contain a single
float or vector value over a given point in time (see **FIGURE A.4** and **FIGURE A.5**).

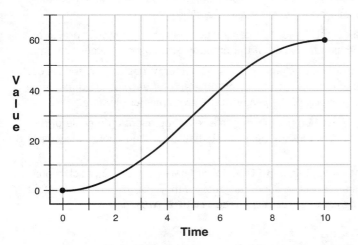

FIGURE A.4   A float constant curve is just a single curve used to define a property.

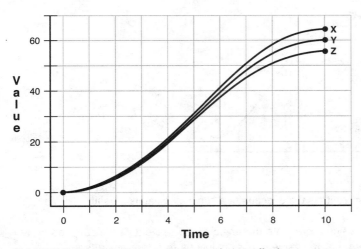

FIGURE A.5   A vector constant curve is actually three curves—one for each axis.

Constant Curve Properties

ConstantCurve—This is the interpolation curve object. As far as we are concerned, it is
merely a container for the Points array.

Points—This is the array that contains all the points used to define the curve. The array is dynamic, meaning that elements can be added, deleted, inserted, or duplicated. Each point in the array contains the following:

InVal—Graphically speaking, this is the value along the horizontal axis for defining the curve. It is representative of some manner of time.

OutVal—In a Float Constant Curve, this designates the value along the vertical axis of the graph, which defines the value of the property at the given moment in time.

For a Vector Constant Curve, this property is a 3D vector of floats (X, Y, and Z), each representing the values in the vertical axis of the graph for each of the three curves created to define the property of the vector at the given moment in time.

ArriveTangent—For a Float Constant Curve, this value represents the angle of the tangent of the curve as it enters the point. Note that the value is not analogous to a true angle.

For a Vector Constant Curve, this is a 3D vector of floats (X, Y, and Z), each representing the angle of its respective curve tangents as they exit this point. Note that the value is not analogous to a true angle (see **FIGURE A.6**).

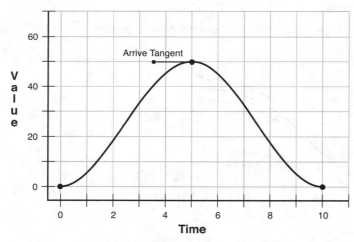

FIGURE A.6   The ArriveTangent controls the direction of a curve as it enters a point.

LeaveTangent—This value represents the angle of the tangent of the curve as it leaves the point. Note that the value is not analogous to a true angle (see **FIGURE A.7**).

For a Vector Constant Curve, this is a 3D vector of floats (X, Y, and Z), each representing the angle of its respective curve tangents as they exit this point. Note that the value is not analogous to a true angle.

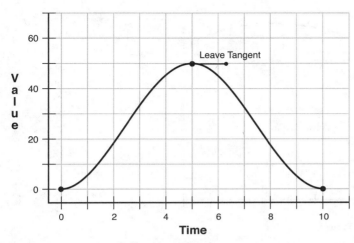

FIGURE A.7   The LeaveTangent controls the direction of a curve as it exits a point.

InterpMode—This controls how the curve progresses from one point to the next as well as how the tangents are used. This property contains the following settings:

CIM_Linear—This mode ignores tangents and forces the curve to follow a straight line from the current point to the next (see **FIGURE A.8**).

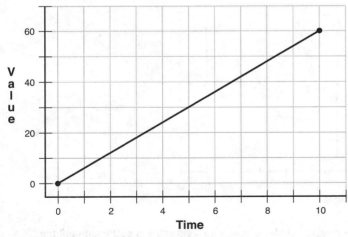

FIGURE A.8   A linear curve will appear like so.

CIM_CurveAuto—This mode sets the tangents automatically to create a smooth curve from the previous point through the current point and on to the next point (see **FIGURE A.9**).

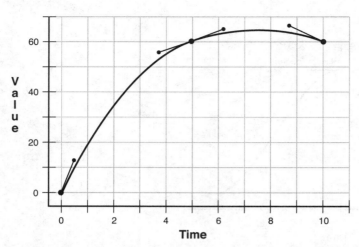

FIGURE A.9   Auto tangents cause a smooth entrance and exit of each point by the curve.

CIM_Constant—This mode creates a stepped curve, meaning that the curve continues at the value of the current point until it reaches the next point (see **FIGURE A.10**).

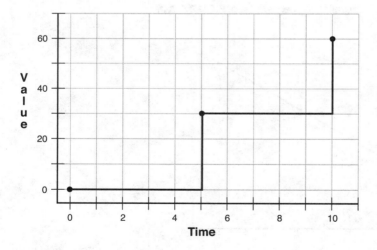

FIGURE A.10   A stepped curve creates "holds" in which a single value is sustained until the next point.

CIM_CurveUser—This mode lets the user determine the tangent values, but requires that both the arriving and leaving tangents be the same (see **FIGURE A.11**).

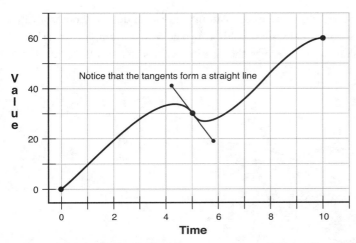

FIGURE A.11   User curves can be edited, but maintain fluid tangency from the in-tangent to the out-tangent.

CIM_CurveBreak—This mode lets the user set the tangents and provides the ability to have separate arriving and leaving tangents (see **FIGURE A.12**).

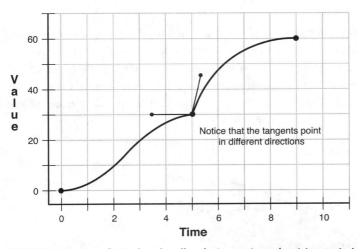

FIGURE A.12   Curve breaks allow in-tangents and out-tangents to have different directions.

Uniform Curves

Just as Uniform distributions specify a value randomly chosen between two limits (Min and Max), a Uniform Curve specifies a value that is randomly selected from between two limit curves. In the case of a Float Uniform Curve, the Max values for all points designate one curve, and the

Min values designate another. Throughout the interpolation, Unreal randomly chooses a value that falls between the two curves. You could visualize this as two curves on a graph with a shaded area in between, wherein the shaded area defines the possible values that could be randomly chosen (see **FIGURE A.13**).

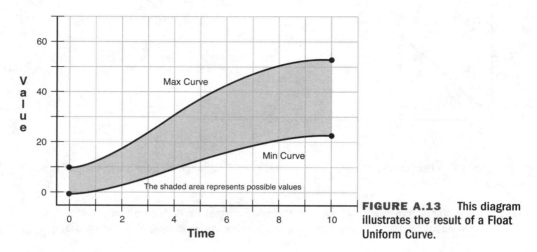

FIGURE A.13   This diagram illustrates the result of a Float Uniform Curve.

Vector Uniform Curves are a bit more complicated, because you have three separate Max values and three separate Min values. This results in a total of six separate curves. Two for each of the axes (X, Y, and Z). However, the general principle is the same. If you consider that each of the three inputs of a vector is simply a float, you can visualize the result as three pairs of curves, with a shaded area in between each pair. The three shaded areas represent the possible values of the three individual axes of the vector (see **FIGURE A.14**).

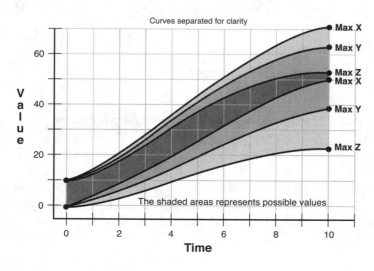

FIGURE A.14   The three overlapping shaded areas represent the result of a Vector Uniform Curve.

Uniform Curve Properties

ConstantCurve—This is the interpolation curve object. As far as we are concerned, it is merely a container for the Points array.

Points—This is the array containing all the points that define the curve. It is a dynamic array, meaning that elements can be added, deleted, inserted, or duplicated. Each point in the array contains the following:

InVal—Graphically speaking, this is the value along the horizontal axis for defining the curve. It is representative of some period of time.

OutVal—For a Float Uniform Curve, this is a 2D vector of floats representing the values in the vertical axis of the Min and Max curves.

X—This is the value of the curve representing the lower bound of the range. Think of it as the Min value.

Y—This is the value of the curve representing the upper bound of the range. Think of it as the Max value.

For a Vector Uniform Curve, the OutVal property is actually defined by two 3D vectors, one for Min and one for Max. The properties within OutVal appear like so:

v1—This is the name of the vector used for the lower bound of the range. Think of this as the Min vector value. Within it you find values for the X, Y, and Z of the vector, used to designate the value of the property for that particular axis at the given moment in time.

v2—This is the name of the vector used for the upper bound of the range. Think of this as the Max vector value. Within it you find values for the X, Y, and Z of the vector, used to designate the value of the property for that particular axis at the given moment in time.

ArriveTangent—For a Float Uniform Curve, this is a 2D vector of floats specifying a tangent angle for the two curves as they approach the current point.

X—This represents the angle of the tangent of the lower-bound curve as it approaches the current point. Note that the value is not analogous to a true angle.

Y—This represents the slope of the tangent of the upper-bound curve as it approaches the current point. Note that the value is not analogous to a true angle.

For a Vector Uniform Curve, this is actually a pair of vectors. Each of the three values within each vector represents the angle of the tangent for the respective curve as it enters the point. Note that the values specified are not analogous to true angles:

v1—This is the name of the vector used for the three tangent angles for the lower-bound curve of the range. Within it you find values for the X, Y, and Z of the vector, used to represent the angle of the tangent for the curve of that particular axis as it enters the given point.

A

v2—This is the name of the vector used for the three tangent angles for the upper-bound curve of the range. Within it you find values for the X, Y, and Z of the vector, used to represent the angle of the tangent for the curve of that particular axis as it enters the given point.

LeaveTangent—For a Float Uniform Curve, this is a 2D vector of floats specifying a tangent angle for the two curves as they exit the current point.

X—This represents the angle of the tangent of the lower-bound curve as it exits the current point. Note that the value is not analogous to a true angle.

Y—This represents the slope of the tangent of the upper-bound curve as it exits the current point. Note that the value is not analogous to a true angle.

For a Vector Uniform Curve, this is actually a pair of vectors. Each of the three values within each vector represents the angle of the tangent for the respective curve as it exits the point. Note that the values specified are not analogous to true angles:

v1—This is the name of the vector used for the three tangent angles for the lower-bound curve of the range. Within it you find values for the X, Y, and Z of the vector, used to represent the angle of the tangent for the curve of that particular axis as it exits the given point.

v2—This is the name of the vector used for the three tangent angles for the upper-bound curve of the range. Within it you find values for the X, Y, and Z of the vector, used to represent the angle of the tangent for the curve of that particular axis as it exits the given point.

InterpMode—This controls how the curve progresses from one point to the next as well as how the tangents are used. This property contains the following settings:

CIM_Linear—This mode ignores tangents and forces the curve to follow a straight line from the current point to the next (see **FIGURE A.15**).

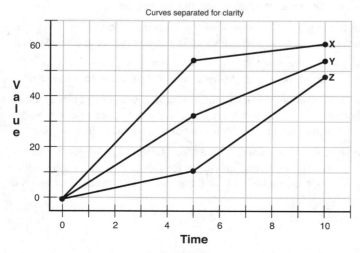

FIGURE A.15   Vector linear curves appear as straight lines.

CIM_CurveAuto—This mode sets the tangents automatically to create a smooth curve from the previous point through the current point and on to the next point (see **FIGURE A.16**).

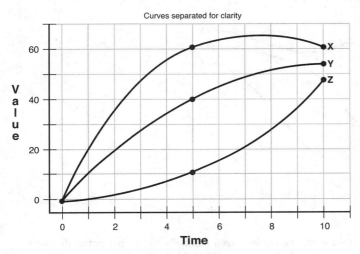

FIGURE A.16   Auto vector curves flow smoothly into and out of the points.

CIM_Constant—This mode creates a stepped curve, meaning that the curve continues at the value of the current point until it reaches the next point (see **FIGURE A.17**).

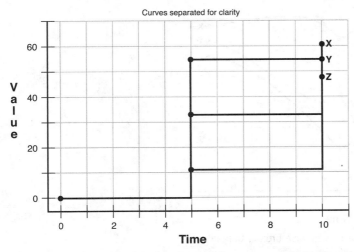

FIGURE A.17   Notice that each of the vector curves holds its value until it reaches the next point.

A

CIM_CurveUser—This mode lets the user determine the tangent values, but requires that both the arriving and leaving tangents be the same (see **FIGURE A.18**).

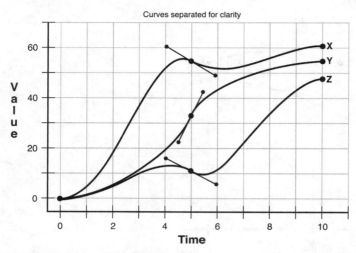

FIGURE A.18   Each of these three vector curves has been manually edited, but notice that their tangents are still straight.

CIM_CurveBreak—This mode lets the user set the tangents and provides the ability to have separate arriving and leaving tangents (see **FIGURE A.19**).

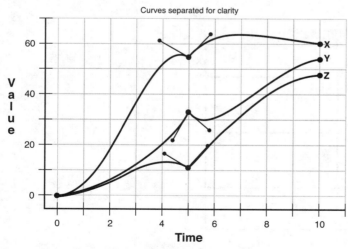

FIGURE A.19   The three vector curves have broken tangents.

bUseExtremes—When true, the value for each axis chosen will either be the Min or the Max.

LockedAxes—See the section "Vector Constant Properties" for an explanation of this property.

MirrorFlags—Allows mirroring the Min/Max values for each component of the value. This property has the following settings:

EDVMF_Same—This setting uses the Max value in place of Min, effectively making it behave like a constant.

EDVMF_Different—This setting uses the values as entered. This is the default.

EDVMF_Mirror—This setting uses the opposite of the Max value in place of the Min value. For example, if Max is set to 30, Min is automatically set to –30.

Parameter Distributions

As mentioned earlier, the purpose of the Float and Vector Parameter distributions is to expose the property containing the distribution so that it can be edited through code, through Kismet, or through Matinee.

One of the most useful functions of this type of distribution is the ability to map a range of input values that is passed in through code, Kismet, or Matinee, to a range of output values that adjusts any incoming value based on the mapping to create an entirely new value that falls within the output values for the property. The user can specify Min and Max for inputs coming in from Matinee, Kismet, and so on, and all incoming values will be clamped within that range. Another Min and Max are specified for the outputs, such that if an input value is equal to the Min input, it will be mapped to the Min output. If, instead, an incoming value is equal to the Max input, it will be mapped to the Max output. Incoming values that fall between the Min and Max inputs are mapped to the corresponding value between the Min and Max outputs (see **FIGURE A.20**).

A good practical example of this would be if you had several particle emitters that were each emitting some type of flame. You want each of the emitters to use a different spawn rate (some things burn better than others, after all), but you also want all the different spawn rates to fade downward and then shut off at the same time, as if someone had turned on a powerful overhead sprinkler system. By setting the ParameterName property for each of these emitters to the same value, you could drive them all with the same Matinee sequence. Then, by adjusting the input and output values for each individual emitter, you could get the behavior you're looking for.

Note that the key difference between Float and Vector Particle Parameter distributions is the fact that Float Particle Parameters use float values whereas Vector Particle Parameters use 3D vectors instead. No other differences exist.

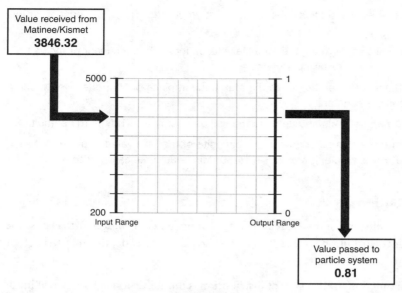

Value received from
Matinee/Kismet
3846.32

5000 ─────────────── 1

200 ─────────────── 0
Input Range   Output Range

Value passed to
particle system
0.81

FIGURE A.20   This diagram illustrates how information from a Kismet sequence can be mapped within an output range.

Particle Parameter Properties

ParameterName—This is the name used to identify this parameter in script, Kismet, Matinee, and so on. If any other properties are using Particle Parameter distributions with the same ParameterName, they will all essentially be "listening" for the same data.

MinInput—This is the lower bound of the range of values passed to the parameter. If values are sent in from Matinee, Kismet, and so on, that are lower than this value, they will be clamped to this value.

MaxInput—This is the upper bound of the range of values passed to the parameter. If values are sent in from Matinee, Kismet, and so on, that are higher than this value, they will be clamped to this value.

MinOutput—This is the lower bound of the mapped value of the distribution. If values are sent in from Matinee, Kismet, and so on, that are equal to MinInput, they will be mapped to this value.

MaxOutput—This is the upper bound of the mapped value of the distribution. If values are sent in from Matinee, Kismet, and so on, that are equal to MaxInput, they will be mapped to this value.

ParaMode—This specifies how the input value should be handled. The property contains the following settings:

DPM_Normal—This causes the input value to be linearly mapped according to the output value range.

DPM_Direct—This causes the input value not to be mapped to the output value range, but instead to be used as is. Essentially, this eliminates range mapping.

DPM_Absolute—This causes the absolute value of the input to be linearly mapped to the output value range.

Constant—This is the value to use for the distribution if the parameter is not set elsewhere, such as through Kismet or Matinee. It also allows for testing and tweaking in Cascade to find the proper values for the output range.

General Performance Cost Comparison

It should be noted that each of the distribution types comes with different costs in terms of performance. Although the difference may be trifling in some instances, we've included a very general outline of the kinds of performance costs you can expect, just as a comparative reference.

The performance costs, from lowest to highest, are as follows:

Constants—Constants are the least-expensive distribution because they only hold a single unchanging value and therefore require no calculation at runtime.

Uniform—Uniforms are just a little bit more expensive than Constants because they require a random calculation in order to function. However, the difference can generally be thought of as negligible. In fact, you'll find that even many professional assets have settings in which the Min and Max values are set to the same number, giving a Uniform the same resulting behavior as a Constant.

Curves—Curves are more expensive than Constants or Uniforms because they require that the curve be evaluated based on certain factors, such as the life of a particle, each time a particle system is updated. This goes double for Uniform Curves, because two curves are actually being calculated, and then a random number must be selected from within those values. It is for this reason that curve-based properties can be cast into Lookup Tables, which are explained in the section "Distribution Baking and Lookup Tables."

Parameters—Although Parameters appear at the end of this list, technically speaking, a Parameter distribution can't really fall within the confines of this list at all. A Parameter's performance cost is dependent upon the complexity of the Kismet sequence, Matinee animation, or UnrealScript that is driving it. However, because of this, Parameters have the *potential* of being the highest-costing distributions available.

A

Distribution Baking and Lookup Tables

As you may have gathered thus far, distributions are very powerful in how they allow the user to manipulate properties over time. However, this power comes at the cost of processing expense. Calculating a value along a curve uses up valuable processing power, as does mapping an output to a random calculation. So naturally, in cases where a user has many different distributions, it would be nice to be able to lighten the load on the engine for calculating the result of these distributions.

To make things easier, Unreal Engine 3 uses the process of baking curves and using Lookup Tables. Essentially, this refers to the curve being evaluated at several points (not just the points used to define the curve) and those values are then placed in a table and stored. These new points are then used to define a much simpler linear curve, which can be quickly referenced during gameplay. The result is much easier on the game engine and therefore faster, but comes at the cost of a loss in precision. Instead of one precise flowing curve, you are essentially left with several linear segments that generally outline the original shape, but are much faster to calculate. You can think of it like being able to use high school pre-algebra instead of college-level calculus. The answers are much easier to understand, but you're dealing with straight lines instead of precise curves (see **FIGURE A.21**).

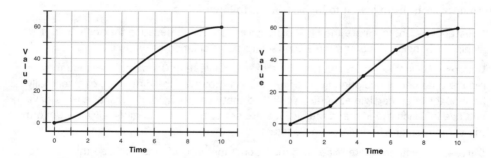

FIGURE A.21   On the left is a smooth unbaked curve, and on the right is a curve with several points being used as references to bake the curve.

Sometimes this loss in precision is unacceptable. Therefore, the user has the option of choosing whether or not to allow the distribution to be baked into a Lookup Table by using the bCanBeBaked property. This property is found at or near the bottom of each distribution property list. In this way, effects that require precise curves can use them, whereas those effects that look acceptable without them can use simplified values from a Lookup Table. You can also toggle Lookup Tables off and on globally using the button in the Main Unreal Editor Toolbar ![icon]. Using this button can help you decide whether or not Lookup Tables are appropriate for a particular effect.

It should be noted that when Lookup Tables are used, any curve-based distributions using only a single point are treated as if they are using a Constant distribution. Also, any Uniform distributions that are using Lookup Tables and have their Min and Max properties set to the same value will also be treated as if they are using a Constant distribution.

Appendix B

The Curve Editor

As you create your gaming assets, you'll sometimes want to change some property or parameter over time, perhaps to animate an asset. These changes are internally graphed onto a curve, in which Time runs along the bottom of the graph and the value of the property runs up the side (see **FIGURE B.1**).

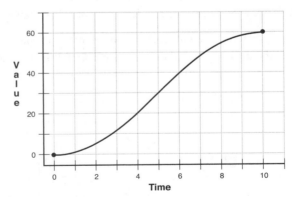

FIGURE B.1 Curve representation

In UnrealEd, you can view and manipulate curves within the Curve Editor. The Curve Editor will appear in two locations: the Cascade Particle Editor and the Matinee System. In each case, its interface and functionality is exactly the same.

In this appendix, we'll walk you through using the Curve Editor. But, before we do, let's take a moment to review a few basic concepts of keyframe-based animation and to learn how curves can be controlled to adjust the animations you create.

Animation Curves

An animation curve is really nothing more than a graphical representation of the change of a property value over time. The final shape of this curve is controlled by two things: keyframes and interpolation curves that connect all the keyframes together.

A *keyframe*—often called a *key* for short in Unreal—is simply the recording of a property's value at a given time. Graphically speaking, you can think of these as the dots in a connect-the-dots game. You could, for example, say that a certain property would have a value of 5 at Time=0, and a value of 10 at Time=3. If you were to plot these two points on your graph, it would look something like **FIGURE B.2**.

Now you know that the property will be one value at a certain time and another value later on. But what happens in between? Fortunately, you don't need to manually designate each and every point along the curve (which is nice; there are an infinite number of points between any two keyframes).

Instead, the computer will do the work for you, creating what are known as *interpolation curves*. If you go back to our connect-the-dots game example, you can think of these as the lines that connect the dots. The great thing is that these lines do not necessarily have to be completely straight as they pass from one key to the next. They can swoop up to the next point, they can meet only at right angles, or they can have a wide variety of other shapes within certain limitations.

Consider, for instance, a curve that started off very flat, but gently became steeper as it approached the next point on the graph (see **FIGURE B.3**). What would be the behavior of such a curve?

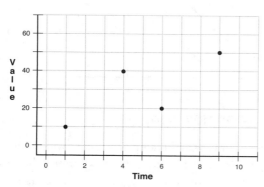

FIGURE B.2   Graphed keyframes

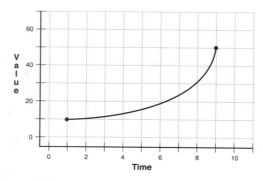

FIGURE B.3   Fast-In curve

This type of curve would define behavior that began with a very slow transition and accelerated, getting faster and faster, right up to the point of the next key. This would be very different from a curve that was simply a straight line connecting the two keys, which would define behavior at a constant rate of change, neither accelerating nor decelerating (see **FIGURE B.4**).

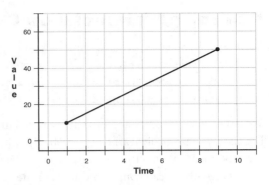

FIGURE B.4   Linear curve

By changing the shape of these curves, you can create a very diverse range of behaviors for your property, all while using the fewest number of keys possible. However, as mentioned previously, there are some limitations. The most important of these is that an animation curve must always evaluate in such a way that if a vertical line were drawn through it at any given point, it would intersect the curve only once. This might sound confusing if you're new to the concept of animation curves, but think about it for a moment. A vertical line on the graph could be used to designate a particular time at a given point, as shown in **FIGURE B.5**.

If the curve were ever allowed to fold back over itself, creating a situation where the vertical line could intersect the curve twice, you would, in effect, have two separate values for the same property at the same time (see **FIGURE B.6**).

This behavior is impossible, and therefore certain shapes for the curve are eliminated.

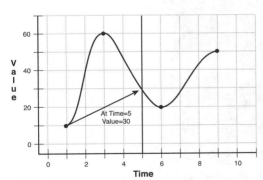

FIGURE B.5   Notice the vertical line designates Time=5.

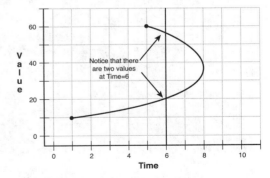

FIGURE B.6   This curve would create two separate property values at the same time.

Controlling Interpolation Curves

So, now that you know generally how an animation curve works, you need to know how you can control its shape in order to get the results you're seeking. This is done in one of two ways: either through the adjustment of *Bezier tangent handles*, which are used to control the angle at which an interpolation curve enters and exits a key; or by changing the type of tangents that the key uses.

We'll start with tangent handles. It helps to first understand what a tangent is. In high school algebra class, you probably learned (or probably will) that a tangent defines the angle of a curve at a given point. That's exactly what we have here. Our point, in this case, is our key. By manipulating these tangents, we can control the angle of the curve at the location of the key.

In UnrealEd's Curve Editor, tangent handles appear as small white lines with a small square handle at the end. By dragging on the small handle, you change the angle at which the tangent intercepts the key, and thereby change the shape of the curve. Also, you'll notice that each key actually contains two handles, one on each side of the key. The handle on the left controls the direction of the curve as it enters the key. The handle on the right controls the direction of the curve as it exits the key (see **FIGURE B.7**).

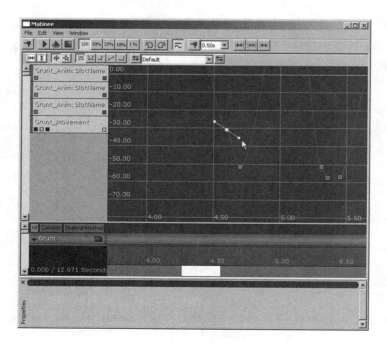

FIGURE B.7   A tangent handle

The second method of controlling a curve involves changing the type of keys used to make the curve. In Unreal, there are five types of keys available to you, as follows:

- Auto
- User
- Break
- Linear
- Constant

Auto

Auto tangents are the default tangent type, and are defined by the computer, rather than being editable by the user. Generally speaking, this type of key creates a very smooth result in which the curve gracefully sweeps from one point to the next (see **FIGURE B.8**). However, this can lead to the problem of overshoot, which we discuss later in this section.

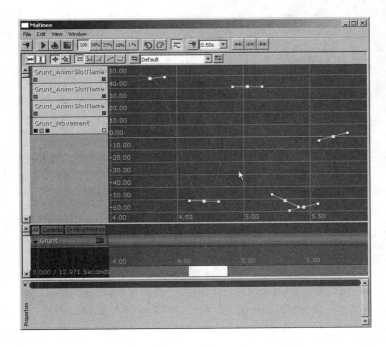

FIGURE B.8   This curve exhibits Auto tangents.

User

User tangents can be adjusted by the designer. This means you can drag on the handle and change the direction at which the curve enters and exits the key. However, as you move the handle, you'll notice that the two handles—the one entering the key and the one exiting it—always remain aligned to one another, appearing as a straight line (see **FIGURE B.9**).

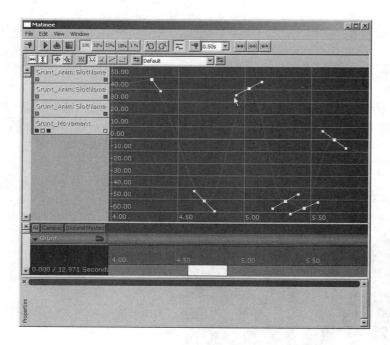

FIGURE B.9   These tangents have been manipulated, meaning they are now User tangents.

Break

Break tangents, like User tangents, can also be adjusted by the designer. However, they differ in that the tangent that enters the key and the one that exits the key will not automatically remain aligned to one another. This means you can point the tangent handles in different directions, which results in a very sharp change in property values over time (see **FIGURE B.10**).

Linear

Linear tangents are by far the most simple, as they merely cause the interpolation curve to create a straight line from one point to the next (see **FIGURE B.11**). The tangents are not editable by the user.

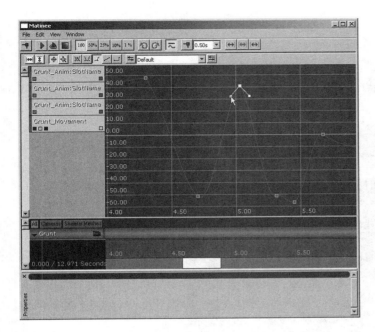

FIGURE B.10   This curve exhibits Break tangents.

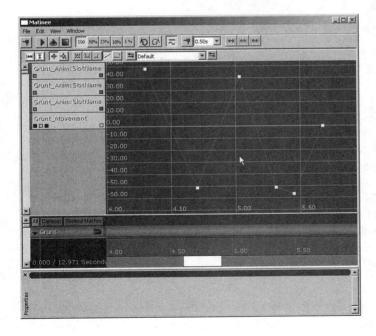

FIGURE B.11   Linear tangents simply cause the curve to create straight lines.

B

Constant

Constant tangents are unique in that they create a stepped curve that will hold the value of the key until the next key comes along in the graph (see **FIGURE B.12**). This is perfect for animating such things as blinking lights, or any other time when you need an instant transition from one value to another.

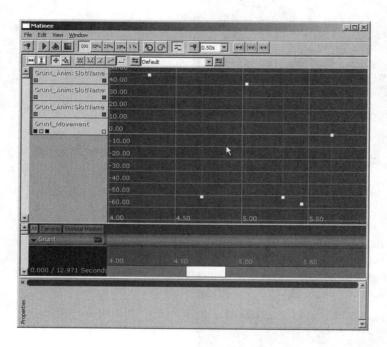

FIGURE B.12   Constant tangents hold the value until the next key comes along.

Curve Editor Interface

The Curve Editor, as mentioned earlier, appears in two key locations in UnrealEd (Matinee and Cascade). It will look and function the same way in both cases. The following is a basic overview of the editor's interface and how it can be navigated. The Curve Editor's interface is divided into three key sections: a toolbar, a curve key list, and the main curve graph.

Curve Editor Toolbar

As with most editors in Unreal, the Curve Editor's toolbar contains a variety of buttons that perform functions that you're going to use most often when working. From left to right, these buttons are listed next.

Fit Visible Tracks Horizontally

Clicking this button zooms the graph view along the horizontal axis (Time), forcing all the visible curves to fit within the horizontal extents.

Fit Visible Tracks Vertically

This button zooms the graph view along the vertical axis (Property value), forcing all the visible curves to fit within the vertical extents.

Pan/Edit Mode

This button toggles on Pan/Edit Mode, which is a navigational mode that still enables you to edit keys and tangents. Navigation of the graph view will be discussed later.

Zoom Mode

This button toggles on Zoom Mode, which enables you to zoom into and out of the graph view.

Auto Curve

This converts any selected keys to use Auto tangents, which were described previously.

User Curve

This converts any selected keys to use User tangents, which were described previously.

Break Curve

This converts any selected keys to use Break tangents, which were described previously.

Linear Curve

This converts any selected keys to use Linear tangents, which were described previously.

Constant Curve

This converts any selected keys to use Constant tangents, which were described previously.

Tabs

Tabs are an aspect of the toolbar that enable you to create your own customized groups of curves, in order to quickly jump to a specific curve or collection of curves.

Create Tab

Clicking this button creates a new tab and displays a dialog where you can input the name of the new tab.

Tab Dropdown [Default ▾]

This dropdown shows a list of all the tabs you've created, enabling you to quickly choose one for editing the curves within.

Delete Tab

This button deletes the current tab from the Tab Dropdown. You cannot delete the default tab. Also, keep in mind that this will not destroy the animation curves within the tab.

Curve Editor Curve Key List

The curve key list provides a scrollable list of all the animated properties within the curve editor, and gives you access to the visibility of the curves for those properties. This list is populated by sending curves into the editor. In Matinee, this is done by clicking the small black square that is visible in the lower-right corner of each animated track (see **FIGURE B.13**). In Cascade, there is a similar black box with a curve icon inside visible on each animatable module.

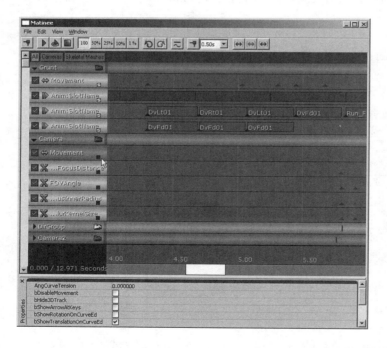

FIGURE B.13   Here you can see the small black box used to send Matinee information to the curve editor.

Visibility Flags

Each entry in the list contains the name of the property being animated, along with a series of small square buttons that control the visibility of each curve in the graph view. The nature of these buttons will change depending on what type of property is being edited, but they all essentially perform the same task: show or hide individual curves.

In the lower-right corner of each entry is a small black box that turns yellow when clicked. This box is the master visibility for the curves of that property. When active, the curve(s) for that property will be visible. When black—or deactivated—the curves cannot be seen.

In the lower-left corner are one to three buttons: red, green, and blue. These control the visibility of individual curves for the property. This is important, especially in the case of vector properties, which have an X, Y, and Z property, because it enables you to control the visibility of individual axes, such as seeing only the X curve. Properties that have only one value show only a red box (X), whereas properties that have an X, Y, and Z value show all three (see **FIGURE B.14**).

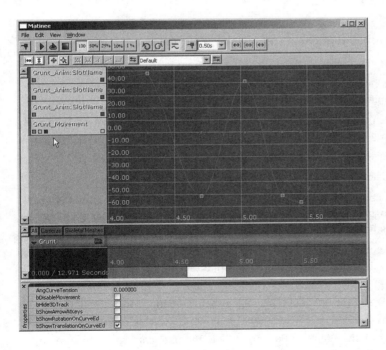

FIGURE B.14   Notice the visibility flags at the bottom of the entry.

B

Curve Editor Graph View

The graph view is where you'll actually get to see and interact with your animation curves. It consists of a simple graphical representation of value and time, with property values running along the vertical axis and time values spanning across the horizontal. It can be zoomed in each axis individually, allowing for easy navigation of various curves.

You can also create keys in this window, as well as relocate keys along the graph. Moving keys vertically change the value of that key, and moving keys horizontally change the time that the key occurs.

Graph View Navigation

The manner in which you navigate the graph view depends on the mode the graph view is in. The two modes available are Pan/Edit Mode and Zoom Mode.

Pan/Edit Mode Navigation

Pan/Edit Mode serves as the graph view's default navigation mode, providing most of your general navigation abilities. It enables you to move around the graph and adjust keys.

Pan—Drag with the left mouse button to pan the view around and see your curves.

Zoom—You can zoom into or out of the graph view by rolling the mouse wheel. Note that this zoom is uniform in the horizontal and vertical axes.

Select Key—You can select a key by left-clicking on it. Doing so will make its Time and Value visible, and will also display that key's tangent handles.

You can toggle a selection by holding Ctrl and clicking multiple keys.

You can marquee select by holding Ctrl and Alt and dragging a selection.

Moving Keys—You can move a key by first selecting it, and then dragging it while holding the Ctrl key. Dragging left and right will change the key's timing. Dragging up and down will control its value.

Adjusting User Tangents—You can adjust the angle of a User or Break tangents by first selecting a key, and then dragging on the small white tangent handle.

It should be noted to those readers who are accustomed to working with animation curves in certain 2D and 3D animation packages that you cannot adjust multiple tangents simultaneously, nor can you change the weighting of a given tangent.

Right-Click Context Menu—While in Pan/Edit Mode, the user can right-click on a key at any time and change its Time or Value.

Key Creation—You can create your own keys along the curve by holding Ctrl and left-clicking anywhere along the curve. You can then use the context menu to change the time and value for the key.

Zoom Mode Navigation

Zoom Mode is a more specialized navigational mode, enabling you to zoom in individually in the horizontal or vertical axes, or both.

Zoom Value (Vertically)—You can zoom vertically without affecting the horizontal axis by dragging with the right mouse button.

Zoom Time (Horizontally)—You can zoom horizontally without affecting the vertical axis by dragging with the left mouse button.

> **NOTE**
>
> You can zoom nonuniformly in the horizontal and vertical directions by holding both mouse buttons.

Preset Curves

As you use the editing tools to create various curves, you may eventually start to realize that you use certain shaped curves over and over. Rather than recreate these curves each time you need one, you can use the preset curve feature to save out a favored curve shape to be reused again and again (see **FIGURE B.15**). On top of this, you can also choose to use a variety of predefined curves, such as sine or cosine waves.

> **NOTE**
>
> At the time of this writing, preset curves are intended for use within Cascade only. In addition, the ability to save your own preset curves is nonfunctional.

Curve presets can be accessed by right-clicking on any of the curves in the Curve Key List. You will see a context menu appear, giving you the ability to remove the curve from the editor entirely, to place a preset curve for it, or to save out the existing curve as a preset for later use.

Choosing the Preset Curve option opens the Preset Curve dialog. This dialog enables you to choose what type of curve you'd like to place, and in which of the available slots for the property you'd like to place it. For example, if you are animating a property, such as the color of a particle in Cascade, you could apply a sine wave curve to the red value, but still control the other two colors manually.

Using the Preset Curve dialog is as simple as choosing the axis to which you'd like to apply the preset, clicking on the dropdown corresponding to that axis, and choosing which curve you want to use.

B

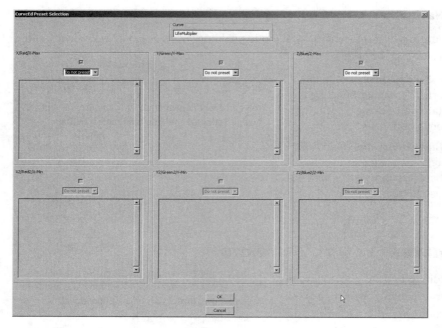

FIGURE B.15   Preset Curve dialog

Available Preset Curve Settings

The following options are available from the Preset Curve dropdowns.

Do Not Preset

This option leaves the curve in its current state, not adding a preset to it.

Cos Wave

This generates a cosine wave over time (see **FIGURE B.16**). When this type of curve is selected, some parameters appear to control the look of the curve. These parameters are as follows:

> **Frequency**—This controls the frequency of the wave as time progresses. At the time of this writing, this is locked to a value between 0 and 1.

> **Scale**—This controls the scale factor of the curve, allowing it to be multiplied by the entered value. As you might know, a sine wave spans between a value of 1 and -1 throughout its life. For example, if you were to set this value to 10, your curve would oscillate between 10 and -10 instead.

Offset—This controls how far you would like to offset the curve once it has been scaled. Say, for example, you wanted a curve that oscillated between 0 and 1; you would need a Scale value of 0.5, which would cause the curve to oscillate between 0.5 and -0.5. You could then set the Offset value to 0.5, which would move the entire curve upwards such that it now oscillated between 0 and 1.

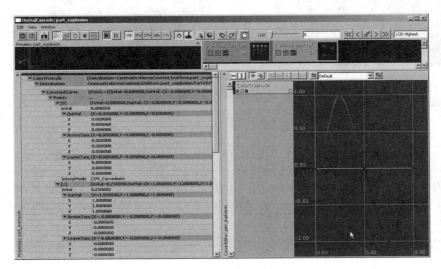

FIGURE B.16   Example of a cosine wave

Sine Wave

This generates a sine wave over time. If this type of curve is selected, the same options described previously for cos waves appear.

Linear Decay

This creates a curve that exhibits linear decay over time (see **FIGURE B.17**). If this type of curve is selected, the following options appear, enabling you to control the setup of the initial curve:

> **NOTE**
>
> Creating a linear decay preset curve will not always result in actual linear decay behavior. This is because the keys that are created are still using Auto tangents. You can solve this problem by selecting each key of the curve and setting their tangent types to Linear.

StartDecay—This is the time at which the decay will start.

StartValue—This is the value at which the curve will begin.

EndDecay—This value sets the time at which the decay will end.

EndValue—This sets the value at which the curve will end.

B

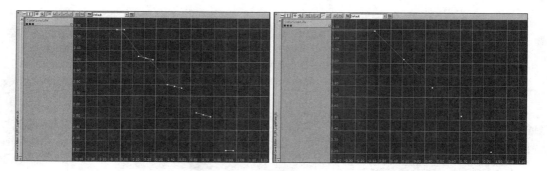

FIGURE B.17   Linear decay curves are not perfectly linear when created. To the right is the same curve with its tangents set to Linear.

User-Set

This option enables the user to load in a pre-curve created earlier. When selecting this type of curve, the UserCurve property appears, enabling you to load in the desirable curve. Please note that these curves appear as objects in the Generic Browser, and that you use the standard Use Current Selection in Browser button to load them in.

Index

c

F

f-stops, 916. *See also* depth
of field
Face Graph
  Options dialog box, 879
  panels, 877
  tabs, 878
FaceFX Studio, 839-840
  Actor panel, 875
  curves, 866-872
  interfaces, 872-882
  links, 850-860
  nodes, 847-850
  phonemes, 840-846
FaceFXBlendMod
  property, 908
FacingFalloffExponent
  property, 191
Fade tracks, adding, 951
fading particles, 289
FalloffExponent property, 678
field of view, 918
files
  INI, 4-5, 556
  UPK, 4
  WAV
    comparing
      SoundCues/
      USounds, 604-611
    importing, 605
FinalAdd expressions, 149
FinalMult expressions, 149
Fit Visible Tracks Horizontally
  button (Curve Editor), 1031
Fit Visible Tracks Vertically
  button (Curve Editor), 1031
FixedRelativeBoundingBox
  property, 273
Flag Cloth, creating, 248

flags, placing, 250
flame effects, 269
FlameGlow emitter, 405
Flames emitter, 401
Float Constant property, 1003
Float Particle Param Track
  property, 408, 463
Float variable, 524
FloatConstantCurve
  Distributions, 289
floats
  constants, 307
  property tracks,
    adding, 959
Fluid Typedata module, 285
FluidCollisionDistance-
  Multiplier property, 395
FluidCollisionResponse-
  Coefficient property, 396
FluidDamping property, 395
FluidDynamicCollision-
  Adhesion property, 396
FluidDynamicCollision-
  Attraction property, 396
FluidDynamicCollision-
  Restitution property, 396
FluidEmitterFluidVelocity-
  Magnitude property, 397
FluidEmitterMaxParticles
  property, 397
FluidEmitterParticleLifetime
  property, 397
FluidEmitterRandomAngle
  property, 397
FluidEmitterRandomPos
  property, 397
FluidEmitterRate
  property, 397
FluidEmitterRepulsion-
  Coefficient property, 397

FluidEmitterShape
  property, 397
FluidEmitterType
  property, 396
FluidExternalAcceleration
  property, 396
FluidForceScale property, 397
FluidFriction property, 164
FluidKernelRadiusMultiplier
  property, 395
FluidMaxParticles
  property, 395
FluidMotionLimitMultiplier
  property, 395
FluidPacketSizeMultiplier
  property, 395
FluidRestDensity
  property, 395
FluidRestParticlesPerMeter
  property, 395
FluidRotationCoefficient
  property, 394
FluidRotationMethod
  property, 394
fluids, emitters, 393-397
FluidSimulationMethod
  property, 396
FluidStaticCollisionAdhesion
  property, 396
FluidStaticCollisionAttraction
  property, 396
FluidStaticCollisionRestitution
  property, 396
FluidStiffness property, 395
FluidViscosity property, 395
Focus Chain, 541-543
focus, 677
FocusDistance property, 678
Focused state, 514
FocusInnerRadius
  property, 678

X–Z

Your purchase of **Mastering Unreal® Technology, Volume II** includes access to a free online edition for 45 days through the Safari Books Online subscription service. Nearly every Sams book is available online through Safari Books Online, along with more than 5,000 other technical books and videos from publishers such as Addison-Wesley Professional, Cisco Press, Exam Cram, IBM Press, O'Reilly, Prentice Hall, and Que.

SAFARI BOOKS ONLINE allows you to search for a specific answer, cut and paste code, download chapters, and stay current with emerging technologies.

Activate your FREE Online Edition at www.informit.com/safarifree

> **STEP 1:** Enter the coupon code: HYDKWWA.

> **STEP 2:** New Safari users, complete the brief registration form.
> Safari subscribers, just log in.

If you have difficulty registering on Safari or accessing the online edition, please e-mail customer-service@safaribooksonline.com

Addison Wesley · Adobe Press · ALPHA · Cisco Press · FT Press · IBM Press · lynda.com · Microsoft Press · New Riders

O'REILLY · Peachpit Press · PRENTICE · Que · SAS Publishing · Sun microsystems · WILEY